# CONTEMPORARY
## Black
## Biography

ISSN-1058-1316

# CONTEMPORARY

## Black

## Biography

### Profiles from the International Black Community

## Volume 87

GALE
CENGAGE Learning

Detroit • New York • San Francisco • New Haven, Conn • Waterville, Maine • London

**Contemporary Black Biography, Volume 87**

**Kepos Media, Inc.: Derek Jacques, Janice Jorgensen, and Paula Kepos, editors**

Project Editor: Margaret Mazurkiewicz

Image Research and Acquisitions: Leitha Etheridge-Sims

Editorial Support Services: Nataliya Mikheyeva

Manufacturing: Dorothy Maki, Rita Wimberley

Composition and Prepress: Mary Beth Trimper, Gary Leach

Imaging: John Watkins

For product information and technology assistance, contact us at
**Gale Customer Support, 1-800-877-4253.**
For permission to use material from this text or product,
submit all requests online at **www.cengage.com/permissions**.
Further permissions questions can be emailed to
**permissionrequest@cengage.com**

*Gale*
27500 Drake Rd.
Farmington Hills, MI, 48331-3535

ISBN-13: 978-1-4144-5852-6
ISBN-10: 1-4144-5852-5

ISSN 1058-1316

This title is also available as an e-book.
ISBN 13: 978-1-4144-6184-7
ISBN-10: 1-4144-6184-4
Contact your Gale sales representative for ordering information.

Printed in Mexico
1 2 3 4 5 6 7 15 14 13 12 11

# Advisory Board

# Contents

**Introduction ix**

**Cumulative Nationality Index 171**

**Cumulative Occupation Index 189**

**Cumulative Subject Index 215**

**Cumulative Name Index 265**

Laz Alonso .............................................................1

    *Rising young actor*

Fred Anderson .......................................................4

    *Experimental jazz saxophonist*

Esther Armah ........................................................7

    *International journalist and author*

Vernon Joseph Baker ............................................9

    *Honored World War II hero*

Herman Branson...................................................13

    *Influential physicist and educator*

Dorothy Brunson...................................................15

    *Respected broadcasting executive*

Lillian Scott Calhoun.............................................18

    *Pioneering journalist*

Barbara-Rose Collins............................................20

    *Controversial U.S. Representative*

Blaise Compaore ..................................................23

    *Longtime president of Burkina Faso*

Stanley Crouch .....................................................26

    *Brilliant and volatile music and social critic*

Ulysses Grant Dailey .............................................31

    *Distinguished surgeon, educator, and hospital administrator*

Gail Devers ...........................................................34

    *Inspiring track star*

Bill Dixon...............................................................38

    *Free jazz trumpeter*

Frederick Douglass................................................41

    *Renowned abolitionist leader*

Kevin Fenton..........................................................46

    *Committed public health official*

Hardy R. Franklin....................................................49

    *Illustrious librarian*

John Trusty Gibson..................................................52

    *Early theater entrepreneur*

Al Goodman ............................................................54

    *Charming R&B vocalist*

Carl Gordon ............................................................56

    *Veteran character actor*

Asamoah Gyan ........................................................59

    *Ghanaian soccer star and musician*

Gary L. Harris .........................................................62

    *Electrical engineering researcher and educator*

Walter Hawkins .......................................................64

    *Grammy Award–winning gospel singer and bishop*

Roy Haynes ............................................................67

    *Acclaimed jazz drummer*

Raymond V. Haysbert Sr. ........................................70

    *Longtime Baltimore business leader*

Santonio Holmes ....................................................73

    *Talented and troubled NFL star*

Iman .......................................................................76

    *Renowned supermodel and cosmetics designer*

Marvin Isley............................................................79

    *Isley Brothers bassist*

Brenda Jackson ......................................................82

    *Top-selling romance writer*

Denise Jefferson.....................................................85

    *Longtime director of the renowned Ailey dance school*

William Layton ........................................................88

    *Distinguished civil servant and historian*

Raphael C. Lee.......................................................91

    *Respected reconstrictive surgeon and bioengineer*

Marvin Lewis ..........................................................94

    *Inspirational NFL coach*

Adrian Matejka............................................98
    Captivating poet
James McBride...........................................100
    Multitalented author and musician
John Mensah.............................................104
    Tough international soccer defender
Paulo Moura.............................................107
    Beloved Brazilian musician
Pius Njawe...............................................109
    Tireless Cameroonian journalist and free press
        advocate
Hildrus A. Poindexter ...............................112
    Trailblazing specialist in tropical medicine
Benny Powell............................................115
    Dedicated jazz trombonist and educator
René Préval .............................................118
    Two-term Haitian president
John Randle..............................................121
    Top NFL defender
J. R. Richard............................................124
    Overpowering MLB pitcher
Frank Robinson ........................................127
    Hall-of-Fame outfielder and manager

Arsenio Rodríguez.....................................132
    Innovative Cuban bandleader
Diana Sands .............................................134
    Award-winning stage actress
Tim Scott..................................................138
    Republican rising star
Shirley Sherrod .........................................141
    Former USDA official
Garry Shider .............................................144
    Popular funk musician
Emmitt Smith ...........................................147
    Pro Football Hall of Fame running back
Michael G. Spencer....................................152
    Prominent engineer and educator
Michael Strautmanis ..................................154
    Trusted White House staffer
Jack Tatum................................................157
    Feared NFL defender
Arthur Walker II.........................................160
    Pioneering astrophysicist
James E. West ..........................................162
    Leading acoustical engineer
John Edgar Wideman...................................164
    Noted chronicler of urban life

# Introduction

*Contemporary Black Biography* provides informative biographical profiles of the important and influential persons of African heritage who form the international black community: men and women who have changed today's world and are shaping tomorrow's. *Contemporary Black Biography* covers persons of various nationalities in a wide variety of fields, including architecture, art, business, dance, education, fashion, film, industry, journalism, law, literature, medicine, music, politics and government, publishing, religion, science and technology, social issues, sports, television, theater, and others. In addition to in-depth coverage of names found in today's headlines, *Contemporary Black Biography* provides coverage of selected individuals from earlier in this century whose influence continues to impact on contemporary life. *Contemporary Black Biography* also provides coverage of important and influential persons who are not yet household names and are therefore likely to be ignored by other biographical reference series. Each volume also includes listee updates on names previously appearing in *CBB*.

## Designed for Quick Research and Interesting Reading

- **Attractive page design** incorporates textual subheads, making it easy to find the information you're looking for.
- **Easy-to-locate data sections** provide quick access to vital personal statistics, career information, major awards, and mailing addresses, when available.
- **Informative biographical essays** trace the subject's personal and professional life with the kind of in-depth analysis you need.
- **To further enhance your appreciation** of the subject, most entries include photographic portraits.
- **Sources for additional information** direct the user to selected books, magazines, and newspapers where more information on the individuals can be obtained.

## Helpful Indexes Make It Easy to Find the Information You Need

*Contemporary Black Biography* includes cumulative Nationality, Occupation, Subject, and Name indexes that make it easy to locate entries in a variety of useful ways.

## Available in Electronic Formats

*Diskette/Magnetic Tape.* Contemporary Black Biography is available for licensing on magnetic tape or diskette in a fielded format. Either the complete database or a custom selection of entries may be ordered. The database is available for internal data processing and nonpublishing purposes only. For more information, call (800) 877-GALE.

*On-line.* Contemporary Black Biography is available on-line through Mead Data Central's NEXIS Service in the NEXIS, PEOPLE and SPORTS Libraries in the GALBIO file and Gale's Biography Resource Center.

## Disclaimer

*Contemporary Black Biography* uses and lists websites as sources and these websites may become obsolete.

## We Welcome Your Suggestions

The editors welcome your comments and suggestions for enhancing and improving *Contemporary Black Biography*. If you would like to suggest persons for inclusion in the series, please submit these names to the editors. Mail comments or suggestions to:

The Editor

Contemporary Black Biography

Gale, Cengage Learning

27500 Drake Rd.

Farmington Hills, MI 48331-3535

Phone: (800) 347-4253

# Laz Alonso

## 1974—

## Film actor

Alonso, Laz, photograph. AP Images/Peter Kramer.

One of the hottest young talents in Hollywood, actor Laz Alonso has already worked with such top directors as Sam Mendes, Spike Lee, and James Cameron. Alonso took an unusual path to acting, starting out as an investment banker on Wall Street before following his dream, but it did not take long for him to build an impressive résumé. Alonso earned high marks for his performance in Lee's World War II picture *Miracle at St. Anna* in 2008, and followed up as the villainous thug Fenix Rise opposite Vin Diesel in the action flick *Fast & Furious* in 2009. Later that year he appeared in the Academy Award–winning sci-fi epic *Avatar,* one of the top-grossing films of all time.

Lazaro Alonso was born on March 25, 1974, in Washington, DC, the only child of immigrants from Cuba. As a boy, he knew that he wanted to act, and he entertained himself by inventing characters, performing scenes, even practicing crying in the bathroom mirror. When he was fourteen, his father died. His mother worked three jobs to earn a living and to pay for Laz's classical piano lessons and, later, his college tuition. Young Laz worked, too, to help make ends meet, which kept him out of trouble. "It ... helped me

stay on the straight-and-narrow because I can't say growing up in D.C. that I was always surrounded by positive role models. Taking care of my family kept me right," he recalled in an interview with *Jet* magazine.

Although his passion was performing, Alonso decided on a more practical career path, studying business and marketing at Howard University. After graduation, he took a job as an investment banker on Wall Street, intending to save enough money to pursue his acting career without financial worries. "I knew deep down in my heart I wasn't going to last too long," he told *Jet*. "It was just a place that was devoid of creativity." After two years, Alonso left to start his own marketing business, and in the evenings, he took acting classes. Before long, he was landing roles in videos and commercials, including Budweiser's memorable "Whassup" television ads in the 1990s, for which he earned an Emmy Award.

Alonso started out on television as the host of the morning show A.M. @ BET, and booked his first acting job on HBO's *Disappearing Acts* with Wesley Snipes. From there, he went on to guest star on series such as *The Practice, Without a Trace, NCIS, Bones, The*

### At a Glance . . .

**B**orn Lazaro Alonso on March 25, 1974, in Washington, DC. *Education:* Howard University, BS in business administration.

**Career:** Actor in film and television roles, 2000—.

**Addresses:** *Agent*—International Creative Management, 10250 Constellation Blvd., 9th Fl., Los Angeles, CA 90067.

*Unit,* and *Southland.* On the big screen, Alonso appeared in small roles in a score of films, including Chris Rock's *Down to Earth* (2001), *All Night Bodega* (2002), *Constantine* (2005), and *All Souls Day: Dio de los Muertos* (2005). His first major feature came in 2005 with *Jarhead,* starring Jamie Foxx and Jake Gyllenhaal, in which he played a soldier stationed in the Persian Gulf, followed by the psychological thriller *Captivity* and then *Stomp the Yard,* both in 2007.

Finally, Alonso landed his breakout role. In 2008 he starred as Corporal Héctor Negrón in Spike Lee's *Miracle at St. Anna,* a film based on the real-life story of Sorentino López, a Puerto Rican soldier who served in an all-black army unit known as the "Buffalo Soldiers" during World War II. Auditioning for the role, Alonso impressed director Lee with his ability to improvise in Spanish, performing two scenes entirely in Spanish. When Lee saw the tape, he called Alonso personally: "Laz, It's Spike Lee. You got the job," the actor recounted to the *New York Daily News.* For Alonso, the chance to work with Lee was a dream come true. "The work that he's done has been so powerful as far as communicating the black experience, and educating not just other races but black people as well," he told *Jet.* "I believe that working with him validates me as a serious actor."

In 2009 Alonso appeared in the blockbuster action flick *Fast & Furious,* the fourth installment of the Vin Diesel series, playing the villain Fenix Rise, Diesel's nemesis. Later that year came James Cameron's 3-D science fiction epic *Avatar,* in which he starred alongside Sam Worthington, Zoe Saldana, and Sigourney Weaver. Alonso played the character of Tsu'tey, a warrior of the Na'vi tribe, part of a humanoid race living on a distant moon. In the film, viewers do not see Alonso in the flesh, but rather a digital counterpart created by attaching tiny cameras to the actor's face to capture his facial expressions. "Working with James, it doesn't feel like you're shooting a movie," Alonso told the New York Daily News, describing his experience with director Cameron. "It feels like you're in a laboratory with Thomas Edison while he's creating a light bulb."

Avatar premiered on December 16, 2009, earning $77 million on its opening weekend and going on to become one of the top-grossing films of all time with more than $760 million in revenue. The movie earned nine Academy Award nominations, including one for best picture. Alonso hoped that his performance in *Avatar* would give him an entrée into the leading man category and more starring roles. "I think that once people see me as a lead, that's when they're really going to see what I can do on film," he told *Jet.*

In 2010 Alonso appeared in the romantic comedy *Just Wright* starring Queen Latifah, and he was slated to perform in the 2011 films *Jumping the Broom* with Angela Bassett and *Straw Dogs* with James Woods. He also signed on to star in the pilot series *Breakout Kings,* about former fugitives who become U.S. marshals, which was set to air on the A&E Network in early 2011.

## Selected works

### Films

*30 Years to Life,* Oasis Entertainment, 2001.
*Down to Earth,* Paramount Pictures, 2001.
*G,* Andrew Lauren Productions, 2002.
*All Night Bodega,* Noé Productions, 2002.
*Leprechaun 2: Back 2 the Hood,* Lions Gate, 2003.
*Hittin' It!,* Lions Gate, 2004.
*All Souls Day: Dio de los Muertos,* IDT Entertainment, 2005.
*Constantine,* Warner Bros., 2005.
*The Tenants,* Millennium Films, 2005.
*Flip the Script,* Vision Films, 2005.
*Issues,* Bullz Eye Productions, 2005.
*Jarhead,* Universal Pictures, 2005.
*The Last Stand,* UpToParr Productions, 2006.
*Stomp the Yard,* Screen Gems, 2007.
*Captivity,* After Dark Films, 2007.
*Bunny Whipped,* Buddha-Cowboy Productions, 2007.
*This Christmas,* Screen Gems, 2007.
*Divine Intervention,* Vision Films, 2007.
*Miracle at St. Anna,* Touchstone Pictures, 2008.
*Fast & Furious,* Universal Pictures, 2009.
*Down for Life,* Por Vida Productions, 2009.
*Avatar,* 20th Century Fox, 2009.
*Just Wright,* Fox Searchlight, 2010.

### Television

*A.M. @ BET,* BET, 2000.
*Disappearing Acts,* HBO, 2000.

## Sources

### Periodicals

*Jet,* November 3, 2008; March 8, 2010.
*New York Daily News,* September 30, 2008.
*Variety,* October 29, 2009.

## *Online*

Cane, Clay, "Fast & Furious Laz Alonso," BET.com, http://www.bet.com/entertainment/News/lazalon sointerview.htm (accessed October 18, 2010).

—Deborah A. Ring

# Fred Anderson

## 1929–2010

### Musician

Fred Anderson was a legendary figure inside Chicago's jazz scene for decades before his death in 2010. The bar owner and saxophonist, whose commitment to experimental jazz helped create a definitive Chicago style and sound, ran the famous Velvet Lounge gathering spot on the city's Near South Side. Whether behind the bar or on stage, Anderson nurtured and promoted several generations of talented musicians, some of whom had even moved to the Windy City to study under him. Arts writer Howard Reich in the *Chicago Tribune* called him the "fire-breathing symbol of everything new, progressive and daring in Chicago jazz."

Anderson, Fred, photograph. James Fraher/Michael Ochs Archives/Getty Images.

### Worked as a Carpet Installer

Like many black Chicagoans of his generation, Anderson was born in the Deep South and came North as a child. His hometown was Monroe, Louisiana, a place he and his mother would leave forever around 1937, when Anderson turned eight years old. At a cousin's place in Chicago, he came across a saxophone and was fascinated by the instrument. He taught himself how to play, but he eventually supplemented his music education with classes at the Roy Knapp Conservatory on Chicago's South Side. Hearing Charlie "Bird" Parker—a rising young sax player out of New York City who was becoming one of the key figures in the development of bebop jazz—at the Pershing Lounge in the 1940s was a pivotal moment in the direction of Anderson's own style.

With a wife and growing family that would eventually include three sons, Anderson could not expect to support his family as a musician, and he spent many years as a carpet installer while playing on the side. Finally, in 1965 he teamed with a few other like-minded musicians in Chicago to establish the Association for the Advancement of Creative Musicians (AACM), an organization that sought to promote and nurture the city's experimental-jazz scene. Turning up at just the right moment on the cultural landscape, the AACM "advocated deep absorption in the jazz tradition and openness to performance art and what would eventually be considered 'world music,'" noted John Fordham in the London *Guardian,* who called the association "an inspiration to many radical Chicago musicians."

*At a Glance . . .*

**B**orn on March 22, 1929, in Monroe, LA; died on June 24, 2010, in Park Ridge, IL; married and divorced; children: Eugene, Michael, Kevin. *Education:* Studied music at the Roy Knapp Conservatory.

**Career:** Saxophonist; worked as a carpet installer in Chicago, 1950s–60s(?); Association for the Advancement of Creative Musicians (AACM), cofounder, 1965; opened the Birdhouse music venue, 1978; bartender and later owner of Tip's Lounge, which Anderson renamed the Velvet Lounge, after 1982; wrote *Exercises for the Creative Musician.*

In the late 1960s Anderson began appearing on releases from Delmark, a Chicago jazz and blues label. "His was a rigorous, demanding brand of jazz improvisation that bridged the bebop idiom of Charlie Parker with the 'free jazz' experiments of the 1960s and thereafter," wrote Reich in the *Chicago Tribune.* "The fast-flying phrases and blues-driven energy of bebop converged with the non-chordal, anything-goes song structures of 'free jazz' in Anderson's best work." The artist, however, never accrued much critical interest outside of his hometown scene until much later in his career. Fordham, writing in the *Guardian,* offered one explanation: "Anderson could microtonally bend notes with an insouciance that brought him accolades from fans and doubts about his competence from skeptics." Fordham continued: "He lasted long enough to see a much more open attitude to music's global vocabularies prevail, but it was a tough slog. The comfort zone of his club, the Velvet Lounge, and its hip audiences saw him through long periods of it."

### Bought His Own Bar

Anderson's first foray into the nightclub business was a loft space on Lincoln Avenue that he called the Birdhouse in homage to Charlie Parker. It lasted a year before it was shuttered in 1979. After some recording sessions in Italy with jazz trumpeter Billy Brimfield, he returned to Chicago and found a bartending job at a gritty neighborhood watering hole called Tip's Lounge at 2128 1/2 South Indiana Avenue. When the owner died, Anderson bought the place. It stayed open all day, with Anderson tending bar, but he started a Sunday-night improv series twice a month that soon became a showcase for local jazz musicians interested in the experimental form. Eventually he renamed it the Velvet Lounge after a compliment from a patron about his sax playing. Fellow musicians, especially his AACM cohorts, loved the stage and the ambiance, often playing

there for a token fee, and it was only in the 1990s that Anderson started charging cover at the door.

Under Anderson's watch, the Velvet Lounge became the launching pad for the careers of some significant musicians in the free-jazz scene: bassist Tatsu Aoki, drummer Hamid Drake, and George Lewis, a trombonist. They were all significantly younger than he was, but they looked to him as a mentor. Although he had little formal training himself, Anderson attempted to teach others, coming up with *Exercises for the Creative Musician,* a written work completed with the help of a University of Chicago music student who transcribed his solos, to which Anderson then appended annotations and notes. "My fondest memories of Fred," declared John Corbett in a *Chicago Reader* tribute, "include his big, projecting sound—a tone he honed practicing outdoors as a young player, bouncing notes off buildings—as well as his epic solos, which could stretch as endlessly as the midwestern horizon. Perhaps that's how he earned the nickname the 'Lone Prophet of the Prairie.'"

In the 1990s Anderson helped launch the careers of jazz artists from an even younger generation, such as flautist Nicole Mitchell and saxophonist Ken Vandermark; the latter had moved from Boston to Chicago to immerse himself in the scene anchored by the Velvet Lounge stage. There was also a contingent of Asian-American jazz artists who came to Chicago to play and record with Anderson. George Lewis, the trombonist, went on to become a professor of music at Columbia University and wrote an epic treatise on the AACM's impact, *A Power Stronger Than Itself: The AACM and American Experimental Music.* Aoki, the bassist, went on to cofound the free-jazz group Asian Improv aRts, which he modeled after the AACM.

### Presided Over Chicago Landmark

In his final years Anderson played with his Fred Anderson Trio at the Velvet Lounge and onstage at various Chicago cultural-scene events. In 2006 the bar was targeted for demolition to make way for a condominium project. Anderson's devoted regulars helped him raise funds to move to a new location at 67 E. Cermak Road. The place was such a Chicago institution that it even earned multiple mentions in one episode of NBC's hit medical drama *E.R.,* when the emergency-room doctors and nurses attempt to plan a post-work get-together to listen to jazz at the Velvet Lounge.

In 2009 Anderson was feted with an eightieth birthday concert at the city's spectacular Millennium Park, and he took the stage at his own bar for a well-attended eighty-first birthday event in March of 2010. Less than three months later he made his own E.R. visit, complaining of stomach pains, and suffered a heart attack two days later on June 14. He died on June 24, 2010.

Survivors include his sons Michael and Eugene—the latter an accomplished jazz drummer—along with five grandchildren and six great-grandchildren. He had been divorced many years before, and his son Kevin predeceased him.

Almost immediately there were worries that the Velvet Lounge would be unable to stay afloat without Anderson's boundless dedication, but supporters rallied to rescue it as a way to preserve Anderson's legacy. Chicago radio host Neil Tesser wrote an article on Anderson's impact for the *New York Times* in which he asserted that it would be the city's free-jazz scene that would bear the brunt of Anderson's passing. Anderson's "various roles intertwined," Tesser noted. "His nightclub fostered his bands, and his bands spread his reputation among three generations of Chicago musicians, who revered him and grew protective of him. This synergy is unique to Chicago," Tesser declared, adding that this phenomenon would have been impossible to re-create in places like New York City or Los Angeles. While the United States has "many excellent collegiate jazz programs," Tesser continued, "none teach young musicians how to break the rules, or how to create a new rule book entirely, as true innovators do. For that, they must follow the example of those who have already been there."

## Selected discography

*Another Place,* Moers Music, 1980.
*The Missing Link,* Nessa Records, 1984.
*Birdhouse,* Okka Disk, 1995.
*Fred: Chicago Chamber Music,* Southport, 1997.
*Fred Anderson/DKV Trio,* Okka Disk, 1997.
*The Milwaukee Tapes Vol. 1* (recorded 1980), Unheard Music, 2000.
*Dark Day + Live in Verona 1979,* Atavistic, 2001.
*Duets 2001 Robert Barry and Fred Anderson,* Thrill Jockey, 2001.
*On the Run: Live at the Velvet Lounge,* Delmark, 2001.
*Back at the Velvet Lounge,* Delmark, 2002.
*Back Together Again: Fred Anderson and Hamid Drake,* Thrill Jockey, 2004.

## Sources

### Periodicals

*Chicago Reader,* July 1, 2010.
*Chicago Tribune,* June 24, 2010.
*Daily Herald* (Arlington Heights, IL), August 13, 1999, p. 14.
*Guardian* (London), July 4, 2010.
*New York Times,* June 26, 2010.

### Online

Vega, Lazaro, "A Conversation with Fred Anderson," Jazz Institute of Chicago, http://www.jazzinchicago.org/educates/journal/interviews/conversation-fred-anderson (accessed August 22, 2010).

—Carol Brennan

# Esther Armah

## 1963—

### Journalist, author, radio host

Armah, Esther, photograph. Jemal Countess/Getty Images.

Esther Armah is an award-winning international journalist and author whose work spans print and broadcast media, exploring issues of race, identity, and culture. Born in London to Ghanaian parents, as a child she lived through the trauma of Ghana's 1966 military takeover, an experience that would shape her career. She earned acclaim for her investigative reporting and documentary films for the BBC and has hosted programs on radio and television for the network. In 2006 Armah published her first nonfiction book, *Can I Be Me?*, which was adapted for the New York stage, and a second play, *Forgive Me?*, followed in 2008. Now living in New York and splitting her time among three continents, she is a well-known radio host on WBAI-FM, a frequent commentator on racial issues in the media, and the director of Centric Productions, a creative media company.

Esther Armah was born in 1963 in London, one of five children of parents from Ghana, and spent her early childhood living in that country. In February of 1966, Ghana's civilian government was overturned in a military coup led by General E. K. Kotoka, and Armah's father, a Ghanaian politician, found himself an enemy of the new regime. On the night of the coup, armed soldiers stormed into the Armah house, where Esther—then three years old—her three sisters, and their mother waited in fear; Samuel Armah, whom the police had come for, was out of the country, en route to Vietnam on government business. The Armahs lived under house arrest for two years, until 1968, when they were able to return to London. Armah's father remained in Ghana despite threats against his life; it was fifteen years before the family was reunited.

For Armah, the trauma of her childhood sparked an interest in journalism as she sought to understand her dual identity and what it meant to be black and British. She began her career writing for the *Weekly Journal* in London and then for *West Africa* magazine before turning to broadcast media. Following a stint as a presenter for *Talking Africa,* a weekly radio program on current affairs, she took a job as a researcher at BBC 4 Radio. That led to a job working on the station's legal program, *Law in Action.* For nearly a decade, Armah worked as a radio and television journalist with the BBC, in the roles of investigative reporter, documentary maker, and radio host. On BBC Radio 5 Live,

*At a Glance . . .*

**B**orn in 1963, in London, England; daughter of a Ghanaian politican.

**Career:** BBC, investigative reporter, documentary maker, radio and television host, 1999–2007; Centric Productions, director, 2009—.

**Addresses:** 657 Jefferson Avenue, Brooklyn, NY 11221.

she hosted "Up All Night," a live four-hour talk show on Saturday and Sunday nights, and reported as a correspondent for the BBC World Service.

On television, Armah worked both behind and in front of the camera. She worked as a reporter for BBC1's long-running investigative program *Panorama,* hosted Panorama Interactive, and appeared as a panelist on Sky TV's *Richard Littlejohn Show.* As a reporter, she traveled throughout the United Kingdom, the United States, and Africa, visiting Ghana, Kenya, Lesotho, Nigeria, and South Africa. Her writing has appeared in the *Guardian* newspaper in London, *Essence* magazine in the United States, the *African Journal,* and the *New Ghanaian.*

In 2006 Armah published her first nonfiction book, *Can I Be Me?,* in which she explores her dual African and British identity, the legacy of her family trauma and her father's long absence, and her addiction to approval. The following year, she adapted the book into a one-woman stage play, which was performed to favorable reviews at the Museum of the City of New York. Her second play, *Forgive Me?,* a two-character drama that highlights the cultural conflict between African immigrants and African Americans, had its New York debut in June of 2008 as part of the New Heritage Theater's Roger Furman Playreading Series, followed by a production in 2009 at the Mainstage Theater of the Midtown International Theater Festival.

Armah relocated to New York in 2007, restless in London after her father's passing. There, she was the host of "Wake Up Call," a popular morning show on WBAI-FM, as well as the weekly radio program "Off the Page," which focused on current events in the publishing industry. "I'm here in New York to practice the kind of journalism which is important to me," Armah explained to the *New York Amsterdam News,* noting that she is intrigued by "the detail of the craft, a mix of perspectives as opposed to one that is purely Euro-centric, and one where authority and establishment can be regularly and thoughtfully challenged." Armah also appeared on BET J's *My Two Cents* and in BET's documentary *Hip Hop vs. America Part II.*

In 2009 Armah founded Centric Productions, a creative media company based in New York, London, and Ghana. In 2010 her second book, *The Negotiation,* was in progress.

## Selected works

### Nonfiction

*Can I Be Me?,* iUniverse, 2006.

### Plays

*Can I Be Me?,* 2007.
*Forgive Me?,* 2008.

## Sources

### Books

Armah, Esther, *Can I Be Me?,* iUniverse, 2006.

### Periodicals

*New York Amsterdam News,* July 24, 2008; July 23, 2009.

### Online

"Esther Armah," BBC News, http://news.bbc.co.uk/ 2/hi/programmes/crossing_continents/2892783. stm (accessed September 30, 2010).

—Deborah A. Ring

# Vernon Joseph Baker

## 1919–2010

### U.S. Army soldier

Baker, Vernon Joseph, photograph. AP Images/Barry Kough.

Vernon J. Baker was already one of the most highly decorated African Americans to serve in World War II when, on January 13, 1997, he was awarded the nation's highest military honor, the Congressional Medal of Honor. Although he was honored along with six other black World War II heroes, he was the only living African American soldier to receive the Medal of Honor for his service in that war, the others having died in the more than half century between their accomplishments in the service of their country and the U.S. government's recognition of same. Presenting the medals, President Bill Clinton acknowledged the injustice to which Baker and his fellow veterans had been subjected. "They were denied their nation's highest honor," he said, "but their deeds could not be denied, and they cleared the way to a better world."

### Fought to Join the Army

Vernon Baker was born on December 17, 1919, in Cheyenne, Wyoming. Both his parents were killed in an auto accident when he was four years old. He and his sisters were raised by their grandparents, and in his stern and husky grandfather, Joseph Baker, he found a figure to idolize.

Joseph Baker gave his grandson his first gun as a Christmas present, when the boy was twelve. His grandfather insisted that for every shot the boy fired he must bring home meat for the family. Baker quickly mastered marksmanship. While in high school he worked summers on the Union Pacific railroad. He was twenty when his grandfather died. With limited prospects for employment, he decided to enlist in the army because he had heard he could make a decent living as a quartermaster. When he went to enlist, however, a white recruiting officer told him, "We have no quotas for you people."

Undeterred, Baker tried again. He requested a post with the Quartermaster Corps, then watched the recruiting officer write on his enlistment form, "Infantry." Baker held his tongue, happy just to have been accepted. He married his sweetheart, Leola, on June 25, 1941, and left the next day for basic training.

### Arrived at the Italian Front

After Baker went through basic training in Texas, he

was sent to Officer Candidate School in Georgia. In the Deep South, Baker experienced racial animosity surpassing anything he had encountered in Wyoming. During World War II the army was segregated, and Baker endured harsh discrimination from whites both above and beneath his rank. He was abused by enlisted whites after he was promoted to sergeant; some whites refused to respect his rank or obey orders from him. Commissioned in early 1943 as a second lieutenant, Baker was assigned to the Ninety-Second Infantry Division, named the Buffalo Division, after the African-American "buffalo soldiers" of the Native American wars. Serving in a black unit under white officers rankled the young lieutenant. "The army decided we needed supervision from white Southerners," Baker told Allan Mikaelian, "as if war was plantation work and fighting Germans was picking cotton." He gradually earned the respect of the men under his command by following a simple code he described to Courtland Milloy of the *Washington Post,* "Give respect before you expect it. Treat people the way you want to be treated. Remember the mission. Set the example. Keep going."

Half a million African Americans served overseas during World War II. Baker's unit stayed out of the war until July of 1944, when he landed in Naples, Italy. For several months, he went on night patrols as a platoon leader. By October they had moved north into Tuscany. Under orders to capture a farmhouse near Seravezza, he sent three men ahead of him along the path to the house. All three were killed, and Baker was haunted by his responsibility. Baker himself was wounded in the

same operation. At first, he did not feel the bullet that struck his wrist, and he carried on until his men had taken the house. He woke up in a hospital near Pisa and was out of action for two months.

In early April of 1945, Baker and the Buffalo Division were in the foothills of the Apuan Alps. Joining them was the 442nd Regimental Combat Team, comprising Japanese Americans who had escaped the internment camps by volunteering for the armed services. The Germans were holding Castle Aghinolfi, a mountain fortress dating back to medieval times. Below the castle were three hills that the Americans called hills X, Y, and Z. The U.S. forces launched a major offensive to capture the garrison and suffered heavy casualties as the dug-in Germans repelled several assaults.

## Penetrated Enemy Lines

On April 5, Baker and his men were ordered to attack the castle. Baker started uphill at the head of his platoon before dawn. He took his M-1, but declined to put on his helmet, which impaired his hearing. Soon he spotted two figures crouching in a machine-gun nest. He shot them, and his men advanced. He observed, and destroyed, another machine-gun position and an observation post, and walked on ahead of all his men. As he went, he used wire cutters to destroy the enemy's communication lines.

The castle was now one deep canyon away; Baker had come closer than anyone on his side expected. His company's new commander, Captain Runyon, caught up with him on the hill. A German soldier appeared and tossed a grenade, which failed to explode. Runyon jostled Baker's rifle in his panic, but Baker recovered and shot the fleeing German. In the meantime, Runyon had disappeared.

Baker pressed on alone. He came dangerously near one camouflaged dugout, whose crew had paused for breakfast. He killed these enemy soldiers. Mortar shells began to fall and hit his men. Over the radio, his unit called in for support, but commanders refused to believe that his unit had penetrated so far past enemy lines. Baker found Runyon hiding in a stone house. The captain said he was going back for reinforcements, but he never returned. Later, Baker learned that Runyon had told command that Baker's men had been wiped out.

While waiting for reinforcements, Baker decided to set up a perimeter and attempt to hold their position. This was a fatal error, he admitted in retrospect. After a fierce German counterattack, the unit was down to eight men. Baker collected the dog tags from his dead comrades and watched for the reinforcements until he realized they were not coming. Then he led a retreat back down Hill X, taking out two machine gunners and a tank along the way.

That was Baker's final day in combat. He had lost nineteen of his men, but the attack was a decisive victory. The Germans pulled out that night. One month later, Benito Mussolini and Adolf Hitler were both dead, and the war in Europe was over.

The experience left Baker bitter and angry. He had experienced the futility of warfare. He would never stop regretting the deaths he might have prevented, among the Germans as well as his own men. What rankled him most of all was that he had gotten no thanks, no recognition that his men had surpassed all expectations, and no apology for the failure to send reinforcements.

On July 4, 1945, Baker received the Distinguished Service Cross for his bravery, the nation's second-highest military award. He had been recommended for the Medal of Honor, it turned out, but the paperwork was never forwarded to Washington, and Baker did not learn of it until decades later. Runyon, the officer who abandoned Baker and his men in the thick of the fight, was recommended for that honor instead. As it was, many white soldiers were displeased with the lesser recognition Baker received. After the war, Baker recounted in his memoir, a white colonel demanded that he take off his medal, saying, "Ain't no nigger I ever saw deserved no Distinguished Service Cross." Baker refused the colonel's direct order, potentially risking court-martial for insubordination. Although the incident went no further, Baker never forgot the disrespect he was shown.

Facing uncertain job prospects back home and divorced from his wife, Baker elected to remain in the military after the war. He remained in Italy for two years and reenlisted when his commission expired in 1947. He volunteered for combat duty at the start of the Korean War in 1950, but he was not assigned to a battle unit. The army was preparing for desegregation and needed decorated minority officers such as Baker to assume command positions. When desegregation became effective in 1951, Baker became a company commander in charge of white troops at Fort Campbell, Kentucky.

In 1953 Baker married Fern Brown, a divorcee with two daughters. They moved to California when Baker was transferred to Fort Ord, and there they had another daughter. The final addition to their family was an orphan, half-Korean and half-black, whom Baker adopted while serving in postwar Korea.

After his retirement from the military in 1968, Baker worked for the Red Cross for nearly twenty years counseling military families. Among the places this work took him was Vietnam, during the height of that country's long war. His wife died in 1986, and Baker retired to a small property in a part of rural Idaho that reminded him of his childhood years in Wyoming. He married Heidy Pawlik, a native of Germany, in 1993.

## Recognized for War Service

In the winter of 1996 Baker received a phone call from historian Daniel Gibran, who had been awarded a grant to investigate why no African Americans had received the Medal of Honor for service during World War II. Gibran's study found clear evidence of a racial disparity in the selection of Medal of Honor winners. On Gibran's recommendation, a panel of generals reviewed the records of ten Distinguished Service Cross recipients; that review led to the White House ceremony belatedly honoring Baker and the six deceased veterans. That month Baker was swamped with attention from the news media. One journalist, Ken Olsen of the *Spokane Spokesman-Review,* wrote a series of profiles of Baker, and later collaborated with him on the memoir *Lasting Valor.*

As President Clinton spoke of Baker's heroic actions on the Italian front, Baker's mind returned to Hill X, and to the nineteen men he lost that day. "I didn't cry for myself," during the ceremony, Baker wrote in his memoir. "I had made peace with the anger that burned my soul years earlier. I cried for the real heroes—those men I left behind on that hill, that day in April 1945." While Baker continued to brood over how he could have prevented their deaths, he told the Public Broadcasting System that, to him, receiving the belated Medal of Honor meant "that every black soldier that fought in the Second World War has been vindicated, every one."

In 2004 Baker had emergency surgery to remove a "baseball-sized" brain tumor that nearly killed him. He recovered well from the surgery but was inundated with medical bills. The community and many of Idaho's most prominent politicians came to the local hero's aid, volunteering, fundraising, and assisting Baker in cutting through layers of red tape to access his well-earned Medicare and Veteran's Administration benefits.

After the tumor, Baker was no longer able to pursue his passion for hunting, but he continued to be honored by civic groups and to speak out about his military service, the prejudice he and other soldiers had faced, and his opposition to the war in Iraq. He lost his battle with cancer on July 13, 2010, and was given a hero's burial at Arlington National Cemetery. Ironically, Baker had always insisted that he was no hero—just a soldier who'd done his job to the best of his ability. Although he was a career military officer and famed for his valor in battle, he never forgot the horror of war. "I hope no man, black, white, or any color, ever again has the opportunity to earn the Medal of Honor," he wrote in *Lasting Valor.* "War is not honor. Those who rush to launch conflict, and those who seek to create heroes from it, should remember war's legacy. You have to be there to appreciate its horrors. And die to forget them."

## *Selected writings*

(With Ken Olsen) *Lasting Valor,* Bantam, 1999.

## *Sources*

### *Books*

Mikaelian, Allen, *Medal of Honor,* Hyperion, 2002.
Smith, Larry, *Beyond Glory,* Norton, 2003.

### *Periodicals*

*New York Times,* January 14, 1997; July 15, 2010, p. B17.

*Spokesman-Review,* July 15, 2010; September 24, 2010.
*Washington Post,* May 2, 2004, p. C01.
*Wyoming Tribune-Eagle,* July 17, 2010.

### *Online*

"Idaho: A Portrait—Vernon Baker,"*Public Broadcasting System,* http://idahoptv.org/productions/idahoportrait/about/baker.html (accessed December 9, 2010).

—Roger K. Smith and Derek Jacques

# Herman Branson

## 1914–1995

### Physicist, educator

It is difficult to underestimate Herman Branson's impact on science and American education. Though best known as a physicist, his work often took him into other fields, including biology, biochemistry, and medicine. Long associated with Howard University, where he chaired the physics department for nearly three decades, he later served as president of two other prominent African-American schools, Central State University in Ohio and Lincoln University in Pennsylvania. A tireless advocate for increased minority participation in the sciences, he played a major role in increasing federal support for African-American universities.

Herman Russell Branson was born August 14, 1914, in Pocahontas, Virginia, a small community in the southwestern corner of the state. At some point in his childhood, his family moved to Washington, DC, where he won entrance to Dunbar High School, a segregated institution known nationwide for the stringency of its requirements. The training and dedication of Dunbar's teachers, many of whom held doctorates, helped Branson and his classmates overcome the inadequate funding, out-of-date textbooks, and other disadvantages that beset African-American schools under segregation.

Branson thrived at Dunbar, rising to become valedictorian of his senior class in 1932. Following graduation, he entered the University of Pittsburgh, where he studied for two years. He then transferred to what was known at the time as Virginia State College for Negroes (now Virginia State University), earning a BS

there in 1936. His undergraduate major is more likely to have been chemistry or mathematics than physics, which required expensive lab equipment and was considered an esoteric discipline at the time. After graduation he was offered a physics fellowship by the University of Cincinnati (UC). There he found a mentor in Boris Podolsky, an internationally renowned theoretician who had done extensive work with Albert Einstein. Under Podolsky's direction, Branson completed a doctoral dissertation on x-rays in 1939. The first African American to earn a PhD in a physical science at UC, he was also among the first nationwide to have done so in physics; according to author Daniel J. Kevles, there were no more than "about a dozen blacks" with physics doctorates before World War II. The racism and lack of educational opportunity that kept African Americans out of the sciences would persist for many years. Gradually, however, the situation began to improve, thanks in part to Branson's grassroots efforts to draw other African Americans into science and to support them once they got there.

His own career, meanwhile, was developing quickly. His first post after UC was at Louisiana's Dillard University, an African-American institution with roots stretching back to the late 1860s. After teaching chemistry and math there for two years (1939–41), he moved on to Washington, DC, where he joined the faculty of Howard University, arguably the best-known African-American school in the country. Hired in 1941 as an assistant professor of physics and chemistry and as chair of the physics department, he became a full

## At a Glance . . .

**B**orn Herman Russell Branson on August 14, 1914, in Pocahontas, VA; died June 7, 1995, in Washington, DC; married Corolynne; children: two. *Education:* Virginia State College for Negroes, BS, 1936; University of Cincinnati, PhD, physics, 1939.

**Career:** Dillard University, faculty member in physics and mathematics, 1939–41; Howard University, assistant professor of physics and chemistry, 1941–44, chair of physics department, 1941–68; professor of physics, 1944–68; Central State University, president, 1968–71; Lincoln University, president, 1971–85.

**Memberships:** National Association for Equal Opportunity in Higher Education, co-founder.

**Awards:** Senior Fellowship, National Research Council, 1948–49; honorary doctorates from many institutions, including Drexel University, 1982, and Northeastern University, 1985.

professor of physics three years later. He remained department chair for twenty-seven years (1941–68).

In addition to teaching and mentoring, Branson did research on a wide variety of topics, many of them related to larger issues in biology and medicine. By studying the physical structure of proteins and cells, he was able to make important contributions to the treatment of sickle-cell anemia, a debilitating, often fatal disease affecting primarily people of African descent. He also completed pioneering studies of the so-called "alpha helix," the most common protein structure. Much of his research in that area took place in 1948–49, when he worked at the California Institute of Technology on a fellowship from the National Research Council. His colleagues in California included the chemist Linus Pauling, who was later acknowledged as the co-discoverer (with Robert Corey) of the alpha helix. That attribution subsequently became highly controversial, largely because of Branson's exclusion. While many details of the discovery are now lost to history, there is little doubt that Branson, who co-authored a 1949 paper on the subject with Pauling and Corey, should have received much more credit than he was given.

Amid his research activities, Branson also worked tirelessly to build Howard's physics department by recruiting students, obtaining specialized equipment, and forging ties with the federal government. The last of these tasks was facilitated by the school's location in Washington and by pressing issues of national defense. During World War II, for example, the government asked him to establish a branch at Howard of the Engineering, Science, and Management War Training program, a national initiative to provide advanced technical training to defense-plant workers and others contributing to the war effort. Similar postwar programs focused above all on atomic fission, a major concern of the federal government during the nuclear arms race that began in the late 1940s.

By the 1960s, Branson's efforts as department chair had begun to draw the attention of administrators at other schools, and in 1968 he was asked to assume the presidency of Central State University, an African-American institution in the Midwest. He remained in that post for three years, stepping down in 1971 to become president of Lincoln University, renowned as the alma mater of poet Langston Hughes and U.S. Supreme Court Justice Thurgood Marshall. During his fourteen-year tenure there, he worked to improve the school's financial position and to strengthen its partnerships with the federal government and the Commonwealth of Pennsylvania.

Branson retired in 1985. He continued his involvement in education, in part by mentoring high school students. The recipient of honorary degrees from many institutions, including Drexel University (1982) and Northeastern University (1985), he died of heart failure at a Washington hospital on June 7, 1995, at the age of eighty. Surviving him were his wife, Corolynne, two children, and hundreds of former students, many of whom had corresponded with him for decades.

## Sources

### Books

Kevles, Daniel J., *The Physicists: The History of a Scientific Community in Modern America,* Knopf, 1977.

### Periodicals

*Jet,* June 26, 1995.
*New York Times,* July 13, 1995.

### Online

"Physicists of the African Diaspora: Herman Branson," University of Buffalo, http://www.math.buffalo.edu/mad/physics/branson_herman.html (accessed November 21, 2010).

—R. Anthony Kugler

# Dorothy Brunson

## 1938—

### Media executive

Dorothy Brunson is a fifty-year veteran of the media industry and the first African-American woman to own and operate radio and television stations in the United States. Brunson "is a dynamic entrepreneur whose hard work, persistence, imagination and business acumen have worked to her advantage in the hardball game of broadcasting," wrote Ken Smikle in *Black Enterprise.* Recognized as one of radio's leading marketing and managerial talents, Brunson is credited with developing the "urban contemporary" radio format, a mix of black and white music for sophisticated audiences that crosses racial barriers.

## Developed the Urban Contemporary Format

Born in rural Georgia and raised in New York City, Brunson graduated from Empire State College with a degree in business and finance. After beginning a career in print media, Brunson switched to the field of broadcasting in 1962. In 1964 she took a job as assistant controller of WWRL-Radio in New York City and was promoted to controller just three months later. She eventually became assistant general manager and acted as the liaison between WWRL and the station's parent company up until her departure in 1970. In 1971 she cofounded Howard Sanders Advertising, one of the first black advertising agencies in the United States. Brunson left with $115,000 in buy-out money the following year and, after a dress shop she'd purchased went out of business, was asked by Inner City Broadcasting (ICB), a start-up company, to organize

investors for its radio stations. After only four months in operation, ICB—which directed WLIB-AM Radio, a black community-oriented station—was over $1 million in debt and Brunson was hired as general manager to turn the station around.

During Brunson's first year at ICB, she reduced the staff size from thirty-five to eight, restructured the station's debt arrangement, and secured a loan to purchase WLIB-FM, the music counterpart of WLIB-AM. Brunson's strategy was to operate both stations with one staff and to broaden the playlist of the FM station so that it played not only established rhythm and blues music but also recordings by white artists with a black audience. Over the next five years this urban contemporary format resulted in a tremendous increase in both listeners and advertising revenues. By 1978 ICB had expanded from a company with $500,000 in annual sales to one that owned seven major-market radio stations, the billing of which exceeded $23 million. According to Simpson, Brunson's urban contemporary sound tapped into a huge and lucrative interracial audience "of the very 12- to 39-year-olds [that] advertisers sought." Brunson commented to Simpson on her objective: "We didn't design it to pioneer anything. We designed urban contemporary to be competitive. Advertisers were only buying black radio for products specifically geared to blacks. We tried to defy the myth and came up with the concept that people at the same economic levels generally purchase goods in a similar fashion."

After her success at ICB, Brunson was ready to establish her own radio empire. In 1979, with $500,000 in venture capital and a $2 million credit line, she purchased WEBB-Radio in Baltimore, Maryland. Over the next seven years Brunson elevated WEBB from number thirty-five to number ten in the ratings. To achieve this, Brunson overcame several difficulties. Shortly after she purchased the station, Brunson learned of the large back taxes owed and of the 600 Federal Communications Commission (FCC) violations amassed by WEBB. Complicating her position further, local stations fiercely opposed Brunson's efforts to establish what they claimed was an unnecessary additional station serving the black community. Meanwhile, neigh-

borhood groups protested Brunson's construction of radio towers in a section of the city where it was believed they would interfere with radio and television reception. Because of all these difficulties, WEBB operated in the red during its first four years. However, investors who were confident in Brunson's ability and proven track record in revitalizing radio stations supplied her with the capital she needed to transform the station. Greg Forest, the vice president of one of the firms that invested in Brunson, told Simpson, "We didn't invest in Dorothy because she was a woman or because she was black but because we thought she knew what she was doing and could make a profit for her and for us.... She's one of the hardest-working people I've ever met."

By 1986 Brunson had succeeded in transforming WEBB into a profitable black community-oriented station. She went on to purchase two more stations, WIGO-Radio in Atlanta, Georgia, and WBMS-Radio in Wilmington, North Carolina, which became part of her burgeoning company, Brunson Communications. She commented to Lloyd Gite in *Essence* of her intent to use the stations "as a propaganda tool, if you will, to enlighten and inform the Black community." She told Simpson that WEBB is known in Baltimore as "the community voice. We do a lot of very positive things like have basketball teams for little kids, a concert, Father's Day awards to highlight the importance of the father." Positive sales figures helped Brunson to fulfill these community roles; after six years of operation WEBB increased its advertising billing from $100,000 to over $800,000, and WIGO more than doubled its revenues during its first few years of operation.

Brunson described herself to Gite as someone who considers "power ... part of my motivation." Revealing her entrepreneurial spirit, she told Smikle that "there's a subliminal comfort in knowing the buck stops with you. You've got to make it or break it." She disclosed to Smikle another motivation: "I want to leave my children and grandchildren with a mentality that says, 'I can fight to get a piece of the American pie.'" By the end of the 1980s Brunson had entered into a food service venture with several other entrepreneurs to operate outlets in airports, aquariums, convention centers, and other public facilities. She was also nominated to the President's Advisory Council, and on three occasions she was a White House panelist in discussions on business and communications.

## Acquired Television Station

In 1989, after four years of hearings, Brunson became the first African-American woman to own a television station. By October of 1990 Bronson had sold all three of her radio stations to raise capital to get the station on the air. In 1992 Brunson Communications acquired the rights to broadcast via WGTW in Philadelphia, Pennsylvania, a frequency that had not been used for over nine years. Rather than hiring expensive lawyers, Brunson did most of the legal research herself to obtain the FCC license at a cost of $400,000, which saved her an estimated $1.5 million. Brunson transferred this frugality to other areas in the business, including acquiring and transporting a new transmitter, which she learned to repair herself, and completing trenching work around the premises.

Brunson recognized that the success of her station was only as good as the people she hired, and common sense and community awareness were prime indicators of worthwhile employees. "The first piece of advice I would give to any small-business person is to teach others in the company how to do what you do," Brunson told Catherine M. Petrini of *Training and Development.* "If you are a business owner, you should never worry about the threat of not having anything to do … it leaves you the time to do what you do best, which is to find new ways for your company to grow."

Brunson's management style was atypical. She never called her employees by their first name. Instead, she preferred to use the person's surname, prefaced by "mister" or "miss." She explained to Nanette Fondas in *Human Resource Planning,* "I find when you call everyone either Mr. or Ms., it works as a great equalizer, and the tendency to establish a pecking order is diminished." When she terminated an employee, Brunson gave the employee the exact reasons for being let go because she felt this helped the individual to become a better worker.

In 1997 Brunson's television station grossed $7 million in ad revenues. A year later the station was building a new production studio to broadcast original programming. Brunson's first new shows included *Health Check* and *Another View,* a current events program with a focus on crime stories. "If you're going to be a player and get recognition," Brunson said to Deni Kasrel of the *Philadelphia Business Journal,* "you have to do something that's going to make people look at what's current." In May of 1999 Brunson launched *48 Talk,* a topical issue debate show with audience and viewer participation.

By 2000 Brunson had gained a reputation as a savvy business forecaster and analyst and was called on to serve as a consultant to other small stations, such as WJYS-TV in Chicago, Illinois, and WDRL-TV in Danville, Virginia. Brunson's goal was to "help them find their niche in terms of how to maximize what they have, especially these independent guys who don't have a lot of money," Brunson said to *Electronic Media's* Jon Lafayette.

## Became a Multimillionaire

In January of 2003 WGTW celebrated its ten-year anniversary, which was now broadcasting in nineteen counties in Delaware, New Jersey, Maryland, and Pennsylvania. According to Deborah Bolling in the *Philadelphia City Paper,* Brunson's estimated net worth was between $60 million and $70 million in 2003. "I always used all of my own money. I didn't borrow money from anyone," Brunson said to Bolling "But then I realized that the return on your investment was greater in television than in radio—with the same amount of work." The following year, now sixty-six years of age, Brunson sold WGTW to Trinity Broadcasting Network for $48 million.

Now semiretired, Brunson still has holdings in two television stations, owns a public relations firm and an insurance company, and serves as executive director of the Maryland Center for Arts and Technology, where she develops workforce training programs for underemployed and unemployed youths aged seventeen to twenty-one years. As an active member of the African Methodist Episcopal Zion Church, Brunson travels frequently to Africa to organize women's groups and to establish schools, clinics, and new businesses. Brunson also helps young African-American women establish their own businesses. "Most of them have already stepped out but don't have a long range processing plan," Brunson said in *Top 100 Minority Business Enterprises 2007.* "I work with them to get access to capital and to network with other people who do the same things." Brunson also lectures widely on many topics in business, economic development, affirmative action, communications, human and women's rights, and religious freedom.

# Sources

### Periodicals

*Baltimore Business Journal,* March 14, 1997, p. 1.
*Black Enterprise,* April 1987, p. 45–46; August 1996, p. 68.
*Chicago Reporter,* November 30, 2009.
*Ebony,* December 1985, p. 152.
*Electronic Media,* February 1, 1999, p. 12.
*Essence,* June 1984.
*Human Resource Planning,* December 1991, p. 312.
*Philadelphia Business Journal,* June 19, 1998, p. 3.
*Philadelphia City Paper,* January 23–29, 2003.
*Top 100 Minority Business Enterprises 2007,* p. 85.
*Training and Development,* September 1992, p. 17.
*Working Woman,* August 1986.

—Michael E. Mueller and Marie O'Sullivan

# Lillian Scott Calhoun

## 1923–2006

### Journalist, public relations executive

Lillian Scott Calhoun was a pioneering journalist who worked in newsrooms in New York and Chicago, bringing attention to minority and civil rights issues and helping to integrate the field of journalism. In the 1960s, as a reporter for the *Chicago Defender,* a leading black-run newspaper, she stirred up controversy with her insightful column "Black and White," arousing the ire of politicians in city hall. In 1965 she became the first black woman ever to work as a reporter for the *Chicago Sun-Times,* and in 1972, she helped found the *Chicago Reporter,* an investigative paper focused on race and poverty. Throughout her career, Calhoun campaigned for black reporters to be treated with the same respect as their white peers, blazing a trail for future generations of black journalists.

Lillian Scott was born on June 25, 1923, in Savannah, Georgia, the youngest of four children of Walter Sanford Scott and his wife Laura. Her father was the founder and president of the Guaranty Life Insurance Company, a post he held for more than fifty years. As a girl, Lillian attended a laboratory school at Ohio State University in Columbus. There she developed an interest in journalism, encouraged by an English teacher who recognized her talent for writing.

After completing her undergraduate degree at Ohio State in 1944, her first job as a reporter was at the *Michigan Chronicle,* a black weekly newspaper based in Detroit, where her sister's husband, Louis Martin, was the editor. In 1945 Martin and his wife, Gertrude, launched the monthly news magazine *Headlines and Pictures,* with Lillian as a roving reporter. A year later,

the trio took the magazine to New York, then the hub of black life in America. They hoped that *Headlines and Pictures* "would do for black news what the *Times* had done for white news," she recalled in an interview with the *Chicago Tribune* in 1976. Though the magazine reached a circulation of more than 20,000, it folded after only a year and a half.

Lillian landed an assignment as the New York correspondent for the *Chicago Defender.* Working out of the paper's Harlem office, she covered everything from politics to social issues to celebrity news; however, she noticed that black reporters were not accorded the same respect as their white colleagues. "I found that filmmakers and Broadway theater operators didn't invite blacks to cover openings as they did whites," she explained to the *Tribune.* "This was wrong, because many black patrons attended those shows." As a result of her campaigning, black journalists began to get opening night invitations.

In 1950 Lillian married Harold Calhoun, whom she had met at Ohio State, and the couple moved to his home state of West Virginia, where her husband set up a law practice. Finding that there were few opportunities for black reporters—let alone a black woman—at the local papers, she set aside her career to raise a family. Almost a decade later, the Calhouns relocated to Chicago, and Lillian returned to journalism, first working in public relations for the Chicago Urban League and then as a reporter for *Ebony* and *Jet* magazines.

## At a Glance . . .

**B**orn Lillian Scott on June 25, 1923, in Savannah, GA; died on January 25, 2006, in New York, NY; daughter of Walter Sanford Scott and Laura (McDowell) Scott; married Harold William Calhoun on September 20, 1950; children: Laura, Harold, Walter, Karen. *Education:* Ohio State University, BA, 1944.

**Career:** *Michigan Chronicle,* reporter, 1944; *Headlines and Pictures,* reporter, 1945–47; *Chicago Defender,* New York correspondent, 1947–50; *Jet* and *Ebony* magazines, associate editor, 1961–63; *Chicago Defender,* columnist and features editor, 1963–65; *Chicago Sun-Times,* 1965–68; *Integrated Education* magazine, managing editor, 1968–71; *Chicago Journalism Review,* columnist, 1969–74; *Chicago Reporter,* founding editor, 1973–76; *Crain's Chicago Business,* columnist, 1978–80; Calmar Communications, president and founder, 1978–93.

**Memberships:** Alpha Gamma Phi; Chicago Network; Chicago Press Club; Society of Midland Authors.

**Awards:** Illinois Associated Press Award, 1966; Outstanding Achievement in Communications, Chicago YMCA, 1984; Victor F. Lawson Award, Community Renewal Society, 1992.

She rejoined the staff of the *Chicago Defender* in 1963, this time as a features editor and columnist, penning the column "Confetti," which covered civil rights issues. That year, she won second prize for feature writing from the National Negro Publishers Association. She left the *Defender* two years later, however, when she was told by her editor that she would have to give up her column because politicians at City Hall did not like what she was writing.

Calhoun joined the staff of the *Chicago Sun-Times* in 1965, becoming the first black woman ever to work in the paper's newsroom. Her article "Why Didn't They Scream?" about Richard Speck, who murdered eight nursing students on one night in 1966, earned her an Illinois Associated Press Award. From 1968 to 1971, Calhoun served as managing editor of the journal *Integrated Education,* a national publication focused on minority education, and from 1969 to 1974, she wrote a column for the *Chicago Journalism Review*

called "Black and White," providing commentary on the media's treatment of racial issues. Her writing also appeared in *Chicago Magazine, Crain's Chicago Business,* and *Reader's Digest.*

In 1972 Calhoun was a founding editor, together with John A. McDermott, of the *Chicago Reporter,* an investigative paper published under the aegis of the Community Renewal Society, a nonprofit mission of the United Church of Christ. Starting out as a four-page, bimonthly newsletter, within two years the *Reporter* had expanded to eight pages and a staff of seven reporters. The newsletter focused on issues of race and poverty and cast a particularly critical eye on corporate discrimination. "We want to pinpoint institutional racism," she explained to *Jet* magazine in 1974, "and show exactly how it works." During her four-year tenure as editor, the *Reporter* won two awards for journalistic excellence.

Calhoun left the newspaper business in 1978 to found her own public relations firm, Calmar Communications, with her sister Gertrude. The sisters' media savvy soon turned the business into one of Chicago's most successful black-owned firms, with revenues of $200,000 in 1981. That year, Calmar inked a $73,000 contract with the Chicago Board of Education to publicize its desegregation plan; other clients included the Chicago Urban League, the Illinois Service Federal Savings and Loan, and Urban Gateways, an arts education organization. "There are not that many black PR firms across the country," Calhoun explained to *Black Enterprise* magazine in 1982. "and as the tenor of the country turns away from minority concerns, the media tend to follow. It become important for black PR firms to get access to the media." Calmar Communications operated until 1993, when Calhoun retired.

In addition to her writing and public relations work, Calhoun also was a commentator for WBBM-AM radio and a producer and program moderator on WLS-AM, both in Chicago. In 1984 she received an award for Outstanding Achievement in Communication from the YMCA, and in 1992 she was honored by the Community Renewal Society with its Victor F. Lawson Award.

Calhoun died of respiratory failure at New York Presbyterian Hospital on June 25, 2006, at the age of 82.

## Sources

### Periodicals

*Black Enterprise,* March 1982.
*Chicago Tribune,* August 5, 1976; January 31, 2006.
*Jet,* December 26, 1974; March 13, 2006.

—Deborah A. Ring

# Barbara-Rose Collins

## 1939—

### Politician

In a city long known for its lively political landscape, Barbara-Rose Collins spent several decades as one of Detroit's most controversy-sparking Democrats. She had several years' worth of experience in the state legislature and on the Detroit City Council when, in 1990, she became the first African-American woman from Michigan to be elected to the U.S. House of Representatives. Voters later returned her to a seat on the city council, but in 2009 she announced she would not run later that year for what would be her sixth term. "I'm 70 years old, and I'm not sure how much longer I have. I want to accomplish some other things," she told *Detroit News* writers Darren A. Nichols and Charlie LeDuff. "My life isn't over, but it's winding down, and I want to put all of my effort into rebuilding the community."

### Relied on Government Assistance

Collins was born Barbara Richardson in Detroit in 1939; she later added her middle name, Rose, to her first name to distinguish her on the ballot. Her father, Lamar, once worked in one of Detroit's humming auto plants before eventually quitting to work as a general contractor. Collins was the first of four children born to Lamar and Versa, and she graduated from the elite Cass Technical High School in 1957.

After high school Collins enrolled in Wayne State University, where she took courses in anthropology and political science. While going to school, she met and eventually married Virgil Gary Collins. The couple had two children; a third child died at the age of two

months. Unable to maintain her studies, Collins was forced to drop out of college. Her plans for a college degree had evaporated, and her marriage followed suit. After her divorce she moved into her grandfather's house on the lower east side of Detroit and supported her children by working as many as three jobs at a time. Despite working multiple jobs and long hours, she was unable to make ends meet, so she applied for and received government assistance and food stamps. Collins eventually settled into a solid job at Wayne State University as a business manager in its Department of Physics.

During the late 1960s Collins became active in the Shrine of the Black Madonna Church, a center of cultural and social consciousness-raising in Detroit that helped boost a new generation of empowered, left-leaning young activists into mainstream politics. The shrine was led by Albert Cleage Jr., who adopted a more Afrocentric name of Jaramogi Abebe Agyeman around this time. In the wake of the disastrous Detroit riots of 1967, residents of what was becoming a majority-black city campaigned long and hard to secure genuine political power. During this period community organizers sought to decentralize the city's public schools via the creation of regional school boards, which gave parents more control over their local schools. Agyeman suggested to Collins that she should run for a seat on one of the newly created school boards. Collins agreed and set about campaigning for a seat. Her efforts proved successful, for in 1970 she won a seat on the Region 1 school board. "I went into politics to change conditions," she said in an *Ebony*

## At a Glance . . .

Born Barbara Rose Richardson on April 13, 1939, in Detroit, MI; daughter of Lamar N. Richardson Sr. (an autoworker and general contractor) and Versa Richardson (a homemaker); married Virgil Gary Collins (a pharmaceutical sales representative), c. 1958 (divorced); married Bruce Simpson Sr.; children: Cynthia Lynn, Christopher Loren. *Politics:* Democrat. *Religion:* Shrine of the Black Madonna Pan-African Orthodox Christian Church. *Education:* Attended Wayne State University.

**Career:** Wayne State University, business manager; Detroit School Board, member, 1971–73; Michigan House of Representatives, representative, 1975–81; Detroit City Council, member, 1982–91, 2002–09; U.S. House of Representatives, representative, 1991–97.

**Memberships:** American Civil Liberties Union; Congressional Black Caucus; Congressional Caucus for Women's Issues; League of Women Voters; National Order of Women Legislators.

**Addresses:** *Home*—2256 Leland St., Detroit, MI 48207.

interview many years later about this time in her life. "I found it was much easier to be a part of the system where the buck stopped at your table, rather than just demonstrating and making demands for your community."

Collins first ran for a seat on the Detroit City Council during the 1973 municipal election, but lost. That election was notable, however, for Coleman A. Young, a labor leader and state senator, was elected as the city's first African-American mayor. From the start, Young proved a feisty, intractable political presence who did much to permanently alter the political landscape of the city, and Collins became one of his staunchest allies. The mayor, in turn, supported Collins's political ambitions and often bestowed on her his crucial public endorsement in her various bids for office.

## Elected to State House

In February of 1974 Collins entered a special election to fill a seat in the Michigan Senate and came in second. Three months later she ran in another special election, this one to fill a vacancy in the Michigan House of Representatives left by the candidate who beat her in the February race, and lost by only sixty-three votes. In August of 1974 Collins entered the Democratic primary race to run for the Michigan House of Representatives, and this time she beat the incumbent by sixty-eight votes. The following November she won the election to represent the twenty-first district in the state legislature.

Collins was elected three more times to the state legislature, where she proved herself an able and effective lawmaker. She served as chair of the Constitutional Revision and Women's Rights Committee, fought hard for funding to help her beleaguered city, and sponsored two significant pieces of legislation: one was a food dating bill that required grocers to label perishable items with a "sell by" date; the second prohibited sexual harassment in the workplace. She was also involved in important changes to Michigan's domestic violence statutes and crusaded to guarantee reproductive rights for all women in the state.

In 1981 Collins ran for and won a seat on the Detroit City Council, at which point she resigned her seat in the state legislature. She served until January of 1991, but her career in municipal politics was less noteworthy than her previous stint as a state lawmaker. For much of the decade Collins held firm to a faction on the nine-member council that consistently sided with Mayor Young's often controversial initiatives. In 1988 she entered the Democratic primary race for Michigan's Thirteenth Congressional District. This was a bold move, for she challenged an icon of Detroit's civil rights era: the former judge George W. Crockett Jr., who had held the seat since 1980. She made a solid showing in that primary race but failed to garner enough votes. Two years later, in 1990, Crockett announced that he was not going to run for a sixth term. Aided by Young's endorsement, Collins won a crowded primary race with 34 percent of the vote and sailed through the November general election by a margin of 80 percent. Sworn into office in January of 1991, she was one of three new African-American females to enter the House of Representatives that year, along with Maxine Waters of California and Eleanor Holmes Norton of the Washington, DC. They joined Cardiss Collins of Illinois to make up the highest number of black women lawmakers in the House in U.S. history.

Collins's most high-profile piece of legislation in Congress was House Resolution 966, the Unremunerated Work Act of 1993. This bill would have compelled the U.S. Bureau of Labor Statistics (BLS) to begin tracking and including the value of unpaid labor—such as housework, child care, elder care, and other unpaid jobs done largely by women—in computing the nation's gross national product. Collins was the lead sponsor of the bill, which gained some notable endorsements from women's groups and labor organizations, but failed to make it pass the committee stage.

## *Battled Local Media*

Collins was regularly reelected to her seat in Congress by her constituents, but her congressional district suffered some of the highest population losses of any district during her tenure. It was eventually redistricted as Michigan's Fifteenth Congressional District, but it still included much of Detroit and some surrounding suburbs. It was known as a hard seat for an incumbent to lose, and at times Collins was reelected with as much as 84 percent of the vote. However, between 1995 and 1996 she was the focus of several negative news stories. One involved a wrongful termination lawsuit filed by her former spokesperson, who claimed she had fired him after his partner died of AIDS. The Office of Fair Employment Practice agreed with the plaintiff and ordered Collins to pay back pay and legal fees to the plaintiff. That story led to other reports that she had an extremely high staff turnover in her office and that she could be extravagantly imperious. For example, she refused to fly coach, and her attendance record for important House votes was revealed to be dismal. During this period the U.S. Department of Justice and the House Ethics Committee launched inquiries into possible misuse of campaign funds and scholarships monies. All of these factors contributed to a heated primary race during the summer of 1996.

Collins and the mainstream Detroit newspapers had had a long running battle dating back to her years on the city council. That war reached a boiling point in July of 1996, when an interview that appeared in one of the metro area's two main dailies, the *Detroit Free Press,* quoted her as saying that "racism is so ingrained in American society that there's nothing I can do about it. I think God is going to have to burn it out of white people," according to *Jet.* The *Jet* story also quoted from the *Free Press* article in which Collins allegedly said, "all white people, I don't believe, are intolerant. That's why I say I love the individuals, but I hate the race."

Even though Collins disputed the *Free Press* quotes, she still lost the August 6 Democratic primary race. Three days later the *Free Press* apologized, printing a front-age retraction admitting that her accusations of being misquoted were indeed correct. According to *Jet,* the taped transcripts of the interview revealed she

had actually said, "I love the individuals, but I don't like the race." The *Free Press* reporter who transcribed the interview was given a three-day suspension, and two editors who failed to fully investigate Collins's initial dispute were reprimanded.

## *Returned to the City Council*

Collins remained out of the public eye for a few years, but returned to politics in 2001 when she won a seat on the Detroit City Council again. She was reelected four years later, serving almost the entire time under a young mayor, Kwame Kilpatrick, whose mother had bested Collins during the 1996 primary race for the U.S. House of Representatives. In 2008 Mayor Kilpatrick was forced to resign from office in the wake of an adultery and perjury scandal, and in 2010 his mother, Carolyn Cheeks Kilpatrick, lost her reelection bid during the August primary race.

A few weeks after celebrating her seventieth birthday in 2009, Collins announced that she would not run again to retain her city council seat. "Almost my whole adult life has been in government, since I was 30 years old," she told Nichols and LeDuff, adding that she may "sit on the banks of the Detroit River and fish while I contemplate my next step."

# Sources

## *Periodicals*

*Black Enterprise,* April 1991, p. 25.
*Congressional Quarterly Weekly Report,* August 8, 1992, p. 2384.
*Crain's Detroit Business,* March 16, 2009, p. 1.
*Detroit News,* May 16, 2009.
*Ebony,* January 1991, p. 104.
*Hispanic,* July 1992, p. 72.
*Jet,* October 22, 1990, p. 38; August 19, 1996, p. 33; September 2, 1996, p. 23.
*Ms.,* May–June 1992, p. 91.
*Nation's Cities Weekly,* December 24, 1990, p. 3.
*New York Times,* December 12, 1991, p. A5; August 6, 1992; August 1, 1996.

—Paula M. Morin and Carol Brennan

# Blaise Compaore

## 1951—

### Army officer, politician

Compaore, Blaise, photograph. AP Images/Richard Drew.

Long a fixture in West African politics, Blaise Compaore has ruled the landlocked, desperately poor nation of Burkina Faso since 1987. An army officer by training, he moved into politics after a successful coup by his colleague Thomas Sankara in 1983. His own coup came four years later. In the decades since, Compaore has transformed himself, at least on paper, into a democrat, holding and winning no less than three elections; the fairness of those contests, however, has been disputed. A pragmatist who has earned some international praise for his efforts to mediate conflicts in nearby nations, he has also been heavily criticized for his own human rights record.

Blaise Compaore (sometimes spelled Compaoré) was born February 3, 1951, in Ouagadougou, by far the largest city in the Upper Volta district of what was then French West Africa. When the French left the region in the early 1960s, the independent nation of Upper Volta was born. Sankara, who made a number of sweeping alterations to the country's institutions, changed its name to Burkina Faso in 1984. Roughly the size of Colorado, it was home to more than fifteen million people as of 2010.

In 1973, at the age of twenty-two, Compaore was accepted as an officer candidate at an international military academy in nearby Cameroon. Competition there was fierce, in part because the army has traditionally been seen throughout West Africa as one of the surest routes to personal and professional success; if a candidate was found wanting at any time, there were dozens more eager to take his place. Compaore, for his part, seems to have done well, for he received his first army commission in 1975. He then traveled to France for further training. On his return, he rose rapidly through the ranks, earning a captain's commission in January of 1982.

The nation's political situation, meanwhile, was deteriorating rapidly. Angered by what they saw as the corrupt and bourgeois policies of President Jean-Baptiste Ouedraogo (or Ouédraogo), Sankara and several close supporters, Compaore included, overturned the regime in the summer of 1983 and announced the beginning of a Marxist revolution. Widely regarded as Sankara's second-in-command, Compaore held the title of minister of state, serving first as a presidential advisor and then as justice minister.

## At a Glance . . .

**B**orn February 3, 1951, in Ouagadougou, French West Africa (later Upper Volta, then Burkina Faso); married Chantal Terrasson. *Military service*: Army of Upper Volta, officer, 1975–83. *Politics*: Congrès pour la Démocratie et le Progrès. *Education*: Completed courses at officer training schools in Cameroon and France, 1970s.

**Career:** Army of Upper Volta, officer, 1975–83, Government of Upper Volta (Burkina Faso after 1984), minister of state, 1983–87, head of state, 1987–91, president, 1991—.

**Memberships:** International Raoul Wallenberg Foundation, honorary member.

**Addresses:** *Office*—c/o Embassy of Burkina Faso, 2340 Massachusetts Ave. NW, Washington, DC 2008-2896.

Several of Sankara's initiatives, including ambitious immunization and reforestation programs, won wide praise from the international community. He was less successful, however, in managing his subordinates. Relations with Compaore, in particular, deteriorated steadily, and in October of 1987 the nation's media abruptly announced Sankara's dismissal from office; it soon emerged that he had been murdered. While Compaore has steadfastly denied any involvement in that crime, there is no question that he was its principal beneficiary. With his charismatic predecessor out of the way, he was able to consolidate his power quickly and effectively. Over the next four years, he seems to have ruled as chief of state, not president, though the latter term was certainly applied to him informally. With the first of his election victories (1991), however, he officially became president.

The 1991 elections offered an early but clear picture of Compaore's tendency to vacillate between democracy and authoritarianism, a dichotomy that has come to characterize much of his political career. On the one hand, the elections came about only because of his insistence on a new constitution that respected democratic institutions and the rule of law. Few observers, on the other hand, considered the vote a fair one. Exasperated by what they felt was rampant favoritism toward Compaore and his coterie, a number of opposition groups boycotted the vote altogether. Given those circumstances, his election by a wide majority was not unexpected. He subsequently won re-election in 1998 and 2005; in the latter race, he finished with no less than eighty percent of the popular vote. Due to

a constitutionally mandated shift from a seven-year to a five-year term, he was scheduled to face the electorate again in November of 2010.

In his first years in power, Compaore concentrated on internal issues. By the early 1990s, however, his domestic position was secure enough to allow him more of a role in regional and international affairs. Here, again, his approach was marked by contradiction. For most of the decade, he had an unenviable reputation in other parts of West Africa, particularly in the small nation of Liberia, then in the throes of a terrible civil war. Under his direction, Burkina Faso provided money, arms, and logistical support to one of the most brutal factions in that conflict, Charles Taylor's National Patriotic Front of Liberia. Given that legacy, many observers were surprised when, Compaore seemed to change course around 1996, acting as a mediator and peacemaker in Liberia and several other nations struggling with civil conflict. Arguably his greatest accomplishment in this regard came in 2007, when a peace deal he helped negotiate was signed by feuding groups in Côte d'Ivoire (Ivory Coast).

As of September of 2010, however, there was some indication that Compaore had not fully renounced the heavy-handed tactics of his earlier years. Even as he was brokering peace elsewhere, he was widely suspected, for example, of fueling a bitter civil war in Sierra Leone. In August of 2000, diplomat Stephen Pattison told Blaine Harden of the *New York Times* that Compaore was sending troops and arms to rebels there, receiving so-called "blood" or "conflict" diamonds in exchange. A spokesperson for the president denied the charges.

In Burkina Faso, meanwhile, Compaore was devoting much of his time to the maintenance of public order. Though that focus made the country more stable than many of its neighbors, there was a significant cost in terms of human rights and social development. Ostensibly a multiparty democracy, the nation remained in many respects an autocracy, with an extensive internal security apparatus and little freedom of the press. Under those circumstances, it was perhaps unsurprising that little progress was being made on a vast array of social, economic, and environmental problems, including illiteracy, unemployment, rapid population growth, and desertification. According to the United Nations' Human Development Index, a broad measure of social and economic progress, in 2009 Burkina Faso ranked one hundred and seventy-seventh; only five nations fared worse.

## Sources

### Periodicals

*New York Times*, November 1, 1989; March 10, 1997; August 1, 2000.

## Online

"Biographie du Président," Government of Burkina Faso, http://www.presidence.bf/index.php (accessed November 21, 2010).

"Human Development Report 2009," United Nations Development Programme, 2009, http://hdr.undp. org/en/media/HDR_2009_EN_Complete.pdf (accessed November 21, 2010).

"The World Factbook: Burkina Faso," Central Intelligence Agency, November 9, 2010, https://www. cia.gov/library/publications/the-world-factbook/ geos/uv.html (accessed November 21, 2010).

—R. Anthony Kugler

# Stanley Crouch

## 1945—

### Writer, social critic

Crouch, Stanley, photograph. Mario Ruiz/Time Life Pictures/Getty Images.

Essayist Stanley Crouch is one of the most controversial cultural commentators of his age and one of the most influential music critics in the history of jazz. As a founder of Jazz at Lincoln Center, and mentor to the program's artistic director, Wynton Marsalis, Crouch has shaped public opinion of an entire musical genre in a manner that few critics could hope for or imagine. His essays and newspaper column have given Crouch platforms to criticize some of the most revered names and ideas in African American culture, making the roster of his enemies as distinguished as his admirers. His idiosyncratic and confrontational intellect has made Crouch a MacArthur Foundation "genius" grant recipient and two-time National Book Critics Circle Award finalist.

## Swept up in Black Militant Movement

Born in 1945 in South Central Los Angeles, Stanley Crouch was a bookish child. Asthma forced him to spend much of his childhood indoors, time Crouch spent devouring American literature and developing an obsession for jazz that would last his lifetime. Crouch's father, a drug addict who was in jail at the time of his birth, was not in the picture most of the time; Stanley and his siblings were raised by their mother, Emma Bea, a domestic worker who insisted that her children be acquainted with the works of William Shakespeare and who taught Stanley to read before he started school. "She was an aristocrat in that strange American way that has nothing to do with money," Crouch told the New Yorker's Robert Boynton.

After high school, Crouch studied at a pair of junior colleges, but did not earn a degree. He worked raising funds for the Student Nonviolent Coordinating Committee (SNCC), a civil rights organization, and he became interested in drama and poetry, particularly the works revolutionary writer LeRoi Jones, better known as Amari Baraka. After the Watts riots of 1965, the community around Crouch radicalized, and the idea of a non-violent civil rights movement began to be replaced with the more militant attitudes of black nationalism. "I was very impressed by the nationalist business for a while," he told Helen Dudar of the Wall Street Journal. "It had a certain appeal that stuff always has—it simplified the world. And all the ambiguities of human conduct don't have to

**B**orn December 14, 1945, in Los Angeles, CA; son of James and Emma Bea (a maid) Crouch. Married Samerna (divorced); daughter Dawneen; married Gloria Nixon (a sculptor). *Education:* Attended East Los Angeles Junior College and Southwest Junior College.

**Career:** Worked for Student Nonviolent Coordinating Committee, c. 1964; member of Watts Repertory Theatre Company, 1965–67; Pitzer College, poet-in-residence, beginning 1968, became member of faculty of Black Studies Center; instructor in English, Pomona College, until 1975; staff writer, *Village Voice*, New York City, 1980–88; artistic consultant, Jazz at Lincoln Center, 1987—; contributing editor, *New Republic*, 1990–95(?); columnist, *New York Daily News*, 1995—; columnist, *Jazz Times,* 2001–03.

**Awards:** Whiting Foundation Writers' Award, 1991; Fellowship, MacArthur Foundation, 1993.

**Addresses:** *Home*—New York, NY. *Agent*—Georges Borchardt Agency, 136 E. 57th St., New York, NY 10022.

be addressed. If you have two people in a store and one is selling superiority while the other is selling equality, the person selling superiority is going to have a line around the block. That is the appeal of Black Nationalism: it is saying that black people are superior and white people are inferior."

## Gained Notice for His Poetry

In the aftermath of the riots, arts programs sprung up in South Central Los Angeles, and Crouch was drawn to them. He participated in poetry workshops and joined Studio Watts, a theater repertory in which he performed and wrote plays. He also became close with Studio Watts's leader, poet Jayne Cortez. Crouch described her influence to Boynton: "I'd never met anyone with that kind of aesthetic commitment, who'd drawn a line in the dirt and said, 'I am an artist.'" It was an example Crouch would strive to follow throughout his life. Cortez also introduced Crouch to the works of Ralph Ellison.

Eventually, Crouch's poetry attracted enough attention that, despite his lack of a college degree, in 1968 he was invited to teach at Pitzker College as a poet-in-residence. In short order, he became a full-time faculty

member in the Claremont Colleges system, first in Black Studies and later in the English department of another Claremont school, Pomona College. At Pomona, Crouch wrote and put on plays designed to shock audiences, both black and white; he published a collection of poems, *Ain't No Ambulances for No Nigguhs Tonight*; and made an impression on a roster of students that included the likes of movie producer Lynda Obst, playwright George C. Wolfe, New Age guru Marianne Williamson, engineer W. Cedric Johnson, and poet Garrett Hongo. Just a few years older than the people he was teaching, Crouch lived among students and sometimes carried on relationships with them. One of those relationships led to Crouch's first marriage.

While he was at Claremont, Crouch's obsession with jazz took on a new form. He had taught himself how to play the drums in the mid-1960s, and now decided it was time to form a band. The band, Black Music Infinity, played in the avant-garde style that was popular at the time. With a terrific ear for musicianship, Crouch selected four band-mates who would all go on to successful careers as performers. All of them, that is, except Crouch. "The problem was that I couldn't really play," he admitted to Boynton. "Since I was doing this avant-garde stuff, I didn't have to be all that good, but I was a real knucklehead. If I hadn't been so arrogant and had just spent a couple of years on rudiments, I'd have taken it over, man—no doubt about it."

## Moved to New York CIty

Regardless, by 1975 Crouch was tired of the academic life. Along with Black Music Infinity's tenor saxophonist, David Murray, Crouch moved to New York, hoping that he would prove himself there as a musician or as a writer.

At first Crouch embraced the subsistence lifestyle of East Village arts scene. He handled jazz bookings at a club where he sometimes worked as bouncer. He also wrote book and music reviews, promoting avant-garde performers. However, during this period Crouch's worldview began to shift. Poet Larry Neal had introduced Crouch to critic and author Albert Murray in 1970. Crouch and Murray quickly found that they shared a passion for jazz and literature, but wildly divergent politics. "[W]e never talked about black power but I had some awareness he was involved with that sort of thing," Murray told Alice Steinbach of the *Baltimore Sun*. "I thought he was too smart to be wasted on that kind of stuff."

Once Crouch moved to New York, the influence of Murray and likeminded Harlem resident Ralph Ellison grew. Murray and Ellison shared a view of race relations that emphasized assimilation over separatism. They argued, in Murray's words, that "the so-called black and so-called white people of the United States resemble nobody else in the world so much as they resemble each other," and that the greater good fell with blacks and whites pulling together behind their shared American identity rather than emphasizing their differences.

Crouch came to accept Murray as more than just a mentor, but as someone who was "far more my father than the fellow whose blood runs through my veins," as Crouch later wrote in *The All-American Skin Game.* He embraced not only Murray's political philosophy, but also his aesthetic approach, which favored traditional jazz over the avant-garde and jazz/rock fusion movements that were then ascendant. By the time Crouch became the first full-time black staff member at the left-leaning *Village Voice,* he had gone from being a member of the black militant and avant-garde jazz movements to being one of both movements' harshest critics.

## Became the "Hanging Judge" of Criticism

Although the change in Crouch's opinions had been gradual, many of his friends felt betrayed by his new views and artistic sensibilities. Many avant-garde performers Crouch had once championed now received poor notices in the *Voice,* and Amari Baraka, who once inspired Crouch's interest in poetry and drama, was "intellectually irresponsible" and "one of the greatest disappointments of his era" in one of Crouch's *Voice* columns.

As Crouch's portfolio grew from arts criticism to commenting on news and politics, more and more of his former fellow travelers expressed their outrage, calling him a sell-out, a traitor, an Uncle Tom. Speaking to Boynton, critic Bell Hooks claimed Crouch had "seen that it pays off when you kiss the ass of white supremacy." Crouch gave as well as he got, and no figure was too big or too revered to escape the jab of his pen. He dismissed Toni Morrison's Pulitzer Prize–winning novel, *Beloved,* as "protest pulp fiction," and "a melodrama lashed to the structural conceits of a miniseries." He labeled filmmaker Spike Lee a "nappy-headed Napoleon" and Nation of Islam leader Louis Farrakhan a "nutcase."

With black nationalism ebbing in the era of Ronald Reagan, Crouch found a new and lasting enemy in the nascent hip hop movement. Hip hop seemed as if it had been created specifically to irritate Crouch: as a musical aesthete, he deplored the lack of musicianship rappers displayed, and as a social critic, he was repulsed by the messages in rap lyrics. "It's either an infantile self-celebration or anarchic glamorization of criminal behavior," he told Lynda Richardson of the *New York Times.* "I don't see what's good about it."

Crouch's rhetorical jabs at rap made him a whole new host of enemies, but it was a physical jab that got him

in trouble. Crouch came to blows with another *Voice* staffer during an argument about hip hop, and the newspaper fired him. According to Boynton, after his dismissal Crouch broke down in tears, worried that his inability to control his temper had just cost him his career.

Time would prove his concerns overblown. "The two best things that ever happened to me were being fired by the *Voice* and being hired by the *Voice,* in that order," he told Boynton. He made a good living freelancing, and in 1990 became a contributing editor at the *New Republic.* A collection of his *Voice* columns, *Notes of a Hanging Judge,* won Crouch strong notices, a National Book Critics Circle Award nomination, and a Whiting Foundation fellowship. In 1993 Crouch received a prestigious MacArthur Foundation "genius" grant, and in 1995 his second collection of essays, titled *The All-American Skin Game,* was published to acclaim. The O. J. Simpson case and murder trial raised Crouch to a new level of celebrity, as the writer was a sought-after commentator in the twenty-four-hour television coverage that attended the racially polarized proceedings. His new public profile briefly won Crouch a part-time spot as a commentator on *60 Minutes* and fueled his third collection of essays, *Always in Pursuit.*

## Co-Founded Jazz at Lincoln Center

In 1980 the same year he took his job at the Voice, Crouch met Wynton Marsalis. Marsalis was then a young trumpeter with Art Blakey's band; Crouch was immediately impressed with Marsalis's technique, even though he "didn't hear much jazz" in the compositions the youngster was playing. Crouch invited Marsalis to his apartment for dinner, where the two had a wide-ranging conversation about jazz and its history. Enthused by Marsalis's intellect and curiosity, Crouch sent him home with some albums and a copy of Murray's book, *Stomping the Blues.* An important mentorship had begun, one in which Crouch would open Marsalis to the possibilities presented by Duke Ellington, Louis Armstrong, Ornette Coleman, and others.

Crouch considered that, by the early 1980s, jazz as he knew it was in peril. The experimentation of the 1970s had stretched the genre to formlessness; meanwhile jazz was losing talent to funk and jazz-rock fusion, which performers hoped would be more popular and lucrative. Although Crouch and Murray were forcefully espousing their views on the aesthetics and future of jazz, there was only so much they as critics could accomplish. Having a world-class musical talent like Marsalis on their side changed everything. Marsalis turned out to not only be an apt pupil, but also an eloquent advocate for Crouch and Murray's views on jazz. Marsalis was able to influence performers, by his example as well as his words. As Marsalis's prominence in the jazz community grew, so did the ranks of "neoclassical" performers of traditional jazz.

For jazz to thrive, Crouch and his associates felt, it would need institutional support of the sort classical music enjoyed. The opportunity came when Lincoln Center approached Crouch and Marsalis about organizing a series of jazz concerts during the cultural center's slow summer season. With the help of New York City political insider Gordon Davis, Jazz at Lincoln Center went from an annual concert series to a yearlong program and eventually became a full department at Lincoln Center, equivalent to the Metropolitan Opera, New York City Ballet, or the New York Philharmonic. Marsalis served as the new organization's artistic director, and Crouch as its artistic consultant. The Jazz at Lincoln Center Orchestra toured the world, and its Essentially Ellington High School Jazz Band Program aimed to teach youngsters around the country the fundamentals of jazz. Crouch personally petitioned the mayor of New York for space in a new development at Columbus Circle to build a home for Jazz at Lincoln Center, thought to feature the first concert space in the world built specifically for jazz performance.

All this progress did not come without controversy. One of Crouch's most famous ideas was that jazz was a metaphor for American democracy—individuals working in concert, listening to each other and improvising within a structure. Ironically, the main complaint about Jazz at Lincoln Center was that it was undemocratic, that Crouch, Marsalis, and Murray used their influence to exclude voices with which they disagreed, presenting only their viewpoint of jazz with no room for dissent. Despite the many claims that Crouch was a self-hating Uncle Tom, many of those who felt excluded by Jazz at Lincoln Center's program were white and European performers who didn't fit into the aesthetic of traditional jazz espoused by Crouch.

Crouch's views on jazz received a substantial boost when filmmaker Ken Burns produced Jazz, a ten-part documentary on the history of jazz in 2001. Crouch, Marsalis, and Murray—whom Burns jokingly called the "evil triumvirate" in an interview with Newsweek—consulted on the project and were prominently featured on screen as "talking head" commentators. Burns's narrative for Jazz would largely follow the triumvirate's traditionalist views. Those views were now jazz's official story.

### Clashed Violently with Critics

Crouch's career was marked by long-gestating projects. As of November of 2010, his multivolume biography of saxophonist Charlie Parker—a project Crouch started in 1982—remained unpublished. Similarly, Crouch's debut as a novelist was long awaited. In the mid-1990s there was a sprawling work in development called First Snow in Kokomo, which Boynton claimed contained "every thought that Stanley Crouch has ever had." The first novel that actually arrived in 2000, Don't the Moon Look Lonesome, was set on a somewhat smaller scale. It was a tale of romance between jazz musicians, told from the perspective of a blonde singer from South Dakota, whose relationship with a black tenor saxophonist is imperiled by their racial differences. Given the polarizing nature of its author, it came as no surprise that reviews of Don't the Moon Look Lonesome were mixed. Washington University professor Gerald Early called it "Perhaps the best chronicle of jazz and American life ever written." In the New York Times James Campbell praised the novel's "sympathetic" intentions, but ultimately declared that "rhythm is what is missing from this novel." However, the strongest salvo came from novelist Dale Peck, writing in the New Republic, who dismissed Don't the Moon Look Lonesome as "a terrible novel, badly conceived, badly executed, and put forward in bad faith; reviewing it is like shooting fish in a barrel." Peck didn't like a single word of the novel, not even its dedication.

Peck's review was, ironically, the same type of in-your-face provocation at which Stanley Crouch excelled. As much a rejection of Crouch's world view as of his novel, Peck insisted that Crouch "wasn't just a bad novelist," but something more sinister, and that his rhetoric "lacked the sophistication" of the hip hop performers he reviled. Despite a reputation for savoring the blood sport of debate with his detractors, Crouch seemed bothered by Peck's review, calling him a "troubled queen" to Heather Caldwell of Salon.com. However, when Crouch ran into Peck at a New York City eatery, he shook the critic's hand...and then slapped him across the face with his other hand.

This incident, combined with the assault that got him fired from the Voice, and another bout of fisticuffs after the first annual Jazz Journalist Association Awards ceremony, have earned Crouch a reputation as one of the most paradoxical figures in American letters, as troubling as he is thought-provoking. While pillorying hip hop for its celebration of thuggishness, he resorts to physical violence and intimidation against critics; while decrying the vulgarity of pop culture, he indulges in scatological name-calling, for example, denouncing talk show host Tavis Smiley in a column for the Daily Beast website as a "deluded teenager in love with the smell of his own piss."

Despite the controversies, Crouch continued to be a top critic and social commentator. In 1995 his columns began appearing in the New York Daily News, and he was a contributing writer in publications such as the Daily Beast and the Jazz Times. In 2006 he published his first book dedicated to jazz criticism, Considering Genius. As of December of 2010, his autobiography of Charlie Parker, Kansas City Lightning, was pending publication.

# Selected works

*Ain't No Ambulances for No Nigguhs Tonight,* R. W. Baron, 1972.

*Notes of a Hanging Judge,* Oxford University Press, 1990.

*The American Skin Game, or The Decoy of Race: The Long and the Short of It,* Pantheon, 1995.

*Always In Pursuit: Fresh American Perspectives,* Pantheon, 1997.

*Don't the Moon Look Lonesome,* Pantheon, 2000.

*The Artificial White Man: Essays on Authenticity,* Basic, 2004.

*Considering Genius: Writing on Jazz,* Basic, 2006.

# Sources

## Periodicals

*Baltimore Sun,* December 31, 1995.
*Booklist,* August 1, 2006.
*Nation,* May 21, 1990, pp. 710–11.
*New Republic,* May 22, 2000, p. 36.
*Newsweek,* January 8, 2001, p. 58.
*New Yorker,* November 6, 1995, pp. 95–115, May 22, 2000, p. 92.
*New York Times,* August 29, 1993, section 4, p. 7, April 30, 2000.
*Time,* June 12, 1995, p. 35.
*Village Voice,* May 13, 2003, July 20, 2004.
*Wall Street Journal,* November 29, 1991, p. A5.

## Online

"Wake Up, Tavis Smiley," *Daily Beast,* April 23, 2010, http://www.thedailybeast.com/blogs-and-stories/2010-04-23/wake-up-tavis-smiley/ (accessed November 23, 2010).

"Blues for Clement Greenberg," *Jerry Jazz Musician,* May 4, 2003, http://www.jerryjazzmusician.com/mainHTML.cfm?page=greenberg.html# (accessed November 23, 2010).

"Pecked," *Salon.com,* July 24, 2002, http://www.salon.com/books/feature/2002/07/24/peck (accessed November 23, 2010).

—Simon Glickman and Derek Jacques

# Ulysses Grant Dailey

## 1885–1961

### Surgeon, editor, professor, administrator

As one of the first African Americans to be internationally recognized in the field of medicine, Dr. Ulysses Grant Dailey broke all racial barriers during the early part of the twentieth century. After receiving his doctorate of medicine from Northwestern University, Dailey went on to excel in surgery. During the early part of his career he also worked as a teacher of anatomy and physiology, with many of his students achieving levels of excellence in their areas of expertise. When he was elected to the International Board of Trustees of the International College of Surgeons, he became an ambassador of American medicine, in which he played an integral role in helping to improve the health care systems in countries throughout the world.

Dailey was born in Donaldsonville, Louisiana, in 1885 to Tony and Missouri Dailey. His parents separated a few years after his birth, and Dailey was brought up by his mother in an atmosphere of books and music. Dailey's early schooling was split between Donaldsonville, Chicago, Illinois, and Fort Worth, Texas.

While a student at Fort Worth High School, Dailey became the office boy for Dr. Ernest L. Stephens, a white practicing physician and professor in the medical department of Fort Worth University. When the typhoid epidemic struck the city, Dailey accompanied Stephens on his house calls, assisting him with routine tasks. Stephens was so impressed with Dailey's intelligence and focus that he encouraged Dailey to pursue a career in medicine. Dailey enrolled in Straight College (now Dillard University) to earn his bachelor's degree and, after several conversations with the dean, was accepted into the Northwestern University Medical School in 1902. Even though he was the youngest of the 150 students in his class and had to work his way through medical school, Dailey did so well that Peter T. Burns, the director of the anatomical laboratory, hired him as his assistant in 1903. Dailey worked alongside Burns for two years, and in 1906 he earned his doctorate of medicine, coming fifth in his class.

Following graduation, Dailey became an assistant demonstrator of anatomy at Northwestern University. Dailey's high score on a highly competitive civil service exam earned him a place as an ambulance surgeon for the Chicago Department of Health in 1907. He held this position until 1909 and, according to the January of 1950 issue of the *Journal of the National Medical Association,* Dailey gained a reputation as "one of the most efficient and best-liked surgeons in the service."

In 1907 Dailey joined Provident Hospital in Chicago, where he was appointed gynecologist of the dispensary. The following year was a turning point for Dailey when the pioneering black surgeon, Daniel Hale Williams, hired him as his surgical assistant. With Williams as his mentor, Dailey gained invaluable experience assisting in operations and preparing lectures, articles, and papers. That same year Dailey joined the National Medical Association (the black counterpart of the American Medical Association), a society in which he enjoyed a rich and lasting relationship throughout his career. He served as president of the organization from 1915 to 1916, and from 1910 to 1949 he was a member of the editorial board of the *Journal of the*

## At a Glance . . .

**B**orn on August 3, 1885, in Donaldsonville, LA; died on April 22, 1961, in Chicago, IL; son of Tony Hannah Dailey (bartender) and Missouri (Johnson) Dailey (teacher and dressmaker); married Eleanor Jane Curtis, 1916; children: Ulysses Jr., Eleanor. *Education:* Dillard University (formerly Straight College); Northwestern University Medical School, MD, 1906.

**Career:** Northwestern University, assistant demonstrator of anatomy, 1906–07; Chicago Department of Health, ambulance surgeon, 1907–09; Provident Hospital Dispensary, gynecologist, 1907–17; Provident Hospital Training School, anatomy and physiology instructor, 1909–17; Chicago Medical College, experimental surgery instructor, 1916–17; Provident Hospital, surgical nursing instructor, 1920–25; Dailey Hospital and Sanitarium, founder and head, 1926–32; Provident Hospital, senior attending surgeon, 1932, became senior consulting surgeon and senior attending surgeon emeritus; *Journal of the National Medical Association*, editorial board, 1910–43, associate editor, 1943–48, editor-in-chief, 1948–49; U.S. Department of State, visiting surgeon in Pakistan, 1952.

**Memberships:** National Medical Association (president, 1915–16); John A. Andrew Clinical Society; American Board of Surgery; American Medical Association; American College of Surgeons; International College of Surgeons; Institute of Medicine of Chicago; International Board of Trustees, International College of Surgeons; National Order of Honor and Merit, Haitian Government.

**Awards:** Honorary ScD, Howard University, 1947; Distinguished Service Award, National Medical Association, 1949; Honorary ScD, Northwestern University, 1955.

*National Medical Association,* becoming associate editor from 1943 to 1948 and editor in chief from 1948 to 1949. In 1949 the National Medical Association honored him with the Distinguished Service Award.

From 1909 to 1917 Dailey was also an instructor of anatomy and physiology at the Provident Hospital

Training School. During this time he left briefly in 1912 to pursue postgraduate study in surgical subjects in Paris and Berlin. From 1916 to 1917 he served as an instructor of experimental surgery at the Chicago Medical College. From 1920 to 1925 Dailey taught surgical nursing at Provident Hospital, and in 1925 he returned to Europe for seven months to study in medical centers and hospitals in London, Manchester, Leeds, Paris, Vienna, and Rome. When he returned from Europe, he purchased two houses in Chicago and established the Dailey Hospital and Sanitarium.

During its six years of operation, Dailey Hospital earned a reputation as a facility that performed numerous safe and successful surgical procedures on black patients. Due in part to the Great Depression, Dailey closed the hospital in 1932 and returned to Provident Hospital, where he was appointed senior attending surgeon before going on to become the hospital's senior consulting surgeon and head of its resident training program.

Throughout his career, Dailey trained a number of African-American surgeons who went on to positions of great responsibility within the medical community. He assisted in the formation of several postgraduate facilities in the southern United States, where he regularly held surgical clinics and educational lectures in institutions such as Meharry Medical College in Nashville, Tennessee, and the John A. Andrew Clinical Society in Tuskegee, Alabama. He was also the featured lecturer for numerous medical organizations, including the first Hale-McMillan Lecture at Meharry Medical College, the Cheatham Memorial Lecture of the Mound City Medical Society in St. Louis, the Austin M. Curtis Memorial Lecture at Howard University, and the Cassasa Memorial Lecture at Harlem Hospital, New York.

In 1935 Dailey became a charter member of the International College of Surgeons (ICS). In this capacity he made several extended trips to Pakistan, India, Japan, and other countries where he held surgical clinics, gave lectures to undergraduate and graduate students, and promoted better health care systems. In 1952 he was elected to the International Board of Trustees of the ICS and embarked on a three-year world tour with other surgeons as emissaries of the organization. Under the auspices of the U.S. Department of State Dailey returned to Pakistan in 1952, where he served as a visiting surgeon and established a chapter of the ICS in Karachi. The following year he accompanied Albert Schweitzer on a five-day trip to Schweitzer's Forest Hospital in Lambaréné, Gabon. In 1954 the Haitian government ordained Dailey an officer of the National Order of Honor and Merit.

Dailey retired from his position at Provident Hospital in 1952 and from active practice in 1956. The following year Dailey and his wife, Eleanor, moved to Port-au-Prince, Haiti, where they hoped to spend their retirement. However, in less than two years Dailey was forced to return to Chicago due to ill health and in April of 1961 he died of heart failure. He was survived by his wife and their adopted twins born in 1919, Ulysses Grant Jr. and Eleanor.He Hekdfjkjd

## *Selected writings*

"Total Congenital Absence of the Veriform Appendix in Man," *Surgery, Gynecology, and Obstetrics,* October 1910, pp. 413–16.

"The Future of the Negro in Medicine," *Journal of the National Medical Association,* July–September 1929.

"Proposals with Reference to the Idea of a Negro College of Surgeons," *Journal of the National Medical Association,* March 1942.

"Diagnostic Problems Relating to Appendicitis," *Journal of the National Medical Association,* March 1957.

## *Sources*

### *Periodicals*

*Journal of the National Medical Association,* March 1943, pp. 64–65; January 1950, pp. 39–40; July 1961, p. 432.

—Marie O'Sullivan

# Gail Devers

## 1966—

### Track and field athlete, entrepreneur

Devers, Gail, photograph. Matthew Stockman/Getty Images.

Gail Devers is among the fastest combination female sprinters and hurdlers in history. Over the course of her competitive career, Devers has succeeded through a rare blend of power, speed, and intense concentration. "I never know where I am in a race," Devers was quoted as saying in the *New York Times*. "When I cross the finish line, I wait for someone to say, 'Gail Devers, you won' or 'Gail Devers, you lost.'" This ability to block out distractions is part of the formula that has resulted in so many of Devers's triumphs.

Even though Devers's accomplishments as an athlete are unquestioned, she is perhaps best known for having overcome a serious illness that almost rendered her permanently disabled. Early in her career, she was diagnosed with Graves' disease, a dangerous thyroid condition. She battled the ailment for two years, intent on pursuing her dreams of athletic glory. Devers eventually overcame her condition and made a dramatic return to competition, establishing herself as one of the leading female track and field performers in the world. Initially known primarily as a hurdler, she stunned audiences with her victory in the 100-meter sprint at the 1992 Olympics in Barcelona, Spain. Devers later won gold in two more events at the 1996 Olympics in Atlanta, and she continued to compete at the highest level well into the twenty-first century.

### Drew Strength from Her Religion

A deeply religious woman, Devers believes that God played a vital role in defeating her illness and helping her realize her potential as an athlete. Her faith was established at an early age. Devers was born on November 19, 1966, in Seattle, Washington, and grew up in San Diego, California. She was the daughter of Reverend Larry Devers, a Baptist pastor. Regarding her childhood, Devers told *Sports Illustrated,* "We were a Leave It to Beaver family.... We had picnics, rode bikes and played touch football together. We did Bible studies together." She began winning gold medals during her adolescence; while attending Sweetwater High School in National City, her outstanding performance on the women's track team helped the school win the San Diego sectional track and field team title. In 1984, at the age of seventeen, Devers won the 100-meter dash and 100-meter hurdles at the state high school track and field

## At a Glance . . .

**B**orn Yolanda Gail Devers, November 19, 1966, in Seattle, WA; daughter of Larry (a minister) and Alabe Devers (a teacher's aide); married Ron Roberts, 1988 (divorced, 1991); married Mike Phillips; children: Karsen. *Education:* University of California at Los Angeles, BA, sociology, 1988.

**Career:** Won 100-meter dash and 100-meter hurdles in California high school state championships, 1984; earned berth on U.S. Olympic team, 1988; set American record and earned silver medal in 100-meter hurdles, World Track & Field Championships, 1991; won gold medal (100-meter dash) at Olympics in Barcelona, Spain, 1992; ran world's fastest time in 100-meter hurdles, 1992 and 1993; won gold medal (60-meter dash) at World Indoor Track & Field Championships, 1993; won gold medals (100-meter dash, 100-meter hurdles) at World Track & Field Championships, 1993; set American indoor record in 50-meter dash and world record in 60-meter dash, 1993; won 21 of 23 races in hurdles and sprints, 1993; ran world's fastest time in 100-meter dash, 1993; won gold medals in the 100-meter dash and the 400-meter relay at Olympics in Atlanta, Georgia, 1996; competed in 2000 Olympics in Sydney, Australia and 2004 Olympics in Athens, Greece.

**Awards:** U.S. Women's Athlete of the Year, Track & Field News, 1993; runner-up, World Women's Athlete of the Year, Track & Field News, 1993; Visa USA Track and Field Humanitarian Athlete of the Year, 1999.

**Addresses:** *Office*—c/o United States Olympians Association, 1750 East Boulder St., Colorado Springs, CO 80909-5764. *Agent*—Arluck Promotions, 940 Lincoln Road, Suite 305, Miami Beach, FL 33139.

championships, while also placing second in the long jump.

While attending UCLA, Devers's development as a runner made a quantum leap under the coaching of Bob Kersee, the husband of Devers's closest friend, the renowned athlete Jackie Joyner-Kersee. Kersee identified Devers's immense potential and put her on a grueling training regimen. Quoted in *Track & Field News,* Devers said, "I loved doing six or seven events in a meet because I was the first to start and the last to finish and there was no time in between to just sit around." Initially, she concentrated on becoming a sprinter and had no intention of attempting the hurdles due to her small size. Under Kersee's guidance, however, she soon changed her mind. By 1988 Devers had become one of the top female hurdlers in the United States, setting a national record of 12.61 seconds in the 100-meter hurdles while qualifying to compete in the event at the 1988 Olympics in Seoul, Korea. That year, she married Ron Roberts.

## Battled a Devastating Illness

Just as Devers appeared to be approaching her peak as an athlete, however, she began to suffer from a variety of physical problems. After earning a spot on the U.S. Olympic team, she found herself plagued by frequent muscle pulls and tired legs, making it difficult for her to complete simple workouts. Devers's problems took their toll at Seoul, where she produced her slowest time in the 100-meter hurdles since high school and failed to qualify for the finals. Soon after she began suffering from impaired hearing, memory loss, migraine headaches, and convulsions. Her hair began falling out and, by January 1989, she had lost nearly twenty-three pounds, her frame becoming so slight that she had to wear children's clothing.

Over the next two and a half years, Devers visited more than a dozen physicians. A number of doctors told her she was simply training too hard, while others thought she had diabetes. Meanwhile, Devers's condition worsened, her list of symptoms expanding to include vision loss and nearly perpetual menstrual bleeding. At one point she seriously considered ending her track career. "I felt like a washed-up athlete, and I began to doubt I could ever again compete at my former level," she explained in *Family Circle.* But Kersee convinced her to stay with it.

Following an almost two-year layoff, Devers tested her condition in a minor track meet in 1990, but she performed poorly. Then in the fall of that same year, a team physician at UCLA with whom she had a chance meeting finally solved the mystery. The physician noticed that Devers's eyes were bulging and that she had a goiter on her throat, both of which are symptoms of a thyroid condition. Subsequent tests revealed that Devers was afflicted with Graves' disease, an autoimmune disorder resulting from an overactive thyroid gland. She was told that her condition had progressed almost to a cancerous state and was perhaps only weeks away from malignancy.

Because the beta-blocker medication for the disease was prohibited by the Olympic Committee as an illegal substance for athletes, Devers elected to receive radiation. Several weeks of intensive treatment resulted in a dramatic improvement in her symptoms, prompting her to think that she was cured. New problems erupted in early 1991, however, among them severely painful blood blisters on the soles of her feet and between her toes. Devers told *Family Circle,* "The pain was so excruciating that I sometimes crawled because it hurt too much to walk."

Devers went to a podiatrist, who wrongly diagnosed the condition as a severe case of athlete's foot. Eventually, the pain of walking became so great that her parents had to carry her around her apartment. Devers began to believe that she might never walk again; at one point a doctor told her that she might have to have her feet amputated. After seeking a second opinion, Devers discovered that the problems with her extremities and skin were simply side effects from the radiation. The radiation had also completely destroyed her thyroid gland, forcing Devers to be placed on a lifetime regimen of daily medication.

## Fought to Regain Top Form

About a month after completing her radiation regimen, Devers had regained most of her former health, although she continued to suffer from sensitivity to the sun and occasional skin-related problems. Once she regained her ability to walk, she resumed training at UCLA. Her first workout was a slow walk around the track, wearing only socks because shoes still hurt her feet. Devers proceeded rapidly to jogging and sprinting workouts, and in March of 1991 she qualified for the prestigious TAC (The Athletics Congress) Meet to be held that June. At the TAC Meet she won the 100-meter hurdles, recording the fastest time by an American woman that year.

The following summer, Devers took second place in the 100-meter hurdles at the World Championships in Tokyo, Japan; two weeks later, she set a new American record in the event at a meet in Berlin, Germany. As she was achieving tremendous success in track, however, Devers's three-year marriage to Ron Roberts was falling apart. She explained in *Family Circle* that, because of her illness, "I had lost touch with myself. My only desire was to be alone.... I felt if I could just get back to running, I would find Gail again."

As the 1992 Olympics in Barcelona approached, Kersee convinced Devers to put more effort into the 100-meter dash, since he had always felt that her greatest potential was as a sprinter. With her physical problems behind her, Devers trained harder than ever and made the 1992 Olympic team in both the 100-meter dash and the 100-meter hurdles. At the Olympics, however, Devers nearly suffered another disastrous setback. While stepping into the starting blocks for the quarter finals in the 100 meters, she temporarily lost all feeling in her feet. Despite fears that her illness was flaring up again, Devers ultimately made it to the finals. She then shocked everyone by posting the best

time of her career, winning the gold medal and beating second-place finisher Julie Cuthbert of Jamaica by only .01 seconds.

Devers's surprise victory led to some suspicion that she was using performance-enhancing drugs; there was no evidence, however, and the rumors were soon dispelled. Still, the ecstasy of victory turned to agony five days later. Running in the finals of the hurdles event, Devers caught one of the barriers with her foot, tripped, and fell across the finish line. The fall dropped her to fifth place, ruining her chances of becoming the second woman in Olympic history to win gold medals in both the hurdles and the 100-meter dash.

Still, her Olympic performance had solidified her position as the fastest woman in the world. Devers dominated the indoor track season in 1993, as she shifted her focus from hurdling to sprinting. For the year, she lost only one indoor sprint in eight races. Her achievement was especially impressive since she had paid little attention to indoor running prior to that year. She set an American record of 6.99 seconds in the 60-meter dash at the USA/Mobil Indoor Track and Field Championships in New Jersey in February, and in March she sped to a world-record time of 6.95 seconds while winning the event at the World Indoor Championships in Toronto, Canada.

## Maintained Her Commitment to Winning

The strain from her grueling indoor season eventually caught up with Devers, and in the spring of 1993 she battled a hamstring injury as she began her outdoor training. She bounced back quickly and was in peak condition for the World Outdoor Track and Field Championships in Stuttgart, Germany, that August, where she won titles in both the 100-meter hurdles and the 100-meter dash. Her victory over Merlene Ottey of Jamaica in the dash was so close that it took the judges three minutes to confirm Devers as the winner. The head of the Jamaican team protested the decision, but Devers's victory was upheld. Earning three major titles in 1993, Devers finished the year with a phenomenal 21 victories in 23 races. She also ran the fastest times in both the 100-meter dash and 100-meter hurdles that year.

Gail Devers's return to running glory—from being on the verge of having her feet amputated to winning an Olympic gold medal in just eighteen months—was widely regarded as the greatest comeback story in the history of track and field. Few athletes, male or female, had ever demonstrated her rare combination of great physical skill and steadfastness in the face of debilitating setbacks. At the time, Devers gave much of the credit to God. In *Family Circle* Devers noted, "My family and friends gave me tremendous support, but faith in God and myself kept me going. I don't wish what I've been through on anyone, but I'm a stronger, more determined person because of it. After conquering Graves' disease, I know there's no hurdle I can't get over."

Even after reaching the summit of her sport, Devers remained committed to competitive running. After several more years of intensive training, she qualified for the U.S. women's track team at the 1996 Summer Olympics in Atlanta, where she won gold medals in both the 100-meter dash and the 400-meter relay. She once again fell short in the finals of the 100-meter hurdles, however, finishing in fourth place. At around this time, Devers created the Gail Devers Foundation. In addition to raising money for various charity organizations, the foundation was also dedicated to offering scholarships and mentoring programs to elementary school students in Los Angeles.

In 2000 Devers earned a chance to compete at the Olympic Games in Sydney, Australia, where she advanced to the semi-final round of the 100-meter hurdles; however, a nagging hamstring injury prevented her from racing in her semi-final heat, and she went home without a medal. Devers returned to Olympic competition at the 2004 summer games in Athens. She managed to advance to the semi-finals of the 100-meter dash despite a calf injury, but she failed to finish her opening heat in the 100-meter hurdles. A year after racing in Athens, Devers gave birth to a daughter, Karsen, with her second husband, Mike Phillips.

Devers remained active in competition into her early 40s. In February of 2007, she won the 60-meter hurdles at the Millrose Games in New York City; her time, 7.86 seconds, was the fastest in the world at that point of the season. As she adapted to life after competitive track, Devers remained involved in numerous charity activities, speaking engagements, and business ventures. In addition to launching a clothing line, Devers and her husband formed Phil Prod LLC, a maker of fitness products. Toward the end of the 2000s, Devers also became involved with promotional activities for the Provisions Resort Guyana, a luxury beach vacation destination.

## Sources

### Books

Woolum, Janet, *Outstanding Women Athletes: Who They Are and How They Influenced Sports in America,* Oryx Press, 1998, pp. 105–07.

### Periodicals

*Atlanta Journal-Constitution,* June 21, 2006, p. C2.
*Essence,* May 1993, p. 96.
*Family Circle,* May 18, 1993, pp. 21–23.
*Idaho State Journal,* February 3, 2007, p. 14.
*Jet,* August 17, 1992, pp. 51–52.
*Miami Herald,* August 3, 2008, p. 12D.
*New York Times,* August 2, 1992, Section 8, pp. 1, 4; February 24, 1993, p. B14; February 27, 1993, pp. 29, 32; March 13, 1993, p. 32; August 17, 1993, pp. B9, B13.
*Philadelphia Inquirer,* February 4, 2006, p. D9.
*San Diego Union-Tribune,* January 27, 2006, p. D1; February 27, 2006, p. D3.
*Sporting News,* August 17, 1992, p. 5.
*Sports Illustrated,* August 10, 1992, pp. 18–19; May 10, 1993, pp. 41–3.
*Track & Field News,* October 1992, pp. 52–3; November 1993, 4pp. 36–7, 48–49; February 1994, pp. 10–11, 14, 17.

### Online

"Gail Devers," Arluck Promotions, http://www.arluckpromotions.com/athlete-management/detail/gail-devers/ (accessed November 2, 2010).
"Gail Devers," SR/Olympic Sports, http://www.sports-reference.com/olympics/athletes/de/gail-devers-1.html (accessed November 2, 2010).
"Members of the Board," Provisions Resort Guyana, http://www.provisionsresortguyana.com/ (accessed November 2, 2010).
"World and Olympic Champion Devers—Athlete, Charity Worker, Coach and Agent," Beijing 2008, http://en.beijing2008.cn/18/36/article214003618.shtml (accessed November 2, 2010).

—Ed Decker and Stephen Meyer

# Bill Dixon

## 1925–2010

### Jazz trumpeter, composer, educator

Trumpeter Bill Dixon was a key figure in the avant-garde or free jazz movement of the 1960s, making his mark as a player, composer, organizer, and educator. As a musician, Dixon is best known for his collaborations with jazz saxophonist Archie Shepp and with pianist Cecil Taylor, whose influential 1966 album *Conquistador* showcased the trumpeter's lyrical style. Dixon had an even greater influence, though, as a champion of free jazz and avant-garde musicians. His 1964 "October Revolution in Jazz," the first-ever festival of free jazz, helped bring attention to the nascent genre. From the 1970s to the 1990s, Dixon was a prolific composer of small-group, orchestral, and solo trumpet music. A faculty member at Bennington College for nearly three decades, Dixon founded the Black Music Division there and mentored generations of contemporary jazz musicians.

William Robert Dixon was born on Nantucket Island, Massachusetts, on October 5, 1925, the oldest of five children. In the early 1930s, his family relocated to Brooklyn and then to Harlem. In high school Dixon began playing the trumpet, inspired to take up the instrument after seeing Louis Armstrong perform at Harlem's Lafayette Theatre, but his primary interest was in painting and the visual arts. In 1944 he enlisted in the U.S. Army, serving in Germany during the last year of World War II. It was not until he returned, at the age of twenty, that he committed himself to formal music studies, taking advantage of the GI Bill to enroll at the Hartnett Conservatory of Music in Manhattan.

By the late 1940s, Dixon was performing in clubs around New York City, playing with like-minded young jazz musicians such as bassist Wilbur Ware, pianist Cecil Taylor, and later saxophonist Archie Shepp. Meanwhile, he held a day job as a secretary at the United Nations, organizing the UN's Jazz Society in 1953. In the early 1960s, Dixon and Shepp formed a quartet that recorded an album on the Savoy label in 1962 and toured Europe. In 1963 they were joined by Danish saxophonist John Tchicai, and the group became known as the New York Contemporary Five, with Dixon as its arranger.

Dixon was a practitioner and a champion of the emerging genre of avant-garde or free jazz, then known simply as "The New Thing." Free jazz, which was most closely associated with the innovations of Ornette Coleman and Cecil Taylor in the 1950s and John Coltrane in the 1960s, sought to get beyond the conventions of bebop and modal jazz by discarding such traditional elements as fixed chord changes and tempos. Free jazz was more improvisational in style, and the sound often was unconventional. Dixon, for instance, "evolved a signature sound of slow-moving, low-end melody lines, often expressed through understated half-valve slurs, expressive growls, vocalized sounds and dramatic vibrato," explained John Fordham of the *Guardian*. "I no longer felt the need to be playing the standard literature within the vernacular. I felt that you can't improve on that, so there must be something else," Dixon said in a 2001 interview with Graham Lock. "We did a lot of crazy things in those

*At a Glance . . .*

**B**orn William Robert Dixon on October 5, 1925, in Nantucket, MA; died on June 16, 2010, in North Bennington, VT; son of William LeRoy Dixon and Louise Wade; partner of Sharon Vogel; children: Claudia Dixon, William R. Dixon, Jr. (deceased), William R. Dixon II. *Military service:* U.S. Army, 1944–46. *Education:* Hartnett Conservatory of Music, 1946–51.

**Career:** Bennington College, lecturer in music, 1968–96.

**Awards:** Musician of the Year, *Jazz Magazine,* 1976; Giancarlo Testoni Award, Discographical Society for Best Recordings of the Year, 1981; BMI Jazz Pioneer Award, 1984; Vision Festival Lifetime Recognition Award, 2007.

days, trying to formulate a way of thinking for yourself."

Avant-garde artists had a hard time landing gigs on the commercial nightclub circuit, however, and the music press had few kind words for free jazz—in fact, many jazz critics were openly hostile to the new genre. "I've never understood why they had to be so hateful," Dixon recalled to *Jazz Times.* "What were they afraid of? We weren't going to take over the world." In response, Dixon began to recruit coffeehouses in Greenwich Village as performance venues, and in 1964, he organized the "October Revolution in Jazz," a four-day concert and discussion series at the Cellar Café on West 91st Street in Manhattan. The first-ever festival of free jazz featured more than 20 groups, mostly little-known artists such as pianists Paul Bley and Sun Ra, drummer Milford Graves, bassist David Izenson, and the Albert Ayler trio. The event helped draw attention to free jazz and proved that there was an audience for the new sound. Buoyed by the success of the "October Revolution," Dixon formed the Jazz Composers Guild in 1965, a short-lived cooperative that sought to give musicians, rather than club owners and record companies, control over their music.

Dixon was fascinated by the rhythms and movement of dance, and in 1965 he began a long creative partnership with dancer and choreographer Judith Dunn; the two debuted their work "Pomegranate" at the Newport Jazz Festival. The next year, Dixon made a notable appearance on Cecil Taylor's classic free jazz album *Conquistador,* and in 1967, he released his first solo work, *Intents and Purposes,* on RCA. At the same time, he founded the Free Conservatory of the University of the Streets, a music education program for inner-city youth in New York. In 1968 Dixon joined Dunn at Bennington College in Vermont. Although he intended to teach for only a few years, he remained on the faculty for nearly three decades, until his retirement in 1996. He founded the Black Music Division there in 1973, developing his own theory and performance curriculum, and served as mentor to a number of contemporary jazz musicians, including alto saxophonist Marco Eneidi and drummer Jackson Krall.

In the 1980s Dixon returned to the studio, recording small-group pieces, orchestral music, and solo trumpet works. For the Italian label Soul Note, he produced a series of solo albums, including *In Italy* (1980), *November 1981* (1981), *Sons of Sisyphus* (1988), and *Vade Mecum* (1993), as well as *Papyrus* (1998) with British percussionist Tony Oxley. On the self-produced six-disc set *Odyssey,* released in 2001, Dixon documented his solo trumpet compositions from the 1970s to the 1990s, many unaccompanied or with little backing. Dixon expressed concern about the genocide in Darfur, Sudan, on the album *17 Musicians in Search of a Sound,* which was recorded at the 2007 Vision Festival in New York City and released the following year. He continued to compose and perform well into his eighties, issuing the small-group records *Bill Dixon and Exploding Star Orchestra* in 2008 and *Tapestries for a Small Orchestra* in 2009.

Dixon made his last concert appearance at a music festival in Victoriaville, Quebec, in May of 2010. On June 16 of that year, he died at his home in North Bennington, Vermont, at the age of 84.

# Selected recordings

## As leader

*Archie Shepp—Bill Dixon Quartet,* Savoy, 1962.
*Bill Dixon 7-tette/Archie Shepp and the New York Contemporary 5,* Savoy, 1964.
*Intents and Purposes,* RCA-Victor, 1966.
*Considerations 1 & 2,* Fore, 1976.
*In Italy, Vol. 1 & 2,* Soul Note, 1980.
*November 1981,* Soul Note, 1981.
*Thoughts,* Soul Note, 1985.
*Sons of Sisyphus,* Soul Note, 1988.
*Vade Mecum, Vol. 1 & 2,* Soul Note, 1993.
*Papyrus, Vol. 1 & 2,* Soul Note, 1998.
*Odyssey,* Archive Editions, 2001.
*17 Musicians in Search of a Sound: Darfur,* AUM Fidelity, 2008.
*Bill Dixon with Exploding Star Orchestra,* Thrill Jockey, 2008.
*Tapestries for Small Orchestra,* Firehouse 12, 2009.

## As a sideman

Cecil Taylor, *Conquistador,* Blue Note, 1966.
Franz Koglman, *Opium for Franz,* Pipe, 1977.

*The Enchanted Messenger: Live from Berlin Jazz Festival,* Soul Note, 1966.

(With Cecil Taylor and Tony Oxley) *Taylor/Dixon/ Oxley,* Victo, 2002.

*Bill Dixon/Aaron Siegel/Ben Hall: Weight/ Counterweight,* Brokenresearch, 2009.

# *Sources*

### *Books*

Young, Ben, compiler, *Dixonia: A Bio-Discography of Bill Dixon,* Greenwood Press, 1998.

### *Periodicals*

*Guardian* (London), July 23, 2010.
*Jazz Times,* May 2001.
*New York Times,* June 22, 2007; June 19, 2010.
*Times* (London), June 30, 2010.

### *Online*

Kelsey, Chris, "Bill Dixon," All Music Guide, http:// www.allmusic.com/artist/bill-dixon-p6406 (accessed October 19, 2010).

—Deborah A. Ring

# Frederick Douglass

## 1817(?)–1895

### Activist, abolitionist

The remarkable life of Frederick Douglass came to a sudden end in February of 1895, when he suffered a heart attack at his home in Anacosta Heights, Maryland. That the most prominent of black abolitionists of the pre–Civil War era had died of age-related causes is in itself somewhat astonishing, given that racial prejudice and hostility toward those who had fought to end slavery in the United States ran high and had even slain a sitting president. An escaped slave who emerged during the 1840s as an eloquent speaker, Douglass became one of the civil rights movement's first black leaders. He was also a newspaper publisher, an author of several volumes of autobiography, and a U.S. minister to Haiti.

Douglass, Frederick, photograph. Library of Congress/Getty Images.

### Was Born a Slave

Douglass was born in Tuckahoe, Maryland, in about 1817. His mother was Harriet Bailey, but he had little contact with her before her death in 1825, when he was eight years old. He was raised by his grandparents, Betsy and Isaac, who he recalled in his 1855 memoir *My Bondage and My Freedom* as being quite advanced in age. His grandmother made handcrafted nets for catching fish. "It was a long time before I knew myself to be a slave. I knew many other things before I knew that…. but, as I grew larger and older, I learned by degrees the sad fact, that the 'little hut,' and the lot on which it stood, belonged not to my dear old grandparents, but to some person who lived a great distance off, and who was called, by grandmother, 'OLD MASTER.'"

Douglass believed that his father was the overseer on the plantation where his mother had toiled. Around 1824 his grandmother took him to Colonel Edward Lloyd's plantation, introduced him to some children she said were his family, and then slipped away. The man who may have been his father, Captain Aaron Anthony, had a daughter named Lucretia. Douglass became one of many slaves on the plantation, though his first jobs involved tending to cattle and assisting Miss Lucretia, as he called her. He shared quarters with other slaves, recalling that "I was kept almost in a state of nudity; no shoes, no stockings, no jacket, no trowsers; nothing but coarse sackcloth or two-linen, made into a sort of shirt, reaching down to my knees," he wrote in *My Bondage and My Freedom*. "The great difficulty was, to keep warm during the night. I had no bed. The pigs in the

## At a Glance . . .

**B**orn Frederick Augustus Washington Bailey on c. February 14, 1817, in Tuckahoe, MD; died on February 20, 1895, in Anacosta Heights, MD; son of Harriet Bailey (a slave); married Anna Murray, 1838 (died 1882); married Helen Pitts (an activist and journalist), 1884; children (with Murray): Rosetta, Lewis Henry, Frederick Jr., Charles Remond, Annie. *Religion:* African Methodist Episcopal.

**Career:** Born into slavery; escaped from a Baltimore shipyard, 1838; Massachusetts Anti-Slavery Society, agent, beginning 1841; lectured against slavery in Great Britain, 1845–47; *The North Star* (later *Frederick Douglass' Paper*), founder and editor, 1847–63; *Douglass' Monthly,* publisher and editor, 1859–63; *New National Era,* publisher and editor, 1870–74; U.S. marshal for the District of Columbia, 1877–81; Recorder of Deeds, District of Columbia, 1881–86; U.S. minister to Haiti, 1889–91.

pen had leaves, and the horses in the stable had straw, but the children had no beds. They lodged anywhere in the ample kitchen. I slept, generally, in a little closet, without even a blanket to cover me. In very cold weather, I sometimes got down the bag in which corn-meal was usually carried to the mill, and crawled into that."

Lucretia married Thomas Auld, and in 1826 Douglass was sent to live with Thomas's brother, Hugh, and his wife, Sophia, in Baltimore. He described this as a dramatically fortunate turn of events in his life because urban slaveholders gave their slaves decent clothes to wear, fed them well, and rarely abused them. Even "Miss Sophy," as he called his new mistress, was kind to him and began teaching him to read—until Hugh informed her that it was illegal for slaves to read and write in Maryland. By this time Douglass had learned from elders that he and all the other blacks he knew were descendants of a people who had been kidnapped from a faraway land. He also learned that elsewhere in the United States there were places that did not permit slavery.

Even though Hugh Auld had expressly forbidden his wife from teaching Douglass to read, the youngster convinced others to help him decipher the letters of the alphabet. "The more I read, the more I was led to abhor and detest slavery, and my enslavers," he wrote in *My Bondage and My Freedom.* "'Slaveholders,' thought I, 'are only a band of successful robbers, who left their homes and went into Africa for the purpose of stealing and reducing my people to slavery.'" Within a few years he had saved fifty cents to purchase a copy of *The Columbian Orator,* a collection of famous speeches from history.

In 1833, when he was sixteen years old, Douglass was relocated once again, this time under Thomas Auld's jurisdiction, to the Eastern Shore lands where he had been born. His rebellious streak and unhappiness at leaving the comfortable urban life was obvious, so Auld sent him to live with a notorious "slavebreaker" named Covey, who starved and beat Douglass and the other slaves under his charge. One day, while feeding the horses in the stable, Douglass was attacked by Covey, who tried to tie his legs together. Douglass knew this was likely in preparation for receiving a beating, so he resisted with an intensity that he did not realized he possessed. At first he merely defended himself against Covey's blows, but when the slavebreaker called for help, Douglass managed to kick the second assailant in the ribs. After a two-hour struggle, Covey was exhausted, but "I felt as I had never felt before," Douglass wrote in *My Bondage and My Freedom.* "It was a resurrection from the dark and pestiferous tomb of slavery… I had reached the point, at which I was not afraid to die. This spirit made me a freeman in fact, while I remained a slave in form. When a slave cannot be flogged he is more than half free."

### Made Flight to Freedom

Douglass was returned to Thomas Auld, and after a failed escape attempt he was finally sent back to the Aulds in Baltimore. There he learned how to caulk ships, which was a valuable skill at a time. His wages went to the Aulds, but the work permitted him some degree of autonomy. At the busy docks Douglass also saw free black men, many of whom were sailors aboard European-owned ships.

In *The Narrative of the Life of Frederick Douglass, an American Slave, Written by Himself,* which was published in 1845, Douglass did not recount the details of how he escaped in 1838 because he did not want to give his enemies any clues about who had helped him. More than a quarter-century later, in a revised autobiography that appeared in 1881, he finally divulged the details of his flight. He explained that during the 1830s free blacks in Maryland were required to carry identification papers, which could be loaned out to escaped slaves to help them reach freedom. "I had one friend—a sailor—who owned a sailor's protection, which answered somewhat the purpose of free papers—describing his person, and certifying to the fact that he was a free American sailor," he wrote in the 1881 memoir. "It called for a man much darker than myself, and close examination of it would have caused my arrest at the start. In order to avoid this fatal scrutiny on the part of the railroad official, I had arranged with Isaac Rolls, a hackman, to bring my baggage to the train just on the moment of its starting, and jumped upon the car myself when the train was already in motion. Had I gone into the station and offered to purchase a ticket, I should have been instantly and carefully examined, and undoubtedly arrested."

Douglass made his way North, to freedom, with those papers in hand. Twenty-four hours later he was in New York City, but friendless and fearful of asking for help. He slept in a barrel on the wharf one night, but a sailor on Centre Street took pity on him, gave him shelter, and even introduced him to antislavery activists who were able to help him. Shortly thereafter, Douglass's fiancé—a free black woman in Baltimore named Anna Murray—joined him in New York and the two were married by a Presbyterian minister. From there they moved north to New Bedford, Massachusetts, which was a major center of the shipbuilding and whaling trades.

### Became Celebrity Lecturer

Douglass hoped to earn a living as a caulker once again, but he settled for a job tending the furnace of a brass foundry. It was in New Bedford that he came across the famous newspaper of the abolitionist movement, *The Liberator*, published by William Lloyd Garrison, and became involved in a local African Methodist Episcopal church, where he occasionally told his story to others. During the summer of 1841 he was invited to address the annual meeting of the Massachusetts Anti-Slavery Society. That address launched his career as a public speaker and as one of the era's most famous antislavery advocates, and he began traveling throughout New England to speak at abolitionist meetings. When he addressed some students at Harvard College, they encouraged him to write a memoir, which resulted in him writing *The Narrative of the Life of Frederick Douglass, an American Slave, Written by Himself*. Published by the American Anti-Slavery Society, the book was widely read throughout the North.

However, the book also exposed him to fugitive slave hunters who wanted to capture and return him to Thomas Auld. In August of 1845 he was forced to flee the United States and spend two years crisscrossing the British Isles on a popular lecture tour. It proved so lucrative that Douglass was able to buy his freedom from Auld in 1847 for $700.

When he returned to the United States, Douglass moved his family to Rochester, New York, to establish his own abolitionist newspaper. The first issue of *North Star* appeared in December of 1847. Its name was a reference to the bright star that helped guide slaves along the Underground Railroad as they made their way north to freedom. In September of 1848 the *Liberator* published Douglass's open letter to Thomas Auld on the occasion of the ten-year anniversary of his escape. Even though he had attained both material comfort and impressive renown by then, Douglass

wrote that looking at his four children asleep in their cozy beds made him recall his own youth. "I remember the chain, the gag, the bloody whip, the deathlike gloom overshadowing the broken spirit of the fettered bondman, the appalling liability of his being torn away from wife and children, and sold like a beast in the market," he wrote in the letter to Auld, according to *My Bondage and My Freedom*. He also wondered about his family, and what had become of them. "I would write to them, and learn all I want to know of them, without disturbing you in any way, but that, through your unrighteous conduct, they have been entirely deprived of the power to read and write," Douglass railed. "You have kept them in utter ignorance, and have therefore robbed them of the sweet enjoyments of writing or receiving letters from absent friends and relatives. Your wickedness and cruelty committed in this respect on your fellow-creatures, are greater than all the stripes you have laid upon my back, or theirs."

Douglass and Garrison had actually parted ways over ideology: the radical Garrison asserted that the U.S. Constitution enshrined the practice of slavery, but Douglass, after a careful reading of the document, maintained that it instead protected all who lived in the United States. Garrison also espoused separation from the slaveholding states of the South entirely, which Douglass believed would bring terrible harm to an estimated four million slaves there, because an autonomous South would forever be a country free to make its own laws governing slavery. One of the most stirring speeches Douglass gave during his long career was in July of 1852 in Rochester, New York. Titled "What to the Slave Is the Fourth of July?" he explained to an enrapt audience that any slave who heard the marching bands, fireworks, and general undercurrent of jubilation every year in celebration of the country's independence from the British Crown did not share in the revelry, because that holiday "reveals to him, more than all other days in the year, the gross injustice and cruelty to which he is the constant victim."

### Served a Number of Presidents

During the 1850s the debate about slavery intensified and spilled over into violence. Douglass was briefly associated with the radical abolitionist John Brown, who led a disastrous raid on a federal arsenal at Harper's Ferry, Virginia, in 1859 in an attempt to arm the slaves of the South and instigate a mass rebellion. Douglass was forced to leave the country for a time, but returned when one of his daughters died unexpectedly. During the 1860 presidential campaign he endorsed Abraham Lincoln of the Republican Party, and civil war broke out a few weeks after Lincoln's inauguration in March of 1861. By this point Douglass had merged his *North Star* newspaper with another paper to establish *Frederick Douglass' Paper*, and had also launched *Douglass' Monthly*.

In January of 1862, at the height of the civil war, the magazine ran Douglass's article "What Shall Be Done with the Slaves If Emancipated?" In it, he repeated some of the arguments voiced by Northerners about the potentially disastrous appearance of four million newly freed blacks in America—that "they would all come to the North; they would not work; they would become a burden upon the State, and a blot upon society; they'd cut their masters' throats; they would cheapen labor, and crowd out the poor white laborers from employment; their former masters would not employ them, and they would necessarily become vagrants, paupers and criminals, over-running all our alms houses, jails and prisons." Douglass, in his eloquent style, contended that the "answer is, do nothing with them; mind your business, and let them mind theirs. Your *doing* with them is their greatest misfortune. They have been undone by your doings, and all they now ask, and really have need of at your hands, is just to let them alone…. Let us stand upon our own legs, work with our own hands, and eat bread in the sweat of our own brows. When you, our white fellow-countrymen, have attempted to do anything for us, it has generally been to deprive us of some right, power or privilege which you yourself would die before you would submit to have taken from you."

Douglass was critical of President Lincoln's policies and those of the Union Army, but he agreed to recruit black soldiers after the 1863 Emancipation Proclamation. Nearly 200,000 blacks served the Union cause, including one of Douglass's sons. The Confederate army surrendered on April 9, 1865, and two days later Lincoln publicly espoused Douglass's long hoped-for promise of black suffrage. Then on April 14 Lincoln was shot while attending a theater performance in Washington and died the next day. This was the first assassination of a president in U.S. history, "a new crime, a pure act of malice," Douglass recalled in his 1881 autobiography. "No purpose of the rebellion was to be served by it. It was the simple gratification of a hell-black spirit of revenge. But it has done good after all. It has filled the country with a deeper abhorrence of slavery and a deeper love for the great liberator."

After President Ulysses S. Grant was sworn into his second term in office, he appointed Douglass to serve as an assistant secretary during a diplomatic mission to Santo Domingo, which later became the nation of Haiti. At the time there was talk of annexing the entire island of Hispaniola as a place where freed American slaves might settle. His tenure there was brief and Douglass returned to Washington in 1872. President Grant then named him to a seat on the Territorial Council of the District of Columbia. In 1877 President Rutherford B. Hayes made Douglass a U.S. marshal for the District of Columbia, making him the first African American to hold that law enforcement post. In 1881 President James A. Garfield named him to the post of Recorder of Deeds for the District of Columbia, a job he held until 1886. When President Benjamin Harrison took office in 1889, he appointed Douglass as the U.S. minister to Haiti, a post he held for two years. Douglass

remained active in the women's suffrage movement up until the day he died. On February 20, 1895, he collapsed while recounting the events of the day to his wife, Helen, at their home in Anacosta Heights.

Douglass's first wife, Anna, died in 1882, and his second marriage to Helen Pitts, a white journalist and women's rights activist, engendered a great deal of controversy. His surviving daughter and three sons all opposed the union and contested his last will and testament in which Douglass had specified that the house, Cedar Hill, should go to his widow. Helen borrowed money from the National Association of Colored Women to purchase the property, and it later became a focus of African-American historic preservation groups. In 1988 it was designated a National Historic Site.

Now a museum that honors Douglass's life and work, Cedar Hill displays many personal items, household furniture, and valuable antiques of a man whose prized possession as a teenager was a fifty-cent book of speeches. One of the most unusual artifacts is a set of curtain tiebacks that were deliberately fashioned to resemble the ball-and-chain shackles used to tie slaves together on the auction block, complete with studded iron ball weights to prevent them from running. "No man can put a chain about the ankle of his fellow man," he told a civil rights gathering in 1883, "without at last finding the other end fastened about his own neck."

## Selected writings

*The Narrative of the Life of Frederick Douglass, an American Slave, Written by Himself,* Anti-Slavery Office, 1845.

*My Bondage and My Freedom,* Miller, Orton, and Mulligan, 1855.

"What Shall Be Done with the Slaves If Emancipated?," *Douglass' Monthly,* January 1862.

*Life and Times of Frederick Douglass,* Park Publishing Company, 1881.

*Why Is the Negro Lynched?,* J. Whitby and Sons, 1895.

*Frederick Douglass: Selected Speeches and Writings,* Lawrence Hill Books, 1999.

## Sources

### Books

Kendrick, Paul, and Stephen Kendrick, *Douglass and Lincoln: How a Revolutionary Black Leader and a Reluctant Liberator Struggled to End Slavery and Save the Union,* Walker and Company, 2008.

### Periodicals

*American Heritage,* Winter 2009, p. 36.
*New York Times,* April 22, 1876.

**Online**

"Frederick Douglass," WinningTheVote.org, http://winningthevote.org/FDouglass.html (accessed October 12, 2010).

"Frederick Douglass: Online Resources," Library of Congress, http://www.loc.gov/rr/program/bib/douglass/ (accessed October 12, 2010).

"Frederick Douglass National Historic Site," National Parks Service, U.S. Department of the Interior, http://www.nps.gov/frdo/ (accessed October 12, 2010).

—Carol Brennan

# Kevin Fenton

## 1966—

### Epidemiologist, public health official

Fenton, Kevin, photograph. Alex Wong/Getty Images.

Dr. Kevin Fenton is director of the National Center for HIV/AIDS, Viral Hepatitis, STD, and TB Prevention at the U.S. Centers for Disease Control and Prevention in Atlanta, Georgia. As one of the nation's top public health officials, Fenton is a vigorous supporter of the campaign to urge all Americans to undergo testing for the human immunodeficiency virus (HIV), the infection that causes acquired immune deficiency syndrome, or AIDS. Since taking over at the agency in 2005, he has also emerged as a leading voice in warning African Americans that their demographic is disproportionately affected by HIV/AIDS. "Don't just think about yourself. Encourage others," he told Margena A. Christian in *Jet* about the battle to reduce those numbers. "We all have to be engaged in this fight. We can't depend on one person to end this epidemic. We have to do this collectively."

Fenton was born in Scotland in 1966 but grew up in Jamaica. His father, Sydney Fenton, was an educator and head of the science department at Excelsior High School in Kingston, the Jamaican capital. His mother, Carmen Fenton, was a nurse at the hospital attached to the University of the West Indies (UWI), where Fenton began his studies as a computer science major but later opted to enter its medicine program. He was elected class president of UWI Medical School during the 1985–86 term, and he went on to complete residencies at Cornwall Regional Hospital in Montego Bay and at the University College Hospital in Kingston. For a time, he worked as a government doctor in the town of Lucea, which prompted him to extend his training into advanced public health issues.

In 1992 Fenton earned his master's degree in public health from the esteemed London School of Hygiene and Tropical Medicine, and he also pursued and completed a doctorate in epidemiology at University College of London. By mid-decade he was serving as a lecturer in HIV epidemiology at an agency attached to the Royal Free and University College Medical School in London. In the United Kingdom, health care is provided to all residents under the government-run National Health Service (NHS), which also funds an array of research and monitoring agencies. One of these is the Communicable Disease Surveillance Centre, where Fenton was hired as senior lecturer and honorary consultant epidemiologist. He was one of the lead researchers on Britain's second major public

## At a Glance . . .

**B**orn Kevin Andrew Fenton on December 19, 1966, in Scotland; son of Sydney (an educator) and Carmen (a nurse) Fenton. *Education:* Earned MD from the University of the West Indies Medical School; London School of Hygiene and Tropical Medicine, MPH, 1992; University College (London), Ph.D., epidemiology.

**Career:** Completed residencies at Cornwall Regional Hospital in Montego Bay and University College Hospital in Kingston, Jamaica; worked as a medical officer in Lucea, Jamaica; Royal Free and University College Medical School, Medical Research Council Coordinating Center for the Epidemiological Study of AIDS, lecturer in HIV epidemiology, after 1995; National Health Service, Communicable Disease Surveillance Centre, senior lecturer and honorary consultant epidemiologist, after 1998; became a public health registrar, 1999; Health Protection Agency, senior lecturer in epidemiology and public health, after 1999, director of its HIV and Sexually Transmitted Infections (STI) Department, after 2002; Centers for Disease Control and Prevention, director of National Syphilis Elimination Effort, January 2005–November 2005, director of National Center for HIV, STD, and TB Prevention (renamed National Center for HIV/AIDS, Viral Hepatitis, STD, and TB Prevention in 2007), 2005–.

**Addresses:** *Office*—National Center for HIV/AIDS, Viral Hepatitis, STD, and TB Prevention, Centers for Disease Control and Prevention, 1600 Clifton Rd., Atlanta, GA 30333.

health study, the National Survey of Sexual Attitudes and Lifestyles, in 2000 and 2001.

In 2002 Fenton was promoted to director of the Health Protection Agency HIV and Sexually Transmitted Infections (STI) Department within the NHS's Communicable Disease Surveillance Centre. This post would be similar to the one he would later take in the United States with the CDC: he monitored data and issued warnings about the new rate of HIV infections, which in Britain's case were attributed to an influx of sex workers from the countries of the former Eastern bloc.

Fenton joined the CDC in January of 2005 as director of its National Syphilis Elimination Effort. Later that

year he was appointed the new director of the CDC's National Center for HIV, STD, and TB Prevention. In 2007 his agency was renamed the National Center for HIV/AIDS, Viral Hepatitis, STD, and TB Prevention. Its mission is to reduce and eliminate the rates of preventable diseases like AIDS, tuberculosis, and viral hepatitis, and Fenton's role is to raise awareness about the high-risk behaviors that cause these diseases.

Fenton was not the first black scientist to run the vast public-health agency—Dr. Helene Gayle was the inaugural director of the National Center for HIV, STD, and TB Prevention when it was created in 1995—but he followed his predecessors' path in speaking eloquently about the high rate of infection among certain segments of the U.S. population, particularly African Americans. Annual public-health data collected by the CDC shows that while African Americans make up 12 percent of U.S. population, a black male in America is seven times more likely to test positive for HIV; African-American women are fifteen times more likely to test positive. The rate of new infections is also alarmingly high for African Americans under the age of thirty. "What we are seeing is a concentration of the epidemic among the poor, among ethnic minorities and racial minorities in the United States," Fenton told George Curry in the *New Pittsburgh Courier* in 2009. "We're seeing populations which have been historically and traditionally hard to reach and more difficult to serve."

After Barack Obama took office, Fenton assumed a prominent role in the Obama White House's "Act Against AIDS" campaign in 2009, which rallied support from the National Association for the Advancement of Colored People (NAACP) and the National Council of Negro Women. He also supported the CDC's decade-old National Black HIV/AIDS Awareness Day, which occurs every February 7, and National HIV Testing Day on June 27. In an article he wrote for Essence.com in 2010, Fenton noted that in the thirty years since the first AIDS cases alarmed public-health officials around the globe, the mortality rate has slowed thanks to advances in prevention and treatment, but "the reality is that HIV continues to be costly and deadly," he asserted. "We need to wake up to the fact that HIV is in every corner of our community— affecting our fathers and mothers, those in the prime of their lives as well as our youth. And, more than this, we need to take action to protect ourselves and our loved ones—that means knowing our HIV status, consistently and correctly using condoms or practicing abstinence."

In 2006 Fenton was profiled in the *Advocate,* a U.S. publication aimed at gay, lesbian, bisexual, and transgender readers. It was one of the few media citations to mention that Fenton is openly gay, but he stressed that his sexual orientation was irrelevant. "My primary driver is as a committed public-health physician and epidemiologist who's worked in the field for many years," he told journalist Sean Kennedy. "Yes, there are many factors that will influence my day-to-day relationships—the drive I bring to the work and the commitment I have—but I'd rather focus on the job at hand and my qualifications to do it."

## *Sources*

### *Periodicals*

*Advocate,* April 11, 2006, p. 4.
*Jamaica Observer,* January 15, 2006.
*Jet,* June 30, 2008, p. 28.
*New York Times,* March 13, 2008; September 12, 2008.

### *Online*

"The CDC Leaders: Kevin Fenton, MD, PhD," Centers for Disease Control and Prevention, http://www. cdc.gov/about/leadership/leaders/fenton.htm (accessed August 23, 2010).

Curry, George, "Official Says 'Down Low' Men Not Responsible for High HIV Rates among Black Women," New Pittsburgh Courier.com, October 8, 2009, http://newpittsburghcourieronline.com/index.php?option=com_content&view=article&id=466 (accessed August 23, 2010).

Fenton, Dr. Kevin, "Breaking the Deadly Cycle of HIV among Black Youth," Essence.com, February 7, 2010, http://www.essence.com/lifestyle/health/commentary_breaking_the_deadly_cycle_of.php (accessed August 23, 2010).

### *Other*

*The Russ Parr Show* (transcript), June 21, 2010, www.cdc.gov/nchhstp/newsroom/docs/TheRuss-ParrShowTranscript.pdf.

—Carol Brennan

# Hardy R. Franklin

## 1929–2004

## Librarian

Hardy R. Franklin's early love of books led him to an illustrious career in library science. From 1974 to 1997 he served as director of the District of Columbia's public library system, one of the largest in the nation. Toward the end of that career he was elected president of his profession's largest and most influential organization, the American Library Association. In both roles Franklin was a champion of the library's function as a vital part of a free, democratic society. As he himself was living testament, Franklin knew that a library with even a modest collection could have an enormous impact on the youngsters in the community it served.

### Was Turned Away from Library

Franklin was born in Rome, Georgia, in 1929, into the deeply segregated world of the American South in the pre–civil rights era. One of four children born to his mother, who worked as a domestic, and a father who later managed to buy the barbershop where he had worked for many years, Franklin began working himself at the age of ten, when a local white family hired him at the rate of $2 per day to read to and entertain their six-year-old son. In that capacity he visited his hometown public library dozens of times. Then, on a spring day in 1939, the young Franklin went to the library—alone this time—to read his favorite book. "You can't come here by yourself," the white librarian told him, as Franklin recalled later in the *Washington Post*. Franklin's father explained to him that he should "understand that this is part of life," Franklin remembered, but being turned away from the library only

heightened the young boy's thirst for literature. "I wanted to read all of the books that I could," he said.

In 1945 Franklin graduated from the Colored Main School in Rome and entered Morehouse College in Atlanta. His parents had been determined to send all four of their children to college, and they did; his mother had taken a correspondence course to become a licensed practical nurse, which brought in a much higher salary than her previous job as a domestic. At Morehouse Franklin majored in sociology and befriended a young Rev. Martin Luther King Jr. After earning his degree he taught school and worked as a school librarian in Conyers, Georgia, until he was drafted into the U.S. Army in 1953.

At the time, the United States was winding down its war on the Korean peninsula against Communist North Korean and Chinese forces but still maintained a strong presence on the Japanese island of Okinawa. Franklin was assigned to oversee an adjutant general's library on a base there during his two-year stint in the military. Upon his discharge he enrolled in the master's degree in library science (MLS) program at Atlanta University, graduating in 1956 and moving to the New York City area to begin his career in the profession.

### Earned Doctorate in Library Science

Franklin had been hired by the Brooklyn Public Library system as a branch librarian for an outpost in the

## At a Glance . . .

Born on May 9, 1929, in Rome, GA; died of complications from Alzheimer's disease and diabetes on August 22, 2004, in Washington, DC; son of John (a barber) and Josephine (a domestic and licensed practical nurse) Franklin; married Jarcelyn Fields (a librarian; died, 1985), married Barbara Washington (an attorney), 1987; children: Hardy R. "Petey" Jr., stepdaughter Regan Hayes. *Military service:* U.S. Army, 1953–55. *Religion:* African Methodist Episcopal (AME). *Education:* Morehouse College, BA, 1950; Atlanta University, MLS, 1956; Rutgers University, PhD, 1971.

**Career:** Rockdale County Board of Education, teacher and librarian, 1950–53; teacher and librarian in Okinawa, Japan; Brooklyn Public Library, began as librarian, 1956, became branch librarian, 1957(?), young adult coordinator, 1961–64, senior community coordinator, 1964–68; Queens College, City University of New York (CUNY), assistant professor, library science department, 1971–74; District of Columbia Public Library, director, 1974–97.

**Memberships:** American Library Association, council member, 1979–83, vice president, 1992–93, president, 1993–94; D.C Library Association, vice president, 1991–92, president, 1992–93.

**Awards:** National Endowment for the Humanities grant, 1970–71; Distinguished Public Service Award, D.C. Public School Library Association, 1979; Allie Beth Martin Award, Public Library Association, 1983; Distinguished Service Award, D.C. Library Association, 1990; Distinguished Alumnus Award, Rutgers University Library School Alumni Association, 1992.

interest in retooling public libraries to serve communities in transition. He also began writing articles for professional publications while serving as an assistant professor in the library science department of Queens College of the City University of New York (CUNY).

The District of Columbia Public Library system (DCPL) was an ailing collection of rundown facilities when it offered Franklin the directorship in 1974. He took charge of a 650,000-volume library system beset by staff shortages and a hiring freeze; most of its satellite branches were located either in storefronts or unattractive rental properties. His greatest successes as director over the next 23 years include fixing the DCPL's financial woes, opening more appealing branch locations, and expanding the holdings to 2.5 million volumes. He also worked with a private nonprofit group, the Friends of DCPL, and the DC Public Library Foundation to improve the system's resources and better serve the community.

Many of Franklin's triumphs as DCPL director over the years were credited to his skilled courting of both the politicians who controlled funding for the system and the patrons who used it. Generations of library users in the District of Columbia grew up with the automated Dial-A-Story, a free 24-hour telephone service that went into operation in the mid-1970s. The DCPL was also among the first major urban library systems to install theft-protection equipment, create an online catalog for its holdings, and offer a popular videotape-rental service.

### Elected to Lead the ALA

Franklin also had a long record of involvement with the American Library Association (ALA), the leading organization for his profession. Over the years he had become a member of the ALA's Committee on the Recruitment of Public Librarians, the Public Library Association Urban Public Library Issues Committee, and its Black Caucus. In 1979 he took a seat on the ALA executive council, and a decade later he was named head of the District of Columbia Library Association. He entered a tightly contested 1992 race for ALA president and was elected to lead the 52,000-member organization for a one-year term beginning the following year.

Franklin spent his year as ALA president promoting programs designed to take advantage of new technologies and make them more accessible to library patrons, particularly young people and the disadvantaged. One example of this was a young-adult multimedia room created at DCPL that he envisioned as a model for other public libraries as "a gathering place for teenagers," he explained to the *Washington Post*. "It is designed to bridge the gap between the children's section and the adult-use area." As ALA president, Franklin also appointed a commission to identify the

Bedford-Stuyvesant neighborhood. Five years later he became coordinator of young adult services, eventually becoming community coordinator for outreach services for the system. Back in the mid-1960s this was a new position, and Franklin was given relatively free reign to design programs he thought could best serve the community. His efforts spurred him to pursue a doctorate in his field from Rutgers University. The title of his 1971 dissertation—"The Relationship between Adult Communication Practices and Public Library Use in a Northern, Urban, Black Ghetto"—reflected his

50 best programs for youth nationwide and to cite them in the ALA's house publication, as well as to award $500 each to the top ten programs. The activities of the commission and the awards were funded by a $20,000 grant from the Margaret Alexander Edwards Trust. Among the top ten award winners were the Male Mentoring/Read Aloud Partners (R.A.P.) Program of the Hall and Robert Taylor Homes Branches of the Chicago Public Library; the Youth-at-Risk Outreach Project of the Alameda County Library in Fremont, California; and the Teen Advisory Council of the B. B. Comer Memorial Public Library of Sylacauga, Alabama.

As the end of his tenure as ALA president neared, Franklin campaigned for unfettered access to the burgeoning new world of cyberspace. It was a time when Vice President Al Gore, as part of the administration of Bill Clinton, was trumpeting the coming of an "information superhighway" and pressuring telecommunications companies to upgrade their technology so that they could provide affordable access to the Internet for all American households. The major corporate players, and their lobbyists, initially resisted this, and Franklin took up the sword for library professionals, who were eager to provide computers and access to the World Wide Web to their patrons. "A truly remarkable system will make this information technology affordable and accessible to every citizen," he wrote in a July of 1994 *Washington Post* editorial. "Assuming that our government cannot afford to provide a computer and linkage for every household, as the French government does, there is only one sure way to create such a system. Every public library must be connected to the information superhighway."

### Resigned Suddenly from DCPL

After his tenure as ALA president came to an end, Franklin returned to his post as DCPL director. He resigned suddenly in January of 1997 as news of some internal scandals came to light: two DCPL executives had filed sexual harassment charges against him, with allegations dating back to the late 1970s, which triggered a formal investigation by the District of Columbia Department of Human Rights. "Word of the accusations against Franklin came as a shock to the library field," noted a *Library Journal* article that appeared in October of 1997. "Throughout what can only be classified as a stellar career, Franklin, a pioneer of black librarianship, forged a name for himself in the profession." After his resignation, a grand jury indicted him on unrelated charges that came to light after a massive audit of the District of Columbia municipal government. Franklin was found guilty of submitting expense

reports to both the ALA and the DCPL during his 1993–94 term as ALA president, and he was ordered to pay back $24,000. He was also sentenced to five months of house arrest, but at the time, he was sixty-nine years old, walked with a cane, and had already suffered a stroke. His attorney, noted a *Washington Post* article by Bill Miller, "maintained that the double-billing was an honest mistake caused by the two jobs and aggravated by poor accounting procedures at the library, and that it was not the result of any scheme."

Since 1971 Franklin suffered from diabetes, a chronic condition that had also afflicted his mother. In addition, he eventually was diagnosed with Alzheimer's disease, and on August 22, 2004, at the age of seventy-five, he died from complications from both diseases. Surviving him were his second wife, attorney Barbara Washington, and a son by his first marriage to Jarcelyn Fields, who died of multiple sclerosis in 1985. Obituary notices mentioned the troubles that had brought Franklin's career to an abrupt and discomforting end, but his true legacy remained the DCPL's success during his 23 years as director. "Two and one-half million people used the D.C. library facilities last year," he told Marcia Mazur in *Diabetes Forecast* in 1992. "That means more people used the D.C. Public Library than attended all the Washington Redskins football games, Bullets basketball games, and Washington Capitals hockey games, added to all those who attended concerts at the Kennedy Center."

## Sources

### Books

Dennis, Thomison, *A History of the American Library Association,* American Library Association, 1978.

### Periodicals

*American Libraries,* July/August 1992, pp. 600–01; September 1993, p. 779; February 1994, p. 200; April 1994, pp. 370, 374; May 1994, p. 467.
*Diabetes Forecast,* February 1992, p. 22.
*Jet,* July 6, 1992, p. 24; July 26, 1993, p. 57.
*Library Journal,* April 1, 1992, pp. 75–83; February 15, 1997, p. 91; October 1, 1997, p. 14.
*New York Times,* February 23, 1997.
*USA Today,* June 1, 1994, p. 10A.
*Washington Post,* January 13, 1994, sec. DC, pp. 1–2; July 27, 1994, p. A27; September 18, 1998, p. B1; August 27, 2004, p. B6.

—Nicholas Patti and Carol Brennan

# John Trusty Gibson

## 1878–1937

### Theater owner, producer, entrepreneur

Theater owner and entrepreneur John Trusty Gibson was a pioneer in the development of black theatrical entertainment in Philadelphia during the 1910s and 1920s. As the owner of the New Standard and Dunbar theaters, located on Philly's South Side, he was the king of the African-American theater business in the city. His clubs drew the top black performers of the era, including bandleaders Louis Armstrong and Duke Ellington and singers Bessie Smith and Ethel Waters. The ventures made Gibson, who was known as the "Little Giant" for his diminutive stature, the richest African American in Philadelphia. Like many businessmen of the time, he was devastated financially by the stock market crash of 1929, and he was forced to sell his theaters by the end of the decade.

Gibson was born on February 4, 1878, in Baltimore, Maryland, the son of George Henry and Elizabeth (Johns) Gibson. He attended the city's public schools, although it is unclear whether he graduated. He spent two years studying at Baltimore's Morgan College Preparatory School (now Morgan State University), and in 1928, the school granted him an honorary degree. In the 1890s, Gibson moved to Philadelphia, where he worked a variety of jobs, including peddling meat, upholstering chairs, and weaving, and tried his hand at several business ventures, all of which were unsuccessful.

In 1910 Gibson joined with local real estate entrepreneur Samuel Reading as part owner of the North Pole Theatre, an aging, unprofitable movie and vaudeville house. A little over a year later, Gibson bought out

Reading for $800 and became sole proprietor of the theater, making him the first African-American theater owner in Philadelphia. Although Gibson turned the North Pole into a moderately profitable business, renaming it the Auditorium, the venue suffered from a poor location, and its physical structure was a shambles.

Gibson closed the North Pole in 1914 and invested in the Standard Theatre, a larger and more modern venue located at Twelfth and South streets, in an upper-middle-class section of town. The new theater was easily accessible to street traffic, and it boasted an impressive exterior with lights that could be seen from a distance. Its interior was decorated in the gaudy style of the era, decked out in gold, purple, and shades of rose.

The New Standard catered to both black and white audiences. It featured vaudeville acts, musical stage shows, and popular music and became a regular stop for the top black performers of the day, including comedians Bylow and Ashes, singers Bessie Smith and Ethel Waters, Erma C. Miller's Brown Skinned Models (known as the "Black Rockettes"), and the jazz bands of Louis Armstrong and Duke Ellington. Many entertainers got their start at the New Standard, such as the Whitmore Sisters, a popular vaudeville act. Gibson also functioned as a producer for a time, presenting *The Chocolate Box Review* for two seasons in 1924 and 1925.

Gibson's club was one of the hottest black theaters in the country, in the same league as the legendary

Lafayette Theatre in Harlem, the Pekin Theater in Chicago, and the Howard Theatre in Washington, DC. The *Philadelphia Tribune,* the city's black newspaper, called Gibson the "creator of the world's largest theater owned by a Negro," according to Errol G. Hill and James V. Hatch's *A History of African American Theatre.* The New Standard brought in weekly receipts of $12,000, making Gibson the richest African American in the city. He bought an estate in the suburbs that he named "Elmira," for his wife Ella, and kept a second home in West Philadelphia. He also was the first African American businessman in the city to make significant investments in property, buying an apartment house, a row of houses, and several tenement buildings.

At just 5 feet, 3 inches tall and weighing 110 pounds, Gibson became known as the "Little Giant." In addition to his entrepreneurial activities, he also was active in civic life, serving as a director of Douglass Hospital and a trustee of Morgan College, to which he donated $5,000. He was a member of the Chamber of Commerce, the Board of Trade, the Broad Street Association, and the Citizen's Republican Club, an association of black Republicans.

Gibson's success with the New Standard inspired competition. In 1919 black entrepreneurs E. C. Brown and A. F. Stevens purchased the Dunbar Theatre, which featured vaudeville shows and dramatic performances. Financial difficulties forced them to sell the theater to Gibson in 1921 for $120,000, however, and the venue became known as Gibson's Dunbar Theatre. The Dunbar was a part of the Theater Owners' and Bookers Association circuit, which brought in national touring acts. That year, Gibson was named the association's representative for the eastern region.

Despite an impressive lineup of performers, the Dunbar lost money, and Gibson kept it afloat with his profits from the New Standard. The theater was in a bad location, at Broad and Lombard streets, and black audiences refused to attend. Gibson also experienced a series of labor problems at the Dunbar: In its opening year, the National Association of Colored Stage Employees charged that Gibson was reluctant to hire African Americans, and musicians in the house orchestra walked out when they did not received the 50 percent raise that they had demanded. In 1927 Gibson changed the name of the theater from the Dunbar to the Gibson Theatre in a last attempt to breathe life into the club, but to no avail.

The stock market crash of 1929 was disastrous for Gibson and spelled his financial ruin. He was forced to sell the Dunbar at a loss to white investors, who renamed the theater the Lincoln. In 1931 he closed the New Standard, which became the Burns & Russell Company, a resident musical stock company. He lived in poverty for the rest of his life, and died at his home in West Philadelphia—his only remaining asset—on June 12, 1937, at the age of 61.

## Sources

### Books

Gates, Henry Louis Jr., and Evelyn Brooks Higginbotham, eds., *Harlem Renaissance Lives: From the African American National Biography,* Oxford University Press, 2009.

Hill, Errol G., and James V. Hatch, *A History of African American Theatre,* Cambridge University Press, 2003.

Smith, Jessie Carney, Millicent Lownes Jackson, and Linda T. Wynn, *Encyclopedia of African American Business,* Greenwood Press, 2006.

### Online

"Dunbar Theatre," ExplorePAHistory.com, http://explorepahistory.com/hmarker.php?markerid=538 (accessed September 22, 2010).

"Standard Theatre," ExplorePAHistory.com, http://explorepahistory.com/hmarker.php?markerid=459 (accessed September 22, 2010).

—Deborah A. Ring

# Al Goodman

## 1943–2010

### R&B vocalist

With a rich baritone and considerable personal charm, vocalist Al Goodman enjoyed a long career at the forefront of rhythm and blues. A native of Mississippi, he first came to prominence in the late 1960s as a member of the Moments, a vocal trio known for lush, highly polished harmonies. After a string of major hits, the group disbanded in the late 1970s, only to re-form as Ray, Goodman & Brown (RGB). Though changing musical tastes eventually affected the trio's album sales, their live shows remained popular well into the twenty-first century.

One of seven children, Willie Albert Goodman was born in Jackson, Mississippi, on March 30, 1943. He began singing early, performing regularly with an *a capella* group while still in high school. Encouraged by that experience to make music his career, he moved to the New York City area in his late teens. While singing with various groups in his spare time, he supported himself as a sound mixer at All Platinum Studios, a producer of soul and other types of R&B. Based in the New York suburb of Englewood, New Jersey, All Platinum had been co-founded by Sylvia Robinson, a singer, entrepreneur, and impresario. It was Robinson who gave Goodman the biggest break of his career. One day in the late 1960s, while she was working with the Moments, then a relatively new group, she heard him singing casually while he worked. Delighted with his voice, she offered him a spot on the group's roster. Joining him there were fellow vocalists Billy Brown and Johnny Moore; when the latter left in about 1970, he was replaced by Harry Ray, a change that resulted in

the Moments' longest-lasting and most definitive lineup.

By the end of the 1960s, Goodman and his partners were working hard to establish themselves in a crowded and highly competitive field. In 1970 they had their biggest hit, "Love on a Two-Way Street." A bittersweet ballad, it had actually been released several years earlier by a different Moments lineup. It was the re-recorded and re-mixed 1970 version, however, that raced up *Billboard* magazine's R&B and pop charts, reaching number one on the first and number three on the second. It eventually sold more than a million copies.

Over the next eight years, the Moments enjoyed a string of hits, notable among them 1973's "Sexy Mama" and 1975's "Look at Me (I'm in Love)," both of which reached the top five on *Billboard*'s R&B chart; the latter spent a week at number one. As the decade progressed, however, it became clear that the emergence of disco was damaging the popularity of the slower, more complex songs in which the Moments specialized. Though the disco fad proved short-lived, its effects contributed to a growing tension between the trio and Stang Records, the All Platinum subsidiary that served as their label. By 1978 the situation had deteriorated to such an extent that the Moments chose to disband rather than remain under Stang's control. Simply leaving was not an option, because All Platinum owned the rights to the group's name. To reassert control over their own careers, therefore, Goodman and his partners had to disband, re-form under a new name, and find a new label.

## At a Glance . . .

Born Willie Albert Goodman on March 30, 1943, in Jackson, MS; died July 26, 2010, in Hackensack, NJ; son of Albert Goodman and Ethel Adams Goodman; married Alice Lewis (divorced), Henrietta Young; children: five.

**Career:** All Platinum Studios (Englewood, NJ), sound mixer, mid-1960s; The Moments (R&B group), vocalist, late 1960s–1978; Ray, Goodman & Brown (R&B group), vocalist, 1979–2010.

By 1979 they had a new name—Ray, Goodman & Brown—and a new label, Polydor. The self-titled album they released that year revitalized their careers. A major success both critically and commercially, *Ray, Goodman & Brown* spawned several hits, the largest of which, "Special Lady," reached number one on the R&B chart. Two of Goodman's daughters later told Mike Kerwick of the Hackensack, New Jersey, *Record* that the song was one of his favorites.

The first half of the 1980s brought a number of smaller hits, but demand for RGB's classic style, particularly among radio executives, continued to decline. Though disco was no longer a threat, rap and hip-hop were growing rapidly. Following their last appearance on the R&B charts in 1986, Ray, Goodman & Brown shifted their focus from the recording studio to the concert hall. By playing intimate venues across the nation, the trio was able to reconnect with their most loyal fans, many of whom traveled long distances to see them. Exhausting though it was, their touring schedule enabled them to remain together long after their last hit. After Ray's death in 1992, Goodman and Brown named Keith Owens as his replacement; the group's name did not change.

After spending most of the 1990s on tour, RGB returned to the recording studio in the early 2000s, singing backup on "You Don't Know My Name," a 2003 hit by vocalist Alicia Keys. They also released several new albums, producing many of the tracks themselves. During this period a studio fire destroyed most of the master recordings Goodman had made over the course of his career. The disaster cost him hundreds of thousands of dollars in lost royalties. He died in July of 2010.

## Selected discography

### Singles

The Moments, "Love on a Two-Way Street," 1970.
The Moments, "Sexy Mama," 1973.
The Moments, "Look at Me (I'm in Love)," 1975.
Ray, Goodman & Brown, "Special Lady," 1979.
Alicia Keys, "You Don't Know My Name," 2003.

### Albums

The Moments, *Moments With You,* Stang, 1976.
Ray, Goodman & Brown, *Ray, Goodman & Brown* (includes "Special Lady"), Polydor, 1979.
Ray, Goodman & Brown, *Ray, Goodman & Brown II,* Polydor, 1980.
Ray, Goodman, & Brown, *Intimate Moments,* Orpheus, 2003.

## Sources

### Periodicals

*New York Times,* July 29, 2010.
*Record* (Hackensack, NJ), July 30, 2010.

### Online

Quan, Denise, "Soul Singer Al Goodman Dies," CNN, July 28, 2010, http://edition.cnn.com/2010/SHOWBIZ/Music/07/28/goodman.death/index.html#fbid=hEbd5JmPF2x (accessed November 21, 2010).
"Ray, Goodman & Brown," SoulWalking.co.uk, http://www.soulwalking.co.uk/Ray,%20Goodman%20&%20Brown.html (accessed November 21, 2010).

—R. Anthony Kugler

# Carl Gordon

## 1932–2010

### Theater film and television actor

Character actor Carl Gordon is best remembered for his role as the proud patriarch Andrew "Pop" Emerson on the FOX comedy series *Roc* in the 1990s. Although the show was short-lived, lasting only three seasons, it was notable for broadcasting live during its second and third seasons, the first television program to do so since the 1950s. Gordon, who came to acting late in life after stumbling through a string of unsatisfying jobs, made his Broadway debut at the age of thirty-six, in *The Great White Hope* with James Earl Jones, and went on to appear in more than sixty plays with the Negro Ensemble Company in New York. On Broadway, he originated the role of Doaker in August Wilson's *The Piano Lesson,* and later performed in a revival of the playwright's *Ma Rainey's Black Bottom* with Whoopi Goldberg. In a career spanning more than three decades, he appeared in a half dozen films and had scores of television appearances to his credit.

Rufus Carl Gordon Jr. was born on January 20, 1932, in Goochland, Virginia. When he was an infant, his family relocated to Brooklyn, where he grew up in the Bedford-Stuyvesant neighborhood, raised by his mother and grandmother. A bright student, he attended the well-regarded Boys' High School and was offered a track scholarship at a North Carolina college, but he turned it down to enlist in the U.S. Air Force. "My childhood dreams were not about being an actor," Gordon explained to the Richmond Times-Dispatch in 1992. "No, I dreamed about becoming an electrical engineer, and I thought the Air Force would give me experience, then pay for me to go to school."

Gordon served four years in the Air Force during the Korean War, learning sheet-metal-working skills. Returning to New York, he went to work for the Lockheed Corporation as a sheet metal engineer, but the company soon left town. With a family to support, Gordon took a job at the Brooklyn department store Abraham and Straus, eventually working his way up to foreman and moonlighting at the U.S. Postal Service. On the job, Gordon overheard his coworkers talking about their lost dreams and the things they should have done with their lives. Thinking about his own life—in his thirties, he was twice divorced and stuck in an unfulfilling job—he saw that it was a shambles, and wondered what he should do. "One night I got so depressed I actually began to cry," he recounted to the *New York Times* in 1992. Asking for God's guidance, "At that moment, some spirit in me said, 'Try acting.'"

Though he had seen only one play in his life—Langston Hughes's *Simply Heaven* in 1952—Gordon decided to become an actor. He enrolled at the Gene Frankel Theater Workshop, where he was the oldest student, as well as the only African American and the only one without a college degree. Careful about the roles he chose, he slowly built a career. "I won't do anything that's derogatory to my race or involves a lot of profanity," he told the Richmond Times-Dispatch.

In 1967 Gordon appeared in the national tour of Happy Ending/Day of Absence, a pair of one-act plays by Douglas Turner Ward, founder of the Negro Ensemble Company. The next year, he landed his first role on Broadway as a replacement in *The Great White Hope* with James Earl Jones, and went on to

## At a Glance . . .

**B**orn Rufus Carl Gordon Jr. on January 20, 1932, in Goochland, VA; died on July 20, 2010, in Jetersville, VA; children: Rufus Carl III, Gloria, Candise, Demethress, Yvette, Jasmine. *Military service:* U.S. Air Force.

**Career:** Negro Ensemble Company, 1960s–80s; film and television actor, 1970s–2010.

perform in the Melvin Van Peebles musical *Ain't Supposed to Die a Natural Death* in 1971. During the late 1960s through the 1980s, he performed in more than sixty productions with Ward's Negro Ensemble Company, including *Kongi's Harvest* (1968), *Sugar Mouth Sam Don't Dance No More* (1975), and *Zooman and the Sign* (1981). In 1990 Gordon originated the role of Doaker in August Wilson's Pulitzer Prize–winning play *The Piano Lesson,* a part that he later reprised in a television adaptation for CBS in 1995.

Though Gordon established himself on the stage, it was his television work that made him famous. In 1991 he joined the cast of *Roc,* a situation comedy about a working-class family in Baltimore that ran on FOX for three seasons. The show starred Broadway colleague Charles S. Dutton as sanitation worker Roc Emerson, with Gordon as his father, Andrew "Pop" Emerson, a retired Pullman porter. Gordon's character was sort of a black Archie Bunker, adorning his home with pictures of Malcolm X and claiming that Boston Celtics star Larry Bird was too good a player to be a white man. "Larry Bird was born and bred in Harlem. His real name is Abdul Mustafa," he declared in one episode.

For the second and third seasons of *Roc,* producers made the unusual decision to broadcast live, becoming the first television show to do so since the 1950s. The choice was influenced by the presence of so many veteran stage actors in the cast—not only Dutton and Gordon, but also Ella Joyce and Rocky Carroll, who played Roc Emerson's wife and brother, respectively. "We're still fresh from the stage, and working in front of a live audience is food for us," Gordon told the *New York Times.* "It's not … a gimmick." As the series progressed, it began to take on a more dramatic tone, tackling social issues such as gang violence, drug use, and the struggles of African Americans.

After *Roc* ended in 1994, Gordon made guest appearances on episodes of *Hangin' with Mr. Cooper, Malcolm & Eddie, The Practice, ER, JAG,* and *Law & Order,* among other series. In 2003 he played the role of Cutler in the Broadway revival of August Wilson's *Ma Rainey's Black Bottom* with Whoopi Goldberg,

and in 2007, he appeared in a production of Wilson's *Joe Turner's Come and Gone* at the Living Word Stage Company in Richmond, Virginia. He has several films to his credit, including *Gordon's War* (1973), John Sayles's *Brother from Another Planet* (1984), and *No Mercy* (1986).

Gordon died of non-Hodgkin's lymphoma at his home in Jetersville, Virginia, on July 23, 2010, at the age of 78.

# Selected works

## Theater

*Happy Ending/Day of Absence,* national tour, 1967.
*Kongi's Harvest,* Negro Ensemble Company, New York, 1968.
*The Great White Hope,* Alvin Theatre, New York, 1968–70.
*Ain't Supposed to Die a Natural Death,* Ethel Barrymore Theatre, New York, 1971, Ambassador Theatre, New York, 1971–72.
*Sugar Mouth Sam Don't Dance No More,* Negro Ensemble Company, New York, 1975.
*Welcome to the Black River,* Negro Ensemble Company, New York, 1975.
*In an Upstate Motel,* Negro Ensemble Company, New York, 1981.
*Zooman and the Sign,* Negro Ensemble Company, New York, 1981.
*Prince,* Negro Ensemble Company, New York, 1988–89.
*Sally,* Negro Ensemble Company, New York, 1988–89.
*The Piano Lesson,* Walter Kerr Theatre, New York, 1990–91.
*Ma Rainey's Black Bottom,* Royale Theatre, New York, 2003.
*Joe Turner's Come and Gone,* Living Word Stage Company, Richmond, VA, 2007.

## Television

*Disaster on the Coastliner,* ABC, 1979.
*The Murder of Mary Phagan* (television movie), NBC, 1988.
*Roc,* 1991–94.
*The Piano Lesson* (television movie), CBS, 1995.
*The Wedding* (television movie), ABC, 1998.
*Love Songs* (television movie), Showtime, 1999.

## Films

*Gordon's War,* 20th Century Fox, 1973.
*The Bingo Long Traveling All-Stars & Motor Kings,* Universal Pictures, 1976.
*Violated,* Vestron Video, 1984.
*The Brother from Another Planet,* Anarchist's Convention Films, 1984.
*No Mercy,* TriStar Pictures, 1986.
*Better Than Ever,* Artist View Entertainment, 1997.

## *Sources*

### *Periodicals*

*New York Times,* August 23, 1991; February 8, 1992; July 23, 2010.
*Richmond Times-Dispatch,* June 27, 1992; February 11, 2007; July 26, 2010.

—Deborah A. Ring

# Asamoah Gyan

## 1985—

### Professional soccer player

Gyan, Asamoah, photograph. Paul Gilham/FIFA via Getty Images.

By 2010, Ghanaian forward Asamoah Gyan had become one of the rising stars in international soccer. Renowned for his athleticism and goal-scoring creativity, Gyan has achieved consistent success both for the Ghana national team and for various professional soccer clubs in Europe. He was catapulted to global stardom during the 2010 World Cup in South Africa, scoring three goals in the tournament and leading Ghana to the round of eight for the first time in the team's history. Although Gyan is also remembered for having missed a crucial penalty kick in Ghana's quarterfinal loss to Uruguay, he was widely hailed for playing a key role in Ghana's surprising run, and was eventually voted the Best African Player of the tournament in a poll sponsored by the Féderation International de Football Association (FIFA), the sport's principal governing body. In addition to his celebrated speed and agility as a player, Gyan is also an accomplished musician, songwriter, and rapper, and has released an album in his native Ghana.

Gyan was born in the Ghanaian capital of Accra on November 22, 1985. As a boy, he became a fan of English soccer team Manchester United, idolizing the squad's legendary forward, Erin Cantona. Cantona's goal-scoring abilities helped lead Manchester United to four Premier League titles during the mid-1990s, while inspiring the young Ghanaian's budding soccer aspirations. Gyan launched his professional career in 2003, playing for both the Liberty Professionals, a club based in Accra, and for the Ghana national team. He first began his rise to prominence in 2004, when he joined FC Modena of Italy's B League. Gyan played in 27 games for FC Modena in 2004–05, scoring seven goals. During this time, Gyan was also a member of the Ghana national team at the 2004 Olympic Games in Athens. The following year, he scored five goals in four appearances with the Ghana team.

In 2005–06, Gyan scored eight goals in 25 games with FC Modena. At season's end, he joined the Ghana national team at the FIFA World Cup in Germany. He made headlines in a qualifying match against the Czech Republic, when he scored a goal only 68 seconds into the game. It was Ghana's first goal ever in World Cup play, and it was the fastest goal of the entire tournament. More importantly, it proved the deciding goal of the match, helping Ghana achieve a major upset over

## At a Glance . . .

**B**orn Asamoah Gyan on November 22, 1985, in Accra, Ghana.

**Career:** Liberty Professionals Accra, forward, 2003; Udinese Calcio (Italy), forward, 2003–04, 2006–08; FC Modena (Italy), forward, 2004–05; Stade Rennais (France), forward, 2008–10; Sunderland AFC (England), forward, 2010—; Ghana Football Association, forward, 2003—; played for Ghana in Olympic games, 2004; played in World Cup as member of the Ghana national team, 2006 and 2010.

**Awards:** Voted best African Player, 2010 FIFA World Cup; nominated for a Ballon d'Or, 2010.

**Addresses:** *Office*—c/o Sunderland Association Football Club, The Sunderland Stadium of Light, Sunderland, SR5 1SU, England.

a highly touted Czech team, which was ranked second in the world entering the World Cup. After the World Cup, Gyan was promoted to Udinese Calcio, FC Modena's affiliate team in the Italian A League. Gyan enjoyed continued success in his first year with his new squad, scoring eight goals in 25 games for the 2006–07 season.

Unfortunately, Gyan's rise to the upper echelon of European soccer was repeatedly delayed during the next several years, as he fell victim to a string of injuries. In 2007–08 he played only 13 games for Udinese Calcio, scoring a mere three goals. During this time Gyan also saw limited play with the Ghana team, appearing in only four games in both 2007 and 2008. Gyan's inability to perform soon drew the ire of the nation's fans, and at one point he threatened to quit in the middle of the 2008 Africa Cup of Nations tournament. In 2008 Gyan joined Stade Rennais of the French league; his first season with his new team was a disappointment, however, as he scored only one goal in 16 games. Gyan also sparked controversy in late 2009, when his refusal to participate in an exhibition match against Angola elicited scathing critiques in the local press.

Gyan gradually returned to form in 2010. In January he scored the deciding goal against Nigeria in the Africa Cup competition, sending Ghana to the finals. That summer, Gyan emerged as one of the elite players at the World Cup in South Africa. He helped Ghana become the first African team to win at the tournament, defeating Serbia with a late penalty kick. In the

team's three group round games, Gyan was named player of the match twice. Gyan later scored the deciding goal in the team's hard-fought victory over the United States in the round of sixteen, and was in a position to send Ghana to its first World Cup semifinals in the team's next match against Uruguay. Gyan missed a free kick as regular time expired, however, and Ghana ultimately lost the match on penalty kicks. Although Gyan wept after the match ended, he remained positive in the days following Ghana's defeat. "It was a major disappointment. I was a broken man but these things happen in football and I have to move on," Gyan told the BBC. "I know when all is said and done that I had a good tournament. It is unfortunate it ended the way it did but that is past now."

Gyan's performance at the 2010 World Cup quickly transformed him into one of the world's elite players. Less than two months after missing the fateful penalty kick against Uruguay, Gyan received a lucrative offer to play for the Sunderland Association Football Club (AFC) of the English Premier League, in a deal worth roughly £13 million ($20 million) over four years. Although the contract was the largest in the team's history, Gyan's signing gave Sunderland an elite scorer, as well as a powerful personality. As coach Steve Bruce told the *Northern Echo* on September 11, 2010: "He is going to be a real handful to manage but a nice handful. He will be a crowd favourite just the way he is." Meanwhile, Gyan's accomplishments at the World Cup continued to earn him accolades. In late October 2010, Gyan was one of only twenty-three players to be nominated for FIFA's Ballon d'Or, an annual award given to the world's best player.

Over the years Gyan has also earned a reputation as a locker room leader. He is known for his charisma and sense of humor and has often taken on the roll of unofficial psychologist to his teammates, intent on helping them reduce the stress of playing soccer at the highest level. As he told Ian Murtagh in the September 10, 2010, edition of the *Daily Star* (Northern Ireland): "I'm somebody who makes people happy. I know how to psyche myself and others. I take the pressure off them because I'm a funny guy."

## Sources

### Periodicals

*Africa News,* November 20, 2009; June 26, 2010.
*Daily Local News* (West Chester, PA), June 14, 2010, pp. 17, 21.
*Daily Star* (Northern Ireland), September 10, 2010, pp. 62, 63.
*Daily Telegraph* (London), September 10, 2010, p. 7.
*Evening Standard* (London), June 14, 2010.
*Express* (Scotland), June 14, 2010, pp. 58, 59.
*Herald* (Harare), July 7, 2010.
*Irish Times,* January 29, 2010, p. 18.
*New York Times,* July 3, 2010, p. 7.

*Northern Echo,* September 7, 2010, p. 46.

*Observer* (London), June 27, 2010, p. 2.

*Sunday Mail* (Queensland, Australia), July 4, 2010, p. 98.

*Westerly Sun* (RI), June 18, 2006, p. 11.

### Online

"2010 Africa Cup of Nations Player Profile: Asamoah Gyan," MTN Football,http://nationscup. mtnfootball.com/live/content.php?Item_ID=26320 (accessed October 28, 2010).

"Asamoah Gyan," FIFA.com, http://www.fifa.com/ worldcup/players/player=208353/profile.html (accessed October 28, 2010).

"Asamoah Gyan," Soccerbase, http://www.soccer-base.com/players_details.sd?playerid=42865 (accessed October 28, 2010).

"Gyan, Asamoah," National Football Teams, http:// www.national-football-teams.com/v2/player.php?id =2660 (accessed October 28, 2010).

"Gyan: I Was a Broken Man," GhanaWeb, July 7, 2010, http://www.ghanaweb.com/GhanaHome Page/SportsArchive/artikel.php?ID=185640 (accessed October 28, 2010).

"Gyan's Nomination Excites Ghana," Ghana Football Association, http://www.ghanafa.org/news/2010 10/5156.php (accessed October 28, 2010).

—Stephen Meyer

# Gary L. Harris

## 1953—

### Engineer, professor

In 1980 Gary L. Harris became the first African American to earn a doctorate in electrical engineering from Cornell University, one of the leading U.S. colleges for graduate engineering programs. Since then Harris has spent his career teaching at Howard University in Washington, DC, where he is credited with building the school's electrical engineering and materials science program. He is also a leading U.S. researcher in the materials that are used in the semiconductor industry.

Harris was born in Denver, Colorado, in 1953 and demonstrated a knack for electronics at an early age. He told Crystal R. Chissell in *U.S. Black Engineer and IT* that "I started repairing televisions" while still in middle school. "I got a novice ham license and started studying electronics." The ham license was granted by the Federal Communications Commission, and in order to earn it Harris had to demonstrate a proficiency in Morse code at a minimum rate of eight words per minute. He enrolled in Cornell University and earned his bachelor of science degree in electrical engineering in 1975. He stayed on to complete a master's degree in his field a year later, and then became the first black student to be awarded a doctorate in electrical engineering at Cornell in 1980. His friend and classmate, Michael G. Spencer, became the first African American to earn that distinction in the field of electro-physics at Cornell the following year.

Harris's impressive record at Cornell helped him to win a spot as a visiting scientist with the U.S. Naval Research Laboratory in Washington, DC, and he also worked for the computer giant IBM Corporation during his summers off before he arrived at Howard University in 1981. Both he and Spencer had been hired by Dr. Eugene N. DeLoatch, the chair of Howard's Department of Electrical Engineering, to work at its relatively new Rockwell Solid State Electronics Laboratory. The lab was founded in 1977 with initial funding from Rockwell International Corp. "Rockwell was trying to improve their image at the time," Harris explained to Chissell. "One of the researchers there got the idea of putting a first class research facility at a couple of black schools so that they could get into research." He also noted that both he and Spencer had turned down job offers from the private sector to instead come to Howard. "I came with the idea that we could build this into a giant," he told Chissell. He added that he and Spencer "made a decision to come down here together and put together a critical mass of people so that we could cause an explosion—of the technology and the materials."

The six-thousand-square-foot Rockwell lab had a bare-bones staff when Harris and Spencer arrived, but was full of expensive, high-tech research equipment thanks to Rockwell's leadership in the field of high-tech electronics. The duo began work on important research into semiconductors, a field known as "microelectronics" back then, and were joined by a third black research scientist, Dr. Keith Jackson, in 1983. In an article about the trio and Howard's Rockwell lab that appeared in a 1986 issue of *Black Enterprise*, Gwen McKinney noted that "of the total pool of American

## At a Glance . . .

**B**orn Gary Lynn Harris on June 24, 1953, in Denver, CO; son of Norman Harris and Gladys Harris; married Jennifer Dean, 1984; children: Jamie. *Education:* Cornell University, BS, electrical engineering, 1975, MS, electrical engineering, 1976, PhD, electrical engineering, 1980.

**Career:** U.S. Naval Research Laboratory, Washington, DC, visiting scientist, 1981–82; Lawrence Livermore National Laboratory, consultant after 1984; Howard University, assistant professor, 1981–87, associate professor, 1987–92, professor of electrical engineering and materials science, 1992—; Howard University, associate vice president for research, 1996–98; Howard University, Materials Science Research Center of Excellence, director, 1999—.

**Memberships:** American Association for the Advancement of Science; American Ceramic Society; American Physical Society; Institute of Electrical and Electronic Engineers; Materials Research Society; National Society of Black Engineers; Optical Society of America.

**Awards:** American Council of Education Citations, 1987—; Apple Fellow, Inter-University Consortium for Educational Computing, 1988; Excellence in Teaching Award, Howard University, 1992; Scientist of the Year Award, National Society of Black Engineers; Sigma Xi; Tau Beta Phi; Who's Who in Black America.

**Addresses:** *Office*—Howard University, Department of Electrical and Computer Engineering, 2400 Sixth St. NW, Washington, DC 20059.

electrical engineers who hold doctoral degrees, only 50 of the 250,000 are black." Harris, Spencer, and Jackson worked to recruit as many electrical engineers and physicist as possible to join them at the lab, and they did so with the help of important research grants from the National Aeronautics and Space Administration's Jet Propulsion Laboratory, the National Science Foundation, and IBM. Much of their work focused on improving the capacity of microchips and laser beams that were used in electronics and in weapons and aircraft systems. Their efforts also yielded important advances in devices that were used in prosthetic limbs.

Harris concentrated on gallium arsenide and silicon carbide, both of which are highly conductive materials used in semiconductors. He secured a large grant from the Solar Energy Research Institute to design a Monolithic Gallium Concentration Spectral Splitter, and in interviews during the 1980s he predicted that gallium arsenide and other high-tech materials would have wide-ranging consumer applications in the next few decades, including flat-screen televisions and what was described as a wristwatch-sized device that was both a radio and a calculator—the theoretical ancestor of the twenty-first century smartphone.

Harris rose at Howard from the post of assistant professor to full professor. In 1987 the Rockwell lab facility severed its ties with Rockwell and became the Materials Science Research Center of Excellence with the help of a $5 million research grant from the National Science Foundation. For a time, Harris served as head of the Department of Electrical and Computer Engineering. During the early 1990s he was part of a committee at the school that issued recommendations for modernizing the undergraduate engineering program. "We're not as good as we should be, but we're not as bad as some people think," he told *Washington Post*'s Brooke A. Masters. "This president has made a commitment to physical facilities … which is good because that had been neglected. It's a positive thing, long overdue." A year later, in 1994, that same president of Howard University, Franklyn G. Jenifer, resigned in the wake of a series of crises at the school involving accusations of financial mismanagement and of support for Louis Farrakhan's Nation of Islam religious organization. "Howard has a great tradition," Harris told Steven A. Holmes in the *New York Times*. "But you can't live on tradition. You have to live on productivity and effort."

Harris continues to teach and conduct research as Howard. His research still focuses on compounds such as gallium arsenide and silicon carbide. "Technology can only advance as far as our understanding of materials," he said in an interview with James Longo for the journal *USBE/HE Professional*. "When you cut through everything and look at the most fundamental thing that is common with some product or reality, the most fundamental thing is the materials. You can't bake a good cake unless you have good flour and good dough."

# Sources

## Periodicals

*Black Enterprise*, August 1986, pp. 44–46.
*New York Times*, December 14, 1994, p. B10.
*U.S. Black Engineer and IT*, 1986, pp. 21–23.
*USBE/HE Professional*, Spring 1990, pp. 12–13.
*Washington Post*, December 20, 1993, p. A1.

—Carol Brennan

# Walter Hawkins

## 1949–2010

### Gospel singer, music producer, minister

Hawkins, Walter, photograph. Moses Robinson/WireImage.

Walter Hawkins was an ordained bishop and one of contemporary gospel music's most legendary and beloved figures. His musical contributions include the widely acclaimed *Love Alive* series and feature the world-renowned Love Center Choir. With a prolific catalog that spans nearly four decades, Hawkins's songs are gospel standards that are sung in churches from coast to coast. "I can go a lot of places with my music that I can't go as a pastor and vice versa," Hawkins once said. "The purpose of both is getting the message out to people." Besides recording his own music, Hawkins collaborated with many notable artists, including Diahann Carroll, Jennifer Holliday, Jeffrey Osborne, the Williams Brothers, and Earth, Wind & Fire, and his songs have been recorded by superstars such as Aretha Franklin, Van Morrison, and MC Hammer.

Hawkins was born in Oakland, California, in 1949. Even though he dropped out of high school, he eventually earned his general education diploma and entered the University of California, Berkeley, to pursue a master's of divinity degree. As a teenager, Hawkins and his brother, Edwin, began playing at events and singing in the youth choir at the Ephesians Church of God in Christ in Berkeley. In 1968 Edwin was the choir director when the choir recorded the album *Let Us Go into the House of the Lord* to raise money to attend a convention in Washington, DC. Much to the choir's surprise, one of album's tracks, "Oh Happy Day," went on to sell over a million copies the following year, rose to number four in the U.S. pop charts, and became a major gospel crossover hit. The song's success also launched Walter's musical career as he toured with the choir (now known as the Edwin Hawkins Singers) before setting out on his own.

In 1970 Hawkins married Tramaine Davis, with whom he had two children, Walter and Trystan. The couple later divorced, but they remained close friends and continued to record together throughout their respective careers. While Edwin's music was more secular, Walter's was pure gospel, and the ministry was the power behind his music. Hawkins recorded his first album, *Do Your Best,* while studying for his divinity degree in 1972. Even though largely unknown in later years, the album did attract the attention of a *Billboard* review: "Walter Hawkins is a pianist of enviable accomplishments while his vocal prowess is in no way disput-

### At a Glance . . .

**B**orn Walter Lee Hawkins on May 18, 1949, in Oakland, CA; died July 11, 2010, in Ripon, CA; married Tramaine Davis, 1970 (divorced); children: Walter, Trystan. *Religion:* Church of God in Christ. *Education:* University of California, Berkeley, MDiv.

**Career:** Love Center Ministries, Inc., founder and minister, 1973–2010; Church of God in Christ, ordained bishop, 1992; Coda Records, owner and recording artist, 2005–10.

**Awards:** Two Dove Awards, Gospel Music Association, 1978, for *Love Alive II;* Grammy Award for best gospel performance, 1980, for *The Lord's Prayer;* Governor's Award for Creative Excellence and Outstanding Achievement, San Francisco Chapter of the Recording Academy, 2003; Gospel Music's Lifetime Heritage Award; Gospel Music Hall of Fame Museum Award; Stellar Award for Traditional Gospel Album of the Year, 2006, for *A Song in My Heart;* Christian Music Hall of Fame, 2007.

able. He's gathered around him an exceptional crew of sidemen and vocalists and the total effect is completely invigorating."

Hawkins began holding Bible study discussions in his home, and in 1973 he founded the Love Center Church and the Love Center Choir in East Oakland, California. Two years later Hawkins and the Love Center Choir recorded the album *Love Alive,* which featured two of the most popular gospel songs of the decade—"Goin' up Yonder" and "Changed"—and sold 300,000 copies. *Love Alive II* followed in 1978, selling 290,000 copies and winning two Dove Awards from the Gospel Music Association. During the 1980s Hawkins also produced albums for a number of artists, including Tramaine, his sister Lynette, and his cousin Shirley Miller. Even though he would eventually be nominated for nine Grammy Awards throughout his entire career, he only won one in 1980 for best performance on the album *The Lord's Prayer.* That same year he also preformed at the Grammy Awards ceremony.

In 1990 *Love Alive III* sold more than a million copies and featured the radio hits "There's a War Going On," " I Love You, Lord," and "He'll Bring You Out." *Love Alive IV* was released that same year. The album was nominated for a Grammy and topped *Billboard's* gospel chart for more than thirty-nine weeks. In 1992

Hawkins was ordained bishop of Love Center Ministries, a church that eventually grew to include more than a thousand members.

The last installment in the *Love Alive* series, *Love Alive V: 25th Anniversary Reunion,* was released in 1998. The two-disc album celebrated Hawkins's twenty-fifth anniversary as a recording artist and minister and reunited the Love Center Choir with his cousins, siblings, and Tramaine. Hawkins wrote seven of the ten tracks on the first disc, with the ballad "Marvelous" becoming a commercial success, and gathered all of his favorite recordings on the second disc. In 2005 Hawkins released his final solo CD, *A Song in My Heart,* which earned him a Stellar Award for Traditional Gospel Album of the Year in 2006.

Hawkins was inducted into the Christian Hall of Fame in 2007. The following year his health began to fail and he ended up having surgery for pancreatic cancer. Though weakened by illness, he still managed to stage a multicity Hawkins family reunion concert tour with Edwin, Tramaine, and Lynette and to perform at the Kennedy Center with a gospel choir and the National Symphony Orchestra. Hawkins died at his home in Ripon, California, in July of 2010. According to Liz Gonzalez in the *Oakland Tribune,* over two thousand people attended a musical tribute and funeral that was held at Oakland's historic Paramount Theatre shortly after Hawkins's passing. "We are not here today because Walter died, we are here today because he lived," the Reverend Carlton Pearson said during the tribute. "We don't really die, we transcend. Walter's footprints are all over us."

## Selected discography

*Love Alive,* Compendia Music Group, 1975.
*Love Alive II,* Light Records, 1978.
*Love Alive III,* A&M, 1990.
*Love Alive IV,* Malaco, 1990.
*Love Alive V: 25th Anniversary Reunion,* Gospocentric Records, 1998.
*A Song in My Heart,* Coda, 2005.

## Sources

### Periodicals

Associated Press, July 12, 2010.
*Billboard,* October 1972.
*Daily Variety,* July 15, 2010, p. 9.
*New York Times,* July 14, 2010, p. A25.
*Oakland Tribune,* July 21, 2010.
*Washington Post,* July 12, 2010.

### Online

"Gospel Legend Walter Hawkins Passes," Blackvoicenews.com, http://www.blackvoicenews.com/news/

44712-gospel-legend-walter-hawkins-passes.html (accessed October 19, 2010).

"The Man, the Music, the Ministry," Walter Hawkins Memorial Foundation, July 15, 2010, http:// walterhawkinsmemorialfoundation.org/about (accessed October 19, 2010).

—Marie O'Sullivan

# Roy Haynes

## 1925—

### Jazz drummer

Drummer Roy Haynes has had an extraordinary career in jazz. For more than six decades, the Massachusetts native has been at the forefront of that genre, collaborating with such giants as saxophonists John Coltrane and Charlie Parker, trumpeter Miles Davis, vocalist Sarah Vaughn, and pianist Chick Corea. One of very few Americans ever to be knighted by the government of France, he has been releasing acclaimed albums under his own name since the 1950s.

The son of immigrants from the Caribbean island of Barbados, Roy Owen Haynes was born March 13, 1925, in Roxbury, a Boston neighborhood that has long served as the center of that city's African-American community. Jazz was part of his life from a very early age. The influence of his older brother Douglas, a trumpet player, was considerable in this regard, for it was through his sibling's records that Haynes was first exposed to the work of bandleaders Duke Ellington and Count Basie, pianist Art Tatum, and other seminal figures. Fascinated by rhythms of all kinds, he quickly gravitated toward the drums, playing them in his high school band and in small groups around Boston. By the mid 1940s, his talents had drawn the attention of bandleader Luis Russell, who

Haynes, Roy, photograph. Barbara Zanon/Getty Images.

hired him for a series of gigs at the Savoy Ballroom in New York.

Haynes thrived in New York. After two years with Russell, he joined a small group led by the saxophonist Lester Young, with whom he stayed until 1949. In a 2006 interview with Ben Ratliff of the *New York Times,* he spoke of Young with obvious affection, noting, in particular, the way the saxophonist allowed him to set the group's tone. "I was always feeding him that thing," he told Ratliff, referring to the ride cymbal, a standard feature on most drum sets. "I was swinging with him. It wasn't particularly hard swinging; we were moving, you know, trying to paint a picture."

After his stint with Young came a somewhat unsettled but extremely productive period. Between 1949 and 1953, Haynes worked with both Parker and Davis, two of the primary forces behind bebop, the impressionistic, improvisatory style that was just beginning to transform the world of jazz. He then joined the backup band for Vaughn, remaining with her for about five years. Already an international star, she brought Haynes to Europe for the first time in his life. His experiences there, particularly in Paris, helped inspire

**At a Glance . . .**

**B**orn Roy Owen Haynes on March 13, 1925, in Boston, MA; son of an oil company worker.

**Career:** Independent drummer, 1940s—; played with Luis Russell, 1945–47, Lester Young, 1947–49, Charlie Parker, 1949(?)–53(?), Miles Davis, 1949(?)–53(?), Sarah Vaughn, 1953(?)–58(?), Billie Holiday, 1959, Stan Getz, 1960s, John Coltrane, 1960s, Gary Burton, 1960s, Chick Corea, 1968—, and many others.

**Awards:** Best Contemporary Jazz Record (for *Te Vou!*), National Association of Independent Record Distributors, 1996; Chevalier dans l'Ordre des Arts et des Lettres, Government of France, 1996.

**Addresses:** *Office*—c/o Francis Dreyfus Music, 26 Avenue Kléber, 75016 Paris, France.

his nascent solo career. His 1954 recording *Busman's Holiday,* the first major album to be released under his own name, was followed two years later by *Jazz Abroad*; both were recorded in Europe. These quickly became classics, as did a number of his subsequent releases, most notably 1962's *Out of the Afternoon,* which Steven McDonald of AllMusic.com called "a delightful mix of techniques in arrangement and performance," adding, "Haynes' drumming is absolutely wonderful here, lightly dancing around the other instruments."

By the time *Out of the Afternoon* appeared, Haynes was again working in a wide variety of backup bands. After leaving Vaughn, he played briefly in 1959 with the iconic vocalist Billie Holiday, then at the end of her life, and more extensively with saxophonist Stan Getz. While Getz had a long and distinguished career, he was at his peak in the early 1960s, issuing a number of groundbreaking albums within the space of a few years. Haynes's drums can be heard on several of these, particularly 1961's *Focus,* which Peter Watrous of the *New York Times* once described as a "masterwork." It was also around this time that Haynes became involved with Coltrane, often filling in for that saxophonist's regular drummer, Elvin Jones. Though Coltrane and Getz had very different styles, Haynes moved between them with ease.

In the second half of the 1960s, Haynes found himself drawn, like many of his peers, toward a harder sound based, in part, on the riffs and rhythms of rock and roll. Much of his early work in this new style, dubbed "fusion," was done with Corea and the vibraphonist Gary Burton, both of whom had worked with him in

Getz' band. His partnership with Corea proved particularly enduring; more than thirty years after their completion of a major album, Corea's *Now He Sings, Now He Sobs* (1968), they were still playing together regularly.

The 1970s found Haynes working on a variety of eclectic projects. In addition to his ongoing collaborations with Corea, he returned to his roots through several prominent gigs with the trumpeter and bandleader Dizzy Gillespie, whose career stretched back to the 1930s. He also began to devote more attention to his solo career, which he had put on hold for several years in the late 1960s. After a string of well-received albums in the 1970s, he took a break again in the 1980s, with only one major release in that decade, the 1986 live album *True or False.* He returned to the recording studio with a renewed sense of purpose in the 1990s, issuing a number of albums in rapid succession. One of these, 1996's *Te Vou!,* was named the year's Best Contemporary Jazz Record by the National Association of Independent Record Distributors. It was also in that year that the French government named him a "chevalier," or knight, in the Order of Arts and Letters, a honor reserved for those deemed to have made a unique contribution to French culture.

As he passed his eightieth birthday in 2005, Haynes showed relatively few signs of slowing down. Asked by Dan King of the Web site All About Jazz to reflect on his career, he responded with modesty and a strong sense of gratitude. "We're all just human beings trying to play the music," he told King in 2003, adding, "I've been very fortunate to live this long and to play and innovate."

## Selected discography

*Busman's Holiday,* EmArcy, 1954.
*Jazz Abroad,* Verve, 1956.
Stan Getz, *Focus,* Verve, 1961.
*Out of the Afternoon,* Impulse!, 1962.
Chick Corea, *Now He Sings, Now He Sobs,* Blue Note, 1968.
*Hip Ensemble,* Mainstream, 1971.
*Live at the Riverbop,* EPM, 1979.
*True or False,* Evidence, 1986.
*Te Vou!,* Dreyfus, 1994.
*Fountain of Youth,* Dreyfus, 2004.
*Whereas,* Dreyfus, 2006.
*A Life in Time: The Roy Haynes Story,* Dreyfus, 2007.

## Sources

### Periodicals

*New York Times,* June 7, 1991; March 10, 2006.

### Online

McDonald, Steven, "*Out of the Afternoon*: Review,"

AllMusic.com, http://www.allmusic.com/cg/amg.dll?p=amg&sql=10:dxfuxq9gld0e (accessed November 21, 2010).

"Roy Haynes," Dreyfus Records, http://www.disques dreyfus.com/catalogue/haynes-roy.html (accessed November 21, 2010).

Yanow, Scott, "Roy Haynes: Biography," AllMusic.com, http://allmusic.com/cg/amg.dll?p=amg&sql=11:fnftxqr5ldke~T1 (accessed August 10, 2010).

—R. Anthony Kugler

# Raymond V. Haysbert Sr.

## 1920–2010

### Business executive

Haysbert, Raymond V., Sr., photograph. AP Images/John Mummert.

Raymond V. Haysbert Sr. was one of Baltimore's most respected civic leaders. Haysbert was a successful executive with the Parks Sausage Company for many years, which in 1969 became Wall Street's first publicly traded firm under black ownership. His influence and commitment to his adopted hometown touched multiple generations of Baltimore citizens and aided in the rise of Maryland political figures such as Kweisi Mfume, who would go on to lead the Congressional Black Caucus.

During World War II Haysbert trained at Tuskegee College to become one of the legendary Tuskegee Airmen. This was more formally known as the 332nd Fighter Group of the U.S. Army Air Forces and was the first all-black fighter squadron at a time when the U.S. military was still dramatically segregated by race. Haysbert and his Tuskegee brethren racked up a phenomenally successful combat record, flying 1,587 missions and downing 400 enemy aircraft. After the war, Haysbert returned to take a teaching job at Wilberforce University.

Haysbert grew up in hardscrabble-poor circumstances in Cincinnati, Ohio, where he was born in 1920 as one of eight children in his family. Three of his younger siblings died during his childhood. As a young man, he worked at a coal company to help pay for tuition at Wilberforce University, a private historically black college. At one point he was forced to drop out because of financial hardship, so he took another job as a janitor at a water treatment plant. However, he eventually went on to earn an undergraduate degree in mathematics from the university and then a second bachelor's degree in business administration from Central State University.

In 1952 Henry Green Parks, a Dayton-raised entrepreneur, persuaded Haysbert to move to Baltimore to help run the sausage company he had founded a year earlier on the site of a former dairy plant. Haysbert agreed and became the accountant and office manager of Parks Sausage Company, which eventually became a Baltimore landmark and a source of pride for its status as a successful, black-owned business in the city. Its sage-and-pepper sausage was considered a local specialty, but Haysbert and others at the company met with resistance from grocery store owners, who would deliberately let its products spoil because they disliked dealing with a black-run firm.

Under the leadership of Parks and Haysbert, the company nevertheless expanded into a regional favorite, and in 1969 Parks Sausage became the first black-owned firm to become a publicly traded company on Wall Street. This happened when the company floated $1.5 million in newly created stock shares on the National Association of Securities Dealers Automated Quotation board to raise capital for further growth.

Haysbert rose to the post of executive vice president of Parks Sausage, and in 1977 Parks sold the still-thriving company to the Norin Corporation, a Miami-based conglomerate, for $5 million. At the time of the sale, Parks Sausage was the seventh-largest black-owned company in the United States, and one of only two publicly traded companies under African-American ownership—the other was Johnson Publishing of Chicago. During the summer of 1980 Norin sold Parks Sausage to the Canellus Company, a subsidiary of Canadian Pacific Enterprises Ltd. A few months later, Haysbert led a group of investors who bought back the company and returned it to being privately held.

Haysbert became president of Parks Sausage in 1985 and oversaw a period of phenomenal success for the company. It landed key wholesale accounts by supplying sausage toppings for Domino's Pizza and Pizza Hut, and annual sales neared the $30 million mark by the end of the decade. His leadership skills earned him National Minority Entrepreneur of the Year honors from the U.S. Department of Commerce in 1991.

By that point, however, Haysbert had been forced to make some difficult decisions that would eventually spell doom for the company. During the late 1980s local officials ordered Parks Sausage to move out of its downtown Baltimore location near the old passenger-rail station. The area was then cleared for the construction of Camden Yards, the new baseball stadium for the Baltimore Orioles. Parks Sausage built a new plant at Druid Park Drive and Reisterstown Road, deliberately staying inside the city, but construction of the new facility plunged the company into debt. Then the company lost both pizza accounts to competitors. In 1996 the company was forced to file for bankruptcy protection and close the plant. The sausage-making started up again a few months later when Haysbert and his son, Reginald, who were co-owners, struck a deal to sell Parks Sausage to Franco Harris, a former Pittsburgh Steeler whose post-football career included several savvy business acquisitions.

Haysbert was traumatized by the bankruptcy and layoffs, and he took the entirety of the blame. "After all is said and done, I made the decisions," he told *Baltimore Business Journal* writer Adam Katz-Stone in 1998. "And if it didn't work, it must have been because I made the wrong decisions." However, Haysbert had an impressive track record of service in other ways to the Baltimore community, which at one time was one of the most segregated urban pockets of the United States. In 1954 his fund-raising and political-organizing skills helped a young attorney named Harry Cole to become the first black to be elected to the Maryland State Senate, and he also worked on Henry Parks's campaign for a seat on the Baltimore City Council a few years later. Haysbert cofounded Helping to Unite Baltimore, a community organization that established neighborhood-watch patrols and demanded a more diverse police force. He was also a pivotal local figure in quelling unrest in Baltimore following the Reverend Martin Luther King Jr.'s assassination in 1968. Long active in the Greater Baltimore Urban League, he was chosen to chair its board of directors in 2001 in a last-minute bid to rescue its ailing finances, which he did.

Haysbert died of congestive heart failure in May of 2010 at Baltimore's Union Memorial Hospital at the age of ninety. Days later, an overflow crowd of mourners came to pay their respects to the longtime head of Parks Sausage. One of those who spoke at his memorial service was Kweisi Mfume, whom Haysbert had met when Mfume was a young black activist during the early 1970s. He went from a seat on the Baltimore City Council to representing Maryland in the U.S. House of Representatives. Mfume praised Haysbert's leadership skills, which were always secondary to his business goals. According to Jacques Kelly in the *Baltimore Sun,* Haysbert liked to remind Mfume, "'Never forget, if you win the rat race, you are still a rat.'"

## *Sources*

### *Periodicals*

*Baltimore Business Journal,* September 4, 1998, p. 29.
*Baltimore Sun,* May 24, 2010; June 2, 2010.
*Black Enterprise,* August 1995, p. 108.
*New York Times,* May 28, 2010.
*Reading Eagle* (Reading, PA), June 14, 1992, p. B4.

### *Online*

Shen, Fern, "Raymond V. Haysbert: The Hard-Won Wisdom of a Baltimore Trail Blazer," Baltimore Brew, May 26, 2010, http://www.baltimorebrew.com/2010/05/26/raymond-v-haysbert-the-hard-won-wisdom-of-a-baltimore-trail-blazer/ (accessed October 14, 2010).

—Carol Brennan

# Santonio Holmes

## 1984—

### Professional football player

Holmes, Santonio, photograph. Al Pereira/Getty Images.

Santonio Holmes is among the most talented, and troubled, wide receivers in professional football. Possessed with what Pittsburgh Post-Gazette writer Ron Cook has described as "big-play capabilities," Holmes is known for his exceptional speed and ball-catching abilities, and is frequently viewed as the most dangerous threat on the field by opposing defenses. A standout talent at Ohio State University, Holmes is perhaps most famous for making the game-winning catch for the Pittsburgh Steelers in Super Bowl XLIII, a feat that helped earn him MVP honors for the game. In spite of his quick rise to success, however, Holmes has also experienced his share of problems over the course of his football career, including multiple arrests on charges ranging from drug possession to domestic assault. Holmes's off-field issues eventually became too much of a distraction for the Steelers, who traded him to the New York Jets following the 2009–10 season.

Holmes traveled a great distance to achieve NFL stardom. He was born on March 3, 1984, in Belle Glade, Florida. He was raised by his mother, Patricia Brown. Holmes's hometown was known as Muck City, a reference to the area's rich, damp soil, which was ideal for raising sugar cane. For many of the city's residents, the nickname had more ominous connotations. Growing up in the city's notorious Okeechobee Center projects, Holmes was exposed to extreme poverty and crime in his early years; several members of his extended family were drug dealers, and Holmes himself began selling drugs on the street when he was only seven years old. As he later recounted in interviews, it wasn't unusual for his mother's apartment to be broken into, or for them to find bullet holes in their front door. Eventually, his mother moved the family to a safer neighborhood, with the hope of providing Holmes and his brothers with the opportunity to break away from their rough origins.

Because his mother worked a full-time job, Holmes also assumed a high level of responsibility at a young age. The oldest of four boys, Holmes woke up early on school days to help his brothers got ready for school; in the afternoons, he prepared snacks and managed the household while waiting for his mother to get home from work. These circumstances did little to slow Holmes's development as an elite athlete. By the time he reached high school, Holmes had emerged as a

## At a Glance . . .

**B**orn Santonio Holmes on March 3, 1984, in Belle Glade, FL; son of Patricia Brown and Santonio Holmes Sr.; children: T.J., Santonio III, Nicori, Saniya. *Education:* Attended Ohio State University, 2002–05.

**Career:** Pittsburgh Steelers, wide receiver, 2006–10; New York Jets, wide receiver, 2010—.

**Awards:** First-team All-Big Ten Conference, 2005; Most Valuable Player, Super Bowl XLIII, 2009.

**Addresses:** *Office*—c/o New York Jets, 1 Jets Dr., Florham Park, NJ 07932.

talented football and basketball player, while also excelling at track. While attending Glades Central High School, Holmes led his football squad to two state championships, won a state title with the track team, and made it to the state finals as a member of the varsity basketball team. In his senior football season, Holmes caught ten touchdown passes and amassed 33 total receptions, averaging nearly 30 yards per catch. During this time, Holmes also became father to his first son, T.J.

Upon graduating from high school, Holmes entered Big Ten powerhouse Ohio State. He began his college career as a redshirt freshman, practicing with the football team while remaining ineligible to play. By his sophomore year, Holmes had emerged as a serious offensive weapon for the Buckeyes, amassing 26 receptions in only his first four games as a full-time starter. His breakout performance came in a September 11, 2004, game against Marshall University, in which Holmes made ten catches, scored two touchdowns, and amassed 224 yards, the second most for a receiver in Ohio State history. Opponents soon began double-teaming the dangerous wideout, and by the end of the season Holmes's production had decreased considerably. Holmes returned to form his junior year, leading the Buckeyes with 977 receiving yards on 53 receptions, while scoring 11 touchdowns. At the same time, Holmes was also one of the best punt returners in college football, averaging 12.8 yards per return in 2005. While in college, Holmes also fathered another son.

Following his junior year, Holmes declared his eligibility for the 2006 NFL draft. He was selected by the Pittsburgh Steelers as the twenty-fifth pick of the first round. Shortly after signing his first professional contract, however, Holmes found himself in trouble with the law. In May of 2006, Holmes was arrested for disorderly conduct in Miami Beach. Less than a month later, he was arrested again on charges of assault and domestic violence, following an altercation with the mother of his newborn daughter, Shaniya. Although Holmes pled innocent to the charges, his behavior became a matter of serious concern for Steelers head coach Bill Cowher, who was quoted as saying he was "not real happy" with his new wide receiver's off-field conduct. In spite of these troubles, Holmes played in all 16 regular season games for the Steelers his rookie season, catching 49 passes and averaging 16.8 yards per catch. Holmes also achieved success as a punt and kickoff returner; in a December 17 game against the Carolina Panthers, he returned a punt 65 yards for a touchdown. Still, Holmes never took his success for granted. At the end of his rookie season, he even had the words "Muck City" tattooed across the knuckles of both hands, as a tribute to his humble beginnings.

By his second season with the Steelers, Holmes had become one of the team's starting receivers. In 2007 he led all NFL wideouts by averaging 18.1 yards per catch, on 52 receptions and 942 total yards. Holmes continued to showcase his tremendous abilities the following year, quickly becoming the team's second leading receiver, with 22 receptions through the first six games. In late October, however, Holmes's progress was once again derailed, after he was arrested for possession of marijuana. Although the charges were eventually dropped, the incident sparked fresh concerns about the receiver's off-field conduct. After serving a one-game suspension, Holmes returned to the starting lineup, helping lead the Steelers to a Super Bowl matchup against the Arizona Cardinals. Holmes delivered a legendary performance in the title game, amassing 131 yards on nine receptions. He saved his biggest catch for last, snagging a pass in the corner of the end zone for the decisive touchdown with less than a minute left in the game. Holmes's feats garnered him the Super Bowl MVP award and elevated him to nationwide fame.

Still, trouble continued to plague Holmes even after he reached pro football's pinnacle. In March of 2010, Holmes was involved in an altercation at an Orlando bar, in which a woman accused him of throwing a glass of liquor at her face. Although Holmes denied the charges, the incident proved too much for the Steelers, and within a month he was traded to the New York Jets. While many felt the change in scenery would help Holmes, his first season with the Jets quickly became mired in controversy. In October of 2010, sports agent Josh Luchs revealed that Holmes had been given money by another agent while a student at Ohio State, in strict violation of NCAA rules. Once again, Holmes denied the allegations. Still his implication in the scandal was ill-timed. As he adjusted to a new offensive system, and new teammates, it was clear that he would also need to contend with yet more unwelcome scrutiny as the season progressed.

# Sources

## Periodicals

*Charlotte Observer,* February 2, 2009, p. 4C.
*Columbus Dispatch,* August 9, 2005, p. 1C.
*Independent* (Massillon, OH), June 20, 2006.
*Miami Herald,* January 27, 2009.
*Orlando Sentinel,* March 30, 2010.
*Pittsburgh Post-Gazette,* April 30, 2006, p. C7; June 26, 2006, p. B6; August 16, 2007, p. C1; October 25, 2008, p. A1; November 15, 2009, p. A1.
*Pittsburgh Tribune-Review,* December 4, 2006; June 10, 2009.
*Plain Dealer* (Cleveland), September 16, 2004, p. D1.

*St. Petersburg Times,* February 3, 2009, p. 1C.
*Star Tribune* (Minneapolis), October 9, 2010, p. 4C.
*Wisconsin State Journal,* October 21, 2010, p. B6.

## Online

"Flashback: Ohio State vs. Marshall 2004," Eleven Warriors, September 1, 2010, http://www.elevenwarriors.com/2010/09/flashback-ohio-state-vs-marshall-2004 (accessed October 29, 2010).
"Santonio Holmes," Pro-Football-Reference.com, http://www.pro-football-reference.com/players/H/HolmSa00.htm (accessed October 29, 2010).

—Stephen Meyer

# Iman

## 1955—

### Fashion model, actor, cosmetic designer

Iman, photograph. Mike Coppola/FilmMagic.

The Somali-born, former supermodel known simply as Iman is often described as one of the world's most beautiful women. Tall, lithe, and graceful, she arrived on the fashion scene in 1975 and went on to have a successful career as one of the world's highest-paid models during the late 1970s and 1980s. She accrued a small fortune, then went on to launch a cosmetics company that became a lucrative second career for her. In 1992 she married one of rock's most iconic figures, David Bowie, and they remain one of the most sought-after celebrity couples at top-tier society galas. "I feel like the best is yet to come," Iman told a cosmetics industry crowd in 2005, according to Haven Thompson in *W* magazine. "Women of color have been accepted not as exotic birds but as beauties."

### Fled to Kenya

Iman was born in 1955 in Mogadishu, an Indian Ocean port city that five years later became the capital of a newly united and independent Somalia. Her mother, Marian, named her "Iman," a traditional masculine name in Somali culture, to reduce some of the discrimi-

nation she would likely face. Iman's father was a diplomat whose job assignments brought the family of five children to settle in Egypt, Saudi Arabia, and Sudan, but their home base was a white house on one of the most beautiful beaches along the Indian Ocean.

Iman's parents were progressive. Somalia was a predominantly Muslim country and her father was permitted to take up to four wives, but he chose not to. However, the country's deep political and religious divisions began to create irreparable turmoil, and in 1969 there was a military coup. Soon after that middle-class educated Somalians who had been part of the old-guard elite began disappearing, and Iman's parents feared that they, too, would be jailed by the new regime. A few months later, her mother "woke us up in the middle of the night and told us we were leaving but to take nothing," she told Leslie Bennetts in a 2007 *Town and Country* interview. "We crossed the border into Kenya with nothing but the clothes on our backs."

Cut off from his well-paying government post, Iman's father struggled to support the family in Kenya. Iman worked as a waitress and translator while taking classes

*At a Glance . . .*

**B**orn Iman Mohamed Abdulmajid on July 25, 1955, in Mogadishu, Somalia; daughter of Mohamed Abdulmajid (a diplomat) and Marian Abdulmajid (a nurse); married Spencer Haywood (a professional basketball player), 1977 (divorced, 1987); married David Bowie (a musician), 1992; children: (with Haywood) Zulekha; (with Bowie) Alexandria Zahra. *Education:* Attended University of Nairobi; graduated from New York University.

**Career:** Signed to Wilhelmina Models, 1975; actress, 1979—; Iman Cosmetics, founder and chief executive officer, 1994—; launched I-Iman Makeup, 2000; launched I-Iman Skincare, 2003.

**Awards:** Fashion Icon Award, Council of Fashion Designers of America, 2010.

**Addresses:** *Home*—New York, NY. *Office*—Impala, Inc., 363 Seventh Ave., Ste. 8, New York, NY 10001-3904.

at the University of Nairobi, and she also married a hotel manager when she was just seventeen—a decision that her parents vehemently opposed. The union lasted just three months, and Iman was back in school one day when a well-known American photographer, Peter Beard, stopped her on the street. "I thought he was trying to pick me up," Iman recalled to Bennetts. "He said, 'Have you ever been photographed?'—as if, because I was African, I would never have seen a camera. But then he said the key words: 'I'll pay you!' I said, 'How much?' He said, 'How much do you want?' I said, 'I need a year's tuition—$8,000.' He said, 'Okay.'"

Beard was a high-profile name entrenched inside New York City's thrumming cultural scene, and he had become a favorite freelance photographer among fashion editors such as Diana Vreeland, though he had spent much of his career photographing animals in the wild in Africa. Beard was nevertheless a tastemaker who did much to introduce the stunning beauty of the African landscape to Western eyes, and when he brought some of the test sheets he had taken of Iman back to New York he told editors he had found her in the grasslands herding cattle. Wilhelmina Cooper, the founder of Wilhelmina Models, contacted Iman and invited her to come to New York City, and she jumped at the chance. "I thought I could go to the U.S. and come back before my parents found out, so I forged

some papers and went," she told Bennetts. At the time, a Somali female had to be twenty-one years old to secure a visa or obtain permission from her father or husband.

## Launched Career with Blaze of Publicity

Iman arrived in New York City during the summer of 1975, when city sanitation workers had briefly walked off the job. "The city was filthy, and more than the stench of the garbage, I smelled danger—everywhere," she wrote in her 2001 memoir *I Am Iman*. "I thought to myself, This is worse than a Third World country!" Beard and Cooper worked together to generate some buzz about their discovery, which included the tale that Iman was a cattle herder. There was also a shambolic press conference in which she pretended not to speak English—though she spoke that language as well as her original Somali, plus French, Italian, and Arabic. She quickly became the hottest new model on the scene. Her parents discovered her actual whereabouts when she appeared in *Newsweek* magazine.

As a top model in high demand, Iman could command stunning fees from designers such as Yves Saint Laurent and Thierry Muglier, both of whom gave her credit as being an creative inspiration. "She has this amazing skin—it sets off color and clothes in a way white women couldn't do," the iconic women's clothing designer Calvin Klein told Teri Agins in the *New York Times*. "On the runway, she exuded style. She was an actress, a natural. She knew how to sell the clothes better than anybody." Yet, as Iman recalled in her memoir, being feted as an exotic beauty had its downside. "There were definitely mixed feelings about me in the African-American community. Who did I think I was? How could I claim to represent the standard of Black beauty? I would walk into a room and nobody would bother to whisper their insults," she wrote. Many people also assumed her stately bearing came with an equally high-handed attitude. "So I worked twice as hard to be friendly, to break down the preconceptions," she wrote. "This took a lot of effort, because I'm not really the sort of person who goes out of her way to explain herself."

Iman's modeling career nearly ended in 1983, when she was injured in a serious automobile wreck while riding in a New York City taxicab. She suffered a dislocated shoulder and three broken ribs as well as injuries to her collarbone and famed cheekbones, one of which required reconstructive surgery. After she fully recovered, Iman entered into a deal to market a line of authentic African fabrics called kikois. She also ventured into film and television, making her big-screen debut in *The Human Factor,* a 1979 British spy thriller that starred Richard Attenborough and John Gielgud. In 1985 she appeared in *Out of Africa* and on the top-rated series *The Cosby Show* and *Miami Vice* in guest roles.

### *Married the Former "Ziggy Stardust"*

For most of the 1980s Iman was married to the star athlete Spencer Haywood, a professional basketball player. The couple had one daughter, Zulekha, before their marriage ended in divorce in 1987. Iman's hairdresser set her up on a date with David Bowie in 1990, and the two were wed in a civil ceremony in Lausanne, Switzerland, in 1992. In November of that year Iman lost a long custody battle with Haywood over their daughter. Zulekha grew up on the east side of Detroit, attended college in Michigan, and went on to work for her mother's cosmetics company. That venture took shape in 1994, when Iman realized that the foundation formulas she made for herself might prove an ideal business opportunity. Her line was launched at J.C. Penney department stores, which carried it exclusively for several years. In 2000 she established I-Iman, a couture cosmetics line for all women that was sold at Sephora cosmetics stores. In 2004 she inked a deal with Procter & Gamble Beauty to manufacture and distribute both lines.

In 2008 Iman was one of a number of prominent names in the fashion industry who chastised both American and European designers for the lack of women of color in runway shows and in print advertising. She and her best friend of three decades, the modeling-agency pioneer Bethann Hardison, set up a series of panel discussions in New York City that fall. Their work was chronicled by the *Vogue* writer Norman Jean Roy in an article that bore the title "Is Fashion Racist?" The article recounted that at the panel discussions some industry professionals confessed that model bookers were told by designers, "We're not [using] black models this season." As Iman pointed out to Roy, "in any other industry that would be a racist remark, and you would be taken to court for it!"

In 2010 Iman was presented with the Fashion Icon Award from the Council of Fashion Designers of America. She and Bowie live in New York City, where they keep a relatively low profile. Iman rarely hesitates to step forward for a good cause, however, and over the years she has worked with a number of organizations that provide aid to Africa. In October of 1992 she visited Somalia for the first time in more than twenty years to make *Somalia Diary,* a documentary film about famine in her native country. She has also worked with Keep a Child Alive, which provides medi-

cation to children with AIDS in Africa. "Africa is in the mess it's in mostly because of our governments, which have let us down repeatedly," she told Bennetts, adding that finding a way to help those in need while avoiding the tangle of civil war, corruption, and mismanagement in many of the countries has been personally frustrating. "Then you think, 'If not I—the African—then who?'.... As an African, I feel like, there but for the grace of God there I go. There is nothing special about me. It was just pure luck. We're talking about modeling, for God's sake! It's not like I earned it."

## Selected works

### Books

*I Am Iman,* Universe Publishers, 2001.
(With Tia Williams) *The Beauty of Color: The Ultimate Beauty Guide for Skin of Color,* Putnam, 2005.

### Films

*The Human Factor,* Sigma Productions, 1979.
*Out of Africa,* Mirage Enterprises, 1985.
*No Way Out,* Orion Pictures Corporation, 1987.
*Surrender,* Cannon Group, 1987.
*House Party 2,* New Line Cinema, 1991.
*Star Trek VI: The Undiscovered Country,* Paramount Pictures, 1991.
*Exit to Eden,* Savoy Pictures, 1994.
*The Deli,* Golden Monkey Pictures, 1997.

## Sources

### Periodicals

*Black Enterprise,* November 1994.
*Essence,* January 1988; November 2001, p. 82.
*Harper's Bazaar,* February 2002, p. 210.
*New York Times,* June 4, 2010.
*People,* May 4, 1992; May 18, 1992; May 8, 2000.
*Town and Country,* June 2007, p. 174.
*Vogue,* October 1989; December 1992; July 2008, p. 134.
*W,* October 2009, p. 72.
*WWD,* March 3, 2000.

—Marjorie Burgess, Christine Miner Minderovic, and Carol Brennan

# Marvin Isley

## 1953–2010

### R&B bassist and vocalist

Isley, Marvin, photograph. GAB Archive/Redferns.

One of the most enduringly popular bands in the history of rhythm and blues, the Isley Brothers had dozens of hits between the late 1950s and the mid-2000s. Playing a major role in their success over much of that period was bassist Marvin Isley, one of the multi-generational group's younger members. Together with guitarist Ernie Isley and keyboardist Chris Jasper, Marvin created the melodic rhythms behind many of the ensemble's best-known songs, including "Fight the Power Part 1." In later life, he became a prominent advocate for diabetes awareness.

Born August 18, 1953, in Cincinnati, Ohio, Isley was surrounded by music from infancy. At the time of his birth, his parents, a professional singer and a church pianist, were already organizing four of his older siblings—Ronald, Rudolph, Vernon, and O'Kelly—into a gospel quartet. After Vernon's death in an accident in 1955, the group, known even then as the Isley Brothers, turned increasingly from gospel to R&B. In 1959 they hit the charts for the first time with "Shout," an energetic, highly danceable song that quickly became one of the genre's standards. Over the next fourteen years, they recorded extensively, both for their own

label, T-Neck, and for larger companies like Motown. While virtually all of their work was well received, major stardom eluded them until 1973, when they were joined officially by Marvin, Ernie, and Jasper, a brother-in-law. At the time, Marvin was a student at C. W. Post College, a division of Long Island University. Though his new responsibilities represented a major commitment, he was able to complete his studies on time, earning a bachelor's degree in music in 1976.

Marvin and the other new members immediately transformed the Isley Brothers' trademark sound, moving it from the realm of classic soul into the harder, faster style known as funk. The group's first release as a sextet—the aptly titled *3+3* (1973)–has often been described as a funk masterpiece. Two years later came an equally acclaimed follow-up, *The Heat Is On*. Included on it was a two-part song called "Fight the Power," the first portion of which reached the top ten on *Billboard* magazine's list of the nation's best-selling R&B singles. Over the next five years, the group had more than a dozen hits. While many of their R&B peers resisted the influence of other styles, the Isleys cheerfully incorporated rock and roll's guitar riffs and disco's dance-friendly beats

## At a Glance . . .

**B**orn August 18, 1953, in Cincinnati, OH; died June 6, 2010, in Chicago, IL; son of a vocalist and a pianist; married Sheila Felton, 1992; children: three. *Education:* C. W. Post College, BA, music, 1976.

**Career:** Isley Brothers (musical group), bassist and vocalist, 1973–84 and 1990(?)–96(?); Isley Jasper Isley (musical group), bassist and vocalist, 1984–late 1980s.

**Memberships:** American Diabetes Association.

**Awards:** Inducted into the Rock and Roll Hall of Fame and Museum, 1992, as a member of the Isley Brothers.

into their own music. While that strategy was successful in the mid-to-late 1970s, it caused some difficulty several years later, when the nation's music fans, in a dramatic shift, began to reject anything associated even tangentially with disco.

That change in taste contributed, in turn, to an increase in tension within the group. Like most large ensembles, the Isley Brothers were no strangers to occasional differences of opinion. Until the mid-1980s, those situations were always handled adroitly. In 1984, however, a serious rift developed, and the younger members—Marvin, Ernie, and Jasper—left to form a new group called Isley Jasper Isley (IJI). Over the next three years, IJI released several major albums, the most successful of which, 1985's *Caravan of Love,* reached number three on *Billboard*'s R&B chart; its title song, meanwhile, spent three weeks at the top of the magazine's list of "Hot R&B/Hip-Hop Singles and Tracks." By the end of 1987, however, the group's momentum had begun to cool noticeably, and they soon disbanded. Marvin and Ernie then joined Ronald in a new version of the Isley Brothers.

As the reconstituted group performed around the nation in the 1990s, they found to their surprise and delight that young people were still embracing their music. Too young to remember the release of "Fight the Power Part 1," these new fans had generally discovered the Isley Brothers through hip-hop, a genre based, in part, on cleverly mixed samples of older songs. Inspired by that innovation, Marvin and his brothers began collaborating extensively with producers and performers well versed in the new style, among them R. Kelly and Keith Sweat. The result was 1996's *Mission to Please,* which Stephen Thomas Erlewine of AllMusic.com called "a testament to the [brothers'] talents" and to "their far-reaching influence."

Just as the album was being released, however, Marvin's daily life was dramatically altered by diabetes. He

had been diagnosed with that affliction many years earlier but had paid it little attention until 1996, when his symptoms worsened to such an extent that he was no longer able to perform on stage or in the recording studio; he eventually lost both legs and the use of one arm. Though these setbacks forced his retirement from the Isley Brothers, he remained active in other ways, often speaking publicly about his experiences with a disease that has long had a disproportionate impact among African Americans. In an extended interview with the *Atlanta Journal-Constitution*'s Patricia Guthrie in 2001, he talked frankly about his initial refusal to acknowledge the seriousness of his condition. "If I … understood diabetes like I understood music, maybe these things wouldn't have happened," he speculated, referring to the loss of his limbs and other complications. He refused, however, to dwell on the past, choosing instead to move forward by educating others. "I'm going to tell as many people as possible [about diabetes]," he vowed to Guthrie. "That's what's important to me now."

In the spring of 2010, it became clear that his long battle with the disease was coming to an end. On June 6 of that year, he died at a hospice in Chicago at the age of fifty-six. Surviving him were three children and his wife of eighteen years, Sheila Felton Isley.

## Selected discography

### Singles

Isely Brothers, "Fight the Power Part 1," 1975.
Isely Jasper Isely, "Caravan of Love," 1985.

### Albums

Isely Brothers, *3+3,* Sony, 1973.
Isely Brothers, *The Heat is On* (includes "Fight the Power Part 1"), T-Neck, 1975.
Isely Brothers, *Showdown,* Columbia, 1978.
Isley Jasper Isley, *Caravan of Love* (includes "Caravan of Love"), Epic, 1985.
Isely Brothers, *Mission to Please,* Island, 1996.

## Sources

### Periodicals

*Atlanta Journal-Constitution,* May 7, 2001.
*Los Angeles Times,* June 9, 2010.
*New York Times,* June 7, 2010.

### Online

Ankeny, Jason, "The Isley Brothers: Biography," All-Music.com, http://allmusic.com/cg/amg.dll?p=amg&sql=11:fifyxqe5ldae~T1 (accessed August 8, 2010).
Erlewine, Stephen Thomas, "*Mission to Please*: Re-

view," AllMusic.com, http://allmusic.com/cg/amg.
dll?p=amg&sql=10:3zfoxqehldse (accessed August
10, 2010).

"The Isley Brothers Biography," Rock and Roll Hall of
Fame and Museum, http://rockhall.com/inductees/
the-isley-brothers/bio/ (accessed November 21,
2010).

—R. Anthony Kugler

# Brenda Jackson

## 1953—

### Romance novelist

Romance novelist Brenda Jackson cannot seem to get enough of happy endings. In June of 2010, she celebrated the publication of *Hidden Pleasures,* her seventy-fifth book in just fifteen years. When she began publishing in 1995, she was among the first romance writers to feature black heroes and heroines in her novels, catering to a burgeoning market for ethnic or multicultural romance literature. Jackson was the first African-American writer to have a book published under the Silhouette Desire imprint, and the first to make the *New York Times* best-seller list with a romance. Today, she is the top-selling black romance writer in the United States.

She was born Brenda Streater in 1953 in Jacksonville, Florida. When she was a girl, her mother often read her fairy tales, and as a teenager, she fell in love with tales of romance. "I grew up thinking this was how love was supposed to be," she told *Publishers Weekly.* "Boy meets girl, they fall in love. Yeah, they have issues along the way, but they are together forever after." She began inventing her own romances in the eighth grade, writing stories over the weekend to share with her classmates on Monday morning. But after being reprimanded by the principal when her friends were caught reading her stories in class, she put her writing aside.

Her own life reads something like a fairy tale. At the age of fourteen, she met her high school sweetheart, Gerald Jackson, though her parents would not allow her to date him until she turned sixteen. Just before her sixteenth birthday, Gerald gave her a "going steady" ring, which she wears to this day. They married when she was nineteen and had two sons together.

After graduating from high school in 1972, Jackson took a job at State Farm Insurance. In her off hours she began reading Harlequin romance novels for escape, but she found them unsatisfying, frustrated by the lack of African-American characters. "I could do this," she told herself, she recalled in an interview with Jennifer Coates of *Romance in Color.* Her husband encouraged her to start writing again and signed her up for a romance writers conference. Meeting other writers gave her the inspiration she needed, and she began crafting stories in the evenings and on weekends. She shared her stories with her coworkers, who encouraged her to publish them.

In the 1980s Jackson approached several publishers, but none was interested in stories featuring "ethnic" characters. Finally, in 1994, she landed a deal with Kensington Publishing, which was launching a new line of romance fiction featuring African-American characters. Her first book, *Tonight and Forever,* was published the following year. The novel introduced the Madaris family—brothers Justin, Dex, and Clayton—whose saga she would continue over the course of sixteen more books, including *Eternally Yours* (1997), *Whispered Promises* (1999), *True Love* (2000), *Unfinished Business* (2004), and *Slow Burn* (2007), right up to 2010's *Sensual Confessions.*

In all, Jackson has written six family series, also chronicling the Steele, Jeffries, Montgomery, Bennett/Masters and Westmoreland clans. The Madaris and Westmoreland series are both her longest and her most popular sagas. Reviewer Gwendolyn Osbourne of *Ro-*

her own husband. "I look at my husband as a very strong African American male. He is supportive and centers his life around his family," she said. "When I think of my life, I think of it as a romance."

Even after publishing a dozen books over the course of a decade, Jackson never considered her writing anything more than a hobby. Every day she woke at 3:00 in the morning and wrote until it was time to go to work, then continued again in the evening, never missing a deadline. In 2008 Jackson signed a lucrative five-year deal with Kimani, a leading publisher of African-American romance fiction, which finally allowed her to retire from State Farm and write full time. In 2010 alone, she was slated to release ten books.

Jackson has earned scores of awards for her writing, including EMMA (Ethnic Multicultural Media Academy) awards for author of the year (2004, 2005, 2006) and career achievement (2006), the *Shades of Romance* Reader's Choice Award for multicultural romance author of the year (2001, 2004), and the Vivien Stephens Career Achievement Award for excellence in romance novel writing (2001). She is a founding member of the national organization Women Writers of Color and belongs to the First Coast Chapter of the Romance Writers of America.

## Selected writings

*Tonight and Forever,* Pinnacle, 1995.
*A Valentine Kiss Anthology,* Pinnacle, 1996.
*Eternally Yours,* Pinnacle, 1997.
*One Special Moment,* BET Arabesque, 1998.
*Fire and Desire,* BET Arabesque, 1999.
*Whispered Promises,* BET Arabesque, 1999.
*Secret Love,* BET Arabesque, 2000.
*True Love,* BET Arabesque, 2000.
*A Family Reunion,* St. Martin's, 2001.
*Surrender,* BET Arabesque, 2001.
*Delaney's Desert Sheikh,* Silhouette, 2002.
*Perfect Timing,* Dafina, 2002.
*Ties That Bind,* St. Martin's, 2002.
*Perfect Fit,* Kensington, 2003.
*Thorn's Challenge,* Silhouette Books, 2003.
*A Little Dare,* Silhouette Books, 2003.
*The Savvy Sistahs,* St. Martin's Griffin, 2003.
*Scandal between the Sheets,* Silhouette Books, 2004.
*Stone Cold Surrender,* Silhouette Books, 2004.
*Riding the Storm,* Silhouette Books, 2004.
*The Playa's Handbook,* St. Martin's Griffin, 2004.
*The Midnight Hour,* St. Martin's, 2004.
*A Whole Lotta Love,* Signet-Penguin, 2004.
*Unfinished Business,* St. Martin's, 2004.
*Let's Get It On,* Silhouette Books, 2004.
*Jared's Counterfeit Fiancée,* Silhouette Books, 2005.
*The Chase Is On,* Silhouette Books, 2005.
*Big Girls Don't Cry,* Signet, 2005.
*The All Night Man,* St. Martin's Griffin, 2005.
*No More Playas,* St. Martin's Griffin, 2005.

*mance Reader* noted that Jackson "doesn't merely write novels ... she organizes reunions that reconnect her readers with the solid, multifaceted characters they have come to know and care about." Jackson's other connecting books include the "Special Woman" series—*Living Large* (2003), *A Whole Lotta Love* (2004), and *Big Girls Don't Cry* (2005)—which feature plus-sized heroines, and the "Bachelor in Demand" series of two novels, *Bachelor Untamed* (2009) and *Bachelor Unleashed* (2010).

A hallmark of Jackson's work is her portrayal of strong, family-centered heroes. "I want [readers] to have an appreciation and acknowledgment for a strong and loving man," she told *Romance in Color.* She admits that many of her male protagonists are modeled after

*The Durango Affair,* Silhouette Books, 2006.
*Ian's Ultimate Gamble,* Silhouette Books, 2006.
*Solid Soul,* Kimani, 2006.
*Night Heat,* Kimani, 2006.
*Seduction, Westmoreland Style,* Silhouette Books, 2007.
*Risky Pleasures,* Kimani, 2007.
*In Bed with Her Boss,* Kimani, 2007.
*What a Woman Wants,* St. Martin's Griffin, 2007.
*Stranded with the Tempting Stranger,* Silhouette, 2007.
*Slow Burn,* St. Martin's, 2007.
*Spencer's Forbidden Passion,* Silhouette, 2007.
*Taming Clint Westmoreland,* Silhouette, 2008.
*Her Little Black Book,* St. Martin's Griffin, 2008.
*Cole's Red-Hot Pursuit,* Silhouette, 2008.
*Irresistible Forces,* Kimani, 2008.
*Just Desserts,* Kimani, 2008.
*The Object of His Protection,* Kimani, 2008.
*Quade's Babies,* Silhouette, 2008.
*Secret Love,* Kimani, 2009.
*Essence of Desire,* Madaris, 2009.
*Fire and Desire,* Kimani, 2009.
*Tall, Dark … Westmoreland,* Silhouette, 2009.
*Surrender,* Kimani, 2009.
*Temperatures Rising,* Kimani, 2009.
*Some Like It Hot,* St. Martin's Griffin, 2009.
*Taste of Passion,* St. Martin's, 2009.
*Intimate Seduction,* Kimani, 2009.
*One Night with a Wealth Rancher,* Silhouette, 2009.
*Bachelor Untamed,* Silhouette, 2009.
*Westmoreland's Way,* Kimani, 2009.

*Tis the Season … for Romance,* Madaris, 2009.
*Wrapped in Pleasure,* Madaris, 2010.
*Ravished by Desire,* Kimani, 2010.
*Hot Westmoreland Nights,* Silhouette, 2010.
*Hidden Pleasures,* Kimani, 2010.
*Bachelor Unleashed,* Kimani, 2010.
*Sensual Confessions,* Kimani, 2010.
*Spontaneous,* Harlequin, 2010.

## *Sources*

### *Periodicals*

*Florida Times-Union,* February 14, 1999.
*New York Daily News,* May 23, 2006.
*Publishers Weekly,* May 3, 2010.

### *Online*

"Brief History of Brenda Jackson," http://www.brendajackson.net/page/brief-history-brenda-jackson (accessed October 21, 2010).
Coates, Jennifer, "Author of the Month: Brenda Jackson," *Romance in Color,* http://www.romanceincolor.com/authormthjacksonB.htm (accessed October 21, 2010).
Osbourne, Gwendolyn, review of *One Special Moment,* Romance Reader, http://www.theromancereader.com/jackson-one.html (accessed October 21, 2010).

—Deborah A. Ring

# Denise Jefferson

## 1944–2010

### Dancer, educator

Jefferson, Denise, photograph. Astrid Strawiarz/Getty Images.

Dancer and educator Denise Jefferson is remembered as the longtime director of the renowned Ailey School, the training arm of the Alvin Ailey American Dance Theater. Hand-picked by Ailey to lead the school in 1984, she served as its director for more than two and a half decades, helping to carry on the choreographer's mission to make dance accessible to all after his death in 1989. Under her leadership, enrollment at the Ailey School expanded to more than 3,500 students, and today it is regarded as one of the premier training programs in modern dance. As director, Jefferson mentored thousands of young dancers, who have gone on to careers in some of the most prestigious companies in the world.

Denise Adele Jefferson was born on November 1, 1944, in Chicago, Illinois, the oldest of two daughters of a local pediatrician. Jefferson and her sister attended the well-regarded University of Chicago Laboratory Schools and began taking music and dance lessons as young girls. The Jeffersons were active patrons of the arts, regularly attending plays at the Goodman Theatre and performances of the Chicago Ballet and the Chicago Symphony. At the age of eight, after begging her mother to take ballet lessons, Jefferson enrolled in classes with Edna McRae, one of the top teachers in the city.

Although Jefferson had the talent to become a ballerina, her teachers stressed that it would be a difficult career path because there were so few African Americans in professional dance companies at the time. "Ballet seemed to be an exciting world, but ... I had never seen anyone who wasn't white in a ballet company," she told *Dance Magazine* in 1999. Instead, Jefferson headed east to Wheaton College in Norton, Massachusetts, to study French, with an eye toward becoming an interpreter. There, she joined the dance company to get out of the school's gym requirement and had her first introduction to modern dance, a genre she knew little about. She was thrilled: "Wait a minute. This is real technique. There's something really quite beautiful here," she recalled in a 2000 interview with the *Boston Globe*.

The following year, Jefferson attended a master class with Donald McKayle, a leading African-American choreographer, at the New England Conservatory in Boston. The experience was transformative. "I remember hearing this deep, powerful voice," she told *Dance*

*Magazine.* "I looked into the room and saw this gorgeous black man. It seemed like I could do everything he asked us to do, and ballet had never been like that for me. There was this incredible connection: I felt free and powerful and I just loved it." During the summer of 1963, she participated in an intensive dance program at the American Dance Festival at Connecticut College in New London, where modern dance pioneers Martha Graham and José Limon were in residence. "That did it. There were performances every night, and I was taking five technique classes a day. And was hungry for it," Jefferson remembered, according to the *Boston Globe.*

Jefferson completed her studies at Wheaton in 1965 and went on to earn a master's degree in French at New York University. Meanwhile she began taking classes at the Martha Graham Center of Contemporary Dance, receiving a scholarship after her first year. She began her professional career with the Pearl Lang Dance Theater, run by Pearl Lang, a teacher at the Graham School.

By the early 1970s, after marrying and giving birth to a daughter and then suffering a serious knee injury, Jefferson began to shift from performance to teaching, which she loved. She started out teaching dance at the American Dance Center, the school founded by African-American choreographer Alvin Ailey in 1969 and then joined the faculty of New York University's Tisch School of the Arts. In 1974 she was offered a full-time position at Ailey's school, and in 1984 Ailey hand-picked her to be its director, a position she would hold for the next twenty-six years.

Following Ailey's death in 1989, Jefferson, together with artistic director Judith Jamison and Sylvia Waters,

director of Ailey II, the company's junior ensemble, formed a triumvirate of women who were charged with continuing the choreographer's mission of making dance accessible to all. To that end, the school's curriculum emphasized a diverse mix of genres, including (Lester) Horton- and (Martha) Graham-based modern dance techniques, ballet, jazz, and West African dance. "The individual is unique and special, and we are here to celebrate that and help the dancers discover that," Jefferson explained to the *Christian Science Monitor* in 1992.

Under Jefferson's leadership, enrollment at the school increased from 125 to more than 3,500 in 2010, with a faculty of 75 teaching 160 classes per week. Jefferson also expanded the range of classes offered by the school to include seven levels of training for children as young as three and a professional division with four different study tracks. In 1998 Jefferson worked with Fordham College at Lincoln Center to establish a unique joint bachelor of fine arts program, the first degree of its kind to be offered by a liberal arts institution. Nearly 90 percent of the dancers in the Alvin Ailey company were trained at the school, while others have gone on to careers with well-known troupes such as the Martha Graham Dance Company, the Mark Morris Dance Group, and the Ballet National de España.

In addition to teaching, Jefferson was a member of the board of directors of the National Association of Schools of Dance, serving as its president from 2004 to 2006, the Elisa Monte Dance Company in New York, and the nonprofit organization Career Transitions for Dancers. She also was the vice chair of the Association for Blacks in Dance, a panelist for the Dance Program of the New York State Council on the Arts, and a trustee of Wheaton College.

On July 17, 2010, Jefferson died at the age of sixty-five, after a battle with ovarian cancer. In her memory, the Ailey School established the Denise Jefferson Scholarship Fund to provide tuition for aspiring young dancers. Jefferson's daughter, Francesca Harper, followed in her footsteps to become a dancer and choreographer.

# Sources

## Periodicals

*Boston Globe,* November 26, 2000.
*Chicago Tribune,* July 20, 2010.
*Christian Science Monitor,* February 24, 1992.
*Dance Magazine,* December 1999.
*New York Times,* July 20, 2010.

## Online

The Ailey School, http://www.theaileyschool.edu/ (accessed October 21, 2010).

Amoruso, Susan, "Ailey's Grand Dame of Dance," DanceTeacher.com, http://www.dance-teacher.com /content/aileys-grand-dame-dance (accessed October 21, 2010).

—Deborah A. Ring

# William Layton

## 1915–2007

### Government administrator, nonprofit administrator, historian, author

Throughout his long and distinguished career in public service, William Layton's love for his country was obvious. Born into a prominent family that had been living as freedmen in Virginia since the eighteenth century, he once described himself, in comments included in a biographical profile on the Web site of the National Visionary Leadership Project, as "one-hundred-percent American and one-thousand-percent Virginian." Following his retirement from civil service, he became a noted author and independent historian.

William Wendell Layton was born on July 17, 1915, in Hanover, a small town in central Virginia. His father, William Brown Layton, was a teacher and school administrator who became superintendent of what was then known as the Negro Reformatory of Virginia. A gifted student who was writing poetry by the age of eight, the younger Layton attended Armstrong High School, a segregated institution in the nearby city of Richmond, and then Pennsylvania's Lincoln University. A sociology major, he spent much of his time studying ways to improve the nation's racial climate.

A pivotal moment in Layton's life came in January of 1933, when he traveled with his family to Washington, DC, to witness the inauguration of President Franklin Delano Roosevelt. Amid the gloom of the Depression, Roosevelt's determination and resolute good cheer impressed him deeply, and he returned home with a new faith in the ability of government to address a wide range of social ills.

Upon receipt of his bachelor's degree in 1937, Layton moved on to graduate school at Tennessee's Fisk University, like Lincoln a predominately African-American institution. His master's degree in sociology there came in the late 1930s; he later did additional graduate work at Michigan State University. His career began shortly after leaving Fisk, when he joined the Nashville (Tennessee) public school system as an administrator. After several years in that role, he moved in 1942 to Columbus, Ohio, where he began working for the Urban League (UL), one of the nation's oldest organizations devoted to civil rights and African-American empowerment. Over the next seventeen years, he held a variety of posts there and at the UL branch in Muskegon, Michigan, rising to become executive director of the latter. His performance eventually drew the attention of the Michigan Civil Rights Commission, which named him director of education and community services in 1959. Six years later, word of his growing expertise in civil rights issues had reached federal officials, who persuaded him to leave Michigan for Washington, where he joined the Department of Agriculture. As director of contract compliance there, he was responsible for ensuring that private companies doing business with the Department adhered to its stipulations, including many recently enacted civil rights regulations. He remained in that post until 1971, when he moved on to become director of the affirmative action program at the Federal Reserve, the nation's central bank. In that capacity, he played a major role in increasing minority employment throughout the Reserve system and in the banking industry as a whole. Though he stepped down in 1977, he

## At a Glance . . .

**B**orn William Wendell Layton on July 17, 1915, in Hanover, VA; died September 12, 2007, in Washington, DC; son of William Brown Layton (a teacher and school administrator) and Mary Amanda Sully Layton; married Phoebe Anderson, early 1940s; children: three. *Education:* Lincoln University, BA, sociology, 1937; Fisk University, MA, sociology, late 1930s; further graduate work at Michigan State University, 1950s(?).

**Career:** Nashville (TN) Public Schools, administrator, late 1930s–early 1940s; Urban League, variety of positions, including executive director of Muskegon, MI, branch, 1942–59; Michigan Civil Rights Commission, director of education and community services, 1959–65; U.S. Department of Agriculture, director of contract compliance, 1965–71; U.S. Federal Reserve, director of affirmative action program, 1971–77, consultant, 1977–81; historian, 1981–2007, author, 1996–2007.

**Memberships:** Fort Collier Civil War Center, cofounder; Shenandoah Arts Council, board member; U.S. Capitol Historical Society, Columbia Historical Society (later known as the Historical Society of Washington, DC), McCormick Civil War Institute.

continued to serve the Reserve as a consultant until 1981, when he retired to focus on his family and on one of his great loves: American history.

Layton's fascination with history began in childhood, when he spent many hours learning about his forebears. In Millwood, Virginia, a small town roughly one hundred and ten miles from his birthplace in Hanover, there was a farmhouse that had been in the family since at least 1871. Upon retiring there in the 1980s, he immersed himself in the region's past, focusing in particular on the tumultuous Civil War era. As his expertise grew, he began to write short essays. While many of these concerned the war and other nineteenth-century subjects, he also wrote frequently and movingly of the Depression and the civil rights struggle, often connecting these to earlier moments in the nation's past and to episodes from his own life. In 1996 he collected several dozen of his favorite pieces and published them as *Layton Looks at Life: 42 Penetrating Looks into the Reality of Living in America's Past, Present, and Future.* Because the volume was self-published, it lacked the marketing

resources that typically bring a book to public attention. Word of mouth, however, brought Layton a small but enthusiastic group of readers. A follow-up volume, *More Of—Layton Looks at Life,* appeared in 2001.

In the course of his history studies, Layton became an avid connoisseur of old documents. Items that had been in his family for decades formed the basis of his collection. Added to these were documents he found at garage sales, flea markets, and antique stores. By the 1990s, he had amassed several thousand items, many of them offering a unique perspective on slavery, emancipation, the Civil War, segregation, and the civil rights movement. A large proportion of it was eventually placed on microfilm by the National Archives and Records Administration, a federal agency. He also donated many documents to museums and research facilities around the country.

On September 12, 2007, at the age of ninety-two, Layton died of Parkinson's disease at his home in Washington. Survivors included his wife of more than sixty-five years, Phoebe Anderson Layton, two daughters, and a number of grandchildren and great-grandchildren; a third daughter predeceased him. Joining his family to mourn his passing were dozens of fellow history enthusiasts, many of whom had met him through the U.S. Capitol Historical Society, the Columbia Historical Society (later known as the Historical Society of Washington, DC), and Shenandoah University's McCormick Civil War Institute. Though he worked tirelessly for all of those organizations, his most significant effort as a volunteer was probably the work he did on behalf of Virginia's Fort Collier Civil War Center, a nonprofit group he co-founded. Fort Collier, an extensive network of earthwork fortifications, would likely have been lost to development if Layton and his colleagues had not arranged its purchase in 2002.

## Selected writings

*Layton Looks at Life: 42 Penetrating Looks into the Reality of Living in America's Past, Present, and Future,* self-published, 1996.
*More Of—Layton Looks at Life,* self-published, 2001.

## Sources

### Periodicals

*Washington Post,* September 19, 2007; October 21, 2007.

### Online

"Fort Collier Civil War Center, Inc.," Fort Collier Civil War Center, http://www.fortcollier.com/fccwc.htm (accessed September 3, 2010).
Layton, William W., "The Spring of 1863—A Call to

Arms," Smithsonian Associates, http://civilwarstud ies.org/articles/Vol_2/william-layton.shtm (accessed August 22, 2010).

"William Layton: National Visionary," National Vision-ary Leadership Project, http://www.visionarypro ject.org/laytonwilliam/ (accessed August 22, 2010).

—R. Anthony Kugler

# Raphael C. Lee

## 1949—

### Biomedical engineer, physician

Dr. Raphael C. Lee is a renowned reconstructive surgeon and biomedical engineer affiliated with the University of Chicago Hospitals. He holds a number of posts there, among them director of the Electrical Trauma Unit, which is the leading U.S. site for treating electrical shock victims. Much of Lee's pioneering research over the course of his career has focused on repairing tissue-damage injuries caused by contact with high-voltage electricity or lightning strikes.

Lee was born in Sumter, South Carolina, in 1949. He grew up in a family of five children and was once turned away from the Sumter public library during the height of the civil rights movement's efforts to desegregate the South. At the University of South Carolina he studied electrical engineering, where he became fascinated by the technological advancements in harnessing electro-magnetic radiation power via laser devices. Laser beams had scores of practical applications, but Lee was drawn to their use in medicine. That led him to enroll in a dual program at Philadelphia's Temple University School of Medicine and Drexel University, from which he earned his medical degree and a master of science in engineering in 1975.

For the next few years Lee divided his time between Chicago and Boston. He was a resident in surgery at the University of Chicago Hospitals while also pursuing a doctor of science degree in bioelectrical engineering at the Massachusetts Institute of Technology. In 1981, the same year he began a second residency at Massachusetts General Hospital, he was awarded one of the first-ever MacArthur fellowships. These fellowships are the so-called genius grants bestowed by the John D. and Catherine T. MacArthur Foundation to U.S. citizens who are emerging as leaders in science, the creative arts, and various academic fields. Lee's grant, which was dispersed over a five-year period, totaled $172,000, and he used some of it to establish the Center for Advanced Medicine, a private practice for plastic surgery, in Chicago in 1983.

Lee won the MacArthur fellowship for his research on tissue regeneration. As a resident in reconstructive surgery, he had treated burn victims and was intrigued by the human body's response to severe tissue damage. However, a few cases he saw were burns from high-voltage power wires or the rare lightning strike, and in these instances the body responded much differently than it did after the more typical thermal burns. Lee's research established that electrical shocks, while burning the skin and first layers, caused a different type of tissue damage over the next several days following an injury.

Lee and his research colleagues presented their findings at the 1987 conference of the Engineering in Medicine and Biology Society of the Institute of Electrical and Electronics Engineers. Their work demonstrated that the actual cells that make up the human body suffer structural damage after electrical shock because of electroporation, meaning that the electrical current permeates cell membranes and hampers their regenerative function. This is why victims of high-voltage electricity or lightning strikes show varying patterns of medical issues in the days following being

## At a Glance . . .

**B**orn Raphael Carl Lee on October 29, 1949, in Sumter, SC; son of Jean Marie Langston Lee; married; two children. *Education:* University of South Carolina, BS, electrical engineering, 1971; Temple University School of Medicine, MD, and Drexel University, MS, engineering, both 1975; Massachusetts Institute of Technology, ScD, bioelectrical engineering, 1979.

**Career:** University of Chicago Hospitals, resident in surgery, 1975–81; Massachusetts General Hospital, resident in surgery, 1981–83; Center for Advanced Medicine, founder and surgeon, 1983—; University of Chicago, faculty member, 1989—; University of Chicago, Electrical Trauma Unit, director; Avocet Polymer Technologies, Inc., cofounder and chief scientist, 1996—; RenaCyte BioMolecular Technologies, cofounder and chief scientist; Maroon Biotech, cofounder and chief scientist, 2002—.

**Memberships:** American Association for the Advancement of Science; American Association of Plastic Surgeons; American College of Surgeons; American Institute of Medical and Biological Engineers; Fellow of the International College of Surgeons; Institute for Electrical and Electronic Engineers.

**Awards:** John D. and Catherine T. MacArthur Fellowship, 1981; Searle Scholar Award, 1985.

**Addresses:** *Office*—Center for Advanced Medicine, 5758 S. Maryland Ave., Chicago, IL 60637.

shocked; the breakdown of tissue leads to infections, amputations, and even damage to the central nervous system.

Searching for a strategy to reverse the effects of electroporation, Lee was watching his young daughter blow bubbles one day and realized that the pretty, ephemeral soap bubble might provide a solution to the problem of cell membrane damage. "You can put your finger in there and pull it out," he said of a soap bubble in an interview with Ingfei Chen in the *Palm Beach Post*, "and an instant after that, it's filled." The permeable but quickly repaired bubble is the result of surfactants, the name given to a class of chemical compounds that are used in soap, detergents, cosmetics, and scores of other products.

In 1992 Lee released the findings from another round of studies using the surfactant poloxamer 188 (P188). P188 is a synthetic compound that is used as an emulsifying agent by blood banks and is known to be relatively nontoxic. His experiments used the muscle tissue of laboratory rats. After shocking the tissue cells with electricity and watching under a microscope as they became instantly unstable, Lee was pleased to see that a quick application of P188 meant that the outer membranes of the cells closed back up much more quickly—just like a permeable soap bubble does.

By this point in his career Lee was holding dual positions at the University of Chicago in its medical center's Department of Plastic and Reconstructive Surgery and in the school's Biomechanics Group of the Department of Organismal Anatomy and Biology. He also headed the hospital's Electrical Trauma Unit, which had been established a decade or so before he returned to Chicago in 1989. This is a special clinic for victims of high-voltage encounters or lightning strikes with its own intensive care medical aircraft on permanent standby to pick up newly injured patients anywhere in the continental United States and bring them to the unit within a critical six-hour period.

It took several years for Lee and the University of Chicago to receive permission from the U.S. Food and Drug Administration to begin actual clinical trials of P188 on patients, and several more years for the first actual treatment. Even among the medical community at top-ranked facilities like his own there was skepticism about the supposed cell-repairing properties of P188. Burn and emergency specialists "thought it was just a gimmick," he told Lydialyle Gibson in the *University of Chicago Magazine*. "It seemed impossible to people that you could apply a polymer and reverse trauma." He recalled one meeting with some of the leading decision makers at the University of Chicago's Pritzker School of Medicine to pitch his application for further funding. "These were smart old guys," he recalled, "who looked at new ideas" regularly. "I took my bottle of Mr. Bubbles in there, and I showed it to them," he told Gibson. "I don't think they believed me at all."

In 2006 Lee was interviewed on the twenty-fifth anniversary of the first MacArthur Foundation fellowships. *Chicago Tribune*'s Charles Storch asked Lee if he had experienced any professional setbacks because he won such a prestigious honor so early in his career. Lee conceded that the fellowship was bestowed "before I contributed very much.... [M]any assumed the award to be simply the consequence of affirmative action and probably lacking in merit. I don't get that sense anymore."

At the University of Chicago Lee holds the Paul S. and Ailene T. Russell Professorship in Surgery, Medicine, Organismal Biology and Anatomy. He is a member of the American Institute of Medical and Biological Engineers, the American College of Surgeons, the American Association of Plastic Surgeons, the American Association for the Advancement of Science, and several other professional bodies, and occasionally provides expert-witness testimony in legal cases involving capital punishment by means of the electric chair or the use of tasers by law enforcement authorities. Lee is also the cofounder and principal scientist of three biotech companies that search for other ways to utilize P188's membrane-healing properties.

## Selected works

(Editor, with Ernest G. Cravalho and John Francis Burke) *Electrical Trauma: The Pathophysiology, Manifestations, and Clinical Management,* Cambridge University Press, 1992.

(Editor, with Mary Capelli-Schellpfeffer and Kathleen M. Kelley) *Electrical Injury: A Multidisciplinary Approach to Prevention, Therapy, and Rehabilitation,* New York Academy of Sciences, 1994.

(Editor, with Chin-tu Chen, J.-X Shih, and Min-Ha Zhong) *Occupational Electrical Injury and Safety: An International Symposium,* New York Academy of Sciences, 1999.

(Editor, with Florin Despa and Kimm J. Hamann) *Cell Injury: Mechanisms, Responses, and Repair,* New York Academy of Sciences, 2005.

## Sources

### Periodicals

*Chicago Tribune,* September 14, 2006.
*Crain's Chicago Business,* June 25, 2001, p. 15; November 5, 2007, p. 84.
*Palm Beach Post,* March 13, 1994.
*University of Chicago Magazine* February 1, 2006.

### Online

"Raphael C. Lee, MD, ScD, DSc (Hon)," University of Chicago Medical Center, http://www.uchospitals.edu/physicians/raphael-lee.html (accessed October 15, 2010).

"Raphael Lee," HistoryMakers.com, May 23, 2003, http://www.thehistorymakers.com/programs/dvl/files/Lee_Ralphaelb.html (accessed October 15, 2010).

—Carol Brennan

# Marvin Lewis

## 1958—

### Football coach

Lewis, Marvin, photograph. Andy Lyons/Getty Images.

When he was named head coach of the Cincinnati Bengals on January 14, 2003, Marvin Lewis became the seventh African American to hold the position of head coach in the modern National Football League (NFL). The promise shown by his distinguished career as an assistant coach was fulfilled when he reversed the fortunes of a team that had been a perennial basement dweller in league rankings. Part of Lewis's success as a coach rested on his genuinely inspirational qualities; he was a living example of the power of hard work, and his life was an all-American success story.

Marvin Lewis was born in McDonald, Pennsylvania, in the state's steelmaking region outside Pittsburgh, on September 23, 1958. Lewis remembered that his father, who worked in a steel mill and often spent his days swinging a sledgehammer at iron ore, would come home and rest his sore elbows on pillows. Lewis's mother was a registered nurse and later a nurse practitioner. His family instilled in him a strong work ethic. One uncle became a Pulitzer Prize–winning newspaper photographer. As a high school student, Lewis worked summers on a garbage truck and spent plenty of time at church as the first youth Sunday

school superintendent in the history of the First Baptist Church.

### Became Senior Class President

Local youths could dream of a way out of the steel industry; McDonald's Fort Cherry High School had an impressive football program that also produced future San Diego Chargers head coach Marty Schottenheimer and several other NFL players and coaches. A quarterback in midget football, Lewis took to sports immediately, joining the football, baseball, and wrestling teams, and often changing out of his garbage collecting clothes and into his team uniform on his way to practices or games. He excelled as a safety and quarterback on the football field and became president of his senior class.

Lewis planned to attend Purdue University in West Lafayette, Indiana, but he changed his mind when he heard about an open football scholarship at faraway Idaho State University, in Boise, and applied, hoping to save his parents his tuition bills. He was admitted and began studying engineering, his determination to succeed strengthened after spending a summer working at

## At a Glance . . .

**B**orn on September 23, 1958, in McDonald, PA; son of Marvin Lewis Sr. (a steelworker and foreman), and Vanetta Lewis (a nurse); married Peggy; children: Whitney, Marcus. *Education:* Idaho State University, BS, physical education, 1981; Idaho State University, MS, athletic administration, 1982.

**Career:** Idaho State University, linebackers coach, 1981–84; Long Beach State University, assistant coach, 1985–86; University of New Mexico, assistant coach, 1987–89; University of Pittsburgh, assistant coach, 1990–91; Pittsburgh Steelers, linebackers coach, 1992–95; Baltimore Ravens, defensive coordinator, 1996–2001; Washington Redskins, assistant head coach and defensive coordinator, 2002; Cincinnati Bengals, head coach, 2003—.

**Memberships:** Marvin Lewis Community Fund, founder.

**Awards:** Inductee, Idaho State Hall of Fame, 2001; Associated Press NFL Coach of the Year, 2009.

**Addresses:** *Office*—Cincinnati Bengals, One Paul Brown Stadium, Cincinnati, OH 45202. *Web*—http://www.marvinlewis.org/.

a steel mill's coke ovens back in Pennsylvania and sweating in the blast of their 2,800-degree temperatures. Too small to dream of a professional career himself, he continued to pursue football with a passion and began to dream of becoming an NFL coach.

His father, Marvin Lewis Sr., who had hoped for a stable career in the engineering profession for his son, did not take this news well. But Lewis—according to Chick Ludwig of the *Dayton Daily News*—convinced his father by telling him to think back on his thirty-one years in the mills: "Daddy, you go into that mill every day and you hate that job. I want to do what I love to do," Lewis said. Fresh out of Idaho State, where he won All-Big Sky Conference honors three times as a linebacker, quarterback, and safety (in 1978, 1979, and 1980), Lewis was hired as a graduate assistant in 1981 by his alma mater at an annual salary of $10,000.

### Hired as Assistant Coach

Coaching Idaho State's linebackers in his first year,

Lewis got a taste of the satisfaction the profession could bring when the Idaho State Bengals notched a 12–1 record and won the National Collegiate Athletic Association's Division 1-AA championship. He stayed on as an assistant coach at Idaho State through 1984 (having earned a master's degree in athletic administration in 1982) and then moved on to assistant coach posts at Long Beach State University in California (1985–86), the University of New Mexico (1987–89), and the University of Pittsburgh (1990–91).

That powerhouse coaching job in his home area put Lewis within reach of a pro coaching slot, and in 1992 he was hired as a linebackers coach by the Pittsburgh Steelers. His Steelers squads from 1992 to 1995 spawned several NFL defensive stars, and in 1996 he was hired by the Baltimore Ravens as defensive coordinator even though head coach Brian Billick originally wanted someone else for the position. Once again Lewis proved himself: the Ravens' defense steadily improved, and the defensive team on the 2000 squad, which won the Super Bowl, set a record for fewest points allowed (165) in a 16-game season and is considered one of the best in NFL history. In 2002 Lewis became defensive coordinator and assistant head coach with the Washington Redskins.

Although NFL teams had interviewed Lewis for head coaching jobs several times, he had been passed over. The biggest heartbreaker came in 2002, when Tampa Bay Buccaneers general manager Rich McKay offered the team's head coach slot to Lewis but was overruled by the team's owners. Discouraged, Lewis nevertheless turned down a $7.5 million offer to coach football at Michigan State University in order to keep pursuing his goal. Finally he was hired in 2003 for $1.5 million a year to coach the Cincinnati Bengals, which in 2002 had amassed a dismal record of 2 wins and 14 losses, worst in the history of the franchise. The team's last winning record had come in 1990.

### Took Visible Role in Cincinnati

In Cincinnati, Lewis became a popular and charismatic figure; some even credited him as a calming force in a city torn by deep-rooted racial unrest. Appearing at a ribbon-cutting ceremony for a new downtown public library shortly after his arrival, he became a fixture at civic functions and was an energetic speechmaker who drew on his small-town roots and experiences. He often spoke out against the crudeness that was endemic to the game of football, on one occasion urging league officials to take action against players who intimidated others by spitting on them. Married and the father of one daughter and one son, Lewis was the voice and face of the Bengals to an unusual degree. Bengals president Mike Brown, previously notorious for his detailed management style, turned not only football decisions but also day-to-day management chores such as staff hires and even the choice of training-camp location over to Lewis.

Shaking up the Bengals squad and recruiting a mixture of veteran free agents and talented young players, Lewis delivered impressive results in his first year as Bengals coach. Although the team lost its first three games, the Bengals bounced back to finish with an 8–8 record. They had a chance to make the NFL playoffs for the first time since 1990, but lost their final game. In the words of the *Washington Post*, "Marvin Lewis restored the dignity of the Cincinnati Bengals" in his debut campaign. After the season, the Bengals were named the most improved team in the league, while Lewis placed second in the NFL Coach of the Year voting.

The Bengals went 8–8 once again in 2004 as Lewis took a chance on rookie quarterback Carson Palmer. The offense jelled toward the end of the year, but, ironically in view of Lewis's wealth of defensive experience, it was the Bengals defense that struggled. Still, Lewis had clearly built the nucleus of a potential playoff contender, and his position as Bengals coach seemed secure. "You can't worry about the bad days getting in the way of the good days that are coming," Lewis told the *Columbus Dispatch*. "You keep your eyes focused on what you're trying to get done. You work at it and work at it, and if things aren't to your liking, you work at changing them."

### Established a Winning Tradition

Entering the 2005 season, Lewis believed he had finally put the Bengals in a position to contend for the playoffs. Speaking to *USA Today* in September of that year, Lewis summed up the new mentality of his team, declaring that "accepting mediocrity is the one thing, more than anything, that you can't do." The Bengals ultimately met their coach's challenge. The team finished the 2005 regular season with a record of 11–5, winning the AFC North Division and earning its first trip to the playoffs in a decade and a half. The team's success was sparked primarily by its offensive firepower, as the Bengals amassed 421 points in 2005, good for fourth in the league. Although the Bengals were ultimately defeated by perennial rival Pittsburgh in the wildcard round of the playoffs, its strong regular season seemed a promise of a new era in Cincinnati football.

The Bengals ultimately failed to capitalize on their successful 2005 campaign, however, as Lewis presided over mediocre records of 8–8and 7–9 in 2006 and 2007, respectively. The low point in Lewis's tenure with the Bengals came in 2008, when the team finished 4–11–1, and were outscored by their opponents 264–204. The Bengals bounced back a year later, compiling a 10–6 record, best in the AFC North, while also earning their second playoff spot in five years. Cincinnati once again failed to advance far into the postseason, however, falling to the New York Jets in the wildcard round, 24–14. Lewis was contrite about the team's performance at the end of the season. "I do

need to apologize that I haven't gotten us over the hump, and I haven't gotten us beyond where we've been," he stated in his final news conference of the year. "That's my job and my focus, to get us beyond that. And we'll get started on that very quickly."

In spite of this early playoff exit, Lewis's leadership during the regular season received widespread praise throughout the league, and he was named the 2009 NFL Coach of the Year by the Associated Press. Responding to the honor, Lewis deflected attention away from his personal contributions to the team's success, citing the importance of the organization as a whole. "To me, this is more a recognition of the organization, for the coaching staff and the hard work they've done, and for the players," he told the *Dallas Morning News*. By the beginning of the 2010 season, Lewis had tied the organization's record for longest stretch as head coach. With 56 wins in his first seven seasons, Lewis ranked second among all Bengals coaches.

The Bengals faltered during the early part of the 2010 season, dropping five of their first seven games. In a press conference following an October 24 defeat to the Atlanta Falcons, Lewis assumed his share of responsibility for the team's early struggles. "As we move forward, I've got to do a better job of coaching our guys so that we're executing and playing poised under pressure," he told the press. Lewis also expressed optimism about the team's prospects for the rest of the season. "We are still in Week 6, so we have time to get back there," he asserted. Having already led the Bengals to two playoff appearances in seven years, Lewis had every reason to believe that the team would remain competitive for years to come.

## Sources

### Periodicals

*Buffalo News*, December 17, 2004, p. B1.
*Columbus Dispatch*, January 15, 2003, p. E1; February 4, 2003, p. E1; September 12, 2004, p. F5; November 10, 2004, p. D4; November 14, 2004, p. E13; December 12, 2004, p. E1; January 9, 2005, p. E11.
*Dallas Morning News*, January 17, 2010, p. C11.
*Dayton Daily News*, April 20, 2003, p. C1.
*Denver Post*, August 31, 2003, p. CC7.
*Pittsburgh Post-Gazette*, February 12, 2002; November 21, 2004, p. D4.
*St. Louis Post-Dispatch*, December 21, 2003, p. E1.
*Toronto Star*, January 12, 2010, p. S6.
*USA Today*, December 29, 2003, p. C7; September 9, 2005, p. 4E.
*Washington Post*, November 10, 2004, p. D4.

**Online**

"Cincinnati Bengals," Pro-Football-Reference.com, http://www.pro-football-reference.com/teams/cin/ (accessed October 31, 2010).

"Coaches: Marvin Lewis," Cincinnati Bengals, http://www.bengals.com/team/coaches/Lewis_Marvin/ c40f7ac1-81b7-415d-8563-f5b309dc83c3

(accessed October 31, 2010).

"Marvin Lewis Press Conference Transcript," Cincinnati Bengals, October 25, 2010, http://www.bengals.com/news/article-1/Marvin-Lewis-Press-Conference-Transcript/cee0a4ae-56bd-4c11-9b16-a8dc1744addd (accessed October 31, 2010.)

—James M. Manheim and Stephen Meyer

# Adrian Matejka

## 1971(?)—

## Writer, professor

Poet Adrian Matejka has won critical acclaim for verse that incorporates the rhythms of modern life and African-American idiom to deliver a crisp literary effect. His second collection, *Mixology,* was chosen as one of the 2008 winners of the coveted National Poetry Series award and was published the following year by Penguin Books. Matejka's verse, wrote Aaron Belz in the *St. Louis Post-Dispatch,* "reads like poetry, but it riffs like hip-hop."

Matejka was born during the early 1970s in Nuremberg, Germany, to a white mother and an African-American father who was a U.S. Army drill sergeant at the time. His mother pursued her career as an artist, and his father would later appear as a dancer on *Soul Train,* a Saturday-afternoon urban-music showcase that was a television staple for much of the 1970s and 1980s across the United States. Matejka grew up in both California and in the Indianapolis area, where he attended high school. His first formal encounters with poetry, he later recalled, were uninspiring, but he went on to enroll in Indiana University, where his Pulitzer Prize–writing teacher, Yusef Komunyakaa, encouraged him to pursue a career as a writer.

Matejka earned a master of fine arts degree from Southern Illinois University, Carbondale, and won a 2002 and 2003 fellowship from the Cave Canem Workshop, which supports African-American poets. His verse began to appear in *American Poetry Review, Indiana Review, Prairie Schooner,* and *Callaloo,* among other literary journals. He also became an assistant professor of English language and literature at Southern Illinois University, Edwardsville. Alice James Books, a nonprofit publisher that is affiliated with the University of Maine, Farmington, published his first volume of verse in 2003.

Most of the poems in *The Devil's Garden* dealt with Matejka's experiences as a biracial American who is often mistaken for a member of another ethnic group. "Part autobiography, part lyric abstraction, this collection gives voice to a multiracial, multiethnic experience that reconciles a range of cultural values," asserted Gregory Pardlo in an assessment for *Black Issues Book Review.* The debut work also earned a strong recommendation from *Library Journal*'s Daniel L. Guillory. "Matejka's theme is the devilish perversity of a white society that leaves him anguished" enough to become physically ill, Guillory wrote.

The National Poetry Series is an arts awards program that was initially funded by the novelist James Michener during the late 1970s. It seeks to promote the work of new poets, whose work might not otherwise be discovered via the traditional literary-journal and book-publishing route. A panel of experienced judges selects five works each year, and in 2008 Matejka's second volume, *Mixology,* was chosen for the honor. That led to a publishing contract with Penguin Books, which issued *Mixology* in 2009. The poems in this volume draw on pop culture, history, and even television reality shows, all of which provided Matejka with rich inspiration. His verse contains references to Spike Lee, Flava Flav, Thomas Jefferson, modern art, jazz music, and even the street strut known as the "pimp limp." In the

*At a Glance . . .*

**B**orn c. 1971, in Nuremberg, Germany; son of an army officer and a painter; married Stacey Lynn Brown (a writer); children: Marley. *Education:* Indiana University, BA; Southern Illinois University, Carbondale, MFA.

**Career:** Southern Illinois University, Edwardsville, assistant professor of English language and literature; named to the William and Margaret Going Award Endowed Professorship, 2010; *River Styx Magazine* poetry reading series, codirector.

**Awards:** Cave Canem Black Poetry workshop, fellow, 2002, 2003; National Poetry Series winner, National Poetry Society, 2008.

**Addresses:** *Home*—Edwardsville, IL. *Office*—Southern Illinois University, Department of English Language and Literature, Peck Hall 3206, Box 1431, Edwardsville, IL 62026. *Web*—www.adrianmatejka.com/.

poem "Do the Right Thing," Matejka reveals a difficult moment when he once met Lee, the highly regarded but feisty filmmaker. Matejka asked Lee to autograph his t-shirt, and "he edited me like one / of his characters: Why you care? / You ain't even black." Belz commended this poem in particular. "Powerful and exact, this image is like many others in the book: seemingly tossed off, almost disposable, but chillingly accurate," Belz wrote.

In January of 2010 Matejka was nominated for an NAACP Image Award by the National Association for the Advancement of Colored People. He traveled to Los Angeles for the awards ceremony and hoped to meet fellow nominee Denzel Washington, who was nominated that year for his role in the film *The Taking of Pelham 123* (2009). "He gets a shout out in one of the poems in 'Mixology' ('Domo Arigato, Mr. Mulatto') and I'd like to give him a copy," Matejka was quoted as saying in a PRWeb Newswire press release that announced the NAACP honor.

Matejka did not win that year's Image Award in his field—Nikki Giovanni and her latest work, *Bicycles,* won the honor—but the experience raised his profile and brought some attention to the Edwardsville campus of Southern Illinois University. At Edwardsville, he teaches creative writing courses and serves as poetry editor for *Sou'wester,* the school's literary journal. Later in 2010 he was awarded the William and Margaret Going Award Endowed Professorship. His wife, Stacey Lynn Brown, also teaches at the school. The couple have a daughter, Marley.

As a teacher, Matejka remembers his own first experiences with the literary form that became his calling. They were the sonnets of William Shakespeare, and while he later came to appreciate their flow, he realizes that the ways in which educators present material to their students can make a world of difference. Some of his poems have been selected for inclusion in a program run by Arts in Transit, a public transportation improvement project in St. Louis. "There's a disconnect between the way poetry's taught and the way it's experienced," he told Jane Henderson in the *St. Louis Post-Dispatch.* "Writers who are successful are engaging in a discourse with the world around them."

## Selected works

*The Devil's Garden,* Alice James Books, 2003.
*Mixology,* Penguin Books, 2009.

## Sources

### Periodicals

*Black Issues Book Review,* May–July 2004, p. 50.
*Library Journal,* October 1, 2003, p. 80.
PRWeb Newswire, January 26, 2010.
*St. Louis Post-Dispatch,* March 8, 2009, p. F1; May 31, 2009, p. D7.

### Online

Klausing, Jessica, "Poet Adrian Matejka Reads Work at UWG," WestGeorgian.com, February 9, 2010, http://www.thewestgeorgian.com/poet-adrian-matejka-reads-work-at-uwg-1.1121360 (accessed October 15, 2010).

—Carol Brennan

# James McBride

## 1957—

## Writer, musician

McBride, James, photograph. Matt Carr/Getty Images.

Writer James McBride possesses a talent for spinning compelling tales out of real-life events. In 2008 filmmaker Spike Lee turned McBride's 2002 novel *Miracle at St. Anna* into a major motion picture, and the author also won solid reviews that same year for his second novel, *Song Yet Sung.* Yet the former newspaper reporter and part-time jazz musician may be best known for his debut book, *The Color of Water: A Black Man's Tribute to His White Mother.* This dual account features both his recollections and those of his Polish-born Jewish mother, Ruth McBride Jordan, whose remarkable life story is detailed within; the book spent nearly two years on the *New York Times* bestseller list.

### Eighth of Twelve Children

McBride's own life story is equally improbable and carries a drift of cinematic flourish: he was born in 1957 in New York City, but his father, a Baptist minister named Andrew D. McBride, died of lung cancer when Ruth McBride was pregnant with him, her eighth child of the twelve she would bear in all. Ruth—born Ruchel Zylska near Gdansk, Poland—was

the daughter of an Orthodox Jewish rabbi and had emigrated to the United States when she was an infant. She grew up in a small Virginia town where anti-Semitism was still rampant in the 1930s, and as a Jew she was unable to attend her own high school graduation because it was held in a Christian church. In the early 1940s she moved to New York City and met McBride's father, who was a musician at the time but eventually became a Baptist minister.

Even in mid-century Brooklyn, McBride's family was an anomaly, both for his parents' mixed-race marriage and the growing number of biracial children they had. They first lived in public housing in Red Hook, a forgotten corner of Brooklyn, but later moved to the more middle-class area of St. Albans, Queens. "Whenever she stepped out of the house with us she went into a sort of mental zone where her attention span went no farther than the five kids trailing her," McBride would later write in *The Color of Water.* "She had absolutely no interest in a world that seemed incredibly agitated by our presence. The stares and remarks, the glances and cackles that we heard as we walked about the world went right over her head."

## At a Glance . . .

**B**orn James C. McBride on September 11, 1957, in New York, NY; son of Andrew McBride (a minister) and Ruth McBride Jordan (a homemaker); stepson of Hunter Jordan (a furnace stoker) married; three children. *Education:* Oberlin College, BA, 1979; Columbia University, MA, 1979.

**Career:** Worked variously as a jazz saxophonist, composer, and producer; staff writer for the *Washington Post, Boston Globe,* and *People,* 1979–87; jazz saxophonist, composer, and producer, after 1987; head of a twelve-piece jazz R&B band; freelance writer for publications including *Essence, Rolling Stone, National Geographic,* and the *New York Times;* distinguished writer in residence, New York University.

**Awards:** Stephen Sondheim Award, American Music Festival, 1993; Richard Rodgers Award, American Academy of Arts and Letters, 1996; Anisfield-Wolf Award for Literary Excellence, and Notable Book of the Year, American Library Association, both 1997; honorary doctorate, Whitman College.

**Addresses:** *Office*—James McBride, PO Box 829, New York, NY 10108. *Web*—www.jamesmcbride.com.

Ruth McBride was a strict parent and was determined that all of her children would attend college. When McBride was still quite young, his widowed mother married another African-American man, Hunter Jordan, who worked as a furnace tender for the New York City Housing Authority, and had four more children with him. As a teen, McBride was an indifferent student but musically gifted, and he managed to get into Oberlin College in Ohio, where he earned his degree in music composition in 1979. He returned to New York City to enter Columbia University's prestigious graduate school of journalism. After that, he had little trouble landing plum posts at top newspapers like the *Boston Globe,* where in 1981 he wrote the Mother's Day tribute column that would launch his career as an author. He recounted his mom's extraordinary life story, and the *Globe* was subsequently deluged with letters from readers. He considered turning her story into book form, but at first she would not agree to work on the project.

### Became *New York Times* Bestseller

McBride's mother finally agreed to provide an oral history of her life for inclusion in a book, partly with the hope of reuniting with a long-lost sister. The result was *The Color of Water,* published by Riverhead Books in 1996. As its pages reveal, Ruth willfully shed every aspect of her past when she moved to the North. She was a white Jewish woman married to a black man at a time when such unions were relatively rare, but she proved to be an independent-minded person and a leader as well. "I stayed on the black side because that was the only place I could stay," she asserted in the book. "The few problems I had with black folks were nothing compared to the grief white folks dished out. With whites it was no question. You weren't accepted to be with a black man and that was that."

In the book McBride sketches his childhood in St. Albans, Queens, a predominantly white neighborhood, and his bafflement over his mother's heritage. She sidestepped issues of color, denying that she was white, and sometimes told her children that she was simply light-skinned. Once, McBride recalls, he asked her what color God was, and she told him, "God is the color of water. Water doesn't have a color." In the book he also recalls that by the age of ten, he had become nervous about going out in public with her in black neighborhoods, for she would sometimes be taunted; this was the height of the Black Power era, and at times he feared for her life. Still, she tried to instill in her children a sense that in the end, one's skin color was unimportant. He recalls an image of his mother riding her bike on neighborhood errands, with "her complete non-awareness of what the world thought of her, a nonchalance in the face of what I perceived to be imminent danger from blacks and whites who disliked her for being a white person in a black world. She saw none of it."

*The Color of Water* garnered accolades and topped the *New York Times* bestseller list in paperback form in September of 1997; it would remain on the top nonfiction sales rankings for the next 108 weeks. Hettie Jones, writing in the *Washington Post,* deemed it "as lively as a novel, a well-written, thoughtful contribution to the literature on race." In the *New York Times,* H. Jack Geiger found the story of the McBride clan inspiring. "The triumph of the book—and of their lives—is that race and religion are transcended in these interwoven histories by family love, the sheer force of a mother's will and her unshakable insistence that only two things really mattered: school and church," Geiger asserted.

Despite the success of his debut, McBride was somewhat perplexed by the reaction the work received from some African Americans. "When my book first came out, no blacks came to the readings. I was surprised," he told Esther Iverem, a *Washington Post* writer. "A black woman called a radio talk show and said, 'Why should we lionize this white woman?'" McBride noted that other readers "don't see it as a story about race. They see it as a story about a woman who defied the odds and insisted that her children be raised right."

## Wove Tale of Black WWII Soldiers

McBride moved on to fiction for his next work. He had long been fascinated by the predominantly African-American 92nd Division of the U.S. Army, nicknamed the "Buffalo Soldiers," which dated back to 1866. Two uncles, a cousin, and some friends of his parents had served in it, and he originally wrote a story about a group of them who find a group of Jews recently liberated from a concentration camp. He was unhappy with the finished manuscript, however, as he told *Houston Chronicle* writer Fritz Lanham. "It failed miserably," McBride said. "I just didn't feel qualified to write about the Holocaust." To rescue the plot, he traveled to Italy to research the American military presence there after a Fascist alliance between Italian dictator Benito Mussolini and Nazi Germany fell apart during World War II, when Italy surrendered to U.S.-led Allied troops in 1943. McBride spent eight months in Italy and visited a Tuscan village demolished by the retreating German soldiers, where 560 villagers were killed in the Roman Catholic church in St. Anna di Stazzema. "When I went to the church, you could almost smell it—the spirit of the place was so eerie," the writer told Lanham. "The hundreds of souls that departed heavenward from right there. You could feel it."

That moving experience gave McBride the inspiration to write his 2002 novel *Miracle at St. Anna.* The World War II story presents a fictional account of several members of the 92nd Division who become separated from their unit in the Italian countryside and find themselves behind enemy lines. The quartet of men under Lieutenant Stamps are members of an American army that is still segregated, but fighting for American principles. There is an illiterate Southerner, Sam Train, of immense size but as kindly as he is large. Hector Negron is Puerto Rican and can translate for the Italians they meet, who have never before seen an African American. There is also a Kansas City preacher and con man, Bishop Cummings. He flirts with the Italian women, and in response to comments by his fellow troops derides the value system under which they all live. "The great white father sends you out here to shoot Germans so he can hang you back in America for looking at his woman wrong," Bishop rails. "You think that's fair?"

Train, who carries around the head of a statue that he believes makes him invisible, befriends a mute and homeless Italian youth who he believes is an angel. Six-year-old Angelo, meanwhile, thinks of his protector as a "chocolate giant." As the Nazis close in for a fight, Italian partisans attempt to engage the Americans in a plot to root out a local traitor. Angelo knows the identity of the turncoat, for he is revealed to be the sole survivor of the St. Anna massacre. "As he slowly reveals the answers, McBride weaves his third-person narrative seamlessly among the soldiers and Italian peasants, many of whom emerge as well-rounded characters—no mean feat for a novel that tomes in at under 300 pages," opined *Black Issues Book Review* critic Clifford Thompson, who also termed it "a moving, sad, ultimately joyful novel that delivers on the promise of *The Color of Water.*" *Entertainment Weekly*'s Bruce Fretts commended the fiction debut as a "strikingly cinematic novel" that "flows along with cool, clean prose," and proves itself, in the end, "profoundly spiritual but rarely preachy."

That cinematic quality also attracted filmmaker Spike Lee, who acquired the film rights and hired McBride to adapt it for the screen. As Lee confessed in an interview with *Ebony*'s Habbiette Cole, when he first read *Miracle at St. Anna* he immediately envisioned it on the screen. "The way he writes is in images and it is very much cinema. So right away I knew that I could make this into a film. It's not just because it's about Black soldiers.... it's just a great story and I liked that it was not a typical war story. And ... I loved James' deep belief in the Almighty, a higher being and how He affects things—that's where miracles come from." Touchstone Pictures gave *Miracle at St. Anna* a generous promotional rollout in September of 2008, but some critics faulted a storyline they felt could have used some judicious editing and better pacing.

## Slave Haunted by Prophetic Visions

By then McBride had finished his second novel, *Song Yet Sung,* which was critically praised. Set in 1850, its plot hinges upon a fugitive slave, Liz Spocott, who is captured and held in a tavern jail on Maryland's Eastern Shore, where she learns about the Underground Railroad from another captive. She leads a breakout, flees into the woods, and begins to make her way to freedom. The mysterious sentences her fellow detainee uttered reveal themselves to be part of "the code," the allegorical phrases and secretive but symbolic actions that a runaway must use to communicate with those who will help him to freedom, which in Liz's case is less than a hundred miles north at the border of Pennsylvania. As reviewer Pam Houston noted in *O: The Oprah Magazine,* "the Code is also an instrument of deep faith, affirming the existence of God and the possibility of freedom—reasons to live in unlivable times—and McBride makes us see why men died rather than reveal it." Critiquing the novel for the *Christian Science Monitor,* Kendra Nordin commended McBride for crafting a tale of American slavery in which "not one scene is spent on a Southern plantation with stereotypes of cruel white masters and cowering black slaves."

In an unusual narrative device, Liz is plagued by dreams in which she can see the future, and she reveals some details of them to others. In these visions, she claims, there are "young black men in great cities who shot one another from horseless carriages, and of fat children who cried of starvation and ran from books like they were poison." On Liz's trail is a legendary fugitive-slave hunter, Denwood Long, who is lured out of retirement in part because of the notoriety attached to Liz as ringleader of the escape. McBride spoke with Sarah Seltzer for a *Publishers Weekly* interview and discussed the strange visions of the future that Liz sees in her dreams. "I thought, what would a slave who was transported to New York tomorrow think?," he reflected. "We've become the people we've dreaded, a consumer society.... That's why Denwood Long is important, because he realizes we're all slaves to something."

In addition to his writing career, McBride is also an accomplished jazz saxophonist and composer. He has written or performed with Anita Baker, Grover Washington Jr., and Jimmy Scott. In 2007 he wrote a lengthy essay for *National Geographic* in which he confessed his longstanding aversion to modern urban musical genres like hip-hop and rap. These styles originated in neighborhoods not far from his own, at a time when he was also coming of age in the late 1970s and early 1980s, but for more than a quarter century he avoided "that music the way you step over a crack in the sidewalk. I heard it pounding out of cars and alleyways from Paris to Abidjan.... I high-stepped away from that music for 26 years because it was everything I thought it was, and more than I ever dreamed it would be, but mostly, because it held everything I wanted to leave behind." As he wrote in the essay, however, by investigating rap music's scholarly links to African-American culture—it hearkens back to the call-and-response of gospel and to the trickster tales spun by West African griots—he learned to appreciate it. The essay was later published in the Bantam anthology *Best African American Essays: 2009.* "At its best, hip-hop lays bare the empty moral cupboard that is our generation's legacy," he wrote. "This music that once made visible the inner culture of America's greatest social problem, its legacy of slavery, has taken the dream deferred to a global scale."

*The Color of Water* remains an enduringly appealing read. In 2004 it was published in its entirety in serial format inside the *New York Times'* Metro section, and two years later Riverhead issued a tenth anniversary edition. McBride's mother died at the age of eighty-eight in January of 2010. All twelve of her children had graduated from college, and she herself went on to earn her own degree in social work from Temple University in 1986, the year she turned sixty-five. Her original intent in agreeing to the book—reuniting with a long-lost sister—came to fruition, while a cousin of McBride's from his Jewish side heard about *The Color of Water* on National Public Radio and contacted McBride's brother. Having struggled for so long with his heritage, McBride is grateful for the gifts it brought him. "[As a child] I didn't want to be white.... I would have preferred that Mommy were black," he wrote in *The Color of Water.* "Now, as a grown man I feel privileged to have come from two worlds. My view of the world is not merely that of a black man, but that of a black man with something of a Jewish soul."

## Selected writings

*The Color of Water: A Black Man's Tribute to His White Mother* (memoir), Riverhead Books, 1996, tenth anniversary edition, Riverhead Books, 2006.
*Miracle at St. Anna* (novel), Riverhead Books, 2002.
*Song Yet Sung* (novel), Riverhead Books, 2008.
"Hip-hop Planet," in *Best African American Essays: 2009,* edited by Gerald Early and Debra Dickerson, Bantam, 2009.

## Sources

### Periodicals

*Black Issues Book Review,* March–April 2002, p. 29.
*Christian Science Monitor,* February 5, 2008, p. 14.
*Ebony,* October 2008, p. 84.
*Entertainment Weekly,* September 26, 1997, p. 71; March 1, 2002, p. 72.
*Houston Chronicle,* March 17, 2002, p. 18.
*National Geographic,* April 2007, p. 100.
*New York Times,* March 31, 1996; March 2, 2008, p. 14; January 18, 2010.
*O: The Oprah Magazine,* February 2008.
*People,* November–December 1984, p. 3; April 1, 1996, p. 38; February 25, 2002, p. 41.
*Publishers Weekly,* October 30, 1995, p. 24; February 5, 1996, p. 36; March 17, 1997, p, 17; August 14, 2000, p. 196; November 26, 2001, p. 36; January 7, 2008, p. 34.
*Washington Post,* January 14, 1996, p. X4; May 21, 1996, p. B2; December 13, 1997, p. C1.

—Carol Brennan

# John Mensah

## 1982—

### Professional soccer player

Mensah, John, photograph. Jamie Squire/FIFA via Getty Images.

John Mensah is widely regarded as one of the toughest defenders in international soccer. Nicknamed the "Rock of Gibraltar," Mensah has anchored the defense for Ghana's national team in two World Cup tournaments, while playing in more than fifty international matches over the course of his young career. Mensah's coach with British team Sunderland AFC, Steve Bruce, once described him as the "best defender" he'd ever coached. Despite his immense talent, Mensah has battled injuries for much of his career, limiting his ability to remain on the field. As a result, he has struggled to find a steady home as a professional, playing for eight different European teams over a ten-year span.

John Mensah was born in Obuasi, Ghana, on November 29, 1982. As a teenager he received a scholarship to attend Sam Okyere Academy, a training institute for the nation's most promising young soccer players. During his early career, Mensah was given the nickname "Rock of Gibraltar" by his minister, the Reverend Joseph Koshy, in tribute to his talents on the field. Mensah soon emerged as one of his country's top young defenders, attracting interest from professional teams in Europe. At the age of eighteen, Mensah was recruited by FC Bologna of the Italian league, which promptly loaned him to Swiss club AC Bellinzona, with the hope of providing him the opportunity to gain valuable playing experience.

Mensah played two seasons with AC Bellinzona, logging twenty-two games in 2000–01. His exemplary play in Switzerland earned him a spot on Ghana's Under-20 national team. He served as the team's starting center back during its surprising run to the 2001 FIFA World Youth Championship Final; Ghana ultimately lost the title match to Argentina. After the tournament, Mensah joined FC Genoa of the Italian B League. He played in twenty-four games during the 2001–02 season, scoring three goals. A year later, Mensah advanced to Italy's elite A League, when he signed a deal to play for Chieva Verona. Injuries soon derailed the defender's progress, however, and he saw limited play in his three seasons in Verona. During this period, Mensah also played for Ghana in the 2004 Summer Olympics in Athens.

In spite of his persistent struggles to stay on the field, Mensah was still one of Europe's most highly touted defenders. In January of 2006 he left Italy to play on

### At a Glance . . .

**B**orn John Mensah on November 29, 1982, in Obuasi, Ghana. *Religion:* Methodist.

**Career:** MBC Accra, defender, 1999; AC Bellinzona (Switzerland), defender, 1999–2001; FC Genoa (Italy), defender, 2001–02; Chievo Verona (Italy), defender, 2002–04, 2004–05; FC Modena (Italy), defender, 2003–04; US Cremonese (Italy), defender, 2005–06; Stade Rennais (France), defender, 2005–08; Olympique Lyonnais (France), defender, 2008–09; Sunderland AFC (England), defender, 2009—; Ghana Football Association, defender, 2001—; played for Ghana in Olympic games, 2004; played in World Cup as member of the Ghana national team, 2006 and 2010.

**Addresses:** *Office*—c/o Sunderland Association Football Club, The Sunderland Stadium of Light, Sunderland, SR5 1SU, England.

loan for French club Stade Rennais; three months later, he signed a three-year contract to play for Rennes full time. At around this time, he competed in the African Nations Cup as part of the Ghana national team. Mensah's high quality of play ultimately earned him a place on the tournament's All-Star Team. In the summer of 2006, he played for Ghana in the World Cup, helping his home nation advance to the tournament's round of sixteen.

After the World Cup, Mensah resumed playing for Stade Rennais. His positive impact on his new professional team quickly became evident. In its first eighteen games with Mensah in the lineup, Stade Rennais allowed only twelve goals, an average of only 0.66 goals per game; in six games it played without him, the team gave up thirteen goals, or 2.66 per game. By the beginning of the 2006–07 season, Mensah was widely regarded as one of the top defenders in the French 1 League. In November of 2006, the nation's leading soccer magazine, *France Football,* ranked Mensah the top player in the French League. In January of 2008, he was named the team's captain.

Mensah's performance with Rennes eventually attracted the interest of other clubs. In July of 2008, after fielding interest from several British clubs, he signed a five-year contract with Olympique Lyonnais, the reigning champions of the French League, in a deal worth €8.4 million. The celebrated defender was soon hampered by a new wave of health issues, however, and by October of 2008 he had played in only five of Lyon's first fourteen matches; for the year, Mensah played in

only twelve games, as he contended with nagging injuries to his back and groin. In 2009 Mensah joined Sunderland AFC of the British Premier League, as part of a loan arrangement with Lyon. He played in sixteen games for Sunderland over the course of 2009–10, scoring one goal.

Mensah continued to battle injuries during this period, as problems with his thigh and hamstring significantly reduced his playing time. While leading the Sunderland defense, Mensah was also involved in several critical World Cup qualifying matches with Ghana, eventually helping his national team secure a berth in the summer 2010 tournament in South Africa. At the same time, however, persistent health problems ultimately prevented him from participating in the 2010 African Cup of Nations, raising serious doubts about his ability to play for the national team in the World Cup. Even in the face of these lingering injury concerns, Mensah's proven ability as a defender made him a valuable commodity in the British Premier League, and by spring 2010 Sunderland coach Steve Bruce went public with his desire to secure Mensah to a long-term deal with the team.

Mensah managed to regain his form in time for the 2010 World Cup, leading Ghana past the group round for the second consecutive tournament. In the round of sixteen, Mensah's stingy defense helped Ghana defeat a dangerous American team, 2–1, sending the Black Stars to their first ever appearance in the final eight of a World Cup tournament. Following the victory over the United States, Mensah publicly expressed his pride in the team's accomplishments. "All of Africa is looking to us now," the defender was quoted as saying in the June 28, 2010, edition of the *Sun* (England). Mensah went on to predict a Ghanaian victory over their next opponent, Uruguay: "We aren't at all worried about Uruguay. We weren't worried about the USA. We played them and won, and we are going to do the same again." Although Ghana ultimately lost its match against the Uruguayans, the team's impressive run helped further Mensah's reputation as one of the world's top defenders.

Even though Sunderland coach Steve Bruce wanted to sign Mensah to a contract extension, the defender's injury-plagued history was still a major concern to the club, and by the beginning of the 2010–11 season, he was once again with the Black Cats on temporary loan. With renewed dedication to an intensive physical therapy regimen, however, the Rock of Gibraltar hoped to finally meet the high expectations that had followed him since his teen years, while also finding a long-term home on one of Europe's elite teams.

## Sources

### Periodicals

*Africa News,* July 22, 2008; July 23, 2008; October 28, 2008; July 1, 2010.

*Northern Echo,* September 16, 2009, p. 53; October 14, 2009, p. 50; March 27, 2010, p. 28; September 8, 2010, p. 58.

*Sun* (England), June 28, 2010, pp. 4, 5.

*Times* (London), August 17, 2009, p. 3.

### Online

"John Mensah," ESPN Soccernet, http://soccernet. espn.go.com/player/_/id/86303/john-mensah?cc =5901 (accessed October 29, 2010).

"John Mensah," FIFA.com, http://www.fifa.com/ worldcup/players/player=184560/profile.html (accessed October 29, 2010).

"John Mensah: The Rock of Gibraltar," johntherock5. com, http://www.johntherock5.com/jr5.php?@= Bio (accessed October 29, 2010).

"Mensah, John," National Football Teams, http:// www.national-football-teams.com/v2/player.php?id =2670 (accessed October 29, 2010).

—Stephen Meyer

# Paulo Moura

## 1932–2010

### Clarinetist, saxophonist, composer

One of Brazil's most famous—and most beloved—musicians, Paulo Moura was renowned above all for his versatility. Equally talented on both the clarinet and the saxophone, he moved easily from one style to another, often playing classical compositions, jazz, popular dance music, and traditional folk songs in the space of a single afternoon. Winner of a Latin Grammy Award in 2000, he had a major role in fostering the growing popularity of Brazilian music across the globe.

One of ten children, Moura was born July 15, 1932, in São José do Rio Prêto, a sizable city in the northwestern corner of the Brazilian state of São Paulo. His father, Pedro Moura, was a carpenter and part-time musician who dreamed of organizing his family into an orchestra. Paulo was given a clarinet about the age of nine, and by the time he reached his teens he was accompanying his father at local gigs. Soon thereafter, the family moved hundreds of miles to Rio de Janeiro, where, in about 1950, he won entrance to the National School of Music. Moura thrived there, focusing on classical music and music theory. According to Alvaro Neder of AllMusic.com, he completed his program in only two years, less than a third of the time normally required. Despite the intensity of his formal studies, he also found time to master the saxophone and to immerse himself in Rio's rich musical heritage. In the city's many dance halls, for example, he developed an abiding love for songs in the *bossa nova, samba,* and *choro* (or *chorinho*) styles. North American jazz affected him deeply as well.

All of those influences can be seen at various points in his career. His first jobs in Rio were undoubtedly in the streets and dance halls. Once he had established a reputation at the School of Music, he found work in jazz clubs and classical orchestras. By the mid-1950s, his performance in the latter had drawn the attention of record executives at Columbia, which issued his first recording, a rendering of the nineteenth-century composer Niccolò Paganini's "Moto Perpetuo" ("Perpetual Motion"). It was partly on the strength of that record, as well as on his increasingly extensive work with local radio stations, that he was hired in 1959 as the lead clarinetist in the orchestra of Rio's Municipal Theater. He retained that position for the next nineteen years.

One of the attractions of orchestra work is that it often leaves time for other gigs. Moura took full advantage of that flexibility, playing with a variety of smaller ensembles throughout the 1960s and 1970s. Many of these engagements were with American jazz stars, who had begun visiting Brazil in large numbers in the late 1950s. Eager to draw inspiration from the nation's music, they often hired local musicians for gigs in Rio and other Brazilian locales. Moura served in many of these backup bands, working with such luminaries as the vocalists Ella Fitzgerald and Lena Horne. In doing so, he established a reputation as a leading practitioner of the *bossa nova* style, hitherto little known outside Brazil. Characterized by complex harmonies and rich, guitar-based orchestration, *bossa nova* appealed deeply to many American jazz stars, who set off an international craze for the new style when they returned home. As a result, Moura and several of his

## At a Glance . . .

**B**orn July 15, 1932, in São José do Rio Prêto, Brazil; died July 12, 2010, in Rio de Janeiro, Brazil; son of Pedro Moura (a carpenter and musician); married Halina Grynberg; children: two. *Education:* National School of Music (Rio de Janeiro, Brazil), seven-year program completed, early 1950s.

**Career:** Independent musician, late 1940s–2010; National Theater (Rio de Janeiro, Brazil), first clarinetist, 1959–78.

**Awards:** Latin Grammy Award (Best Brazilian Roots/Regional Album, for *Pixinguinha*), 2000.

friends, among them composer Antonio Carlos Jobim and pianist Sergio Mendes, suddenly found themselves in great demand around the world. In November of 1962, for example, he and Mendes appeared at New York City's Carnegie Hall in a concert later regarded as a pivotal moment in the development of jazz from classic 1950s bebop to the more eclectic sounds of later decades. Nearly as significant in this regard was Moura's work on a 1962 album by the American saxophonist Cannonball Adderley. Together with *Getz/Gilberto* (1963), an iconic collaboration between saxophonist Stan Getz and guitarist João Gilberto, *Cannonball's Bossa Nova* did much to bring Brazilian music to the attention of jazz fans worldwide.

After Carnegie Hall, Moura spent roughly fifteen years balancing his responsibilities at the National Theater with his growing involvement in jazz around the globe. He toured extensively, visiting Greece in 1971, the United States in 1975, and Japan in 1976. He also spent a great deal of time in the recording studio, working both on his own albums and on others'. Among his most notable solo works in this period was 1976's *Confusão Urbana, Suburbana e Rural*, a compelling mixture of jazz, *samba*, and *choro* rhythms. Its release prompted many new offers from concert promoters and record executives, and to handle these he stepped down from the National Theater in 1978.

The 1980s and 1990s were, in the eyes of many fans, among the most vibrant and productive years of Mou-

ra's career. Much of his work in this era involved the addition of jazz motifs to folk songs and other traditional melodies. In 1998, for example, he released *Pixinguinha*, an album made up of songs by the composer of that name, a figure "considered," in the words of the *New York Times*' Larry Rohter, "the father of Brazilian popular music." At the first Latin Grammy Awards, held two years later in Los Angeles, *Pixinguinha* was named Best Brazilian Roots/Regional Album.

Though Moura's health began to decline after the turn of the twenty-first century, he continued to perform and record. Shortly after the release of his last major album (2009's *AfroBossaNova*), he was hospitalized with terminal cancer. Surrounded by friends and family, including his wife Halina and two children, he made the most of his final days, playing in an intimate "jam session" just hours before his death in Rio on July 12, 2010. "I have the feeling that he was trying to say goodbye, and to give his friends a blessing," guitarist Marcello Gonçalves said of that final concert, in a conversation with Tom Phillips of the London *Guardian*. "It was a farewell, but a farewell on a high."

## Selected works

*Moto Perpetuo*, Columbia, 1956.
Cannonball Adderley, *Cannonball's Bossa Nova*, Riverside, 1962.
*Confusão Urbana, Suburbana e Rural*, BMG, 1976.
*Pixinguinha*, Blue Jackel, 1998.
*AfroBossaNova*, Biscoito Fino, 2009.

## Sources

### Periodicals

*Guardian* (London), July 20, 2010.
*New York Times*, July 18, 2010.

### Online

Dacks, David, "Seu Jorge Remembers Fallen Brazilian Music Pioneer Paulo Moura," Exclaim.ca, July 14, 2010, http://www.exclaim.ca/articles/generalarticlesynopsfullart.aspx?csid1=145&csid2=844&fid1=48081 (accessed August 12, 2010).
Neder, Alvaro, "Paulo Moura: Biography," AllMusic.com, http://allmusic.com/cg/amg.dll?p=amg&sql=11:f9ftxql5ldje~T1 (accessed August 12, 2010).

—R. Anthony Kugler

# Pius Njawe

## 1957–2010

### Journalist, newspaper publisher, activist

Njawe, Pius, photograph. AP Images/Themba Hadebe.

One of Africa's most distinguished journalists, Pius Njawe of Cameroon spent more than three decades in a tireless fight for democracy and freedom of the press. The founder of his nation's first fully independent newspaper, *Le Messager,* he doggedly publicized corruption, catastrophic pollution, and other major problems. Angered by his exposés, the government of President Paul Biya subjected him to a horrifying campaign of harassment and intimidation, but even torture failed to shake his determination. "He was a pioneer," Stephen W. Smith of Duke University told Adam Nossiter of the *New York Times* in 2010, shortly after Njawe's untimely death in a car accident. "He put his whole life into being a journalist. It came out of his pores."

Pius Noumeni Njawe (also spelled Njawé) was born under the colonial authority of France on March 4, 1957, roughly three years before Cameroon's independence. His birthplace was Babouantou, a small community several hundred miles north of Douala, a major port on the nation's Atlantic coast. By his sixteenth birthday, he was working as a paperboy for *Seeds Africa,* a regional periodical. After about two years there, he moved on in 1974 to become a reporter for *La Gazette,* a local paper in Douala. Despite draconian press restrictions, Njawe immediately began filing controversial stories, particularly regarding the country's oil industry, a subject that would maintain his interest—and his indignation—for the rest of his career. Though Cameroon has an abundance of oil, the revenues generated from its sale have not been shared with the vast bulk of the population. The environmental damage associated with its extraction, meanwhile, has been enormous. Njawe's detailed reports on those problems infuriated the government of Ahmadou Ahidjo, Biya's predecessor, and in 1976 he was arrested. That detention, though relatively brief, marked the start of an ominous campaign of intimidation; over the next thirty-four years, he was arrested more than one hundred and twenty times.

After five years as a reporter, Njawe left *La Gazette* in 1979 to establish a paper of his own, *Le Messager* ("*The Messenger*"). Only twenty-two at the time, he was the youngest newspaper publisher on the continent. Despite the notoriously difficult financial and logistical challenges associated with a new publication,

*At a Glance . . .*

**B**orn Pius Noumeni Njawe (or Njawé) on March 4, 1957, in Babouantou, Cameroon (then the French colony of Cameroun); died July 12, 2010, outside Norfolk, VA; married twice; first wife, Jane, died 2002; children: eight.

**Career:** *La Gazette* (Douala, Cameroon), reporter, 1974–79; *Le Messager* (Douala, Cameroon), founder and publisher, 1979–2010.

**Memberships:** Cameroon Organization for Press Freedom, founder; Justice and Jane (road safety organization), founder.

**Awards:** Golden Pen of Freedom, World Newspaper Association, 1993; named a World Press Freedom Hero, International Press Institute, 2000.

*Le Messager* thrived, largely on the basis of Njawe's reputation for journalistic integrity. As the paper grew, however, so did the government's efforts to silence it, despite an ostensible repeal of press restrictions by President Biya in the mid-1980s. Frustrated by his refusal to bow to pressure, the government banned *Le Messager* outright in 1992 and forced its founder into exile in nearby Benin. On his arrival there, he simply resumed publishing. A year later, he was allowed to return to Cameroon, but the harassment continued, and in 1998 he was sentenced to two years in prison for disseminating information the government alleged was false. Though he was pardoned after ten months, the treatment he received from his jailers—treatment he recorded and published—was widely condemned as torture. Fortunately, he was able to rely on the devoted assistance of friends and colleagues. The support of journalists outside Cameroon proved particularly important in this regard, for it was their repeated inquiries about his case that seem to have persuaded President Biya to release him.

Amid the demands of his work, Njawe also lent his support to a variety of important causes. Many of these, not surprisingly, involved grassroots efforts to reduce government interference in the press and other fragile institutions: in 1993, for example, he founded the Cameroon Organization for Press Freedom. Perhaps his most visible advocacy work concerned road safety. Like many of its neighbors, Cameroon has long had an unusually high rate of traffic fatalities, due in part to inadequate ambulance services, poorly maintained infrastructure, and lax regulation. Though he wrote a number of editorials on the subject in the

1980s and 1990s, it was not until a tragic accident in 2002 that Njawe became a dedicated safety activist. In September of that year, his wife Jane died of injuries sustained when a oncoming bus, trying to pass another vehicle on a narrow road, struck her car. According to a statement Njawe later gave the World Health Organization (WHO), his wife might well have survived with adequate medical treatment. As it was, her death spurred him to create Justice and Jane, a volunteer organization that uses education and publicity to improve the safety of Cameroon's roads. In his comments to WHO, he called the work "my way of honoring Jane," adding, "I will do anything to honour her memory."

Njawe's activism, combined with his courage and good humor in the face of near-constant harassment, brought him a number of awards and honors. Among the most prominent of these were the World Newspaper Association's Golden Pen of Freedom in 1993 and designation as a "World Press Freedom Hero" by the International Press Institute (IPI) in 2000. In an accompanying citation, later quoted by Adam Bernstein of the *Washington Post*, the IPI called him "Cameroon's most beleaguered journalist and one of Africa's most courageous fighters for press freedom."

In the summer of 2010, Njawe traveled to Washington, DC, for a series of meetings with a group of Cameroonian exiles and political activists. On July 12, he was taking a break to visit relatives in nearby Virginia when his car was hit by a truck outside the city of Norfolk; he was killed instantly. Surviving him were eight children, his second wife, and hundreds of close colleagues from the world of journalism. In a tribute on the IPI's Web site, fellow journalist Wangethi Mwangi of Kenya called Njawe "the quintessential torch bearer of the free press campaign not just in his native land but also in Africa."

## Sources

### Periodicals

*New York Times*, November 12, 1996; July 14, 2010.
*Observer* (London), July 18, 2010.
*Washington Post*, July 15, 2010.

### Online

McKenzie, Alison Bethel, "Timeline: Pius Njawe, 1957–2010," International Press Institute, July 14, 2010, http://www.freemedia.at/singleview/5052/ (accessed August 20, 2010).
Njawe, Pius, "Jane Njawe: Died in a Road Traffic Crash: 16 September 2002," World Health Organization, 2007, http://www.who.int/features/2007/faces/jane/en/print.html (accessed August 19, 2010).
"Tributes to Pius Njawe: 1957–2010," International

Press Institute, July 13, 2010, http://www.
freemedia.at/site-services/singleview-master/5051/
(accessed August 21, 2010).

—R. Anthony Kugler

# Hildrus A. Poindexter

## 1901–1987

### Physician, public health director

Physician Hildrus Poindexter made invaluable contributions to the field of public health as a specialist in tropical medicine. During his career of more than five decades, he traveled to dozens of countries in Latin America, the Caribbean, Africa, Southeast Asia, and the Pacific Islands, where he made careful scientific observations of tropical diseases and implemented prevention and treatment programs to reduce their incidence. A dedicated public servant in the U.S. Public Health Service, he was commended by President John F. Kennedy in 1963. As the first African American ever to earn both a medical degree and a doctorate, Poindexter helped blaze a trail for future generations of black doctors and medical researchers.

Hildrus Augustus "Gus" Poindexter was born on May 10, 1901, in Shelby County near Memphis, Tennessee, the sixth of eleven children of tenant farmers Fred and Luvenia Gilberta (Clarke) Poindexter. He first became interested in medicine at the age of five, after observing a local black physician and seeing the respect he was accorded. At the age of fifteen he sold the horse and chickens that his parents gave him to set up in farm life in order to attend Swift Memorial College, a Presbyterian secondary school for blacks in Rogersville in eastern Tennessee. There, he excelled in mathematics, Greek, Latin, and biblical studies and taught summer school to elementary students.

Poindexter's teachers arranged for him to attend Lincoln University, a historically black college in Pennsylvania. He financed his education by working in the nearby coal mines, tutoring divinity students in Greek

and Latin, and working summers in factories and hotels. At Lincoln, Poindexter was a standout athlete—nicknamed "Pig Iron," he was an All-American guard for the football team and won the Central Intercollegiate Athletic Association championship in shot put. He graduated cum laude in June of 1924, and the same month married Ruth Viola Grier.

To raise money for his medical school education, Poindexter and his wife moved to Oxford, North Carolina, where he taught for a year at Mary Potter High School and worked as a Pullman porter. He entered the two-year program at Dartmouth College Medical School in New Hampshire and performed well enough to earn himself a spot in the third-year class at Harvard Medical School. At Harvard, Poindexter was one of only three of African-American students in his class.

During his studies at Dartmouth and Harvard, Poindexter developed an interest in tropical medicine, and he hoped to work in the area of public health. He applied for a post at a U.S. government laboratory in Manila but was rejected because of his race. Instead, he accepted a ten-week internship at the John A. Andrew Hospital at the Tuskegee Institute in Alabama, one of the few facilities that was open to blacks wishing to pursue postgraduate training. While there, he conducted an epidemiological survey and developed a health education program in Bullock County, Alabama, a poor and predominantly African-American settlement. On a two-year fellowship from the Rockefeller Foundation, Poindexter went on to Columbia Univer-

## At a Glance . . .

**B**orn Hildrus Augustus Poindexter on May 10, 1901, near Memphis, TN; died on April 21, 1987, in Clinton, MD; son of Fred and Luvenia Gilberta (Clarke) Poindexter; married Ruth Viola Grier on June 11, 1924; children: Patchechole Ojo. *Military service:* U.S. Army, 1943–46. *Education:* Lincoln University, BA, 1924; Harvard University, MD, 1929; Columbia University, MS, 1930, PhD, 1932, MPH (master of public health), 1937.

**Career:** Howard University College of Medicine, assistant professor of bacteriology, preventive medicine, and public health, 1931–36, professor and department head, 1936–43; U.S. Public Health Service, medical officer and director, 1947–65; Howard University College of Medicine, professor of community health practice, 1965–87.

**Memberships:** American Board of Microbiology; American Board of Preventive Medicine and Public Health; American Society of Tropical Medicine; Medico-Chirurgical Society of the District of Columbia; National Medical Association; Omega Psi Phi; Society of Tropical Medicine and Hygiene.

**Awards:** Bronze Star Medal, U.S. Army, 1945; Knight Commander of the Order of African Humane Redemption, government of Liberia, 1948; Career Award, National Civil Service League, 1963; Distinguished Service Medal, National Medical Association, 1964; Meritorious Award, U.S. Public Health Service, 1965; Human Service Award, National Graduate University, 1975.

sity, earning a doctorate in bacteriology and parasitology in 1932, and later a master's degree in public health in 1937. Notably, Poindexter was the first African American to earn both a medical degree and a doctorate.

In 1931 Poindexter joined the faculty at Howard University Medical College in Washington, DC, as an assistant professor of bacteriology, preventive medicine, and public health, and in 1936 he became head of that department. The following year, he returned to the field to conduct epistemological studies in Alabama and Mississippi, where he identified malnutrition, insect-borne disease, and syphilis as the most pressing health problems in the rural South. Between 1938 and 1943, research fellowships took him to South America, Puerto Rico, the Virgin Islands, and other islands in the Caribbean to study tropical diseases.

When the United States entered World War II in 1941, expertise in tropical medicine was much in demand, but few specialists were eligible for military service. Poindexter registered for the draft but was deferred because he was training other physicians. In 1943, at the age of forty-two, he enlisted in the U.S. Army Medical Corps as a volunteer, with the rank of major. He served in the South Pacific, joining the headquarters unit of the 93rd Infantry Division in the Solomon and Bougainville islands, where malaria threatened Allied troops. Poindexter implemented a program that significantly reduced malarial infection, receiving the Bronze Star for his efforts.

In January of 1947 Poindexter left the army as a lieutenant colonel and joined the U.S. Public Health Service. His first assignment took him to the West African nation of Liberia, as part of a foreign aid program developed by the Harry S. Truman administration to help the Liberian government improve sanitation planning and control infectious diseases. He handled all aspects of health care, including training health providers, developing disease prevention and treatment programs, and conducting research. From 1948 to 1953 Poindexter served as senior medical officer at the U.S. embassy in the capital city of Monrovia.

Poindexter served his next tour in Southeast Asia, where he was chief of health and sanitation for the U.S. Operation in Vietnam, Cambodia, and Laos. First stationed in the North in Hanoi and then in the South in Saigon, he was in charge of health care for refugees from the Battle of Dien Bien Phu. He left the country before the beginning of the Vietnam War. Poindexter's other tours included service in Surinam (1956–58), Iraq (1958–59), Libya (1959–61), and Sierra Leone (1962–64). During his tour in Iraq, he was a professor of preventive medicine at the Royal Baghdad Medical College.

In 1965, at the age of sixty-five, Poindexter retired from public service and returned to Howard University as a part-time professor of community health practice. He continued his teaching and research for the next two decades, training Peace Corps volunteers and working as a special consultant to the U.S. State Department and the U.S. Agency for International Development. In the latter capacity, he did a six-month tour of duty in Nigeria in 1965.

Poindexter received many accolades for his contributions to public health. In 1963 President John F. Kennedy presented him with the National Civil Service League Career Service Award, and in 1964, the National Medical Association honored him with the

19th Distinguished Service Award. The U.S. Public Health Service recognized his many years of service in 1965 with the Meritorious Award.

In 1949 Poindexter became the first African American to be admitted to the American Society of Tropical Medicine—he had been denied membership in 1934 because of his race—and went on to serve as vice president of the organization's Washington, DC, chapter and a trustee of the national body. He was the founder of the Tropical Medicine Laboratory and a certified specialist of the American Board of Microbiology and the American Board of Preventive Medicine and Public Health.

After suffering a heart attack, Poindexter died on April 21, 1987, in Clinton, Maryland, at the age of eighty-five. In his honor, the Black Caucus of Health Workers established the Hildrus A. Poindexter Award, which is given annually to a public health practitioner who has made a difference in the field of public health through his or her accomplishments, service, and dedication.

## Selected works

*My World of Reality: An Autobiography,* Balamp Publishing, 1973.

## Sources

### Books

Nercessian, Nora N., *Against All Odds: The Legacy of Students of African Descent at Harvard Medical School Before Affirmative Action, 1950–1968,* Puritan Press, 2004.

### Periodicals

*Journal of the National Medical Association,* May 1973, 243–47.
*Lincoln Lion,* Summer 1987.
*Washington Post,* April 25, 1987.

—Deborah A. Ring

# Benny Powell

## 1930–2010

### Jazz trombonist, music educator

Powell, Benny, photograph. AP Images/Garet Cobb.

Trombonist Benny Powell dedicated his life to jazz. A native of Louisiana, he is probably best remembered for his tenure with the Count Basie Orchestra (CBO) and other "big band" ensembles. Equally significant, however, was his work in a variety of small groups, both as a sideman and as a leader. He was also a highly regarded teacher. Longtime colleague Randy Weston once described him, in comments quoted by Claire Noland of the *Los Angeles Times,* as "the most incredible, spiritual person I know."

way to pay for lessons. He progressed rapidly, and at the age of fourteen he had his first professional gig, an orchestra concert for members of the armed services. His performance at that event, held at a United Service Organizations (USO) club in New Orleans, pleased his employers and earned him a longer-term assignment.

In high school, meanwhile, Powell excelled, completing all the requirements for his diploma by the age of sixteen. He then entered Alabama's State Teachers College, a seg-

Born March 1, 1930, in New Orleans, Benjamin Gordon Powell Jr. was drawn to that city's rich musical heritage at a very early age. In a 1997 interview with Bob Bernotas of the *Online Trombone Journal,* he recalled watching a trombonist march in one of the parades for which New Orleans has long been known. "I was fascinated by this shiny instrument and this guy marching down the street playing it," he told Bernotas. "I couldn't take my eyes off of him." He nevertheless began on the drums, switching to the trombone about the age of twelve, when he received one from an uncle. Though his widowed mother, a domestic worker, often struggled to make ends meet, she determinedly found a

regated institution known for the strength of its music program. His stay there proved a short one, however, for he quickly won a job with the bandleader King Kolax. After touring with Kolax through the South and West, he joined the orchestras of Ernie Fields and Lionel Hampton. His work with those ensembles, in turn, drew the attention of Basie, who hired him in 1951. Their association would last for the next twelve years. A demanding, meticulous leader, Basie only rarely allowed his players the freedom of a long solo; to be granted one, as Powell was at a recording session in 1955, was a sign of strong approval. The song, "April in Paris," subsequently became a jazz standard.

## At a Glance . . .

**B**orn Benjamin Gordon Powell Jr. on March 1, 1930, in New Orleans, LA; died June 26, 2010, in New York, NY; son of a domestic worker; divorced; children: one. *Education:* Attended State Teachers College (later Alabama State University), 1940s.

**Career:** Independent trombonist, 1940s–2010; Count Basie Orchestra, trombonist, 1951–63; Thad Jones—Mel Lewis Jazz Orchestra, trombonist, 1966–70; *Merv Griffin Show,* trombonist, 1970–78; New School for Jazz and Contemporary Music, faculty member, 1994–2010.

**Memberships:** Jazzmobile.

Then one of the most prominent bands in the world, the CBO toured constantly, often appearing before heads of state. In 1961, for example, it performed at the inauguration of U.S. President John F. Kennedy, an event Powell often described as a highlight of his career. By that time, however, he was also beginning to feel somewhat constricted by the big band format. In 1963 he left Basie to pursue other opportunities. Most of these were with quartets and quintets, though he also had a number of short-term assignments with Broadway musicals and with vocalists, including Frank Sinatra and Joe Williams. In 1966 he joined the Thad Jones—Mel Lewis Jazz Orchestra, a group that, despite its name, generally eschewed the big band format in favor of improvisations and extended solos. He remained there until 1970, when he left to join the house orchestra for television's *Merv Griffin Show,* a well-paying gig that required only a portion of his time, giving him the freedom to focus on other projects. The program's move from New York to Los Angeles in the early 1970s brought him to California, where he remained for a little more than a decade. After leaving Griffin in 1978, he worked for several years in the many clubs and recording studios in Los Angeles before returning to New York, where he began his partnership with Weston, a pianist known for mixing cutting-edge jazz with traditional African rhythms.

Powell's busy schedule hindered his solo career for many years, and it was not until the early 1980s that he began to release albums under his own name. The first of these, 1982's *Coast to Coast,* "displays the kind of versatility that stood Benny in such good stead in a turbulent musical world," wrote David Jacoby of the music Web site Yehoodi.com. Three more major albums followed; all won strong reviews, particularly 2008's *Nextep,* which Adam Greenberg of AllMusic.com praised for its "sparkling solos."

By the early 1990s, Powell was increasingly recognized as one of the elder statesmen of jazz. By all accounts a warm, gregarious person, he especially enjoyed mentoring younger players, guiding them in practical matters as well as musical ones. His efforts in this area were formally recognized in 1994, when he was offered a faculty position at New York's New School for Jazz and Contemporary Music. Aside from occasional breaks for touring and other commitments, he taught there for the rest of his life. He also volunteered regularly with Jazzmobile, a New York institution dedicated to jazz education.

Powell had several serious health issues over the years, notably including two kidney transplants in the 1990s. By the end of that decade he had made a full recovery, and the 2000s were among the most productive years of his career. In addition to his teaching duties, his albums, and his ongoing work with Weston, he performed regularly with saxophonist Jimmy Heath and other luminaries. By 2010, however, his health was again deteriorating, and in June of that year he entered a New York hospital for surgery on his back and spinal cord. Serious complications ensued, and on June 26, 2010, he died at the age of eighty. Surviving him were a daughter, several grandchildren, and legions of fans. At a memorial service at New York's St. Peter's Church, a succession of speakers described his life as one well lived. Their words echoed his own comments to Bernotas more than a decade earlier. Asked then to reflect on the course of his career, he had replied, "I am doubly blessed to be able to make my livelihood for 50 years playing trombone only. I never had any jobs as a waiter, taxi driver, any of that stuff. ... It's fantastic."

## Selected discography

### Singles

Count Basie Orchestra, "April in Paris," 1955.

### Albums

*Coast to Coast,* Trident, 1982.
*Why Don't You Say Yes Sometime?* Inspire, 1991.
*The Gift of Love,* Faith, 2003.
*Nextep,* Origin, 2008.

## Sources

### Periodicals

*New York Times,* July 3, 2010.
*Los Angeles Times,* July 10, 2010.

### Online

Bernotas, Bob, "An Interview With Benny Powell," Online Trombone Journal, 1997 (revised 1998), http://www.trombone.org/articles/library/benny-powell-int.asp (accessed August 4, 2010).

Dupont, David, "Benny Powell: Biography," AllMusic. com, http://allmusic.com/cg/amg.dll?p=amg&sql =11:39fixqrgld0e~T1 (accessed August 4, 2010).

Greenberg, Adam, "*Nextep*: Review," AllMusic.com, http://allmusic.com/cg/amg.dll?p=amg&sql=10: hxfoxz9kldae (accessed August 5, 2010).

Jacoby, David, "Benny Powell's 75th Birthday Celebration!!!" Yehoodi.com, March 4, 2005, http:// yehoodi.com/comment/71079/benny-powell-s-75 th-birthday-celebration/ (accessed August 5, 2010).

"Powell, Benny," New School for Jazz and Contemporary Music, http://www.newschool.edu/jazz/faculty. aspx?id=11090 (accessed August 4, 2010).

—R. Anthony Kugler

# René Préval

## 1943—

### Agronomist, civil servant, entrepreneur, politician

Préval, René, photograph. Thony Belizaire/AFP/Getty Images.

René Préval became president of Haiti for the second time in 2006. The Caribbean nation, the poorest in the Western Hemisphere, has long faced a number of immense problems, including high unemployment, high infant mortality, near total deforestation, and illiteracy. All of these were made worse in January of 2010, when a devastating earthquake killed several hundred thousand people and left the capital, Port-au-Prince, in ruins. An agronomist by training, Préval enjoyed considerable goodwill, particularly abroad. He also faced criticism, however, for allegedly failing to move fast enough on a number of critical reforms.

The son of Claude Préval, an agronomist who rose to become the country's minister of agriculture, René Garcia Préval was born in Port-au-Prince on January 17, 1943. Much of his childhood was spent in the northern district of Marmelade, where his father's family had a farm. After high school, he was able to study in Europe. At the Colllege of Gembloux and the Catholic University of Louvain, both in Belgium, he took a range of courses in science and agronomy, and he later studied at the University of Pisa in Italy.

The 1960s seem to have been a challenging period for Préval and his family, thanks in large part to the repressive policies of Fran͵ois "Papa Doc" Duvalier, who ruled Haiti as self-proclaimed "president for life" from 1957 to 1971. Because Préval's father had served in the administration of Duvalier's predecessor, Paul Magloire, the entire family was considered politically suspect. Forced into exile, Préval moved to central Africa, working there for the United Nations as an agronomist and administrator. In about 1970 he moved to New York City, where he supported his family with a variety of jobs, most of them unrelated to his training. His return to Haiti came in 1975, four years after the death of Duvalier. Though the country was still in the firm grip of his family, with power having passed to the president's son Jean-Claude ("Baby Doc"), political conditions had stabilized enough to allow Préval to obtain a civil service post at the Ministry of Mining and Energy.

Political conditions, meanwhile, were deteriorating again. The younger Duvalier's ouster in 1986 was accompanied by widespread rioting and economic turmoil. Like many other well-educated Haitians,

## At a Glance . . .

**B**orn René Garcia Préval on January 17, 1943, in Port-au-Prince, Haiti; son of Claude Préval (an agronomist and government minister) and Céline Talleyrand Préval; divorced twice; married Elisabeth Delatour, 2009; children: two. *Politics:* Lavalas, then Fwon Lespwa ("Hope Front"). *Education:* Studied at the College of Gembloux (Belgium), the Catholic University of Louvain (Belgium), and the University of Pisa (Italy), 1960s–1970s(?).

**Career:** United Nations, agronomist and administrator, 1960s(?)–early 1970s(?); Republic of Haiti, civil servant, 1975–1980s; bakery co-founder and executive, 1988–91; Republic of Haiti, prime minister, 1991–93 (in exile after September 1991), presidential advisor, 1993–94; Economic and Social Assistance Fund (Haiti), general director, 1994–95(?); Republic of Haiti, president, 1996–2001; entrepreneur, 2001–06; Republic of Haiti, president, 2006—.

**Addresses:** *Office*—c/o Embassy of Haiti, 2311 Massachusetts Ave. NW, Washington, DC 20008.

Préval tried to ease the suffering of his compatriots. Of his various efforts in this area, the most prominent was a bread distribution program that he began shortly after co-founding a bakery in the capital in 1988. According to David Adams of the *St. Petersburg* (Florida) *Times,* the program fed as many as twenty-five thousand children, many of whom came from an orphanage run by Jean-Bertrand Aristide, a Catholic priest who quickly became the agronomist's political mentor. Winner of the 1990 presidential race, Aristide named Préval his prime minister upon taking office the following year.

Préval's first months in the spotlight were difficult ones. As he struggled to gain experience in the day-to-day business of running a nation, domestic opposition mounted, and in September of 1991, after less than a year in office, the Aristide administration fell in a coup. Most of its senior members, the president and prime minister included, then fled to Washington, DC, where they set up a government in exile. Préval remained the country's prime minister, at least in the eyes of the international community, until 1993, when he stepped down to become an advisor to Aristide. With the help of troops from the United States, the two returned home the following year. By that time, however, their relationship had deteriorated, and Préval left the administration to become general director of the Eco-

nomic and Social Assistance Fund, a development initiative sponsored by the World Bank and other international organizations. He left that position a short time later, after it became clear that he was going to be nominated for president by Lavalas, Aristide's party. Constitutionally barred from seeking a second consecutive term, Aristide responded to his protege's sudden rise by leaving Lavalas, taking many supporters with him.

Emotions ran high on all sides throughout the campaign. The election, held in December of 1995, brought Préval nearly eighty-eight percent of the vote. Turnout was relatively low, however, and in the months following his inauguration in May of 1996, he found himself facing a formidable opposition, both in the nation's parliament (known as the National Assembly) and in the streets. He nevertheless managed to put through a number of economic reforms, most of them involving the privatization of state-owned enterprises. He also won praise for his efforts to begin prosecuting police officers and other officials accused of corruption and human rights violations. Though some progress was made, Haiti's court system remained, as of 2010, wholly unequipped to handle more than a small fraction of the allegations brought before it. Only a handful of public officials had faced trial, and even fewer had been convicted.

In retrospect, the greatest achievement of Préval's first term may have been its stability. After the turmoil of the mid-1990s, a relative calm gradually returned to Port-au-Prince and other cities. Arguably the clearest sign of that stability came in 2001, when he left office quietly at the end of his term; he was the first president in the long, coup-ridden history of independent Haiti to ever have done so. Constitutionally barred, as Aristide had been, from seeking a second consecutive term, he retired to his family farm in Marmelade, where he began an agricultural cooperative and assisted a number of local development projects. Aristide, who returned to office, was deposed in another coup in 2004. Amid the chaos that resulted, Préval was asked to leave his farm and run for the presidency again. He agreed, and in February of 2006 he won another five-year term, this time on the ticket of Fwon Lespwa ("Hope Front" in Haitian Creole), a new coalition with a left-wing orientation. The election results were controversial, with many reports of fraud and ballot stuffing. The country's electoral commission, however, eventually declared Préval the winner with fifty-one percent of the vote. His inauguration took place the following May.

As of September of 2010, it was still too early to assess Préval's performance in his second term, which had been dominated by natural disasters. A series of tropical storms in 2008 left much of the country in ruins; less than two years later came the even more devastating earthquake. By necessity, therefore, Préval had to focus most of his attention on obtaining the international aid needed to keep millions of citizens fed and housed. While his efforts in this area met with considerable success, many of the country's longer-term needs were neglected, while its political institutions remained mired in corruption and paralyzing disunity.

## Sources

### Periodicals

*St. Petersburg Times* (Florida), February 7, 2006.
*New York Times,* June 19, 2010.

### Online

"Biography of His Excellency René Préval, President of Haiti," Embassy of Haiti (Washington, DC), http://www.haiti.org/index.php?option=com_content&view=article&id=50&Itemid=117 (accessed September 8, 2010).

"René Garcia Préval," Pan American Health Organization, http://www.paho.org/english/d/csu/CVRen%C3%A9Pr%C3%A9val.pdf (accessed September 8, 2010).

"René Préval," NYTimes.com, January 14, 2010, http://topics.nytimes.com/topics/reference/timestopics/people/p/rene_preval/index.html?scp=1-spot&sq=rene%20preval&st=cse (accessed September 8, 2010).

—R. Anthony Kugler

# John Randle

## 1967—

### Professional football player

Randle, John, photograph. Tom Dahlin/Getty Images.

A member of the Pro Football Hall of Fame, John Randle was among the NFL's most dominant defensive players of the 1990s. Randle played the bulk of his career with the Minnesota Vikings, where he emerged as one of the top defenders of his generation, while anchoring one of the most stifling defensive units in the league. Originally considered too small to play professional football, Randle quickly established a new standard for the position of defensive tackle, bringing unprecedented quickness and agility to the defensive line. A pass rush specialist, Randle recorded 137.5 sacks over the course of his career, a record for a defensive lineman.

John Randle's path to NFL stardom was far from conventional. He was born in Hearne, Texas, on December 12, 1967, and grew up in nearby Mumford. The youngest of three boys, Randle was raised by his single mother, Martha Randle, who worked two jobs in order to support the family. A large, formidable woman, Martha Randle believed strongly in the importance of discipline and hard work, values that she strove to pass onto her children. Indeed, these qualities would later become the core of John Randle's identity as an NFL player.

Randle attended Hearne High School, where he developed into a standout defensive lineman. After graduating, he was recruited to play at Baylor University. He failed to meet the school's academic requirements, however, and ultimately enrolled at Trinity Valley Community College. Randle made the most of his opportunity at Trinity Valley, earning a place on the All-Conference team and helping his team become one of the top ten pass defenses in the country. After playing two seasons at the junior college level, Randle transferred to Division II school Texas A&I University, where he earned widespread recognition as one of the division's star defensive players. In his senior year, Randle logged twenty sacks from the defensive end position.

In spite of his prodigious talent, Randle was largely ignored by professional scouts in the months leading up to the 1990 NFL draft. The biggest concern surrounding the standout defensive end was his size. Just over six feet tall and weighing 240 pounds, Randle was significantly smaller than the average defensive lineman in the NFL, making many teams wary of his ability to produce at the highest level. Even with his speed and aggressiveness as a pass rusher, Randle went undrafted

### At a Glance . . .

**B**orn John Anthony Randle on December 12, 1967, in Hearne, TX; son of Edward Wilson (a mechanic) and Martha Randle (a maid and farm laborer); married Candace; children: Jonathan, Ryann. *Education:* Attended Trinity Valley Community College, 1986–87; attended Texas A&I University (now Texas A&M University-Kingsville), 1987–90.

**Career:** Minnesota Vikings, defensive tackle and defensive end, 1990–2000; Seattle Seahawks, defensive tackle, 2001–03.

**Awards:** Named first team All-Pro, 1993–98; named first team All-NFC, 1993–98; named All-AFC, 2001; selected to seven Pro Bowl teams; inducted into College Football Hall of Fame, 2009; inducted into NFL Hall of Fame, 2010.

**Addresses:** *Home*—Medina, MN. *Office*—c/o Pro Football Hall of Fame, 2121 George Halas Dr. NW, Canton, OH 44708.

1997 regular season, Randle became a free agent. After receiving lucrative offers from various teams throughout the league, Randle ultimately decided to stay with the Vikings, signing a new five-year contract worth $32.5 million. The deal made Randle the highest paid defensive player in NFL history. Randle's first season under his new contract didn't disappoint the Minnesota fans. His 10.5 sacks helped lead the Vikings to a regular season record of 15–1, and the team came within a field goal of playing in the Super Bowl, ultimately losing to the Atlanta Falcons in the Conference title game.

Over the course of the 1990s, Randle played in six straight Pro Bowls, while also earning first-team All Pro status six times. Between 1991 and 1998, Randle amassed a staggering 84.5 sacks, most in the NFL during that span. Randle's consistent dominance during the 1990s earned a place on the NFL's All-Decade team. Throughout these years, Randle also achieved a reputation for his durability; between 1993 and 2000, he started 133 consecutive games while playing in 176 straight games. During his time with the Vikings, Randle led the team in sacks nine times.

Following the 2000 regular season, after 11 years with the Vikings, Randle signed a contract with the Seattle Seahawks. He started 14 games for the Seahawks in 2001, recording 11 sacks. His performance that year earned him the seventh Pro Bowl selection of his career. By the next season, however, Randle's physical health began to deteriorate. He played only 12 games in 2002, as he battled knee injuries for much of the season. Although Randle played the entire 2003 season for the Seahawks, he started only nine games, recording 5.5 sacks and 12 tackles. Shortly after the season ended, Randle announced his retirement. He ended his NFL career with 137.5 sacks, along with 471 tackles, over 14 seasons.

In addition to his dominance as a player, Randle also earned a reputation as a strong locker room presence during his NFL career, leading through his passion and dedication to hard work. With the conclusion of his career, Randle eventually settled in Medina, Minnesota with his wife, Candace, and their two children. In 2010, on his second year of eligibility, Randle was voted into the Pro Football Hall of Fame. With his election, he became only the 14th undrafted player in NFL history to earn the league's most prestigious honor.

that year, leaving him no choice but to try to earn a roster spot on a team as a free agent. He ultimately tried out for the Minnesota Vikings, impressing the coaching staff with his work ethic and raw talent. By the beginning of the 1990 NFL season, Randle had signed with the Vikings, in a deal worth $65,000 a year.

By 1991 Randle emerged as the team's starting defensive end, recording 9.5 sacks and 58 tackles for the season. The turning point in his career came in 1992, when Dennis Greene took over as coach of the Vikings, and Tony Dungy became the team's defensive coordinator. Dungy moved Randle to the defensive tackle position, where he soon thrived. For the season, Randle sacked the opposing quarterback 11.5 times, the first of eight consecutive seasons in which he recorded at least ten sacks. Randle's performance during the 1992 season earned him a spot in his first Pro Bowl. A year later, Randle recorded 12.5 sacks and 59 tackles, while being named to the first team All-NFL.

By the mid-1990s, Randle had developed into one of the league's elite defensive players. He recorded 13.5 sacks in 1994, the second highest total in the league. Randle's best performance came in 1997, when he led the NFL with a career-high 15.5 sacks; Randle's sack total that year placed him within the NFL's all-time top 50 for sacks in a single season. At the conclusion of the

## Sources

### Periodicals

*Dallas Morning News*, January 7, 2000, p. 6B.
*Philadelphia Inquirer*, February 14, 1998, p. C1.
*USA Today*, October 26, 1994, p. 10C; February 18, 1998, p. 1C; February 20, 1998, p. 6C.
*Washington Times*, June 20, 2003, p. C7.

## Online

Craig, Mark, "Undrafted Randle Gets Call to Hall," The Olympian, August 7, 2010, http://www.theolympian.com/2010/08/07/1329096/undrafted-randle-gets-call-to.html (accessed October 31, 2010).

Farnsworth, Clare, "Randle Remembers," Seattle Seahawks News, February 8, 2010, http://www.seahawks.com/news/articles/article-1/Randle-Remembers/8ce9c7c3-fd25-4e09-8707-27984b63b741 (accessed October 31, 2010).

Flores, David, "Randle's Trademark Work Ethic Led Him to Stardom," Kens5.com, http://www.kens5.com/sports/football/DAVID-FLORES-Tough-childhood-drove-Randle-on-football-field-84664712.html (accessed October 31, 2010).

"John Randle," Facebook.com, http://www.facebook.com/pages/John-Randle/103108823062873 (accessed October 31, 2010).

"John Randle," Pro Football Hall of Fame, http://www.profootballhof.com/hof/member.aspx?player_id=278 (accessed October 31, 2010).

"John Randle," Pro-Football-Reference.com, http://www.pro-football-reference.com/players/R/RandJo00.htm (accessed October 31, 2010).

"John Randle Goes from Trinity Valley Community College to NFL Hall of Fame," National Junior College Athletic Association, August 8, 2010, http://www.njcaa.org/newsArticle.cfm?articleId=11901 (accessed October 31, 2010).

Kindervater, David, "John Randle: Small Town Kid's Dream Comes True," bleacher report, August 7, 2010, http://bleacherreport.com/articles/431413-john-randle-small-town-kids-dream-comes-true (accessed October 31, 2010).

"Relentless John Randle Ready to Enter Hall of Fame," USA Today, August 6, 2010, http://www.usatoday.com/sports/football/nfl/2010-08-06-john-randle-hall_N.htm (accessed October 31, 2010).

—Stephen Meyer

# J. R. Richard

## 1950—

### Professional baseball player, minister

Richard, J. R., photograph. Rich Pilling/MLB Photos via Getty Images.

In the late 1970s, J.R. Richard was among the most feared right-handed pitchers in major league baseball. A member of a Houston Astros rotation that included future Hall-of-Famer Nolan Ryan, Richard possessed a dominating fastball that routinely topped 100 miles per hour, as well as a devastating slider. Richard's physical size was a major factor in his success. At six feet, eight inches tall, Richard was an imposing figure on the mound, overpowering opposing batters with his high delivery. As Pittsburgh Pirates outfielder Dave Parker once told *Sports Illustrated*: "He looks like he's 10 feet away from you instead of 60. It causes you to lean a little bit and makes you think you have to swing the bat quicker." Richard's teammate, Hall-of-Fame second baseman Joe Morgan, once called him the greatest pitcher he'd ever witnessed.

Just as he was emerging as one of the game's most fearsome starters, however, Richard was dealt a devastating setback. In July 1980, Richard suddenly collapsed during a routine throwing session in Houston and was rushed to the hospital. Doctors soon discovered that Richard had suffered a catastrophic stroke; although he fought to regain his form, he never played major league baseball again. Struck down in his prime, Richard struggled with depression and other health issues for years; for a brief period in the early 1990s, he was homeless. With the help of an old friend, Richard eventually climbed his way back to respectability, becoming a church minister and devoting his life to charity work.

James Rodney Richard was born on March 7, 1950, in Vienna, Louisiana. His father, Clayton, was a lumber grader, while his mother, Lizzie, worked as a cook in a cafeteria. He attended Lincoln High School in Ruston, Louisiana, where he excelled at both baseball and basketball. As the school's star pitcher, Richard never lost a game during his four-year high school career; his senior year, he didn't allow a single earned run the entire season. In one memorable game, Richard hit four home runs while simultaneously pitching a shutout; the final score was 48–0. At the same time, Richard was a dominant basketball player, and by his senior year he had more than 200 college scholarship offers. He opted for baseball instead, and in 1969 the Houston Astros selected Richard with the second overall pick of the amateur draft.

## At a Glance . . .

**B**orn James Rodney Richard on March 7, 1950, in Vienna, LA; son of Clayton and Lizzie Richard; married: Carolyn (divorced); married Zemphery Volcy, 1988 (divorced); children: Zanna, six others. *Religion:* Baptist.

**Career:** Houston Astros, pitcher, 1971–80; Now Testament Church, Houston, minister.

**Awards:** Named to National League All-Star Team, 1980; inducted into Louisiana Sports Hall of Fame, 1988.

**Addresses:** *Office*—c/o Now Testament Church, 3401 Anderson Rd., Houston, TX 77053.

For the next two years, Richard toiled in the Astros minor league system. Although he showed flashes of dominance as a strikeout pitcher, he also struggled with his command, as problems with his technique delayed his progress. He earned his first big break September 1971, when he was called up to the majors to pitch the second game of a doubleheader against the San Francisco Giants. He struck out 15 in his major league debut, allowing two earned runs en route to a complete game victory. In spite of this early promise, Richard struggled with consistency for much of the early 1970s, and he spent the next several seasons moving back and forth between the minors and the majors.

Richard finally established himself as an Astros regular in 1975, when he started 31 games, compiling a 12–10 record and striking out 176; that year he also led the National League in walks (138) and wild pitches (20). By the following year, Richard had developed into one of the most effective pitchers in baseball. He won 20 games in 1976, throwing 14 complete games, striking out 214, and finishing the season with an earned run average of 2.75. Richard continued to assert his dominance over the remainder of the 1970s. In 1978 he became the first right-handed pitcher in National League history to strike out more than 300 batters in a single season. In 1979 Richard collected 313 strikeouts, most in the National League. That year, Richard also led the league in earned run average (2.71), strikeouts per nine innings pitched (9.6), and hits allowed per nine innings (6.8).

Entering the 1980 season, Richard appeared poised to take his game to an even higher level. Over the first two months of the season he compiled a 10–4 record while striking out 119. Although he began to suffer from arm fatigue in early July, he shook off his health concerns to start the All-Star game for the National League, striking out three batters in two innings of work. As the Astros prepared for the second half of the season, Richard was widely regarded to be the leading candidate for the Cy Young Award.

In the ensuing weeks, however, Richard's season, and career, began to unravel. In his next start against the Atlanta Braves, Richard complained of nausea and fatigue during the early part of the game, and he even struggled to read his catcher's signs behind the plate. By the fourth inning, he was unable to continue pitching and was taken out of the game. Two days later, he was placed on the disabled list. In the midst of Richard's struggles, several members of the Houston press questioned the pitcher's desire to complete, while some of his own teammates accused him of lying about his condition.

Medical tests soon revealed that Richard had developed a blood clot in his neck. Although the condition was considered serious, doctors determined that the clot had stabilized, and that Richard's throwing arm had developed a secondary flow of blood circulation in the interim, making it possible for him to resume pitching quickly. Following the advice of his physicians, Richard undertook a light training regimen, remaining in Houston while the team embarked on a nine-game road trip. On July 30, after complaining of coldness in his arm during a throwing session with former teammate Wilbur Howard, he suffered a massive stroke. After nine hours of emergency surgery, Richard's condition stabilized.

Over the next two years Richard attempted a comeback, pitching for a brief period in the Astros minor league system. He never regained his previous form, however, and was finally released in 1983. Soon after retiring, Richard briefly worked as a car salesman, but he quit after only three months. The pitcher struggled to earn a living over the next several years and eventually slipped into a severe depression. In the mid-1980s he divorced his wife, Carolyn, with whom he had five children. In 1990 Richard filed for bankruptcy. Three years later, Chris Clark, a longtime friend of the former pitcher, found Richard living in a homeless encampment under a Houston overpass.

A short time later, Richard began to turn his life around. With Clark's help, Richard managed to find a steady job in the public relations department of a local asphalt firm. At around this time, Richard met Reverend Floyd Lewis of the Now Testament Church. Devoutly religious early in his life, Richard became close to Lewis, who eventually ordained him as a minister. In his work with the Now Testament Church, Richard also devoted much of his time to helping the homeless and mentoring inner city children.

## *Sources*

### *Periodicals*

*Chicago Sun-Times,* August 23, 1987, p. 85.
*Houston Chronicle,* February 4, 1990, p. 1.
*Sports Illustrated,* September 4, 1978, pp. 66–68; August 18, 1980, pp. 12–17; March 1, 1981, pp. 26–31; March 23, 1998, p. 15.
*Times-Picayune* (New Orleans), July 9, 2002, p. 1.
*Wichita Falls Times Record News,* March 30, 2003, p. D1.

### *Online*

"J.R. Richard," Baseball-Reference.com, http://www.baseball-reference.com/players/r/richaj.01.shtml (accessed November 3, 2010).
Spence, Blaine, "From Unhittable to Homeless: The J.R. Richard Story," bleacher report, http://bleacherreport.com/articles/217945-from-unhittable-to-homeless-the-jr-richard-story (accessed November 3, 2010).

—Stephen Meyer

# Frank Robinson

## 1935—

### Professional baseball player, manager, executive

Frank Robinson had already enjoyed a Hall of Fame career as a baseball player when he became the first African American manager in major league history. In a 21-year playing career, spent primarily with the Cincinnati Reds and Baltimore Orioles, the slugging outfielder belted 586 home runs, which at that time was the fourth-highest career total in the game's history. As infamous for his temper and intensity as he was famous for his bat, Robinson won two World Series and was the only player ever named Most Valuable Player (MVP) in both the National League (NL) and the American League (AL). At the end of his career Robinson broke the color barrier by becoming the manager of the Cleveland Indians, the first African American to hold such a post in Major League history. He would manage fifteen more years, winning the AL Manager of the Year award in 1989. In addition, he would make his mark as a top executive with the office of the commissioner of baseball. Robinson was inducted into the National Baseball Hall of Fame in 1982.

### Faced Fast Pitches and Bigotry

Frank Robinson was born in Beaumont, Texas, in

Robinson, Frank, photograph. Michael Kovac/FilmMagic.

1935, the youngest of ten children in a single-parent household. Robinson's father deserted the family when he was an infant, and his mother struggled to provide her children with basic necessities. When Robinson was four his mother moved the family to Oakland, California. There he grew up, determined to be a professional baseball player despite what seemed like insurmountable odds.

"I never really knew my own father," Robinson told *Sports Illustrated.* "But it didn't bother me. My mother, my brothers and sisters. I was always right in the middle of a bunch of bigger boys, and they'd rough me up and give me information. They were always keeping my feet on the ground, making me see the outlook from other sides." Living in a mixed-race neighborhood of West Oakland, Robinson spent most of his waking hours on the sandlot, playing baseball and planning his future in the major leagues. Robinson's devotion to baseball continued into high school, where he played third base and even pitched a game or two. He also played basketball with future Boston Celtics star Bill Russell.

Right out of high school Robinson signed with the

## At a Glance . . .

**B**orn August 31, 1935, in Beaumont, TX; son of Frank and Ruth (Shaw) Robinson; married Barbara Ann Cole, October 28, 1961; children: Frank Kevin, Nichelle. *Education:* Attended Xavier University.

**Career:** Professional baseball player, 1956–77. Cincinnati Reds, player, 1956–65; Baltimore Orioles, player, 1966–71, coach, 1978–80, 1985–87, manager, 1988–91, assistant to general manager, 1991–1995; Los Angeles Dodgers, player, 1972; California Angels, player, 1973–74, coach, 1977; Cleveland Indians, player, 1974–77, manager, 1975–77; San Francisco Giants, manager, 1981–84; Montreal Expos, manager, 2002–04; Washington Nationals, manager, 2005–06; Major League Baseball, consultant to the Commissioner, 1997–2000, vice president of on-field operations, 2000–02, special advisor, 2007–09; senior vice president of baseball operations, 2010—.

**Awards:** Named National League Rookie of the Year, 1956; member of All-Star Team, 1957, 1959, 1961, 1962, 1965, 1966, 1967, 1968, 1969, 1970, 1971, 1974; named National League Most Valuable Player, 1961; named American League Most Valuable Player, 1966; uniform number retired by Baltimore Orioles, 1972, and by Cincinnati Reds, 1998; inducted into National Baseball Hall of Fame, 1982; named American League Manager of the Year, 1989; received Presidential Medal of Freedom, 2005.

**Addresses:** *Office*—Major League Baseball, 245 Park Avenue, New York, NY 10167.

Cincinnati Reds organization. He was sent to the Class C team in Ogden, Utah, for the 1953 season. The California-raised Robinson quickly found much to dislike in Ogden. The only movie theater in town did not admit blacks, and most of the restaurants were segregated as well. Nevertheless, Robinson shone on the field, batting .348, leading his team in home runs, and hitting twenty doubles and six triples. When he requested a move from third base to the outfield, his defense improved as well.

Robinson found himself in an even more tense racial situation in 1954 and 1955, when he played in the South Atlantic League. Fans in cities such as Macon,

Georgia, and Columbia, South Carolina, hurled abuse at the young player, and it got under his skin. By the time he was called to the Cincinnati Reds in 1956 he was, as he told *Sports Illustrated,* "quiet and withdrawn," both afraid and unwilling to associate with his teammates. On the field, however, his first major league season was nothing short of dazzling. He batted .290 with 83 runs batted in (RBI) and hit a rookie record-tying 26 home runs. He was voted National League Rookie of the Year and was talked about as a sure prospect for superstardom.

## Became Star People Loved to Hate

By 1961, when Robinson helped the Reds win their first pennant in two decades, he was one of the most detested men in baseball. His aggressive use of spikes on the base path and his penchant for hitting blistering home runs did not endear him to his opponents. So much animosity developed between Robinson and the Reds' general manager Bill DeWitt that Robinson threatened to retire in 1962, but even amidst the tension Robinson was able to compile remarkable statistics. In 1961 he batted .323 with 37 home runs, and in 1962 he hit a phenomenal .342 with 39 homers and 136 RBI. He was voted the National League Most Valuable Player (MVP) in 1961 and was paid a then-record salary in excess of $60,000. But problems continued between Robinson and the Cincinnati front office, so in the offseason of 1965 the Reds traded their star to the Baltimore Orioles.

Some observers hinted darkly that at the age of thirty, Robinson was past his prime. Those observers could not have been more wrong. Robinson had the best year of his career in 1966, setting a career high in home runs with forty-nine and winning the triple crown by leading the league in batting average, homers, and RBI. With Robinson's potent bat in the middle of the lineup, Baltimore ran away with the pennant. In the World Series against the Los Angeles Dodgers, Robinson set the tone in the first game, launching two-run home run against Don Drysdale in his first at bat. The home run gave the Orioles the lead, kicking off a four-game sweep in which the Orioles never trailed.

It was the first World Series championship ever for the Orioles, and soon after they won, Robinson was named American League MVP. He was the first baseball star ever to win MVP in both the National League and the American League. The Orioles raised Robinson's salary to $100,000 per year and filled their promotional materials with Robinson highlights, including a monumental home run that completely cleared Baltimore's Memorial Stadium.

Robinson's tenure with the Orioles would be the happiest of his playing career. In Baltimore he assumed a leadership role and began to study the managing techniques of Earl Weaver. All told, Robinson helped the Orioles to win four pennants and two World Series titles in five years, while simultaneously becoming the 11th player in major league history to hit 500 home runs. Robinson's years in Baltimore saw another important step in his career as well. In the off-season he began managing the Santurce Cangrejeros (Crabbers), a top team in the Puerto Rican winter league. Early in 1969 Robinson brought the winter league pennant to Santurce and earned his first Manager of the Year honors.

## Hired as MLB's First Black Manager

Robinson, whose 586 career home runs put him fourth on the all-time list, made no secret of his managerial ambitions as his playing career wound down. While with the Los Angeles Dodgers and then the California Angels, he often expressed the desire to play for an organization that would be willing to track him into a management or front office position. The difficulty was that in the mid-1970s blacks were well represented on the field as players but had yet to make any inroads into executive positions with the clubs. Robinson's wish came true in 1975, when he moved to the Cleveland Indians, first as a player-manager and then simply as the manager. Robinson's desire to manage was so strong his managerial salary his first season was just $20,000—which was all that the Indians were willing to offer him to manage above his guaranteed salary as a player.

Well aware that he was making history, Robinson chose to downplay his role as a racial pioneer, asking instead to be judged simply on his team's performance. He managed the Indians until 1977, pushing their record over .500 during the 1976 season. He was fired after a round of intense clubhouse bickering and rumors that he was aloof toward his less talented players. Robinson answered the charges in a *Sports Illustrated* feature. "They say catchers or .200 hitters or minor league players make the best managers, because they are 'students of the game' and are understanding of difficult situations," he said. "I've heard just the opposite from top players. 'How can that guy tell me what to do?' they say. 'How can he understand me when he has never been at the level I'm at?'"

Chafing at the innuendos that surrounded his Cleveland days, Robinson returned to Baltimore as first-base coach under his former manager, Earl Weaver. In 1980 he was given a second chance to manage, this time in the National League with the San Francisco Giants. Robinson led the Giants to back-to-back winning years in 1980 and 1981. In 1982 Robinson led a team that had been left for dead with a sub-.500 record at the start of August back into the pennant race, coming within one game of the division lead in the last week of the season. Despite this success, conflicts developed once again. Robinson was curt with the press, short of patience with some of his younger players, and stymied by an uncooperative front office. He was fired in 1984.

Robinson told the *Los Angeles Times*: "After I was fired for the second time as manager, I think I finally got a different perspective on myself. After I looked at myself and the way I'd lived, maybe I was wrong more than I was right. Maybe it's not the way you look at yourself, but the way other people see you." The baseball legend subjected himself to a close self-analysis that he said improved his managerial skills in the long run. "I studied Frank Robinson," he concluded, "putting things in order and deciding this is what Frank Robinson wants to accomplish and this is who he wants to be."

## Managed the Orioles

Robinson brought a new attitude back to the Baltimore Orioles when he took over as manager six games into the 1988 season. Baltimore had already lost its first six games and was on the way to a record-setting season-opening streak of losses that seemed to set the tone for the season. By October of 1988 the Orioles had suffered 101 losses. Some observers felt it would take years for the team to rebound. Robinson refused to adopt a defeatist attitude, or cast blame on others in the Orioles' organization. Instead he hired batting coach Tom McCraw and pitching coach Al Jackson to help him tutor a team of relatively raw youngsters.

The 1989 Orioles, an array of rookies, players who had been released by other clubs, and struggling pitchers, began to mesh early in the spring and dominated first place in the American League East until well into September, losing a pennant bid in the next-to-last game of the season. A team that had been 54–101 in 1988 improved to 87–75 in 1989, and Robinson was the unanimous choice for American League Manager of the Year. Robinson told the *Washington Post*: "When I took over, there was a job to be done, to help rebuild the organization and build a solid contender. The job is not done, and I want to finish that work. We want to be respected contenders every year."

Unfortunately for Robinson, the Orioles slumped to under .500 in 1990 for a fifth place finish. When the team began 1991 at 13–24 under Robinson, he was relieved of his duties as manager. Although he was dismissed as manager, by the terms of his contract Robinson stayed with the Orioles, serving as one of the two chief lieutenants to general manager Roland Hemond. The position gave Robinson input in the Orioles' roster decisions, as well as a role in the planning of the Orioles' new ballpark and spring training facilities.

However, after a few years in the Orioles' front office, Robinson's hopes of being Hemond's successor were dashed. The club was sold to a new owner, who wanted to put his own management team in place. In 1995 Robinson was let go from his front office position and found himself out of baseball for the first time in more than forty years.

## Became Baseball's Dean of Discipline

At the age of sixty, Robinson was not ready for retirement. When Cincinnati Reds owner Marge Schott was suspended from baseball on charges of making racist and anti-Semitic remarks in 1996, Robinson lobbied for the job of running the franchise in her absence. He tried to secure jobs as a manager, coach, or front office executive, to no avail. "It's not like I'm looking to be given anything," he told Murray Chass of the *New York Times*. "I have something to offer. That's the tough part. People are told: 'You don't have experience. You haven't put in time.' They can't say that about me."

In 1997 Robinson became a consultant to baseball Commissioner Bud Selig. Robinson was also put in charge of the Arizona Fall League, a developmental league for promising young players. By 1999 Robinson was happy enough working at the commissioner's office that he turned down a coaching position with the Chicago Cubs, offered by one of his former protégés, Don Baylor. The following year, Robinson was promoted to the post of Vice President of On-Field Operations. The new position put Robinson in charge of disciplining players throughout the majors for on-field incidents, with broad authority to hand out suspensions to any player, coach or manager who misbehaved.

Robinson quickly proved to be a harsh disciplinarian. As a player, he was one of the career leaders in being hit by pitches; now, he had little tolerance for players who charged the mound after they were brushed back by opposing pitchers. In April of 2000 he handed out eighty-two games' worth of suspensions to sixteen members of the Chicago White Sox and Detroit Tigers who had been involved in a brawl. It was the largest total penalty handed out for one incident, until later that season, when members of the Dodgers charged into the stands to scuffle with Cubs fans at Wrigley Field, resulting in a total of eighty-four games' worth of suspensions and $72,000 in fines. Although Robinson's drastic penalties were often reduced or overturned on appeal, his actions sent a clear signal that baseball would not tolerate violence on the field of play.

## Returned to Manage Montreal Expos

Robinson would only remain in that Vice President post for two years. In 2002 Selig turned to Robinson with a new challenge: managing the Montreal Expos. The Expos franchise had fallen upon hard times, and Major League Baseball (MLB) had taken ownership of the team, with an eye to selling it to a new owner who would move the team out of Canada. From Robinson's perspective, his job was cut out for him: for half a decade, the Expos had been one of the worst teams in the majors, and the outgoing owners had gutted the franchise, trading away many of the team's most talented players in the interest of reducing payroll.

The task was almost too much for Robinson. According to Chass, in July of 2002 the manager was so fed up with his team's lackadaisical play that he quit during a team meeting, tearing off his jersey and throwing it away in disgust. The players talked him into taking back his resignation the following day. Under Robinson's guidance, the Expos finished the season strong, going 17–10 in September to secure a second-place finish in the National League East division, and the team's first winning season since 1996.

Robinson had taken the Expos job on terms that he would only manage for one season. However, at the end of 2002 MLB had made few inroads to finding a buyer for the team, and Robinson decided to stay on. The 2003 season presented new challenges, as MLB decided that the Expos would play half their "home" games in Puerto Rico. The resulting travel schedule was brutal for both the players and their manager. In mid-June, the team was in second place with an excellent 39–26 record and in line for a spot in the playoffs. However, Robinson saw that even though the season was not even halfway over, his team was exhausted. "I said [to the bench coach], 'The air has gone out.' You could just see it. You could feel it," Robinson told Dan Connolly of the *Baltimore Sun*. The team slumped, finishing with the same record (83–79) as they had in 2002, but falling to fourth place. The following season, the floor fell out from under the Expos, and the team finished in last place with 95 losses.

## Became First Manager of Washington Nationals

For Robinson, there was a silver lining to the Expos' abysmal 2004 season. On September 29, 2004, hours before the Expos' final game of the season in Montreal, MLB announced that it was moving the team to Washington, DC. In 2005 Robinson returned to the dugout as the first manager of the newly minted Washington Nationals. The team responded to the change of scenery, winning as many games as they lost, but in a very competitive division, that was not enough to keep them out of last place.

The 2006 season was probably the most emotional of Robinson's managerial career. During Spring Training, he won a very public battle of wills with star Alfonso Soriano over his decision to move Soriano from second base to the outfield. On May 25, Robinson was forced to remove catcher Matt LeCroy in the middle of an inning during a game against the Houston Astros. LeCroy had been helpless in the face of the Astros' base runners all game long, allowing seven stolen bases and committing two throwing errors. Despite the necessity of the move, removing a catcher in the middle of an inning was a breach of baseball etiquette that an old school manager like Robinson did not make lightly. In his post-game press conference, tears streamed down his face as Robinson discussed the humiliation to which he'd subjected his player. "I feel for him," the manager was quoted as saying by the *Associated Press.* "And I hope the fans understand. And I just appreciate him hanging in there as long as he did."

Robinson's emotions would run high again toward the end of the season. In June of 2006 MLB finally sold the franchise to a group led by investor Tom Lerner. Once again, the ownership change meant personnel changes, and with the team mired in last place for the third straight year, there was no chance that Robinson would be asked to return as manager. The Nationals held a day in his honor at the end of the season, then let him go.

Robinson returned to work at the commissioner's office in 2007, as a special assistant to the executive vice president for baseball operations, Jimmie Lee Solomon. In 2010 he was promoted to the position of senior vice president of baseball operations, a position in which he was charged with overseeing major league umpires. He remains one of the most venerated players in the history of the Orioles and Reds franchises, both of which honored him by retiring his uniform number. In 2005, the Nationals' inaugural season in Washington, Robinson received the Presidential Medal of Freedom, the highest honor given by the executive branch of the U.S. government.

## Selected works

(With Al Silverman) *My Life Is Baseball,* Doubleday, 1968.

(With Barry Steinbach) *Extra Innings,* Doubleday, 1989.

## Sources

### Books

Vincent, Faye, *We Would Have Played for Nothing: Baseball Stars of the 1950s and 1960s Talk About the Game They Loved,* Simon & Schuster, 1988.

### Periodicals

*Baltimore Sun,* June 7, 1994, p. C1; July 10, 1994, p. C11; August 7, 1994, p. C8; February 22, 2002; April 3, 2005; October 1, 2006.
*Ebony,* September 1966; June 1981.
*Look,* May 5, 1970.
*Los Angeles Times,* April 16, 1989; July 6,1989; August 6, 1989.
*Newsweek,* October 14, 1974.
*New York Times,* April 20, 1997; November 23, 1999; July 19, 2002.
*Sports Illustrated,* June 17, 1963; February 3, 1969; October 5, 1970; October 21, 1974; March 24, 1975; July 4, 1977; June 19, 1989.
*Time,* October 14, 1974.
*Washington Post,* November 2, 1989.

### Online

"Frank Robinson Rejoins Commissioner's Office" *The Biz of Baseball,* March 2, 2007, http://www.bizof-baseball.com/index.php?option=com_content&view=article&id=816:frank-robinson-rejoins-com-missioners-office&catid=30:mlb-news&Itemid=42 (accessed November 29, 2010).

—Mark Kram and Derek Jacques

# Arsenio Rodríguez

## 1911–1970

### Guitarist, percussionist, bandleader, composer

Rodríguez, Arsenio, photograph. Frank Driggs Collection/Getty Images.

Few performers have had a greater impact on the course of Cuban music than Arsenio Rodríguez. Known as "The Marvelous Blind One" (El Ciego Maravilloso), he overcame the loss of his sight in childhood to become a leading percussionist and a master of the six-string guitar known as the *tres*. He is probably best remembered, however, as the bandleader whose adaptations of tradition resulted in *son montuno*, an innovative style that set the stage, in turn, for salsa, now one of the most popular forms of music in the world. He is also sometimes credited with the creation of mambo, a related style that sparked an international dance craze in the 1950s.

Rodríguez's birth name, widely reported to have been Ignacio Arsenio Travieso Scull, has been the subject of some controversy. He was born in 1911 in Güira de Macurijes, a small community in a rural area of Matanzas Province, southeast of Havana, Cuba's capital. Like many of his neighbors, he was the descendant of slaves from the Congo, a vast region in central Africa. Though slavery had been abolished in Cuba in the late nineteenth century, racial intolerance and widespread poverty made life difficult for former slaves and their families. Many clung tenaciously—and bravely, given the racial climate—to Congolese traditions, particularly in music. By the time of Rodríguez's birth, Matanzas was known for rearing musicians well versed in the rhythms and melodies of central Africa.

Given that rich heritage, Rodríguez's decision to become a professional musician was not surprising. In light of his disability, however, it was almost inevitable, for at the time music was virtually the only occupation open to the blind. He began by playing with a variety of ensembles in and around his hometown. The most significant of these early gigs came with a group called the Boston Sextet (*El Sexteto Boston*), with whom he was performing regularly by the early 1930s. He also had steady work as a freelance composer. By the middle of the decade, as his songs began to appear on Cuban radio, he found himself in demand among club owners in Havana. In about 1940 he formed a group under his own name and began to lay the groundwork for *son montuno*.

*Son,* a rhythmic, guitar-based style, had deep roots in Cuba's rural heartland. Rodríguez's essential innovation involved mixing several new instruments into the

*At a Glance . . .*

**B**orn in 1911 in Güira de Macurijes, Matanzas Province, Cuba; birth name may have been Ignacio Arsenio Travieso Scull; died December 30(?), 1970, in Los Angeles, CA.

**Career:** Independent musician, 1920s–1970; independent recording artist, 1930s–1970.

**Awards:** International Latin Music Hall of Fame, 1999.

*son* band's traditional lineup. These additions included a piano, an expanded brass section, and a conga drum, a powerful symbol of his own ethnic heritage. Though congas and other African drums had been used at private gatherings in Cuba for several centuries, they were excluded from dance halls and nightclubs, largely because of racial prejudice. That Rodríguez seems to have escaped any adverse consequences for bringing the conga into those venues can probably be attributed more to his growing popularity than to any change in social attitudes. It is clear, in any event, that the added instrumentation revolutionized the *son,* transforming it so radically that it became a new genre, *son montuno.*

The new sound's heavier beat made it especially popular among dancers, and it was not long before Rodríguez's compositions were heard in clubs and dance halls outside Cuba. Residents of New York City, in particular, embraced *son montuno,* and in the early 1940s he traveled there for an extended series of gigs. On his return to Cuba, he found political conditions deteriorating rapidly. Growing class tensions, in particular, made life difficult for professional musicians, who generally came from the lower classes but depended on the wealthy for employment. To escape that increasingly awkward situation, Rodríguez eventually moved back to the United States, settling permanently there by the mid-1950s.

By that point, however, the period of his greatest popularity was probably behind him. His biggest hit, "Life Is a Dream" ("La Vida Es Un Sueño"), came in 1947. Though his ongoing experiments with various band lineups, including the addition of flutes and saxophones, resulted in innovative, strikingly original recordings, these were not always appreciated by club owners and record executives, who generally preferred more predictable music. His status as a neglected pioneer was also apparent in the birth of salsa and mambo, both of which had their origins in *son mon-*

*tuno.* Both genres received wide exposure on television, a medium Rodríguez, because of his disability, was unable to utilize as effectively as many of his peers.

The 1960s proved a particularly difficult period. Though salsa's growth was explosive, Rodríguez struggled to obtain bookings, due in part to what author David F. Garcia called "his alienation from the large community of Cuban political exiles in Miami and the Northeast." That alienation, in turn, was rooted in "racial tensions" and Rodríguez's "suspicion of all Cuban political orientations." Few were surprised, therefore, when he moved in the late 1960s from New York to California, where he had had some success with Hispanic audiences several years earlier. He had little opportunity to revive his career there, however, for on December 30 (some sources say December 31), 1970, he died in Los Angeles in relative obscurity. In the decades since, there has been a resurgence of interest in his music, and much of his work from the 1940s and 1950s has been reissued. Of one of those collections, 2008's *El Alma de Cuba,* Ben Ratliff of the *New York Times* wrote, "If you a guitar player, it will make you want to play. If you are a dancer, it will make you want to dance. [Rodríguez] makes you begin to hear rhythm as he does; he improves you."

## Selected discography

"La Vida Es Un Sueño," 1947.
*El Alma de Cuba,* Tumbao, 2008.

## Sources

### Books

Garcia, David F., *Arsenio Rodríguez and the Transnational Flows of Latin Popular Music,* Temple University, 2006.
Sublette, Ned, *Cuba and Its Music: From the First Drums to the Mambo,* Chicago Review, 2004.

### Periodicals

*New York Times,* March 17, 2008.

### Online

"Arsenio Rodriguez," AfroCubaWeb, http://afrocubaweb.com/arsenioRodríguez.htm (accessed August 18, 2010).
Herman, Nick, "Arsenio Rodríguez: Biography," All Music.com, http://allmusic.com/cg/amg.dll?p=amg&sql=11:fifqxqw5ld0e~T1 (accessed August 18, 2010).

—R. Anthony Kugler

# Diana Sands

## 1934–1973

### Stage television and film actress

Sands, Diana, photograph. AP Images.

Award-winning stage actress Diana Sands is best remembered for her role as Beneatha Younger in Lorraine Hansberry's classic drama *A Raisin in the Sun,* which she originated on Broadway in 1959 and reprised in the 1961 Hollywood film. The role, her first on Broadway, earned Sands critical acclaim and made her an overnight success. In an era when opportunities for African-American actors and actresses were few, Sands refused to be typecast in "black" parts. She was outspoken in her advocacy of color-blind casting and took on classic roles usually reserved for white actresses, including Cleopatra, Phaedra, and Joan of Arc. In 1964 she broke the "color barrier" in theater when she starred opposite Alan Alda in the Off-Broadway comedy *The Owl and the Pussycat* in a part written for a white actress. The theater mourned the loss of a great actress at her death from cancer at age thirty-nine.

Diana Patricia Sands was born on August 22, 1934, in the Bronx, New York, one of three children of Rudolph Thomas Sands Jr., a carpenter, and his wife Shirley, a milliner. When she was a girl, her parents moved the family to suburban Elmsford in Westchester County, where she attended elementary school. A dramatic

child, at the age of seven she decided that she wanted to be an actress, inspired by Canada Lee's performance in the 1941 film *Native Son.* Feeling the burden of racial discrimination in the predominantly white suburbs, her parents opted to move back to the city, settling in Manhattan. There, Sands attended the famed High School of Performing Arts as a drama major. Upon her graduation in 1952, she was voted best actress in her class.

### Refused to be Typecast

Sands threw herself into acting, singing, and dancing lessons, studying under acting coach Michael Howard and legendary African-American director Lloyd Richards, among others. In 1953 she made her theatrical debut as Juliet in the Off-Broadway production *An Evening with Will Shakespeare* at the Caravan Theatre and, later that year, appeared in Arnold Perl's *The World of Sholem Aleichem.* The next summer, she played the role of Jenny Hill in a revival of George Bernard Shaw's comedy *Major Barbara* at the Greenwich Mews Theatre, one of the first venues in New York to feature integrated casts.

## At a Glance . . .

**B**orn Diana Patricia Sands on August 22, 1934, in New York City, NY; died on September 21, 1973, in New York City, NY; daughter of Rudolph Thomas Sands Jr. and Shirley Walker; married Lucien Happersberger in 1964 (divorced 1967).

**Career:** Stage, television, and film actress, 1953–73.

**Awards:** Best Actress of the Month, *Off-Broadway* magazine, 1959; Outer Critics Circle Award for Best Supporting Actress (for *A Raisin in the Sun*), 1959; Most Promising Actress of 1959, *Variety* magazine critics poll; International Artist Award, 1961 (for *A Raisin in the Sun*); Theatre World Award, 1963–64; OBIE Award for distinguished performance, 1964 (for *The Living Premise*).

The young actress struggled to make ends meet, working as a key-punch operator for the utility company Con Edison and holding other odd jobs in between stage roles. Despite the financial difficulty, Sands made a decision early in her career to accept only quality roles, refusing to be shunted into stereotypical "black" parts. "I can't take acting jobs which are degrading to Negroes in order to prosper, or even to live," she told the *New York Times* in a 1964 interview. "I've been told that I'm naive, even childish, to say this, but I think that there must be a few producers who believe in the same things, who have the same principles as I do."

Sands toured with the Repertory Group of the Pantomime Art Theatre in 1955, and in March of the next year, she appeared in a pair of one-act plays, *Mary and the Fairy* and *Fortunato,* at the Club Cinema. Other stage work followed, including *The Man with the Golden Arm* (1956) at the Cherry Lane Theatre, *The Land Beyond the River* (1958) at the Greenwich Mews, and *The Egg and I* at the Jan Hus Auditorium (1958), for which she was named "Best Actress of the Month" by *Off-Broadway* magazine.

### Made Her Debut on Broadway

Feeling that her career was not progressing as she would like, and frustrated by the dearth of quality roles for black actresses, Sands considered giving up acting. Initially, she refused an audition for the role of Beneatha Younger in a stage adaptation of Lorraine Hansberry's novel *A Raisin in the Sun,* despite the producers' encouragement. Finally, though, she agreed, and the role marked her Broadway debut.

*A Raisin in the Sun* opened at the Ethel Barrymore Theatre on March 11, 1959. Notably, it was the first play written by a black woman to be produced on Broadway, and the first Broadway show to have a black director, Lloyd Richards. The cast included star Sidney Poitier as Walter Lee Younger; Ruby Dee as Ruth, his wife; Sands as his naive younger sister, Beneatha; and Claudia McNeil as Lena "Mama" Younger. The production met with critical acclaim and was named best play of the 1958–1959 season by the New York Drama Critics' Circle. For her portrayal of Beneatha, Sands won an Outer Critics Circle Award for best supporting actress, and in a poll of *Variety* magazine critics, she was named most promising actress of 1959. After the show's Broadway run, which lasted 530 performances, Sands joined the national tour in 1960–61. She reprised her role in the 1961 Hollywood film adaptation, which also starred Poitier, earning an International Artist Award for her performance.

Despite the success of *Raisin,* Sands had difficulty finding a suitable follow-up role on Broadway. She returned to off-Broadway theater, performing in *Another Evening with Harry Stoones* at the Gramercy Arts Theatre in 1961. The next year, she had roles in *Brecht on Brecht* at the Theatre de Lys and *Black Monday* and the Vandam. Later in 1962, she returned to Broadway in Peter Feibleman's *Tiger, Tiger, Burning Bright,* a play about a troubled black family in New Orleans. Directed by Joshua Logan, the show also featured *Raisin* co-star Claudia McNeil, as well as Alvin Ailey and Cicely Tyson. Sands earned a Theatre World Award in 1962–63 for her performance.

In 1964 Sands had a banner year. First, she starred in James Baldwin's award-winning play *Blues for Mister Charlie* at the ANTA (American National Theatre and Academy) Theatre on Broadway. Playing the role of Juanita, the girlfriend of a black man who is murdered by a white shopkeeper, she delivered a moving soliloquy in the final act that was the highlight of the critically acclaimed drama. Writing for the *New York Times,* critic Joanne Stang described Sands's performance as "an unparalleled tour de force," while Howard Taubman praised her "shattering emotion." She earned a Tony Award nomination for best featured actress in a play.

### Broke the "Color Barrier" in Theater

Later that year, Sands appeared again at the ANTA Theatre in Bill Manhoff's two-person play *The Owl and the Pussycat,* opposite Alan Alda. Although the role had been written to be played by a white actress, no alteration was made to the script to explain the racial difference. Producer Philip Rose was quick to defend his casting choice: "There's not a line in this play about the racial problem. It is simply a play dealing with the specific problems of this boy and this girl," he told the *New York Times.* "What we're doing is breaking the color barrier. ... I'm hoping that the audience, after a while, will not see color on the stage at all." The low-budget production was a hit, earning Sands her second Tony nomination.

While she waited for her next Broadway gig to come along, Sands took on the classics in regional theater. In 1967 she starred as Cleopatra in George Bernard Shaw's *Caesar and Cleopatra* at Theatre Atlanta, played the title role in *Phaedra* at the Theater of the Living Word in Philadelphia, and appeared in Shakespeare's Antony and Cleopatra in MacArthur Park in Los Angeles. In 1968 she returned to New York, where she joined the Lincoln Center Repertory Company for two plays. First, she appeared in Shaw's *Saint Joan,* in which she played the sixteen-year-old French martyr Joan of Arc—a bold bit of casting hailed, but a role that was hailed by critics as her greatest performance. Later that year, she portrayed Cassandra in Jean Giraudoux's *Tiger at the Gates.*

Sands appeared twice more on Broadway, in Joseph Heller's *We Bombed in New Haven* at the Ambassador Theatre and Lanford Wilson's *The Gingham Dog* at the John Golden Theatre, before giving up on the stage. Though she had worked tirelessly to open doors for herself and other black actresses, she still felt the pain of discrimination. "I think progress is being made, but it's so slow, so slow," she had told the *New York Times* in 1964, a sentiment she held to. "Integration in the theater is like integration everywhere else. People want to go about it gradually. But there are so many fine, talented young people ready now. How can you ask them to wait ten or fifteen years, when it will be too late?"

Although Sands was best known as a stage actress, she also worked in film and television throughout her career. She had a memorable guest spot on the series *East Side/West Side* in 1963 that earned her an Emmy nomination, and appeared on episodes of *The Outer Limits, Dr. Kildare, I Spy,* and *The Fugitive,* among others. Sands was slated to star in the 1974 film *Claudine* opposite James Earl Jones, but health problems forced her to back out. Instead, she recommended her friend Diahann Carroll, who was later nominated for an Academy Award for the role.

A lifelong chain smoker, Sands was diagnosed with lung cancer in the summer of 1973. She underwent surgery to remove the tumor, but the cancer already had spread, and she remained hospitalized. Sands died three weeks later, on September 19, at the age of thirty-nine. In a tribute published in the *New York Times,* legendary actor Ossie Davis reflected on Sands's place in the American theater. "Out there she became what America is not yet prepared to let black women be within their private lives: invulnerable, inviolate, invincible!"

## Selected works

### Theater

*An Evening with Will Shakespeare,* Caravan Theatre, New York, 1953.
*The World of Sholem Aleichem,* Barbizon Plaza Theatre, New York, 1953.
*Major Barbara,* Greenwich Mews Theatre, New York, 1954.
*Mary and the Fairy/Fortunato,* Club Cinema, New York, 1956.
*The Man with the Golden Arm,* Cherry Lane Theatre, New York, 1956.
*A Land Beyond the River,* Greenwich Mews Theatre, New York, 1957.
*The Egg and I,* Jan Hus Auditorium, New York, 1958.
*A Raisin in the Sun,* Ethel Barrymore Theatre, New York, 1959, Belasco Theatre, New York, 1959–60.
*Another Evening with Harry Stoones,* Gramercy Arts Theatre, New York, 1961.
*Black Monday,* Vandam Theatre, New York, 1962.
*Brecht on Brecht,* Theatre de Lys, New York, 1962.
*Tiger, Tiger, Burning Bright,* Booth Theatre, New York, 1962.
*The Living Premise,* Premise Theatre, New York, 1963.
*Blues for Mister Charlie,* ANTA Playhouse, New York, 1964.
*The Owl and the Pussycat,* ANTA Playhouse, New York, 1964–65, Royale Theatre, New York, 1965, Criterion Theatre, London, 1966.
*Caesar and Cleopatra,* Theatre Atlanta, Atlanta, GA, 1967.
*Phaedra,* Theatre of Living Arts, Philadelphia, 1967.
*Antony and Cleopatra,* MacArthur Park, Los Angeles, 1967.
*Wait Until Dark,* Tappan Zee Playhouse, Nyack, NY, 1967.
*Saint Joan,* Vivian Beaumont Theatre at Lincoln Center, New York, 1967–68.
*Tiger at the Gates,* Vivian Beaumont Theatre at Lincoln Center, New York, 1968.
*We Bombed in New Haven,* Ambassador Theatre, New York, 1968.
*The Gingham Dog,* John Golden Theatre, New York, 1969.

### Films

*Four Boys and a Gun,* Security Pictures, 1957.
*A Raisin in the Sun,* Columbia Pictures, 1959.
*An Affair of the Skin,* Zenith International. 1963.
*Ensign Pilver,* Warner Bros., 1964.
*The Landlord,* United Artists, 1970.
*Doctors' Wives,* Columbia Pictures, 1971.
*Georgia, Georgia,* Jorkel Productions, 1972.
*Willy Dynamite,* Universal Pictures, 1974.
*Honeybaby, Honeybaby,* Kelly/Jordan Enterprises, 1974.

# Sources

## Periodicals

*Ebony,* February 1965; January 1974.
*New York Times,* April 24, 1964; May 10, 1964; November 15, 1964; November 19, 1964; August 14, 1967; December 31, 1967; September 30, 1973.

—Deborah A. Ring

# Tim Scott

## 1965—

### Politician, business owner

Scott, Tim, photograph. AP Images/Bruce Smith.

Tim Scott's staunch conservative views helped him to become the first black Republican to be elected to the South Carolina House of Representatives in more than a hundred years. The Charleston native went on to gather impressive state and national Republican Party support for his 2010 campaign to represent South Carolina in Congress, defeating a passel of other Republican candidates in the June primary race. "To know my story is to understand that there were people who had no reason to step up to the plate and help me, but who did," Scott told *New York Times*'s Katharine Q. Seelye about his Christian faith, which has deeply influenced his political beliefs. "I want to serve the community because the community helped me."

Scott was born in Charleston in 1965 to parents who divorced when he was still in elementary school. His father, Ben, was in the U.S. Air Force and stationed in Colorado for some years, while in South Carolina Scott's mother, Frances, worked long hours as a nurse's aide. With two children to support, she often clocked double shifts, leaving the boys to fend for themselves for more than sixteen hours a day. By the time Scott reached high school, he was known to

teachers and classmates alike as a perennial goof-off and was failing several classes by then. He did, however, hold down a job at a local cinema. The movie house was located next door to a Chick-Fil-A restaurant—a popular fast-food chain in the South—and Scott loved the french fries there. John Moniz, the franchise owner, befriended Scott and sought to impart some important life lessons before he suffered a fatal heart attack just a few years later. Moniz was a conservative Christian who stressed the importance of self-reliance gleaned from the series of motivational books by Zig Ziglar, which Scott started to read.

Moniz died when Scott was seventeen. Overwhelmed by the loss, the teenager sat down and wrote a mission statement for his life, setting a goal of having a similar positive impact on the lives of one billion people. He also laid out a series of five-year plans for his schooling and future career. By the time he graduated from high school, he had improved his grades enough to win a partial football scholarship to Presbyterian College, but he later transferred to Charleston Southern University, where he earned his undergraduate degree in political science in 1988.

## At a Glance . . .

**B**orn Timothy Eugene Scott on September 19, 1965, in Charleston, SC; son of Ben Scott Sr. and Frances Scott (a nurse's aide). *Politics:* Republican. *Education:* Attended Presbyterian College; Charleston Southern University, BS, political science, 1988.

**Career:** Tim Scott Allstate, owner and principal insurance agent; Pathway Real Estate Group, LLC, founding partner; Charleston County Council, member, 1995–2008; South Carolina House of Representatives, representative, 2008—.

**Addresses:** *Home*—Charleston, SC. *Office*—South Carolina Republican Party, PO Box 12373, Columbia, SC 29211.

Over the next few years Scott became a local business leader in Charleston. He owned an Allstate insurance office and was partners in a real estate firm before winning election to the Charleston County Council in 1995. Even though there had been many black Democrats elected to local and state office since the reforms of the civil rights movement, African Americans in the Republican Party remained a rarity well into the twenty-first century in the South, and Scott's victory in the Charleston County election attracted some notice. For example, Strom Thurmond, a U.S. senator from South Carolina, invited Scott to cochair his 1996 reelection campaign, which Scott accepted.

Scott's close ties to the state Republican Party helped him take the lead in a 2008 race for a seat in the South Carolina House of Representatives. He first won the June Republican primary for House District 117, but because this district is so heavily Republican, he was a shoe-in for the November race, and he ran unopposed. There were other African-American lawmakers in the state house, but Scott was sworn in as the sole black member of the Republican delegation.

In 2009 Scott began raising money for a campaign to secure the Republican Party nomination for lieutenant governor in the 2010 gubernatorial race. However, in February of 2010 he announced he was leaving that race and would instead run for a seat in Congress from South Carolina's First Congressional District. The congressional district was a Republican stronghold, one that encompassed the city of Charleston and some pricey shoreline real estate. Scott entered a crowded primary race that included two Republicans with famous South Carolina names: Paul Thurmond, the son of the now-deceased Strom Thurmond, and Carroll Campbell III, the son of the former South Carolina

governor. Scott was the leader in the June 8 primary, taking 32 percent of the vote, and then he ran against Thurmond, the second-place finisher, in a June 22 runoff. Scott won that contest with 68 percent of the vote, which garnered some national attention.

For the November ballot, Scott faced a retired postal worker who had never won political office despite numerous attempts. With that almost-assured win, Scott was poised to become South Carolina's first African-American Republican Party delegate in Congress since 1897. "This race is about the size of the federal government, eliminating that size and getting us closer to the constitutional mandate of a smaller, less intrusive government," he told Patrik Jonsson in the *Christian Science Monitor*, stressing his conservative platform. "We have strayed so far away from those enumerated powers that we don't even know what they look like anymore."

The 2010 midterm elections became a battleground for an arch-conservative wing of the U.S. political spectrum that was loosely organized into the so-called Tea Party movement. Galvanized into action by President Barack Obama's 2008 election and subsequent efforts by the White House and a Democratic-controlled Congress to revive the moribund U.S. economy and provide health care for all citizens, the Tea Party members were dramatically anti-tax and against such federal spending programs. Their supporters were predominantly white, and Scott appeared on CNN's *John King, USA* a few weeks after his primary win to discuss some recent embarrassing incidents that showed some Tea Party supporters displaying dramatically racist opinions. "When you have folks on the fringes that show up at rallies, how you respond to those folks is less important, in my opinion, than is what your focus on your issues are," he told King. "Ultimately, the Tea Party stands on the values of limited government, fiscal responsibility and free markets. This is a party that helped me win 68 percent of the vote, to earn the Republican nominee. To talk about the Tea Party as a racist group of folks is wrong."

# Sources

## Periodicals

*Christian Science Monitor*, June 15, 2010.
*New York Times*, June 25, 2010.
*Newsweek*, June 30, 2010.
*Post and Courier* (Charleston, SC), February 8, 2010.
*The State* (Columbia, SC), June 12, 2008.
*Washington Times*, August 9, 2010.

## Other

"Oil Cap Test; White House Meeting; Cheney Heart Surgery; Economic Stimulus Plan" (transcript), *John King, USA*, July 14, 2010, http://archives.cnn.

com/TRANSCRIPTS/1007/14/jkusa.01.html
(accessed October 15, 2010).

—Carol Brennan

# Shirley Sherrod

## 1948—

### Government official

Sherrod, Shirley, photograph. AP Images/Manuel Balce Ceneta.

Shirley Sherrod was an unknown, state-level official with the U.S. Department of Agriculture (USDA) during the summer of 2010 when she found herself enmeshed in a distasteful media attack that ultimately resulted in the loss of her job. Remarks Sherrod had made a few months earlier became the basis of a deceptively edited story on conservative news outlets, and Sherrod caved in to pressure and tendered her resignation. Within a day, however, the full transcript of her remarks were made public, and Tom Vilsack, the U.S. secretary of agriculture, personally apologized to Sherrod at a press conference. "This is a good woman," said Vilsack, according to a *New York Times* report. "She's been put through hell and I could have and should have done a better job."

### Lost Father to a Racist Neighbor

Sherrod was born in 1948 in Baker County, Georgia, a place with a long history of civil rights violations against African-American families. Her father, Hosie Miller, was a farmer and a deacon in their local Baptist church. She was one of five daughters and her mother was pregnant with a sixth child when in March of 1965 three cows belonging to a white neighbor had wandered off. The man confronted Hosie and accused him of taking them. Sherrod's father protested and told the man that he was going contact the local authorities to straighten out the matter. When he turned to walk away, the neighbor shot him in the back. Three people had witnessed the shooting, but an all-white grand jury declined to indict the neighbor.

The tragedy occurred during Sherrod's final year of high school. The following year she had just started taking classes at Fort Valley State College when she received a phone call from home. "They called and told me that a bunch of white men had gathered outside of our home and burned the cross one night," Sherrod recalled during a speech in March of 2010 for a Georgia National Association for the Advancement of Colored People (NAACP) chapter, a speech that later became the basis for a conservative news media attack. "One of my sisters got on the phone [to call] other black men in the county. And it wasn't long before they had surrounded these white men. And they had to keep one young man from actually using his gun on one of them. You probably would have read about it had that happened that night. But they actually allowed those men to leave."

Throughout her teens Sherrod had dreamed of leaving the South forever, but "on the night of my father's death I felt I had to do something," she said during her the NAACP speech. "I couldn't just let his death go without doing something in answer to what happened. I made the commitment on the night of my father's death, at the age of 17, that I would not leave the South, that I would stay in the South and devote my life to working for change." At Fort Valley, Sherrod became involved in the Student Nonviolent Coordinating Committee's efforts in Albany, Georgia, a town that had been the focus of an intense civil rights campaign since 1961. Her future husband, Charles Sherrod, was one of the leaders of the Albany movement, and she eventually transferred to Albany State University, where she earned a bachelor's degree in sociology.

## Spent Career Aiding Rural Farms

In 1969 Sherrod and her husband, along with several other black activists, were the founding members of the New Communities Land Trust, a collective farm enterprise that was modeled on the highly successful kibbutz collectives of Israel. Their fifty-seven-hundred-acre farm in Lee County, Georgia, became one of the biggest parcels of land under African-American ownership during the early 1970s. It soldiered on for many years, consistently failing to win vital federal and state agriculture loans designed to help struggling American farms. However, by 1985 Sherrod and the other members finally decided to shut down the farm. Twelve years later Sherrod and several other black farmers joined a class-action suit against the USDA that successfully demonstrated that government officials had denied loans to black farmers. In all, more than $1 billion was eventually paid out to black farmers.

During her NAACP speech, Sherrod recounted her experiences as the head of the Georgia office of the Federation of Southern Cooperatives, a job she took in 1985. She noted that a year after she took the job a white farmer came to her for assistance. "He took a long time talking, but he was trying to show me he was superior to me," she said. "I know what he was doing. But he had come to me for help. What he didn't know—while he was taking all that time trying to show me he was superior to me—was I was trying to decide just how much help I was going to give him."

Sherrod went on to say that she put the farmer in touch with a white attorney who handled such cases. "About seven days before that land would have been sold at the courthouse steps, the farmer called me and said the lawyer wasn't doing anything. And that's when I spent time there in my office calling everybody I could think of to try to see—help me find the lawyer who would handle this," she recalled. "Working with him made me see that it's really about those who have versus those who don't, you know. And they could be black, and they could be white; they could be Hispanic. And it made me realize then that I needed to work to help poor people—those who don't have access the way others have."

## Forced to Resign Because of Remarks

When her speech was first aired four months later, on July 19, the second half of her comments were not included in the footage. Headlined "Video Proof: The NAACP Awards Racism" on the website Biggovernment.com, which is run by the conservative blogger Andrew Breitbart, the story included a clip that only showed the first part of Sherrod's tale of the 1986 incident. Fox News picked up the story, and one of the cable news channel's highest-rated hosts, Bill O'Reilly, called for Sherrod to resign from her post as Georgia

State Director of Rural Development, which she had held for a year by that point. Other news sources ran the story, and the NAACP formally condemned Sherrod's remarks and called for her resignation. By the evening of July 19 Sherrod had decided, after fielding several phone calls, to e-mail her letter of resignation to a deputy undersecretary at the USDA.

On July 20 the wife of the white farmer contacted CNN and defended Sherrod's reputation, saying that Sherrod had helped them and that they had become friends. Then the owner of the video company that had taped the footage of the NAACP banquet at which Sherrod spoke contacted news outlets and explained that Sherrod's comments were taken out of context. He even provided the full copy of her speech. When both parts of her speech were presented together, unedited, both the media and the public made an about-face. Later that same day Benjamin Jealous, the head of the NAACP, publicly apologized to Sherrod, as did O'Reilly. On July 21 Vilsack appeared visibly mortified at a press conference in which he fielded tough questions from reporters and said that he had offered to rehire Sherrod at the USDA in a new post, as deputy director of the Office of Advocacy and Outreach.

On July 22 Sherrod appeared on CNN's prime-time news roundup, *John King, USA,* in a lengthy interview segment. When asked by King if she would like to say anything to Breitbart, she replied, "I'd tell him he's a liar. He knew exactly what effect that would have on … the conservative racist people he's dealing with. That's why I started getting the hate mail, and that's why I started getting the hate calls. He got the effect he was looking for." She confirmed that President Barack Obama had called her and extended his apologies for the fracas and that she had declined Vilsack's offer of another USDA job. "I'm at a place where I just need to get out of this frenzy, go home, and get my grandchildren," she told King, "and get to the point where I can think."

## Sources

### Periodicals

*Atlanta Journal-Constitution,* July 22, 2010, p. A1. *New York Times,* July 22, 2010; July 25, 2010.

### Online

Dreyfuss, Joel, "Shirley Sherrod, the Media and Conservative Fantasies," TheRoot.com, July 21, 2010, http://www.theroot.com/print/42801 (accessed October 13, 2010).

"Shirley Sherrod: Address at the Georgia NAACP 20th Annual Freedom Fund Banquet," American Rhetoric, March 27, 2010, http://www.americanrhetoric.com/speeches/shirleysherrodnaacpfreedom.htm (accessed October 13, 2010).

"Video Proof: The NAACP Awards Racism," Biggovernment.com, July 19, 2010, http://biggovernment.com/abreitbart/2010/07/19/video-proof-the-naacp-awards-racism2010/ (accessed October 13, 2010).

### Other

"Apology from the President; Approval Ratings," *John King, USA* (transcript), CNN, July 22, 2010.

—Carol Brennan

# Garry Shider

## 1953–2010

### Musician

Shider, Garry, photograph. Jay West/WireImage/Getty Images.

Garry Shider's career in music was irrevocably tied to that of George Clinton. As the guitarist and songwriter for Clinton's raucous and highly influential Parliament-Funkadelic, and later as the musical director for Clinton's equally successful P-Funk All-Stars, Shider helped define a science fiction–inspired and counterculture-inflected sound that influenced several later generations of black musical genres. "Shider's presence was integral to Funkadelic's identity, for his strong throat (his father was a preacher), versatile guitar chops, unmistakable diaper garb, and hysterics onstage made his vibe central to the Funkadelic experience," wrote Rickey Vincent in the 1996 book *Funk: The Music, the People, and the Rhythm of the One*. Vincent also asserted that "Clinton and his associates drew such far-reaching scope for their silly stories and cartoon characters that one can conceive of their works as folklore, and perhaps some of the first postindustrial black American mythology."

Shider was born in Plainfield, New Jersey, in 1953, a town that Clinton had moved to from his native North Carolina. During the early 1960s Shider and his brother, Kevin, formed the gospel group the Shider-

ettes, which opened for big-name gospel acts that came through town. Shider gained some of his first performing experiences as an opener or backup singer for the Mighty Clouds of Joy, the Five Blind Boys, Shirley Caesar, and other top religious-music acts. By the time Shider entered his teens, Clinton was working as a barber in Plainfield, and Shider frequented the barbershop with his friends because of Clinton's emerging status as a local singer.

In 1969, at the height of the Vietnam War and after several race-related urban disturbances in American cities, Shider moved to Canada with his friend Cordell "Boogie" Mosson. They settled in Toronto, a hub of the counterculture. He and Mosson began playing together as United Soul, and Clinton, after having had limited success as a doo-wop group called George Clinton and the Parliaments, made his way north of the border and was surprised to find a solid R&B act fronted by two guys from his hometown. By this point Clinton was beginning to transform himself into a full-fledged funk maestro, forming an outfit he called Funkadelic that, after some legal issues, was signed to another label as Parliament. Clinton had some contacts in Detroit, Michigan, so he shifted his operation there. He con-

### At a Glance . . .

**B**orn Garry Marshall Shider on July 24, 1953, in Plainfield, NJ; died of cancer on June 16, 2010, in Upper Marlboro, MD; son of Jesse Shider (a minister); married Linda (a singer/songwriter), c. 1978; children: Garrett, Marshall.

**Career:** The Shiderettes, singer, early 1960s; Parliament-Funkadelic, guitarist, vocalist, songwriter, and producer, after 1972; P-Funk All Stars, musical director, guitarist, vocalist, songwriter, and producer.

**Awards:** Inducted into the Rock and Roll Hall of Fame, 1997.

vinced Shider and Mosson to come to Detroit and record, and they cut two singles that were released by Westbound Records in 1972 under the name U.S. Music with Funkadelic. Clinton actually planned to produce a full-length record with United Soul, but the project was abandoned and Shider and Mosson instead signed on with Parliament-Funkadelic, as the dual bands were jointly known.

Parliament-Funkadelic's original guitarist, Tal Ross, had left the group, so Shider joined a guitar lineup that was fronted by Eddie Hazel. A few talented musicians from James Brown's group had also joined by that point, and Funkadelic's 1972 *America Eats Its Young* was the first LP to fully showcase the Parliament-Funkadelic lineup. Shider shared vocals on a few of the tracks, but he shined more brightly on Funkadelic's 1973 release *Cosmic Slop*. He sang the lead on the title track, about a struggling mother of five who resorts to prostitution to feed and shelter her children.

Clinton managed to reclaim the Parliament name after some legal wrangling and signed it to Casablanca Records. Shider was part of the lineup for *Up for the Down Stroke* in 1974, and played guitar and sang vocals on a pair of Parliament releases in 1975: *Chocolate City* and *Mothership Connection*. That second LP gave the band their first gold-selling single, "Give up the Funk (Tear the Roof off the Sucker)." Besides being a massive hit during the summer of 1976, the track also served as a sonic calling card for the entire funk genre.

*The Clones of Dr. Funkenstein* followed in 1976, and then a live recording that was taped during two shows in Los Angeles and Oakland, California, in 1977 showcased the dazzling virtuosity of the Parliament-

Funkadelic experience. Shider and his bandmates took to the stage with lavish props and special effects, often playing five- or six-hour shows. As Funkadelic, they released *One Nation under a Groove* on the Warner Brothers label, whose title track became another massive hit for the group on the *Billboard* Hot Soul Singles chart. Shider co-wrote the song, which spent several weeks as number 1 before it was bumped by Chaka Khan's "I'm Every Woman."

Parliament-Funkadelic were huge during the 1970s, but they appeared at a unique juncture in the pop-music timeline. "The racially formatted radio that persists to this day took shape just as Funkadelic started to hit, ensuring that most white listeners perceived the P-Funk phenomenon as merely freaky dance pop (which it was), not as restlessly radical art rock (which it also was)," wrote Joe Gore in *Guitar Player*. Furthermore, Clinton's "Mothership" proved too small to contain the clashing egos of some of the members, a few of whom departed to start their own projects. Clinton held the remaining members together under the name P-Funk All-Stars and appointed Shider to serve as the musical director. The guitarist played on Clinton's enormously successful 1982 solo record *Computer Games,* which yielded "Atomic Dog," a number 1 hit on the *Billboard* Hot R&B Singles chart during the spring of 1983. Shider also appeared on *Urban Dancefloor Guerillas,* which was released in 1983.

Like the other members of Parliament-Funkadelic, Shider favored outlandish stage costumes. He often played in a large diaper, which earned him the nickname "Diaper Man." After the demise of Clinton's original lineup, he went on to play with bands formed by Eddie Hazel and Bootsy Collins. Occasionally, he appeared with the house band on *Saturday Night Live* and with Paul Shaffer's band on *The Late Show with David Letterman.* He released "Beautiful," a solo single for MCA Records, in 1988 and *Diaper Man: The Second Coming,* a full-length solo record for Raw Funk Records, in 2002. In 2009 the original tracks that he and Mosson had recorded in 1971 for a planned United Soul release were finally issued as *U.S. Music with Funkadelic* on Westbound Records.

In March of 2010 Shider was diagnosed with brain and lung cancer. He died at his home in Upper Marlboro, Maryland, on June 16, 2010. With his wife, Linda, he had two sons, Garrett and Marshall. "I'm sure if he had the choice, he would have passed on a tour bus," Garrett told the Associated Press correspondent Bruce Shipkowski, "because he loved playing music, playing for the fans." Garrett also said that he hoped to get a movie project off the ground that would recount his father's life story. "People know about his talent," he said, "but I want them to know about the great man he was."

## Selected discography

### Singles

(As U.S. Music with Funkadelic) "I Miss My Baby," Westbound Records, 1972.

(As U.S. Music with Funkadelic) "Baby I Owe You Something Good," Westbound Records, 1972.

"Beautiful" (solo), MCA Records, 1988.

### Albums

(With Funkadelic) *America Eats Its Young,* Westbound Records, 1972.

(With Funkadelic) *Cosmic Slop,* Westbound Records, 1973.

(With Parliament) *Up for the Down Stroke,* Casablanca Records, 1974.

(With Parliament) *Chocolate City,* Casablanca Records, 1975.

(With Parliament) *Mothership Connection,* Casablanca Records, 1975.

(With Parliament) *The Clones of Dr. Funkenstein,* Casablanca Records, 1976.

(With Funkadelic) *One Nation under a Groove,* Warner Brothers, 1978.

(With P-Funk All-Stars) *Urban Dancefloor Guerillas,* Uncle Jam/CBS Records, 1983.

*Diaper Man: The Second Coming* (solo), Raw Funk Records, 2002.

*U.S. Music with Funkadelic,* Westbound Records, 2009.

## Sources

### Books

Vincent, Rickey, *Funk: The Music, the People, and the Rhythm of the One,* St. Martin's Griffin, 1996.

### Periodicals

*Associated Press,* June 18, 2010.
*Guardian* (London), June 29, 2010, p. 35.
*Guitar Player,* April 1996, p. 84.
*New York Times,* June 21, 2010.
*Times* (London) June 30, 2010, p. 47.

### Online

McCall, Tris, "Joyful Tribute to Garry Shider, Master of Funk," NJ.com, July 13, 2010, http://www.nj.com/entertainment/music/index.ssf/2010/07/joyful_tribute_to_kevin_shider.html (accessed October 14, 2010).

—Carol Brennan

# Emmitt Smith

## 1969—

**Professional football player, television analyst, real estate developer**

Smith, Emmitt, photograph. Al Messerschmidt/Getty Images.

Hall of Fame running back Emmitt Smith is arguably the greatest offensive player in NFL history. The league's all-time leading rusher, Smith amassed 18,355 running yards over the course of his 13-year career, while scoring a record 164 rushing touchdowns. Smith was the NFL's most dominant back throughout the 1990s, earning eight Pro Bowl selections, leading the Dallas Cowboys to three Super Bowl titles and winning league MVP honors in 1994. In the five-year span between 1991 and 1995, Smith led the NFL in rushing four times. As Peter King put it in *Sports Illustrated,* "The thing that turns Smith on the most is his desire to be a tremendous player, and that's refreshing. He wants to make a mark on this game that few players will *ever* equal." Few would dispute that he succeeded in doing just that.

At *every* level throughout his illustrious career—high school, college, and professional—Smith ranked among the very best. His consistent achievement as a running back came not from blinding speed or extra strength, but rather from an instinctive feel for the game and an uncanny ability to read and respond to every shift in the opposing defense. "I know I'm not the fastest guy around," Smith told *Sports Illustrated,* while still at the height of his professional career. "And I know I'm not the strongest guy, either. It doesn't bother me at all. I see myself as being able to get the job done." He added: "If you want to get through a hole bad enough, you'll get through it." Former Cowboys offensive coordinator Norv Turner once related *Sports Illustrated*: "Emmitt rarely makes a play that makes you go, Wow! It's his total package. His great games are games where he just wears you down, play after play, over and over. This is what great runners do. They dominate games. And nobody dominates games in the NFL like Emmitt has recently."

### Born to Play Football

Emmitt James Smith III was born in 1969, one of five children of Emmitt Smith Jr., a Pensacola bus driver who spent his weekends playing semi-pro football with a local Florida league, and Mary Smith. When he was an infant, his mother could calm him by turning on televised football games. In *Sports Illustrated,* Mary Smith recalled watching her oldest son "just sort of rocking in his little swing, but watching everything" as the action unfolded on the screen. Gifted with athletic potential from an early age, Smith spent hours of his youth playing backyard football with the neighbor children and his older cousins. *Sports Illustrated* contributor Rick Telander noted: "Little Emmitt always played with older kids because of his athletic skills; he had the balance to walk forever on neighborhood fences and curbs without falling off; he was the Gale Sayers of the local youth league."

At the age of seven Smith joined an organized football program, the mini-mite division of the Salvation Army Optimists League. While other children experimented with various hobbies and extracurricular activities, young Smith stuck to football. *Sports Illustrated* writer Paul Zimmerman observed: "When you ask [Smith] the standard questions about how he avoided getting involved with drugs and street gangs and the usual teenage trouble, he gives you a strange look and says, 'It never occurred to me.'" Gangs held no appeal for Emmitt Smith. He was too busy keeping in shape and building his strength and endurance.

The public high school nearest to the Smith home was Escambia High. Before Smith arrived, the Escambia Gators had not compiled a winning season in twenty-one years. In an article published in *Sports Illustrated*, Gators coach Dwight Thomas, who arrived at Escambia in 1983—the same year as Smith—described the program as "the most negative, apathetic, losing environment I've ever been in, ever." That was about to change. Thomas vividly recalled his first encounter with Emmitt Smith: "All the other kids were acting like kids, fooling around, taking nothing seriously. Then a boy in neat, pressed clothes walks up to me and shakes my hand. 'Hi, Coach Thomas,' he said. 'I'm Emmitt.' So confident, so gracious. I have three children, and I just hope they can be like him. And I don't mean anything about athletics."

Coach Thomas described the game plan he developed for Smith at Escambia. "For four years we did three things, and won two state championships doing them," the coach said. "Hand the ball to Emmitt, pitch the ball to Emmitt, throw the ball to Emmitt. It was no secret. Everyone knew we were going to get the ball to him. It was just a question of how." Smith led Escambia to a four-year record of 42–7 while rushing for a phenomenal 8,804 yards.

By the end of his senior season, Smith was ranked second-highest in total yardage in the history of high school football. As Telander pointed out, "Smith was so unstoppable in high school that an entire defensive unit once showed up with his number, 24, taped on their helmets." During his senior year Smith was named National Player of the Year by *Parade* magazine.

It is quite possible that Smith could have been the all-time rushing record-holder at the high school level; however, the idea of breaking records was not uppermost in his mind, nor in the mind of his coach. Often Smith was pulled out of games, along with the rest of Escambia's first string, once a victory was assured. Then he would sit on the bench and cheer the other players on. In *Sports Illustrated*, Thomas described his star player as "unselfish, special, never complained about anything."

Ironically, for all the hype surrounding his high school career, Smith had not particularly impressed the college scouts. A few of them dismissed him as too small and too slow to perform well at the college level. One such scout told *Sports Illustrated*: "[Smith's] a lugger, not a runner. The thing is that sportswriters blew him all out of proportion." Not everyone agreed with that assessment. The young running back earned a full scholarship to the University of Florida, where scouts and coaches alike predicted a stellar career for him.

## Proved the Skeptics Wrong

Smith promptly proved their most spectacular predictions true. In his very first game as a Florida freshman, Smith gained 224 yards on 39 carries, a single-game rushing record at that university. The University of Florida handily beat favored University of Alabama in that match, and the national "Emmitt watch" began. As the 1987 college season progressed, Smith became the only freshman in history to gain 100 or more yards per game in seven games. Telander wrote that Smith "displayed a running style that defies easy description. He darted, slithered and followed his blockers, and squeezed yard after yard out of plays that didn't have any yards in them. He didn't look especially fast or powerful or blindingly deceptive, yet he couldn't be stopped." It is almost unheard of for a freshman to be in the running for the Heisman Trophy, yet Smith made the top ten in balloting after his first year with the squad.

Smith conquered college level football just as he had high school level football. By his junior year he had been named All-America and All-Southeast Conference three times. He had also established 58 school records, including a career rushing mark of 3,928 yards. Zimmerman described Smith as "an incredible yardage machine, having rushed for more than 100 yards in 25 of his 34 games at Florida, and in 70 out of 83 high school and college games combined."

One big question remained: could Smith take his success on to the professional ranks? Once again he was faced with a chorus of detractors. "Too slow," a New York Giants scout told *Sports Illustrated*. Others thought him too small or too weak to hold his own against professional defenders. Smith felt otherwise. In 1990, as a college junior, he declared himself eligible for the pro football draft.

One of the clubs that took immediate interest in Smith was the Dallas Cowboys. The Cowboys had just come off a 1–15 season under new coach, Jimmy Johnson, and were looking to rebuild the team from bottom to top, relying upon younger players. Joe Brodsky, a scout for Dallas, told *Sports Illustrated*: "You had to be an idiot not to recognize the talent there. What I did find out, though, was the kind of person [Smith] was: played in pain, never missed a workout, not a nick-and-bump guy who'd miss a lot of practice time, an extra-good worker and not a complainer." Brodsky

added that he told Coach Johnson that Smith "will take your breath away, and you won't get it back until he scores." In the first round of the 1990 draft, Johnson made a trade with the Pittsburgh Steelers for the seventeenth pick; he promptly chose Smith. Back home in Pensacola, Smith celebrated with his family and friends.

Reflecting on the 1990 draft, Dallas coach Johnson commented in *Sports Illustrated*: "Emmitt had been our fourth-rated player in the entire draft. Our owner, Jerry Jones, went on the radio that night and mentioned it, and when it was time to talk contract, Emmitt's agent reminded him of that. Which I'm sure is one reason why he held out for the whole training camp." The Cowboys' executives, including the owner, quickly discovered that Smith intended to fight for the very best contract possible. Negotiations with the rookie running back dragged on nearly until the beginning of the season, and Smith came to his new team without the benefit of summertime game preparations. Nevertheless, he became the starting running back just two games into the 1990 season.

Johnson was reluctant to use Smith at first. By midseason, however, the coach realized he had acquired a whole new offensive arsenal—Emmitt Smith on the ground, Emmitt Smith on the short pass, Emmitt Smith for the touchdown. By the end of the 1990 season, Smith had compiled 937 rushing yards and eleven rushing touchdowns. He was named NFL Offensive Rookie of the Year by the Associated Press. As Zimmerman put it, "he wasn't quite the yardage machine he'd been in high school and college, but he was getting there."

## Rose to Peak of NFL Stardom

Smith blossomed in his second year with Dallas, leading the NFL in rushing with 1,563 yards. Just 22 at the time of this accomplishment, he became the youngest player in the history of the NFL to gain more than 1,500 yards in a season. The 1991 Cowboys, a far cry from the lackluster squad of just two years earlier, finished with an 11–5 record and a playoff victory against the Chicago Bears. In that wild card playoff game, Smith rushed for 105 yards against a team that had never in history allowed a running back to gain more than 100 yards in a post-season game. Dallas's 1991 season ended with a playoff defeat to the Detroit Lions.

In 1992 Smith again led the league in rushing, becoming only the ninth player in history to win back-to-back rushing titles. The runner set a new Cowboys record with 1,713 yards for the season, as Dallas posted a 13–3 record and took first in the NFC East. After trouncing both the Philadelphia Eagles and the San Francisco 49ers in the playoffs, the Cowboys advanced into Super Bowl XXVII against the favored Buffalo

Bills. By this time the nation was watching young Emmitt Smith, who had become the first player to win the rushing title and go to both the Super Bowl and the Pro Bowl in the same season.

Super Bowl XXVII was an absolute romp for the Cowboys. They beat Buffalo 52–17, prompting sports writers to label the Dallas team a "new dynasty" and the "team of the decade" for the 1990s. For his part, Smith became the first Cowboys player ever to rush for more than 100 yards in a Super Bowl, with a 108-yard total on 22 carries.

Smith's first contract expired in 1993, and as the new season neared he clashed with the Cowboys' owner about how much he was worth. Once again he missed training camp, and entering the regular season he still didn't have a contract. Dallas lost its first two games that year, while Smith sat at home in Pensacola watching them on television. Finally, after the second defeat, Cowboys' owner Jerry Jones offered Smith a four-year, $13.6 million deal, including a $4 million signing bonus. Relieved that his long holdout was over, Smith eagerly rejoined the Cowboys and proceeded to help turn their season around. The contract made Smith, just 24, the highest paid running back in football history.

No football team has ever gone 0–2 and come back to win a Super Bowl, but Dallas was so improved after Smith's return to the offense that the Cowboys finished the 1993 season in a divisional first-place tie with the New York Giants. In the first week of 1994 the Cowboys met the Giants in a divisional showdown to determine NFC East first place (carrying an automatic home field advantage throughout the playoffs). This game, perhaps more than any other, highlighted the singular talents that had already made Smith famous. Despite a serious separation of the shoulder sustained early in the second half, he was eager to remain in the game. In the end he earned 168 yards on 32 carries, another 61 yards on 10 pass receptions, and handled the ball on 42 of Dallas's 70 offensive plays. The Cowboys went on to win the game 16–13 in overtime. In the process, Smith became the fourth player in NFL history to win three straight NFL rushing titles, joining Hall-of-Famers Steve Van Buren, Jim Brown, and Earl Campbell.

Despite battling his shoulder separation and a nagging hamstring injury, Smith dominated the 1994 NFL postseason. In the Cowboys' 38–21 NFC Championship win over the San Francisco 49ers, Smith earned 88 yards rushing and 85 yards receiving, with two touchdowns—and then left the game with ten minutes to play. Just a week later he earned Super Bowl MVP honors with a 30-carry, 132-yard, two-touchdown romp in Super Bowl XXVIII. The Cowboys had been trailing the Buffalo Bills at half time, but rebounded to win the game with some timely defensive receptions, as well as Smith's third- and fourth-quarter rushing. At

game's end the new Super Bowl MVP was mobbed by his teammates, Dallas coach Jimmy Johnson, and Cowboys owner Jerry Jones. Smith also finished the 1993–94 season as the league MVP.

"Who knows what kind of mileage Smith will leave behind him?" Zimmerman asked in *Sports Illustrated.* Entering the 1994 season, Smith began to ponder his NFL legacy. "I think about it all the time," the player told *Sports Illustrated.* "I'm chasing after legends, after Walter Payton and Tony Dorsett and Jim Brown and Eric Dickerson, after guys who made history. When my career's over, I want to have the new kids, the new backs, say, 'Boy, we have to chase a legend to be the best.' And they'll mean Emmitt Smith." At the same time, Smith conceded that the biggest obstacle to his ambition was the threat of injuries. Still, he didn't care to dwell upon the negative. "I play with the hand dealt to me," he said. "I look at the future and wonder what it'll be like. Eventually, I'm going to have arthritis. Eventually, I know I'll have to live with pain. That's part of all this. I want to do everything in football—and in life—that I can. I still believe, no matter how many times I carry the ball, that I can be one of those guys who walks away from the game whole. If I stay healthy, I think I've got a great chance of accomplishing what I want to accomplish." Asked about his abilities elsewhere in *Sports Illustrated,* Smith concluded: "The way I see it, my talent came from God. What I add is my desire. I have great desire."

### Shattered NFL Records

Arguably the best performance of Smith's career came in 1995, when he gained 1,773 rushing yards and 2,148 total yards from scrimmage, while scoring 25 touchdowns—all career highs. For the season he averaged a career-best 110.8 yards per game, while leading the Cowboys to their third Super Bowl title in four years. In the spring of 1996, Smith achieved a very personal milestone, when he finally completed his BS degree at the University of Florida. That August, Smith signed an eight-year contract extension worth $48 million; the deal included a signing bonus of $15 million, an NFL record. Smith's production dropped off in 1996, however, as he battled injuries to his neck, knee, and ankle.

Smith continued to struggle in 1997, amassing only 1,074 rushing yards, his lowest total since his rookie season; even worse for the consummate team player, the Cowboys failed to make the playoffs that year, posting its worst record since 1990. Smith returned to form in 1998, gaining 1,332 yards and helping lead the Cowboys back to the playoffs. That year, Smith also set a new NFL record when he scored his 125th career rushing touchdown. Smith remained highly productive the following season, when he gained 1,397 rushing yards, while scoring 13 touchdowns.

Entering the new decade, the 31-year-old Smith showed no signs of slowing down. In 2000 he ran for more than 100 yards in six games, while averaging 4.1 yards per carry. Although Smith gained only 1,021 rushing yards in 2001, it marked the 11th consecutive season in which he ran for more than 1,000 yards, an NFL record. His performance began to slip the following year, however, as he gained 975 yards and scored only five touchdowns. In February of 2003, the Cowboys released Smith. A month later, he signed a two-year deal to play for the Arizona Cardinals. Smith posted the worst season of his career in 2003, gaining only 256 rushing yards in ten games. He rebounded somewhat in 2004, starting 15 games for the Cardinals, en route to 937 rushing yards. At the conclusion of the season, Smith announced his retirement.

After retiring from football, Smith shifted his focus to the real estate business. In 2005 he joined legendary Cowboys quarterback Roger Staubach to create Smith/Cypress Partners, a real estate development firm. Three years later, Smith co-founded a new commercial real estate company, ESmith Legacy, Inc. Throughout these years, Smith continued to earn recognition for his accomplishments on the football field. In September of 2005 Smith was named to the Dallas Cowboys Ring of Honor, inducted alongside Troy Aikman and Michael Irvin, his teammates from the Super Bowl Championship teams. In February of 2010 Smith received the NFL's highest honor when he was elected into the Pro Football Hall of Fame.

## Sources

### Periodicals

*Dallas Morning News,* January 25, 1996, p. 3B; May 5, 1996, p. 1A; August 24, 2000, p. 1H; August 22, 2002, p. 6F; October 28, 2002, p. 36B; October 30, 2002, p. 6B; May 22, 2005, p. 1D; April 1, 2010, p. C9.

*Ebony,* October 1993, p. 50.

*Fort Worth Star-Telegram,* August 7, 2010, p. CC.

*Gazette* (Montreal), November 9, 1998, p. F8.

*International Herald Tribune,* February 8, 2010, p. 10.

*Jet,* January 31, 1994, p. 47.

*New York Times,* September 17, 1993; December 13, 1996, p. B1; February 4, 2005, p. D4.

*Sports Illustrated,* November 16, 1987; October 21, 1991; September 7, 1992; September 27, 1993; January 10, 1994, pp. 34–38; January 31, 1994, p. 14.

*Toronto Star,* August 16, 1996, p. C3.

*USA Today,* July 19, 2001, p. 3C; March 27, 2003, p. 1C.

Additional information for this sketch was taken from Associated Press releases dated September 17 and 18, 1993.

### Online

"Emmitt Smith," Pro-Football-Reference.com, http://www.pro-football-reference.com/players/S/SmitEm00.htm (accessed November 3, 2010).

ESmith Legacy, Inc., http://www.esmithlegacy.com/ (accessed November 3, 2010).

Official Website of Emmitt Smith, http://www.emmittsmith.com/ssp/home/ (accessed November 3, 2010).

—Mark Kram and Stephen Meyer

# Michael G. Spencer

## 1952—

### Engineer, professor

Michael G. Spencer graduated from Cornell University in 1981 with a doctorate in electro-physics and became the first African-American student at the school to earn the highest degree in his field. He spent several years at Howard University with his former Cornell classmate, Gary L. Harris, and later returned to his alma mater as a professor of electrical and computer engineering.

Spencer was born in Detroit, Michigan, in 1952 when his mother, Laura, was attending law school at Wayne State University. His father, Thomas, was also an attorney and for a time his parents were partners in a Detroit law firm that handled workers' compensation claims. His father died in 1956, and Laura returned with her only child to the city where she grew up, Washington, DC. During the mid-1960s Laura became a staff attorney with the U.S. Department of Housing and Urban Development, and she eventually rose to become deputy director of the department's equal opportunity program.

Spencer showed an early aptitude for electronics. "In junior high, I worked on a science project and tried to build an ultrasonic demonstration device," he told *Black Enterprise*'s Gwen McKinney in 1986. "It didn't work too well, but I won third place." He enrolled in Cornell University and graduated with a bachelor's degree in engineering in 1974. The following year he earned a master's degree in engineering. In 1981 he graduated with a doctorate in electro-physics.

Spencer's work experience began at General Electric's Syracuse, New York, facility, while he was an under-graduate at Cornell. From 1974 to 1977 he designed electronic equipment for Bell Laboratories in Whippany, New Jersey. In 1981 he returned to Howard University as an assistant professor, where he joined Harris. Both had been hired by the school's Department of Electrical Engineering at a time when Howard was recruiting talented young electrical engineering graduates to staff its new Rockwell Solid State Electronics Laboratory.

The Rockwell lab was quite large, at six thousand square feet, and stocked with the latest high-tech research tools. Spencer and Harris quickly gained prominence for their findings in the field of what was then called "microelectronics." In 1983 they were joined by a third black research scientist, Dr. Keith Jackson, and all three worked on improving the capacity and durability of semiconductors and microchips. In her article about the Rockwell lab, McKinney cited the scarcity of African Americans with advanced degrees in electrical engineering and physics. She also discussed the efforts by Spencer, Harris, and Jackson to recruit as many engineers and physicists as possible to join them at the lab.

Spencer and his colleagues at Rockwell lab won significant research grants from the National Aeronautics and Space Administration's Jet Propulsion Laboratory, the National Science Foundation, and IBM. At the time, their work focused on improving the capacity of microchips and laser beams that were used in electronics and in weapons and aircraft systems, including the controversial Strategic Defense Initiative, an antimissile de-

## At a Glance . . .

**B**orn Michael Gregg Spencer on March 9, 1952, in Detroit, MI; son of Thomas Spencer (an attorney) and Laura (Lee) Spencer (an attorney and government official); divorced; three children. *Education:* Cornell University, BS, electrical engineering, 1974, MS, electrical engineering, 1975, PhD, electro-physics, 1981.

**Career:** Intern with General Electric, 1972, 1973; Bell Laboratories, designer of electronic equipment, 1974–77; Howard University, assistant professor, 1981, associate professor, 1985; Howard University, Materials Science Research Center of Excellence, director, 1989–99; Cornell University, professor of electrical and computer engineering and assistant dean, after 2002; Widetronix Inc., Ithaca, New York, cofounder and chief scientist, 2003—.

**Memberships:** Institute of Electrical and Electronic Engineers; National Society of Black Engineers; National Science Foundation.

**Awards:** Presidential Young Investigator Award, National Science Foundation, 1985; Alan Berman Research Publication Award, Naval Research Laboratories, 1986; Outstanding Faculty Award, White House Initiative on Historically Black Colleges and Universities, 1988; NASA Certificate of Recognition, 1992.

**Addresses:** *Office*—Cornell University, Professor, Department of Electrical and Computer Engineering, 418 Phillips Hall, Ithaca, NY 14853.

fense program for the nation during the cold war. "This area of research in solid state microelectronics is very exciting," Spender told Crystal R. Chissell in *U.S. Black Engineer and IT.* "In some cases it encompasses chemistry, material science, solid state physics, and electrical engineering. That always presents some challenging problems."

In 1985 Spencer became an associate professor at Howard, the same year he won a Presidential Young Investigator Award from the National Science Foundation. He was also working on bringing new graduate students into the field. "We don't have a lot of Black electrical engineers who have considered graduate school," he told Chissell. "Sometimes financial constraints or other things decide the issue for them. Traditionally we have been underrepresented in engineering as a whole.... That's why I think it's very important that a place like Howard, a Black institution, has a graduate program so that students can actually see what that's all about."

In 1987 the Rockwell lab evolved into the Howard University Materials Science Research Center of Excellence, and Spencer was its director from 1989 to 1999. In 2002 he returned to Cornell, where he rose to the position of assistant dean and professor in its College of Engineering. In 2003 he was a cofounder of Widetronix Inc., in Ithaca, which used some of the technologies developed at Cornell to make long-lasting betavoltaic batteries.

Spencer still confers with Harris on a project set up by the National Science Foundation. Each runs his respective school's program within the National Nanotechnology Infrastructure Network, which develops advanced technologies using molecular and atom-sized particles. In 2010 Widetronix received more than $2 million in funding from the Solar Energy Consortium and the U.S. Department of Defense to work on new types of batteries using silicon carbide, which was one of the semiconductor compounds that he and Harris had worked with during the mid-1980s. "The engine that drives this country, and the world, is technology and engineering," Spencer told McKinney. "In a very real sense, our work is where people will go and where business will go."

## Sources

### Periodicals

*Black Enterprise,* August 1986, pp. 44–46.
*Ebony,* October 1994, p. 132.
*U.S. Black Engineer and IT,* 1986, pp. 21–23.
*USBE/HE Professional,* Spring 1990, pp. 12–13.
*Washington Post,* January 22, 2004, p. B7.

### Online

Ju, Anne, "Cornell-Developed Battery Technology Company Receives $2.2 Million in Federal Funds," Chronicle Online, May 4, 2010, http://www.news. cornell.edu/stories/May10/WidetronixAward.html (accessed October 14, 2010).
"Michael G. Spencer," Cornell University School of Electrical and Computer Engineering, http://people. ece.cornell.edu/spencer/ (accessed October 14, 2010).

—Carol Brennan

# Michael Strautmanis

## 1969—

## Government official

Strautmanis, Michael, photograph. Alex Wong/Getty Images.

Michael Strautmanis serves as chief of staff to Valerie Jarrett, who is one of President Barack Obama's most trusted advisers. Strautmanis himself is part of a tight-knit circle of friends of Barack and Michelle Obama, a connection that stretches back to a time during the early 1990s, when he and Michelle worked at the same Chicago law firm. In an interview with Mike Dorning and Christi Parsons in the *Chicago Tribune* three months before his historic 2008 election, Obama described himself and Strautmanis as "good, good friends." Obama said, "It predates me being involved in politics or him being involved in politics. I'm older than him so I serve an older-brother role…. I hope he feels I've been there for him, and he's certainly been a very loyal and terrifically helpful colleague."

Strautmanis was born in Chicago in 1969 and spent his first years living on the city's South Side. His mother was a teacher who eventually married a Latvian-American man who worked at the same school. The couple settled in Chicago's North Side and Strautmanis took his stepfather's Latvian surname. He attended St. Ignatius College Preparatory School, which was consistently ranked as one of the top private schools in the city, and initially set his sights on a performing arts career. He appeared in plays with the highly regarded Black Ensemble Theater Company and enrolled at the University of Illinois as a theater major. He eventually switched to advertising and earned his undergraduate degree in 1991.

During his college years, Strautmanis worked as a bike messenger. His favorite delivery stops were at the posh offices of major corporate law firms in the Loop, "these glittering buildings in downtown Chicago, and when you're a kid growing up in Chicago, these are the most important buildings in your life," he told Dorning and Parsons about the iconic skyline landmarks. "I thought, 'This must be the best place to be.'" Shortly before his college graduation, he landed a job as a paralegal at Sidley Austin, one of the major corporate law firms in the United States.

Strautmanis worked for Michelle, a Chicago native who had graduated from Princeton University and then earned her Harvard Law School degree in 1988. At the law firm, Michelle was assigned to mentor Barack, a Harvard Law student who had won one of Sidley Austin's prestigious summer associate slots. The two began dating in earnest after Barack graduated with his law degree from Harvard and moved to Chicago to begin a career as a community organizer and a University of Chicago Law School professor. Strautmanis first met Barack around this time.

As a boss, Michelle quickly intuited Strautmanis's intellectual gifts and encouraged him to enroll in law school. He entered the University of Illinois College of Law. By then Michelle and Barack had married and Strautmanis's former boss had followed her own mentor, Valerie Jarrett, from private practice into public service with a job inside the administration of Richard M. Daley, the mayor of Chicago.

After earning his law degree in 1994, Strautmanis established a private practice, but he eventually abandoned that path. He worked on the 1996 Clinton-Gore campaign, then moved to Washington, DC, in 1998 to take a job with the U.S. Agency for International Development as chief of staff to its general counsel. He left that post to work for an up-and-coming Democrat from Chicago, Rod R. Blagojevich, who was then serving in the U.S. House of Representatives. Straut-

manis was Blagojevich's legislative director between 1999 and 2001 before moving on to a post with the American Association for Justice, a lobbyist group for trial lawyers.

By this point Barack Obama had gained some political experience in the Illinois Senate, and he made a bid for one of the state's two U.S. Senate seats in 2004. Obama won the seat, and he offered Strautmanis a job as chief counsel and deputy chief of staff. He served in that role for three years, working with representatives of major U.S. labor unions and African-American interest groups, before joining the Obama for America presidential campaign as senior counsel. Strautmanis's name, along with that of Jarrett and a few other longtime friends from the Obamas' early Chicago years, was often mentioned as part of the Obama family's close-knit cadre whose personal and professional ties overlapped. Political analysts theorized that this was one of the key reasons that Obama's impressively managed campaign stayed so consistently focused on its message. Both Obama and Jarrett spoke highly of him, and in the 2008 interview with Dorning and Parsons, Strautmanis described himself as Obama's "translator, telling people, 'Yes, he has a different approach. He's serious about change. This is what it means.'"

Obama was elected to the White House in November of 2008. Strautmanis moved onto the official transition team, and four weeks after the historic win President-elect Obama announced that Jarrett would become White House senior adviser and assistant to the president for public liaison and intergovernmental affairs and that Strautmanis would serve as Jarrett's chief of staff. In 2009 the Office of Public Liaison and Intergovernmental Affairs, which reaches out to various interest groups to carry out the administration's political goals, was renamed the Office of Public Engagement and Intergovernmental Affairs. As chief of staff, Strautmanis works closely with Obama, Jarrett, and Christina M. Tchen, another former Chicago attorney who serves as Obama's director of public engagement.

Strautmanis keeps a low profile, but he did tangle once with the Alaska governor and 2008 Republican vice presidential candidate Sarah Palin during the campaign on a hot-button issue. The topic was Obama's proposed strategy to give all Americans full medical coverage. Strautmanis and his wife, Damona, have three children, including a son diagnosed with an autism-spectrum disorder. Palin asserted that her youngest son, born with Down syndrome, would lose coverage under Obama's health care plan, and Strautmanis disagreed with that. He noted that the current Republican administration had trumpeted the idea of a self-sufficient "ownership society," which Strautmanis claimed boiled down to "you are on your own," according to Kristina Chew, who reported on the policy debate for the website Autism Vox. "I felt that as far back as this moment I had a responsibility to advocate for, work for, not only my child, but all of us."

## Sources

### Periodicals

*Chicago Tribune,* August 10, 2008.
*Nation's Cities Weekly,* November 23, 2009, p. 5.
*New York Times Magazine,* August 10, 2008.

### Online

Chew, Kristina, "A Statement from Mike Strautmanis, Obama's Chief Counsel," Autism Vox, September 3, 2008, http://blisstree.com/live/a-statement-from-mike-strautmanis-obamas-chieft-counsel/?utm_source=blisstree&utm_medium=web&utm_campaign=b5hubs_migration (accessed October 15, 2010).
"Mike Strautmanis," WhoRunsGov.com, August 25, 2010, http://www.whorunsgov.com/Profiles/Mike_Strautmanis (accessed October 15, 2010).

—Carol Brennan

# Jack Tatum

## 1948–2010

### Professional football player

Tatum, Jack, photograph. Michael Zagaris/Getty Images.

During the 1970s, free safety Jack Tatum was among the NFL's most feared defensive players. Remembered as "the Assassin" for his punishing hits, Tatum was an intimidating presence in the Oakland Raiders backfield, anchoring a stout defense that helped the team win a Super Bowl title in 1977. While Tatum earned widespread renown as a player throughout his career, he arguably remains best known for his devastating collision with New England Patriots wide receiver Darryl Stingley in a 1978 exhibition game. The blow broke two vertebrae in Stingley's spine and left the wide receiver paralyzed from the neck down. Tatum was vilified in the press for years after the incident, in part because he adamantly refused to apologize for his role in Stingley's injury. In spite of his notoriety, Tatum was surprisingly quiet off the field, and his teammates and close friends consistently attested to the easygoing, gentle nature of his character.

Tatum was born in Cherryville, North Carolina, in 1948, and raised in Passaic, New Jersey. He began his football career at Eastside High School and later transferred to Passaic High School, where he played both fullback and linebacker. Although he excelled on the offensive side of the ball, it was as a defender that he attracted the most attention, developing a reputation throughout the state for his tackling skills and ferocious hits. Over the course of three years at Passaic, Tatum's team went 24–2–1, winning the New Jersey state championship in 1964. In his senior year, Tatum amassed 187 tackles as a linebacker, while also rushing for 1,421 yards on offense. His accomplishments earned him All-American honors in 1966.

After his final season at Passaic, Tatum was widely recruited by colleges. He eventually received a scholarship to attend Ohio State University, where he played under celebrated Buckeyes coach Woody Hayes. Although Tatum was highly touted for both his offensive and defensive abilities, the coaching staff soon elected to have him play exclusively on defense. Tatum started on the varsity squad all three years at Ohio State and quickly emerged as one of the best defensive players in the nation. He played a key role in Ohio State's national championship victory in 1968, was named first-team All-Big Ten three consecutive years, and was a two-time All-American.

## At a Glance . . .

**B**orn John David Tatum on November 18, 1948, in Cherryville, NC; died July 27, 2010, in Oakland, CA; son of Lewis (a steel welder) and Annie Mae (a domestic) Tatum; married Denise; children: Dorian, Samuel, Jestynn. *Education:* Attended Ohio State University, 1968–71.

**Career:** Oakland Raiders, free safety, 1971–79; Houston Oilers, free safety, 1980.

**Memberships:** Jack Tatum Fund for Youthful Diabetes, founder.

**Awards:** Named first-team All-Big Ten, 1968–70; named All-American, 1969 and 1970; Pro Bowl selection, 1973–75; named first-team All-Conference, Pro Football Weekly, 1973 and 1975; named second-team All-NFL, Associated Press, 1974; named first-team All-Conference, UPI, 1974, 1975, and 1977; named first-team All-Conference, Sporting News, 1975, 1976, and 1977; five-time All Pro selection.

Upon leaving Ohio State, Tatum joined the Oakland Raiders as the nineteenth pick of the 1971 NFL draft. Tatum made an indelible impression in his very first professional game, when he knocked two Baltimore Colts players out of the game with his hard-hitting tackles. Tatum quickly became the anchor of the Oakland defense during the 1970s, earning notoriety throughout the league for his aggressiveness and ruthless hits. In 1977 Tatum helped lead the Raiders to their first Super Bowl victory, a 32–14 triumph over the Minnesota Vikings. Tatum's reputation soon became severely tarnished, however, after his infamous hit on Darryl Stingley. In the aftermath of the incident, Tatum became a symbol of excessive violence in professional football. His notoriety spread even further with the publication of his 1980 memoir, *They Call Me Assassin,* a work co-authored with Bill Kushner. In the book, Tatum defended his aggressive playing style and described some of his injury-inflicting hits. At one point in the narrative, he boasts, "I like to believe that my best hits border on felonious assault." Nowhere in the work does Tatum express any remorse for his hit on Stingley.

Tatum played a total of nine seasons for the Raiders. In 1980 he joined the Houston Oilers, where he played as a backup. He finished his career with thirty-seven interceptions, played in three Pro Bowls, and was named All-Pro five times. Toward the end of his playing years, Tatum married his long-time girlfriend, Denise;

the couple would eventually have two sons and a daughter. In 1989 Tatum and Kushner teamed up to author a new book, *They Still Call Me Assassin: Here We Go Again.* In 1996 the duo published a new book, *Final Confessions of NFL Assassin Jack Tatum.* While promoting the work, Tatum invited Darryl Stingley, the man he had paralyzed nearly two decades earlier, to join him for a public appearance. Stingley refused. "If Tatum couldn't even once come to see me in 18 years … couldn't lift a phone once in those 18 years and call me, what could he want now?" Stingley told the *Philadelphia Inquirer.*

In 1997 Tatum stoked further controversy when he petitioned the NFL for disability payments of more than $150,000 a year as compensation for the psychological damage he had suffered in the aftermath of the Stingley incident. The request outraged both NFL executives and the Players Association and was ultimately denied. By this time, Tatum was struggling with numerous health problems, including diabetes. In 2003 he contracted a staph infection in his right leg; the lower portion of the leg was eventually amputated. A short time later, Tatum founded the Jack Tatum Fund for Youthful Diabetes, dedicated to raising money for research into the disease.

During the last decade of his life, Tatum garnered a wave of renewed recognition for his accomplishments on the football field. In 2001 Ohio State football coach Jim Tressel established the Jack Tatum Hit of the Week Award, an acknowledgment given to the defensive player who delivered the most impressive collision in the team's weekly game. In 2008 Tatum's uniform number was retired by his high school alma mater in Passaic; he was only the third player in the school's history to receive that honor. For much of this period, Tatum was also a member of the NFL's Uniform Code Enforcement Team—or "fashion police"—a group dedicated to ensuring that players adhered to the league's policies concerning appropriate dress.

Jack Tatum died of a heart attack on July 27, 2010. In a statement issued shortly after his death, Ohio State football coach Jim Tressel declared, "We have lost one of our greatest Buckeyes." As Angela Woodall reported in the *Alameda Times-Star,* Tatum was buried wearing an Oakland Raiders neckband beneath his dark suit jacket.

## Selected works

(With Bill Kushner) *They Call Me Assassin,* Everest House, 1980.

(With Bill Kushner) *They Still Call Me Assassin: Here We Go Again,* Regal Productions & Pub., 1989.

(With Bill Kushner) *Final Confessions of NFL Assassin Jack Tatum,* Quality Sports, 1996.

# Sources

## Periodicals

*Alameda Times-Star,* August 4, 2010.
*Daily News* (New York), July 28, 2010, p. 67.
*Los Angeles Times,* July 28, 2010, p. AA1.
*National Post* (Canada), July 28, 2010, p. S1.
*New York Times,* January 24, 1997, p. B12; July 28, 2010, p. 21.
*Philadelphia Inquirer,* October 19, 1996, p. C5.
*The Record* (Hackensack, NJ), November 28, 2008, p. S1.

## Online

Carrillo, David, "Jack Tatum #32: The Man, the Legend, the 'Assassin,'" Raiderdrive.com, http://www.raiderdrive.com/jack_tatum_the_legend.htm (accessed October 27, 2010).

De Vries, Jack, "Jack Tatum Comes Home," Clifton Merchant Magazine, November 24, 2008, http://cliftonmerchantmagazine.blogspot.com/2008/11/jack-tatum-comes-home.html (accessed October 27, 2010).

"Jack Tatum," Pro-Football-Reference.com, http://www.pro-football-reference.com/players/T/TatuJa00.htm (accessed October 27, 2010).

—Stephen Meyer

# Arthur Walker II

## 1936–2001

### Physicist, professor

Arthur Walker II, a nationally recognized expert on astrophysics, was a Stanford University professor of applied physics from 1974 until his death in 2001. His field of expertise was extreme ultraviolet astronomy, and his innovative research led to the first solar telescopes being deployed in space in 1987. The first detailed images of the solar corona, the sun's outermost atmosphere, were captured by Walker's x-ray and thin film telescopes and were featured on the cover of the September 30, 1988, issue of *Science* magazine. He is also credited with playing a vital role in the advancement of traditionally underrepresented groups in the sciences and fighting against racial and gender discrimination at Stanford.

Walker was the only child born to Cuthbert and Hilda Walker in Cleveland, Ohio, in 1936. His paternal and maternal families considered education to be the key to achieving success. His paternal grandfather, James Henry, was a schoolmaster in Barbados, and his wife, Millicent, encouraged their eight children to excel in school. During the early 1900s Cuthbert immigrated to New York to study at the City College of New York and work for Eerie Railroad. When Eerie Railroad moved its headquarters to Cleveland during the 1930s, Cuthbert followed the company, completed his law degree at John Marshall Law School, and met his future wife, Hilda. Hilda was the daughter of Ormand Forte, who also emigrated from Barbados to the United States with his wife, Ida, to study at Macalester College in St. Paul, Minnesota, and work for Hanna Steel in Cleveland, Ohio.

Recognizing their son's passion for science, Walker's

parents encouraged him to take the entrance exam for the Bronx High School of Science, which he passed. While a student at the prestigious high school, one of Walker's teachers tried to discourage him from pursuing a career in the sciences, suggesting that the field in the United States was fairly closed to blacks. Hilda would have none of it. "She paid a visit to the school and told [the teacher] in no uncertain terms that her son would study whatever he wishes," Walker's wife, Victoria, said to James Glanz in the *New York Times*. After high school Walker enrolled at the Case Institute of Technology in Cleveland, where he earned his bachelor of science degree in physics with honors in 1957. He completed his master's degree in 1958 and his doctorate in astrophysics in 1962 from the University of Illinois. His dissertation was on the use of radiation to produce pi mesons, the particles that bind protons and neutrons together in the atomic nucleus. For his research, Walker used powerful x-rays that broke down helium to produce the particles, and his interests soon turned to x-rays and ultraviolet radiation from the sun.

From 1962 to 1965 Walker served as a first lieutenant in the U.S. Air Force and was assigned to the Air Force Weapons Laboratory, where he developed instrumentation for the rocket launch of satellites to measure radiation in the Earth's magnetic field. This work set Walker firmly on the path of space-based research, and when he left the service in 1965 he joined the Aerospace Corporation's Space Physics Laboratory. His experiments at the laboratory focused on solar physics and upper atmospheric physics. In collaboration with

## At a Glance . . .

**B**orn Arthur Bertram Cuthbert Walker II on August 24, 1936, in Cleveland, OH; died on April 29, 2001, in Stanford, CA; son of Cuthbert Walker (a lawyer) and Hilda (Forte) Walker (a social worker and Sunday school teacher); married Victoria; children: Heather, stepsons Nigel, Eric. *Military service:* U.S. Air Force, 1962–65. *Education:* Case Institute of Technology, BS, physics, 1957; University of Illinois, MS, 1958; University of Illinois, PhD, astrophysics, 1962.

**Career:** Aerospace Corporation, Space Physics Laboratory, technical staff member, 1965–73, Space Astronomy Program, director, 1971–73; Stanford University, associate professor of applied physics, 1974–82, professor of applied physics, 1982–2001.

**Memberships:** Center for Space Science and Astrophysics; Hansen Experimental Physics Laboratory; Observatories Council of the Association of Universities for Research in Astronomy's Board of Directors; Sigma Xi; Tau Beta Pi Engineering Honor Society.

**Awards:** Distinguished Public Service Medal, National Aeronautics and Space Administration, 2000.

H. R. Rugge, Walker developed the first satellite borne x-ray spectrometer to study the x-ray spectrum of the solar corona. He also served as director of the Astronomy Program from 1971 to 1973, when he left to teach at Stanford University.

Walker was attracted to Stanford due to its reputation for having one of the most distinguished African-American faculties of any major research university. He was aware that the number of minorities with doctorates in the sciences nationwide was seriously lacking; however, he believed that qualifications were not the only factor limiting diversity within the sciences. As a result, throughout his tenure at Stanford he fought to guarantee that qualified minority candidates at both the student and faculty levels were seriously considered. He mentored many students who majored in physics and applied physics and played a significant role in producing minorities and women with doctorates in physics between 1978 and 1988. Many of Walker's students went on to hold prominent positions in a variety of fields, such as Sally Ride, who became the first American woman in space when she flew aboard the space

shuttle *Challenger* in 1983. "He instilled confidence, and made me believe that I could accomplish what I set out to accomplish," Ride said to Glanz.

During his career Walker served on several national committees, including the National Academy of Science's Space Studies Board, the National Science Foundation's (NSF) Astronomy Advisory Committee, and NASA's Astrophysics Council and the Advanced Solar Observatory Science Working Group. He served on the Observatories Council of the Association of Universities for Research in Astronomy's Board of Directors and on the Astronomy Subcommittee of the NSF Division of Mathematical and Physical Sciences. He also presided over the National Conference of Black Physics Students and collaborated with a team of scientists in the development of the Transition Edge Sensor, an x-ray microcalorimeter detector for astronomical imaging.

In September of 2000 Stanford University held a celebration to honor Walker's achievements in education and innovative research. During the event NASA officials awarded Walker the Distinguished Public Service Medal—the highest honor for nongovernmental individuals. At the reception, it was acknowledged that Walker's introductory course on Observational and Laboratory Astronomy inspired dozens of students to pursue a career in physics, who might otherwise have chosen a different path. Following his death in April of 2001, the Arthur B. C. Walker II Memorial Scholarship Fund was established. According to Stanford University's Department of Physics, the fund was established "for the promotion of greater inclusion of ethnic minorities and women in the Sciences."

## Sources

### Periodicals

*New York Times,* May 9, 2001.

### Online

"Arthur BC Walker II, Professor, Physics," Stanford University School of Humanities and Sciences, Department of Physics, 2010, http://www.stanford.edu/dept/physics/people/faculty/walker_ii_arthur.html (accessed October 19, 2010).

"Arthur Bertram Cuthbert Walker, Jr.," Physicists of the African Diaspora, 2008, http://www.math.buffalo.edu/mad/physics/walker_arthurbc.html (accessed October 19, 2010).

"Arthur Walker II, Professor," SFGate.com, May 6, 2001, http://articles.sfgate.com/2001-05-06/news/17599434_1_arthur-walker-ii-magnetic-field-cleveland-professor-walker (accessed October 19, 2010).

—Marie O'Sullivan

# James E. West

## 1931—

### Acoustical engineer, inventor, educator

It is difficult to imagine how today's advanced communications networks would function without the work of James E. West. One of the world's leading acoustical engineers, he is renowned above all for co-developing the electret microphone, a small, low-cost device now found in the vast majority of telephones and voice recorders. A longtime employee of Bell Labs in New Jersey, he is also known for his strong support of programs designed to facilitate minority participation in engineering and the sciences.

James Edward West, known as Jim to friends and family, was born February 10, 1931, in a rural area of Prince Edward County, Virginia. One of several children born to Samuel and Matilda West, he was fascinated by technology from a very early age. "If I had a screwdriver and a pair of pliers, anything that could be opened was in danger," he once recalled, according to "Physicists of the African Diaspora," a Web site maintained at the University of Buffalo (UB). "I had this need to know what was inside." A pivotal moment in West's training came when he was about eight, when he received a strong electric shock from a radio he had repaired. Far from discouraging further experiments, the episode fueled his curiosity, particularly about electricity.

Though West's parents encouraged his interest in engineering and science for many years, they began to have misgivings when he approached college, because they knew that opportunities for African Americans in those fields were almost nonexistent. They therefore urged him to go into medicine, where more jobs were available. He agreed, enrolling in Virginia's Hampton Institute (later Hampton University) as a premedical student. His plans changed, however, when he was drafted by the U.S. Army for wartime service in Korea, where he saw combat and received a Purple Heart. By the time he returned home, he had decided that it would be a mistake to ignore the subjects he loved, however difficult the employment situation might prove. He therefore transferred to Philadelphia's Temple University, where he majored in physics.

Temple proved a wise choice for West, for it was not far from Bell Labs (BL), then one of the few research institutions in the country willing to hire African Americans. Offered an undergraduate internship there in the mid-1950s, he was hired full time upon completion of his undergraduate degree in 1957. As an joint venture between the Western Electric Company, a leading manufacturer of telephone equipment, and AT&T, BL focused much of its attention on the study of acoustics, and it was to that field that West was assigned. By the early 1960s, he had joined colleague Gerhard M. Sessler on a particularly challenging problem. While existing microphones worked fairly well, they were heavy, expensive, and powered by batteries. West and Sessler's goal was nothing less than the creation of a thoroughly new microphone design, one that could be replicated easily and cheaply. In 1962 they succeeded.

Though the new microphone differed from the older "condenser" models in a number of ways, the most important innovation was the use of electret, a material that can hold a permanent electric charge, thereby

## At a Glance . . .

**B**orn James Edward West on February 10, 1931, in Prince Edward County, VA; son of Samuel West (a porter and entrepreneur) and Matilda West (a schoolteacher); married Marlene; children: four. *Military service:* U.S. Army, early 1950s. *Education:* Temple University, BA, physics, 1957.

**Career:** Bell Labs, acoustical engineer, 1957–2001; Johns Hopkins University, research professor, 2002—.

**Memberships:** Acoustical Society of America, past president.

**Awards:** Inventor of the Year, New Jersey Inventors Hall of Fame, 1995; National Academy of Engineering, 1998; National Inventors Hall of Fame, 1999; Gold Medal Award, Acoustical Society of America, 2006.

**Addresses:** *Office*—Department of Electrical and Computer Engineering, Johns Hopkins University, 3400 N. Charles Street, Baltimore, MD 21218.

Wideman, John Edgar, photograph. ULF Andersen/Getty Images.

avoiding the need for batteries. By combining the electret with a very thin teflon film, West and Sessler were able to create a device that converted the air-pressure fluctuations that constitute sound into transmissible electrical impulses. Once patent protection was obtained (1964), Bell Labs licensed the invention, known technically as an "electroacoustic transducer," for wide-scale use. The Acoustical Society of America (ASA) estimated in 2006 that annual production exceeded two billion units, making it one of the most common electrical devices in the world.

Though the microphone was by far the most prominent of West's inventions at BL, it was only one of the more than one hundred patents he earned there. He also authored or co-authored more than two hundred scientific papers and was a driving force behind the establishment of the AT&T Corporate Research Fellowship Program (CRFP), one of the oldest and largest minority-recruitment initiatives in the research community. As a co-founder of CRFP, West had a hand in facilitating the careers of hundreds of minority scientists and engineers. The Web site BlackInventor.com termed his efforts in this area "perhaps his most significant contributions" to science.

After more than forty years of service, West left BL in 2001. He declined to retire, however, choosing instead to enter the world of academia. In 2002 he joined the faculty of Johns Hopkins University (JHU) in Baltimore, Maryland. Though he had offers from several other institutions, he chose JHU, in part, because it encouraged the kind of cross-disciplinary collaboration he had found useful in his earlier post. "I discovered," he told Phil Sneiderman Homewood of the *JHU Gazette* in 2003, "that Johns Hopkins was a lot like Bell Labs, where the doors were always open and we were free to collaborate with researchers in other disciplines. I like the fact that I won't be locked into one small niche here."

As a research professor in JHU's department of electrical and computer engineering, West was involved in a variety of research projects, including efforts to reduce ambient noise at a local hospital and to improve sound transmission in the fast-growing field of teleconferencing. As of 2010, his most prominent project was his research into the electrical charges that arise when certain materials are subjected to mechanical pressure. Though the phenomenon, called piezoelectricity, has been studied for several centuries, the increasingly rapid development of composite materials in the twenty-first century promised to revolutionize its use in industry. Much of West's work focused on altering those composites to enhance their piezoelectric attributes.

An enthusiastic mentor to students and younger colleagues, West won a host of awards over the years, including induction into the National Academy of Engineering in 1998 and the National Inventors Hall of Fame in 1999. He was also the recipient of the ASA's 2006 Gold Medal Award. In the citation that accompanied that honor, he was called "a sterling colleague, collaborator, friend, and mentor," as well as "an extraordinary human being."

## Sources

### Periodicals

*JHU Gazette,* January 13, 2003.

### Online

Busch-Vishniac, Ilene J., Gary W. Elko, and Gerhard M. Sessler, "Gold Medal Award – 2006: James E. West," Acoustical Society of America, 2006, http://asa.aip.org/encomia/gold/west.html (accessed August 15, 2010).
"James West," BlackInventor.com, http://www.blackinventor.com/pages/jameswest.html (accessed August 15, 2010).
"Physicists of the African Diaspora: James E. West," University of Buffalo, http://www.math.buffalo.edu/mad/physics/west_jamese.html (accessed August 15, 2010).

—R. Anthony Kugler

# John Edgar Wideman

## 1941—

## Author, educator

Wideman, John Edgar, photograph. Ulf Andersen/Getty Images.

John Edgar Wideman is one of the leading chroniclers of life in urban black America. An author who intertwines ghetto experiences with experimental fiction techniques and personal history with current and historical events, Wideman is the only artist who has won the prestigious PEN/Faulkner Award for literature twice. His provocative works depict the widening chasm between the urban poor and the largely white power structure in the United States, as well as the deep personal conflicts engendered in African Americans who succeed in penetrating that power structure. *Washington Post Book World* reviewer Jonathan Yardley noted that Wideman makes clear in his books that "moving out of the ghetto into the white world is a process that requires excruciating compromises, sacrifices and denials, that leaves the person who makes the journey truly at home in neither the world he has entered nor the world he has left."

Wideman is a prolific writer who has been publishing books since he was twenty-six. His body of work includes novels, short story collections, and nonfiction. Wideman is also a contributor of articles, essays, book reviews, and poetry to several periodicals, including

*American Poetry Review, Negro Digest, Black American Literature Forum,* the *New Yorker, Vogue, Esquire, Emerge,* the *New York Times Magazine, Black World, American Scholar, Gentleman's Quarterly,* the *New York Times Book Review, North American Review,* and the *Washington Post Book World.*

Much of his fiction explores events and personalities from the Homewood section of Pittsburgh, the all-black neighborhood in which he grew up. His stories reveal several generations of Homewood residents, including those who have left the area in triumph or tragedy. Indeed, suggests Wideman, the "triumph" of leaving home is hollow unless one retains the spirit and the culture of the community left behind. For Wideman, an Oxford-trained scholar, that process of absorbing a community and relating its history artistically has provided grist for complex explorations of family relationships, isolation, and the search for self.

Wideman told the *Washington Post*: "My novels and the essays attempt to exploit the inherent tension between what is fictional and what is factual, and to illuminate how unsteady and unpredictable the relation-

## At a Glance . . .

**B**orn John Edgar Wideman on June 14, 1941, in Washington, DC; son of Edgar and Bette Wideman; married Judith Ann Goldman, 1965; children: Daniel Jerome, Jacob Edgar, Jamila Ann. *Education:* University of Pennsylvania, BA, 1963; New College, Oxford University, BPhil, 1966.

**Career:** Howard University, Washington, DC, teacher of American literature, summer, 1965; University of Pennsylvania, Philadelphia, PA, 1966–74, began as instructor, professor of English, 1974, director of Afro-American studies program, 1971–73; University of Wyoming, Laramie, WY, professor of English, 1974–86; University of Massachusetts—Amherst, Amherst, MA, professor of English, beginning 1986, named distinguished professor, 2001; Brown University, Asa Messer professor and professor of Africana Studies and English, 2002—. Made U.S. Department of State lecture tour of Europe and the Near East, 1976; Phi Beta Kappa lecturer, 1976; visiting writer and lecturer at numerous colleges and universities; has also served as administrator/teacher in a curriculum planning, teacher-training institute sponsored by National Defense Education Act.

**Memberships:** Association of American Rhodes Scholars (member of board of directors and of state and national selection committees); American Studies Association (council, 1980–81); Modern Language Association, American Academy of Arts and Sciences, Phi Beta Kappa.

**Awards:** Rhodes Scholar, Oxford University, 1963; Kent fellow, University of Iowa, 1966; Young Humanist fellow, 1975; National Book Award nomination, 1984, for *Brothers and Keepers*; PEN/Faulkner awards, 1984, for *Sent for You Yesterday*, and 1991, for *Philadelphia Fire*; Du Sable Museum Prize, 1985; John Dos Passos Prize, 1986; National Magazine Editors Prize, 1987; honorary degree from University of Pennsylvania, 1986; Lannan Literary fellowship, 1991; American Book Award, Before Columbus Foundation, 1991, for *Philadelphia Fire*; MacArthur fellow, MacArthur Foundation, 1993; James Fenimore Cooper Prize, 1996, for *The Cattle Killing*; Rea Prize, Dungannon Foundation, 1998; *Readers' Digest/ Lila Wallace* grant, 1999; O. Henry Award, 2000; New England Book Award, New England Booksellers Association, 2001, for *Hoop Roots: Basketball, Race, and Love*; Nonfiction Honor Book, Black Caucus Award, American Library Association, 2002, for *Hoop Roots: Basketball, Race, and Love*; grant, National Endowment Humanities; Chancellor's Medal, University of Massachusetts; African American fiction award, Ballantine Books, 2010.

**Addresses:** *Office*—Department of Africana Studies, Brown University, Box 1904, 155 Angell St., Providence, RI 02912.

ship is. I'm trying to remind people of what Ralph Ellison said about the uncertainties that lie within your certainties." This tension between fiction and fact is a hallmark of Wideman's writing. It has helped him to address his own personal tragedies, including the life-term prison sentences of his son and his brother. In interviews the author says little about his brother, Robby, who is serving time in Pennsylvania as an accessory to murder, or about his son Jacob, convicted in 1988 in the stabbing death of another teenager. The dual tragedies loom large in Wideman's art, however, as he seeks to understand life's bitter twists of fate. "I'm not putting up my life as material to explain anything to anyone," the author told the *Washington Post.* "I'll put it this way. It's a formulation. My life is a closed book. My fiction is an open book. They may seem like the same book—but I know the difference."

Wideman, the oldest of five children, was born in Washington, DC, in 1941. Before his first birthday, his family moved to Pittsburgh, where his great-great-great grandmother, a fugitive slave, had settled in the mid-nineteenth century. Wideman's father, Edgar, worked hard at several jobs simultaneously but was unable to provide economic security for the growing family. As Chip Brown noted in *Esquire* magazine, "Edgar earned a living as a paperhanger, a welder, a waiter in the cafeteria at Kauffman's department store; for all his doubling up on jobs, he was never able to break the barriers of class and race and economics, and his ambition to be a dentist fell by the wayside." His own perilous fortunes notwithstanding, Edgar Wideman encouraged his children to pursue excellence in everything they did. John became an honor student and an athlete, with dreams of playing professional basketball.

John Wideman's youth was spent in the Homewood district of Pittsburgh, a neighborhood that included many members of his extended family. From a young age he delivered newspapers on upper class Negley Avenue, a "lily white" region where he felt like an "intruder," according to a Wideman essay in the *New York Times Book Review.* If he was an intruder, he was determined to make his presence known. During his high school years, his family moved to a suburb called Shadyside so he could attend highly ranked Peabody High School. There he earned top grades and became class president and captain of the basketball team. He graduated first in his class in 1959.

"When my family moved to Shadyside so I could attend 'better' schools and we were one of only three or four black families in the neighborhood, I learned to laugh with the white guys when we hid in a stairwell outside Liberty School gym and passed around a 'nigarette,'" Wideman recalled in the *New York Times Book Review.* "I hated it when a buddy took a greedy, wet puff, 'nigger-lipping' a butt before he passed it on to me. Speaking out, identifying myself with the group being slurred by these expressions, was impossible. I had neither the words nor the heart. I talked the talk and walked the walk of the rest of my companions."

## Entered the University of Pennsylvania

Wideman attended the University of Pennsylvania on scholarship from 1959 until 1963. One of only six black students at the Ivy League college, he became well known for his basketball skill as well as his exposition talents. *Washington Post* correspondent Paul Hendrickson pointed out that, as a Penn basketball star, Wideman "made All-Ivy, he made Big Five Basketball Hall of Fame. He was among the last of the great 6-foot-2 forwards, before forwards became 7-footers—a leaper who could mix it up underneath and take rebounds off players three and four inches bigger than he was." Wideman excelled off-court as well, winning the university's creative writing prize and being elected to Phi Beta Kappa.

During his senior year at Penn, Wideman applied for and won a Rhodes Scholarship to Oxford University. He was the first African American in more than a half-century to earn the important academic award. National recognition came from *Look* magazine, where a profile of Wideman ran in 1963. A professor quoted in the article warned that Wideman would have to be "careful," that now he was a "symbol." Many times over the ensuing years, John Edgar Wideman would ask himself just what it was he symbolized.

In his 1984 memoir *Brothers and Keepers,* Wideman wrote of his student days: "Just two choices as far as I could tell: either/or. Rich or poor. White or black. Win or lose. I figured which side I wanted to be on when the Saints came marching in…. To succeed in the white man's world you must become like the man and the man sure didn't claim no bunch of nigger relatives in Pittsburgh." As his family's circumstances forced them back into Homewood, Wideman persevered at Oxford. He studied English literature and philosophy and wrote a thesis on eighteenth-century narrative techniques. In 1966 he returned to the United States for a year's fellowship study at the Iowa Writers' Workshop, the nation's best-known proving ground for would-be novelists. He also married Judith Goldman, a fellow Penn graduate.

While still in his twenties Wideman began publishing fiction. His first novel, *A Glance Away,* appeared in 1967, followed by *Hurry Home* in 1970 and *The Lynchers* in 1973. All three books deal with black protagonists who are confused and controlled by their pasts, and who are, at the very least, highly ambivalent about white society. As early as *Hurry Home* Wideman began to explore the importance of cultural history to self-awareness and the role that family ties and friendships serve in promoting peace of mind.

Throughout the period when his first three novels appeared, Wideman was teaching literature at the University of Pennsylvania. There he was asked to present a course on black writing, and he delved deeply into black literature for the first time. The experience was enlightening—a catalyst to his own work—and eventually the course became the nucleus of the university's Afro-American studies program, which Wideman chaired in 1972 and 1973. Another catalyst to Wideman's work was the death of his grandmother, back in Homewood, in 1973. After the funeral, Wideman and his family reminisced about the history of the family in Homewood, going back many generations, almost to the founding of the neighborhood. From that conversation and others remembered from his childhood, Wideman fashioned his best-known work to date.

## Wrote the Homewood Trilogy

Wideman wrote most of his books and stories about Homewood while living in the prairie town of Laramie, Wyoming. He accepted a teaching position at the university there in late 1974. "It was hard to admit to myself that I'd just begun learning how to write," he commented in the *Atlanta Constitution.* "I realized that the core of the language and culture that nurtured me had hardly been touched by my writing." A creative explosion occurred while he was in Laramie, and by the mid-1980s Wideman had released *Damballah, Hiding Place,* and *Sent for You Yesterday,* a series of interrelated stories and novels now known as the "Homewood Trilogy." Ranging from the nineteenth century to the present, the Homewood Trilogy explores the various lives of descendants of Sybela Owens, a slave who ran North to Pittsburgh with her white husband.

Enthusiastic reviews followed the publication of each of the Homewood Trilogy installments. "Mr. Wideman has used a narrative laced with myth, superstition and dream sequences to create an elaborate poetic portrait of the lives of ordinary black people," wrote Mel Watkins in the *New York Times Book Review.* "He has written tales that can stand on their own, but that assume much greater impact collectively. The individual 'parts,' or stories, as disparate as they may initially seem, form a vivid and coherent montage of black life over a period of five generations…. These books once again demonstrate that John Wideman is one of America's premier writers of fiction." In the *American Book Review,* Wilfred D. Samuels concluded: "By going home to Homewood, Wideman has found a voice for his work and consequently a means of celebrating Afro-American culture and further validating the Afro-American experience in literature."

*Sent for You Yesterday,* the third part of the Homewood Trilogy, was awarded the PEN/Faulkner fiction prize in 1984. The work treats the themes of creativity, imagination, and cultural bonds as means to transcend despair and socially sanctioned economic discrimination.

The novel *Hiding Place* deals with a young boy on the

run from a petty robbery turned deadly. The situation is very similar to the circumstances surrounding the incarceration of Robby Wideman. Robby, the author's younger brother, was sentenced in 1976 to life in prison for his part in a larceny/murder case. Wideman sought to understand his brother's plight, publishing *Brothers and Keepers,* in 1984. The book attempts to address the difficult questions of "success" and "failure" on white society's terms as well as the sense of guilt Wideman felt about his brother's fate. Nominated for the National Book Critics' Circle Award, *Brothers and Keepers* brought Wideman national acclaim. He was profiled on *60 Minutes* and became a sought-after essayist and commentator on the particular dilemmas faced by black artists.

Tragedy struck again in 1986. Wideman's second son, Jacob, fatally stabbed a fellow camper during an outing in Arizona. Both boys were sixteen. Facing the death penalty, Jacob Wideman agreed to plead guilty and was sentenced instead to life in prison. John Wideman has steadfastly refused to comment on the case in interviews. "I don't like to talk about it," he said. "On the advice of lawyers, I don't talk about it. I've had all kinds of unpleasant experiences because, of course, the journalists smell the blood and feel it is their responsibility to go after it.... I don't talk about it." Not surprisingly, however, the theme of an incarcerated or missing son has permeated Wideman's fiction since the tragic events in 1986.

## Won His Second PEN/Faulkner Award

Wideman won his second PEN/Faulkner Award for the controversial novel *Philadelphia Fire,* an angry extrapolation on the 1985 bombing of a black religious cult's Philadelphia headquarters. The actual bombing, ordered by W. Wilson Goode, then mayor of Philadelphia, killed a dozen people and incinerated several blocks of low-income housing. The incident occurred on Osage Avenue, where Wideman had lived while teaching at Penn. The author told the *Washington Post* that he wanted to "pry the event loose from that collective amnesia that's settled on it.... I want people to re-imagine it, rethink this goddam fire." Wideman's imaginative re-telling of the fire includes direct references to Jacob in prison and an oblique, unfulfilled search for a child seen running from the blaze. A *Washington Post* reviewer called the book "199 pages of conflagration, a lyric and confusing and riveting and ragged work of fiction that does and does not concern the 1985 ... disaster, in which a bomb from a state police helicopter was dropped on a back-to-nature cult." In the *Bloomsbury Review,* Mark Hummel concluded of *Philadelphia Fire*: "Despite the tough questions and the deep-rooted pain, the novel is about survival. While hope is distant, Wideman asks us to hold on. And while his own words seem—to him—heavy, even cumbersome, all he has left, they bring meaning to events apparently beyond meaning."

While a professor of literature and creative writing at the University of Massachusetts at Amherst, Wideman at mid-life wrestled with more dilemmas—artistic, personal, and social—than most people encounter in a lifetime. In *Fatheralong: A Meditation on Fathers and Sons, Race and Society,* Wideman explored the complex dynamics in the father-son relationship, interwoven with memories of his strained relationship with his own father and his troubles with his son. Hendrickson wrote: "You keep wondering how he can even function in this unspoken, surreal, Kafka walking dream, let alone get the garbage out on Tuesdays and compose beautiful sentences."

Many of Wideman's pieces in the 1990s offered a pessimistic view of race relations and a warning that the widening gap between white society and the minority underclass may result in serious social disruption. In an interview with the *Washington Post,* the author said he hoped to wage "a little war to beat back the direction the culture is going." His novel, *The Cattle Killing,* published in 1996, interwove his childhood in Philadelphia, the plight of urban blacks in the late eighteenth century, and a South African Xhosa tribe. Critics found that the novel lacked coherency but still praised Wideman's lyrical storytelling style. In 1998 came *Two Cities,* the story of Kassima, a woman grieving the loss of two sons to gang-related crimes, and her struggle to find peace and happiness in Philadelphia and Pittsburgh. Concerning his fiction writing, Wideman concluded in the *New York Times Book Review*: "When I write I want to show how simple acts, simple words can be transformed to release their spiritual force. This is less a conscious esthetic to be argued or analyzed than a determination to draw from the unique voices of Homewood's people the means for documenting the reality of their attitudes and emotions. I want to trace the comings and goings of my people on the invisible plane of existence where so much of the substance of black life resides."

## Moved to Brown University

In 2001 Wideman served as editor of a compilation of inspirational stories from well-known and lesser-known authors. *My Soul Has Grown Deep: Classics of Early African-American Literature* featured twelve pieces offering messages of hope from eighteenth- and nineteenth-century writers, including Phyllis Wheatley, Sojourner Truth, W. E. B Dubois, and Booker T. Washington. In his memoir, *Hoop Roots: Basketball, Race, and Love,* Wideman used one of his first loves, basketball, as a backdrop to study race relations, family tensions, and black American culture during his lifetime.

Wideman moved to Brown University in 2002 to assume the position of Asa Messer professor and professor of Africana Studies and English. In a ten-story collection published in 2005, *God's Gym,* Wideman once again explored the theme of basketball, as well as black icons, death, and suicide. One story dealt with a young man sentenced to life in prison and brought to the surface the pain the author has carried with him since his own son's incarceration in 1988. "The full range of Wideman's talents are on display here," said a *Publishers Weekly* contributor.

Wideman's first novel in ten years, *Fanon,* published in 2008, traced the life of Franz Fanon, philosopher, psychiatrist, political activist, and author of *The Wretched of the Earth.* Reviews of this ambitious blend of fiction, biography, and memoir were mixed, with *Booklist*'s Vanessa Bush writing that Wideman's book was "filled with poetic imagery and a thrilling love of language," while Jonathan Liu of the *New York Observer* deemed the work "showoffy."

An invitation by *O Magazine* to contribute a 500-word story for a microfiction section started Wideman thinking about digital publishing. Citing changes in the publishing business and a desire to have more control over the publishing process, in 2010 Wideman made the decision to self-publish. Influenced by his son, Daniel, a writer who also worked for the print-on-demand service Lulu.com, Wideman released was *Briefs, Stories for the Palm of the Mind,* which the author described as a collection of "microstories" in which the fictional storytellers are eavesdroppers and diarists. Reprints of *Hurry Home* and *The Lynchers* soon followed. Wideman wrote in *Publishers Weekly in May of 2010,* "Print on demand could create the sort of arena I'd like my fiction to enter, a virtual niche where I can deposit a book without fearing it will disappear overnight, a space where I can watch it, tend it if I choose, extend for years its chance to gather an audience." As Wideman considered all the possibilities that the digital age presented, he posed the question, "Can books regain more of the jazzlike spontaneity and improvisation vital to speech, that ancient fire of live, face-to-face exchange?"

## Selected writings

### Novels

*A Glance Away,* Harcourt, 1967.
*Hurry Home,* Harcourt, 1970.
*The Lynchers,* Harcourt, 1973.
*Hiding Place,* Avon, 1981.
*Sent for You Yesterday,* Avon, 1983.
*Reuben,* H. Holt, 1987.
*Philadelphia Fire,* H. Holt, 1990.
*A Glance Away, Hurry Home, and The Lynchers: Three Early Novels by John Edgar Wideman,* H. Holt, 1994.
*The Cattle Killing,* Houghton Mifflin, 1996.
*Two Cities,* Houghton Mifflin, 1998.
*Fanon,* Houghton Mifflin, 2008.

### Short Stories

*Damballah,* Avon, 1981.

*The Homewood Trilogy* (includes *Damballah, Hiding Place,* and *Sent for You Yesterday* ), Avon, 1985.
*Fever,* H. Holt, 1989.
*The Stories of John Edgar Wideman,* Pantheon, 1992.
*God's Gym,* Houghton Mifflin, 2005.
*Briefs, Stories for the Palm,* Lulu Press, 2010.

### Nonfiction

*Brothers and Keepers: A Memoir,* H. Holt, 1984.
(With others) *Malcolm X: In Our Own Image* (essays), edited by Joe Wood, St. Martin's, 1992.
*Fatheralong: A Meditation on Fathers and Sons, Race and Society,* Pantheon, 1994.
(With Mumia Abu-Jamal) *Live from Death Row,* Addison Wesley, 1995.
*Hoop Roots: Basketball, Race, and Love,* Houghton Mifflin, 2001.

### As editor

*My Soul Has Grown Deep: Classics of Early African-American Literature,* Running Press, 2001.
*The Best of the Drue Heinz Literature Prize,* University of Pittsburgh Press, 2001.

## Sources

### Books

Bell, Bernard W., *The Afro-American Novel and Its Tradition,* University of Massachusetts Press, 1987, pp. 281–338.
Mbalia, Doreathea D., *John Edgar Wideman: Reclaiming the African Personality,* Associated University Press, 1995.
O'Brien, John, editor, *Interviews with Black Writers,* Liveright, 1973, pp. 213–23.
TuSmith, Bonnie, and Keith E. Byerman, editors, *Critical Essays on John Edgar Wideman,* University of Tennessee Press, 2006.

### Periodicals

*American Book Review,* July–August 1982, pp. 12–13.
*Atlanta Constitution,* December 3, 1989, p. L1.
*Atlanta Journal,* June 7, 1992, p. N8.
*Bloomsbury Review,* March 1991, p. 1.
*Boston Globe,* June 14, 1992, p. B40.
*Chicago Tribune,* July 9, 1992, p. TEMPO-1.
*Esquire,* August 1989, pp. 122–32; September 1992, pp. 149–56.
*Publishers Weekly,* May 3, 2010, p. 56(1).
*Progressive,* April 2008, p. 33(3).
*Nation,* October 4, 1986, pp. 321-22.
*New York Times,* July 21, 1992, p. C15; October 7, 2010, p. A39.
*New York Times Book Review,* April 11, 1982, pp. 6, 21; May 15, 1983, pp. 13, 41; January 13, 1985, p. 1.

*North American Review,* June 1988, p. 60-61.
*O, The Oprah Magazine,* March 2007, p. 202(3).
*People,* February 11, 1985, p. 121.
*Publishers Weekly,* November 17, 1989, pp. 37-38.
*Washington Post,* May 12, 1984, p. C1; October 15, 1990, p. B1; May 3, 1991, p. B1; August 9, 1992, p. 15.
*Washington Post Book World,* July 3, 1983, pp. 1-2; October 21, 1984; November 15, 1987, p. 7; October 7, 1990, pp. 6, 12.

**Online**

"John Edgar Wideman: Professor of Africana Studies, Creative Writing," Brown University, http://www.brown.edu/Departments/Africana_Studies/people/wideman_john.html (accessed October 14, 2010).
McWhorter, John, "Empty Seat While Back? I Wish!" Philly.com-The Inquirer Daily News, http://www.philly.com/dailynews/opinion/20101013_Empty_Seat_While_Black_I_wish.html (accessed October 13, 2010).

—Anne Janette Johnson and Marie O'Sullivan

# Cumulative Nationality Index

*Volume numbers appear in **bold***

## American

Aaliyah **30**
Aaron, Hank **5**
Aaron, Quinton **82**
Abbott, Robert Sengstacke **27**
Abdul-Jabbar, Kareem **8**
Abdur-Rahim, Shareef **28**
Abele, Julian **55**
Abernathy, Ralph David **1**
Aberra, Amsale **67**
Abu-Jamal, Mumia **15**
Ace, Johnny **36**
Adams, Eula L. **39**
Adams, Floyd, Jr. **12**
Adams, Jenoyne **60**
Adams, Johnny **39**
Adams, Leslie **39**
Adams, Oleta **18**
Adams, Osceola Macarthy **31**
Adams, Sheila J. **25**
Adams, Yolanda **17, 67**
Adams-Campbell, Lucille L. **60**
Adams Earley, Charity **13, 34**
Adams-Ender, Clara **40**
Adderley, Julian "Cannonball" **30**
Adderley, Nat **29**
Adebimpe, Tunde **75**
Adkins, Rod **41**
Adkins, Rutherford H. **21**
Adu, Freddy **67**
Agyeman, Jaramogi Abebe **10, 63**
Ailey, Alvin **8**
Akil, Mara Brock **60, 82**
Akon **68**
Al-Amin, Jamil Abdullah **6**
Albright, Gerald **23**
Alcorn, George Edward, Jr. **59**
Alert, Kool DJ Red **33**
Alexander, Archie Alphonso **14**
Alexander, Clifford **26**
Alexander, Elizabeth **75**
Alexander, Joyce London **18**
Alexander, Khandi **43**
Alexander, Margaret Walker **22**
Alexander, Sadie Tanner Mossell **22**
Alexander, Shaun **58**
Ali, Hana Yasmeen **52**
Ali, Laila **27, 63**
Ali, Muhammad **2, 16, 52**
Ali, Rashied **79**
Ali, Tatyana **73**
Allain, Stephanie **49**
Allen, Betty **83**

Allen, Byron **3, 24**
Allen, Claude **68**
Allen, Debbie **13, 42**
Allen, Dick **85**
Allen, Ethel D. **13**
Allen, Eugene **79**
Allen, Lucy **85**
Allen, Marcus **20**
Allen, Ray **82**
Allen, Robert L. **38**
Allen, Samuel W. **38**
Allen, Tina **22, 75**
Allen, Will **74**
Allen-Buillard, Melba **55**
Alonso, Laz **87**
Alston, Charles **33**
Amaker, Norman **63**
Amaker, Tommy **62**
Amaki, Amalia **76**
Amerie **52**
Ames, Wilmer **27**
Ammons, James H. **81**
Amos, Emma **63**
Amos, John **8, 62**
Amos, Wally **9**
Anderson, Anthony **51, 77**
Anderson, Carl **48**
Anderson, Charles Edward **37**
Anderson, Eddie "Rochester" **30**
Anderson, Elmer **25**
Anderson, Fred **87**
Anderson, Jamal **22**
Anderson, Lauren **72**
Anderson, Marian **2, 33**
Anderson, Michael P. **40**
Anderson, Mike **63**
Anderson, Norman B. **45**
Anderson, Reuben V. **81**
Anderson, William G(ilchrist) **57**
Andrews, Benny **22, 59**
Andrews, Bert **13**
Andrews, Raymond **4**
Andrews, Tina **74**
Angelou, Maya **1, 15**
Ansa, Tina McElroy **14**
Anthony, Carmelo **46**
Anthony, Wendell **25**
apl.de.ap **84**
Appiah, Kwame Anthony **67**
Archer, Dennis **7, 36**
Archer, Lee, Jr. **79**
Archie-Hudson, Marguerite **44**
Ardoin, Alphonse **65**
Arenas, Gilbert **84**

Arkadie, Kevin **17**
Armstrong, Govind **81**
Armstrong, Louis **2**
Armstrong, Robb **15**
Armstrong, Vanessa Bell **24**
Arnez J **53**
Arnold, Tichina **63**
Arnwine, Barbara **28**
Arrington, Richard **24**
Arroyo, Martina **30**
Artest, Ron **52**
Asante, Molefi Kete **3**
Ashanti **37**
Ashe, Arthur **1, 18**
Ashford, Calvin, Jr. **74**
Ashford, Emmett **22**
Ashford, Evelyn **63**
Ashford, Nickolas **21**
Ashley-Ward, Amelia **23**
Ashong, Derrick **86**
Asim, Jabari **71**
Atkins, Cholly **40**
Atkins, Erica **34**
Atkins, Juan **50**
Atkins, Russell **45**
Atkins, Tina **34**
Aubert, Alvin **41**
Auguste, Donna **29**
Austin, Gloria **63**
Austin, Jim **63**
Austin, Junius C. **44**
Austin, Lovie **40**
Austin, Patti **24**
Autrey, Wesley **68**
Avant, Clarence **19, 86**
Avery, Byllye Y. **66**
Ayers, Roy **16**
Babatunde, Obba **35**
Babyface **10, 31, 82**
Bacon-Bercey, June **38**
Badu, Erykah **22**
Bahati, Wambui **60**
Bailey, Buster **38**
Bailey, Chauncey **68**
Bailey, Clyde **45**
Bailey, DeFord **33**
Bailey, Philip **63**
Bailey, Radcliffe **19**
Bailey, Xenobia **11**
Baines, Harold **32**
Baiocchi, Regina Harris **41**
Baker, Anita **21, 48**
Baker, Augusta **38**

Baker, Dusty **8, 43, 72**
Baker, Ella **5**
Baker, Gwendolyn Calvert **9**
Baker, Houston A., Jr. **6**
Baker, Josephine **3**
Baker, LaVern **26**
Baker, Matt **76**
Baker, Maxine B. **28**
Baker, Thurbert **22**
Baker, Vernon Joseph **65, 87**
Baldwin, Cynthia A. **74**
Baldwin, James **1**
Ballance, Frank W. **41**
Ballard, Allen Butler, Jr. **40**
Ballard, Hank **41**
Baltimore, Richard Lewis, III **71**
Bambaataa, Afrika **34**
Bambara, Toni Cade **10**
Bandele, Asha **36**
Banks, Ernie **33**
Banks, Jeffrey **17**
Banks, Michelle **59**
Banks, Paula A. **68**
Banks, Tyra **11, 50**
Banks, William **11**
Banner, David **55**
Baquet, Dean **63**
Baraka, Amiri **1, 38**
Barbee, Lloyd Augustus **71**
Barber, Ronde **41**
Barber, Tiki **57**
Barboza, Anthony **10**
Barclay, Paris **37**
Barden, Don H. **9, 20**
Barker, Danny **32**
Barkley, Charles **5, 66**
Barlow, Roosevelt **49**
Barnes, Ernie **16, 78**
Barnes, Melody **75**
Barnes, Roosevelt "Booba" **33**
Barnes, Steven **54**
Barnett, Amy Du Bois **46**
Barnett, Etta Moten **56**
Barnett, Marguerite **46**
Barney, Lem **26**
Barnhill, David **30**
Barrax, Gerald William **45**
Barrett, Andrew C. **12**
Barrett, Jacquelyn **28**
Barrino, Fantasia **53**
Barrow, Willie T. **85**
Barry, Marion S(hepilov, Jr.) **7, 44**
Barthé, Earl **78**
Barthe, Richmond **15**

Basie, Count 23
Basquiat, Jean-Michel 5
Bass, Charlotta Spears 40
Bass, Karen 70
Bassett, Angela 6, 23, 62
Baszile, Jennifer 79
Bates, Daisy 13
Bates, Karen Grigsby 40
Bates, Peg Leg 14
Bath, Patricia E. 37
Batiste, Alvin 66
Battle, Kathleen 70
Baugh, David 23
Baylor, Don 6
Baylor, Helen 36
Beach, Michael 26
Beal, Bernard B. 46
Beals, Jennifer 12
Beals, Melba Patillo 15
Bearden, Romare 2, 50
Beasley, Jamar 29
Beasley, Phoebe 34
Beatty, Talley 35
Bechet, Sidney 18
Beckford, Tyson 11, 68
Beckham, Barry 41
Belafonte, Harry 4, 65
Belgrave, Cynthia 75
Belgrave, Marcus 77
Bell, Darrin 77
Bell, Derrick 6
Bell, James "Cool Papa" 36
Bell, James A. 50
Bell, James Madison 40
Bell, Michael 40
Bell, Robert Mack 22
Bellamy, Bill 12
Bellamy, Terry 58
Belle, Albert 10
Belle, Regina 1, 51
Belton, Sharon Sayles 9, 16
Benberry, Cuesta 65
Benét, Eric 28, 77
Benham, Robert 78
Ben-Israel, Ben Ami 11
Benjamin, Andre 45
Benjamin, Regina 20, 75
Benjamin, Tritobia Hayes 53
Bennett, Estelle 77
Bennett, George Harold "Hal" 45
Bennett, Gwendolyn B. 59
Bennett, Lerone, Jr. 5, 84
Benson, Angela 34
Bentley, Lamont 53
Berry, Edwin C. 81
Berry, Halle 4, 19, 57
Berry, Bertice 8, 55
Berry, Chuck 29
Berry, Fred "Rerun" 48
Berry, Mary Frances 7
Berry, Moses 84
Berry, Theodore 31
Berrysmith, Don Reginald 49
Bethune, Mary McLeod 4
Betsch, MaVynee 28
Bettis, Jerome 64
Betts, Keter 85
Betts, R. Dwayne 86
Bevel, James L. 75
Beverly, Frankie 25
Beyoncé 39, 70
Bibb, Eric 49
Bibb, Henry and Mary 54

Bickerstaff, Bernie 21
Big Daddy Kane 79
Biggers, John 20, 33
Biggers, Sanford 62
Billops, Camille 82
bin Wahad, Dhoruba 85
Bing, Dave 3, 59, 78
Birch, Adolpho A., Jr. 85
Birch, Glynn R. 61
Bishop, Sanford D., Jr. 24
Bivins, Michael 72
Black, Albert 51
Black, Barry C. 47
Black, Joe 75
Black, Keith Lanier 18, 84
Black Thought 63
Blackburn, Robert 28
Blackman, Toni 86
Blackmon, Brenda 58
Blackshear, Leonard 52
Blackwell, David 79
Blackwell, Kenneth, Sr. 61
Blackwell, Robert D., Sr. 52
Blackwell, Unita 17
Blacque, Taurean 58
Blair, Jayson 50
Blair, Paul 36
Blake, Asha 26
Blake, Charles E. 82
Blake, Eubie 29
Blake, James 43
Blakey, Art 37
Blanchard, Terence 43
Bland, Bobby "Blue" 36
Bland, Eleanor Taylor 39
Blanks, Billy 22
Blanks, Deborah K. 69
Blanton, Dain 29
Blassingame, John Wesley 40
Blaylock, Ronald 86
Blayton, Jesse B., Sr. 55
Bleu, Corbin 65
Blige, Mary J. 20, 34, 60
Blockson, Charles L. 42
Bloomer, George 86
Blow, Charles M. 73
Blow, Kurtis 31
Bluford, Guy 2, 35
Bluitt, Juliann S. 14
Bobb, Robert C. 83
Bobo, Lawrence 60
Bogle, Donald 34
Bogues, Tyrone "Muggsy" 56
Bolden, Buddy 39
Bolden, Charles Frank, Jr. 7, 78
Bolden, Frank E. 44
Bolden, Tonya 32
Bolin, Jane 22, 59
Bolton, Terrell D. 25
Bolton-Holifield, Ruthie 28
Bond, Beverly 53
Bond, J. Max, Jr. 76
Bond, Julian 2, 35
Bonds, Barry 6, 34, 63
Bonds, Bobby 43
Bonds, Margaret 39
Bonet, Lisa 58
Bontemps, Arna 8
Booker, Cory Anthony 68
Booker, Simeon 23
Borders, James 9
Bosh, Chris 85
Bosley, Freeman, Jr. 7

Boston, Kelvin E. 25
Boston, Lloyd 24
Bow Wow 35
Bowe, Riddick 6
Bowen, Ruth 83
Bowman, Bertie 71
Bowser, Yvette Lee 17
Boyd, Edward 70
Boyd, Gerald M. 32, 59
Boyd, Gwendolyn 49
Boyd, John W., Jr. 20, 72
Boyd, Melba Joyce 86
Boyd, T. B., III 6
Boykin, Keith 14
Boyz II Men 82
Bradley, David Henry, Jr. 39
Bradley, Ed 2, 59
Bradley, J. Robert 65
Bradley, Jennette B. 40
Bradley, Thomas 2, 20
Brady, Wayne 32, 71
Brae, C. Michael 61
Braithwaite, William Stanley 52
Branch, William Blackwell 39
Brand, Elton 31
Brandon, Barbara 3
Brandon, Terrell 16
Brandy 14, 34, 72
Branham, George, III 50
Branson, Herman 87
Brashear, Carl 29
Brashear, Donald 39
Braugher, Andre 13, 58
Braun, Carol Moseley 4, 42
Brawley, Benjamin 44
Braxton, Brad 77
Braxton, Toni 15, 61
Brazile, Donna 25, 70
Bridges, Ruby 77
Bridges, Sheila 36
Bridges, Todd 37
Bridgewater, Dee Dee 32
Bridgforth, Glinda 36
Briggs, Curtis 84
Brimmer, Andrew F. 2, 48
Briscoe, Connie 15
Briscoe, Marlin 37
Britt, Donna 28
Broadbent, Hydeia 36
Brock, Lou 18
Brock, Roslyn McCallister 86
Bromery, Randolph Wilson 85
Bronner, Nathaniel H., Sr. 32
Brooke, Edward 8
Brooks, Tyrone 59
Brooks, Aaron 33
Brooks, Avery 9
Brooks, Derrick 43
Brooks, Golden 62
Brooks, Gwendolyn 1, 28
Brooks, Hadda 40
Brooks, Mehcad 62
Broonzy, Big Bill 82
Brower, William 49
Brown, Angela M. 54
Brown, Anne 76
Brown, Anthony G. 72
Brown, Antron 85
Brown, Bobby 58
Brown, Byrd 49
Brown, Byron W. 72
Brown, Cecil M. 46
Brown, Charles 23

Brown, Chris 74
Brown, Chuck 78
Brown, Clarence Gatemouth 59
Brown, Claude 38
Brown, Clifford 86
Brown, Cora 33
Brown, Corrine 24
Brown, Cupcake 63
Brown, Donald 19
Brown, Eddie C. 35
Brown, Elaine 8
Brown, Ernest 80
Brown, Erroll M. 23
Brown, Foxy 25
Brown, George Leslie 62
Brown, Homer S. 47
Brown, James 15, 60
Brown, James 22
Brown, Janice Rogers 43
Brown, Jesse 6, 41
Brown, Jesse Leroy 31
Brown, Jim 11
Brown, Joe 29
Brown, Joyce F. 25
Brown, Lee Patrick 1, 24
Brown, Les 5
Brown, Lloyd Louis 42
Brown, Marie Dutton 12
Brown, Mike 77
Brown, Nappy 73
Brown, Oscar, Jr. 53
Brown, Patrick "Sleepy" 50
Brown, Robert 65
Brown, Ron 5
Brown, Sterling Allen 10, 64
Brown, Tony 3
Brown, Uzee 42
Brown, Vivian 27
Brown, Warren 61
Brown, Wesley 23
Brown, Willa 40
Brown, Willard 36
Brown, Willie 7, 85
Brown, Zora Kramer 12
Browne, Roscoe Lee 66
Broyard, Anatole 68
Broyard, Bliss 68
Bruce, Blanche Kelso 33
Bruce, Bruce 56
Bruce, Isaac 26
Brunson, Dorothy 1, 87
Bryan, Ashley F. 41
Bryant, Cullen 81
Bryant, John 26
Bryant, John R. 45
Bryant, Kobe 15, 31, 71
Bryant, Wayne R. 6
Bryant, William Benson 61
Buchanan, Ray 32
Buckley, Gail Lumet 39
Buckley, Victoria (Vikki) 24
Bullard, Eugene 12
Bullins, Ed 25
Bullock, Steve 22
Bully-Cummings, Ella 48
Bumbry, Grace 5
Bunche, Ralph J. 5
Bunkley, Anita Richmond 39
Burgess, John 46
Burgess, Marjorie L. 55
Burke, Selma 16
Burke, Solomon 31, 86
Burke, Yvonne Brathwaite 42

Burks, Mary Fair **40**
Burleigh, Henry Thacker **56**
Burnett, Charles **16, 68**
Burnim, Mickey L. **48**
Burns, Eddie **44**
Burns, Ursula **60**
Burnside, R.L. **56**
Burrell, Tom **21, 51**
Burris, Chuck **21**
Burris, Roland W. **25, 75**
Burroughs, Margaret Taylor **9**
Burrows, Stephen **31**
Burrus, William Henry "Bill" **45**
Burt-Murray, Angela **59**
Burton, LeVar **8**
Burwell, Bryan **83**
Busby, Jheryl **3, 74**
Bush, Gordon **82**
Bush, Reggie **59**
Butler, George, Jr. **70**
Butler, Jerry **26**
Butler, Leroy, III **17**
Butler, Louis **70**
Butler, Octavia **8, 43, 58**
Butler, Paul D. **17**
Butts, Calvin O., III **9**
Butts, Cassandra **78**
Bynoe, Peter C. B. **40**
Bynum, Juanita **31, 71**
Byrd, Donald **10**
Byrd, Eugene **64**
Byrd, Michelle **19**
Byrd, Robert **11**
Cadoria, Sherian Grace **14**
Caesar, Shirley **19**
Cage, Byron **53**
Cain, Herman **15**
Caldwell, Benjamin **46**
Caldwell, Earl **60**
Caldwell, Jim **81**
Caldwell, Kirbyjon **55**
Calhoun, Lillian Scott **87**
Callender, Clive O. **3**
Calloway, Cab **14**
Cameron, James **80**
Camp, Kimberly **19**
Campanella, Roy **25**
Campbell, Bebe Moore **6, 24, 59**
Campbell, Bill **9, 76**
Campbell, Donald J.**66**
Campbell, E. Simms **13**
Campbell, Mary Schmidt **43**
Campbell-Martin, Tisha **8, 42**
Canada, Geoffrey **23**
Canady, Alexa **28**
Cannon, Katie **10**
Cannon, Nick **47, 73**
Cannon, Reuben **50**
Cara, Irene **77**
Carr, Johnnie **69**
Carr, Keela **74**
Cardozo, Francis L. **33**
Carew, Rod **20**
Carey, Mariah **32, 53, 69**
Cargill, Victoria A. **43**
Carr, Kurt **56**
Carr, Leroy **49**
Carroll, Diahann **9**
Carroll, L. Natalie **44**
Carroll, Rocky **74**
Carruthers, George R. **40**
Carson, André **69**
Carson, Benjamin **1, 35, 76**

Carson, Johnnie **85**
Carson, Julia **23, 69**
Carson, Lisa Nicole **21**
Carter, Anson **24**
Carter, Benny **46**
Carter, Betty **19**
Carter, Butch **27**
Carter, Cris **21**
Carter, Joe **30**
Carter, Joye Maureen **41**
Carter, Kenneth **53**
Carter, Majora **77**
Carter, Mandy **11**
Carter, Nell **39**
Carter, Pamela Lynn **67**
Carter, Regina **23**
Carter, Robert L. **51**
Carter, Rubin **26**
Carter, Stephen L. **4**
Carter, Vince **26**
Carter, Warrick L. **27**
Cartey, Wilfred **47**
Cartiér, Xam Wilson **41**
Carver, George Washington **4**
Cary, Lorene **3**
Cary, Mary Ann Shadd **30**
Cash, Rosalind **28**
Cash, Swin **59**
Cashin, Sheryll **63**
CasSelle, Malcolm **11**
Catchings, Tamika **43**
Catlett, Elizabeth **2**
Catto, Octavius V. **83**
Cayton, Horace **26**
Cedric the Entertainer **29, 60**
Cee-Lo **70**
Chadiha, Jeffri **57**
Chamberlain, Wilt **18, 47**
Chambers, Julius **3**
Chamillionaire **82**
Chaney, John **67**
Chapman, Nathan A., Jr. **21**
Chapman, Tracy **26**
Chappell, Emma **18**
Chappelle, Dave **50**
Charles, Ray **16, 48**
Charleston, Oscar **39**
Chase, Debra Martin **49**
Chase, Leah **57**
Chase-Riboud, Barbara **20, 46**
Chatard, Peter **44**
Chavis, Benjamin **6**
Cheadle, Don **19, 52**
Checker, Chubby **28**
Cheeks, Maurice **47**
Chenault, John **40**
Chenault, Kenneth I. **4, 36**
Cherry, Deron **40**
Chesnutt, Charles **29**
Chestnut, J. L., Jr. **73**
Chestnut, Morris **31**
Chideya, Farai **14, 61**
Childress, Alice **15**
Chineworth, Mary Alice **79**
Chinn, May Edward **26**
Chisholm, Samuel **32**
Chisholm, Shirley **2, 50**
Christian, Barbara T. **44**
Christian, Spencer **15**
Christian-Green, Donna M. **17**
Christie, Angella **36**
Christie, Ron **83**
Chuck D **9**

Churchwell, Robert, Sr. **76**
Ciara **56**
Ciara, Barbara **69**
Clack, Zoanne **73**
Claiborne, Loretta **34**
Clark, Celeste **15**
Clark, Joe **1**
Clark, Kenneth B. **5, 52**
Clark, Mamie Phipps **79**
Clark, Mattie Moss **61**
Clark, Patrick **14**
Clark, Septima **7**
Clark-Cole, Dorinda **66**
Clarke, Cheryl **32**
Clarke, Hope **14**
Clarke, John Henrik **20**
Clarke, Kenny **27**
Clark-Sheard, Karen **22**
Clash, Kevin **14**
Clay, Bryan **57, 74**
Clay, William Lacy **8**
Clayton, Constance **1**
Clayton, Eva M. **20**
Clayton, Mayme Agnew **62**
Clayton, Xernona **3, 45**
Claytor, Helen **14, 52**
Cleage, Pearl **17, 64**
Cleaver, Eldridge **5**
Cleaver, Emanuel **4, 45, 68**
Cleaver, Kathleen **29**
Clemente, Rosa **74**
Clements, George **2**
Clemmons, Reginal G. **41**
Clemons, Clarence **41**
Clemons, Michael "Pinball" **64**
Clendenon, Donn **26, 56**
Cleveland, James **19**
Cliff, Michelle **42**
Clifton, Lucille **14, 64**
Clifton, Nathaniel "Sweetwater" **47**
Clinton, George **9**
Clyburn, James E. **21, 71**
Clyburn, Mignon **78**
Coachman, Alice **18**
Coates, Ta-Nehisi **76**
Cobb, Jewel Plummer **42**
Cobb, W. Montague **39**
Cobb, William Jelani **59**
Cobbs, Price M. **9**
Cochran, Johnnie **11, 39, 52**
Cockrel, Kenneth V., Jr. **79**
Cockrel, Kenneth Vern, Sr. **79**
Cohen, Anthony **15**
Colbert, Virgis William **17**
Cole, Johnnetta B. **5, 43**
Cole, Keyshia **63**
Cole, Lorraine **48**
Cole, Nat "King" **17**
Cole, Natalie **17, 60, 84**
Cole, Rebecca **38**
Coleman, Bessie **9**
Coleman, Donald **24, 62**
Coleman, Gary **35, 86**
Coleman, James E., Jr. **79**
Coleman, Ken **57**
Coleman, Leonard S., Jr. **12**
Coleman, Mary **46**
Coleman, Michael B. **28, 79**
Coleman, Ornette **39, 69**
Coleman, Wanda **48**
Coleman, William F., III **61**
Coleman, William T. **76**
Colemon, Johnnie **11**

Coles, Alice **80**
Colescott, Robert **69**
Collins, Albert **12**
Collins, Barbara-Rose **7, 87**
Collins, Bootsy **31**
Collins, Cardiss **10, 80**
Collins, Janet **33, 64**
Collins, Lyn **53**
Collins, Marva **3, 71**
Collins, Patricia Hill **67**
Collins, Paul **61**
Colston, Hal **72**
Colter, Cyrus J. **36**
Coltrane, Alice **70**
Coltrane, John **19**
Coltrane, Ravi **71**
Combs, Sean "Puffy" **17, 43**
Comer, James P. **6**
Common **31, 63**
Compton-Rock, Malaak **86**
Cone, James H. **3, 82**
Coney, PonJola **48**
Connerly, Ward **14**
Conyers, John, Jr. **4**
Conyers, Monica **85**
Conyers, Nathan G. **24, 45**
Cook, Charles "Doc" **44**
Cook, (Will) Mercer **40**
Cook, Samuel DuBois **14**
Cook, Suzan D. Johnson **22**
Cook, Toni **23**
Cook, Will Marion **40**
Cooke, Marcia **60**
Cooke, Marvel **31**
Cooper, Andrew W. **36**
Cooper, Andy "Lefty" **63**
Cooper, Anna Julia **20**
Cooper, Barry **33**
Cooper, Charles "Chuck" **47**
Cooper, Chuck **75**
Cooper, Cynthia **17**
Cooper, Edward S. **6**
Cooper, Evern **40**
Cooper, Helene **74**
Cooper, J. California **12, 85**
Cooper, Lisa **73**
Cooper, Margaret J. **46**
Cooper, Michael **31**
Cooper Cafritz, Peggy **43**
Copeland, Michael **47**
Coppola, Imani Francesca **82**
Corbi, Lana **42**
Corley, Tony **62**
Cornelius, Don **4**
Cornish, Sam **50**
Cornwell, Edward E., III **70**
Cortez, Jayne **43**
Corthron, Kia **43**
Cortor, Eldzier **42**
Cosby, Bill **7, 26, 59**
Cosby, Camille **14, 80**
Cose, Ellis **5, 50**
Cotter, Joseph Seamon, Sr. **40**
Cottrell, Comer **11**
Counter, S. Allen **74**
Cowans, Adger W. **20**
Cowboy Troy **54**
Cox, Bryan **83**
Cox, Ida **42**
Cox, Joseph Mason Andrew **51**
Cox, Renée **67**
Cox, William E. **68**
Craig, Carl **31, 71**

Craig-Jones, Ellen Walker **44**
Crawford, Hank **77**
Crawford, Randy **19**
Cray, Robert **30**
Creagh, Milton **27**
Crennel, Romeo **54**
Crew, Rudolph F. **16**
Crew, Spencer R. **55**
Crichlow, Ernest **75**
Crite, Alan Rohan **29**
Croal, N'Gai **76**
Crocker, Frankie **29**
Crockett, George W., Jr. **10, 64**
Croom, Sylvester **50**
Cross, Dolores E. **23**
Crothers, Scatman **19**
Crouch, Andraé **27**
Crouch, Stanley **11, 87**
Crowder, Henry **16**
Cruse, Harold **54**
Crutchfield, James N. **55**
Cullen, Countee **8**
Cullers, Vincent T. **49**
Culpepper, Daunte **32, 85**
Cummings, Elijah E. **24**
Cuney, William Waring **44**
Cunningham, Evelyn **23, 85**
Cunningham, Randall **23**
Currie, Betty **21**
Currie, Ulysses **73**
Curry, George E. **23**
Curry, Mark **17**
Curry, Michael **85**
Curtis, Christopher Paul **26**
Curtis-Hall, Vondie **17**
Da Don, Polow **86**
Daemyon, Jerald **64**
Dailey, Ulysses Grant **87**
Daly, Marie Maynard **37**
Dandridge, Dorothy **3**
Dandridge, Ray **36**
Dandridge, Raymond Garfield **45**
D'Angelo **27**
Daniels, Lee **36, 76**
Daniels-Carter, Valerie **23**
Danner, Margaret Esse **49**
Dantley, Adrian **72**
Dara, Olu **35**
Darden, Calvin **38**
Darden, Christopher **13**
Dash, Damon **31**
Dash, Julie **4**
Dash, Leon **47**
Datcher, Michael **60**
David, Keith **27**
Davidson, Jaye **5**
Davidson, Tommy **21**
Davis, Allison **12**
Davis, Altovise **76**
Davis, Angela **5**
Davis, Anthony **11**
Davis, Arthur Paul **41**
Davis, Artur **41**
Davis, Belva **61**
Davis, Benjamin O., Jr. **2, 43**
Davis, Benjamin O., Sr. **4**
Davis, Bing **84**
Davis, Charles T. **48**
Davis, Chuck **33**
Davis, Danny K. **24, 79**
Davis, Ed **24**
Davis, Eisa **68**
Davis, Ernie **48**

Davis, Erroll B., Jr. **57**
Davis, Frank Marshall **47**
Davis, Gary **41**
Davis, George **36**
Davis, Gordon J. **76**
Davis, Guy **36**
Davis, James E. **50**
Davis, Mike **41**
Davis, Miles **4**
Davis, Milt **74**
Davis, Nolan **45**
Davis, Ossie **5, 50**
Davis, Piper **19**
Davis, Ruth **37**
Davis, Shani **58, 84**
Davis, Terrell **20**
Davis, Thulani **61**
Davis, Tyrone **54**
Davis, Viola **34, 76**
Dawes, Dominique **11**
Dawkins, Wayne **20**
Dawn, Marpessa **75**
Dawson, Andre **85**
Dawson, Matel "Mat," Jr. **39**
Dawson, Michael C. **63**
Dawson, Rosario **72**
Dawson, William Levi **39**
Day, Leon **39**
Days, Drew S., III **10**
de Lavallade, Carmen **78**
de Passe, Suzanne **25**
De Priest, Oscar Stanton **80**
De Shields, André **72**
De Veaux, Alexis **44**
De' Alexander, Quinton **57**
Dean, Mark E. **35**
Deas, Gerald **85**
DeBaptiste, George **32**
DeCarava, Roy **42, 81**
Deconge-Watson, Lovenia **55**
Dee, Merri **55**
Dee, Ruby **8, 50, 68**
Deezer D **53**
DeFrantz, Anita **37**
Deggans, Eric **71**
DeJongh, John, Jr. **85**
Delaney, Beauford **19**
Delaney, Joe **76**
Delaney, Joseph **30**
Delany, Bessie **12**
Delany, Martin R. **27**
Delany, Sadie **12**
Delany, Samuel R., Jr. **9**
Delco, Wilhemina **33**
DeLille, Henriette **30**
Dellums, Ronald **2, 81**
DeLoach, Nora **30**
Delsarte, Louis **34**
Demby, William **51**
Dennard, Brazeal **37**
Dent, Thomas C. **50**
DePreist, James **37**
DeVard, Jerri **61**
Devers, Gail **7, 87**
Devine, Loretta **24**
Dickens, Helen Octavia **14, 64**
Dickenson, Vic **38**
Dickerson, Debra J. **60**
Dickerson, Eric **27**
Dickerson, Ernest R. **6, 17**
Dickey, Eric Jerome **21, 56**
Diddley, Bo **39, 72**
Diesel, Vin **29**

Diggs, Charles C. **21**
Diggs, Taye **25, 63**
Diggs-Taylor, Anna **20**
Dillard, Godfrey J. **45**
Dinkins, David **4**
Divine, Father **7**
Dixon, Bill **87**
Dixon, Dean **68**
Dixon, Ivan **69**
Dixon, Julian C. **24**
Dixon, Margaret **14**
Dixon, Sharon Pratt **1**
Dixon, Sheila **68**
Dixon, Willie **4**
DMX **28, 64**
Dobbs, Mattiwilda **34**
Doby, Lawrence Eugene, Sr. **16, 41**
Dodson, Howard, Jr. **7, 52**
Dodson, Owen Vincent **38**
Doley, Harold, Jr. **26**
Domino, Fats **20**
Donald, Arnold Wayne **36**
Donaldson, Jeff **46**
Donegan, Dorothy **19**
Dorrell, Karl **52**
Dorsey, Lee **65**
Dorsey, Thomas **15**
Dortch, Thomas W., Jr. **45**
Dougherty, Mary Pearl **47**
Douglas, Aaron **7**
Douglass, Frederick **87**
Dourdan, Gary **37**
Dove, Rita **6, 78**
Dove, Ulysses **5**
Downing, Will **19**
Draper, Sharon Mills **16, 43**
Dre, Dr. **10, 14, 30**
Drew, Alvin, Jr. **67**
Drew, Charles Richard **7**
Drexler, Clyde **4, 61**
Driskell, David C. **7**
Driver, David E. **11**
Drummond, William J. **40**
Du Bois, David Graham **45**
du Cille, Michel **74**
DuBois, Shirley Graham **21**
DuBois, W. E. B. **3**
Ducksworth, Marilyn **12**
Dudley, Edward R. **58**
Due, Tananarive **30**
Duggins, George **64**
Duke, Bill **3**
Duke, George **21**
Dukes, Hazel Nell **56**
Dumars, Joe **16, 65**
Dumas, Henry **41**
Dunbar, Paul Laurence **8**
Dunbar-Nelson, Alice Ruth Moore **44**
Duncan, Michael Clarke **26**
Duncan, Tim **20**
Duncan, Todd **76**
Dungey, Merrin **62**
Dungy, Camille **86**
Dungy, Tony **17, 42, 59**
Dunham, Katherine **4, 59**
Dunlap, Ericka **55**
Dunn, Jerry **27**
Dunner, Leslie B. **45**
Dunnigan, Alice Allison **41**
Dunston, Georgia Mae **48**
Duplechan, Larry **55**
Dupri, Jermaine **13, 46**

Durant, Kevin **76**
Durham, Bobby **73**
Dutton, Charles S. **4, 22**
Dworkin, Aaron P. **52**
Dwight, Edward **65**
Dye, Jermaine **58**
Dyson, Michael Eric **11, 40**
Early, Gerald **15**
Earthquake **55**
Easley, Annie J. **61**
Ebanks, Michelle **60**
Eckstine, Billy **28**
Edelin, Ramona Hoage **19**
Edelman, Marian Wright **5, 42**
Edley, Christopher **2, 48**
Edley, Christopher F., Jr. **48**
Edmonds, Terry **17**
Edmonds, Tracey **16, 64**
Edmunds, Gladys **48**
Edwards, Donna **77**
Edwards, Esther Gordy **43**
Edwards, Harry **2**
Edwards, Herman **51**
Edwards, Lena Frances **76**
Edwards, Melvin **22**
Edwards, Teresa **14**
Edwards, Willarda V. **59**
El Wilson, Barbara **35**
Elder, Larry **25**
Elder, Lee **6**
Elder, Lonne, III **38**
Elders, Joycelyn **6**
Eldridge, Roy **37**
Elise, Kimberly **32**
Ellerbe, Brian **22**
Ellington, Duke **5**
Ellington, E. David **11**
Ellington, Mercedes **34**
Elliott, Missy "Misdemeanor" **31**
Elliott, Sean **26**
Ellis, Charles H., III **79**
Ellis, Clarence A. **38**
Ellis, Dock **78**
Ellis, Jimmy **44**
Ellison, Keith **59**
Ellison, Ralph **7**
Elmore, Ronn **21**
Emanuel, James A. **46**
Emeagwali, Dale **31**
Ephriam, Mablean **29**
Epperson, Sharon **54**
Epps, Archie C., III **45**
Epps, Mike **60**
Epps, Omar **23, 59**
Ericsson-Jackson, Aprille **28**
Ervin, Anthony **66**
Ervin, Clark Kent **82**
Erving, Julius **18, 47**
Escobar, Damien **56**
Escobar, Tourie **56**
Esposito, Giancarlo **9**
Espy, Mike **6**
Estes, Rufus **29**
Estes, Simon **28**
Estes, Sleepy John **33**
Eubanks, Kevin **15**
Eugene-Richard, Margie **63**
Europe, James Reese **10**
Evans, Darryl **22**
Evans, Etu **55**
Evans, Faith **22**
Evans, Harry **25**
Evans, Mari **26**

Evans, Warren C. 76
Eve 29
Everett, Francine 23
Evers, Medgar 3
Evers, Myrlie 8
Ewing, Patrick 17, 73
Fabio, Sarah Webster 48
Fabre, Shelton 71
Fair, Ronald L. 47
Faison, Donald 50
Faison, Frankie 55
Faison, George 16
Falana, Lola 42
Falconer, Etta Zuber 59
Fargas, Antonio 50
Farley, Christopher John 54
Farmer, Art 38
Farmer, Forest J. 1
Farmer, James 2, 64
Farmer-Paellmann, Deadria 43
Farr, Mel 24
Farrakhan, Louis 2, 15
Farrell, Herman D., Jr. 81
Farris, Isaac Newton, Jr. 63
Fattah, Chaka 11, 70
Faulk, Marshall 35
Fauntroy, Walter E. 11
Fauset, Jessie 7
Favors, Steve 23
Fax, Elton 48
Feelings, Muriel 44
Feelings, Tom 11, 47
Felix, Allyson 48
Felix, Larry R. 64
Feemster, Herbert 72
Fennoy, Ilene 72
Fenty, Adrian 60
Ferguson, Roger W. 25
Ferguson, Ronald F. 75
Ferrell, Rachelle 29
Fetchit, Stepin 32
Fiasco, Lupe 64
Fielder, Cecil 2
Fielder, Prince Semien 68
Fields, C. Virginia 25
Fields, Cleo 13
Fields, Evelyn J. 27
Fields, Felicia P. 60
Fields, Julia 45
Fields, Kim 36
50 Cent 46, 83
Files, Lolita 35
Fils-Aimé, Reggie 74
Fine, Sam 60
Finner-Williams, Paris Michele 62
Fishburne, Laurence 4, 22, 70
Fisher, Ada Lois Sipuel 76
Fisher, Ada M. 76
Fisher, Antwone 40
Fisher, Gail 85
Fitzgerald, Ella 1, 18
Flack, Roberta 19
Flanagan, Tommy 69
Flavor Flav 67
Fleming, Erik R. 75
Fleming, Raymond 48
Fletcher, Arthur A. 63
Fletcher, Bill, Jr. 41
Fletcher, Geoffrey 85
Flo Rida 78
Flowers, Sylester 50
Flowers, Vonetta 35
Floyd, Elson S. 41

Forbes, Calvin 46
Forbes, James A., Jr. 71
Ford, Cheryl 45
Ford, Clyde W. 40
Ford, Harold E(ugene) 42
Ford, Harold E(ugene), Jr. 16, 70
Ford, Jack 39
Ford, Johnny 70
Ford, Nick Aaron 44
Ford, Wallace 58
Forman, James 7, 51
Forrest, Leon 44
Forrest, Vernon 40, 79
Forté, John 74
Forte, Linda Diane 54
Foster, Andrew 79
Foster, Ezola 28
Foster, George "Pops" 40
Foster, Henry W., Jr. 26
Foster, Jylla Moore 45
Foster, Marie 48
Fowler, Reggie 51
Fox, Vivica A. 15, 53
Foxx, Anthony 81
Foxx, Jamie 15, 48
Foxx, Redd 2
Francis, Norman (C.) 60
Franklin, Aretha 11, 44
Franklin, C. L. 68
Franklin, Hardy R. 9, 87
Franklin, J. E. 44
Franklin, John Hope 5, 77
Franklin, Kirk 15, 49
Franklin, Shirley 34, 80
Frazer, Jendayi 68
Frazier, E. Franklin 10
Frazier, Joe 19
Frazier, Kevin 58
Frazier, Oscar 58
Frazier-Lyde, Jacqui 31
Freelon, Nnenna 32
Freeman, Aaron 52
Freeman, Al, Jr. 11
Freeman, Charles 19
Freeman, Harold P. 23
Freeman, Leonard 27
Freeman, Marianna 23
Freeman, Morgan 2, 20, 62
Freeman, Paul 39
Freeman, Yvette 27
French, Albert 18
Friday, Jeff 24
Fryer, Roland G. 56
Fudge, Ann (Marie) 11, 55
Fudge, Marcia L. 76
Fulani, Lenora 11
Fuller, A. Oveta 43
Fuller, Arthur 27
Fuller, Blind Boy 86
Fuller, Charles 8
Fuller, Howard L. 37
Fuller, Hoyt 44
Fuller, Meta Vaux Warrick 27
Fuller, S.B. 13
Fuller, Solomon Carter, Jr. 15
Fuller, Vivian 33
Funderburg, I. Owen 38
Funnye, Capers C., Jr. 73
Fuqua, Antoine 35
Futch, Eddie 33
Gaines, Brenda 41
Gaines, Clarence E., Sr. 55
Gaines, Ernest J. 7

Gaines, Grady 38
Gaines, Lloyd 79
Gaiter, Dorothy J. 80
Gaither, Alonzo Smith (Jake) 14
Gaither, Israel L. 65
Gamble, Kenny 85
Gantt, Harvey 1
Gardere, Jeffrey 76
Gardner, Chris 65
Gardner, Edward G. 45
Garner, Erroll 76
Garnett, Kevin 14, 70
Garrett, James F. 78
Garrett, Joyce Finley 59
Garrison, Zina 2
Garvin, Gerry 78
Gary, Willie E. 12
Gaskins, Eric 64
Gaskins, Rudy 74
Gaspard, Patrick 84
Gaston, Arthur George 3, 38, 59
Gaston, Cito 71
Gaston, Marilyn Hughes 60
Gates, Henry Louis, Jr. 3, 38, 67
Gates, Sylvester James, Jr. 15
Gaye, Marvin 2
Gaye, Nona 56
Gayle, Addison, Jr. 41
Gayle, Helene D. 3, 46
Gaynor, Gloria 36
Gentry, Alvin 23
George, Eddie 80
George, Nelson 12
George, Zelma Watson 42
Gervin, George 80
Gibbs, Marla 86
Gibson, Althea 8, 43
Gibson, Bob 33
Gibson, Donald Bernard 40
Gibson, John Trusty 87
Gibson, Johnnie Mae 23
Gibson, Josh 22
Gibson, Kenneth Allen 6
Gibson, Ted 66
Gibson, Truman K., Jr. 60
Gibson, Tyrese 27, 62
Gibson, William F. 6
Giddings, Paula 11
Gidron, Richard D. 68
Gilbert, Christopher 50
Gill, Gerald 69
Gill, Johnny 51
Gill, Turner 83
Gilles, Ralph 61
Gillespie, Dizzy 1
Gilliam, Frank 23
Gilliam, Joe 31
Gilliam, Sam 16
Gilliard, Steve 69
Gilmore, Marshall 46
Gilpin, Charles Sidney 81
Ginuwine 35
Giovanni, Nikki 9, 39, 85
Gist, Carole 1
Givens, Adele 62
Givens, Robin 4, 25, 58
Givhan, Robin Deneen 72
Glanville, Douglas Metunwa 82
Glover, Corey 34
Glover, Danny 1, 24
Glover, Donald 85
Glover, Keith 79
Glover, Nathaniel, Jr. 12

Glover, Savion 14
Goapele 55
Goines, Donald 19
Goings, Russell 59
Goldberg, Whoopi 4, 33, 69
Golden, Marita 19
Golden, Thelma 10, 55
Goldsberry, Ronald 18
Golson, Benny 37
Golston, Allan C. 55
Gomes, Peter J. 15
Gomez, Jewelle 30
Gomez-Preston, Cheryl 9
Goode, Mal 13
Goode, W. Wilson 4
Gooden, Dwight 20
Gooding, Cuba, Jr. 16, 62
Goodman, Al 87
Goodnight, Paul 32
Gorden, W. C. 71
Gordon, Bruce S. 41, 53, 82
Gordon, Carl 87
Gordon, Dexter 25
Gordon, Ed 10, 53
Gordone, Charles 15
Gordon-Reed, Annette 74
Gordy, Berry, Jr. 1
Goss, Carol A. 55
Goss, Tom 23
Gossett, Louis, Jr. 7
Gotti, Irv 39
Gourdine, Meredith 33
Gourdine, Simon 11
Grace, George H. 48
Graham, Lawrence Otis 12
Graham, Lorenz 48
Graham, Stedman 13
Graham, Trevor 84
Granderson, Curtis 66
Granger, Lester B. 75
Grant, Augustus O. 71
Grant, Bernie 57
Grant, Gwendolyn Goldsby 28
Granville, Evelyn Boyd 36
Gravely, Samuel L., Jr. 5, 49
Graves, Butch 77
Graves, Denyce Antoinette 19, 57
Graves, Earl G. 1, 35
Gray, Darius 69
Gray, F. Gary 14, 49
Gray, Farrah 59
Gray, Fred 37
Gray, Ida 41
Gray, Macy 29
Gray, William H., III 3
Gray, Willie 46
Gray, Yeshimbra "Shimmy" 55
Greaves, William 38
Greely, M. Gasby 27
Green, A. C. 32
Green, Al 13, 47, 74
Green, Darrell 39, 74
Green, Dennis 5, 45
Green, Grant 56
Green, Isaac H. 79
Green, Jonathan 54
Greene, Jimmy 74
Greene, Joe 10
Greene, Maurice 27, 77
Greene, Petey 65
Greene, Richard Thaddeus, Sr. 67
Greenfield, Eloise 9
Greenhouse, Bunnatine "Bunny" 57

Greenlee, Sam 48
Greenwood, Monique 38
Gregory, Ann 63
Gregory, Dick 1, 54
Gregory, Frederick 8, 51
Gregory, Wilton 37
Grier, David Alan 28
Grier, Mike 43
Grier, Pam 9, 31, 86
Grier, Roosevelt 13
Griffey, Ken, Jr. 12, 73
Griffin, Anthony 71
Griffin, Bessie Blout 43
Griffin, Johnny 71
Griffin, LaShell 51
Griffith, Mark Winston 8
Griffith, Yolanda 25
Griffith-Joyner, Florence 28
Grimké, Archibald H. 9
Grist, Reri 84
Grooms, Henry R(andall) 50
Guillaume, Robert 3, 48
Guinier, Lani 7, 30
Gumbel, Bryant 14, 80
Gumbel, Greg 8
Gunn, Moses 10
Gurira, Danai 73
Guru 84
Guy, George "Buddy" 31
Guy, Jasmine 2
Guy, Rosa 5
Guy-Sheftall, Beverly 13
Guyton, Tyree 9
Gwynn, Tony 18, 83
Haddon, Dietrick 55
Hageman, Hans 36
Hageman, Ivan 36
Hailey, JoJo 22
Hailey, K-Ci 22
Hale, Clara 16
Hale, Lorraine 8
Haley, Alex 4
Haley, George Williford Boyce 21
Hall, Aaron 57
Hall, Alvin D. 86
Hall, Arsenio 58
Hall, Arthur 39
Hall, Elliott S. 24
Hall, Juanita 62
Hall, Kevan 61
Hall, Lloyd A. 8
Halliburton, Warren J. 49
Ham, Cynthia Parker 58
Hamblin, Ken 10
Hamburg, Beatrix 84
Hamburg, Margaret 78
Hamer, Fannie Lou 6
Hamilton, Anthony 61
Hamilton, Samuel C. 47
Hamilton, Lisa Gay 71
Hamilton, Virginia 10
Hamlin, Larry Leon 49, 62
Hammond, Fred 23
Hammonds, Evelynn 69
Hammons, David 69
Hampton, Fred 18
Hampton, Henry 6
Hampton, Lionel 17, 41
Hancock, Herbie 20, 67
Handy, W. C. 8
Haney, Lee 77
Hannah, Marc 10
Hansberry, Lorraine 6

Hansberry, William Leo 11
Hardaway, Anfernee (Penny) 13
Hardaway, Tim 35
Hardin Armstrong, Lil 39
Harding, Vincent 67
Hardison, Bethann 12
Hardison, Kadeem 22
Hare, Nathan 44
Harkless, Necia Desiree 19
Harmon, Clarence 26
Harold, Erika 54
Harper, Ben 34, 62
Harper, Frances Ellen Watkins 11
Harper, Hill 32, 65
Harper, Michael S. 34
Harrell, Andre 9, 30
Harrington, Oliver W. 9
Harris, Alice 7
Harris, Barbara 12
Harris, Barry 68
Harris, Bill 72
Harris, Carla A. 67
Harris, Corey 39, 73
Harris, E. Lynn 12, 33
Harris, Eddy L. 18
Harris, Gary L. 87
Harris, James 79
Harris, Jay T. 19
Harris, Kamala D. 64
Harris, Leslie 6
Harris, Lyle Ashton 83
Harris, Marcelite Jordon 16
Harris, Mary Styles 31
Harris, Monica 18
Harris, Patricia Roberts 2
Harris, Richard E. 61
Harris, Robin 7
Harris, Sylvia 70
Harris-Lacewell, Melissa 81
Harrison, Alvin 28
Harrison, Calvin 28
Harrison, Charles 72
Harsh, Vivian Gordon 14
Hart, Alvin Youngblood 61
Harvard, Beverly 11
Harvey, Steve 18, 58
Harvey, William R. 42
Haskins, Clem 23
Haskins, James 36, 54
Hassell, Leroy Rountree, Sr. 41
Hastie, William H. 8
Hastings, Alcee L. 16
Hatcher, Richard G. 55
Hatchett, Glenda 32
Hathaway, Donny 18
Hathaway, Isaac Scott 33
Hathaway, Lalah 57
Hawkins, Augustus F. 68
Hawkins, Coleman 9
Hawkins, Erskine 14
Hawkins, La-Van 17, 54
Hawkins, Screamin' Jay 30
Hawkins, Steven 14
Hawkins, Tramaine 16
Hawkins, Walter 87
Hayden, Carla D. 47
Hayden, Palmer 13
Hayden, Robert 12
Hayes, Bob 77
Hayes, Cecil N. 46
Hayes, Dennis 54
Hayes, Isaac 20, 58, 73
Hayes, James C. 10

Hayes, Roland 4
Hayes, Teddy 40
Haygood, Wil 83
Haynes, George Edmund 8
Haynes, Marques 22
Haynes, Roy 87
Haynes, Trudy 44
Haysbert, Dennis 42
Haysbert, Raymond V., Sr. 87
Haywood, Gar Anthony 43
Haywood, Jimmy 58
Haywood, Margaret A. 24
Hazel, Darryl B. 50
Healy, James Augustine 30
Heard, Gar 25
Heard, Nathan C. 45
Hearns, Thomas 29
Hedgeman, Anna Arnold 22
Height, Dorothy I. 2, 23, 78
Hemphill, Essex 10
Hemphill, Jessie Mae 33, 59
Hemsley, Sherman 19
Henderson, Cornelius Langston 26
Henderson, David 53
Henderson, Fletcher 32
Henderson, Gordon 5
Henderson, Jeff 72
Henderson, Rickey 28, 78
Henderson, Stephen E. 45
Henderson, Thelton E. 68
Henderson, Wade J. 14
Henderson, Zelma 71
Hendrix, Jimi 10
Hendryx, Nona 56
Hendy, Francis 47
Henries, A. Doris Banks 44
Henry, Aaron 19
Henry, Clarence "Frogman" 46
Henry, Troy 85
Henson, Darrin 33
Henson, Matthew 2
Henson, Taraji P. 58, 77
Herbert, Bob 63
Hercules, Frank 44
Herenton, Willie W. 24, 81
Herman, Alexis M. 15
Hernandez, Aileen Clarke 13
Hernton, Calvin C. 51
Hickman, Fred 11
Higginbotham, A. Leon, Jr. 13, 25
Higginbotham, Jay C. 37
Higginsen, Vy 65
Hightower, Dennis F. 13
Hill, Andrew 66
Hill, Anita 5, 65
Hill, Bonnie Guiton 20
Hill, Calvin 19
Hill, Donna 32
Hill, Dulé 29
Hill, Grant 13
Hill, Hugh Morgan 83
Hill, Janet 19
Hill, Jesse, Jr. 13
Hill, Lauryn 20, 53
Hill, Leslie Pinckney 44
Hill, Marc Lamont 80
Hill, Oliver W. 24, 63
Hillard, Terry 25
Hillary, Barbara 65
Hilliard, Asa Grant, III 66
Hilliard, David 7
Hilliard, Earl F. 24
Hilliard, Wendy 53

Hilson, Keri 84
Himes, Chester 8
Hinderas, Natalie 5
Hine, Darlene Clark 24
Hines, Earl "Fatha" 39
Hines, Garrett 35
Hines, Gregory 1, 42
Hinton, Milt 30
Hinton, William Augustus 8
Hoagland, Everett H. 45
Hobson, Julius W. 44
Hobson, Mellody 40
Hogan, Beverly Wade 50
Holder, Eric H., Jr. 9, 76
Holder, Laurence 34
Holdsclaw, Chamique 24
Holiday, Billie 1
Holland, Endesha Ida Mae 3, 57
Holland, Kimberly N. 62
Holland, Robert, Jr. 11
Holland-Dozier-Holland 36
Holloway, Brenda 65
Hollowell, Donald L. 57
Holmes, Amy 69
Holmes, Clint 57
Holmes, Hamilton E. 82
Holmes, Larry 20, 68
Holmes, Santonio 87
Holmes, Shannon 70
Holt, Lester 66
Holt, Nora 38
Holt Baker, Arlene 73
Holton, Hugh, Jr. 39
Holyfield, Evander 6
Honeywood, Varnette P. 54
Honoré, Russel L. 64
Hooker, John Lee 30
hooks, bell 5
Hooks, Benjamin L. 2, 85
Hooks, Robert 76
Hope, John 8
Hopkins, Bernard 35, 69
Hopkins, Lightnin' 83
Horn, Shirley 32, 56
Horne, Frank 44
Horne, Lena 5, 86
Horton, Andre 33
Horton, James Oliver 58
Horton, Suki 33
House, Son 8
Houston, Charles Hamilton 4
Houston, Cissy 20, 83
Houston, Whitney 7, 28, 83
Howard, Ayanna 65
Howard, Desmond 16, 58
Howard, Juwan 15
Howard, M. William, Jr. 26
Howard, Michelle 28
Howard, Ryan 65
Howard, Sherri 36
Howard, Terrence Dashon 59
Howlin' Wolf 9
Howroyd, Janice Bryant 42
Hoyte, Lenon 50
Hrabowski, Freeman A., III 22
Hubbard, Arnette Rhinehart 38
Hubbard, Freddie 75
Hudlin, Reginald 9, 86
Hudlin, Warrington 9
Hudson, Cheryl 15
Hudson, Ernie 72
Hudson, Jennifer 63, 83
Hudson, Wade 15

Huff, Leon **86**
Huggins, Edie **71**
Huggins, Larry **21**
Huggins, Nathan Irvin **52**
Hughes, Albert **7**
Hughes, Allen **7**
Hughes, Cathy **27**
Hughes, Ebony **57**
Hughes, Langston **4**
Hughley, D. L. **23, 76**
Hull, Akasha Gloria **45**
Humphrey, Bobbi **20**
Humphries, Frederick **20**
Hunt, Richard **6**
Hunter, Alberta **42**
Hunter, Clementine **45**
Hunter, Torii **43**
Hunter-Gault, Charlayne **6, 31**
Hurston, Zora Neale **3**
Hurt, Byron **61**
Hurt, Mississippi John **84**
Hurtt, Harold **46**
Hutch, Willie **62**
Hutcherson, Hilda Yvonne **54**
Hutchinson, Earl Ofari **24**
Hutson, Jean Blackwell **16**
Hyde, Cowan F. "Bubba" **47**
Hyman, Earle **25, 79**
Hyman, Phyllis **19**
Ice Cube **8, 30, 60**
Iceberg Slim **11**
Ice-T **6, 31**
Iman, Chanel **66**
Ifill, Gwen **28**
Imes, Elmer Samuel **39**
India.Arie **34**
Ingram, James **84**
Ingram, Rex **5**
Innis, Roy **5**
Irvin, Michael **64**
Irvin, Monford Merrill **31**
Irvin, Vernon **65**
Irving, Larry, Jr. **12**
Irvis, K. Leroy **67**
Isaacs, John **76**
Isley, Marvin **87**
Isley, Ronald **25, 56**
Iverson, Allen **24, 46**
Ivey, Phil **72**
Ja Rule **35**
Jackson, Alexine Clement **22**
Jackson, Alphonso R. **48**
Jackson, Brenda **87**
Jackson, Earl **31**
Jackson, Edison O. **67**
Jackson, Frank G. **76**
Jackson, Fred James **25**
Jackson, George **14**
Jackson, George **19**
Jackson, Hal **41**
Jackson, Isaiah **3**
Jackson, Jamea **64**
Jackson, Janet **6, 30, 68**
Jackson, Jermaine **79**
Jackson, Jesse **1, 27, 72**
Jackson, Jesse, Jr. **14, 45, 81**
Jackson, Joe **78**
Jackson, John **36**
Jackson, Judith D. **57**
Jackson, Lisa **77**
Jackson, Mae **57**
Jackson, Mahalia **5**
Jackson, Mannie **14**

Jackson, Mary **73**
Jackson, Maynard **2, 41**
Jackson, Michael **19, 53, 76**
Jackson, Millie **25**
Jackson, Milt **26**
Jackson, Rampage **83**
Jackson, Randy **40**
Jackson, Reggie **15**
Jackson, Samuel **8, 63**
Jackson, Sheneska **18**
Jackson, Shirley Ann **12**
Jackson, Tito **81**
Jackson, Tom **70**
Jackson, Vera **40**
Jackson Lee, Sheila **20**
Jacob, John E. **2**
Jacobs, Regina **38**
Jacquet, Illinois **49**
Jaheim **58**
Jakes, Thomas "T.D." **17, 43**
Jamal, Ahmad **69**
Jamerson, James **59**
James, Charles H., III **62**
James, Daniel, Jr. **16**
James, Donna A. **51**
James, Etta **13, 52**
James, G. Larry **74**
James, Juanita **13**
James, LeBron **46, 78**
James, Rick **19**
James, Sharpe **23, 69**
James, Skip **38**
Jamison, Judith **7, 67**
Jarreau, Al **21, 65**
Jarrett, Valerie **73**
Jarrett, Vernon D. **42**
Jarvis, Charlene Drew **21**
Jarvis, Erich **67**
Jarvis, Kristen **85**
Jasper, Kenji **39**
Jay-Z **27, 69**
Jazzy Jeff **32**
Jealous, Benjamin **70**
Jefferson, Blind Lemon **81**
Jefferson, Denise **87**
Jefferson, William J. **25, 72**
Jeffries, Leonard **8**
Jemison, Mae C. **1, 35**
Jemison, Major L. **48**
Jenifer, Franklyn G. **2**
Jenkins, Beverly **14**
Jenkins, Ella **15**
Jenkins, Ray **77**
Jennings, Lyfe **56, 69**
Jerkins, Rodney **31**
Jeter, Claude **75**
Jeter, Derek **27**
Jimmy Jam **13**
Joe, Yolanda **21**
John, Daymond **23**
Johns, Vernon **38**
Johnson, Angela **52**
Johnson, Avery **62**
Johnson, Beverly **2**
Johnson, Buddy **36**
Johnson, Charles **1, 82**
Johnson, Charles S. **12**
Johnson, Clifford "Connie" **52**
Johnson, Earvin "Magic" **3, 39**
Johnson, Eddie Bernice **8**
Johnson, Eunice W. **83**
Johnson, George E. **29**
Johnson, Georgia Douglas **41**

Johnson, Hank, Jr. **80**
Johnson, Harry E. **57**
Johnson, Harvey, Jr. **24, 82**
Johnson, J. J. **37**
Johnson, Jack **8**
Johnson, James Weldon **5**
Johnson, Je'Caryous **63**
Johnson, Jeh C. **76**
Johnson, Jeh Vincent **44**
Johnson, John H. **3, 54**
Johnson, Johnnie **56**
Johnson, Katherine (Coleman
  Goble) **61**
Johnson, Kevin **70**
Johnson, Larry **28**
Johnson, Levi **48**
Johnson, Lonnie **85**
Johnson, Lonnie G. **32**
Johnson, Mamie "Peanut" **40**
Johnson, Mat **31**
Johnson, Michael **13**
Johnson, Mordecai Wyatt **79**
Johnson, Norma L. Holloway **17**
Johnson, R. M. **36**
Johnson, Rafer **33**
Johnson, Robert **2**
Johnson, Robert L. **3, 39**
Johnson, Robert T. **17**
Johnson, Rodney Van **28**
Johnson, Sheila Crump **48**
Johnson, Shoshana **47**
Johnson, Virginia **9**
Johnson, William Henry **3**
Johnson-George, Tamara **79**
Jolley, Willie **28**
Jones, Absalom **52**
Jones, Alex **64**
Jones, Bill T. **1, 46, 80**
Jones, Bobby **20**
Jones, Booker T. **84**
Jones, Carl **7**
Jones, Caroline **29**
Jones, Clara Stanton **51**
Jones, Cobi N'Gai **18**
Jones, Cullen **73**
Jones, Donell **29**
Jones, Doris W. **62**
Jones, E. Edward, Sr. **45**
Jones, Ed "Too Tall" **46**
Jones, Edith Mae Irby **65**
Jones, Edward P. **43, 67**
Jones, Elaine R. **7, 45**
Jones, Elvin **14, 68**
Jones, Emil, Jr. **74**
Jones, Etta **35**
Jones, Eugene Kinckle **79**
Jones, Frederick McKinley **68**
Jones, Gayl **37**
Jones, Hank **57, 86**
Jones, Ingrid Saunders **18**
Jones, James Earl **3, 49, 79**
Jones, Jonah **39**
Jones, K. C. **83**
Jones, Lois Mailou **13**
Jones, Lou **64**
Jones, Marion **21, 66**
Jones, Merlakia **34**
Jones, Orlando **30**
Jones, Paul R. **76**
Jones, Quincy **8, 30**
Jones, Randy **35**
Jones, Robert G. **81**
Jones, Sam **85**

Jones, Sarah **39**
Jones, Sharon **86**
Jones, Thad **68**
Jones, Thomas W. **41**
Jones, Van **70**
Jones, Wayne **53**
Jones, William A., Jr. **61**
Joplin, Scott **6**
Jordan, Barbara **4, 78**
Jordan, Eddie **82**
Jordan, Eddie **83**
Jordan, June **7, 35**
Jordan, Michael **6, 21**
Jordan, Montell **23**
Jordan, Vernon E. **3, 35**
Joseph, Kathie-Ann **56**
Josey, E. J. **10**
Joyce, Dru **81**
Joyner, Marjorie Stewart **26**
Joyner, Matilda Sissieretta **15**
Joyner, Tom **19**
Joyner-Kersee, Jackie **5**
Julian, Percy Lavon **6**
July, William **27**
Just, Ernest Everett **3**
Justice, David **18**
Kaigler, Denise **63**
Kaiser, Cecil **42**
Kandi **83**
Kani, Karl **10**
Karenga, Maulana **10, 71**
Karim, Benjamin **61**
Kaufman, Monica **66**
Kay, Ulysses **37**
Kearney, Janis **54**
Kearse, Amalya Lyle **12**
Kee, John P. **43**
Keene, John **73**
Keflezighi, Meb **49**
Keith, Damon J. **16, 74**
Keith, Floyd A. **61**
Kelis **58**
Kelley, Cliff **75**
Kelley, Elijah **65**
Kelley, Malcolm David **59**
Kellogg, Clark **64**
Kelly, Patrick **3**
Kelly, R. **18, 44, 71**
Kem **47**
Kendrick, Erika **57**
Kendricks, Eddie **22**
Kennedy, Adrienne **11**
Kennedy, Florynce **12, 33**
Kennedy, Randall **40**
Kennedy-Overton, Jayne Harris **46**
Kenney, John A., Jr. **48**
Kenoly, Ron **45**
Kenyatta, Robin **54**
Kerry, Leon G. **46**
Keyes, Alan L. **11**
Keys, Alicia **32, 68**
Khan, Chaka **12, 50**
Khanga, Yelena **6**
Kid Cudi **83**
Kidd, Jason **86**
Kidd, Mae Street **39**
Killens, John O. **54**
Killings, Debra **57**
Killingsworth, Cleve, Jr. **54**
Kilpatrick, Carolyn Cheeks **16**
Kilpatrick, Kwame **34, 71**
Kimbro, Dennis **10**
Kimbro, Henry A. **25**

Kimbro, Warren 76
Kincaid, Bernard 28
Kincaid, Jamaica 4
King, Alonzo 38
King, B. B. 7
King, Barbara 22
King, Bernice 4, 81
King, Colbert I. 69
King, Coretta Scott 3, 57
King, Dexter 10
King, Don 14
King, Gayle 19
King, Martin Luther, III 20
King, Martin Luther, Jr. 1
King, Preston 28
King, Reatha Clark 65
King, Regina 22, 45
King, Robert Arthur 58
King, Robert Hillary 84
King, Teresa 80
King, Woodie, Jr. 27
King, Yolanda 6
Kirby, George 14
Kirk, Ron 11, 75
Kitt, Eartha 16, 75
Kitt, Sandra 23
Kittles, Rick 51
Kitwana, Bakari 86
Klugh, Earl 59
Knight, Etheridge 37
Knight, Gladys 16, 66
Knight, Marie 80
Knight, Suge 11, 30
Knowles, Tina 61
Knowling, Robert E., Jr. 38
Knox, Simmie 49
Knuckles, Frankie 42
Komunyakaa, Yusef 9
Kong, B. Waine 50
Kool Moe Dee 37
Kotto, Yaphet 7
Kountz, Samuel L. 10
Kravitz, Lenny 10, 34
KRS-One 34
K-Swift 73
Kunjufu, Jawanza 3, 50
La Salle, Eriq 12
LaBelle, Patti 13, 30
Lacy, Sam 30, 46
Ladd, Ernie 64
Ladner, Joyce A. 42
Lafontant, Jewel Stradford 3, 51
Lampkin, Daisy 19
Lampley, Oni Faida 43, 71
Lane, Charles 3
Lane, Vincent 5
Langford, Larry P. 74
Langhart Cohen, Janet 19, 60
Lanier, Bob 47
Lanier, Willie 33
Lankford, Ray 23
Larkin, Barry 24
Larrieux, Amel 63
Lars, Byron 32
Larsen, Nella 10
Laryea, Thomas Davies, III 67
Lashley, Bobby 63
Lassiter, Roy 24
Lathan, Sanaa 27
Latimer, Lewis H. 4
Lattimore, Kenny 35
LaVette, Bettye 85
Lavizzo-Mourey, Risa 48

Lawless, Theodore K. 8
Lawrence, Jacob 4, 28
Lawrence, Martin 6, 27
Lawrence, Robert H., Jr. 16
Lawrence-Lightfoot, Sara 10
Lawson, Jennifer 1, 50
Layton, William 87
Leadbelly 82
Leary, Kathryn D. 10
Leavell, Dorothy R. 17
Ledisi 73
Lee, Annie Frances 22
Lee, Barbara 25
Lee, Bertram M., Sr. 46
Lee, Canada 8
Lee, Consuela 84
Lee, Debra L. 62
Lee, Eric P. 79
Lee, Joe A. 45
Lee, Joie 1
Lee, Leslie 85
Lee, Malcolm D. 75
Lee, Raphael C. 87
Lee, Spike 5, 19, 86
Lee-Smith, Hughie 5, 22
Leevy, Carrol M. 42
Leffall, Lasalle, Jr. 3, 64
Legend, John 67
Leggs, Kingsley 62
Leland, Mickey 2
Lemmons, Kasi 20
Lennox, Betty 31
LeNoire, Rosetta 37
Lenox, Adriane 59
Leon, Kenny 10
Leonard, Buck 67
Leonard, Sugar Ray 15
Leslie, Lisa 16, 73
Lester, Bill 42, 85
Lester, Julius 9
Lesure, James 64
LeTang, Henry 66
Letson, Al 39
Levert, Eddie 70
Levert, Gerald 22, 59
Lewis, Ananda 28
Lewis, Aylwin 51
Lewis, Butch 71
Lewis, Byron E. 13
Lewis, Carl 4
Lewis, David Levering 9
Lewis, Delano 7
Lewis, Edmonia 10
Lewis, Edward T. 21
Lewis, Emmanuel 36
Lewis, Henry 38
Lewis, John 2, 46, 83
Lewis, Marvin 51, 87
Lewis, Norman 39
Lewis, Oliver 56
Lewis, Ramsey 35, 70
Lewis, Ray 33
Lewis, Reginald F. 6
Lewis, Samella 25
Lewis, Shirley A. R. 14
Lewis, Terry 13
Lewis, Thomas 19
Lewis, William M., Jr. 40
Lewis-Thornton, Rae 32
Ligging, Alfred, III 43
Ligon, Glenn 82
Lil' Kim 28
Lil Wayne 66, 84

Liles, Kevin 42
Lincoln, Abbey 3
Lincoln, C. Eric 38
Lindsey, Tommie 51
Lipscomb, Mance 49
LisaRaye 27
Lister, Marquita 65
Liston, Sonny 33
Little, Benilde 21
Little, Floyd 86
Little, Robert L. 2
Little Milton 36, 54
Little Richard 15
Little Walter 36
Littlepage, Craig 35
LL Cool J 16, 49
Llewellyn, J. Bruce 13, 85
Lloyd, Earl 26
Lloyd, John Henry "Pop" 30
Lloyd, Reginald 64
Locke, Alain 10
Locke, Attica 85
Locke, Eddie 44
Lofton, James 42
Lofton, Kenny 12
Logan, Onnie Lee 14
Logan, Rayford W. 40
Lomax, Michael L. 58
Long, Eddie L. 29
Long, Huey 79
Long, Loretta 58
Long, Nia 17
Long, Richard Alexander 65
Lopes, Lisa "Left Eye" 36
Lorde, Audre 6
Lott, Ronnie 9
Louis, Errol T. 8
Louis, Joe 5
Loury, Glenn 36
Love, Darlene 23
Love, Ed 58
Love, Laura 50
Love, Nat 9
Love, Reggie 77
Lovell, Whitfield 74
Lover, Ed 10
Loving, Alvin, Jr. 35, 53
Loving, Mildred 69
Lowe, Herbert 57
Lowe, Sidney 64
Lowery, Joseph 2
Lowery, Myron 80
Lowry, A. Leon 60
Lucas, John 7
Lucie, Lawrence 80
Lucien, Jon 66
Luckett, Letoya 61
Lucy, William 50
Lucy Foster, Autherine 35
Ludacris 37, 60
Luke, Derek 61
Lumbly, Carl 47
Lumet, Jenny 80
Lyles, Lester Lawrence 31
Lymon, Frankie 22
Lynch, Shola 61
Lyons, Henry 12
Lyttle, Hulda Margaret 14
Mabley, Moms 15
Mabrey, Vicki 26
Mabry, Marcus 70
Mac, Bernie 29, 61, 72
Mackey, Biz 82

Mackey, Nathaniel 75
Madhubuti, Haki 7, 85
Madison, Joseph E. 17
Madison, Paula 37
Madison, Romell 45
Mahal, Taj 39
Mahorn, Rick 60
Maitreya, Sananda 85
Majette, Denise 41
Major, Clarence 9
Majors, Jeff 41
Malco, Romany 71
Mallett, Conrad, Jr. 16
Mallory, Mark 62
Malone, Annie 13
Malone, Karl 18, 51
Malone, Maurice 32
Malone, Moses 79
Malone Jones, Vivian 59
Malveaux, Floyd 54
Malveaux, Julianne 32, 70
Manigault, Earl "The Goat" 15
Manigault-Stallworth, Omarosa 69
Manley, Audrey Forbes 16
Manning, Frankie 78
Marable, Manning 10
March, William Carrington 56
Mariner, Jonathan 41
Marino, Eugene Antonio 30
Mario 71
Marrow, Queen Esther 24
Marsalis, Branford 34
Marsalis, Delfeayo 41
Marsalis, Wynton 16
Marsh, Henry, III 32
Marshall, Bella 22
Marshall, Kerry James 59
Marshall, Paule 7, 77
Marshall, Thurgood 1, 44
Martin, Darnell 43, 78
Martin, Helen 31
Martin, Jesse L. 31
Martin, Louis E. 16
Martin, Roberta 58
Martin, Roland S. 49, 84
Martin, Ruby Grant 49
Martin, Sara 38
Mase 24
Mason, Felicia 31
Mason, Herman, Jr. 83
Mason, Ronald 27
Massaquoi, Hans J. 30
Massenburg, Kedar 23
Massey, Brandon 40
Massey, Walter E. 5, 45
Massie, Samuel Proctor, Jr. 29
Master P 21
Matejka, Adrian 87
Mathis, Greg 26
Mathis, Johnny 20
Matthews, Mark 59
Matthews Shatteen, Westina 51
Maxey, Randall 46
Maxis, Theresa 62
Maxwell 20, 81
May, Derrick 41
Mayfield, Curtis 2, 43
Mayhew, Martin R. 76
Mayhew, Richard 39
Maynard, Nancy Hicks 73
Maynard, Robert C. 7
Maynor, Dorothy 19
Mayo, Whitman 32

Mays, Benjamin E. 7
Mays, Leslie A. 41
Mays, William G. 34
Mays, Willie 3
Mayweather, Floyd, Jr. 57
MC Breed 75
M.C. Hammer 20, 80
MC Lyte 34
McAdoo, Bob 75
McAnulty, William E., Jr. 66
McBride, Bryant 18
McBride, Chi 73
McBride, James 35, 87
McCabe, Jewell Jackson 10
McCall, H. Carl 27
McCall, Nathan 8
McCann, Renetta 44
McCarthy, Sandy 64
McCarty, Osceola 16
McCauley, Gina 76
McClendon, Lisa 61
McClinton, Marion Isaac 77
McClurkin, Donnie 25
McCoo, Marilyn 53
McCoy, Elijah 8
McCrary Anthony, Crystal 70
McCray, Nikki 18
McCullough, Geraldine 58, 79
McDaniel, Hattie 5
McDaniel, Randall Cornell 81
McDaniels, Ralph 79
McDonald, Audra 20, 62
McDonald, Erroll 1
McDonald, Gabrielle Kirk 20
McDougall, Gay J. 11, 43
McDuffie, Dwayne 62
McEwen, Mark 5
McFadden, Bernice L. 39
McFarlan, Tyron 60
McFarland, Roland 49
McFerrin, Bobby 68
McGee, Charles 10
McGee, James D. 74
McGee, James Madison 46
McGill, Anthony 76
McGlowan, Angela 64, 86
McGrady, Tracy 80
McGriff, Fred 24
McGriff, Jimmy 72
McGruder, Aaron 28, 56
McGruder, Robert 22, 35
McGuire, Raymond J. 57
McHenry, Donald F. 83
McKay, Claude 6
McKay, Nellie Yvonne 17, 57
McKee, Lonette 12
McKenzie, Vashti M. 29
McKinney, Cynthia 11, 52, 74
McKinney, Nina Mae 40
McKinney-Whetstone, Diane 27
McKinnon, Isaiah 9
McKissack, Leatrice 80
McKissick, Floyd B. 3
McKnight, Brian 18, 34
McLean, Jackie 78
McLeod, Gus 27
McMillan, Rosalynn A. 36
McMillan, Terry 4, 17, 53
McMurray, Georgia L. 36
McNabb, Donovan 29
McNair, Ronald 3, 58
McNair, Steve 22, 47, 79
McNeil, Lori 1

McPhail, Sharon 2
McPherson, David 32
McPherson, James Alan 70
McQueen, Butterfly 6, 54
McRae, Carmen 77
McRae, Hal 84
McWhorter, John 35
Meadows, Tim 30
Meek, Carrie 6, 36
Meek, Kendrick 41
Meeks, Gregory 25
Mehretu, Julie 85
Mell, Patricia 49
Melton, Frank 81
Melton, Harold D. 79
Memphis Minnie 33
Mengestu, Dinaw 66
Mercado-Valdes, Frank 43
Meredith, James H. 11
Merkerson, S. Epatha 47, 83
Metcalfe, Ralph 26
Method Man 81
Mfume, Kweisi 6, 41
Micheaux, Oscar 7
Michele, Michael 31
Mickelbury, Penny 28
Miles, Buddy 69
Millender-McDonald, Juanita 21, 61
Miller, Bebe 3
Miller, Cheryl 10, 74
Miller, Dorie 29
Miller, Larry G. 72
Miller, Marcus 84
Miller, Reggie 33
Miller, Warren F., Jr. 53
Miller, Wentworth 75
Miller-Travis, Vernice 64
Millines Dziko, Trish 28
Millner, Denene 76
Mills, Florence 22
Mills, Joseph C. 51
Mills, Sam 33
Mills, Stephanie 36
Mills, Steve 47
Milner, Ron 39
Milton, DeLisha 31
Minaj, Nicki 86
Mingo, Frank 32
Mingus, Charles 15
Minor, DeWayne 32
Mitchell, Arthur 2, 47
Mitchell, Brian Stokes 21
Mitchell, Corinne 8
Mitchell, Elvis 67
Mitchell, Kel 66
Mitchell, Leona 42
Mitchell, Loften 31
Mitchell, Nicole 66
Mitchell, Parren J. 42, 66
Mitchell, Russ 21, 73
Mitchell, Sam 82
Mitchell, Stephanie 36
Mo', Keb' 36
Mohammed, Nazr 64
Mohammed, W. Deen 27
Mokae, Zakes 80
Monáe, Janelle 86
Monica 21
Mo'Nique 35, 84
Monk, Art 38, 73
Monk, Thelonious 1
Monroe, Bryan 71
Monroe, Mary 35

Montgomery, Tim 41
Moody, James 83
Moody-Adams, Michele 76
Moon, Warren 8, 66
Mooney, Paul 37
Moore, Barbara C. 49
Moore, Chante 26
Moore, Dorothy Rudd 46
Moore, Gwendolynne S. 55
Moore, Harry T. 29
Moore, Jessica Care 30
Moore, Johnny B. 38
Moore, Juanita 83
Moore, LeRoi 72
Moore, Melba 21
Moore, Minyon 45
Moore, Shemar 21
Moore, Undine Smith 28
Moore, Wes 86
Moorer, Michael 19
Moose, Charles 40
Morgan, Garrett 1
Morgan, Gertrude 63
Morgan, Irene 65
Morgan, Joe Leonard 9
Morgan, Rose 11
Morgan, Tracy 61
Morial, Ernest "Dutch" 26
Morial, Marc H. 20, 51
Morris, Garrett 31
Morris, Greg 28
Morris, Raheem 77
Morrison, Sam 50
Morrison, Toni 2, 15, 86
Morrison, Vanessa 84
Morton, Azie Taylor 48
Morton, Jelly Roll 29
Morton, Joe 18
Mos Def 30
Moses, Edwin 8
Moses, Gilbert 12
Moses, Robert Parris 11
Mosley, Shane 32
Mosley, Walter 5, 25, 68
Moss, Carlton 17
Moss, J. 64
Moss, Otis, Jr. 72
Moss, Otis, III 72
Moss, Preacher 63
Moss, Randy 23
Mossell, Gertrude Bustill 40
Moten, Etta 18
Motley, Archibald, Jr. 30
Motley, Constance Baker 10, 55
Motley, Marion 26
Moton, Robert Russa 83
Mourning, Alonzo 17, 44
Moutoussamy-Ashe, Jeanne 7
Mowry, Jess 7
Mowry, Tamera 79
Mowry, Tia 78
Moyo, Karega Kofi 36
Moyo, Yvette Jackson 36
Muhammad, Ava 31
Muhammad, Elijah 4
Muhammad, Jabir Herbert 72
Muhammad, Khallid Abdul 10, 31
Mullen, Harryette 34
Mullen, Nicole C. 45
Murphy, Eddie 4, 20, 61
Murphy, John H. 42
Murphy, Laura M. 43
Murray, Albert L. 33

Murray, Cecil 12, 47
Murray, Eddie 12
Murray, Lenda 10
Murray, Pauli 38
Murray, Tai 47
Murrell, Sylvia Marilyn 49
Muse, Clarence Edouard 21
Musiq 37, 84
Mya 35
Myers, Walter Dean 8, 70
Myles, Kim 69
Nabrit, Samuel Milton 47
Nagin, C. Ray 42, 57
Nance, Cynthia 71
Nanula, Richard D. 20
Napoleon, Benny N. 23
Nas 33
Nash, Diane 72
Nash, Joe 55
Nash, Johnny 40
Nash, Niecy 66
Nash, Shannon King 84
Naylor, Gloria 10, 42
Ndegeocello, Meshell 15, 83
Neal, Elise 29
Neal, Larry 38
Neal, Mark Anthony 74
Neal, Raful 44
Neals, Otto 73
Nelly 32
Nelson, Jill 6, 54
Nelson Meigs, Andrea 48
Neville, Aaron 21
Neville, Arthel 53
Newcombe, Don 24
Newkirk, Pamela 69
Newman, David 76
Newman, Lester C. 51
Newsome, Ozzie 26
Newton, Huey 2
Ne-Yo 65
Ngaujah, Sahr 86
Nicholas, Denise 82
Nicholas, Fayard 20, 57
Nicholas, Harold 20
Nichols, Nichelle 11
Nissel, Angela 42
Nix, Robert N. C., Jr. 51
N'Namdi, George R. 17
Noble, Gil 76
Noble, Ronald 46
Norman, Christina 47
Norman, Jessye 5
Norman, Maidie 20
Norman, Pat 10
Norris, Michele 83
Norton, Eleanor Holmes 7
Norton, Meredith 72
Notorious B.I.G. 20
Nottage, Lynn 66
Nugent, Richard Bruce 39
Nunn, Annetta 43
Nutter, Michael 69
Obadele, Imari 84
Obama, Barack 49, 74
Obama, Michelle 61
Odetta 37, 74
Odom, Lamar 81
Oglesby, Zena 12
Ogletree, Charles, Jr. 12, 47
O'Grady, Lorraine 73
Ojikutu, Bayo 66
Ojikutu, Bisola 65

Ol' Dirty Bastard 52
Olden, Georg(e) 44
O'Leary, Hazel 6
Oliver, Jerry 37
Oliver, Joe "King" 42
Oliver, John J., Jr. 48
Oliver, Kimberly 60
Oliver, Pam 54
O'Neal, Ron 46
O'Neal, Shaquille 8, 30
O'Neal, Stanley 38, 67
O'Neil, Buck 19, 59
Onyewu, Oguchi 60
Orange, James 74
Orlandersmith, Dael 42
Orman, Roscoe 55
Ormes, Jackie 73
Osborne, Jeffrey 26
Osborne, Na'taki 54
Otis, Clarence, Jr. 55
Otis, Clyde 67
Ouattara, Morou 74
Owens, Helen 48
Owens, Jack 38
Owens, Jesse 2
Owens, Major 6
Owens, Terrell 53
Pace, Betty 59
Pace, Orlando 21
Packer, Daniel 56
Packer, Will 71
Packer, Z. Z. 64
Page, Alan 7
Page, Clarence 4
Page, Greg 78
Page, Inman 82
Paige, Rod 29
Paige, Satchel 7
Painter, Nell Irvin 24
Palmer, Keke 68
Palmer, Rissi 65
Palmer, Violet 59
Parham, Marjorie B. 71
Parish, Robert 43
Parker, Candace 74
Parker, Charlie 20
Parker, Jim 64
Parker, Kellis E. 30
Parker, Maceo 72
Parker, Nicole Ari 52
Parker, Pat 19
Parker, Ray, Jr. 85
Parker, Star 70
Parks, Bernard C. 17
Parks, Gordon 1, 35, 58
Parks, Rosa 1, 35, 56
Parks, Suzan-Lori 34, 85
Parr, Russ 51
Parsons, James 14
Parsons, Richard Dean 11, 33
Paterson, Basil A. 69
Paterson, David A. 59
Patrick, Deval 12, 61
Patterson, Floyd 19, 58
Patterson, Frederick Douglass 12
Patterson, Gilbert Earl 41
Patterson, J. O., Jr. 80
Patterson, Louise 25
Patterson, Mary Jane 54
Patton, Antwan 45
Patton, Paula 62
Paul, Chris 84
Payne, Allen 13

Payne, Donald M. 2, 57
Payne, Ethel L. 28
Payne, Freda 58
Payne, Ulice 42
Payne, William D. 60
Payton, Benjamin F. 23
Payton, John 48
Payton, Walter 11, 25
Peck, Carolyn 23
Peete, Calvin 11
Peete, Holly Robinson 20
Peete, Rodney 60
Pena, Paul 58
Pendergrass, Teddy 22, 83
Peoples, Dottie 22
Perez, Anna 1
Perkins, Edward 5
Perkins, James, Jr. 55
Perkins, Marion 38
Perkins, Pinetop 70
Perkins, Tony 24
Perren, Freddie 60
Perrineau, Harold, Jr. 51
Perrot, Kim 23
Perry, James 83
Perry, Laval 64
Perry, Lowell 30
Perry, Tyler 40, 54
Perry, Warren 56
Person, Waverly 9, 51
Peters, Margaret 43
Peters, Matilda 43
Petersen, Frank E. 31
Peterson, James 38
Peterson, James 81
Peterson, Jesse Lee 81
Peterson, Marvin "Hannibal" 27
Petry, Ann 19
Phifer, Mekhi 25
Phillips, Charles E., Jr. 57
Phillips, Helen L. 63
Phillips, Joseph C. 73
Phillips, Teresa L. 42
Phipps, Wintley 59
Pickens, James, Jr. 59
Pickett, Bill 11
Pickett, Cecil 39
Pierce, Elijah 84
Pierce, Harold 75
Pierce, Paul 71
Pierre, Percy Anthony 46
Pincham, R. Eugene, Sr. 69
Pinchback, P. B. S. 9
Pinckney, Bill 42
Pinckney, Sandra 56
Pindell, Howardena 55
Pinder, Jefferson 77
Pinderhughes, John 47
Pinkett, Randal 61
Pinkett Smith, Jada 10, 41
Pinkney, Fayette 80
Pinkney, Jerry 15
Pinkston, W. Randall 24
Pinn, Vivian Winona 49
Piper, Adrian 71
Pippen, Scottie 15
Pippin, Horace 9
Pitts, Byron 71
Pitts, Derrick 77
Pitts, Robb 84
Pitts, Leonard, Jr. 54, 85
Player, Willa B. 43
Pleasant, Mary Ellen 9

Pleasure P 84
Plessy, Homer Adolph 31
P.M. Dawn 54
Poindexter, Hildrus A. 87
Poitier, Sidney 11, 36
Poitier, Sydney Tamiia 65
Polite, Carlene Hatcher 82
Pollard, Fritz 53
Pope.L, William 72
Porter, James A. 11
Porter, Terry 75
Potter, Myrtle 40
Pough, Terrell 58
Pounder, CCH 72
Poussaint, Alvin F. 5, 67
Poussaint, Renee 78
Powell, Adam Clayton, Jr. 3
Powell, Benny 87
Powell, Bud 24
Powell, Colin 1, 28, 75
Powell, Debra A. 23
Powell, Kevin 31, 74
Powell, Maxine 8
Powell, Michael 32
Powell, Mike 7
Powell, Renee 34
Powell, William J. 82
Power, Will 83
Pratt, Awadagin 31
Pratt, Geronimo 18
Pratt, Kyla 57
Preer, Evelyn 82
Premice, Josephine 41
Pressley, Condace L. 41
Preston, Billy 39, 59
Price, Florence 37
Price, Frederick K.C. 21
Price, Glenda 22
Price, Hugh B. 9, 54
Price, Kelly 23
Price, Leontyne 1
Price, Richard 51
Pride, Charley 26
Primus, Pearl 6
Prince 18, 65
Prince, Richard E. 71
Prince, Ron 64
Prince, Tayshaun 68
Prince-Bythewood, Gina 31, 77
Pritchard, Robert Starling 21
Procope, Ernesta 23
Procope, John Levy 56
Prophet, Nancy Elizabeth 42
Prothrow-Stith, Deborah 10
Pryor, Rain 65
Pryor, Richard 3, 24, 56
Puckett, Kirby 4, 58
Pugh, Charles 81
Purdie, Bernard 77
Purnell, Silas 59
Puryear, Martin 42
Putney, Martha S. 75
Quarles, Benjamin Arthur 18
Quarles, Norma 25
Quarterman, Lloyd Albert 4
Queen Latifah 1, 16, 58
?uestlove 74
Quigless, Helen G. 49
Quince, Peggy A. 69
Quivers, Robin 61
Rabb, Maurice F., Jr. 58
Radcliffe, Ted 74
Ragin, Derek Lee 84

Rahman, Aishah 37
Raines, Franklin Delano 14
Rainey, Ma 33
Ralph, Sheryl Lee 18
Ramsey, Charles H. 21, 69
Rand, A. Barry 6
Randall, Alice 38
Randall, Dudley 8, 55
Randle, John 87
Randle, Theresa 16
Randolph, A. Philip 3
Randolph, Linda A. 52
Randolph, Willie 53
Rangel, Charles B. 3, 52, 85
Raoul, Kwame 55
Rapier, James T. 82
Rashad, Ahmad 18
Rashad, Phylicia 21
Raspberry, William 2
Raven 44
Rawlinson, Johnnie B. 79
Rawls, Lou 17, 57
Ray, Charlotte E. 60
Ray, Gene Anthony 47
Ray J 86
Razaf, Andy 19
Reagon, Bernice Johnson 7
Reagon, Toshi 76
Reason, J. Paul 19
Record, Eugene 60
Reddick, Lance 52
Reddick, Lawrence Dunbar 20
Redding, Ann Holmes 77
Redding, J. Saunders 26
Redding, Louis L. 26
Redding, Otis 16
Redman 81
Redman, Joshua 30
Redmond, Eugene 23
Redwood, John Henry 78
Reed, A. C. 36
Reed, Ishmael 8
Reed, Jimmy 38
Reed, Kasim 82
Reed, Willis, Jr. 86
Reed Hall, Alaina 83
Reems, Ernestine Cleveland 27
Reese, Della 6, 20
Reese, Milous J., Jr. 51
Reese, Pokey 28
Reese, Tracy 54
Reeves, Dianne 32
Reeves, Gregory 49
Reeves, Martha 85
Reeves, Rachel J. 23
Reeves, Triette Lipsey 27
Reid, Antonio "L.A." 28
Reid, Irvin D. 20
Reid, Senghor 55
Reid, Tim 56
Reid, Vernon 34
Reverend Ike 79
Reynolds, Harold 77
Reynolds, Star Jones 10, 27, 61
Rhames, Ving 14, 50
Rhimes, Shonda Lynn 67
Rhoden, Dwight 40
Rhoden, William C. 67
Rhodes, Jewell Parker 84
Rhodes, Ray 14
Rhone, Sylvia 2
Rhymes, Busta 31
Ribbs, Willy T. 2

Ribeau, Sidney 70
Ribeiro, Alfonso 17
Rice, Condoleezza 3, 28, 72
Rice, Constance LaMay 60
Rice, Jerry 5, 55
Rice, Jim 75
Rice, Linda Johnson 9, 41
Rice, Louise Allen 54
Rice, Norm 8
Rice, Susan E. 74
Richard, J. R. 87
Richards, Beah 30
Richards, Hilda 49
Richards, Sanya 66
Richardson, Desmond 39
Richardson, Donna 39
Richardson, Julieanna 81
Richardson, LaTanya 71
Richardson, Laura 81
Richardson, Nolan 9
Richardson, Rupert 67
Richardson, Salli 68
Richie, Leroy C. 18
Richie, Lionel 27, 65
Richmond, Mitch 19
Rideau, Iris 46
Ridley, John 69
Riggs, Marlon 5, 44
Riles, Wilson C. 79
Riley, Helen Caldwell Day 13
Riley, Rochelle 50
Ringgold, Faith 4, 81
Riperton, Minnie 32
Rivers, Doc 25, 81
Rivers, Eugene F., III 81
Roach, Max 21, 63
Roberts, Darryl 70
Roberts, Deborah 35
Roberts, Kimberly Rivers 72
Roberts, Lillian 83
Roberts, Marcus 19
Roberts, Mike 57
Roberts, Robin 16, 54
Roberts, Roy S. 14
Robertson, Gil L., IV 85
Robertson, Oscar 26
Robeson, Eslanda Goode 13
Robeson, Paul 2
Robinson, Aminah 50
Robinson, Bill "Bojangles" 11
Robinson, Bishop L. 66
Robinson, Cleo Parker 38
Robinson, David 24
Robinson, Eddie G. 10
Robinson, Eugene 77
Robinson, Fatima 34
Robinson, Fenton 38
Robinson, Frank 9, 87
Robinson, Jackie 6
Robinson, LaVaughn 69
Robinson, Malcolm S. 44
Robinson, Matt 69
Robinson, Max 3
Robinson, Patrick 19, 71
Robinson, Rachel 16
Robinson, Randall 7, 46
Robinson, Reginald R. 53
Robinson, Sharon 22
Robinson, Shaun 36
Robinson, Smokey 3, 49
Robinson, Spottswood W., III 22
Robinson, Sugar Ray 18
Robinson, Sylvia 79

Robinson, Will 51, 69
Roble, Abdi 71
Roby, Kimberla Lawson 86
Roche, Joyce M. 17
Rochon, Lela 16
Rochon, Stephen W. 78
Rock, Chris 3, 22, 66
Rock, The 29, 66
Rodgers, Johnathan 6, 51
Rodgers, Rod 36
Rodman, Dennis 12, 44
Rodriguez, Jimmy 47
Rodriguez, Cheryl 64
Rogers, Alan G. 72
Rogers, Jimmy 38
Rogers, Joe 27
Rogers, Joel Augustus 30
Rogers, John W., Jr. 5, 52
Roker, Al 12, 49
Roker, Roxie 68
Rolle, Esther 13, 21
Rollins, Charlemae Hill 27
Rollins, Howard E., Jr. 16
Rollins, Jimmy 70
Rollins, Sonny 37
Rose, Anika Noni 70
Rose, Derrick 82
Ross, Charles 27
Ross, Diana 8, 27
Ross, Don 27
Ross, Isaiah "Doc" 40
Ross, Rick 79
Ross, Tracee Ellis 35
Ross-Lee, Barbara 67
Roundtree, Dovey 80
Roundtree, Richard 27
Rowan, Carl T. 1, 30
Rowell, Victoria 13, 68
Roxanne Shante 33
Roy, Kenny 51
Rubin, Chanda 37
Rucker, Darius 34, 74
Rudolph, Maya 46
Rudolph, Wilma 4
Ruffin, Josephine St. Pierre 75
Ruffins, Kermit 85
Ruley, Ellis 38
Run 31, 73, 75
Rupaul 17
Rush, Bobby 26, 76
Rush, Bobby 78
Rush, Otis 38
Rushen, Patrice 12
Rushing, Jimmy 37
Russell, Bill 8
Russell, Brenda 52
Russell, Herman Jerome 17
Russell, Nipsey 66
Russell-McCloud, Patricia A. 17
Rust, Art, Jr. 83
Rustin, Bayard 4
RZA 80
Saar, Alison 16
Saar, Betye 80
Sabathia, CC 74
St. Jacques, Raymond 8
Saint James, Synthia 12
St. John, Kristoff 25
St. Julien, Marlon 29
St. Patrick, Mathew 48
Saldana, Zoe 72
Sallee, Charles 38
Salter, Nikkole 73

Salters, Lisa 71
Samara, Noah 15
Sample, Joe 51
Sampson, Charles 13
Sanchez, Sonia 17, 51
Sanders, Angelia 86
Sanders, Barry 1, 53
Sanders, Bob 72
Sanders, Deion 4, 31
Sanders, Joseph R., Jr. 11
Sanders, Malika 48
Sanders, Pharoah 64
Sanders, Satch 77
Sands, Diana 87
Sanford, Isabel 53
Santamaria, Mongo 81
Santiago-Hudson, Ruben 85
Sapp, Marvin 74
Sapp, Warren 38
Sapphire 14
Satcher, David 7, 57
Savage, Augusta 12
Sawyer, Eugene 81
Sayers, Gale 28
Sayles Belton, Sharon 9, 16
Scantlebury-White, Velma 64
Schmoke, Kurt 1, 48
Schuyler, George Samuel 40
Schuyler, Philippa 50
Scott, C(ornelius) A(dolphus) 29
Scott, David 41
Scott, George 55
Scott, Harold Russell, Jr. 61
Scott, Hazel 66
Scott, Jill 29, 83
Scott, John T. 65
Scott, "Little" Jimmy 48
Scott, Milton 51
Scott, Robert C. 23
Scott, Stuart 34
Scott, Tim 87
Scott, Wendell Oliver, Sr. 19
Scurry, Briana 27
Seals, Son 56
Sears, Leah Ward 5, 79
Sears, Stephanie 53
Sebree, Charles 40
Seele, Pernessa 46
Sengstacke, John 18
Sermon, Erick 81
Serrano, Andres 3
Shabazz, Attallah 6
Shabazz, Betty 7, 26
Shabazz, Ilyasah 36
Shadd, Abraham D. 81
Shakur, Afeni 67
Shakur, Assata 6
Shakur, Tupac 14
Shakur, Yusef 85
Shange, Ntozake 8
Shank, Suzanne F. 77
Shannon, Randy 82
Sharper, Darren 32
Sharpton, Al 21
Shavers, Cheryl 31
Shaw, Bernard 2, 28
Shaw, William J. 30
Sheard, Kierra "Kiki" 61
Sheffield, Gary 16
Shell, Art 1, 66
Shelton, Paula Young 86
Shepherd, Sherri 55
Sherrod, Clayton 17

Sherrod, Shirley 87
Shider, Garry 87
Shinhoster, Earl 32
Shipp, E. R. 15
Shippen, John 43
Shirley, George 33
Shockley, Ann Allen 84
Short, Bobby 52
Short, Columbus 79
Shorter, Wayne 75
Showers, Reggie 30
Shropshire, Thomas B. 49
Shuttlesworth, Fred 47
Sidibe, Gabourey 84
Sifford, Charlie 4, 49
Sigur, Wanda 44
Silas, Paul 24
Silver, Horace 26
Simmons, Bob 29
Simmons, E. Denise 79
Simmons, Gary 58
Simmons, Henry 55
Simmons, Jamal 72
Simmons, Kimora Lee 51, 83
Simmons, Russell 1, 30
Simmons, Ruth J. 13, 38
Simone, Nina 15, 41
Simpson, Carole 6, 30
Simpson, Lorna 4, 36
Simpson, O. J. 15
Simpson, Valerie 21
Simpson-Hoffman, N'kenge 52
Sims, Howard "Sandman" 48
Sims, Lowery Stokes 27
Sims, Naomi 29, 79
Sinbad 1, 16
Singletary, Mike 4, 76
Singleton, John 2, 30
Sinkford, Jeanne C. 13
Sir Mix-A-Lot 82
Sisqo 30
Sissle, Noble 29
Sister Souljah 11
Sizemore, Barbara A. 26
Skinner, Kiron K. 65
Sklarek, Norma Merrick 25
Slater, Rodney E. 15
Slaughter, John Brooks 53
Sledge, Percy 39
Sleet, Moneta, Jr. 5
Slice, Kimbo 73
Slim Thug 86
Slocumb, Jonathan 52
Slyde, Jimmy 70
Smalls, Robert 82
Smaltz, Audrey 12
Smiley, Rickey 59
Smiley, Tavis 20, 68
Smith, Anna Deavere 6, 44
Smith, B(arbara) 11
Smith, Barbara 28
Smith, Bessie 3
Smith, Bruce 80
Smith, Bruce W. 53
Smith, Cladys "Jabbo" 32
Smith, Clarence O. 21
Smith, Damu 54
Smith, Danyel 40
Smith, Dr. Lonnie 49
Smith, Emmitt 7, 87
Smith, Greg 28
Smith, Hilton 29
Smith, Ian 62

Smith, Jaden **82**
Smith, Jane E. **24**
Smith, Jessie Carney **35**
Smith, John L. **22**
Smith, Joshua **10**
Smith, Kemba **70**
Smith, Lonnie Liston **49**
Smith, Lovie **66**
Smith, Malcolm A. **75**
Smith, Mamie **32**
Smith, Marie F. **70**
Smith, Marvin **46**
Smith, Mary Carter **26**
Smith, Morgan **46**
Smith, Nate **49**
Smith, Ozzie **77**
Smith, Princella **86**
Smith, Randy **81**
Smith, Rick **72**
Smith, Roger Guenveur **12**
Smith, Stephen A. **69**
Smith, Stuff **37**
Smith, Tasha **73**
Smith, Trixie **34**
Smith, Tubby **18, 83**
Smith, Vincent D. **48**
Smith, Will **8, 18, 53**
Smith, Willi **8**
Smythe Haith, Mabel **61**
Sneed, Paula A. **18**
Snipes, Wesley **3, 24, 67**
Snoop Dogg **35, 84**
Snow, Samuel **71**
Snowden, Frank M., Jr. **67**
Solomon, Jimmie Lee **38**
Somi **85**
Sommore **61**
Southern, Eileen **56**
Southgate, Martha **58**
Sowell, Thomas **2**
Sparks, Jordin **66**
Spaulding, Charles Clinton **9**
Spearman, Leonard H. O., Sr. **81**
Spears, Warren **52**
Spector, Ronnie **77**
Speech **82**
Spencer, Anne **27**
Spencer, Michael G. **87**
Spigner, Archie **81**
Spikes, Dolores **18**
Spiller, Bill **64**
Sprewell, Latrell **23**
Spriggs, William **67**
Stackhouse, Jerry **30**
Staley, Dawn **57**
Stallings, George A., Jr. **6**
Stampley, Micah **54**
Stanford, John **20**
Stanford, Olivia Lee Dilworth **49**
Stanton, Alysa **78**
Stanton, Robert **20**
Staples, Brent **8**
Staples, Mavis **50**
Staples, "Pops" **32**
Stargell, Willie **29**
Staton, Candi **27**
Staton, Dakota **62**
Staupers, Mabel K. **7**
Stearnes, Norman "Turkey" **31**
Steave-Dickerson, Kia **57**
Steele, Claude Mason **13**
Steele, Lawrence **28**
Steele, Michael **38, 73**

Steele, Shelby **13, 82**
Steinberg, Martha Jean "The
    Queen" **28**
Stephens, Charlotte Andrews **14**
Stew **69**
Steward, David L. **36**
Steward, Emanuel **18**
Stewart, Alison **13**
Stewart, Ella **39**
Stewart, James "Bubba," Jr. **60**
Stewart, Kordell **21**
Stewart, Maria W. Miller **19**
Stewart, Paul Wilbur **12**
Stewart, Tonea Harris **78**
Sticky Fingaz **86**
Still, William Grant **37**
Stingley, Darryl **69**
Stinson, Denise L. **59**
Stith, Charles R. **73**
Stokes, Carl **10, 73**
Stokes, Louis **3**
Stone, Angie **31**
Stone, Chuck **9**
Stone, Sly **85**
Stone, Toni **15**
Stoney, Michael **50**
Stoudemire, Amaré **59**
Stout, Juanita Kidd **24**
Stout, Renee **63**
Stoute, Steve **38**
Strahan, Michael **35, 81**
Strautmanis, Michael **87**
Strawberry, Darryl **22**
Strayhorn, Billy **31**
Street, John F. **24**
Streeter, Sarah **45**
Stringer, C. Vivian **13, 66**
Stringer, Korey **35**
Stringer, Vickie **58**
Studdard, Ruben **46**
Sudarkasa, Niara **4**
Sudduth, Jimmy Lee **65**
Sugarhill Gang, The **79**
Sullivan, Jazmine **81**
Sullivan, Leon H. **3, 30**
Sullivan, Louis **8**
Sullivan, Maxine **37**
Summer, Donna **25**
Sun Ra **60**
Sundiata, Sekou **66**
Sutphen, Mona **77**
Sutton, Percy E. **42, 82**
Swann, Lynn **28**
Sweat, Keith **19**
Sweet, Ossian **68**
Swoopes, Sheryl **12, 56**
Swygert, H. Patrick **22**
Sykes, Roosevelt **20**
Sykes, Wanda **48, 81**
Syler, Rene **53**
Tademy, Lalita **36**
Tait, Michael **57**
Talbert, David **34**
Talbert, Mary B. **77**
Talley, André Leon **56**
Tamar-kali **63**
Tamia **24, 55**
Tampa Red **63**
Tancil, Gladys Quander **59**
Tanksley, Ann **37**
Tanner, Henry Ossawa **1**
Tate, Eleanora E. **20, 55**
Tate, Larenz **15**

Tatum, Art **28**
Tatum, Beverly Daniel **42, 84**
Tatum, Elinor R. **78**
Tatum, Jack **87**
Tatum, Wilbert **76**
Taulbert, Clifton Lemoure **19**
Taylor, Billy **23**
Taylor, Bo **72**
Taylor, Cecil **70**
Taylor, Charles **20**
Taylor, Ephren W., II **61**
Taylor, Gardner C. **76**
Taylor, Helen (Lavon Hollingshed)
    **30**
Taylor, Jason **70**
Taylor, Jermain **60**
Taylor, Koko **40, 80**
Taylor, Kristin Clark **8**
Taylor, Lawrence **25**
Taylor, Marshall Walter "Major" **62**
Taylor, Meshach **4**
Taylor, Mildred D. **26**
Taylor, Natalie **47**
Taylor, Regina **9, 46**
Taylor, Robert Robinson **80**
Taylor, Ron **35**
Taylor, Susan C. **62**
Taylor, Susan L. **10, 86**
Taylor, Susie King **13**
Teer, Barbara Ann **81**
Terrell, Dorothy A. **24**
Terrell, Mary Church **9**
Terrell, Tammi **32**
Terrell-Kearney, Kim **83**
Terry, Clark **39**
Tharpe, Rosetta **65**
The-Dream **74**
Thigpen, Lynne **17, 41**
Thomas, Alma **14**
Thomas, Arthur Ray **52**
Thomas, Clarence **2, 39, 65**
Thomas, Claudia Lynn **64**
Thomas, Debi **26**
Thomas, Derrick **25**
Thomas, Emmitt **71**
Thomas, Frank **12, 51**
Thomas, Franklin A. **5, 49**
Thomas, Irma **29**
Thomas, Isiah **7, 26, 65**
Thomas, Michael **69**
Thomas, Mickalene **61**
Thomas, Rozonda **34, 78**
Thomas, Rufus **20**
Thomas, Sean Patrick **35**
Thomas, Thurman **75**
Thomas, Trisha R. **65**
Thomas, Vivien **9**
Thomas-Graham, Pamela **29**
Thompson, Bennie G. **26**
Thompson, Cynthia Bramlett **50**
Thompson, Don **56**
Thompson, John Douglas **81**
Thompson, John W. **26**
Thompson, Kenan **52**
Thompson, Larry D. **39**
Thompson, Tazewell **13**
Thompson, Tina **25, 75**
Thompson, William C. **35**
Thoms, Tracie **61**
Thornton, Big Mama **33**
Thornton, Yvonne S. **69**
Thrash, Dox **35**
Thrower, Willie **35**

Thurman, Howard **3**
Thurman, Wallace **16**
Thurston, Baratunde **79**
Thurston, Stephen J. **49**
Till, Emmett **7**
Tillard, Conrad **47**
Tillis, Frederick **40**
Tillman, Dorothy **76**
Tillman, George, Jr. **20**
Timbaland **32**
Tinsley, Boyd **50**
Tirico, Mike **68**
Tisdale, Wayman **50**
Tobias, Channing H. **79**
Tobin, Patricia **75**
Todman, Terence A. **55**
Tolbert, Terence **74**
Toler, Burl **80**
Tolliver, Mose **60**
Tolliver, William **9**
Tolson, Melvin **37**
Tolton, Augustine **62**
Tomlinson, LaDainian **65**
Tonex **54**
Tooks, Lance **62**
Toomer, Jean **6**
Toote, Gloria E.A. **64**
Torres, Gina **52**
Torry, Guy **31**
Touré, Askia (Muhammad Abu Bakr
    el) **47**
Touré, Faya Ora Rose **56**
Toussaint, Allen **60**
Towns, Edolphus **19, 75**
Townsend, Robert **4, 23**
T-Pain **73**
Tresvant, Ralph **57**
Tribbett, Tye **81**
Tribble, Israel, Jr. **8**
Trotter, Donne E. **28**
Trotter, Lloyd G. **56**
Trotter, Monroe **9**
Troupe, Quincy **83**
Trouppe, Quincy Thomas, Sr. **84**
True, Rachel **82**
Trueheart, William E. **49**
Tubbs Jones, Stephanie **24, 72**
Tubman, Harriet **9**
Tucker, C. Delores **12, 56**
Tucker, Chris **13, 23, 62**
Tucker, Cynthia **15, 61**
Tucker, Rosina **14**
Tuckson, Reed V. **71**
Tunie, Tamara **63**
Tunnell, Emlen **54**
Turnbull, Charles Wesley **62**
Turnbull, Walter **13, 60**
Turner, Henry McNeal **5**
Turner, Ike **68**
Turner, Tina **6, 27**
Tyler, Aisha N. **36**
Tyree, Omar Rashad **21**
Tyson, Andre **40**
Tyson, Asha **39**
Tyson, Cicely **7, 51**
Tyson, Mike **28, 44**
Tyson, Neil deGrasse **15, 65**
Uggams, Leslie **23**
Ulmer, James **79**
Underwood, Blair **7, 27, 76**
Union, Gabrielle **31**
Unseld, Wes **23**
Upshaw, Gene **18, 47, 72**

Usher 23, 56
Usry, James L. 23
Ussery, Terdema, II 29
Utendahl, John 23
Valentino, Bobby 62
Van Lierop, Robert 53
Van Peebles, Mario 2, 51
Van Peebles, Melvin 7
Vance, Courtney B. 15, 60
VanDerZee, James 6
Vandross, Luther 13, 48, 59
Vanzant, Iyanla 17, 47
Vaughan, Sarah 13
Vaughn, Countess 53
Vaughn, Gladys Gary 47
Vaughn, Mo 16
Vaughn, Viola 70
Vaughns, Cleopatra 46
Vega, Marta Moreno 61
Velez-Rodriguez, Argelia 56
Verdelle, A. J. 26
Vereen, Ben 4
Verrett, Shirley 66
Vick, Michael 39, 65
Villarosa, Clara 85
Vincent, Marjorie Judith 2
Von Lipsey, Roderick K. 11
Waddles, Charleszetta "Mother" 10, 49
Wade, Dwyane 61
Wade-Gayles, Gloria Jean 41
Wagner, Albert 78
Wagner, Annice 22
Wainwright, Joscelyn 46
Walker, A'lelia 14
Walker, Albertina 10, 58
Walker, Alice 1, 43
Walker, Arthur, II 87
Walker, Bernita Ruth 53
Walker, Cedric "Ricky" 19
Walker, Cora T. 68
Walker, Dianne 57
Walker, George 37
Walker, Herschel 1, 69
Walker, Hezekiah 34
Walker, John T. 50
Walker, Kara 16, 80
Walker, Madame C. J. 7
Walker, Maggie Lena 17
Walker, Margaret 29
Walker, Rebecca 50
Walker, T. J. 7
Walker, Wyatt Tee 80
Wallace, Ben 54
Wallace, Joaquin 49
Wallace, Michele Faith 13
Wallace, Perry E. 47
Wallace, Phyllis A. 9
Wallace, Rasheed 56
Wallace, Sippie 1
Wallace, William 75
Waller, Fats 29
Walters, Ronald 83
Ward, Andre 62
Ward, Benjamin 68
Ward, Douglas Turner 42
Ward, Hines 84
Ward, Lloyd 21, 46
Ware, Andre 37
Ware, Carl H. 30
Warfield, Marsha 2
Warner, Malcolm-Jamal 22, 36
Warren, Michael 27

Warwick, Dionne 18
Washington, Alonzo 29
Washington, Booker T. 4
Washington, Denzel 1, 16
Washington, Dinah 22
Washington, Ebonya 79
Washington, Elsie B. 78
Washington, Fredi 10
Washington, Gene 63
Washington, Grover, Jr. 17, 44
Washington, Harold 6
Washington, Harriet A. 69
Washington, Hayma 86
Washington, Isaiah 62
Washington, James, Jr. 38
Washington, James Melvin 50
Washington, Kenny 50
Washington, Kerry 46
Washington, Laura S. 18
Washington, MaliVai 8
Washington, Mary T. 57
Washington, Patrice Clarke 12
Washington, Pauletta Pearson 86
Washington, Regynald G. 44
Washington, Val 12
Washington, Walter 45
Wasow, Omar 15
Waters, Benny 26
Waters, Ethel 7
Waters, Maxine 3, 67
Waters, Muddy 34
Watkins, Donald 35
Watkins, Joe 86
Watkins, Levi, Jr. 9
Watkins, Perry 12
Watkins, Shirley R. 17
Watkins, Tionne "T-Boz" 34
Watkins, Walter C. 24
Watley, Jody 54
Watson, Bob 25
Watson, Carlos 50
Watson, Diane 41
Watson, Johnny "Guitar" 18
Watt, Melvin 26
Wattleton, Faye 9
Watts, J. C., Jr. 14, 38
Watts, Reggie 52
Watts, Rolonda 9
Wayans, Damien 78
Wayans, Damon 8, 41
Wayans, Keenen Ivory 18
Wayans, Kim 80
Wayans, Marlon 29, 82
Wayans, Shawn 29
Weathers, Carl 10
Weaver, Afaa Michael 37
Weaver, Robert C. 8, 46
Webb, Veronica 10
Webb, Wellington 3, 81
Webber, Chris 15, 30, 59
Webster, Katie 29
Wedgeworth, Robert W. 42
Weeks, Thomas, III 70
Weems, Carrie Mae 63
Weems, Renita J. 44
Wein, Joyce 62
Welburn, Edward T. 50
Welch, Elisabeth 52
Wells, Henrietta Bell 69
Wells, James Lesesne 10
Wells, Mary 28
Wells-Barnett, Ida B. 8
Welsing, Frances Cress 5

Wesley, Dorothy Porter 19
Wesley, Richard 73
Wesley, Valerie Wilson 18
West, Cornel 5, 33, 80
West, Dorothy 12, 54
West, James E. 87
West, Kanye 52
West, Togo D., Jr. 16
Westbrook, Kelvin 50
Westbrook, Peter 20
Westbrooks, Bobby 51
Whack, Rita Coburn 36
Whalum, Kirk 37, 64
Wharton, Clifton R., Jr. 7
Wharton, Clifton Reginald, Sr. 36
Wheat, Alan 14
Whitaker, Forest 2, 49, 67
Whitaker, Mark 21, 47
Whitaker, Pernell 10
White, Armond 80
White, Barry 13, 41
White, Bill 1, 48
White, Charles 39
White, Dondi 34
White, Jesse 22, 75
White, Jessica 83
White, John H. 27
White, Josh 86
White, Josh, Jr. 52
White, Linda M. 45
White, Lois Jean 20
White, Maurice 29
White, Michael Jai 71
White, Michael R. 5
White, Reggie 6, 50
White, Terri 82
White, Walter F. 4
White, Willye 67
White-Hammond, Gloria 61
Whitehead, Colson 77
Whitfield, Fred 23
Whitfield, LeRoy 84
Whitfield, Lynn 18
Whitfield, Mal 60
Whitfield, Norman 73
Whitfield, Van 34
Whitlock, Jason 78
Wideman, John Edgar 5, 87
Wilbekin, Emil 63
Wilbon, Michael 68
Wilder, L. Douglas 3, 48
Wiley, Kehinde 62
Wiley, Ralph 8, 78
Wilkens, J. Ernest, Jr. 43
Wilkens, Lenny 11
Wilkerson, Isabel 71
Wilkins, David 77
Wilkins, Dominique 74
Wilkins, Ray 47
Wilkins, Roger 2, 84
Wilkins, Roy 4
Wilkins, Thomas Alphonso 71
will.i.am 64
Williams, Ann Claire 82
Williams, Anthony 21
Williams, Armstrong 29
Williams, Bert 18
Williams, Billy 86
Williams, Billy Dee 8
Williams, Clarence 33
Williams, Clarence 70
Williams, Clarence, III 26
Williams, Claude 80

Williams, Daniel Hale 2
Williams, David Rudyard 50
Williams, Deniece 36
Williams, Doug 22
Williams, Dudley 60
Williams, Eddie N. 44
Williams, Evelyn 10
Williams, Fannie Barrier 27
Williams, Frederick (B.) 63
Williams, George Washington 18
Williams, Gregory 11
Williams, Hosea Lorenzo 15, 31
Williams, J. Mayo 83
Williams, Joe 5, 25
Williams, John A. 27
Williams, Juan 35, 80
Williams, Ken 68
Williams, Lauryn 58
Williams, Lindsey 75
Williams, Maggie 7, 71
Williams, Malinda 57
Williams, Marco 53
Williams, Mary Lou 15
Williams, Michael L. 86
Williams, Michelle 73
Williams, Montel 4, 57
Williams, Natalie 31
Williams, O. S. 13
Williams, Patricia 11, 54
Williams, Paul R. 9
Williams, Pharrell 47, 82
Williams, Preston Warren, II 64
Williams, Rhonda Y. 86
Williams, Ricky 85
Williams, Robert F. 11
Williams, Ronald A. 57
Williams, Russell, II 70
Williams, Samm-Art 21
Williams, Saul 31
Williams, Serena 20, 41, 73
Williams, Sherley Anne 25
Williams, Stanley "Tookie" 29, 57
Williams, Stevie 71
Williams, Terrie M. 35
Williams, Tony 67
Williams, Vanessa A. 32, 66
Williams, Vanessa L. 4, 17
Williams, Venus 17, 34, 62
Williams, Walter E. 4
Williams, Wendy 62
Williams, William T. 11
Williams, Willie L. 4
Williamson, Fred 67
Williamson, Mykelti 22
Williamson, Sonny Boy 84
Willie, Louis, Jr. 68
Willingham, Tyrone 43
Willis, Bill 68
Willis, Deborah 85
Willis, Dontrelle 55
Wills, Harry 80
Wills, Maury 73
Wilson, August 7, 33, 55
Wilson, Cassandra 16
Wilson, Chandra 57
Wilson, Charlie 31, 77
Wilson, Debra 38
Wilson, Dorien 55
Wilson, Ellis 39
Wilson, Flip 21
Wilson, Gerald 49
Wilson, Jackie 60
Wilson, Jimmy 45

Wilson, Margaret Bush 79
Wilson, Mary 28
Wilson, Nancy 10
Wilson, Natalie 38
Wilson, Phill 9
Wilson, Stephanie 72
Wilson, Sunnie 7, 55
Wilson, Tracey Scott 777
Wilson, William Julius 20
Winans, Angie 36
Winans, BeBe 14
Winans, CeCe 14, 43
Winans, David 77
Winans, Debbie 36
Winans, Marvin L. 17
Winans, Ronald 54
Winans, Vickie 24
Winfield, Dave 5
Winfield, Paul 2, 45
Winfrey, Oprah 2, 15, 61
Winkfield, Jimmy 42
Winslow, Kellen 83
Wisdom, Kimberlydawn 57
Withers, Bill 61
Withers, Ernest C. 68
Withers-Mendes, Elisabeth 64
Witherspoon, John 38
Witt, Edwin T. 26
Wolfe, Ann 82
Wolfe, George C. 6, 43
Womack, Bobby 60
Wonder, Stevie 11, 53
Woodard, Alfre 9
Woodard, Lynette 67
Woodruff, Hale 9
Woodruff, John 68
Woods, Abraham, Jr. 74
Woods, Georgie 57
Woods, Granville T. 5
Woods, Jacqueline 52
Woods, Mattiebelle 63
Woods, Scott 55
Woods, Sylvia 34
Woods, Teri 69
Woods, Tiger 14, 31, 81
Woodson, Carter G. 2
Woodson, Mike 78
Woodson, Robert L. 10
Woodson, Rod 79
Worrill, Conrad 12
Worthy, James 49
Worthy, Kym 84
Wright, Antoinette 60
Wright, Bruce McMarion 3, 52
Wright, Charles H. 35
Wright, Deborah C. 25
Wright, Jeffrey 54
Wright, Jeremiah A., Jr. 45, 69
Wright, Lewin 43
Wright, Louis Tompkins 4
Wright, Nathan, Jr. 56
Wright, Rayfield 70
Wright, Richard 5
Wright, Timothy 74
Wyatt, Addie L. 56
Wynn, Albert R. 25, 77
X, Malcolm 1
X, Marvin 45
Xuma, Madie Hall 59
Xzibit 78
Yancy, Dorothy Cowser 42
Yarbrough, Camille 40
Yarbrough, Cedric 51

Yette, Samuel F. 63
Yoba, Malik 11
York, Dwight D. 71
York, Vincent 40
Young, Al 82
Young, Andrew 3, 48
Young, Charles 77
Young, Coleman 1, 20
Young, Donald, Jr. 57
Young, Jean Childs 14
Young, Jimmy 54
Young, Lee 72
Young, Lester 37
Young, Roger Arliner 29
Young, Whitney M., Jr. 4
Young Jeezy 63
Youngblood, Johnny Ray 8
Youngblood, Shay 32
Zane 71
Zollar, Alfred 40
Zollar, Jawole Willa Jo 28
Zook, Kristal Brent 62

**Angolan**
Bonga, Kuenda 13
dos Santos, José Eduardo 43
Neto, António Agostinho 43
Roberto, Holden 65
Savimbi, Jonas 2, 34

**Antiguan**
McGuire, George Alexander 80
Spencer, Winston Baldwin 68
Williams, Denise 40

**Aruban**
Williams, David Rudyard 50

**Australian**
Freeman, Cathy 29
Mundine, Anthony 56
Rose, Lionel 56

**Austrian**
Kodjoe, Boris 34

**Bahamian**
Christie, Perry Gladstone 53
Ferguson, Amos 81
Ingraham, Hubert A. 19
Pindling, Lynden 81
Spence, Joseph 49

**Barbadian**
Adams, Grantley 82
Arthur, Owen 33
Brathwaite, Kamau 36
Clarke, Austin C. 32
Foster, Cecil 32
Grandmaster Flash 33, 60
Kamau, Kwadwo Agymah 28
Lamming, George 35
Rihanna 65

**Belizean**
Barrow, Dean 69
Jones, Marion 21, 66

**Beninese**
Gantin, Bernardin 70
Hounsou, Djimon 19, 45
Joachim, Paulin 34
Kerekou, Ahmed (Mathieu) 1
Kidjo, Angelique 50
Soglo, Nicéphore 15

Yayi, Boni T. 84

**Bermudian**
Cameron, Earl 44
Gordon, Pamela 17
Smith, Jennifer 21

**Bissau-Guinean**
Sanhá Malam Bacai 84
Vieira, João Bernardo 14, 84

**Botswanan**
Masire, Quett 5
Mogae, Festus Gontebanye 19, 79

**Brazilian**
Brown, Carlinhos 81
Caymmi, Dorival 72
da Silva, Benedita 5
dos Santos, Manuel Francisco 65
Gil, Gilberto 53
Jorge, Seu 73
Machado de Assis 74
Mello, Breno 73
Moura, Paulo 87
Nascimento, Milton 2, 64
Pelé 7
Pitta, Celso 17
Querino, Manuel Raimundo 84
Ronaldinho 69
Silva, Marina 80

**British**
Abbott, Diane 9
Adjaye, David 38, 78
Akinnuoye-Agbaje, Adewale 56
Akomfrah, John 37
Amos, Valerie 41
Anderson, Ho Che 54
Anthony, Trey 63
Appiah, Kwame Anthony 67
Armah, Esther 87
Armatrading, Joan 32
Bailey Rae, Corinne 83
Barnes, John 53
Bassey, Shirley 25
Berry, James 41
Blackwood, Maureen 37
Boateng, Ozwald 35
Boateng, Paul Yaw 56
Breeze, Jean "Binta" 37
Brown, Melanie 73
Campbell, Naomi 1, 31
Carby, Hazel 27
Christie, Linford 8
Coleridge-Taylor, Samuel 75
Crooks, Garth 53
D'Aguiar, Fred 50
David, Craig 31, 53
Davidson, Jaye 5
DeGale, James 74
Edwards, Trevor 54
Ejiofor, Chiwetel 67
Elba, Idris 49
Emmanuel, Alphonsia 38
Equiano, Olaudah 78
Estelle 75
Evans, Diana 72
Fenton, Kevin 87
Ferdinand, Rio 82
Garrett, Sean 57
Gladwell, Malcolm 62
Griffin, Angela 80
Hall, Stuart 78

Hamilton, Lewis 66
Harewood, David 52
Harris, Naomie 55
Haye, David 82
Henriques, Julian 37
Henry, Lenny 9, 52
Holmes, Kelly 47
Ibrahim, Mo 67
Ince, Paul 83
Jamelia 51
James, David 84
Jean-Baptiste, Marianne 17, 46
Jordan, Ronny 26
Julien, Isaac 3
Kay, Jackie 37
King, Oona 27
Kwei-Armah, Kwame 84
Lester, Adrian 46
Lewis, Denise 33
Lewis, Lennox 27
Lewis, Leona 75
Lindo, Delroy 18, 45
Markham, E. A. 37
McGrath, Pat 72
McKinney Hammond, Michelle 51
McQueen, Steve 84
Miller, Wentworth 75
Morris, William "Bill" 51
Newton, Thandie 26
Okonedo, Sophie 67
Oyelowo, David 82
Pitt, David Thomas 10
Rascal, Dizzee 82
Regis, Cyrille 51
Scantlebury, Janna 47
Seacole, Mary 54
Seal 14, 75
Siji 56
Slash 75
Smith, Anjela Lauren 44
Smith, Richard 51
Smith, Zadie 51
Stoutt, H. Lavity 83
Stuart, Moira 82
Taylor, John (David Beckett) 16
Thomason, Marsha 47
Walker, Eamonn 37

**Burkinabé**
Compaore, Blaise 87
Somé, Malidoma Patrice 10

**Burundian**
Ndadaye, Melchior 7
Nkurunziza, Pierre 78
Ntaryamira, Cyprien 8

**Cameroonian**
Ahidjo, Ahmadou 81
Bebey, Francis 45
Beti, Mongo 36
Biya, Paul 28
Eto'o, Samuel 73
Kotto, Yaphet 7
Milla, Roger 2
Njawe, Pius 87
Oyono, Ferdinand 38

**Canadian**
Auguste, Arnold A. 47
Augustine, Jean 53
Bell, Ralph S. 5
Best, Carrie 80
Boyd, Suzanne 52

Brand, Dionne 32
Brathwaite, Fred 35
Brown, Rosemary 62
Brown, Sean 52
Carnegie, Herbert 25
Chanté, Keshia 50
Chong, Rae Dawn 62
Clarke, Austin 32
Clarke, George 32
Cools, Anne 64
Cooper, Afua 53
Cox, Deborah 28
Croal, N'Gai 76
Curling, Alvin 34
Dixon, George 52
Doig, Jason 45
Drake 86
Elliot, Lorris 37
Fiona, Melanie 84
Foster, Cecil 32
Fox, Rick 27
Fuhr, Grant 1, 49
Grand-Pierre, Jean-Luc 46
Hammond, Lenn 34
Harris, Claire 34
Iginla, Jarome 35
Isaac, Julius 34
James, Vanessa 84
Jean, Michaëlle; 70
Jenkins, Fergie 46
Johnson, Ben 1
K'naan 76
Laraque, Georges 48
Lewis, Daurene 72
Mayers, Jamal 39
McKegney, Tony 3
Mollel, Tololwa 38
Neale, Haydain 52
O'Ree, Willie 5
Peterson, Oscar 52
Philip, Marlene Nourbese 32
Reuben, Gloria 15
Richards, Lloyd 2
Rodrigues, Percy 68
Sadlier, Rosemary 62
Salvador, Bryce 51
Scarlett, Millicent 49
Senior, Olive 37
Sparks, Corinne Etta 53
Vanity 67
Verna, Gelsy 70
Weekes, Kevin 67
Williams, Denise 40

**Cape Verdean**
Evora, Cesaria 12
Pereira, Aristides 30

**Caymanian**
Ebanks, Selita 67

**Chadian**
Déby, Idriss 30
Habré, Hissène 6

**Colombian**
Pomare, Eleo 72

**Congolese**
Kabila, Joseph 30
Kintaudi, Leon 62
Kolosoy, Wendo 73
Lumumba, Patrice 33
Mudimbe, V. Y. 61

Nkunda, Laurent 75

**Costa Rican**
McDonald, Erroll 1

**Cuban**
Ferrer, Ibrahim 41
Güines, Tata 69
León, Tania 13
Maceo, Antonio 82
Portuondo, Omara 53
Quirot, Ana 13
Rodríguez, Arsenio 87
Santamaria, Mongo 81
Velez-Rodriguez, Argelia 56

**Dominican (from Dominica)**
Charles, Mary Eugenia 10, 55
Charles, Pierre 52
Skerrit, Roosevelt 72

**Dominican (from Dominican Republic)**
Martinez, Pedro 81
Ortiz, David 52, 82
Sosa, Sammy 21, 44
Virgil, Ozzie 48

**Dutch**
Liberia-Peters, Maria Philomena 12

**Eritrean**
Keflezighi, Meb 49

**Ethiopian**
Aberra, Amsale 67
Afro, Teddy 78
Astatke, Mulatu 81
Bekele, Kenenisa 75
Dibaba, Tirunesh 73
Gabre-Medhin, Tsegaye 64
Gebrselassie, Haile 70
Gerima, Haile 38, 80
Haile Selassie 7
Kebede, Liya 59
Meles Zenawi 3
Mengistu, Haile Mariam 65
Samuelsson, Marcus 53

**Filipino**
apl.de.ap 84

**French**
Baker, Josephine 3
Baldwin, James 1
Baugé, Grégory 86
Bebey, Francis 45
Bonaly, Surya 7
Chase-Riboud, Barbara 20, 46
Dieudonné 67
Fanon, Frantz 44
Henry, Thierry 66
James, Vanessa 84
Kanouté, Fred 68
Noah, Yannick 4, 60
Parker, Tony 75
Tanner, Henry Ossawa 1

**Gabonese**
Bongo, Ali Ben 80
Bongo, Omar 1, 79

**Gambian**
Jammeh, Yahya 23
Peters, Lenrie 43

**German**
Massaquoi, Hans J. 30
Watts, Andre 42

**Ghanaian**
Adu, Freddy 67
Aidoo, Ama Ata 38
Ali, Mohammed Naseehu 60
Annan, Kofi Atta 15, 48
Appiah, Kwame Anthony 67
Armah, Ayi Kwei 49
Atta Mills, John 75
Awoonor, Kofi 37
Bartels, Peggielene 80
DuBois, Shirley Graham 21
Gyan, Asamoah 87
Jawara, Dawda Kairaba 11
Kufuor, John Agyekum 54, 82
Mensah, John 87
Mensah, Thomas 48
Nkrumah, Kwame 3
Rawlings, Jerry 9
Rawlings, Nana Konadu Agyeman 13
Yeboah, Emmanuel Ofosu 53

**Grenadian**
Bishop, Maurice 39
Gairy, Eric Matthew 83
Isaac, Julius 34
Mitchell, Keith 82

**Guinean**
Camara, Moussa Dadis 76
Conté, Lansana 7, 76
Diallo, Amadou 27
Niane, Katoucha 70
Touré, Sekou 6

**Guyanese**
Amos, Valerie 41
Beaton, Norman 14
Burnham, Forbes 66
Carter, Martin 49
Dabydeen, David 48
D'Aguiar, Fred 50
Damas, Léon-Gontran 46
Dathorne, O. R. 52
Griffith, Patrick A. 64
Jagan, Cheddi 16
Lefel, Edith 41
van Sertima, Ivan 25

**Haitian**
Aristide, Jean-Bertrand 6, 45
Auguste, Rose-Anne 13
Beauvais, Garcelle 29
Beauvoir, Max 74
Charlemagne, Manno 11
Christophe, Henri 9
Danticat, Edwidge 15, 68
Delice, Ronald 48
Delice, Rony 48
Jean, Wyclef 20, 86
Jean-Juste, Gérard 78
Jean-Louis, Jimmy 76
Laferriere, Dany 33
Laraque, Paul 67
Laroche, Joseph Philippe Lemercier 85
Magloire, Paul Eugène 68
Pascal-Trouillot, Ertha 3
Peck, Raoul 32
Pierre, Andre 17

Pierre-Louis, Michèle 75
Préval, René 87
Siméus, Dumas M. 25
Verna, Gelsy 70

**Irish**
Adebari, Rotimi 83
Mumba, Samantha 29

**Italian**
Esposito, Giancarlo 9

**Ivorian**
Bedie, Henri Konan 21
Blondy, Alpha 30
Dadié, Bernard 34
De Bankolé, Isaach 78
Drogba, Didier 78
Gbagbo, Laurent 43
Guéï, Robert 66
Houphouët-Boigny, Félix 4, 64
Ouattara 43
Ouattara, Morou 74

**Jamaican**
Ashley, Maurice 15, 47
Barnes, John 53
Barnes, Lloyd 77
Barrett, Lindsay 43
Beenie Man 32
Belafonte, Harry 4
Bennett, Louise 69
Berry, James 41
Bolt, Usain 73
Burning Spear 79
Channer, Colin 36
Cliff, Jimmy 28
Cliff, Michelle 42
Cooper, Afua 53
Cox, Renée 67
Curling, Alvin 34
Dunbar, Sly 34
Ellis, Alton 74
Ewing, Patrick 17, 73
Fagan, Garth 18
Fenton, Kevin 87
Figueroa, John J. 40
Ford, Vincent 75
Garvey, Marcus 1
Golding, Bruce 78
Goodison, Lorna 71
Graham, Trevor 84
Griffiths, Marcia 29
Hammond, Lenn 34
Hearne, John Edgar Caulwell 45
Heavy D 58
James, Marlon 85
Johnson, Ben 1
Johnson, Linton Kwesi 37
Joseph, Kathie-Ann 56
Kong, B. Waine 50
Manley, Edna 26
Manley, Ruth 34
Marley, Bob 5
Marley, Rita 32, 70
Marley, Ziggy 41
McKay, Claude 6
McKenzie, Jaunel 73
Minott, Sugar 86
Moody, Ronald 30
Morrison, Keith 13
Mowatt, Judy 38
Palmer, Everard 37
Patterson, Orlando 4

Patterson, P. J. **6, 20**
Perry, Ruth **19**
Ranglin, Ernest **78**
Reece, E. Albert **63**
Rhoden, Wayne **70**
Rhone, Trevor **80**
Rogers, Joel Augustus **30**
Senior, Olive **37**
Shaggy **31**
Shakespeare, Robbie **34**
Simpson-Miller, Portia **62**
Sinclair, Madge **78**
Steely **80**
Taylor, Karin **34**
Tosh, Peter **9**
White, Willard **53**
Yabby You **83**

**Kenyan**
Cheruiyot, Robert **69**
Juma, Calestous **57**
Kariuki, J. M. **67**
Kenyatta, Jomo **5**
Kibaki, Mwai **60**
Kobia, Samuel **43**
Loroupe, Tegla **59**
Maathai, Wangari **43**
Mazrui, Ali A. **12**
Moi, Daniel Arap **1, 35**
Mutu, Wangechi **44**
Mwangi, Meja **40**
Ngilu, Charity **58**
Ngugi wa Thiong'o **29, 61**
Odinga, Raila **67**
Otunga, Maurice Michael **55**
Tergat, Paul **59**
Wambugu, Florence **42**

**Korean**
Ward, Hines **84**

**Lesothoian**
Mofolo, Thomas **37**

**Liberian**
Conneh, Sekou Damate, Jr. **51**
Cooper, Lisa **73**
Fuller, Solomon Carter, Jr. **15**
Gbowee, Leymah **76**
Keith, Rachel Boone **63**
Perry, Ruth **15**
Sawyer, Amos **2**
Sirleaf, Ellen Johnson **71**
Taylor, Charles **20**
Weah, George **58**

**Malawian**
Banda, Hastings Kamuzu **6, 54**
Kayira, Legson **40**
Muluzi, Bakili **14, 76**

**Malian**
Keita, Salif **83**
Souleymane, Mahamane **78**
Touré, Amadou Toumani **18**

**Martinican**
Césaire, Aimé **48, 69**

**Mozambican**
Chissano, Joaquim **7, 55, 67**
Couto, Mia **45**
Diogo, Luisa Dias **63**
Guebuza, Armando **81**
Machel, Graca Simbine **16**

Machel, Samora Moises **8**
Mutola, Maria **12**

**Namibian**
Mbuende, Kaire **12**
Nujoma, Samuel **10**

**Nigerian**
Abacha, Sani **11, 70**
Abani, Chris **77**
Abiola, Moshood **70**
Abubakar, Abdulsalami **66**
Achebe, Chinua **6**
Ade, King Sunny **41**
Adichie, Chimamanda Ngozi **64**
Ake, Claude **30**
Akinola, Peter Jasper **65**
Akpan, Uwem **70**
Akunyili, Dora Nkem **58**
Amadi, Elechi **40**
Arinze, Francis **19**
Azikiwe, Nnamdi **13**
Babangida, Ibrahim **4**
Bandele, Biyi **68**
Clark-Bekedermo, J. P. **44**
Darego, Agbani **52**
Ekwensi, Cyprian **37**
Emeagwali, Philip **30**
Emecheta, Buchi **30**
Fela **1, 42**
Jonathan, Goodluck **83**
Kuti, Femi **47**
Lawal, Kase L. **45**
Obasanjo, Olusegun **5, 22**
Obasanjo, Stella **32, 56**
Ogunlesi, Adebayo O. **37**
Okara, Gabriel **37**
Okosuns, Sonny **71**
Olajuwon, Hakeem **2, 72**
Olatunji, Babatunde **36**
Olojede, Dele **59**
Olopade, Olufunmilayo Falusi **58**
Onwueme, Tess Osonye **23**
Onwurah, Ngozi **38**
Rotimi, Ola **1**
Sade **15**
Saro-Wiwa, Kenule **39**
Siji **56**
Sowande, Fela **39**
Soyinka, Wole **4**
Tutuola, Amos **30**
Ukpabio, Helen **86**
Wiwa, Ken **67**
Yar'adua, Umaru **69**

**Nigerien**
Tandja, Mamadou **33, 78**

**Norwegian**
Brown, Anne **76**

**Panamanian**
Bailey, Preston **64**
Williams, Juan **35, 80**

**Peruvian**
Baca, Susana **80**

**Polish**
Bridgetower, George **78**

**Puerto Rican**
Schomburg, Arthur Alfonso **9**

**Rhodesian**
Brutus, Dennis **38**

**Russian**
Khanga, Yelena **6**

**Rwandan**
Bizimungu, Pasteur **19**
Habyarimana, Juvenal **8**
Ilibagiza, Immaculée **66**
Kagame, Paul **54**
Rusesabagina, Paul **60**

**St. Kitts and Nevis**
Douglas, Denzil Llewellyn **53**

**Saint Lucian**
Compton, John **65**

**Saudi**
Kalbani, Adil **77**

**Senegalese**
Acogny, Germaine **55**
Akon **68**
Ba, Mariama **30**
Boye, Madior **30**
Diop, Birago **53**
Diop, Cheikh Anta **4**
Diouf, Abdou **3**
Maal, Baaba **66**
Mbaye, Mariétou **31**
Mboup, Souleymane **10**
Ndiaye, Iba **74**
N'Dour, Youssou **1, 53, 79**
Sané, Pierre Gabriel **21**
Sembène, Ousmane **13, 62**
Senghor, Augustin Diamancoune **66**
Senghor, Léopold Sédar **12, 66**
Sy, Oumou **65**
Wade, Abdoulaye **66**

**Sierra Leonean**
Beah, Ishmael **69**
Cheney-Coker, Syl **43**
Jones, Monty **66**
Kabbah, Ahmad Tejan **23**
Koroma, Ernest Bai **84**
Sankoh, Foday **74**

**Somali**
Ahmed, Sharif **80**
Ali, Ayaan Hirsi **58**
Ali Mahdi Mohamed **5**
Dirie, Waris **56**
Farah, Nuruddin **27**
Iman **4, 33, 87**
K'naan **76**
Roble, Abdi **71**

**South African**
Abrahams, Peter **39**
Adams, Paul **50**
Biko, Steven **4**
Brutus, Dennis **38**
Buthelezi, Mangosuthu Gatsha **9**
Butler, Jonathan **28**
Chweneyagae, Presley **63**
Dandala, Mvume **77**
Dube, Lucky **77**
Grae, Jean **51**
Hani, Chris **6**
Head, Bessie **28**
Ka Dinizulu, Mcwayizeni **29**
Kente, Gibson **52**

Khumalo, Leleti **51**
Kuzwayo, Ellen **68**
LaGuma, Alex **30**
Luthuli, Albert **13**
Mabuza, Lindiwe **18**
Mabuza-Suttle, Felicia **43**
Mahlasela, Vusi **65**
Makeba, Miriam **2, 50, 74**
Mandela, Nelson **1, 14, 77**
Mandela, Winnie **2, 35**
Masekela, Barbara **18**
Masekela, Hugh **1**
Mathabane, Mark **5**
Mbeki, Govan A. **80**
Mbeki, Thabo **14, 73**
Mhlaba, Raymond **55**
Mokae, Zakes **80**
Motlanthe, Kgalema **74**
Mphalele, Es'kia (Ezekiel) **40**
Naki, Hamilton **63**
Ngubane, Ben **33**
Nkoli, Simon **60**
Nkosi, Lewis **46**
Ntshona, Winston **52**
Nyanda, Siphiwe **21**
Nzo, Alfred **15**
Plaatje, Sol. T. **80**
Ramaphosa, Cyril **3**
Ramphele, Mamphela **29**
Sisulu, Albertina **57**
Sisulu, Sheila Violet Makate **24**
Sisulu, Walter **47**
Sono, Jomo **86**
Thugwane, Josia **21**
Tutu, Desmond (Mpilo) **6, 44**
Tutu, Nontombi Naomi **57**
Zuma, Jacob **33, 75**
Zuma, Nkosazana Dlamini **34**

**Spanish**
Eto'o, Samuel **73**

**Sudanese**
Bashir, Halima **73**
Bashir, Omar al- **77**
Bol, Manute **1**
Cham, Adongo Agada Akway **77**
Hussein, Lubna **80**
Kiir, Salva **85**
Nour, Nawal M. **56**
Salih, Al-Tayyib **37**
Wek, Alek **18, 63**

**Swazi**
Mswati III **56**

**Swedish**
Hendricks, Barbara **3, 67**
Valdés, Bebo **75**

**Tanzanian**
Kikwete, Jakaya Mrisho **73**
Mkapa, Benjamin W. **16, 77**
Mollel, Tololwa **38**
Mongella, Gertrude **11**
Mwinyi, Ali Hassan **1, 77**
Nyerere, Julius **5**
Rugambwa, Laurean **20**

**Togolese**
Eyadéma, Gnassingbé **7, 52**
Gnassingbé, Faure **67**

Soglo, Nicéphore 15

**Trinidadian**
Anthony, Michael 29
Auguste, Arnold A. 47
Brand, Dionne 32
Carmichael, Stokely 5, 26
Cartey, Wilfred 47
Dymally, Mervyn 42
Guy, Rosa 5
Harris, Claire 34
Hendy, Francis 47
Hercules, Frank 44
Hill, Errol 40
Holder, Geoffrey 78
Lushington, Augustus Nathaniel 56
Nakhid, David 25
Nunez, Elizabeth 62

Primus, Pearl 6
Rudder, David 79
Shorty, Ras, I 47
Toussaint, Lorraine 32
Williams, Eric Eustace 65

**Tunisian**
Memmi, Albert 37

**Ugandan**
Amin, Idi 42
Arac de Nyeko, Monica 66
Atim, Julian 66
Atyam, Angelina 55
Museveni, Yoweri 4
Mutebi, Ronald 25
Obote, Milton 63
Okaalet, Peter 58
Sentamu, John 58

**Upper Voltan**
Sankara, Thomas 17

**West Indian**
Césaire, Aimé 48, 69
Coombs, Orde M. 44
Innis, Roy 5
Kincaid, Jamaica 4
Knight, Gwendolyn 63
Rojas, Don 33
Staupers, Mabel K. 7
Pitt, David Thomas 10
Taylor, Susan L. 10, 86
Walcott, Derek 5

**Zairean**
Kabila, Laurent 20
Mobutu Sese Seko 1, 56
Mutombo, Dikembe 7

Ongala, Remmy 9

**Zambian**
Chiluba, Frederick 56, 80
Kaunda, Kenneth 2
Moyo, Dambisa 76
Mwanawasa, Levy 72
Zulu, Princess Kasune 54

**Zimbabwean**
Chideya, Farai 14
Marechera, Dambudzo 39
Moyo, Lovemore 76
Mugabe, Robert 10, 71
Mukoko, Jestina 75
Muzorewa, Abel 85
Nkomo, Joshua 4, 65
Tsvangirai, Morgan 26, 72
Vera, Yvonne 32

# Cumulative Occupation Index

*Volume numbers appear in **bold***

## Art and design

Abele, Julian **55**
Aberra, Amsale **67**
Adjaye, David **38, 78**
Allen, Tina **22, 75**
Alston, Charles **33**
Amaki, Amalia **76**
Amos, Emma **63**
Anderson, Ho Che **54**
Andrews, Benny **22, 59**
Andrews, Bert **13**
Armstrong, Robb **15**
Ashford, Calvin, Jr. **74**
Bailey, Preston **64**
Bailey, Radcliffe **19**
Bailey, Xenobia **11**
Baker, Matt **76**
Barboza, Anthony **10**
Barnes, Ernie **16, 78**
Barthé, Earl **78**
Barthe, Richmond **15**
Basquiat, Jean-Michel **5**
Bearden, Romare **2, 50**
Beasley, Phoebe **34**
Bell, Darrin **77**
Benberry, Cuesta **65**
Benjamin, Tritobia Hayes **53**
Biggers, John **20, 33**
Biggers, Sanford **62**
Billops, Camille **82**
Blackburn, Robert **28**
Bond, J. Max, Jr. **76**
Brandon, Barbara **3**
Brown, Donald **19**
Brown, Robert **65**
Burke, Selma **16**
Burroughs, Margaret Taylor **9**
Camp, Kimberly **19**
Campbell, E. Simms **13**
Campbell, Mary Schmidt **43**
Catlett, Elizabeth **2**
Chase-Riboud, Barbara **20, 46**
Colescott, Robert **69**
Collins, Paul **61**
Cortor, Eldzier **42**
Cowans, Adger W. **20**
Cox, Renée **67**
Crichlow, Ernest **75**
Crite, Alan Rohan **29**
Davis, Bing **84**
De Veaux, Alexis **44**
DeCarava, Roy **42, 81**
Delaney, Beauford **19**

Delaney, Joseph **30**
Delsarte, Louis **34**
Donaldson, Jeff **46**
Douglas, Aaron **7**
Driskell, David C. **7**
du Cille, Michel **74**
Dwight, Edward **65**
Edwards, Melvin **22**
El Wilson, Barbara **35**
Ewing, Patrick **17, 73**
Fax, Elton **48**
Feelings, Tom **11, 47**
Ferguson, Amos **81**
Fine, Sam **60**
Freeman, Leonard **27**
Fuller, Meta Vaux Warrick **27**
Gantt, Harvey **1**
Garvin, Gerry **78**
Gilles, Ralph **61**
Gilliam, Sam **16**
Golden, Thelma **10, 55**
Goodnight, Paul **32**
Green, Jonathan **54**
Guyton, Tyree **9**
Hammons, David **69**
Harkless, Necia Desiree **19**
Harrington, Oliver W. **9**
Harris, Lyle Ashton **83**
Harrison, Charles **72**
Hathaway, Isaac Scott **33**
Hayden, Palmer **13**
Hayes, Cecil N. **46**
Holder, Geoffrey **78**
Honeywood, Varnette P. **54**
Hope, John **8**
Hudson, Cheryl **15**
Hudson, Wade **15**
Hunt, Richard **6**
Hunter, Clementine **45**
Hutson, Jean Blackwell **16**
Jackson, Earl **31**
Jackson, Mary **73**
Jackson, Vera **40**
John, Daymond **23**
Johnson, Jeh Vincent **44**
Johnson, William Henry **3**
Jones, Lois Mailou **13**
Jones, Paul R. **76**
King, Robert Arthur **58**
Kitt, Sandra **23**
Knight, Gwendolyn **63**
Knox, Simmie **49**
Lawrence, Jacob **4, 28**
Lee, Annie Frances **22**

Lee-Smith, Hughie **5, 22**
Lewis, Edmonia **10**
Lewis, Norman **39**
Lewis, Samella **25**
Ligon, Glenn **82**
Lovell, Whitfield **74**
Loving, Alvin, Jr. **35, 53**
Manley, Edna **26**
Marshall, Kerry James **59**
Mayhew, Richard **39**
McCullough, Geraldine **58, 79**
McDuffie, Dwayne **62**
McGee, Charles **10**
McGruder, Aaron **28, 56**
McQueen, Steve **84**
Mehretu, Julie **85**
Mitchell, Corinne **8**
Moody, Ronald **30**
Morrison, Keith **13**
Motley, Archibald, Jr. **30**
Moutoussamy-Ashe, Jeanne **7**
Mutu, Wangechi **44**
Myles, Kim **69**
Ndiaye, Iba **74**
Neals, Otto **73**
N'Namdi, George R. **17**
Nugent, Richard Bruce **39**
O'Grady, Lorraine **73**
Olden, Georg(e) **44**
Ormes, Jackie **73**
Ouattara **43**
Perkins, Marion **38**
Pierce, Elijah **84**
Pierre, Andre **17**
Pindell, Howardena **55**
Pinder, Jefferson **77**
Pinderhughes, John **47**
Pinkney, Jerry **15**
Piper, Adrian **71**
Pippin, Horace **9**
Pope.L, William **72**
Porter, James A. **11**
Prophet, Nancy Elizabeth **42**
Puryear, Martin **42**
Querino, Manuel Raimundo **84**
Reid, Senghor **55**
Ringgold, Faith **4, 81**
Roble, Abdi **71**
Ruley, Ellis **38**
Saar, Alison **16**
Saar, Betye **80**
Saint James, Synthia **12**
Sallee, Charles **38**
Sanders, Joseph R., Jr. **11**

Savage, Augusta **12**
Scott, John T. **65**
Sebree, Charles **40**
Serrano, Andres **3**
Shabazz, Attallah **6**
Shonibare, Yinka **58**
Simmons, Gary **58**
Simpson, Lorna **4, 36**
Sims, Lowery Stokes **27**
Sklarek, Norma Merrick **25**
Sleet, Moneta, Jr. **5**
Smith, Bruce W. **53**
Smith, Marvin **46**
Smith, Morgan **46**
Smith, Vincent D. **48**
Steave-Dickerson, Kia **57**
Stout, Renee **63**
Sudduth, Jimmy Lee **65**
Tanksley, Ann **37**
Tanner, Henry Ossawa **1**
Taylor, Robert Robinson **80**
Thomas, Alma **14**
Thrash, Dox **35**
Tolliver, Mose **60**
Tolliver, William **9**
Tooks, Lance **62**
VanDerZee, James **6**
Verna, Gelsy **70**
Wagner, Albert **78**
Wainwright, Joscelyn **46**
Walker, A'lelia **14**
Walker, Kara **16, 80**
Washington, Alonzo **29**
Washington, James, Jr. **38**
Weems, Carrie Mae **63**
Wells, James Lesesne **10**
White, Charles **39**
White, Dondi **34**
White, John H. **27**
Wiley, Kehinde **62**
Williams, Billy Dee **8**
Williams, Clarence **70**
Williams, O. S. **13**
Williams, Paul R. **9**
Williams, William T. **11**
Willis, Deborah **85**
Wilson, Ellis **39**
Withers, Ernest C. **68**
Woodruff, Hale **9**

## Business

Abbott, Robert Sengstacke **27**
Abdul-Jabbar, Kareem **8**
Abiola, Moshood **70**

Adams, Eula L. **39**
Adams, Jenoyne **60**
Adkins, Rod **41**
Ailey, Alvin **8**
Akil, Mara Brock **60, 82**
Al-Amin, Jamil Abdullah **6**
Alexander, Archie Alphonso **14**
Allen, Byron **24**
Allen-Buillard, Melba **55**
Ames, Wilmer **27**
Amos, Wally **9**
Archer, Lee, Jr. **79**
Armstrong, Govind **81**
Auguste, Donna **29**
Austin, Gloria **63**
Austin, Jim **63**
Avant, Clarence **19, 86**
Baker, Dusty **8, 43, 72**
Baker, Ella **5**
Baker, Gwendolyn Calvert **9**
Baker, Maxine **28**
Banks, Jeffrey **17**
Banks, Paula A. **68**
Banks, William **11**
Barden, Don H. **9, 20**
Barrett, Andrew C. **12**
Beal, Bernard B. **46**
Beamon, Bob **30**
Beasley, Phoebe **34**
Bell, James A. **50**
Bing, Dave **3, 59, 78**
Blackshear, Leonard **52**
Blackwell, Robert D., Sr. **52**
Blaylock, Ronald **86**
Blayton, Jesse B., Sr. **55**
Bolden, Frank E. **44**
Borders, James **9**
Boston, Kelvin E. **25**
Boston, Lloyd **24**
Bowen, Ruth **83**
Boyd, Edward **70**
Boyd, Gwendolyn **49**
Boyd, John W., Jr. **20, 72**
Boyd, T. B., III **6**
Bradley, Jennette B. **40**
Brae, C. Michael **61**
Bridges, Shelia **36**
Bridgforth, Glinda **36**
Briggs, Curtis **84**
Brimmer, Andrew F. **2, 48**
Bronner, Nathaniel H., Sr. **32**
Brown, Eddie C. **35**
Brown, Les **5**
Brown, Marie Dutton **12**
Brunson, Dorothy **1, 87**
Bryant, John **26**
Burgess, Marjorie L. **55**
Burns, Ursula **60**
Burrell, Tom **21, 51**
Burroughs, Margaret Taylor **9**
Burrus, William Henry **45**
Burt-Murray, Angela **59**
Butler, George, Jr. **70**
Cain, Herman **15**
Caldwell, Earl **60**
Cameron, James **80**
Carter, Pamela Lynn **67**
CasSelle, Malcolm **11**
Chamberlain, Wilt **18, 47**
Chapman, Nathan A., Jr. **21**
Chappell, Emma **18**
Chase, Debra Martin **49**
Chase, Leah **57**

Chenault, Kenneth I. **4, 36**
Cherry, Deron **40**
Chisholm, Samuel J. **32**
Clark, Celeste **15**
Clark, Patrick **14**
Clay, William Lacy **8**
Clayton, Xernona **3, 45**
Clyburn, Mignon **78**
Cobbs, Price M. **9**
Colbert, Virgis William **17**
Coleman, Donald **24, 62**
Coleman, Ken **57**
Combs, Sean "Puffy" **17, 43**
Compton-Rock, Malaak **86**
Connerly, Ward **14**
Conyers, Nathan G. **24**
Cooper, Barry **33**
Cooper, Evern **40**
Corbi, Lana **42**
Cornelius, Don **4**
Cosby, Camille **14, 80**
Cottrell, Comer **11**
Cox, William E. **68**
Creagh, Milton **27**
Cullers, Vincent T. **49**
Daniels-Carter, Valerie **23**
Darden, Calvin **38**
Dash, Darien **29**
Davis, Belva **61**
Davis, Ed **24**
Davis, Erroll B., Jr. **57**
Dawson, Matel, Jr. **39**
de Passe, Suzanne **25**
Dean, Mark **35**
Dee, Merri **55**
Delany, Bessie **12**
Delany, Martin R. **27**
Delany, Sadie **12**
DeVard, Jerri **61**
Diallo, Amadou **27**
Divine, Father **7**
Doley, Harold, Jr. **26**
Donald, Arnold Wayne **36**
Dre, Dr. **10, 14, 30**
Driver, David E. **11**
Ducksworth, Marilyn **12**
Easley, Annie J. **61**
Ebanks, Michelle **60**
Edelin, Ramona Hoage **19**
Edmonds, Tracey **16, 64**
Edmunds, Gladys **48**
Edwards, Trevor **54**
El Wilson, Barbara **35**
Elder, Lee **6**
Ellington, E. David **11**
Evans, Darryl **22**
Evers, Myrlie **8**
Farmer, Forest J. **1**
Farr, Mel **24**
Farrakhan, Louis **15**
Fauntroy, Walter E. **11**
Ferdinand, Rio **82**
50 Cent **46, 83**
Fils-Aimé, Reggie **74**
Fletcher, Alphonse, Jr. **16**
Flowers, Sylester **50**
Ford, Harold E(ugene), Jr. **16, 70**
Forte, Linda Diane **54**
Foster, Jylla Moore **45**
Fowler, Reggie **51**
Franklin, Hardy R. **9**
Friday, Jeff **24**
Fryer, Roland G. **56**

Fudge, Ann **11, 55**
Fuller, S. B. **13**
Funderburg, I. Owen **38**
Gaines, Brenda **41**
Gardner, Chris **65**
Gardner, Edward G. **45**
Garrett, James F. **78**
Gaskins, Rudy **74**
Gaston, Arthur George **3, 38, 59**
Gibson, John Trusty **87**
Gibson, Kenneth Allen **6**
Gibson, Ted **66**
Gidron, Richard D. **68**
Gilles, Ralph **61**
Goings, Russell **59**
Goldsberry, Ronald **18**
Golston, Allan C. **55**
Gordon, Bruce S. **41, 53, 82**
Gordon, Pamela **17**
Gordy, Berry, Jr. **1**
Goss, Carol A. **55**
Goss, Tom **23**
Grace, George H. **48**
Graham, Stedman **13**
Graves, Butch **77**
Graves, Earl G. **1, 35**
Gray, Farrah **59**
Greely, M. Gasby **27**
Green, Isaac H. **79**
Greene, Richard Thaddeus, Sr. **67**
Greenwood, Monique **38**
Griffith, Mark Winston **8**
Grooms, Henry R(andall) **50**
Hale, Lorraine **8**
Hall, Alvin D. **86**
Ham, Cynthia Parker **58**
Hamer, Fannie Lou **6**
Hamilton, Samuel C. **47**
Handy, W. C. **8**
Hannah, Marc **10**
Hardison, Bethann **12**
Harrell, Andre **9, 30**
Harris, Alice **7**
Harris, Carla A. **67**
Harris, E. Lynn **12, 33**
Harris, Monica **18**
Harris, Richard E. **61**
Harvey, Steve **18, 58**
Harvey, William R. **42**
Hawkins, La-Van **17, 54**
Hayden, Carla D. **47**
Haysbert, Raymond V., Sr. **87**
Hazel, Darryl B. **50**
Henderson, Gordon **5**
Henry, Lenny **9, 52**
Henry, Troy **85**
Hightower, Dennis F. **13**
Hill, Bonnie Guiton **20**
Hill, Calvin **19**
Hill, Janet **19**
Hill, Jesse, Jr. **13**
Hobson, Mellody **40**
Holland, Kimberly N. **62**
Holland, Robert, Jr. **11**
Holmes, Larry **20, 68**
Howroyd, Janice Bryant **42**
Hudlin, Warrington **9**
Hudson, Cheryl **15**
Hudson, Wade **15**
Huggins, Larry **21**
Hughes, Cathy **27**
Ibrahim, Mo **67**
Ice Cube **8, 30, 60**

Irvin, Vernon **65**
Jackson, George **19**
Jackson, Joe **78**
Jackson, Mannie **14**
Jackson, Michael **19, 53, 76**
Jakes, Thomas "T. D." **17, 43**
James, Charles H., III **62**
James, Donna A. **51**
James, Juanita **13**
Jenkins, Ray **77**
John, Daymond **23**
Johnson, Earvin "Magic" **3, 39**
Johnson, Eddie Bernice **8**
Johnson, Eunice W. **83**
Johnson, George E. **29**
Johnson, John H. **3, 54**
Johnson, Kevin **70**
Johnson, Robert L. **3, 39**
Johnson, Sheila Crump **48**
Jolley, Willie **28**
Jones, Bobby **20**
Jones, Carl **7**
Jones, Caroline **29**
Jones, Ingrid Saunders **18**
Jones, Quincy **8, 30**
Jones, Thomas W. **41**
Jones, Wayne **53**
Jordan, Michael **6, 21**
Jordan, Montell **23**
Joyner, Marjorie Stewart **26**
Julian, Percy Lavon **6**
Kaigler, Denise **63**
Keith, Floyd A. **61**
Kelly, Patrick **3**
Kendrick, Erika **57**
Kidd, Mae Street **39**
Killingsworth, Cleve, Jr. **54**
Kimbro, Dennis **10**
King, Dexter **10**
King, Don **14**
Knight, Suge **11, 30**
Knowles, Tina **61**
Knowling, Robert E., Jr. **38**
Lane, Vincent **5**
Langhart Cohen, Janet **19, 60**
Lanier, Willie **33**
Laryea, Thomas Davies, III **67**
Lawal, Kase L. **45**
Lawless, Theodore K. **8**
Lawson, Jennifer **1, 50**
Leary, Kathryn D. **10**
Leavell, Dorothy R. **17**
Lee, Annie Frances **22**
Lee, Bertram M., Sr. **46**
Lee, Debra L. **62**
Leonard, Sugar Ray **15**
Lewis, Aylwin **51**
Lewis, Byron E. **13**
Lewis, Delano **7**
Lewis, Edward T. **21**
Lewis, Reginald F. **6**
Lewis, William M., Jr. **40**
Ligging, Alfred, III **43**
Llewellyn, J. Bruce **13, 85**
Long, Eddie L. **29**
Lott, Ronnie **9**
Louis, Errol T. **8**
Lucas, John **7**
Lucy, William **50**
Madison, Paula **37**
Malone, Annie **13**
March, William Carrington **56**
Marshall, Bella **22**

Massenburg, Kedar 23
Master P 21
Matthews Shatteen, Westina 51
Maynard, Robert C. 7
Mays, Leslie A. 41
Mays, William G. 34
M.C. Hammer 20, 80
McCabe, Jewell Jackson 10
McCann, Renetta 44
McCoy, Elijah 8
McDonald, Erroll 1
McGee, James Madison 46
McGuire, Raymond J. 57
McKissack, Leatrice 80
McLeod, Gus 27
McPherson, David 32
Micheaux, Oscar 7
Miller, Larry G. 72
Millines Dziko, Trish 28
Mills, Steve 47
Mingo, Frank 32
Monk, Art 38, 73
Monroe, Bryan 71
Moore, Wes 86
Morgan, Garrett 1
Morgan, Joe Leonard 9
Morgan, Rose 11
Morris, William 51
Moyo, Karega Kofi 36
Moyo, Yvette Jackson 36
Muhammad, Jabir Herbert 72
Nanula, Richard D. 20
Nash, Diane 72
Nelson Meigs, Andrea 48
Nichols, Nichelle 11
Norman, Christina 47
Ogunlesi, Adebayo O. 37
Olojede, Dele 59
O'Neal, Stanley 38, 67
Otis, Clarence, Jr. 55
Ouattara, Morou 74
Packer, Daniel 56
Parham, Marjorie B. 71
Parks, Gordon 1, 35, 58
Parsons, Richard Dean 11, 33
Payton, Walter 11, 25
Peck, Carolyn 23
Perez, Anna 1
Perkins, James, Jr. 55
Perry, Laval 64
Perry, Lowell 30
Phillips, Charles E., Jr. 57
Pierce, Harold 75
Pinckney, Bill 42
Pinkett, Randal 61
Pleasant, Mary Ellen 9
Potter, Myrtle 40
Powell, Maxine 8
Price, Frederick K. C. 21
Price, Hugh B. 9, 54
Procope, Ernesta 23
Procope, John Levy 56
Queen Latifah 1, 16, 58
Quivers, Robin 61
Rand, A. Barry 6
Reeves, Rachel J. 23
Reid, Antonio "L.A." 28
Rhone, Sylvia 2
Rice, Linda Johnson 9, 41
Rice, Norm 8
Richardson, Donna 39
Richie, Leroy C. 18
Rideau, Iris 46

Roberts, Mike 57
Roberts, Roy S. 14
Robertson, Oscar 26
Robeson, Eslanda Goode 13
Robinson, Jackie 6
Robinson, Rachel 16
Robinson, Randall 7, 46
Roche, Joyce M. 17
Rodgers, Johnathan 6, 51
Rodriguez, Jimmy 47
Rogers, John W., Jr. 5, 52
Rojas, Don 33
Ross, Charles 27
Ross, Diana 8, 27
Russell, Bill 8
Russell, Herman Jerome 17
Russell-McCloud, Patricia 17
Saint James, Synthia 12
Samara, Noah 15
Samuelsson, Marcus 53
Sanders, Angelia 86
Sanders, Dori 8
Scott, C. A. 29
Scott, Milton 51
Scott, Tim 87
Sengstacke, John 18
Shakur, Afeni 67
Shank, Suzanne F. 77
Shropshire, Thomas B. 49
Siméus, Dumas M. 25
Simmons, Kimora Lee 51, 83
Simmons, Russell 1, 30
Sims, Naomi 29, 79
Sinbad 1, 16
Smith, B(arbara) 11
Smith, Clarence O. 21
Smith, Jane E. 24
Smith, Joshua 10
Smith, Willi 8
Sneed, Paula A. 18
Spaulding, Charles Clinton 9
Staley, Dawn 57
Stanford, Olivia Lee Dilworth 49
Steinberg, Martha Jean "The
    Queen" 28
Steward, David L. 36
Stewart, Ella 39
Stewart, Paul Wilbur 12
Stinson, Denise L. 59
Stringer, Vickie 58
Sullivan, Leon H. 3, 30
Sutton, Percy E. 42, 82
Taylor, Ephren W., II 61
Taylor, Karin 34
Taylor, Kristin Clark 8
Taylor, Natalie 47
Taylor, Susan L. 10, 86
Terrell, Dorothy A. 24
Thomas, Franklin A. 5, 49
Thomas, Isiah 7, 26, 65
Thomas-Graham, Pamela 29
Thompson, Cynthia Bramlett 50
Thompson, Don 56
Thompson, John W. 26
Tobin, Patricia 75
Tribble, Israel, Jr. 8
Trotter, Lloyd G. 56
Trotter, Monroe 9
Tuckson, Reed V. 71
Tyson, Asha 39
Ussery, Terdema, II 29
Utendahl, John 23
VanDerZee, James 6

Vaughn, Gladys Gary 47
Vaughns, Cleopatra 46
Villarosa, Clara 85
Walker, A'lelia 14
Walker, Cedric 19
Walker, Madame C. J. 7
Walker, Maggie Lena 17
Walker, T. J. 7
Ward, Lloyd 21, 46
Ware, Carl H. 30
Washington, Alonzo 29
Washington, Mary T. 57
Washington, Regynald G. 44
Washington, Val 12
Wasow, Omar 15
Watkins, Donald 35
Watkins, Walter C., Jr. 24
Wattleton, Faye 9
Wein, Joyce 62
Wek, Alek 18, 63
Welburn, Edward T. 50
Wells-Barnett, Ida B. 8
Westbrook, Kelvin 50
Wharton, Clifton R., Jr. 7
White, Linda M. 45
White, Walter F. 4
Wilkins, Ray 47
Williams, Armstrong 29
Williams, Lindsey 75
Williams, O. S. 13
Williams, Paul R. 9
Williams, Ronald A. 57
Williams, Terrie 35
Williams, Walter E. 4
Williams, Wendy 62
Willie, Louis, Jr. 68
Wilson, Phill 9
Wilson, Sunnie 7, 55
Winfrey, Oprah 2, 15, 61
Woods, Jacqueline 52
Woods, Sylvia 34
Woodson, Robert L. 10
Wright, Antoinette 60
Wright, Charles H. 35
Wright, Deborah C. 25
Wright, Rayfield 70
Yoba, Malik 11
Zollar, Alfred 40

**Dance**
Acogny, Germaine 55
Adams, Jenoyne 60
Ailey, Alvin 8
Allen, Debbie 13, 42
Anderson, Lauren 72
Atkins, Cholly 40
Babatunde, Obba 35
Baker, Josephine 3
Bates, Peg Leg 14
Beatty, Talley 35
Brown, Ernest 80
Byrd, Donald 10
Clarke, Hope 14
Collins, Janet 33, 64
Davis, Chuck 33
de Lavallade, Carmen 78
Dove, Ulysses 5
Dunham, Katherine 4, 59
Ellington, Mercedes 34
Fagan, Garth 18
Falana, Lola 42
Glover, Savion 14
Hall, Arthur 39

Henson, Darrin 33
Hines, Gregory 1, 42
Jamison, Judith 7, 67
Jefferson, Denise 87
Johnson, Virginia 9
Jones, Bill T. 1, 46, 80
Jones, Doris W. 62
King, Alonzo 38
LeTang, Henry 66
Manning, Frankie 78
Miller, Bebe 3
Mills, Florence 22
Mitchell, Arthur 2, 47
Moten, Etta 18
Muse, Clarence Edouard 21
Nash, Joe 55
Nicholas, Fayard 20, 57
Nicholas, Harold 20
Nichols, Nichelle 11
Polite, Carlene Hatcher 82
Pomare, Eleo 72
Powell, Maxine 8
Premice, Josephine 41
Primus, Pearl 6
Ray, Gene Anthony 47
Rhoden, Dwight 40
Ribeiro, Alfonso 17
Richardson, Desmond 39
Robinson, Bill "Bojangles" 11
Robinson, Cleo Parker 38
Robinson, Fatima 34
Robinson, LaVaughn 69
Rodgers, Rod 36
Sims, Howard "Sandman" 48
Slyde, Jimmy 70
Spears, Warren 52
Tyson, Andre 40
Vereen, Ben 4
Walker, Dianne 57
Washington, Fredi 10
Williams, Dudley 60
Zollar, Jawole Willa Jo 28

**Education**
Abani, Chris 77
Achebe, Chinua 6
Adams, Leslie 39
Adams-Ender, Clara 40
Adkins, Rutherford H. 21
Aidoo, Ama Ata 38
Ake, Claude 30
Alexander, Margaret Walker 22
Allen, Robert L. 38
Allen, Samuel W. 38
Allen-Buillard, Melba 55
Alston, Charles 33
Amadi, Elechi 40
Ammons, James H. 81
Anderson, Charles Edward 37
Appiah, Kwame Anthony 67
Archer, Dennis 7
Archie-Hudson, Marguerite 44
Aristide, Jean-Bertrand 6, 45
Asante, Molefi Kete 3
Aubert, Alvin 41
Awoonor, Kofi 37
Bacon-Bercey, June 38
Bahati, Wambui 60
Baiocchi, Regina Harris 41
Baker, Augusta 38
Baker, Gwendolyn Calvert 9
Baker, Houston A., Jr. 6
Baldwin, Cynthia A. 74

Ballard, Allen Butler, Jr. 40
Bambara, Toni Cade 10
Baraka, Amiri 1, 38
Barbee, Lloyd Augustus 71
Barboza, Anthony 10
Barnett, Marguerite 46
Barthé, Earl 78
Bath, Patricia E. 37
Batiste, Alvin 66
Beckham, Barry 41
Belgrave, Marcus 77
Bell, Derrick 6
Benberry, Cuesta 65
Benjamin, Tritobia Hayes 53
Berry, Bertice 8, 55
Berry, Mary Frances 7
Bethune, Mary McLeod 4
Biggers, John 20, 33
Black, Albert 51
Blackwell, David 79
Blassingame, John Wesley 40
Blockson, Charles L. 42
Bluitt, Juliann S. 14
Bobo, Lawrence 60
Bogle, Donald 34
Bolden, Tonya 32
Bosley, Freeman, Jr. 7
Boyd, Melba Joyce 86
Boyd, T. B., III 6
Bradley, David Henry, Jr. 39
Branch, William Blackwell 39
Brathwaite, Kamau 36
Braun, Carol Moseley 4, 42
Briscoe, Marlin 37
Bromery, Randolph Wilson 85
Brooks, Avery 9
Brown, Claude 38
Brown, Joyce F. 25
Brown, Sterling Allen 10, 64
Brown, Uzee 42
Brown, Wesley 23
Brown, Willa 40
Bruce, Blanche Kelso 33
Brutus, Dennis 38
Bryan, Ashley F. 41
Burke, Selma 16
Burke, Yvonne Brathwaite 42
Burks, Mary Fair 40
Burnim, Mickey L. 48
Burroughs, Margaret Taylor 9
Burton, LeVar 8
Butler, Paul D. 17
Callender, Clive O. 3
Campbell, Bebe Moore 6, 24, 59
Campbell, Mary Schmidt 43
Cannon, Katie 10
Carby, Hazel 27
Cardozo, Francis L. 33
Carnegie, Herbert 25
Carruthers, George R. 40
Carter, Joye Maureen 41
Carter, Kenneth 53
Carter, Warrick L. 27
Cartey, Wilfred 47
Carver, George Washington 4
Cary, Lorene 3
Cary, Mary Ann Shadd 30
Catlett, Elizabeth 2
Cayton, Horace 26
Chaney, John 67
Cheney-Coker, Syl 43
Clark, Joe 1
Clark, Kenneth B. 5, 52

Clark, Septima 7
Clarke, Cheryl 32
Clarke, George 32
Clarke, John Henrik 20
Clayton, Constance 1
Cleaver, Kathleen Neal 29
Clements, George 2
Clemmons, Reginal G. 41
Clifton, Lucille 14, 64
Cobb, Jewel Plummer 42
Cobb, W. Montague 39
Cobb, William Jelani 59
Cobbs, Price M. 9
Cohen, Anthony 15
Cole, Johnnetta B. 5, 43
Coleman, William F., III 61
Colescott, Robert 69
Collins, Janet 33, 64
Collins, Marva 3, 71
Collins, Patricia Hill 67
Comer, James P. 6
Coney, PonJola 48
Cook, Mercer 40
Cook, Samuel DuBois 14
Cook, Toni 23
Cooper, Afua 53
Cooper, Anna Julia 20
Cooper, Edward S. 6
Cooper Cafritz, Peggy 43
Copeland, Michael 47
Cortez, Jayne 43
Cosby, Bill 7, 26, 59
Cotter, Joseph Seamon, Sr. 40
Cottrell, Comer 11
Counter, S. Allen 74
Cox, Joseph Mason Andrew 51
Cox, William E. 68
Creagh, Milton 27
Crew, Rudolph F. 16
Crew, Spencer R. 55
Cross, Dolores E. 23
Cruse, Harold 54
Cullen, Countee 8
Daly, Marie Maynard 37
Dathorne, O. R. 52
Davis, Allison 12
Davis, Angela 5
Davis, Arthur P. 41
Davis, Charles T. 48
Davis, Erroll B., Jr. 57
Davis, George 36
Davis, Milt 74
Dawson, William Levi 39
Days, Drew S., III 10
Deconge-Watson, Lovenia 55
Delany, Sadie 12
Delany, Samuel R., Jr. 9
Delco, Wilhemina R. 33
Delsarte, Louis 34
Dennard, Brazeal 37
Dickens, Helen Octavia 14, 64
Diop, Cheikh Anta 4
Dixon, Margaret 14
Dodson, Howard, Jr. 7, 52
Dodson, Owen Vincent 38
Donaldson, Jeff 46
Douglas, Aaron 7
Dove, Rita 6, 78
Dove, Ulysses 5
Draper, Sharon Mills 16, 43
Driskell, David C. 7
Drummond, William J. 40
Du Bois, David Graham 45

Dumas, Henry 41
Dunbar-Nelson, Alice Ruth Moore
  44
Dunnigan, Alice Allison 41
Dunston, Georgia Mae 48
Dymally, Mervyn 42
Dyson, Michael Eric 11, 40
Early, Gerald 15
Edelin, Ramona Hoage 19
Edelman, Marian Wright 5, 42
Edley, Christopher 2, 48
Edley, Christopher F., Jr. 48
Edwards, Harry 2
Elders, Joycelyn 6
Elliot, Lorris 37
Ellis, Clarence A. 38
Ellison, Ralph 7
Epps, Archie C., III 45
Evans, Mari 26
Falconer, Etta Zuber 59
Fauset, Jessie 7
Favors, Steve 23
Feelings, Muriel 44
Ferguson, Ronald F. 75
Figueroa, John J. 40
Fleming, Raymond 48
Fletcher, Bill, Jr. 41
Floyd, Elson S. 41
Ford, Jack 39
Foster, Ezola 28
Foster, Henry W., Jr. 26
Francis, Norman (C.) 60
Franklin, Hardy R. 9, 87
Franklin, John Hope 5, 77
Franklin, Robert M. 13
Frazier, E. Franklin 10
Freeman, Al, Jr. 11
Fryer, Roland G. 56
Fuller, A. Oveta 43
Fuller, Arthur 27
Fuller, Howard L. 37
Fuller, Solomon Carter, Jr. 15
Futrell, Mary Hatwood 33
Gaines, Ernest J. 7
Gates, Henry Louis, Jr. 3, 38, 67
Gates, Sylvester James, Jr. 15
Gayle, Addison, Jr. 41
George, Zelma Watson 42
Gerima, Haile 38, 80
Gibson, Donald Bernard 40
Giddings, Paula 11
Gill, Gerald 69
Golden, Marita 19
Gomes, Peter J. 15
Gomez, Jewelle 30
Goodison, Lorna 71
Granville, Evelyn Boyd 36
Greenfield, Eloise 9
Guinier, Lani 7, 30
Guy-Sheftall, Beverly 13
Hageman, Hans and Ivan 36
Hale, Lorraine 8
Hall, Stuart 78
Halliburton, Warren J. 49
Hamburg, Beatrix 84
Hammonds, Evelynn 69
Handy, W. C. 8
Hansberry, William Leo 11
Harding, Vincent 67
Harkless, Necia Desiree 19
Harper, Michael S. 34
Harris, Alice 7
Harris, Barry 68

Harris, Bill 72
Harris, Gary L. 87
Harris, Jay T. 19
Harris, Patricia Roberts 2
Harris-Lacewell, Melissa 81
Harsh, Vivian Gordon 14
Harvey, William R. 42
Haskins, James 36, 54
Hathaway, Isaac Scott 33
Hayden, Carla D. 47
Hayden, Robert 12
Haynes, George Edmund 8
Henderson, Stephen E. 45
Henries, A. Doris Banks 44
Herenton, Willie W. 24, 81
Hill, Andrew 66
Hill, Anita 5, 65
Hill, Bonnie Guiton 20
Hill, Errol 40
Hill, Leslie Pinckney 44
Hill, Marc Lamont 80
Hilliard, Asa Grant, III 66
Hine, Darlene Clark 24
Hinton, William Augustus 8
Hoagland, Everett H. 45
Hogan, Beverly Wade 50
Holland, Endesha Ida Mae 3, 57
Holt, Nora 38
hooks, Bell 5
Hope, John 8
Horton, James Oliver 58
Houston, Charles Hamilton 4
Hoyte, Lenon 50
Hrabowski, Freeman A., III 22
Huggins, Nathan Irvin 52
Hughes, Ebony 57
Hull, Akasha Gloria 45
Humphries, Frederick 20
Hunt, Richard 6
Hutcherson, Hilda Yvonne 54
Hutson, Jean Blackwell 16
Imes, Elmer Samuel 39
Jackson, Edison O. 67
Jackson, Fred James 25
Jackson, Vera 40
Jarrett, Vernon D. 42
Jarvis, Charlene Drew 21
Jarvis, Erich 67
Jefferson, Denise 87
Jeffries, Leonard 8
Jenifer, Franklyn G. 2
Jenkins, Ella 15
Johns, Vernon 38
Johnson, Hazel 22
Johnson, James Weldon 5
Johnson, Katherine 61
Johnson, Mordecai Wyatt 79
Jones, Bobby 20
Jones, Clara Stanton 51
Jones, Edward P. 43, 67
Jones, Gayl 37
Jones, Ingrid Saunders 18
Jones, Lois Mailou 13
Joplin, Scott 6
Jordan, June 7, 35
Josey, E. J. 10
Just, Ernest Everett 3
Karenga, Maulana 10, 71
Kay, Ulysses 37
Keith, Damon J. 16, 74
Kennedy, Florynce 12, 33
Kennedy, Randall 40
Kilpatrick, Carolyn Cheeks 16

Kimbro, Dennis 10
King, Preston 28
King, Reatha Clark 65
Kittles, Rick 51
Komunyakaa, Yusef 9
Kunjufu, Jawanza 3, 50
Ladner, Joyce A. 42
Lawrence, Jacob 4, 28
Lawrence-Lightfoot, Sara 10
Lee, Annie Frances 22
Lee, Joe A. 45
Leevy, Carrol M. 42
Leffall, Lasalle 3, 64
Lester, Julius 9
Lewis, David Levering 9
Lewis, Norman 39
Lewis, Samella 25
Lewis, Shirley A. R. 14
Lewis, Thomas 19
Liberia-Peters, Maria Philomena 12
Lincoln, C. Eric 38
Lindsey, Tommie 51
Locke, Alain 10
Logan, Rayford W. 40
Lomax, Michael L. 58
Long, Loretta 58
Long, Richard Alexander 65
Lorde, Audre 6
Loury, Glenn 36
Loving, Alvin, Jr. 35, 53
Lowry, A. Leon 60
Lucy Foster, Autherine 35
Lyttle, Hulda Margaret 14
Mackey, Nathaniel 75
Major, Clarence 9
Malveaux, Floyd 54
Manley, Audrey Forbes 16
Marable, Manning 10
Markham, E. A. 37
Marsalis, Wynton 16
Marshall, Paule 7, 77
Masekela, Barbara 18
Mason, Herman, Jr. 83
Mason, Ronald 27
Massey, Walter E. 5, 45
Massie, Samuel P., Jr. 29
Matejka, Adrian 87
Mayhew, Richard 39
Maynard, Robert C. 7
Maynor, Dorothy 19
Mayo, Whitman 32
Mays, Benjamin E. 7
McCarty, Osceola 16
McCullough, Geraldine 58, 79
McDaniel, Randall Cornell 81
McKay, Nellie Yvonne 17, 57
McMillan, Terry 4, 17, 53
McMurray, Georgia L. 36
McPherson, James Alan 70
McWhorter, John 35
Meek, Carrie 6
Mell, Patricia 49
Memmi, Albert 37
Meredith, James H. 11
Millender-McDonald, Juanita 21, 61
Mitchell, Corinne 8
Mitchell, Nicole 66
Mitchell, Sharon 36
Mofolo, Thomas Mokopu 37
Mollel, Tololwa 38
Mongella, Gertrude 11
Moody-Adams, Michele 76
Mooney, Paul 37

Moore, Barbara C. 49
Moore, Harry T. 29
Moore, Melba 21
Morrison, Keith 13
Morrison, Sam 50
Morrison, Toni 2, 15, 86
Moses, Robert Parris 11
Moton, Robert Russa 83
Mphalele, Es'kia (Ezekiel) 40
Mudimbe, V. Y. 61
Mullen, Harryette 34
Murray, Pauli 38
Nabrit, Samuel Milton 47
Nance, Cynthia 71
Naylor, Gloria 10, 42
Neal, Larry 38
Neal, Mark Anthony 74
Newkirk, Pamela 69
Newman, Lester C. 51
N'Namdi, George R. 17
Norman, Maidie 20
Norton, Eleanor Holmes 7
Nour, Nawal M. 56
Obadele, Imari 84
Ogletree, Charles, Jr. 12, 47
Ojikutu, Bisola 65
Oliver, Kimberly 60
Onwueme, Tess Osonye 23
Onwurah, Ngozi 38
Owens, Helen 48
Page, Alan 7
Page, Inman 82
Paige, Rod 29
Painter, Nell Irvin 24
Palmer, Everard 37
Parker, Kellis E. 30
Patterson, Frederick Douglass 12
Patterson, Mary Jane 54
Patterson, Orlando 4
Payton, Benjamin F. 23
Perry, Warren 56
Peters, Margaret 43
Peters, Matilda 43
Peterson, James 81
Pickett, Cecil 39
Pinckney, Bill 42
Pindell, Howardena 55
Piper, Adrian 71
Player, Willa B. 43
Porter, James A. 11
Poussaint, Alvin F. 5, 67
Powell, Benny 87
Price, Florence 37
Price, Glenda 22
Price, Richard 51
Primus, Pearl 6
Prophet, Nancy Elizabeth 42
Purnell, Silas 59
Puryear, Martin 42
Putney, Martha S. 75
Quarles, Benjamin Arthur 18
Querino, Manuel Raimundo 84
Quigless, Helen G. 49
Rahman, Aishah 37
Ramphele, Mamphela 29
Reagon, Bernice Johnson 7
Reddick, Lawrence Dunbar 20
Redding, J. Saunders 26
Redmond, Eugene 23
Reid, Irvin D. 20
Rhodes, Jewell Parker 84
Ribeau, Sidney 70
Rice, Condoleezza 3, 28, 72

Rice, Louise Allen 54
Richards, Hilda 49
Riles, Wilson C. 79
Robinson, Sharon 22
Robinson, Spottswood W., III 22
Rodriguez, Cheryl 64
Rogers, Joel Augustus 30
Rollins, Charlemae Hill 27
Ross-Lee, Barbara 67
Russell-McCloud, Patricia 17
Salih, Al-Tayyib 37
Sallee, Charles Louis, Jr. 38
Satcher, David 7, 57
Schomburg, Arthur Alfonso 9
Sears, Stephanie 53
Senior, Olive 37
Shabazz, Betty 7, 26
Shange, Ntozake 8
Shelton, Paula Young 86
Shipp, E. R. 15
Shirley, George 33
Shockley, Ann Allen 84
Simmons, Ruth J. 13, 38
Sinkford, Jeanne C. 13
Sisulu, Sheila Violet Makate 24
Sizemore, Barbara A. 26
Smith, Anna Deavere 6
Smith, Barbara 28
Smith, Jessie Carney 35
Smith, John L. 22
Smith, Mary Carter 26
Smith, Tubby 18, 83
Snowden, Frank M., Jr. 67
Southern, Eileen 56
Sowande, Fela 39
Soyinka, Wole 4
Spearman, Leonard H. O., Sr. 81
Spears, Warren 52
Spikes, Dolores 18
Spriggs, William 67
Stanford, John 20
Steele, Claude Mason 13
Steele, Shelby 13, 82
Stephens, Charlotte Andrews 14
Stewart, Maria W. Miller 19
Stewart, Tonea Harris 78
Stone, Chuck 9
Sudarkasa, Niara 4
Sullivan, Louis 8
Swygert, H. Patrick 22
Talbert, Mary B. 77
Tancil, Gladys Quander 59
Tanksley, Ann 37
Tatum, Beverly Daniel 42, 84
Taylor, Helen (Lavon Hollingshed) 30
Taylor, Susie King 13
Terrell, Mary Church 9
Thomas, Alma 14
Thomas, Michael 69
Thurman, Howard 3
Tillis, Frederick 40
Tobias, Channing H. 79
Toler, Burl 80
Tolson, Melvin 37
Tribble, Israel, Jr. 8
Trueheart, William E. 49
Tucker, Rosina 14
Turnbull, Charles Wesley 62
Turnbull, Walter 13, 60
Tutu, Desmond 6
Tutu, Nontombi Naomi 57
Tutuola, Amos 30

Tyson, Andre 40
Tyson, Asha 39
Tyson, Neil deGrasse 15, 65
Usry, James L. 23
van Sertima, Ivan 25
Vaughn, Viola 70
Vega, Marta Moreno 61
Velez-Rodriguez, Argelia 56
Verna, Gelsy 70
Wade-Gayles, Gloria Jean 41
Walcott, Derek 5
Walker, George 37
Wallace, Michele Faith 13
Wallace, Perry E. 47
Wallace, Phyllis A. 9
Walters, Ronald 83
Washington, Booker T. 4
Watkins, Shirley R. 17
Wattleton, Faye 9
Weaver, Afaa Michael 37
Wedgeworth, Robert W. 42
Wells, Henrietta Bell 69
Wells, James Lesesne 10
Wells-Barnett, Ida B. 8
Welsing, Frances Cress 5
Wesley, Dorothy Porter 19
Wesley, Richard 73
West, Cornel 5, 33, 80
Wharton, Clifton R., Jr. 7
White, Charles 39
White, Lois Jean 20
Wilkens, J. Ernest, Jr. 43
Wilkins, Roger 2, 84
Williams, David Rudyard 50
Williams, Fannie Barrier 27
Williams, Gregory 11
Williams, Patricia 11, 54
Williams, Rhonda Y. 86
Williams, Sherley Anne 25
Williams, Walter E. 4
Wilson, William Julius 22
Woodruff, Hale 9
Woodson, Carter G. 2
Worrill, Conrad 12
Wright, Antoinette 60
Xuma, Madie Hall 59
Yancy, Dorothy Cowser 42
Young, Jean Childs 14
Zook, Kristal Brent 62

**Fashion**
Aberra, Amsale 67
Bailey, Xenobia 11
Banks, Jeffrey 17
Banks, Tyra 11, 50
Barboza, Anthony 10
Beals, Jennifer 12
Beckford, Tyson 11, 68
Boateng, Ozwald 35
Bond, Beverly 53
Boyd, Suzanne 52
Bridges, Sheila 36
Brown, Joyce F. 25
Burrows, Stephen 31
Campbell, Naomi 1, 31
Common 31, 63
Darego, Agbani 52
Dash, Damon 31
Davidson, Jaye 5
De' Alexander, Quinton 57
Delice, Ronald 48
Delice, Rony 48
Dirie, Waris 56

Ebanks, Selita **67**
Evans, Etu **55**
Gaskins, Eric **64**
Gibson, Ted **66**
Givhan, Robin Deneen **72**
Hall, Kevan **61**
Harold, Erika **54**
Henderson, Gordon **5**
Hendy, Francis **47**
Iman **4, 33, 87**
Iman, Chanel **66**
John, Daymond **23**
Johnson, Beverly **2**
Johnson, Eunice W. **83**
Jones, Carl **7**
Kani, Karl **10**
Kebede, Liya **59**
Kelly, Patrick **3**
Kodjoe, Boris **34**
Lars, Byron **32**
Malone, Maurice **32**
McGrath, Pat **72**
McKenzie, Jaunel **73**
Michele, Michael **31**
Niane, Katoucha **70**
Onwurah, Ngozi **38**
Powell, Maxine **8**
Reese, Tracy **54**
Rhymes, Busta **31**
Robinson, Patrick **19, 71**
Rochon, Lela **16**
Rowell, Victoria **13, 68**
Simmons, Kimora Lee **51, 83**
Sims, Naomi **29, 79**
Smaltz, Audrey **12**
Smith, B(arbara) **11**
Smith, Willi **8**
Smythe Haith, Mabel **61**
Steele, Lawrence **28**
Stoney, Michael **50**
Sy, Oumou **65**
Talley, André Leon **56**
Taylor, Karin **34**
Walker, T. J. **7**
Webb, Veronica **10**
Wek, Alek **18, 63**
White, Jessica **83**
Williams, Serena **20, 41, 73**

**Film**

Aaliyah **30**
Aaron, Quinton **82**
Adebimpe, Tunde **75**
Akinnuoye-Agbaje, Adewale **56**
Akomfrah, John **37**
Ali, Tatyana **73**
Allain, Stephanie **49**
Allen, Debbie **13, 42**
Alonso, Laz **87**
Amos, John **8, 62**
Anderson, Anthony **51, 77**
Anderson, Eddie "Rochester" **30**
Andrews, Tina **74**
Armah, Esther **87**
Awoonor, Kofi **37**
Babatunde, Obba **35**
Babyface **10, 31, 82**
Baker, Josephine **3**
Banks, Michelle **59**
Banks, Tyra **11, 50**
Barclay, Paris **37**
Barnett, Etta Moten **56**
Bassett, Angela **6, 23, 62**

Beach, Michael **26**
Beals, Jennifer **12**
Beckford, Tyson **11, 68**
Belafonte, Harry **4, 65**
Bellamy, Bill **12**
Bennett, Louise **69**
Bentley, Lamont **53**
Berry, Fred "Rerun" **48**
Berry, Halle **4, 19, 57**
Beyoncé **39, 70**
Billops, Camille **82**
Bivins, Michael **72**
Blackwood, Maureen **37**
Bleu, Corbin **65**
Bogle, Donald **34**
Bonet, Lisa **58**
Brady, Wayne **32, 71**
Brandy **14, 34, 72**
Braugher, Andre **13, 58**
Breeze, Jean "Binta" **37**
Brooks, Golden **62**
Brooks, Hadda **40**
Brown, Chris **74**
Brown, Jim **11**
Brown, Tony **3**
Browne, Roscoe Lee **66**
Burnett, Charles **16, 68**
Byrd, Michelle **19**
Byrd, Robert **11**
Calloway, Cab **14**
Campbell, Naomi **1, 31**
Campbell-Martin, Tisha **8, 42**
Cannon, Nick **47, 73**
Cannon, Reuben **50**
Cara, Irene **77**
Carroll, Diahann **9**
Carroll, Rocky **74**
Carson, Lisa Nicole **21**
Cash, Rosalind **28**
Cedric the Entertainer **29, 60**
Chase, Debra Martin **49**
Cheadle, Don **19, 52**
Chestnut, Morris **31**
Chong, Rae Dawn **62**
Chweneyagae, Presley **63**
Clash, Kevin **14**
Cliff, Jimmy **28**
Combs, Sean "Puffy" **17, 43**
Cortez, Jayne **43**
Cosby, Bill **7, 26, 59**
Crothers, Scatman **19**
Curry, Mark **17**
Curtis-Hall, Vondie **17**
Dandridge, Dorothy **3**
Daniels, Lee **36, 76**
Dash, Julie **4**
David, Keith **27**
Davidson, Jaye **5**
Davidson, Tommy **21**
Davis, Eisa **68**
Davis, Guy **36**
Davis, Ossie **5, 50**
Davis, Sammy, Jr. **18**
Davis, Viola **34, 76**
Dawn, Marpessa **75**
Dawson, Rosario **72**
De Bankolé, Isaach **78**
de Passe, Suzanne **25**
De Shields, André **72**
Dee, Ruby **8, 50, 68**
Devine, Loretta **24**
Dickerson, Ernest **6, 17**
Diesel, Vin **29**

Dieudonné **67**
Diggs, Taye **25, 63**
Dixon, Ivan **69**
DMX **28, 64**
Driskell, David C. **7**
Duke, Bill **3**
Duncan, Michael Clarke **26**
Dunham, Katherine **4, 59**
Dutton, Charles S. **4, 22**
Earthquake **55**
Ejiofor, Chiwetel **67**
Elder, Lonne, III **38**
Elise, Kimberly **32**
Emmanuel, Alphonsia **38**
Epps, Omar **23, 59**
Esposito, Giancarlo **9**
Evans, Darryl **22**
Everett, Francine **23**
Faison, Donald **50**
Faison, Frankie **55**
Fetchit, Stepin **32**
Fishburne, Laurence **4, 22, 70**
Fisher, Antwone **40**
Fisher, Gail **85**
Fletcher, Geoffrey **85**
Fox, Rick **27**
Fox, Vivica A. **15, 53**
Foxx, Jamie **15, 48**
Franklin, Carl **11**
Freeman, Al, Jr. **11**
Freeman, Morgan **2, 20, 62**
Freeman, Yvette **27**
Friday, Jeff **24**
Fuller, Charles **8**
Fuqua, Antoine **35**
Gaye, Nona **56**
George, Nelson **12**
Gerima, Haile **38, 80**
Gibbs, Marla **86**
Gibson, Tyrese **27, 62**
Givens, Adele **62**
Givens, Robin **4, 25, 58**
Glover, Danny **1, 24**
Glover, Donald **85**
Glover, Savion **14**
Goldberg, Whoopi **4, 33, 69**
Gooding, Cuba, Jr. **16, 62**
Gordon, Dexter **25**
Gordy, Berry, Jr. **1**
Gossett, Louis, Jr. **7**
Gray, F. Gary **14, 49**
Greaves, William **38**
Grier, David Alan **28**
Grier, Pam **9, 31, 86**
Guillaume, Robert **3, 48**
Gunn, Moses **10**
Gurira, Danai **73**
Guy, Jasmine **2**
Hall, Arsenio **58**
Hall, Juanita **62**
Hamilton, Lisa Gay **71**
Hampton, Henry **6**
Hardison, Kadeem **22**
Harewood, David **52**
Harper, Hill **32, 65**
Harris, Leslie **6**
Harris, Naomie **55**
Harris, Robin **7**
Hawkins, Screamin' Jay **30**
Hayes, Isaac **20, 58, 73**
Hayes, Teddy **40**
Haysbert, Dennis **42**
Hemsley, Sherman **19**

Henriques, Julian **37**
Henry, Lenny **9, 52**
Henson, Darrin **33**
Henson, Taraji P. **58, 77**
Hill, Dulé **29**
Hill, Lauryn **20, 53**
Hines, Gregory **1, 42**
Hooks, Robert **76**
Horne, Lena **5, 86**
Hounsou, Djimon **19, 45**
Houston, Whitney **7, 28, 83**
Howard, Sherri **36**
Howard, Terrence **59**
Hudlin, Reginald **9, 86**
Hudlin, Warrington **9**
Hudson, Ernie **72**
Hudson, Jennifer **63, 83**
Hughes, Albert **7**
Hughes, Allen **7**
Hughley, D. L. **23, 76**
Hurt, Byron **61**
Ice Cube **8, 30, 60**
Ice-T **6, 31**
Ingram, Rex **5**
Jackson, George **19**
Jackson, Janet **6, 30, 68**
Jackson, Rampage **83**
Jackson, Samuel **8, 19, 63**
Jean, Michaëlle; **70**
Jean-Baptiste, Marianne **17, 46**
Jean-Louis, Jimmy **76**
Johnson, Beverly **2**
Jones, James Earl **3, 49, 79**
Jones, Orlando **30**
Jones, Quincy **8, 30**
Jorge, Seu **73**
Julien, Isaac **3**
Kelley, Elijah **65**
Keys, Alicia **32, 68**
Khumalo, Leleti **51**
King, Regina **22, 45**
King, Woodie, Jr. **27**
Kirby, George **14**
Kitt, Eartha **16, 75**
Kool Moe Dee **37**
Kotto, Yaphet **7**
Kunjufu, Jawanza **3, 50**
Lane, Charles **3**
Lathan, Sanaa **27**
Lawrence, Martin **6, 27, 60**
Lee, Joie **1**
Lee, Malcolm D. **75**
Lee, Spike **5, 19, 86**
Lemmons, Kasi **20**
LeNoire, Rosetta **37**
Lester, Adrian **46**
Lewis, Samella **25**
Lil' Kim **28**
Lincoln, Abbey **3**
Lindo, Delroy **18, 45**
LisaRaye **27**
LL Cool J **16, 49**
Long, Nia **17**
Love, Darlene **23**
Lover, Ed **10**
Luke, Derek **61**
Lumet, Jenny **80**
Lynch, Shola **61**
Mabley, Jackie "Moms" **15**
Mac, Bernie **29, 61, 72**
Malco, Romany **71**
Marsalis, Branford **34**
Martin, Darnell **43, 78**

Martin, Helen 31
Master P 21
McBride, Chi 73
McDaniel, Hattie 5
McKee, Lonette 12
McKinney, Nina Mae 40
McQueen, Butterfly 6, 54
McQueen, Steve 84
Meadows, Tim 30
Mello, Breno 73
Merkerson, S. Epatha 47, 83
Micheaux, Oscar 7
Miller, Wentworth 75
Mitchell, Elvis 67
Mitchell, Kel 66
Mokae, Zakes 80
Mo'Nique 35, 84
Mooney, Paul 37
Moore, Chante 26
Moore, Juanita 83
Moore, Melba 21
Moore, Shemar 21
Morris, Garrett 31
Morrison, Vanessa 84
Morton, Joe 18
Mos Def 30
Moses, Gilbert 12
Moss, Carlton 17
Murphy, Eddie 4, 20, 61
Muse, Clarence Edouard 21
Nas 33
Nash, Johnny 40
Nash, Niecy 66
Neal, Elise 29
Newton, Thandie 26
Nicholas, Fayard 20, 57
Nicholas, Harold 20
Nichols, Nichelle 11
Norman, Maidie 20
Okonedo, Sophie 67
O'Neal, Ron 46
Onwurah, Ngozi 38
Oyelowo, David 82
Packer, Will 71
Palmer, Keke 68
Parker, Nicole Ari 52
Parks, Gordon 1, 35, 58
Patton, Paula 62
Payne, Allen 13
Peck, Raoul 32
Perrineau, Harold, Jr. 51
Perry, Tyler 54
Phifer, Mekhi 25
Pinkett Smith, Jada 10, 41
Poitier, Sidney 11, 36
Poitier, Sydney Tamiia 65
Pounder, CCH 72
Pratt, Kyla 57
Preer, Evelyn 82
Prince 18, 65
Prince-Bythewood, Gina 31, 77
Pryor, Richard 3, 24, 56
Queen Latifah 1, 16, 58
Ralph, Sheryl Lee 18
Randle, Theresa 16
Reddick, Lance 52
Reuben, Gloria 15
Rhames, Ving 14, 50
Rhimes, Shonda Lynn 67
Rhymes, Busta 31
Richards, Beah 30
Richardson, LaTanya 71
Richardson, Salli 68

Ridley, John 69
Riggs, Marlon 5, 44
Roberts, Darryl 70
Roberts, Kimberly Rivers 72
Robinson, Matt 69
Robinson, Shaun 36
Rochon, Lela 16
Rock, Chris 3, 22, 66
Rock, The 29, 66
Rodrigues, Percy 68
Rolle, Esther 13, 21
Rollins, Howard E., Jr. 16
Rose, Anika Noni 70
Ross, Diana 8, 27
Roundtree, Richard 27
Rowell, Victoria 13, 68
St. Jacques, Raymond 8
St. John, Kristoff 25
Saldana, Zoe 72
Salter, Nikkole 73
Sands, Diana 87
Schultz, Michael A. 6
Scott, Hazel 66
Scott, Jill 29, 83
Sembène, Ousmane 13, 62
Shakur, Tupac 14
Shepherd, Sherri 55
Short, Columbus 79
Sidibe, Gabourey 84
Simpson, O. J. 15
Sinbad 1, 16
Sinclair, Madge 78
Singleton, John 2, 30
Sisqo 30
Smith, Anjela Lauren 44
Smith, Anna Deavere 6, 44
Smith, Jaden 82
Smith, Roger Guenveur 12
Smith, Tasha 73
Smith, Will 8, 18, 53
Snipes, Wesley 3, 24, 67
Souleymane, Mahamane 78
Sullivan, Maxine 37
Sykes, Wanda 48, 81
Tate, Larenz 15
Taylor, Meshach 4
Taylor, Regina 9, 46
Thigpen, Lynne 17, 41
Thomas, Sean Patrick 35
Thompson, Kenan 52
Thurman, Wallace 16
Tillman, George, Jr. 20
Torres, Gina 52
Torry, Guy 31
Toussaint, Lorraine 32
Townsend, Robert 4, 23
True, Rachel 82
Tucker, Chris 13, 23, 62
Tunie, Tamara 63
Turner, Tina 6, 27
Tyler, Aisha N. 36
Tyson, Cicely 7, 51
Uggams, Leslie 23
Underwood, Blair 7, 27, 76
Union, Gabrielle 31
Usher 23, 56
Van Lierop, Robert 53
Van Peebles, Mario 2, 51
Van Peebles, Melvin 7
Vance, Courtney B. 15, 60
Vanity 67
Vereen, Ben 4
Walker, Eamonn 37

Wallace, William 75
Ward, Douglas Turner 42
Warfield, Marsha 2
Warner, Malcolm-Jamal 22, 36
Warren, Michael 27
Warwick, Dionne 18
Washington, Denzel 1, 16
Washington, Fredi 10
Washington, Kerry 46
Waters, Ethel 7
Wayans, Damien 78
Wayans, Damon 8, 41
Wayans, Keenen Ivory 18
Wayans, Kim 80
Wayans, Marlon 29, 82
Wayans, Shawn 29
Weathers, Carl 10
Webb, Veronica 10
Wesley, Richard 73
Whitaker, Forest 2, 49, 67
White, Armond 80
White, Michael Jai 71
Whitfield, Lynn 18
Williams, Billy Dee 8
Williams, Clarence, III 26
Williams, Marco 53
Williams, Russell, II 70
Williams, Samm-Art 21
Williams, Saul 31
Williams, Vanessa A. 32, 66
Williams, Vanessa L. 4, 17
Williamson, Fred 67
Williamson, Mykelti 22
Wilson, Debra 38
Wilson, Dorien 55
Winfield, Paul 2, 45
Winfrey, Oprah 2, 15, 61
Witherspoon, John 38
Woodard, Alfre 9
Wright, Jeffrey 54
Yarbrough, Cedric 51
Yoba, Malik 11

**Government and politics--
international**
Abacha, Sani 11, 70
Abbott, Diane 9
Abiola, Moshood 70
Abubakar, Abdulsalami 66
Achebe, Chinua 6
Adebari, Rotimi 83
Ahidjo, Ahmadou 81
Akunyili, Dora Nkem 58
Ali, Ayaan Hirsi 58
Ali Mahdi Mohamed 5
Amadi, Elechi 40
Amin, Idi 42
Amos, Valerie 41
Annan, Kofi Atta 15, 48
Aristide, Jean-Bertrand 6, 45
Arthur, Owen 33
Atta Mills, John 75
Augustine, Jean 53
Awoonor, Kofi 37
Azikiwe, Nnamdi 13
Babangida, Ibrahim 4
Baker, Gwendolyn Calvert 9
Banda, Hastings Kamuzu 6, 54
Barnes, Melody 75
Barrow, Dean 69
Bartels, Peggielene 80
Bashir, Omar al- 77
Bedie, Henri Konan 21

Berry, Mary Frances 7
Biko, Steven 4
Bishop, Maurice 39
Biya, Paul 28
Bizimungu, Pasteur 19
Boateng, Paul Yaw 56
Bongo, Ali Ben 80
Bongo, Omar 1, 79
Boye, Madior 30
Brown, Rosemary 62
Bunche, Ralph J. 5
Burnham, Forbes 66
Buthelezi, Mangosuthu Gatsha 9
Camara, Moussa Dadis 76
Césaire, Aimé 48, 69
Cham, Adongo Agada Akway 77
Charlemagne, Manno 11
Charles, Mary Eugenia 10, 55
Charles, Pierre 52
Chiluba, Frederick 56, 80
Chissano, Joaquim 7, 55, 67
Christie, Perry Gladstone 53
Christophe, Henri 9
Compaore, Blaise 87
Compton, John 65
Conneh, Sekou Damate, Jr. 51
Conté, Lansana 7, 76
Cools, Anne 64
Curling, Alvin 34
da Silva, Benedita 5
Dadié, Bernard 34
Dandala, Mvume 77
Davis, Ruth 37
Déby, Idriss 30
Diogo, Luisa Dias 63
Diop, Cheikh Anta 4
Diouf, Abdou 3
dos Santos, José Eduardo 43
Douglas, Denzil Llewellyn 53
Ekwensi, Cyprian 37
Eyadéma, Gnassingbé 7, 52
Fela 1, 42
Frazer, Jendayi 68
Gairy, Eric Matthew 83
Gbagbo, Laurent 43
Gnassingbé, Faure 67
Golding, Bruce 78
Gordon, Pamela 17
Grant, Bernie 57
Guebuza, Armando 81
Habré, Hissène 6
Habyarimana, Juvenal 8
Haile Selassie 7
Haley, George Williford Boyce 21
Hani, Chris 6
Houphouët-Boigny, Félix 4, 64
Hussein, Lubna 80
Ifill, Gwen 28
Ingraham, Hubert A. 19
Isaac, Julius 34
Jagan, Cheddi 16
Jammeh, Yahya 23
Jawara, Dawda Kairaba 11
Jean, Michaëlle; 70
Jean, Wyclef 20, 86
Jonathan, Goodluck 83
Ka Dinizulu, Mcwayizeni 29
Kabbah, Ahmad Tejan 23
Kabila, Joseph 30
Kabila, Laurent 20
Kabunda, Kenneth 2
Kagame, Paul 54
Kariuki, J. M. 67

Kenyatta, Jomo **5**
Kerekou, Ahmed (Mathieu) **1**
Kibaki, Mwai **60**
Kiir, Salva **85**
Kikwete, Jakaya Mrisho **73**
King, Oona **27**
Koroma, Ernest Bai **84**
Kufuor, John Agyekum **54, 82**
Laraque, Paul **67**
Lewis, Daurene **72**
Liberia-Peters, Maria Philomena **12**
Lumumba, Patrice **33**
Luthuli, Albert **13**
Maathai, Wangari **43**
Mabuza, Lindiwe **18**
Machel, Samora Moises **8**
Magloire, Paul Eugène **68**
Mandela, Nelson **1, 14, 77**
Mandela, Winnie **2, 35**
Masekela, Barbara **18**
Masire, Quett **5**
Mbeki, Govan A. **80**
Mbeki, Thabo **14, 73**
Mbuende, Kaire **12**
Meles Zenawi **3**
Mengistu, Haile Mariam **65**
Mhlaba, Raymond **55**
Mitchell, Keith **82**
Mkapa, Benjamin W. **16, 77**
Mobutu Sese Seko **1, 56**
Mogae, Festus Gontebanye **19, 79**
Moi, Daniel Arap **1, 35**
Mongella, Gertrude **11**
Motlanthe, Kgalema **74**
Moyo, Dambisa **76**
Moyo, Lovemore **76**
Mswati III **56**
Mugabe, Robert **10, 71**
Mukoko, Jestina **75**
Muluzi, Bakili **14, 76**
Museveni, Yoweri **4**
Mutebi, Ronald **25**
Muzorewa, Abel **85**
Mwanawasa, Levy **72**
Mwinyi, Ali Hassan **1, 77**
Ndadaye, Melchior **7**
Neto, António Agostinho **43**
Ngilu, Charity **58**
Ngubane, Ben **33**
Nkoli, Simon **60**
Nkomo, Joshua **4, 65**
Nkrumah, Kwame **3**
Nkurunziza, Pierre **78**
Ntaryamira, Cyprien **8**
Nujoma, Samuel **10**
Nyanda, Siphiwe **21**
Nyerere, Julius **5**
Nzo, Alfred **15**
Obasanjo, Olusegun **5, 22**
Obasanjo, Stella **32, 56**
Obote, Milton **63**
Odinga, Raila **67**
Okara, Gabriel **37**
Oyono, Ferdinand **38**
Pascal-Trouillot, Ertha **3**
Patterson, P. J. **6, 20**
Pereira, Aristides **30**
Perkins, Edward **5**
Perry, Ruth **15**
Pierre-Louis, Michèle **75**
Pindling, Lynden **81**
Pitt, David Thomas **10**
Pitta, Celso **17**

Préval, René **87**
Ramaphosa, Cyril **3**
Rawlings, Jerry **9**
Rawlings, Nana Konadu Agyeman **13**
Roberto, Holden **65**
Robinson, Randall **7, 46**
Sampson, Edith S. **4**
Sanhá Malam Bacai **84**
Sankara, Thomas **17**
Sankoh, Foday **74**
Savimbi, Jonas **2, 34**
Sawyer, Amos **2**
Senghor, Augustin Diamacoune **66**
Senghor, Léopold Sédar **12, 66**
Silva, Marina **80**
Simpson-Miller, Portia **62**
Sirleaf, Ellen Johnson **71**
Sisulu, Walter **47**
Skerrit, Roosevelt **72**
Skinner, Kiron K. **65**
Smith, Jennifer **21**
Soglo, Nicephore **15**
Soyinka, Wole **4**
Spencer, Winston Baldwin **68**
Tandja, Mamadou **33, 78**
Taylor, Charles **20**
Taylor, John (David Beckett) **16**
Todman, Terence A. **55**
Touré, Amadou Toumani **18**
Touré, Sekou **6**
Tsvangirai, Morgan **26, 72**
Tutu, Desmond (Mpilo) **6, 44**
Van Lierop, Robert **53**
Vieira, João Bernardo **14, 84**
Wade, Abdoulaye **66**
Weah, George **58**
Wharton, Clifton R., Jr. **7**
Wharton, Clifton Reginald, Sr. **36**
Williams, Eric Eustace **65**
Wiwa, Ken **67**
Yar'adua, Umaru **69**
Yayi, Boni T. **84**
Zuma, Jacob G. **33, 75**
Zuma, Nkosazana Dlamini **34**

**Government and politics--U.S.**
Adams, Floyd, Jr. **12**
Adams, Grantley **82**
Ahmed, Sharif **80**
Alexander, Archie Alphonso **14**
Alexander, Clifford **26**
Allen, Claude **68**
Allen, Ethel D. **13**
Allen, Eugene **79**
Archer, Dennis **7, 36**
Arrington, Richard **24**
Avant, Clarence **19, 86**
Baker, Thurbert **22**
Ballance, Frank W. **41**
Baltimore, Richard Lewis, III **71**
Barbee, Lloyd Augustus **71**
Barden, Don H. **9, 20**
Barrett, Andrew C. **12**
Barrett, Jacqueline **28**
Barry, Marion S. **7, 44**
Bass, Karen **70**
Bell, Michael **40**
Bellamy, Terry **58**
Belton, Sharon Sayles **9, 16**
Berry, Edwin C. **81**
Berry, Mary Frances **7**
Berry, Theodore M. **31**

Bethune, Mary McLeod **4**
Bing, Dave **3, 59, 78**
Blackwell, Kenneth, Sr. **61**
Blackwell, Unita **17**
Bobb, Robert C. **83**
Bond, Julian **2, 35**
Booker, Cory Anthony **68**
Bosley, Freeman, Jr. **7**
Bowman, Bertie **71**
Boykin, Keith **14**
Bradley, Jennette B. **40**
Bradley, Thomas **2**
Braun, Carol Moseley **4, 42**
Brazile, Donna **25, 70**
Brimmer, Andrew F. **2, 48**
Brooke, Edward **8**
Brooks, Tyrone **59**
Brown, Anthony G. **72**
Brown, Byrd **49**
Brown, Byron W. **72**
Brown, Cora **33**
Brown, Corrine **24**
Brown, Elaine **8**
Brown, George Leslie **62**
Brown, Jesse **6, 41**
Brown, Lee Patrick **24**
Brown, Les **5**
Brown, Ron **5**
Brown, Willie **7, 85**
Bruce, Blanche K. **33**
Bryant, Wayne R. **6**
Buckley, Victoria (Vicki) **24**
Bunche, Ralph J. **5**
Burke, Yvonne Brathwaite **42**
Burris, Chuck **21**
Burris, Roland W. **25, 75**
Bush, Gordon **82**
Butler, Jerry **26**
Butts, Cassandra **78**
Caesar, Shirley **19**
Campbell, Bill **9, 76**
Cardozo, Francis L. **33**
Carson, André **69**
Carson, Johnnie **85**
Carson, Julia **23, 69**
Carter, Pamela Lynn **67**
Carter, Robert L. **51**
Chavis, Benjamin **6**
Chisholm, Shirley **2, 50**
Christian-Green, Donna M. **17**
Christie, Ron **83**
Clay, William Lacy **8**
Clayton, Eva M. **20**
Cleaver, Eldridge **5**
Cleaver, Emanuel **4, 45, 68**
Clemente, Rosa **74**
Clyburn, James E. **21, 71**
Clyburn, Mignon **78**
Cockrel, Kenneth V., Jr. **79**
Cockrel, Kenneth Vern, Sr. **79**
Coleman, Mary **46**
Coleman, Michael B. **28, 79**
Coleman, William T. **76**
Collins, Barbara-Rose **7, 87**
Collins, Cardiss **10, 80**
Colter, Cyrus J. **36**
Connerly, Ward **14**
Conyers, John, Jr. **4, 45**
Conyers, Monica **85**
Cook, Mercer **40**
Cose, Ellis **5, 50**
Craig-Jones, Ellen Walker **44**
Crockett, George W., Jr. **10, 64**

Cummings, Elijah E. **24**
Cunningham, Evelyn **23, 85**
Currie, Betty **21**
Currie, Ulysses **73**
Davis, Angela **5**
Davis, Artur **41**
Davis, Benjamin O., Jr. **2, 43**
Davis, Benjamin O., Sr. **4**
Davis, Danny K. **24, 79**
Davis, Gordon J. **76**
Davis, James E. **50**
Days, Drew S., III **10**
De Priest, Oscar Stanton **80**
DeJongh, John, Jr. **85**
Delany, Martin R. **27**
Delco, Wilhemina R. **33**
Dellums, Ronald **2, 81**
Diggs, Charles R. **21**
Dinkins, David **4**
Dixon, Julian C. **24**
Dixon, Sharon Pratt **1**
Dixon, Sheila **68**
Dougherty, Mary Pearl **47**
Du Bois, W. E. B. **3**
Dudley, Edward R. **58**
Dukes, Hazel Nell **56**
Dunbar-Nelson, Alice Ruth Moore **44**
Dymally, Mervyn **42**
Easley, Annie J. **61**
Edmonds, Terry **17**
Edwards, Donna **77**
Elders, Joycelyn **6**
Ellison, Keith **59**
Ervin, Clark Kent **82**
Espy, Mike **6**
Farmer, James **2, 64**
Farrakhan, Louis **2**
Farrell, Herman D., Jr. **81**
Fattah, Chaka **11, 70**
Fauntroy, Walter E. **11**
Felix, Larry R. **64**
Fenty, Adrian **60**
Ferguson, Roger W. **25**
Fields, C. Virginia **25**
Fields, Cleo **13**
Fisher, Ada M. **76**
Flake, Floyd H. **18**
Fleming, Erik R. **75**
Fletcher, Arthur A. **63**
Flipper, Henry O. **3**
Ford, Harold E(ugene) **42**
Ford, Harold E(ugene), Jr. **16, 70**
Ford, Jack **39**
Ford, Johnny **70**
Fortune, T. Thomas **6**
Foster, Ezola **28**
Foxx, Anthony **81**
Franklin, Shirley **34, 80**
Franks, Gary **2**
Frazer, Jendayi **68**
Fudge, Marcia L. **76**
Fulani, Lenora **11**
Gantt, Harvey **1**
Garrett, Joyce Finley **59**
Garvey, Marcus **1**
Gaspard, Patrick **84**
Gibson, Johnnie Mae **23**
Gibson, Kenneth Allen **6**
Gibson, William F. **6**
Goode, W. Wilson **4**
Gravely, Samuel L., Jr. **5, 49**
Gray, William H., III **3**

Grimké, Archibald H. **9**
Guinier, Lani **7**, **30**
Haley, George Williford Boyce **21**
Hamer, Fannie Lou **6**
Harmon, Clarence **26**
Harris, Alice **7**
Harris, Patricia Roberts **2**
Harvard, Beverly **11**
Hastie, William H. **8**
Hastings, Alcee L. **16**
Hatcher, Richard G. **55**
Hawkins, Augustus F. **68**
Hayes, James C. **10**
Henderson, Thelton E. **68**
Henry, Aaron **19**
Herenton, Willie W. **24**, **81**
Herman, Alexis M. **15**
Hernandez, Aileen Clarke **13**
Hill, Bonnie Guiton **20**
Hilliard, Earl F. **24**
Hobson, Julius W. **44**
Holder, Eric H., Jr. **9**, **76**
Holmes, Amy **69**
Holt Baker, Arlene **73**
Ifill, Gwen **28**
Irving, Larry, Jr. **12**
Irvis, K. Leroy **67**
Jackson, Alphonso R. **48**
Jackson, Frank G. **76**
Jackson, George **14**
Jackson, Jesse **1**, **27**, **72**
Jackson, Jesse, Jr. **14**, **45**, **81**
Jackson, Lisa **77**
Jackson, Mae **57**
Jackson, Maynard **2**, **41**
Jackson, Shirley Ann **12**
Jackson Lee, Sheila **20**
Jacob, John E. **2**
James, Sharpe **23**, **69**
Jarrett, Valerie **73**
Jarvis, Charlene Drew **21**
Jarvis, Kristen **85**
Jefferson, William J. **25**, **72**
Johnson, Eddie Bernice **8**
Johnson, Hank, Jr. **80**
Johnson, Harvey, Jr. **24**, **82**
Johnson, James Weldon **5**
Johnson, Jeh C. **76**
Johnson, Katherine (Coleman Goble) **61**
Johnson, Kevin **70**
Johnson, Norma L. Holloway **17**
Johnson, Robert T. **17**
Jones, Elaine R. **7**, **45**
Jones, Emil, Jr. **74**
Jordan, Barbara **4**, **78**
Jordan, Vernon **3**, **35**
Kelley, Cliff **75**
Kennard, William Earl **18**
Keyes, Alan L. **11**
Kidd, Mae Street **39**
Kilpatrick, Carolyn Cheeks **16**
Kilpatrick, Kwame **34**, **71**
Kincaid, Bernard **28**
King, Martin Luther, III **20**
Kirk, Ron **11**, **75**
Lafontant, Jewel Stradford **3**, **51**
Langford, Larry P. **74**
Layton, William **87**
Lee, Barbara **25**
Leland, Mickey **2**
Lewis, Delano **7**
Lewis, John **2**, **46**, **83**

Love, Reggie **77**
Lowery, Myron **80**
Majette, Denise **41**
Mallett, Conrad, Jr. **16**
Mallory, Mark **62**
Marsh, Henry, III **32**
Marshall, Bella **22**
Marshall, Thurgood **1**, **44**
Martin, Louis E. **16**
Martin, Ruby Grant **49**
McCall, H. Carl **27**
McGee, James D. **74**
McGee, James Madison **46**
McGlowan, Angela **64**, **86**
McHenry, Donald F. **83**
McKinney, Cynthia **11**, **52**, **74**
McKissick, Floyd B. **3**
Meek, Carrie **6**, **36**
Meek, Kendrick **41**
Meeks, Gregory **25**
Melton, Frank **81**
Meredith, James H. **11**
Metcalfe, Ralph **26**
Mfume, Kweisi **6**, **41**
Millender-McDonald, Juanita **21**, **61**
Mitchell, Parren J. **42**, **66**
Moore, Gwendolynne S. **55**
Moore, Minyon **45**
Morial, Ernest "Dutch" **26**
Morial, Marc H. **20**, **51**
Morton, Azie Taylor **48**
Moses, Robert Parris **11**
Murrell, Sylvia Marilyn **49**
Nagin, C. Ray **42**, **57**
Nix, Robert N.C., Jr. **51**
Norton, Eleanor Holmes **7**
Nutter, Michael **69**
Obama, Barack **49**, **74**
O'Leary, Hazel **6**
Owens, Major **6**
Page, Alan **7**
Paige, Rod **29**
Paterson, Basil A. **69**
Paterson, David A. **59**
Patrick, Deval **12**, **61**
Patterson, J. O., Jr. **80**
Patterson, Louise **25**
Payne, Donald M. **2**, **57**
Payne, William D. **60**
Perez, Anna **1**
Perkins, Edward **5**
Perkins, James, Jr. **55**
Perry, James **83**
Perry, Lowell **30**
Pinchback, P. B. S. **9**
Pitts, Robb **84**
Powell, Adam Clayton, Jr. **3**
Powell, Colin **1**, **28**, **75**
Powell, Debra A. **23**
Powell, Michael **32**
Pugh, Charles **81**
Raines, Franklin Delano **14**
Randolph, A. Philip **3**
Rangel, Charles B. **3**, **52**, **85**
Raoul, Kwame **55**
Rapier, James T. **82**
Reed, Kasim **82**
Reeves, Gregory **49**
Reeves, Martha **85**
Reeves, Triette Lipsey **27**
Rice, Condoleezza **3**, **28**, **72**
Rice, Norm **8**
Rice, Susan E. **74**

Richardson, Laura **81**
Richardson, Rupert **67**
Riles, Wilson C. **79**
Roberts, Lillian **83**
Robinson, Bishop L. **66**
Robinson, Randall **7**, **46**
Rochon, Stephen W. **78**
Rogers, Joe **27**
Ross, Don **27**
Rush, Bobby **26**, **76**
Rustin, Bayard **4**
Sampson, Edith S. **4**
Sanders, Malika **48**
Satcher, David **7**, **57**
Sawyer, Eugene **81**
Sayles Belton, Sharon **9**
Schmoke, Kurt **1**, **48**
Scott, David **41**
Scott, Robert C. **23**
Scott, Tim **87**
Shakur, Assata **6**
Shavers, Cheryl **31**
Shelton, Paula Young **86**
Sherrod, Shirley **87**
Simmons, E. Denise **79**
Simmons, Jamal **72**
Simpson, Carole **6**, **30**
Sisulu, Sheila Violet Makate **24**
Slater, Rodney E. **15**
Smith, Malcolm A. **75**
Smith, Nate **49**
Smith, Princella **86**
Smythe Haith, Mabel **61**
Spearman, Leonard H. O., Sr. **81**
Spigner, Archie **81**
Stanton, Robert **20**
Staupers, Mabel K. **7**
Steele, Michael **38**, **73**
Stokes, Carl **10**, **73**
Stokes, Louis **3**
Stone, Chuck **9**
Stoutt, H. Lavity **83**
Strautmanis, Michael **87**
Street, John F. **24**
Sullivan, Louis **8**
Sutphen, Mona **77**
Sutton, Percy E. **42**, **82**
Terry, Clark **39**
Thomas, Clarence **2**, **39**, **65**
Thompson, Bennie G. **26**
Thompson, Larry D. **39**
Thompson, William C. **35**
Tillman, Dorothy **76**
Todman, Terence A. **55**
Tolbert, Terence **74**
Toote, Gloria E.A. **64**
Towns, Edolphus **19**, **75**
Tribble, Israel, Jr. **8**
Trotter, Donne E. **28**
Tubbs Jones, Stephanie **24**, **72**
Tucker, C. Delores **12**, **56**
Turnbull, Charles Wesley **62**
Turner, Henry McNeal **5**
Usry, James L. **23**
Vaughn, Gladys Gary **47**
Von Lipsey, Roderick K. **11**
Wallace, Phyllis A. **9**
Washington, Harold **6**
Washington, Val **12**
Washington, Walter **45**
Waters, Maxine **3**, **67**
Watkins, Joe **86**
Watkins, Shirley R. **17**

Watson, Diane **41**
Watt, Melvin **26**
Watts, J. C., Jr. **14**, **38**
Weaver, Robert C. **8**, **46**
Webb, Wellington **3**, **81**
Wharton, Clifton R., Jr. **7**
Wharton, Clifton Reginald, Sr. **36**
Wheat, Alan **14**
White, Jesse **22**, **75**
White, Michael R. **5**
Wilder, L. Douglas **3**, **48**
Williams, Anthony **21**
Williams, Eddie N. **44**
Williams, George Washington **18**
Williams, Hosea Lorenzo **15**, **31**
Williams, Maggie **9**, **71**
Williams, Michael L. **86**
Wilson, Margaret Bush **79**
Wilson, Sunnie **7**, **55**
Woods, Abraham, Jr. **74**
Wynn, Albert **25**, **77**
Young, Andrew **3**, **48**

**Law**
Alexander, Clifford **26**
Alexander, Joyce London **18**
Alexander, Sadie Tanner Mossell **22**
Allen, Samuel W. **38**
Amaker, Norman **63**
Anderson, Reuben V. **81**
Archer, Dennis **7**, **36**
Arnwine, Barbara **28**
Bailey, Clyde **45**
Baldwin, Cynthia A. **74**
Banks, William **11**
Barbee, Lloyd Augustus **71**
Barrett, Andrew C. **12**
Barrett, Jacqueline **28**
Baugh, David **23**
Bell, Derrick **6**
Benham, Robert **78**
Berry, Mary Frances **7**
Berry, Theodore M. **31**
Birch, Adolpho A., Jr. **85**
Bishop, Sanford D., Jr. **24**
Bolin, Jane **22**, **59**
Bolton, Terrell D. **25**
Booker, Cory Anthony **68**
Bosley, Freeman, Jr. **7**
Boykin, Keith **14**
Bradley, Thomas **2**
Braun, Carol Moseley **4**, **42**
Brooke, Edward **8**
Brown, Byrd **49**
Brown, Cora **33**
Brown, Cupcake **63**
Brown, Homer S. **47**
Brown, Janice Rogers **43**
Brown, Joe **29**
Brown, Lee Patrick **1**, **24**
Brown, Ron **5**
Bryant, Wayne R. **6**
Bryant, William Benson **61**
Bully-Cummings, Ella **48**
Burke, Yvonne Brathwaite **42**
Burris, Roland W. **25**, **75**
Butler, Louis **70**
Butler, Paul D. **17**
Bynoe, Peter C. B. **40**
Campbell, Bill **9**, **76**
Carter, Pamela Lynn **67**
Carter, Robert L. **51**

Carter, Stephen L. 4
Cashin, Sheryll 63
Chambers, Julius 3
Chestnut, J. L., Jr. 73
Cleaver, Kathleen Neal 29
Clendenon, Donn 26, 56
Cochran, Johnnie 11, 39, 52
Coleman, James E., Jr. 79
Coleman, William T. 76
Colter, Cyrus J. 36
Conyers, John, Jr. 4, 45
Crockett, George W., Jr. 10, 64
Darden, Christopher 13
Davis, Artur 41
Davis, Gordon J. 76
Days, Drew S., III 10
DeFrantz, Anita 37
Diggs-Taylor, Anna 20
Dillard, Godfrey J. 45
Dinkins, David 4
Dixon, Sharon Pratt 1
Edelman, Marian Wright 5, 42
Edley, Christopher 2, 48
Edley, Christopher F., Jr. 48
Ellington, E. David 11
Ephriam, Mablean 29
Ervin, Clark Kent 82
Espy, Mike 6
Evans, Warren C. 76
Farmer-Paellmann, Deadria 43
Feemster, Herbert 72
Fields, Cleo 13
Finner-Williams, Paris Michele 62
Fisher, Ada Lois Sipuel 76
Ford, Wallace 58
Foxx, Anthony 81
Frazier-Lyde, Jacqui 31
Freeman, Charles 19
Gaines, Lloyd 79
Gary, Willie E. 12
Gibson, Johnnie Mae 23
Glover, Nathaniel, Jr. 12
Gomez-Preston, Cheryl 9
Gordon-Reed, Annette 74
Graham, Lawrence Otis 12
Gray, Fred 37
Gray, Willie 46
Greenhouse, Bunnatine 57
Grimké, Archibald H. 9
Guinier, Lani 7, 30
Haley, George Williford Boyce 21
Hall, Elliott S. 24
Harris, Kamala D. 64
Harris, Patricia Roberts 2
Harvard, Beverly 11
Hassell, Leroy Rountree, Sr. 41
Hastie, William H. 8
Hastings, Alcee L. 16
Hatcher, Richard G. 55
Hatchett, Glenda 32
Hawkins, Augustus F. 68
Hawkins, Steven 14
Hayes, Dennis 54
Haywood, Margaret A. 24
Henderson, Thelton E. 68
Higginbotham, A. Leon, Jr. 13, 25
Hill, Anita 5, 65
Hillard, Terry 25
Hills, Oliver W. 24
Holder, Eric H., Jr. 9, 76
Hollowell, Donald L. 57
Holton, Hugh, Jr. 39
Hooks, Benjamin L. 2, 85

Houston, Charles Hamilton 4
Hubbard, Arnette Rhinehart 38
Hunter, Billy 22
Hurtt, Harold 46
Isaac, Julius 34
Jackson, Maynard 2, 41
Jackson Lee, Sheila 20
Johnson, Harry E. 57
Johnson, James Weldon 5
Johnson, Jeh C. 76
Johnson, Norma L. Holloway 17
Jones, Elaine R. 7, 45
Jones, Van 70
Jordan, Eddie 82
Jordan, Vernon E. 3, 35
Kearse, Amalya Lyle 12
Keith, Damon J. 16, 74
Kennard, William Earl 18
Kennedy, Florynce 12, 33
Kennedy, Randall 40
Kibaki, Mwai 60
Kirk, Ron 11, 75
Lafontant, Jewel Stradford 3, 51
Lewis, Delano 7
Lewis, Reginald F. 6
Lloyd, Reginald 64
Majette, Denise 41
Mallett, Conrad, Jr. 16
Mandela, Nelson 1, 14, 77
Marsh, Henry, III 32
Marshall, Thurgood 1, 44
Mathis, Greg 26
McAnulty, William E., Jr. 66
McCrary Anthony, Crystal 70
McDonald, Gabrielle Kirk 20
McDougall, Gay J. 11, 43
McKinnon, Isaiah 9
McKissick, Floyd B. 3
McPhail, Sharon 2
Meek, Kendrick 41
Meeks, Gregory 25
Melton, Harold D. 79
Moose, Charles 40
Morial, Ernest "Dutch" 26
Motley, Constance Baker 10, 55
Muhammad, Ava 31
Murray, Pauli 38
Nance, Cynthia 71
Napoleon, Benny N. 23
Nash, Shannon King 84
Nix, Robert N. C., Jr. 51
Noble, Ronald 46
Norton, Eleanor Holmes 7
Nunn, Annetta 43
Obama, Barack 49, 74
Obama, Michelle 61
Ogletree, Charles, Jr. 12, 47
Ogunlesi, Adebayo O. 37
O'Leary, Hazel 6
Oliver, Jerry 37
Page, Alan 7
Parker, Kellis E. 30
Parks, Bernard C. 17
Parsons, James 14
Parsons, Richard Dean 11, 33
Pascal-Trouillot, Ertha 3
Paterson, Basil A. 69
Patrick, Deval 12
Payne, Ulice 42
Payton, John 48
Perry, Lowell 30
Philip, Marlene Nourbese 32
Pincham, R. Eugene, Sr. 69

Powell, Michael 32
Quince, Peggy A. 69
Ramsey, Charles H. 21, 69
Raoul, Kwame 55
Rawlinson, Johnnie B. 79
Ray, Charlotte E. 60
Redding, Louis L. 26
Reed, Kasim 82
Reynolds, Star Jones 10, 27, 61
Rice, Constance LaMay 60
Richie, Leroy C. 18
Robinson, Bishop L. 66
Robinson, Malcolm S. 44
Robinson, Randall 7, 46
Roundtree, Dovey 80
Russell-McCloud, Patricia 17
Sampson, Edith S. 4
Schmoke, Kurt 1, 48
Sears, Leah Ward 5, 79
Solomon, Jimmie Lee 38
Sparks, Corinne Etta 53
Steele, Michael 38, 73
Stokes, Carl 10, 73
Stokes, Louis 3
Stout, Juanita Kidd 24
Strautmanis, Michael 87
Sutton, Percy E. 42, 82
Taylor, John (David Beckett) 16
Thomas, Arthur Ray 52
Thomas, Clarence 2, 39, 65
Thomas, Franklin A. 5, 49
Thompson, Larry D. 39
Touré, Faya Ora Rose 56
Tubbs Jones, Stephanie 24, 72
Van Lierop, Robert 53
Vanzant, Iyanla 17, 47
Wagner, Annice 22
Wainwright, Joscelyn 46
Walker, Cora T. 68
Wallace, Perry E. 47
Ward, Benjamin 68
Washington, Harold 6
Watkins, Donald 35
Watt, Melvin 26
Wharton, Clifton Reginald, Sr. 36
Wilder, L. Douglas 3, 48
Wilkins, David 77
Williams, Ann Claire 82
Williams, Evelyn 10
Williams, Gregory 11
Williams, Patricia 11, 54
Williams, Willie L. 4
Wilson, Jimmy 45
Worthy, Kym 84
Wright, Bruce McMarion 3, 52
Wynn, Albert 25, 77

**Military**
Abacha, Sani 11, 70
Adams Early, Charity 13, 34
Adams-Ender, Clara 40
Alexander, Margaret Walker 22
Amin, Idi 42
Archer, Lee, Jr. 79
Babangida, Ibrahim 4
Baker, Vernon Joseph 65, 87
Bashir, Omar al- 77
Black, Barry C. 47
Bolden, Charles Frank, Jr. 7, 78
Brashear, Carl 29
Brown, Anthony G. 72
Brown, Erroll M. 23
Brown, Jesse 6, 41

Brown, Jesse Leroy 31
Brown, Willa 40
Bullard, Eugene 12
Cadoria, Sherian Grace 14
Chissano, Joaquim 7, 55, 67
Christophe, Henri 9
Clemmons, Reginal G. 41
Compaore, Blaise 87
Conté, Lansana 7, 76
Cooke, Marcia 60
Davis, Benjamin O., Jr. 2, 43
Davis, Benjamin O., Sr. 4
Drew, Alvin, Jr. 67
Duggins, George 64
Europe, James Reese 10
Eyadéma, Gnassingbé 7, 52
Fields, Evelyn J. 27
Flipper, Henry O. 3
Gravely, Samuel L., Jr. 5, 49
Gregory, Frederick 8, 51
Guéï, Robert 66
Habré, Hissène 6
Habyarimana, Juvenal 8
Harris, Marcelite Jordan 16
Honoré, Russel L. 64
Howard, Michelle 28
Jackson, Fred James 25
James, Daniel, Jr. 16
Johnson, Hazel 22
Johnson, Shoshana 47
Kagame, Paul 54
Kerekou, Ahmed (Mathieu) 1
Kiir, Salva 85
King, Teresa 80
Laraque, Paul 67
Lawrence, Robert H., Jr. 16
Lyles, Lester 31
Maceo, Antonio 82
Magloire, Paul Eugène 68
Matthews, Mark 59
Miller, Dorie 29
Nkunda, Laurent 75
Nyanda, Siphiwe 21
Obasanjo, Olusegun 5, 22
Petersen, Frank E. 31
Powell, Colin 1, 28, 75
Pratt, Geronimo 18
Rawlings, Jerry 9
Reason, J. Paul 19
Rochon, Stephen W. 78
Rogers, Alan G. 72
Scantlebury, Janna 47
Smalls, Robert 82
Snow, Samuel 71
Stanford, John 20
Staupers, Mabel K. 7
Stokes, Louis 3
Touré, Amadou Toumani 18
Von Lipsey, Roderick K. 11
Watkins, Perry 12
West, Togo, D., Jr. 16
Wilson, Jimmy 45
Wright, Lewin 43
Young, Charles 77

**Music**
Aaliyah 30
Ace, Johnny 36
Adams, Johnny 39
Adams, Leslie 39
Adams, Oleta 18
Adams, Yolanda 17, 67
Adderley, Julian "Cannonball" 30

Adderley, Nat **29**
Ade, King Sunny **41**
Adebimpe, Tunde **75**
Afro, Teddy **78**
Akon **68**
Albright, Gerald **23**
Alert, Kool DJ **33**
Ali, Rashied **79**
Allen, Betty **83**
Amerie **52**
Anderson, Carl **48**
Anderson, Fred **87**
Anderson, Marian **2**, **33**
apl.de.ap **84**
Ardoin, Alphonse **65**
Armatrading, Joan **32**
Armstrong, Louis **2**
Armstrong, Vanessa Bell **24**
Arroyo, Marina **30**
Ashanti **37**
Ashford, Nickolas **21**
Ashong, Derrick **86**
Astatke, Mulatu **81**
Atkins, Juan **50**
Austin, Lovie **40**
Austin, Patti **24**
Avant, Clarence **19**, **86**
Ayers, Roy **16**
Babyface **10**, **31**, **82**
Baca, Susana **80**
Badu, Erykah **22**
Bailey, Buster **38**
Bailey, DeFord **33**
Bailey, Philip **63**
Bailey Rae, Corinne **83**
Baiocchi, Regina Harris **41**
Baker, Anita **21**, **48**
Baker, Josephine **3**
Baker, LaVern **26**
Ballard, Hank **41**
Bambaataa, Afrika **34**
Banner, David **55**
Barker, Danny **32**
Barnes, Lloyd **77**
Barnes, Roosevelt "Booba" **33**
Barrino, Fantasia **53**
Basie, Count **23**
Bassey, Shirley **25**
Batiste, Alvin **66**
Battle, Kathleen **70**
Baylor, Helen **36**
Bebey, Francis **45**
Bechet, Sidney **18**
Beenie Man **32**
Belafonte, Harry **4**, **65**
Belgrave, Marcus **77**
Belle, Regina **1**, **51**
Benét, Eric **28**, **77**
Benjamin, Andre **45**
Bennett, Estelle **77**
Bentley, Lamont **53**
Berry, Chuck **29**
Betts, Keter **85**
Beverly, Frankie **25**
Beyoncé **39**, **70**
Bibb, Eric **49**
Big Daddy Kane **79**
Bivins, Michael **72**
Black Thought **63**
Blackman, Toni **86**
Blake, Eubie **29**
Blakey, Art **37**
Blanchard, Terence **43**

Bland, Bobby "Blue" **36**
Bleu, Corbin **65**
Blige, Mary J. **20**, **34**, **60**
Blondy, Alpha **30**
Blow, Kurtis **31**
Bolden, Buddy **39**
Bond, Beverly **53**
Bonds, Margaret **39**
Bonga, Kuenda **13**
Bow Wow **35**
Boyz II Men **82**
Bradley, J. Robert **65**
Brae, C. Michael **61**
Brandy **14**, **34**, **72**
Braxton, Toni **15**, **61**
Bridgetower, George **78**
Bridgewater, Dee Dee **32**
Brooks, Avery **9**
Brooks, Hadda **40**
Broonzy, Big Bill **82**
Brown, Angela M. **54**
Brown, Anne **76**
Brown, Bobby **58**
Brown, Carlinhos **81**
Brown, Charles **23**
Brown, Chris **74**
Brown, Chuck **78**
Brown, Clarence Gatemouth **59**
Brown, Clifford **86**
Brown, Foxy **25**
Brown, James **15**, **60**
Brown, Melanie **73**
Brown, Nappy **73**
Brown, Oscar, Jr. **53**
Brown, Patrick "Sleepy" **50**
Brown, Uzee **42**
Bumbry, Grace **5**
Burke, Solomon **31**, **86**
Burleigh, Henry Thacker **56**
Burning Spear **79**
Burns, Eddie **44**
Burnside, R. L. **56**
Busby, Jheryl **3**, **74**
Butler, George, Jr. **70**
Butler, Jerry **26**
Butler, Jonathan **28**
Caesar, Shirley **19**
Cage, Byron **53**
Calloway, Cab **1**
Campbell-Martin, Tisha **8**, **42**
Cannon, Nick **47**, **73**
Carey, Mariah **32**, **53**, **69**
Carr, Kurt **56**
Carr, Leroy **49**
Carroll, Diahann **9**
Carter, Benny **46**
Carter, Betty **19**
Carter, Nell **39**
Carter, Regina **23**
Carter, Warrick L. **27**
Cartiér, Xam Wilson **41**
Caymmi, Dorival **72**
Cee-Lo **70**
Chamillionaire **82**
Chanté, Keshia **50**
Chapman, Tracy **26**
Charlemagne, Manno **11**
Charles, Ray **16**, **48**
Cheatham, Doc **17**
Checker, Chubby **28**
Chenault, John **40**
Christie, Angella **36**
Chuck D **9**

Ciara **56**
Clark, Mattie Moss **61**
Clark-Cole, Dorinda **66**
Clarke, Kenny **27**
Clark-Sheard, Karen **22**
Clemons, Clarence **41**
Cleveland, James **19**
Cliff, Jimmy **28**
Clinton, George **9**
Cole, Keyshia **63**
Cole, Nat "King" **17**
Cole, Natalie **17**, **60**, **84**
Coleman, Ornette **39**, **69**
Coleridge-Taylor, Samuel **75**
Collins, Albert **12**
Collins, Bootsy **31**
Collins, Lyn **53**
Coltrane, Alice **70**
Coltrane, John **19**
Coltrane, Ravi **71**
Combs, Sean "Puffy" **17**, **43**
Common **31**, **63**
Cook, Charles "Doc" **44**
Cook, Will Marion **40**
Cooke, Sam **17**
Coppola, Imani Francesca **82**
Cortez, Jayne **43**
Count Basie **23**
Cowboy Troy **54**
Cox, Deborah **28**
Cox, Ida **42**
Craig, Carl **31**, **71**
Crawford, Hank **77**
Crawford, Randy **19**
Cray, Robert **30**
Creagh, Milton **27**
Crocker, Frankie **29**
Crothers, Scatman **19**
Crouch, Andraé **27**
Crowder, Henry **16**
Da Don, Polow **86**
Daemyon, Jerald **64**
D'Angelo **27**
Dara, Olu **35**
Dash, Damon **31**
Dash, Darien **29**
David, Craig **31**, **53**
Davis, Anthony **11**
Davis, Gary **41**
Davis, Guy **36**
Davis, Miles **4**
Davis, Sammy, Jr. **18**
Davis, Tyrone **54**
Dawson, William Levi **39**
de Passe, Suzanne **25**
Deezer D **53**
Dennard, Brazeal **37**
Dickenson, Vic **38**
Diddley, Bo **39**, **72**
Dixon, Bill **87**
Dixon, Dean **68**
Dixon, Willie **4**
DJ Jazzy Jeff **32**
DMX **28**, **64**
Dobbs, Mattiwilda **34**
Domino, Fats **20**
Donegan, Dorothy **19**
Dorsey, Lee **65**
Dorsey, Thomas **15**
Downing, Will **19**
Drake **86**
Dre, Dr. **10**, **14**, **30**
Dube, Lucky **77**

Duke, George **21**
Dumas, Henry **41**
Duncan, Todd **76**
Dunner, Leslie B. **45**
Duplechan, Larry **55**
Dupri, Jermaine **13**, **46**
Durham, Bobby **73**
Dworkin, Aaron P. **52**
Earthquake **55**
Eckstine, Billy **28**
Edmonds, Tracey **16**, **64**
Edwards, Esther Gordy **43**
Eldridge, Roy **37**
Ellington, Duke **5**
Elliott, Missy "Misdemeanor" **31**
Ellis, Alton **74**
Escobar, Damien **56**
Escobar, Tourie **56**
Estelle **75**
Estes, Simon **28**
Estes, Sleepy John **33**
Eubanks, Kevin **15**
Europe, James Reese **10**
Evans, Faith **22**
Eve **29**
Evora, Cesaria **12**
Falana, Lola **42**
Farmer, Art **38**
Feemster, Herbert **72**
Fela **1**, **42**
Ferrell, Rachelle **29**
Ferrer, Ibrahim **41**
Fiasco, Lupe **64**
50 Cent **46**, **83**
Fiona, Melanie **84**
Fitzgerald, Ella **8**, **18**
Flack, Roberta **19**
Flanagan, Tommy **69**
Flavor Flav **67**
Flo Rida **78**
Ford, Vincent **75**
Forté, John **74**
Foster, George "Pops" **40**
Foxx, Jamie **15**, **48**
Franklin, Aretha **11**, **44**
Franklin, Kirk **15**, **49**
Freelon, Nnenna **32**
Freeman, Paul **39**
Freeman, Yvette **27**
Fuller, Blind Boy **86**
Fuqua, Antoine **35**
Gaines, Grady **38**
Gamble, Kenny **85**
Garner, Erroll **76**
Garrett, Sean **57**
Gaye, Marvin **2**
Gaye, Nona **56**
Gaynor, Gloria **36**
George, Zelma Watson **42**
Gibson, Althea **8**, **43**
Gibson, Tyrese **27**, **62**
Gil, Gilberto **53**
Gill, Johnny **51**
Gillespie, Dizzy **1**
Ginuwine **35**
Glover, Corey **34**
Goapele **55**
Golson, Benny **37**
Goodman, Al **87**
Gordon, Dexter **25**
Gordy, Berry, Jr. **1**
Gotti, Irv **39**
Grae, Jean **51**

Grandmaster Flash **33, 60**
Graves, Denyce Antoinette **19, 57**
Gray, F. Gary **14, 49**
Gray, Macy **29**
Greaves, William **38**
Greely, M. Gasby **27**
Green, Al **13, 47, 74**
Green, Grant **56**
Greene, Jimmy **74**
Griffin, Johnny **71**
Griffin, LaShell **51**
Griffiths, Marcia **29**
Grist, Reri **84**
Günes, Tata **69**
Guru **84**
Guy, Buddy **31**
Haddon, Dietrick **55**
Hailey, JoJo **22**
Hailey, K-Ci **22**
Hall, Aaron **57**
Hall, Juanita **62**
Hamilton, Anthony **61**
Hammond, Fred **23**
Hammond, Lenn **34**
Hampton, Lionel **17, 41**
Hancock, Herbie **20, 67**
Handy, W. C. **8**
Hardin Armstrong, Lil **39**
Harper, Ben **34, 62**
Harrell, Andre **9, 30**
Harris, Barry **68**
Harris, Corey **39, 73**
Hart, Alvin Youngblood **61**
Hathaway, Donny **18**
Hathaway, Lalah **57**
Hawkins, Coleman **9**
Hawkins, Erskine **14**
Hawkins, Screamin' Jay **30**
Hawkins, Tramaine **16**
Hawkins, Walter **87**
Hayes, Isaac **20, 58, 73**
Hayes, Roland **4**
Hayes, Teddy **40**
Haynes, Roy **87**
Heavy D **58**
Hemphill, Jessie Mae **33, 59**
Henderson, Fletcher **32**
Hendricks, Barbara **3, 67**
Hendrix, Jimi **10**
Hendryx, Nona **56**
Henry, Clarence "Frogman" **46**
Higginbotham, J. C. **37**
Higginsen, Vy **65**
Hill, Andrew **66**
Hill, Lauryn **20, 53**
Hilson, Keri **84**
Hinderas, Natalie **5**
Hines, Earl "Fatha" **39**
Hinton, Milt **30**
Holiday, Billie **1**
Holland-Dozier-Holland **36**
Holloway, Brenda **65**
Holmes, Clint **57**
Holt, Nora **38**
Hooker, John Lee **30**
Hopkins, Lightnin' **83**
Horn, Shirley **32, 56**
Horne, Lena **5, 86**
House, Son **8**
Houston, Cissy **20, 83**
Houston, Whitney **7, 28, 83**
Howlin' Wolf **9**
Hubbard, Freddie **75**

Hudson, Jennifer **63, 83**
Huff, Leon **86**
Humphrey, Bobbi **20**
Hunter, Alberta **42**
Hurt, Mississippi John **84**
Hutch, Willie **62**
Hyman, Phyllis **19**
Ice Cube **8, 30, 60**
Ice-T **6, 31**
India.Arie **34**
Ingram, James **84**
Isley, Marvin **87**
Isley, Ronald **25, 56**
Ja Rule **35**
Jackson, Fred James **25**
Jackson, George **19**
Jackson, Hal **41**
Jackson, Isaiah **3**
Jackson, Janet **6, 30, 68**
Jackson, Jermaine **79**
Jackson, John **36**
Jackson, Mahalia **5**
Jackson, Michael **19, 53, 76**
Jackson, Millie **25**
Jackson, Milt **26**
Jackson, Randy **40**
Jackson, Tito **81**
Jacquet, Illinois **49**
Jaheim **58**
Jamal, Ahmad **69**
Jamelia **51**
Jamerson, James **59**
James, Etta **13, 52**
James, Rick **17**
James, Skip **38**
Jarreau, Al **21, 65**
Jay-Z **27, 69**
Jean, Wyclef **20, 86**
Jefferson, Blind Lemon **81**
Jenkins, Ella **15**
Jennings, Lyfe **56, 69**
Jerkins, Rodney **31**
Jeter, Claude **75**
Jimmy Jam **13**
Johnson, Beverly **2**
Johnson, Buddy **36**
Johnson, J. J. **37**
Johnson, James Weldon **5**
Johnson, Johnnie **56**
Johnson, Lonnie **85**
Johnson, Robert **2**
Johnson-George, Tamara **79**
Jones, Bobby **20**
Jones, Booker T. **84**
Jones, Donell **29**
Jones, Elvin **14, 68**
Jones, Etta **35**
Jones, Hank **57, 86**
Jones, Jonah **39**
Jones, Quincy **8, 30**
Jones, Robert G. **81**
Jones, Sharon **86**
Jones, Thad **68**
Joplin, Scott **6**
Jordan, Montell **23**
Jordan, Ronny **26**
Jorge, Seu **73**
Joyner, Matilda Sissieretta **15**
Joyner, Tom **19**
Kandi **83**
Kay, Ulysses **37**
Kee, John P. **43**
Keita, Salif **83**

Kelis **58**
Kelley, Elijah **65**
Kelly, R. **18, 44, 71**
Kem **47**
Kendricks, Eddie **22**
Kenoly, Ron **45**
Kenyatta, Robin **54**
Keys, Alicia **32, 68**
Khan, Chaka **12, 50**
Kid Cudi **83**
Kidjo, Angelique **50**
Killings, Debra **57**
King, B. B. **7**
King, Coretta Scott **3, 57**
Kitt, Eartha **16, 75**
Klugh, Earl **59**
K'naan **76**
Knight, Gladys **16, 66**
Knight, Marie **80**
Knight, Suge **11, 30**
Knowles, Tina **61**
Knuckles, Frankie **42**
Kolosoy, Wendo **73**
Kool Moe Dee **37**
Kravitz, Lenny **10, 34**
KRS-One **34**
K-Swift **73**
Kuti, Femi **47**
LaBelle, Patti **13, 30**
Larrieux, Amel **63**
Lattimore, Kenny **35**
LaVette, Bettye **85**
Leadbelly **82**
Ledisi **73**
Lee, Consuela **84**
Lefel, Edith **41**
Legend, John **67**
León, Tania **13**
Lester, Julius **9**
Levert, Eddie **70**
Levert, Gerald **22, 59**
Lewis, Ananda **28**
Lewis, Butch **71**
Lewis, Henry **38**
Lewis, Leona **75**
Lewis, Ramsey **35, 70**
Lewis, Terry **13**
Lil' Kim **28**
Lil Wayne **66, 84**
Liles, Kevin **42**
Lincoln, Abbey **3**
Lipscomb, Mance **49**
Lister, Marquita **65**
Little Milton **36, 54**
Little Richard **15**
Little Walter **36**
LL Cool J **16, 49**
Locke, Eddie **44**
Long, Huey **79**
Lopes, Lisa "Left Eye" **36**
Love, Darlene **23**
Love, Ed **58**
Love, Laura **50**
Lover, Ed **10**
Lucie, Lawrence **80**
Lucien, Jon **66**
Luckett, Letoya **61**
Ludacris **37, 60**
Lymon, Frankie **22**
Maal, Baaba **66**
Mahal, Taj **39**
Mahlasela, Vusi **65**
Maitreya, Sananda **85**

Majors, Jeff **41**
Makeba, Miriam **2, 50, 74**
Mario **71**
Marley, Bob **5**
Marley, Rita **32, 70**
Marley, Ziggy **41**
Marrow, Queen Esther **24**
Marsalis, Branford **34**
Marsalis, Delfeayo **41**
Marsalis, Wynton **16**
Martin, Roberta **58**
Martin, Sara **38**
Mary Mary **34**
Mase **24**
Masekela, Hugh **1**
Massenburg, Kedar **23**
Master P **21**
Mathis, Johnny **20**
Maxwell **20, 81**
May, Derrick **41**
Mayfield, Curtis **2, 43**
Maynor, Dorothy **19**
MC Breed **75**
M.C. Hammer **20, 80**
MC Lyte **34**
McClendon, Lisa **61**
McClurkin, Donnie **25**
McCoo, Marilyn **53**
McDaniel, Hattie **5**
McFerrin, Bobby **68**
McGill, Anthony **76**
McGriff, Jimmy **72**
McKee, Lonette **12**
McKinney, Nina Mae **40**
McKnight, Brian **18, 34**
McLean, Jackie **78**
McPherson, David **32**
McRae, Carmen **77**
Memphis Minnie **33**
Method Man **81**
Miles, Buddy **69**
Miller, Marcus **84**
Mills, Stephanie **36**
Minaj, Nicki **86**
Mingus, Charles **15**
Minott, Sugar **86**
Mitchell, Leona **42**
Mitchell, Nicole **66**
Mo', Keb' **36**
Monáe, Janelle **86**
Monica **21**
Monk, Thelonious **1**
Moody, James **83**
Moore, Chante **26**
Moore, Dorothy Rudd **46**
Moore, Johnny B. **38**
Moore, LeRoi **72**
Moore, Melba **21**
Moore, Undine Smith **28**
Morton, Jelly Roll **29**
Mos Def **30**
Moses, Gilbert **12**
Moss, J **64**
Moten, Etta **18**
Moura, Paulo **87**
Mowatt, Judy **38**
Mullen, Nicole C. **45**
Mumba, Samantha **29**
Murphy, Eddie **4, 20, 61**
Murray, Tai **47**
Muse, Clarence Edouard **21**
Musiq **37, 84**
Mya **35**

Nas **33**
Nascimento, Milton **2, 64**
Nash, Johnny **40**
Ndegeocello, Meshell **15, 83**
N'Dour, Youssou **1, 53, 79**
Neal, Raful **44**
Neale, Haydain **52**
Nelly **32**
Neville, Aaron **21**
Newman, David **76**
Ne-Yo **65**
Nicholas, Fayard **20, 57**
Nicholas, Harold **20**
Noah, Yannick **4, 60**
Norman, Jessye **5**
Notorious B.I.G. **20**
Odetta **37, 74**
Okosuns, Sonny **71**
Ol' Dirty Bastard **52**
Olatunji, Babatunde **36**
Oliver, Joe "King" **42**
O'Neal, Shaquille **8, 30**
Ongala, Remmy **9**
Osborne, Jeffrey **26**
Otis, Clyde **67**
OutKast **35**
Owens, Jack **38**
Palmer, Keke **68**
Palmer, Rissi **65**
Parker, Charlie **20**
Parker, Maceo **72**
Parker, Ray, Jr. **85**
Parks, Gordon **1, 35, 58**
Patton, Antwan **45**
Payne, Freda **58**
Pena, Paul **58**
Pendergrass, Teddy **22, 83**
Peoples, Dottie **22**
Perkins, Pinetop **70**
Perren, Freddie **60**
Perry, Ruth **19**
Peterson, James **38**
Peterson, Marvin "Hannibal" **27**
Peterson, Oscar **52**
Phillips, Helen L. **63**
Phipps, Wintley **59**
Pinkney, Fayette **80**
Pleasure P **84**
P.M. Dawn **54**
Portuondo, Omara **53**
Powell, Benny **87**
Powell, Bud **24**
Powell, Maxine **8**
Pratt, Awadagin **31**
Premice, Josephine **41**
Preston, Billy **39, 59**
Price, Florence **37**
Price, Kelly **23**
Price, Leontyne **1**
Pride, Charley **26**
Prince **18, 65**
Pritchard, Robert Starling **21**
Pryor, Rain **65**
Purdie, Bernard **77**
Queen Latifah **1, 16, 58**
?uestlove **74**
Ragin, Derek Lee **84**
Rainey, Ma **33**
Ralph, Sheryl Lee **18**
Randall, Alice **38**
Ranglin, Ernest **78**
Rascal, Dizzee **82**
Ray J **86**

Razaf, Andy **19**
Reagon, Bernice Johnson **7**
Reagon, Toshi **76**
Record, Eugene **60**
Redman **81**
Redman, Joshua **30**
Reed, A. C. **36**
Reed, Jimmy **38**
Reese, Della **6, 20**
Reeves, Dianne **32**
Reeves, Martha **85**
Reid, Antonio "L.A." **28**
Reid, Vernon **34**
Rhoden, Wayne **70**
Rhone, Sylvia **2**
Rhymes, Busta **31**
Richie, Lionel **27, 65**
Rihanna **65**
Riperton, Minnie **32**
Roach, Max **21, 63**
Roberts, Kimberly Rivers **72**
Roberts, Marcus **19**
Robeson, Paul **2**
Robinson, Fenton **38**
Robinson, Reginald R. **53**
Robinson, Smokey **3, 49**
Robinson, Sylvia **79**
Rodríguez, Arsenio **87**
Rogers, Jimmy **38**
Rollins, Sonny **37**
Ross, Diana **8, 27**
Ross, Isaiah "Doc" **40**
Ross, Rick **79**
Roxanne Shante **33**
Rucker, Darius **34, 74**
Rudder, David **79**
Ruffins, Kermit **85**
Run **31, 73**
Run-DMC **31, 75**
Rupaul **17**
Rush, Bobby **78**
Rush, Otis **38**
Rushen, Patrice **12**
Rushing, Jimmy **37**
Russell, Brenda **52**
RZA **80**
Sade **15**
Sample, Joe **51**
Sanders, Angelia **86**
Sanders, Pharoah **64**
Sangare, Oumou **18**
Santamaria, Mongo **81**
Sapp, Marvin **74**
Scarlett, Millicent **49**
Schuyler, Philippa **50**
Scott, George **55**
Scott, Hazel **66**
Scott, Jill **29, 83**
Scott, "Little" Jimmy **48**
Seal **14, 75**
Seals, Son **56**
Sermon, Erick **81**
Shaggy **31**
Shakur, Afeni **67**
Shakur, Tupac **14**
Sheard, Kierra "Kiki" **61**
Shider, Garry **87**
Shirley, George **33**
Short, Bobby **52**
Shorter, Wayne **75**
Shorty, Ras, I **47**
Siji **56**
Silver, Horace **26**

Simmons, Russell **1, 30**
Simone, Nina **15, 41**
Simpson, Valerie **21**
Simpson-Hoffman, N'kenge **52**
Sir Mix-A-Lot **82**
Sisqo **30**
Sissle, Noble **29**
Sister Souljah **11**
Slash **75**
Sledge, Percy **39**
Slim Thug **86**
Sly & Robbie **34**
Smith, Bessie **3**
Smith, Cladys "Jabbo" **32**
Smith, Dr. Lonnie **49**
Smith, Lonnie Liston **49**
Smith, Mamie **32**
Smith, Stuff **37**
Smith, Trixie **34**
Smith, Will **8, 18, 53**
Snoop Dogg **35, 84**
Somi **85**
Southern, Eileen **56**
Sowande, Fela **39**
Sparks, Jordin **66**
Spector, Ronnie **77**
Speech **82**
Spence, Joseph **49**
Stampley, Micah **54**
Stanford, Olivia Lee Dilworth **49**
Staples, Mavis **50**
Staples, "Pops" **32**
Staton, Candi **27**
Staton, Dakota **62**
Steely **80**
Steinberg, Martha Jean "The
    Queen" **28**
Stew **69**
Sticky Fingaz **86**
Still, William Grant **37**
Stone, Angie **31**
Stone, Sly **85**
Stoute, Steve **38**
Strayhorn, Billy **31**
Streeter, Sarah **45**
Studdard, Ruben **46**
Sugarhill Gang, The **79**
Sullivan, Jazmine **81**
Sullivan, Maxine **37**
Summer, Donna **25**
Sun Ra **60**
Sundiata, Sekou **66**
Supremes, The **33**
Sweat, Keith **19**
Sykes, Roosevelt **20**
Tait, Michael **57**
Tamar-kali **63**
Tamia **24, 55**
Tampa Red **63**
Tatum, Art **28**
Taylor, Billy **23**
Taylor, Cecil **70**
Taylor, Koko **40, 80**
Tempations, The **33**
Terrell, Tammi **32**
Terry, Clark **39**
Tharpe, Rosetta **65**
The-Dream **74**
Thomas, Irma **29**
Thomas, Rozonda **34, 78**
Thomas, Rufus **20**
Thornton, Big Mama **33**
Three Mo' Tenors **35**

Thurston, Stephen J. **49**
Tillis, Frederick **40**
Timbaland **32**
Tinsley, Boyd **50**
Tisdale, Wayman **50**
TLC **34**
Tonex **54**
Tosh, Peter **9**
Toussaint, Allen **60**
T-Pain **73**
Tresvant, Ralph **57**
Tribbett, Tye **81**
Turnbull, Walter **13, 60**
Turner, Ike **68**
Turner, Tina **6, 27**
Uggams, Leslie **23**
Ulmer, James **79**
Usher **23, 56**
Valdés, Bebo **75**
Valentino, Bobby **62**
Vandross, Luther **13, 48, 59**
Vanity **67**
Vaughan, Sarah **13**
Vereen, Ben **4**
Verrett, Shirley **66**
Walker, Albertina **10, 58**
Walker, Cedric **19**
Walker, George **37**
Walker, Hezekiah **34**
Wallace, Sippie **1**
Waller, Fats **29**
Warwick, Dionne **18**
Washington, Dinah **22**
Washington, Grover, Jr. **17, 44**
Waters, Benny **26**
Waters, Ethel **7**
Waters, Muddy **34**
Watley, Jody **54**
Watson, Johnny "Guitar" **18**
Watts, Andre **42**
Watts, Reggie **52**
Webster, Katie **29**
Wein, Joyce **62**
Welch, Elisabeth **52**
Wells, Mary **28**
West, Kanye **52**
Whalum, Kirk **37, 64**
White, Barry **13, 41**
White, Josh **86**
White, Josh, Jr. **52**
White, Maurice **29**
White, Willard **53**
Whitfield, Norman **73**
Wilkins, Thomas Alphonso **71**
will.i.am **64**
Williams, Bert **18**
Williams, Clarence **33**
Williams, Claude **80**
Williams, Deniece **36**
Williams, Denise **40**
Williams, J. Mayo **83**
Williams, Joe **5, 25**
Williams, Mary Lou **15**
Williams, Michelle **73**
Williams, Pharrell **47, 82**
Williams, Saul **31**
Williams, Tony **67**
Williams, Vanessa L. **4, 17**
Williamson, Sonny Boy **84**
Wilson, Cassandra **16**
Wilson, Charlie **31, 77**
Wilson, Gerald **49**
Wilson, Jackie **60**

Wilson, Mary 28
Wilson, Nancy 10
Wilson, Natalie 38
Wilson, Sunnie 7, 55
Winans, Angie 36
Winans, BeBe 14
Winans, CeCe 14, 43
Winans, David 77
Winans, Debbie 36
Winans, Marvin L. 17
Winans, Ronald 54
Winans, Vickie 24
Withers, Bill 61
Withers-Mendes, Elisabeth 64
Womack, Bobby 60
Wonder, Stevie 11, 53
Woods, Georgie 57
Woods, Scott 55
Wright, Timothy 74
Xzibit 78
Yabby You 83
Yarbrough, Camille 40
Yoba, Malik 11
York, Vincent 40
Young, Lee 72
Young, Lester 37
Young Jeezy 63

**Religion**
Abernathy, Ralph David 1
Adams, Yolanda 17, 67
Agyeman, Jaramogi Abebe 10, 63
Akinola, Peter Jasper 65
Akpan, Uwem 70
Al-Amin, Jamil Abdullah 6
Anthony, Wendell 25
Arinze, Francis19
Aristide, Jean-Bertrand 6, 45
Armstrong, Vanessa Bell 24
Austin, Junius C. 44
Banks, William 11
Barrow, Willie T. 85
Baylor, Helen 36
Beauvoir, Max 74
Bell, Ralph S. 5
Ben-Israel, Ben Ami 11
Berry, Moses 84
Black, Barry C. 47
Blake, Charles E. 82
Blanks, Deborah K. 69
Bloomer, George 86
Boyd, T. B., III 6
Braxton, Brad 77
Bryant, John R. 45
Burgess, John 46
Butts, Calvin O., III 9
Bynum, Juanita 31, 71
Caesar, Shirley 19
Cage, Byron 53
Caldwell, Kirbyjon 55
Cannon, Katie 10
Cardozo, Francis L. 33
Carr, Kurt 56
Chavis, Benjamin 6
Chineworth, Mary Alice 79
Cleaver, Emanuel 4, 45, 68
Clements, George 2
Cleveland, James 19
Colemon, Johnnie 11
Collins, Janet 33, 64
Coltrane, Alice 70
Cone, James H. 3, 82
Cook, Suzan D. Johnson 22

Crouch, Andraé 27
Dandala, Mvume 77
DeLille, Henriette 30
Divine, Father 7
Dyson, Michael Eric 11, 40
Ellis, Charles H., III 79
Elmore, Ronn 21
Fabre, Shelton 71
Farrakhan, Louis 2, 15
Fauntroy, Walter E. 11
Flake, Floyd H. 18
Forbes, James A., Jr. 71
Franklin, C. L. 68
Franklin, Kirk 15, 49
Franklin, Robert M. 13
Funnye, Capers C., Jr. 73
Gaither, Israel L. 65
Gantin, Bernardin 70
Gilmore, Marshall 46
Gomes, Peter J. 15
Gray, Darius 69
Gray, William H., III 3
Green, Al 13, 47, 74
Gregory, Wilton 37
Grier, Roosevelt 13
Haddon, Dietrick 55
Haile Selassie 7
Harding, Vincent 67
Harris, Barbara 12
Hawkins, Tramaine 16
Hawkins, Walter 87
Hayes, James C. 10
Healy, James Augustine 30
Hooks, Benjamin L. 2, 85
Howard, M. William, Jr. 26
Jackson, Jesse 1, 27, 72
Jakes, Thomas "T. D." 17, 43
Jean-Juste, Gérard 78
Jemison, Major L. 48
Johns, Vernon 38
Jones, Absalom 52
Jones, Alex 64
Jones, Bobby 20
Jones, E. Edward, Sr. 45
Jones, William A., Jr. 61
Kalbani, Adil 77
Karim, Benjamin 61
Kelly, Leontine 33
King, Barbara 22
King, Bernice 4, 81
King, Martin Luther, Jr. 1
Kobia, Samuel 43
Lee, Eric P. 79
Lester, Julius 9
Lewis-Thornton, Rae 32
Lincoln, C. Eric 38
Little Richard 15
Long, Eddie L. 29
Lowery, Joseph 2
Lowry, A. Leon 60
Lyons, Henry 12
Majors, Jeff 41
Marino, Eugene Antonio 30
Maxis, Theresa 62
Mays, Benjamin E. 7
McClurkin, Donnie 25
McGuire, George Alexander 80
McKenzie, Vashti M. 29
Morgan, Gertrude 63
Moss, J 64
Moss, Otis, Jr. 72
Moss, Otis, III 72
Muhammad, Ava 31

Muhammad, Elijah 4
Muhammad, Jabir Herbert 72
Muhammad, Khallid Abdul 10, 31
Muhammad, W. Deen 27
Murray, Cecil 12, 47
Muzorewa, Abel 85
Okaalet, Peter 58
Otunga, Maurice Michael 55
Patterson, Gilbert Earl 41
Patterson, J. O., Jr. 80
Peterson, Jesse Lee 81
Phipps, Wintley 59
Pierre, Andre 17
Powell, Adam Clayton, Jr. 3
Price, Frederick K. C. 21
Redding, Ann Holmes 77
Reems, Ernestine Cleveland 27
Reese, Della 6, 20
Reverend Ike 79
Riley, Helen Caldwell Day 13
Rivers, Eugene F., III 81
Rogers, Alan G. 72
Roundtree, Dovey 80
Rugambwa, Laurean 20
Sapp, Marvin 74
Scott, George 55
Senghor, Augustin Diamancoune 66
Sentamu, John 58
Shabazz, Betty 7, 26
Sharpton, Al 21
Shaw, William J. 30
Shuttlesworth, Fred 47
Slocumb, Jonathan 52
Somé, Malidoma Patrice 10
Stallings, George A., Jr. 6
Stampley, Micah 54
Stanton, Alysa 78
Steinberg, Martha Jean "The Queen" 28
Stith, Charles R. 73
Sullivan, Leon H. 3, 30
Taylor, Gardner C. 76
Thurman, Howard 3
Tillard, Conrad 47
Tolton, Augustine 62
Tonex 54
Tribbett, Tye 81
Turner, Henry McNeal 5
Tutu, Desmond (Mpilo) 6, 44
Ukpabio, Helen 86
Vanity 67
Vanzant, Iyanla 17, 47
Waddles, Charleszetta "Mother" 10, 49
Walker, Hezekiah 34
Walker, John T. 50
Walker, Wyatt Tee 80
Washington, James Melvin 50
Waters, Ethel 7
Watkins, Joe 86
Weeks, Thomas, III 70
Weems, Renita J. 44
White, Reggie 6, 50
White-Hammond, Gloria 61
Williams, Frederick (B.) 63
Williams, Hosea Lorenzo 15, 31
Williams, Preston Warren, II 64
Wilson, Natalie 38
Winans, BeBe 14
Winans, CeCe 14, 43
Winans, Marvin L. 17
Winans, Ronald 54
Woods, Abraham, Jr. 74

Wright, Jeremiah A., Jr. 45, 69
Wright, Nathan, Jr. 56
Wright, Timothy 74
Wyatt, Addie L. 56
X, Malcolm 1
York, Dwight D. 71
Youngblood, Johnny Ray 8

**Science and technology**
Adams-Campbell, Lucille L. 60
Adkins, Rod 41
Adkins, Rutherford H. 21
Alcorn, George Edward, Jr. 59
Alexander, Archie Alphonso 14
Allen, Ethel D. 13
Allen, Will 74
Anderson, Charles Edward 37
Anderson, Michael P. 40
Anderson, Norman B. 45
Anderson, William G(ilchrist) 57
Atim, Julian 66
Auguste, Donna 29
Auguste, Rose-Anne 13
Bacon-Bercey, June 38
Banda, Hastings Kamuzu 6, 54
Bashir, Halima 73
Bath, Patricia E. 37
Benjamin, Regina 20, 75
Benson, Angela 34
Black, Keith Lanier 18, 84
Blackwell, David 79
Bluford, Guy 2, 35
Bluitt, Juliann S. 14
Bolden, Charles Frank, Jr. 7, 78
Branson, Herman 87
Brown, Vivian 27
Brown, Willa 40
Bullard, Eugene 12
Callender, Clive O. 3
Campbell, Donald J. 66
Canady, Alexa 28
Cargill, Victoria A. 43
Carroll, L. Natalie 44
Carruthers, George R. 40
Carson, Benjamin 1, 35, 76
Carter, Joye Maureen 41
Carter, Majora 77
Carver, George Washington 4
CasSelle, Malcolm 11
Chatard, Peter 44
Chinn, May Edward 26
Christian, Spencer 15
Clack, Zoanne 73
Clark, Mamie Phipps 79
Cobb, W. Montague 39
Cobbs, Price M. 9
Cole, Rebecca 38
Coleman, Bessie 9
Coleman, Ken 57
Comer, James P. 6
Coney, PonJola 48
Cooper, Edward S. 6
Cooper, Lisa 73
Cornwell, Edward E., III 70
Counter, S. Allen 74
Dailey, Ulysses Grant 87
Daly, Marie Maynard 37
Davis, Allison 12
Dean, Mark 35
Deas, Gerald 85
Deconge-Watson, Lovenia 55
Delany, Bessie 12
Delany, Martin R. 27

Dickens, Helen Octavia **14, 64**
Diop, Cheikh Anta **4**
Drew, Alvin, Jr. **67**
Drew, Charles Richard **7**
Dunham, Katherine **4, 59**
Dunston, Georgia Mae **48**
Edwards, Lena Frances **76**
Edwards, Willarda V. **59**
Elders, Joycelyn **6**
Ellington, E. David **11**
Ellis, Clarence A. **38**
Emeagwali, Dale **31**
Emeagwali, Philip **30**
Ericsson-Jackson, Aprille **28**
Fennoy, Ilene **72**
Fenton, Kevin **87**
Fields, Evelyn J. **27**
Fisher, Ada M. **76**
Fisher, Rudolph **17**
Flipper, Henry O. **3**
Flowers, Sylester **50**
Foster, Henry W., Jr. **26**
Freeman, Harold P. **23**
Fulani, Lenora **11**
Fuller, A. Oveta **43**
Fuller, Arthur **27**
Fuller, Solomon Carter, Jr. **15**
Gardere, Jeffrey **76**
Gaston, Marilyn Hughes **60**
Gates, Sylvester James, Jr. **15**
Gayle, Helene D. **3, 46**
Gibson, Kenneth Allen **6**
Gibson, William F. **6**
Gilliard, Steve **69**
Gourdine, Meredith **33**
Grant, Augustus O. **71**
Granville, Evelyn Boyd **36**
Gray, Ida **41**
Gregory, Frederick **8, 51**
Griffin, Anthony **71**
Griffin, Bessie Blout **43**
Griffith, Patrick A. **64**
Hall, Lloyd A. **8**
Hamburg, Margaret **78**
Hammonds, Evelynn **69**
Hannah, Marc **10**
Harris, Gary L. **87**
Harris, Mary Styles **31**
Haywood, Jimmy **58**
Henderson, Cornelius Langston **26**
Henson, Matthew **2**
Hillary, Barbara **65**
Hinton, William Augustus **8**
Holmes, Hamilton E. **82**
Howard, Ayanna **65**
Hutcherson, Hilda Yvonne **54**
Ibrahim, Mo **67**
Imes, Elmer Samuel **39**
Irving, Larry, Jr. **12**
Jackson, Lisa **77**
Jackson, Shirley Ann **12**
Jarvis, Erich **67**
Jawara, Dawda Kairaba **11**
Jemison, Mae C. **1, 35**
Jenifer, Franklyn G. **2**
Johnson, Eddie Bernice **8**
Johnson, Lonnie G. **32**
Jones, Edith Mae Irby **65**
Jones, Frederick McKinley **68**
Jones, Monty **66**
Jones, Randy **35**
Jones, Wayne **53**
Joseph, Kathie-Ann **56**

Julian, Percy Lavon **6**
Juma, Calestous **57**
Just, Ernest Everett **3**
Keith, Rachel Boone **63**
Kenney, John A., Jr. **48**
King, Reatha Clark **65**
Kintaudi, Leon **62**
Kittles, Rick **51**
Knowling, Robert E., Jr. **38**
Kong, B. Waine **50**
Kountz, Samuel L. **10**
Laroche, Joseph Philippe Lemercier **85**
Laryea, Thomas Davies, III **67**
Latimer, Lewis H. **4**
Lavizzo-Mourey, Risa **48**
Lawless, Theodore K. **8**
Lawrence, Robert H., Jr. **16**
Lee, Raphael C. **87**
Leevy, Carrol M. **42**
Leffall, Lasalle **3, 64**
Lewis, Daurene **72**
Lewis, Delano **7**
Logan, Onnie Lee **14**
Lushington, Augustus Nathaniel **56**
Lyttle, Hulda Margaret **14**
Madison, Romell **45**
Malveaux, Floyd **54**
Manley, Audrey Forbes **16**
Massey, Walter E. **5, 45**
Massie, Samuel P., Jr. **29**
Maxey, Randall **46**
Mays, William G. **34**
Mboup, Souleymane **10**
McCoy, Elijah **8**
McNair, Ronald **3, 58**
Mensah, Thomas **48**
Miller, Warren F., Jr. **53**
Millines Dziko, Trish **28**
Mills, Joseph C. **51**
Morgan, Garrett **1**
Murray, Pauli **38**
Nabrit, Samuel Milton **47**
Naki, Hamilton **63**
Neto, António Agostinho **43**
Nour, Nawal M. **56**
Ojikutu, Bisola **65**
O'Leary, Hazel **6**
Olopade, Olufunmilayo Falusi **58**
Osborne, Na'taki **54**
Pace, Betty **59**
Perry, Warren **56**
Person, Waverly **9, 51**
Peters, Lenrie **43**
Pickett, Cecil **39**
Pierre, Percy Anthony **46**
Pinn, Vivian Winona **49**
Pitt, David Thomas **10**
Pitts, Derrick **77**
Poindexter, Hildrus A. **87**
Poussaint, Alvin F. **5, 67**
Price, Richard **51**
Prothrow-Stith, Deborah **10**
Quarterman, Lloyd Albert **4**
Rabb, Maurice F., Jr. **58**
Randolph, Linda A. **52**
Reece, E. Albert **63**
Reese, Milous J., Jr. **51**
Riley, Helen Caldwell Day **13**
Robeson, Eslanda Goode **13**
Robinson, Rachel **16**
Roker, Al **12, 49**
Ross-Lee, Barbara **67**

Samara, Noah **15**
Satcher, David **7, 57**
Seacole, Mary **54**
Shabazz, Betty **7, 26**
Shavers, Cheryl **31**
Sigur, Wanda **44**
Sinkford, Jeanne C. **13**
Slaughter, John Brooks **53**
Smith, Ian **62**
Smith, Richard **51**
Spencer, Michael G. **87**
Staples, Brent **8**
Staupers, Mabel K. **7**
Stewart, Ella **39**
Sullivan, Louis **8**
Sweet, Ossian **68**
Taylor, Susan C. **62**
Terrell, Dorothy A. **24**
Thomas, Vivien **9**
Thornton, Yvonne S. **69**
Thurston, Baratunde **79**
Tuckson, Reed V. **71**
Tyson, Neil deGrasse **15, 65**
Walker, Arthur, II **87**
Wambugu, Florence **42**
Washington, Patrice Clarke **12**
Watkins, Levi, Jr. **9**
Wein, Joyce **62**
Welsing, Frances Cress **5**
West, James E. **87**
Westbrooks, Bobby **51**
White-Hammond, Gloria **61**
Wilkens, J. Ernest, Jr. **43**
Williams, Daniel Hale **2**
Williams, David Rudyard **50**
Williams, O. S. **13**
Wilson, Stephanie **72**
Wisdom, Kimberlydawn **57**
Witt, Edwin T. **26**
Woods, Granville T. **5**
Wright, Louis Tompkins **4**
Young, Roger Arliner **29**

**Social issues**
Abbott, Diane **9**
Abbott, Robert Sengstacke **27**
Abernathy, Ralph David **1**
Abu-Jamal, Mumia **15**
Adams, Sheila J. **25**
Agyeman, Jaramogi Abebe **10, 63**
Ake, Claude **30**
Al-Amin, Jamil Abdullah **6**
Alexander, Clifford **26**
Alexander, Sadie Tanner Mossell **22**
Allen, Lucy **85**
Allen, Will **74**
Ali, Muhammad **2, 16, 52**
Allen, Ethel D. **13**
Amaker, Norman **63**
Andrews, Benny **22, 59**
Angelou, Maya **1, 15**
Annan, Kofi Atta **15, 48**
Anthony, Wendell **25**
Appiah, Kwame Anthony **67**
Arac de Nyeko, Monica **66**
Archer, Dennis **7**
Aristide, Jean-Bertrand **6, 45**
Arnwine, Barbara **28**
Asante, Molefi Kete **3**
Ashe, Arthur **1, 18**
Atyam, Angelina **55**

Auguste, Rose-Anne **13**
Autrey, Wesley **68**
Avery, Byllye Y. **66**
Azikiwe, Nnamdi **13**
Ba, Mariama **30**
Baisden, Michael **25, 66**
Baker, Ella **5**
Baker, Gwendolyn Calvert **9**
Baker, Houston A., Jr. **6**
Baker, Josephine **3**
Baker, Thurbert **22**
Baldwin, James **1**
Banks, Paula A. **68**
Barbee, Lloyd Augustus **71**
Barlow, Roosevelt **49**
Barnett, Etta Moten **56**
Barrow, Willie T. **85**
Bass, Charlotta Spears **40**
Bates, Daisy **13**
Beals, Melba Patillo **15**
Bell, Derrick **6**
Bell, Ralph S. **5**
Berry, Bertice **8, 55**
Berry, Edwin C. **81**
Berry, Mary Frances **7**
Berrysmith, Don Reginald **49**
Bethune, Mary McLeod **4**
Betsch, MaVynee **28**
Betts, R. Dwayne **86**
Bevel, James L. **75**
Bibb, Henry and Mary **54**
Biko, Steven **4**
bin Wahad, Dhoruba **85**
Birch, Glynn R. **61**
Black, Albert **51**
Blackwell, Unita **17**
Bobo, Lawrence **60**
Bolin, Jane **22, 59**
Bond, Julian **2, 35**
Bonga, Kuenda **13**
Booker, Cory Anthony **68**
Bosley, Freeman, Jr. **7**
Boyd, Gwendolyn **49**
Boyd, John W., Jr. **20, 72**
Boyd, T. B., III **6**
Boykin, Keith **14**
Bradley, David Henry, Jr. **39**
Braun, Carol Moseley **4, 42**
Bridges, Ruby **77**
Broadbent, Hydeia **36**
Brock, Roslyn McCallister **86**
Brown, Byrd **49**
Brown, Cora **33**
Brown, Eddie C. **35**
Brown, Elaine **8**
Brown, Homer S. **47**
Brown, Jesse **6, 41**
Brown, Jim **11**
Brown, Lee P. **1**
Brown, Les **5**
Brown, Lloyd Louis **10 42**
Brown, Oscar, Jr. **53**
Brown, Tony **3**
Brown, Willa **40**
Brown, Zora Kramer **12**
Brutus, Dennis **38**
Bryant, Wayne R. **6**
Bullock, Steve **22**
Bunche, Ralph J. **5**
Burks, Mary Fair **40**
Burroughs, Margaret Taylor **9**
Butler, Paul D. **17**
Butts, Calvin O., III **9**

Cameron, James 80
Campbell, Bebe Moore 6, 24, 59
Canada, Geoffrey 23
Carby, Hazel 27
Carmichael, Stokely 5, 26
Carr, Johnnie 69
Carr, Keela 74
Carter, Majora 77
Carter, Mandy 11
Carter, Robert L. 51
Carter, Rubin 26
Carter, Stephen L. 4
Cary, Lorene 3
Cary, Mary Ann Shadd 30
Catto, Octavius V. 83
Cayton, Horace 26
Chavis, Benjamin 6
Chestnut, J. L., Jr. 73
Chideya, Farai 14, 61
Childress, Alice 15
Chissano, Joaquim 7, 55, 67
Christophe, Henri 9
Chuck D 9
Clark, Joe 1
Clark, Kenneth B. 5, 52
Clark, Septima 7
Clay, William Lacy 8
Clayton, Mayme Agnew 62
Claytor, Helen 14, 52
Cleaver, Eldridge 5
Cleaver, Kathleen Neal 29
Clements, George 2
Cobbs, Price M. 9
Cole, Johnnetta B. 5, 43
Cole, Lorraine 48
Coles, Alice 80
Collins, Patricia Hill 67
Colston, Hal 72
Comer, James P. 6
Compton-Rock, Malaak 86
Connerly, Ward 14
Conyers, John, Jr. 4, 45
Cook, Toni 23
Cooke, Marvel 31
Cooper, Anna Julia 20
Cooper, Edward S. 6
Cooper, Margaret J. 46
Cosby, Bill 7, 26, 59
Cosby, Camille 14, 80
Cose, Ellis 5, 50
Creagh, Milton 27
Crew, Spencer R. 55
Cruse, Harold 54
Cummings, Elijah E. 24
da Silva, Benedita 5
Davis, Angela 5
Davis, Artur 41
Davis, Danny K. 24
Dawson, Matel, Jr. 39
Dawson, Michael C. 63
DeBaptiste, George 32
Delany, Martin R. 27
Dellums, Ronald 2, 81
Dent, Thomas C. 50
Diallo, Amadou 27
Dickerson, Ernest 6
Dieudonné 67
Diop, Cheikh Anta 4
Dirie, Waris 56
Divine, Father 7
Dixon, Margaret 14
Dodson, Howard, Jr. 7, 52
Dortch, Thomas W., Jr. 45

Douglass, Frederick 87
Drew, Charles Richard 7
Du Bois, W. E. B. 3
DuBois, Shirley Graham 21
Duggins, George 64
Dukes, Hazel Nell 56
Dumas, Henry 41
Dunham, Katherine 4, 59
Early, Gerald 15
Edelin, Ramona Hoage 19
Edelman, Marian Wright 5, 42
Edley, Christopher 2, 48
Edwards, Harry 2
Edwards, Lena Frances 76
Elder, Larry 25
Elders, Joycelyn 6
Ellison, Ralph 7
Esposito, Giancarlo 9
Espy, Mike 6
Eugene-Richard, Margie 63
Europe, James Reese 10
Evers, Medgar 3
Evers, Myrlie 8
Farmer, James 2, 64
Farrakhan, Louis 15
Farris, Isaac Newton, Jr. 63
Fauntroy, Walter E. 11
Fauset, Jessie 7
Fela 1, 42
Fields, C. Virginia 25
Finner-Williams, Paris Michele 62
Flavor Flav 67
Fletcher, Bill, Jr. 41
Forbes, James A., Jr. 71
Forman, James 7, 51
Fortune, T. Thomas 6
Foster, Marie 48
Franklin, C. L. 68
Franklin, Hardy R. 9
Franklin, John Hope 5, 77
Franklin, Robert M. 13
Frazier, E. Franklin 10
Fulani, Lenora 11
Fuller, Arthur 27
Fuller, Charles 8
Gaines, Ernest J. 7
Gamble, Kenny 85
Gardner, Chris 65
Garvey, Marcus 1
Gates, Henry Louis, Jr. 3, 38, 67
Gayle, Helene D. 3
Gbowee, Leymah 76
George, Zelma Watson 42
Gibson, Kenneth Allen 6
Gibson, William F. 6
Gilbert, Christopher 50
Gist, Carole 1
Goldberg, Whoopi 4, 33, 69
Golden, Marita 19
Golston, Allan C. 55
Gomez, Jewelle 30
Gomez-Preston, Cheryl 9
Goss, Carol A. 55
Gossett, Louis, Jr. 7
Graham, Lawrence Otis 12
Granger, Lester B. 75
Gray, Fred 37
Greene, Petey 65
Gregory, Dick 1, 54
Gregory, Wilton 37
Grier, Roosevelt 13
Griffith, Mark Winston 8
Grimké, Archibald H. 9

Guinier, Lani 7, 30
Guy, Rosa 5
Guy-Sheftall, Beverly 13
Hale, Lorraine 8
Haley, Alex 4
Hall, Elliott S. 24
Hall, Stuart 78
Hamblin, Ken 10
Hamer, Fannie Lou 6
Hampton, Fred 18
Hampton, Henry 6
Hani, Chris 6
Hansberry, Lorraine 6
Hansberry, William Leo 11
Harding, Vincent 67
Harper, Frances Ellen Watkins 11
Harrington, Oliver W. 9
Harris, Alice 7
Harris, Leslie 6
Harris, Marcelite Jordan 16
Harris, Patricia Roberts 2
Hastings, Alcee L. 16
Hawkins, Augustus F. 68
Hawkins, Steven 14
Hayes, Dennis 54
Haynes, George Edmund 8
Hedgeman, Anna Arnold 22
Height, Dorothy I. 2, 23, 78
Henderson, Thelton E. 68
Henderson, Wade J. 14
Henderson, Zelma 71
Henry, Aaron Edd 19
Henry, Lenny 9, 52
Hernandez, Aileen Clarke 13
Hernton, Calvin C. 51
Hill, Anita 5, 65
Hill, Jesse, Jr. 13
Hill, Lauryn 20, 53
Hill, Oliver W. 24, 63
Hilliard, Asa Grant, III 66
Hilliard, David 7
Holland, Endesha Ida Mae 3, 57
Holt Baker, Arlene 73
hooks, bell 5
Hooks, Benjamin L. 2, 85
Houston, Charles Hamilton 4
Howard, M. William, Jr. 26
Hoyte, Lenon 50
Hubbard, Arnette Rhinehart 38
Huggins, Nathan Irvin 52
Hughes, Albert 7
Hughes, Allen 7
Hughes, Langston 4
Hunter-Gault, Charlayne 6, 31
Hutchinson, Earl Ofari 24
Hutson, Jean Blackwell 16
Ibrahim, Mo 67
Iceberg Slim 11
Ice-T 6, 31
Ingram, Rex 5
Innis, Roy 5
Irvis, K. Leroy 67
Jackson, Edison O. 67
Jackson, Fred James 25
Jackson, George 14
Jackson, Janet 6, 30, 68
Jackson, Jesse 1, 27, 72
Jackson, Judith D. 57
Jackson, Mahalia 5
Jacob, John E. 2
Jagan, Cheddi 16
James, Daniel, Jr. 16
Jealous, Benjamin 70

Jean, Wyclef 20, 86
Jeffries, Leonard 8
Jenkins, Ray 77
Johnson, Charles S. 12
Johnson, Earvin "Magic" 3, 39
Johnson, James Weldon 5
Johnson, Kevin 70
Jolley, Willie 28
Jones, Cullen 73
Jones, Elaine R. 7, 45
Jones, Eugene Kinckle 79
Jones, Van 70
Jones, William A., Jr. 61
Jordan, June 7, 35
Jordan, Vernon E. 3, 35
Joseph, Kathie-Ann 56
Josey, E. J. 10
Joyner, Marjorie Stewart 26
Joyner, Tom 19
Julian, Percy Lavon 6
Karim, Benjamin 61
Kaunda, Kenneth 2
Keita, Salif 83
Kelley, Cliff 75
Kennedy, Florynce 12, 33
Khanga, Yelena 6
Kidd, Mae Street 39
Kimbro, Warren 76
King, Bernice 4, 81
King, Coretta Scott 3, 57
King, Dexter 10
King, Martin Luther, III 20
King, Martin Luther, Jr. 1
King, Preston 28
King, Robert Hillary 84
King, Yolanda 6
Kitwana, Bakari 86
Kuzwayo, Ellen 68
Ladner, Joyce A. 42
LaGuma, Alex 30
Lampkin, Daisy 19
Lane, Charles 3
Lane, Vincent 5
Laraque, Paul 67
Lee, Canada 8
Lee, Eric P. 79
Leland, Mickey 2
Lester, Julius 9
Lewis, Ananda 28
Lewis, Delano 7
Lewis, Thomas 19
Lewis-Thornton, Rae 32
Little, Robert L. 2
Logan, Rayford W. 40
Long, Eddie L. 29
Lorde, Audre 6
Louis, Errol T. 8
Loving, Mildred 69
Lowery, Joseph 2
Lowry, A. Leon 60
Lucas, John 7
Lucy, William 50
Lucy Foster, Autherine 35
Maathai, Wangari 43
Mabuza-Suttle, Felicia 43
Madison, Joseph E. 17
Makeba, Miriam 2, 50, 74
Malone Jones, Vivian 59
Malveaux, Julianne 32, 70
Mandela, Nelson 1, 14, 77
Mandela, Winnie 2, 35
Manley, Audrey Forbes 16
Marable, Manning 10

Marshall, Paule 7, 77
Marshall, Thurgood 1, 44
Martin, Louis E. 16
Masekela, Barbara 18
Masekela, Hugh 1
Mason, Ronald 27
Mathabane, Mark 5
Maynard, Robert C. 7
Mays, Benjamin E. 7
Mbeki, Thabo 14, 73
McCabe, Jewell Jackson 10
McCarty, Osceola 16
McDougall, Gay J. 11, 43
McKay, Claude 6
McKenzie, Vashti M. 29
McKinney Hammond, Michelle 51
McKissick, Floyd B. 3
McMurray, Georgia L. 36
McQueen, Butterfly 6, 54
McWhorter, John 35
Meek, Carrie 6, 36
Meredith, James H. 11
Mfume, Kweisi 6, 41
Mhlaba, Raymond 55
Micheaux, Oscar 7
Millender-McDonald, Juanita 21, 61
Miller-Travis, Vernice 64
Millines Dziko, Trish 28
Mkapa, Benjamin W. 16, 77
Mongella, Gertrude 11
Moore, Gwendolynne S. 55
Moore, Harry T. 29
Morgan, Irene 65
Morial, Ernest "Dutch" 26
Moses, Robert Parris 11
Moss, Otis, Jr. 72
Mossell, Gertrude Bustill 40
Motley, Constance Baker 10, 55
Moton, Robert Russa 83
Moutoussamy-Ashe, Jeanne 7
Mowry, Jess 7
Muhammad, Elijah 4
Muhammad, Khallid Abdul 10, 31
Mukoko, Jestina 75
Murphy, Laura M. 43
Murray, Pauli 38
Nash, Diane 72
Ndadaye, Melchior 7
Nelson, Jill 6, 54
Newton, Huey 2
Niane, Katoucha 70
Nkoli, Simon 60
Nkrumah, Kwame 3
Noble, Gil 76
Norman, Pat 10
Norton, Eleanor Holmes 7
Nour, Nawal M. 56
Nzo, Alfred 15
Obasanjo, Olusegun 5
Oglesby, Zena 12
Ojikutu, Bisola 65
O'Leary, Hazel 6
Orange, James 74
Ormes, Jackie 73
Osborne, Na'taki 54
Owens, Major 6
Page, Alan 7
Page, Clarence 4
Parker, Kellis E. 30
Parker, Pat 19
Parks, Rosa 1, 35, 56
Parr, Russ 51
Patterson, Frederick Douglass 12

Patterson, Louise 25
Patterson, Orlando 4
Patterson, P. J. 6, 20
Perkins, Edward 5
Perry, James 83
Peterson, Jesse Lee 81
Pitt, David Thomas 10
Pleasant, Mary Ellen 9
Plessy, Homer Adolph 31
Pough, Terrell 58
Poussaint, Alvin F. 5, 67
Powell, Adam Clayton, Jr. 3
Powell, Kevin 31, 74
Pratt, Geronimo 18
Pressley, Condace L. 41
Price, Hugh B. 9, 54
Primus, Pearl 6
Pritchard, Robert Starling 21
Prothrow-Stith, Deborah 10
Quarles, Benjamin Arthur 18
Quigless, Helen G. 49
Ramaphosa, Cyril 3
Ramphele, Mamphela 29
Ramsey, Charles H. 21, 69
Rand, A. Barry 6
Randolph, A. Philip 3
Randolph, Linda A. 52
Rawlings, Nana Konadu Agyeman
   13
Reagon, Bernice Johnson 7
Reed, Ishmael 8
Rice, Louise Allen 54
Rice, Norm 8
Richards, Hilda 49
Richardson, Julieanna 81
Richardson, Rupert 67
Riggs, Marlon 5
Riley, Helen Caldwell Day 13
Rivers, Eugene F., III 81
Roberts, Lillian 83
Robeson, Eslanda Goode 13
Robeson, Paul 2
Robinson, Jackie 6
Robinson, Rachel 16
Robinson, Randall 7, 46
Robinson, Sharon 22
Robinson, Spottswood W., III 22
Roble, Abdi 71
Rodriguez, Cheryl 64
Rowan, Carl T. 1, 30
Rowell, Victoria 13, 68
Ruffin, Josephine St. Pierre 75
Rusesabagina, Paul 60
Rustin, Bayard 4
Sampson, Edith S. 4
Sanders, Malika 48
Sané, Pierre Gabriel 21
Sapphire 14
Saro-Wiwa, Kenule 39
Satcher, David 7, 57
Savimbi, Jonas 2, 34
Sawyer, Amos 2
Sayles Belton, Sharon 9, 16
Scantlebury-White, Velma 64
Seacole, Mary 54
Seale, Bobby 3
Sears, Stephanie 53
Seele, Pernessa 46
Senghor, Léopold Sédar 12
Shabazz, Attallah 6
Shabazz, Betty 7, 26
Shadd, Abraham D. 81
Shakur, Afeni 67

Shakur, Assata 6
Shakur, Yusef 85
Sherrod, Shirley 87
Shinhoster, Earl 32
Shuttlesworth, Fred 47
Sifford, Charlie 4, 49
Simone, Nina 15, 41
Sisulu, Albertina 57
Sisulu, Sheila Violet Makate 24
Sleet, Moneta, Jr. 5
Smith, Anna Deavere 6
Smith, Barbara 28
Smith, Damu 54
Smith, Greg 28
Smith, Kemba 70
Smith, Marie F. 70
Smith, Nate 49
Snowden, Frank M., Jr. 67
Soyinka, Wole 4
Spriggs, William 67
Stallings, George A., Jr. 6
Staupers, Mabel K. 7
Steele, Claude Mason 13
Steele, Shelby 13, 82
Stewart, Alison 13
Stewart, Ella 39
Stewart, Maria W. Miller 19
Stone, Chuck 9
Sullivan, Leon H. 3, 30
Sweet, Ossian 68
Talbert, Mary B. 77
Tate, Eleanora E. 20, 55
Tatum, Wilbert 76
Taulbert, Clifton Lemoure 19
Taylor, Bo 72
Taylor, Mildred D. 26
Terrell, Mary Church 9
Thomas, Arthur Ray 52
Thomas, Franklin A. 5, 49
Thomas, Isiah 7, 26, 65
Thompson, Bennie G. 26
Thompson, Cynthia Bramlett 50
Thurman, Howard 3
Thurman, Wallace 16
Till, Emmett 7
Tobias, Channing H. 79
Toomer, Jean 6
Tosh, Peter 9
Touré, Askia (Muhammad Abu Bakr
   el) 47
Touré, Faya Ora Rose 56
Tribble, Israel, Jr. 8
Trotter, Donne E. 28
Trotter, Monroe 9
Tsvangirai, Morgan 26, 72
Tubman, Harriet 9
Tucker, C. Delores 12, 56
Tucker, Cynthia 15, 61
Tucker, Rosina 14
Tutu, Desmond 6
Tyree, Omar Rashad 21
Van Peebles, Melvin 7
Vanzant, Iyanla 17, 47
Vaughn, Viola 70
Vega, Marta Moreno 61
Velez-Rodriguez, Argelia 56
Vincent, Marjorie Judith 2
Waddles, Charleszetta "Mother" 10,
   49
Walcott, Derek 5
Walker, A'lelia 14
Walker, Alice 1, 43
Walker, Bernita Ruth 53

Wallace, Joaquin 49
Wallace, Michele Faith 13
Wallace, Phyllis A. 9
Wallace, William 75
Washington, Booker T. 4
Washington, Ebonya 79
Washington, Fredi 10
Washington, Harold 6
Washington, Pauletta Pearson 86
Waters, Maxine 3, 67
Wattleton, Faye 9
Wells, Henrietta Bell 69
Wells, James Lesesne 10
Wells-Barnett, Ida B. 8
Welsing, Frances Cress 5
West, Cornel 5, 33, 80
White, Michael R. 5
White, Reggie 6, 50
White, Walter F. 4
White, Willye 67
White-Hammond, Gloria 61
Wilkins, Roy 4
Williams, Armstrong 29
Williams, Evelyn 10
Williams, Fannie Barrier 27
Williams, George Washington 18
Williams, Hosea Lorenzo 15, 31
Williams, Maggie 7, 71
Williams, Montel 4, 57
Williams, Patricia 11, 54
Williams, Robert F. 11
Williams, Stanley "Tookie" 29, 57
Williams, Walter E. 4
Williams, Willie L. 4
Wilson, August 7, 33, 55
Wilson, Margaret Bush 79
Wilson, Phill 9
Wilson, Sunnie 7, 55
Wilson, William Julius 22
Withers, Ernest C. 68
Wiwa, Ken 67
Wolfe, George C. 6, 43
Woodson, Robert L. 10
Worrill, Conrad 12
Wright, Charles H. 35
Wright, Louis Tompkins 4
Wright, Nathan, Jr. 56
Wright, Richard 5
Wyatt, Addie L. 56
X, Malcolm 1
Xuma, Madie Hall 59
Yancy, Dorothy Cowser 42
Yarbrough, Camille 40
Yeboah, Emmanuel Ofosu 53
Yoba, Malik 11
Young, Andrew 3, 48
Young, Jean Childs 14
Young, Whitney M., Jr. 4
Youngblood, Johnny Ray 8
Zulu, Princess Kasune 54

**Sports**
Aaron, Hank 5
Abdul-Jabbar, Kareem 8
Abdur-Rahim, Shareef 28
Adams, Paul 50
Adu, Freddy 67
Alexander, Shaun 58
Ali, Laila 27, 63
Ali, Muhammad 2, 16, 52
Allen, Dick 85
Allen, Marcus 20
Allen, Ray 82

Amaker, Tommy **62**
Amos, John **8, 62**
Anderson, Elmer **25**
Anderson, Jamal **22**
Anderson, Mike **63**
Anderson, Viv **58**
Anthony, Carmelo **46**
Arenas, Gilbert **84**
Artest, Ron **52**
Ashe, Arthur **1, 18**
Ashford, Emmett **22**
Ashford, Evelyn **63**
Ashley, Maurice **15, 47**
Baines, Harold **32**
Baker, Dusty **8, 43, 72**
Banks, Ernie **33**
Barber, Ronde **41**
Barber, Tiki **57**
Barkley, Charles **5, 66**
Barnes, Ernie **16, 78**
Barnes, John **53**
Barnes, Steven **54**
Barney, Lem **26**
Barnhill, David **30**
Baugé, Grégory **86**
Baylor, Don **6**
Beamon, Bob **30**
Beasley, Jamar **29**
Bekele, Kenenisa **75**
Bell, James "Cool Papa" **36**
Belle, Albert **10**
Bettis, Jerome **64**
Bickerstaff, Bernie **21**
Bing, Dave **3, 59, 78**
Bivins, Michael **72**
Black, Joe **75**
Blair, Paul **36**
Blake, James **43**
Blanks, Billy **22**
Blanton, Dain **29**
Bogues, Tyrone "Muggsy" **56**
Bol, Manute **1**
Bolt, Usain **73**
Bolton-Holifield, Ruthie **28**
Bonaly, Surya **7**
Bonds, Barry **6, 34, 63**
Bonds, Bobby **43**
Bonheur, Yannick **84**
Bosh, Chris **85**
Bowe, Riddick **6**
Brand, Elton **31**
Brandon, Terrell **16**
Branham, George, III **50**
Brashear, Donald **39**
Brathwaite, Fred **35**
Briscoe, Marlin **37**
Brock, Lou **18**
Brooks, Aaron **33**
Brooks, Derrick **43**
Brown, Antron **85**
Brown, James **22**
Brown, Jim **11**
Brown, Mike **77**
Brown, Sean **52**
Brown, Willard **36**
Bruce, Isaac **26**
Bryant, Cullen **81**
Bryant, Kobe **15, 31, 71**
Buchanan, Ray **32**
Bush, Reggie **59**
Butler, Leroy, III **17**
Bynoe, Peter C.B. **40**
Caldwell, Jim **81**

Campanella, Roy **25**
Carew, Rod **20**
Carnegie, Herbert **25**
Carter, Anson **24**
Carter, Butch **27**
Carter, Cris **21**
Carter, Joe **30**
Carter, Kenneth **53**
Carter, Rubin **26**
Carter, Vince **26**
Cash, Swin **59**
Catchings, Tamika **43**
Chamberlain, Wilt **18, 47**
Chaney, John **67**
Charleston, Oscar **39**
Cheeks, Maurice **47**
Cherry, Deron **40**
Cheruiyot, Robert **69**
Christie, Linford **8**
Claiborne, Loretta **34**
Clay, Bryan **57, 74**
Clemons, Michael "Pinball" **64**
Clendenon, Donn **26, 56**
Clifton, Nathaniel "Sweetwater" **47**
Coachman, Alice **18**
Coleman, Leonard S., Jr. **12**
Cooper, Andy "Lefty" **63**
Cooper, Charles "Chuck" **47**
Cooper, Cynthia **17**
Cooper, Michael **31**
Copeland, Michael **47**
Corley, Tony **62**
Cottrell, Comer **11**
Cox, Bryan **83**
Crennel, Romeo **54**
Crooks, Garth **53**
Croom, Sylvester **50**
Culpepper, Daunte **32, 85**
Cunningham, Randall **23**
Curry, Michael **85**
Dandridge, Ray **36**
Dantley, Adrian **72**
Davis, Ernie **48**
Davis, Mike **41**
Davis, Milt **74**
Davis, Piper **19**
Davis, Shani **58, 84**
Davis, Terrell **20**
Dawes, Dominique **11**
Dawson, Andre **85**
Day, Leon **39**
DeFrantz, Anita **37**
DeGale, James **74**
Delaney, Joe **76**
Devers, Gail **7, 87**
Dibaba, Tirunesh **73**
Dickerson, Eric **27**
Dixon, George **52**
Doby, Lawrence Eugene, Sr. **16, 41**
Doig, Jason **45**
Dorrell, Karl **52**
dos Santos, Manuel Francisco **65**
Drew, Charles Richard **7**
Drexler, Clyde **4, 61**
Drogba, Didier **78**
Dumars, Joe **16, 65**
Duncan, Tim **20**
Dungy, Tony **17, 42, 59**
Dunn, Jerry **27**
Durant, Kevin **76**
Dye, Jermaine **58**
Edwards, Harry **2**
Edwards, Herman **51**

Edwards, Teresa **14**
Elder, Lee **6**
Ellerbe, Brian **22**
Elliott, Sean **26**
Ellis, Dock **78**
Ellis, Jimmy **44**
Ervin, Anthony **66**
Erving, Julius **18, 47**
Eto'o, Samuel **73**
Ewing, Patrick **17, 73**
Farr, Mel **24**
Faulk, Marshall **35**
Felix, Allyson **48**
Ferdinand, Rio **82**
Fielder, Cecil **2**
Fielder, Prince Semien **68**
Flood, Curt **10**
Flowers, Vonetta **35**
Ford, Cheryl **45**
Foreman, George **1, 15**
Forrest, Vernon **40, 79**
Foster, Andrew **79**
Fowler, Reggie **51**
Fox, Rick **27**
Frazier, Joe **19**
Frazier-Lyde, Jacqui **31**
Freeman, Cathy **29**
Freeman, Marianna **23**
Fuhr, Grant **1, 49**
Fuller, Vivian **33**
Futch, Eddie **33**
Gaines, Clarence E., Sr. **55**
Gaither, Alonzo Smith (Jake) **14**
Garnett, Kevin **14, 70**
Garrison, Zina **2**
Gaston, Cito **71**
Gebrselassie, Haile **70**
Gentry, Alvin **23**
George, Eddie **80**
Gervin, George **80**
Gibson, Althea **8, 43**
Gibson, Bob **33**
Gibson, Josh **22**
Gibson, Truman K., Jr. **60**
Gill, Turner **83**
Gilliam, Frank **23**
Gilliam, Joe **31**
Glanville, Douglas Metunwa **82**
Gooden, Dwight **20**
Gorden, W. C. **71**
Goss, Tom **23**
Gourdine, Meredith **33**
Gourdine, Simon **11**
Graham, Trevor **84**
Granderson, Curtis **66**
Grand-Pierre, Jean-Luc **46**
Gray, Yeshimbra "Shimmy" **55**
Green, A. C. **32**
Green, Darrell **39, 74**
Green, Dennis **5, 45**
Greene, Joe **10**
Greene, Maurice **27, 77**
Gregg, Eric **16**
Gregory, Ann **63**
Grier, Mike **43**
Grier, Roosevelt **1**
Griffey, Ken, Jr. **12, 73**
Griffith, Yolanda **25**
Griffith-Joyner, Florence **28**
Gumbel, Greg **8**
Gwynn, Tony **18, 83**
Gyan, Asamoah **87**
Hamilton, Lewis **66**

Haney, Lee **77**
Hardaway, Anfernee (Penny) **13**
Hardaway, Tim **35**
Harris, James **79**
Harris, Sylvia **70**
Harrison, Alvin **28**
Harrison, Calvin **28**
Haskins, Clem **23**
Haye, David **82**
Hayes, Bob **77**
Heard, Gar **25**
Hearns, Thomas **29**
Henderson, Rickey **28, 78**
Henry, Thierry **66**
Hickman, Fred **11**
Hill, Calvin **19**
Hill, Grant **13**
Hillary, Barbara **65**
Hilliard, Wendy **53**
Hines, Garrett **35**
Holdsclaw, Chamique **24**
Holland, Kimberly N. **62**
Holmes, Kelly **47**
Holmes, Larry **20, 68**
Holmes, Santonio **87**
Holyfield, Evander **6**
Hopkins, Bernard **35, 69**
Horton, Andre **33**
Horton, Suki **33**
Howard, Desmond **16, 58**
Howard, Juwan **15**
Howard, Ryan **65**
Howard, Sherri **36**
Hunter, Billy **22**
Hunter, Torii **43**
Hyde, Cowan F. "Bubba" **47**
Iginla, Jarome **35**
Ince, Paul **83**
Irvin, Michael **64**
Irvin, Monte **31**
Isaacs, John **76**
Iverson, Allen **24, 46**
Ivey, Phil **72**
Jackson, Jamea **64**
Jackson, Mannie **14**
Jackson, Rampage **83**
Jackson, Reggie **15**
Jackson, Tom **70**
Jacobs, Regina **38**
James, David **84**
James, G. Larry **74**
James, LeBron **46, 78**
James, Vanessa **84**
Jenkins, Fergie **46**
Jeter, Derek **27**
Johnson, Avery **62**
Johnson, Ben **1**
Johnson, Clifford "Connie" **52**
Johnson, Earvin "Magic" **3, 39**
Johnson, Jack **8**
Johnson, Kevin **70**
Johnson, Larry **28**
Johnson, Levi **48**
Johnson, Mamie "Peanut" **40**
Johnson, Michael **13**
Johnson, Rafer **33**
Johnson, Rodney Van **28**
Jones, Cobi N'Gai **18**
Jones, Cullen **73**
Jones, Ed "Too Tall" **46**
Jones, K. C. **83**
Jones, Lou **64**
Jones, Marion **21, 66**

Jones, Merlakia **34**
Jones, Randy **35**
Jones, Roy, Jr. **22**
Jones, Sam **85**
Jordan, Eddie **83**
Jordan, Michael **6, 21**
Joyce, Dru **81**
Joyner-Kersee, Jackie **5**
Justice, David **18**
Kaiser, Cecil **42**
Kanouté, Fred **68**
Keflezighi, Meb **49**
Keith, Floyd A. **61**
Kellogg, Clark **64**
Kennedy-Overton, Jayne Harris **46**
Kerry, Leon G. **46**
Kidd, Jason **86**
Kimbro, Henry A. **25**
King, Don **14**
Lacy, Sam **30, 46**
Ladd, Ernie **64**
Lanier, Bob **47**
Lanier, Willie **33**
Lankford, Ray **23**
Laraque, Georges **48**
Larkin, Barry **24**
Lashley, Bobby **63**
Lassiter, Roy **24**
Lee, Canada **8**
Lennox, Betty **31**
Leonard, Buck **67**
Leonard, Sugar Ray **15**
Leslie, Lisa **16, 73**
Lester, Bill **42, 85**
Lewis, Butch **71**
Lewis, Carl **4**
Lewis, Denise **33**
Lewis, Lennox **27**
Lewis, Marvin **51, 87**
Lewis, Oliver **56**
Lewis, Ray **33**
Liston, Sonny **33**
Little, Floyd **86**
Littlepage, Craig **35**
Lloyd, Earl **26**
Lloyd, John Henry "Pop" **30**
Lofton, James **42**
Lofton, Kenny **12**
Loroupe, Tegla **59**
Lott, Ronnie **9**
Louis, Joe **5**
Love, Nat **9**
Love, Reggie **77**
Lowe, Sidney **64**
Lucas, John **7**
Mackey, Biz **82**
Mahorn, Rick **60**
Malone, Karl **18, 51**
Malone, Moses **79**
Manigault, Earl "The Goat" **15**
Mariner, Jonathan **41**
Martinez, Pedro **81**
Master P **21**
Mayers, Jamal **39**
Mayhew, Martin R. **76**
Mays, Willie **3**
Mayweather, Floyd, Jr. **57**
McAdoo, Bob **75**
McBride, Bryant **18**
McCarthy, Sandy **64**
McCray, Nikki **18**
McDaniel, Randall Cornell **81**
McGrady, Tracy **80**

McGriff, Fred **24**
McKegney, Tony **3**
McNabb, Donovan **29**
McNair, Steve **22, 47, 79**
McNeil, Lori **1**
McRae, Hal **84**
Mello, Breno **73**
Mensah, John **87**
Metcalfe, Ralph **26**
Milla, Roger **2**
Miller, Cheryl **10, 74**
Miller, Larry G. **72**
Miller, Reggie **33**
Mills, Sam **33**
Milton, DeLisha **31**
Minor, DeWayne **32**
Mitchell, Sam **82**
Mohammed, Nazr **64**
Monk, Art **38, 73**
Montgomery, Tim **41**
Moon, Warren **8, 66**
Moorer, Michael **19**
Morgan, Joe Leonard **9**
Morris, Raheem **77**
Moses, Edwin **8**
Mosley, Shane **32**
Moss, Randy **23**
Motley, Marion **26**
Mourning, Alonzo **17, 44**
Muhammad, Jabir Herbert **72**
Mundine, Anthony **56**
Murray, Eddie **12**
Murray, Lenda **10**
Mutola, Maria **12**
Mutombo, Dikembe **7**
Nakhid, David **25**
Newcombe, Don **24**
Newsome, Ozzie **26**
Noah, Yannick **4, 60**
Odom, Lamar **81**
Olajuwon, Hakeem **2, 72**
Oliver, Pam **54**
O'Neal, Shaquille **8, 30**
O'Neil, Buck **19, 59**
Onyewu, Oguchi **60**
O'Ree, Willie **5**
Ortiz, David **52, 82**
Owens, Jesse **2**
Owens, Terrell **53**
Pace, Orlando **21**
Page, Alan **7**
Page, Greg **78**
Paige, Satchel **7**
Palmer, Violet **59**
Parish, Robert **43**
Parker, Candace **74**
Parker, Jim **64**
Parker, Tony **75**
Patterson, Floyd **19, 58**
Paul, Chris **84**
Payne, Ulice **42**
Payton, Walter **11, 25**
Peck, Carolyn **23**
Peete, Calvin **11**
Peete, Rodney **60**
Pelé **7**
Perrot, Kim **23**
Perry, Lowell **30**
Peters, Margaret **43**
Peters, Matilda **43**
Phillips, Teresa L. **42**
Pickett, Bill **11**
Pierce, Paul **71**

Pippen, Scottie **15**
Pollard, Fritz **53**
Porter, Terry **75**
Powell, Mike **7**
Powell, Renee **34**
Powell, William J. **82**
Pride, Charley **26**
Prince, Ron **64**
Prince, Tayshaun **68**
Puckett, Kirby **4, 58**
Quirot, Ana **13**
Radcliffe, Ted **74**
Randle, John **87**
Randolph, Willie **53**
Rashad, Ahmad **18**
Ready, Stephanie **33**
Reed, Willis, Jr. **86**
Reese, Pokey **28**
Regis, Cyrille **51**
Reynolds, Harold **77**
Rhoden, William C. **67**
Rhodes, Ray **14**
Ribbs, Willy T. **2**
Rice, Jerry **5, 55**
Rice, Jim **75**
Richard, J. R. **87**
Richards, Sanya **66**
Richardson, Donna **39**
Richardson, Nolan **9**
Richmond, Mitch **19**
Rivers, Doc **25, 81**
Robertson, Oscar **26**
Robinson, David **24**
Robinson, Eddie G. **10, 61**
Robinson, Frank **9, 87**
Robinson, Jackie **6**
Robinson, Sugar Ray **18**
Robinson, Will **51, 69**
Rodman, Dennis **12, 44**
Rollins, Jimmy **70**
Ronaldinho **69**
Rose, Derrick **82**
Rose, Lionel **56**
Rubin, Chanda **37**
Rudolph, Wilma **4**
Russell, Bill **8**
Sabathia, CC **74**
St. Julien, Marlon **29**
Salvador, Bryce **51**
Sampson, Charles **13**
Sanders, Barry **1, 53**
Sanders, Bob **72**
Sanders, Deion **4, 31**
Sanders, Satch **77**
Sapp, Warren **38**
Sayers, Gale **28**
Scott, Stuart **34**
Scott, Wendell Oliver, Sr. **19**
Scurry, Briana **27**
Shannon, Randy **82**
Sharper, Darren **32**
Sheffield, Gary **16**
Shell, Art **1, 66**
Shippen, John **43**
Showers, Reggie **30**
Sifford, Charlie **4, 49**
Silas, Paul **24**
Simmons, Bob **29**
Simpson, O. J. **15**
Singletary, Mike **4, 76**
Slice, Kimbo **73**
Smith, Bruce **80**
Smith, Emmitt **7, 87**

Smith, Hilton **29**
Smith, Lovie **66**
Smith, Ozzie **77**
Smith, Randy **81**
Smith, Rick **72**
Smith, Stephen A. **69**
Smith, Tubby **18, 83**
Solomon, Jimmie Lee **38**
Sono, Jomo **86**
Sosa, Sammy **21, 44**
Spiller, Bill **64**
Sprewell, Latrell **23**
Stackhouse, Jerry **30**
Staley, Dawn **57**
Stargell, Willie **29**
Stearns, Norman "Turkey" **31**
Steward, Emanuel **18**
Stewart, James "Bubba," Jr. **60**
Stewart, Kordell **21**
Stingley, Darryl **69**
Stone, Toni **15**
Stoudemire, Amaré **59**
Strahan, Michael **35, 81**
Strawberry, Darryl **22**
Stringer, C. Vivian **13, 66**
Stringer, Korey **35**
Swann, Lynn **28**
Swoopes, Sheryl **12, 56**
Tatum, Jack **87**
Taylor, Jason **70**
Taylor, Jermain **60**
Taylor, Lawrence **25**
Taylor, Marshall Walter "Major" **62**
Tergat, Paul **59**
Terrell-Kearney, Kim **83**
Thomas, Debi **26**
Thomas, Derrick **25**
Thomas, Emmitt **71**
Thomas, Frank **12, 51**
Thomas, Isiah **7, 26, 65**
Thomas, Thurman **75**
Thompson, Tina **25, 75**
Thrower, Willie **35**
Thugwane, Josia **21**
Tirico, Mike **68**
Tisdale, Wayman **50**
Toler, Burl **80**
Tomlinson, LaDainian **65**
Trouppe, Quincy Thomas, Sr. **84**
Tunnell, Emlen **54**
Tyson, Mike **28, 44**
Unseld, Wes **23**
Upshaw, Gene **18, 47, 72**
Ussery, Terdema, II **29**
Vanessa James and Yannick Bon-
    heur **84**
Vick, Michael **39**
Virgil, Ozzie **48**
Wade, Dwyane **61**
Walker, Herschel **1, 69**
Wallace, Ben **54**
Wallace, Perry E. **47**
Wallace, Rasheed **56**
Ward, Andre **62**
Ward, Hines **84**
Ware, Andre **37**
Washington, Gene **63**
Washington, Kenny **50**
Washington, MaliVai **8**
Watson, Bob **25**
Watts, J. C., Jr. **14, 38**
Weah, George **58**
Weathers, Carl **10**

Webber, Chris 15, 30, 59
Weekes, Kevin 67
Westbrook, Peter 20
Whitaker, Pernell 10
White, Bill 1, 48
White, Jesse 22, 75
White, Reggie 6, 50
White, Willye 67
Whitfield, Fred 23
Whitfield, Mal 60
Wilbon, Michael 68
Wilkens, Lenny 11
Wilkins, Dominique 74
Williams, Billy 86
Williams, Doug 22
Williams, J. Mayo 83
Williams, Ken 68
Williams, Lauryn 58
Williams, Natalie 31
Williams, Ricky 85
Williams, Serena 20, 41, 73
Williams, Stevie 71
Williams, Venus 17, 34, 62
Williamson, Fred 67
Willingham, Tyrone 43
Willis, Bill 68
Willis, Dontrelle 55
Wills, Harry 80
Wills, Maury 73
Wilson, Sunnie 7, 55
Winfield, Dave 5
Winkfield, Jimmy 42
Winslow, Kellen 83
Wolfe, Ann 82
Woodard, Lynette 67
Woodruff, John 68
Woods, Tiger 14, 31, 81
Woodson, Mike 78
Woodson, Rod 79
Worthy, James 49
Wright, Rayfield 70
Yeboah, Emmanuel Ofosu 53
Young, Donald, Jr. 57
Young, Jimmy 54

**Television**

Akil, Mara Brock 60, 82
Akinnuoye-Agbaje, Adewale 56
Alexander, Khandi 43
Ali, Tatyana 73
Allen, Byron 3
Allen, Debbie 13, 42
Allen, Marcus 20
Alonso, Laz 87
Amos, John 8, 62
Anderson, Anthony 51, 77
Anderson, Eddie "Rochester" 30
Andrews, Tina 74
Arkadie, Kevin 17
Arnez J 53
Arnold, Tichina 63
Babatunde, Obba 35
Banks, Michelle 59
Banks, William 11
Barclay, Paris 37
Barden, Don H. 9
Bassett, Angela 6, 23, 62
Beach, Michael 26
Beaton, Norman 14
Beauvais, Garcelle 29
Belafonte, Harry 4, 65
Bellamy, Bill 12
Bennett, Louise 69

Bentley, Lamont 53
Berry, Bertice 8, 55
Berry, Fred "Rerun" 48
Berry, Halle 4, 19, 57
Blackmon, Brenda 58
Blackwood, Maureen 37
Blacque, Taurean 58
Blake, Asha 26
Bleu, Corbin 65
Bonet, Lisa 58
Boston, Kelvin E. 25
Bowser, Yvette Lee 17
Bradley, Ed 2, 59
Brady, Wayne 32, 71
Brandy 14, 34, 72
Braugher, Andre 13, 58
Bridges, Todd 37
Brooks, Avery 9
Brooks, Golden 62
Brooks, Hadda 40
Brooks, Mehcad 62
Brown, Chris 74
Brown, James 22
Brown, Joe 29
Brown, Les 5
Brown, Tony 3
Brown, Vivian 27
Brown, Warren 61
Browne, Roscoe Lee 66
Bruce, Bruce 56
Burnett, Charles 16, 68
Burton, LeVar 8
Byrd, Eugene 64
Byrd, Robert 11
Caldwell, Benjamin 46
Cameron, Earl 44
Campbell, Naomi 1, 31
Campbell-Martin, Tisha 8, 42
Cannon, Nick 47, 73
Cannon, Reuben 50
Cara, Irene 77
Carroll, Rocky 74
Carroll, Diahann 9
Carson, Lisa Nicole 21
Carter, Nell 39
Cash, Rosalind 28
Cedric the Entertainer 29, 60
Chappelle, Dave 50
Cheadle, Don 19, 52
Chestnut, Morris 31
Chideya, Farai 14, 61
Christian, Spencer 15
Ciara, Barbara 69
Clack, Zoanne 73
Clash, Kevin 14
Clayton, Xernona 3, 45
Cole, Nat "King" 17
Coleman, Gary 35, 86
Corbi, Lana 42
Cornelius, Don 4
Cosby, Bill 7, 26, 59
Crothers, Scatman 19
Curry, Mark 17
Curtis-Hall, Vondie 17
Davidson, Tommy 21
Davis, Eisa 68
Davis, Ossie 5, 50
Davis, Viola 34, 76
de Passe, Suzanne 25
De Shields, André 72
Dee, Ruby 8, 50, 68
Deezer D 53
Devine, Loretta 24

Dickerson, Eric 27
Dickerson, Ernest 6
Diggs, Taye 25, 63
Dixon, Ivan 69
Dourdan, Gary 37
Drake 86
Dre, Dr. 10
Duke, Bill 3
Dungey, Merrin 62
Dutton, Charles S. 4, 22
Earthquake 55
Ejiofor, Chiwetel 67
Elba, Idris 49
Elder, Larry 25
Elise, Kimberly 32
Emmanuel, Alphonsia 38
Ephriam, Mablean 29
Epperson, Sharon 54
Erving, Julius 18, 47
Esposito, Giancarlo 9
Eubanks, Kevin 15
Evans, Harry 25
Faison, Donald 50
Faison, Frankie 55
Falana, Lola 42
Fargas, Antonio 50
Fields, Kim 36
Fishburne, Laurence 4, 22, 70
Fisher, Gail 85
Flavor Flav 67
Fox, Rick 27
Foxx, Jamie 15, 48
Foxx, Redd 2
Frazier, Kevin 58
Freeman, Aaron 52
Freeman, Al, Jr. 11
Freeman, Morgan 2, 20, 62
Freeman, Yvette 27
Gaines, Ernest J. 7
Gardere, Jeffrey 76
Garvin, Gerry 78
Gibbs, Marla 86
Gibson, Tyrese 27, 62
Givens, Adele 62
Givens, Robin 4, 25, 58
Glover, Danny 3, 24
Glover, Donald 85
Glover, Savion 14
Goldberg, Whoopi 4, 33, 69
Goode, Mal 13
Gooding, Cuba, Jr. 16, 62
Gordon, Carl 87
Gordon, Ed 10, 53
Gossett, Louis, Jr. 7
Gray, Darius 69
Greely, M. Gasby 27
Greene, Petey 65
Grier, David Alan 28
Grier, Pam 9, 31, 86
Griffin, Angela 80
Guillaume, Robert 3, 48
Gumbel, Bryant 14, 80
Gumbel, Greg 8
Gunn, Moses 10
Gurira, Danai 73
Guy, Jasmine 2
Haley, Alex 4
Hall, Arsenio 58
Hamilton, Lisa Gay 71
Hampton, Henry 6
Hardison, Kadeem 22
Harewood, David 52
Harper, Hill 32, 65

Harrell, Andre 9, 30
Harris, Naomie 55
Harris, Robin 7
Harvey, Steve 18, 58
Hatchett, Glenda 32
Hayes, Isaac 20, 58, 73
Haynes, Trudy 44
Haysbert, Dennis 42
Hemsley, Sherman 19
Henderson, Jeff 72
Henriques, Julian 37
Henry, Lenny 9, 52
Henson, Darrin 33
Henson, Taraji P. 58, 77
Hickman, Fred 11
Hill, Dulé 29
Hill, Lauryn 20, 53
Hill, Marc Lamont 80
Hinderas, Natalie 5
Hines, Gregory 1, 42
Hines, Amy 69
Holt, Lester 66
Hooks, Robert 76
Hounsou, Djimon 19, 45
Howard, Sherri 36
Howard, Terrence 59
Hudson, Ernie 72
Huggins, Edie 71
Hughley, D. L. 23, 76
Hunter-Gault, Charlayne 6, 31
Hyman, Earle 25, 79
Ice-T 6, 31
Ifill, Gwen 28
Ingram, Rex 5
Jackson, George 19
Jackson, Janet 6, 30, 68
Jackson, Randy 40
Jackson, Tom 70
Jarrett, Vernon D. 42
Joe, Yolanda 21
Johnson, Beverly 2
Johnson, Linton Kwesi 37
Johnson, Robert L. 3, 39
Johnson, Rodney Van 28
Jones, Bobby 20
Jones, James Earl 3, 49, 79
Jones, Orlando 30
Jones, Quincy 8, 30
Kandi 83
Kaufman, Monica 66
Kelley, Malcolm David 59
Kennedy-Overton, Jayne Harris 46
Keys, Alicia 32, 68
Kid Cudi 83
King, Gayle 19
King, Regina 22, 45
King, Woodie, Jr. 27
Kirby, George 14
Kitt, Eartha 16, 75
Knight, Gladys 16, 66
Kodjoe, Boris 34
Kotto, Yaphet 7
Kwei-Armah, Kwame 84
La Salle, Eriq 12
LaBelle, Patti 13, 30
Langhart Cohen, Janet 19, 60
Lathan, Sanaa 27
Lawrence, Martin 6, 27, 60
Lawson, Jennifer 1, 50
Lee, Leslie 85
Lemmons, Kasi 20
Lesure, James 64
Lewis, Ananda 28

Lewis, Byron E. **13**
Lewis, Emmanuel **36**
Lil' Kim **28**
Lindo, Delroy **18, 45**
LisaRaye **27**
LL Cool J **16, 49**
Lofton, James **42**
Long, Loretta **58**
Long, Nia **17**
Lover, Ed **10**
Luke, Derek **61**
Lumbly, Carl **47**
Mabrey, Vicki **26**
Mabuza-Suttle, Felicia **43**
Mac, Bernie **29, 61, 72**
Madison, Paula **37**
Malco, Romany **71**
Manigault-Stallworth, Omarosa **69**
Martin, Helen **31**
Martin, Jesse L. **31**
Mathis, Greg **26**
Mayo, Whitman **32**
McBride, Chi **73**
McCoo, Marilyn **53**
McCrary Anthony, Crystal **70**
McDaniel, Hattie **5**
McDaniels, Ralph **79**
McEwen, Mark **5**
McFarland, Roland **49**
McGlowan, Angela **64, 86**
McKee, Lonette **12**
McKenzie, Vashti M. **29**
McKinney, Nina Mae **40**
McQueen, Butterfly **6, 54**
Meadows, Tim **30**
Mello, Breno **73**
Melton, Frank **81**
Mercado-Valdes, Frank **43**
Merkerson, S. Epatha **47, 83**
Michele, Michael **31**
Mickelbury, Penny **28**
Miller, Cheryl **10, 74**
Miller, Wentworth **75**
Mitchell, Brian Stokes **21**
Mitchell, Kel **66**
Mitchell, Russ **21, 73**
Mokae, Zakes **80**
Mo'Nique **35, 84**
Mooney, Paul **37**
Moore, Chante **26**
Moore, Melba **21**
Moore, Shemar **21**
Morgan, Joe Leonard **9**
Morgan, Tracy **61**
Morris, Garrett **31**
Morris, Greg **28**
Morton, Joe **18**
Mos Def **30**
Moses, Gilbert **12**
Moss, Carlton **17**
Mowry, Tamera **79**
Mowry, Tia **78**
Murphy, Eddie **4, 20, 61**
Muse, Clarence Edouard **21**
Myles, Kim **69**
Nash, Johnny **40**
Nash, Niecy **66**
Neal, Elise **29**
Nicholas, Denise **82**
Nichols, Nichelle **11**
Nissel, Angela **42**
Neville, Arthel **53**
Noble, Gil **76**

Norman, Christina **47**
Norman, Maidie **20**
Odetta **37, 74**
Okonedo, Sophie **67**
Oliver, Pam **54**
Onwurah, Ngozi **38**
Orman, Roscoe **55**
Palmer, Keke **68**
Parker, Nicole Ari **52**
Parr, Russ **51**
Payne, Allen **13**
Peete, Holly Robinson **20**
Peete, Rodney **60**
Perkins, Tony **24**
Perrineau, Harold, Jr. **51**
Perry, Lowell **30**
Perry, Tyler **40**
Phifer, Mekhi **25**
Phillips, Joseph C. **73**
Pickens, James, Jr. **59**
Pinckney, Sandra **56**
Pinkett Smith, Jada **10, 41**
Pinkston, W. Randall **24**
Pitts, Byron **71**
Poitier, Sydney Tamiia **65**
Pounder, CCH **72**
Poussaint, Renee **78**
Price, Frederick K. C. **21**
Price, Hugh B. **9, 54**
Prince-Bythewood, Gina **31, 77**
Pugh, Charles **81**
Quarles, Norma **25**
Queen Latifah **1, 16, 58**
Quivers, Robin **61**
Ralph, Sheryl Lee **18**
Randle, Theresa **16**
Rashad, Ahmad **18**
Rashad, Phylicia **21**
Raven **44**
Ray, Gene Anthony **47**
Ray J **86**
Reddick, Lance **52**
Reed Hall, Alaina **83**
Reese, Della **6, 20**
Reid, Tim **56**
Reuben, Gloria **15**
Reynolds, Star Jones **10, 27, 61**
Rhimes, Shonda Lynn **67**
Ribeiro, Alfonso **17**
Richards, Beah **30**
Richardson, Donna **39**
Richardson, LaTanya **71**
Richardson, Salli **68**
Ridley, John **69**
Roberts, Deborah **35**
Roberts, Robin **16, 54**
Robinson, Matt **69**
Robinson, Max **3**
Robinson, Shaun **36**
Rochon, Lela **16**
Rock, Chris **3, 22, 66**
Rodgers, Johnathan **6, 51**
Rodrigues, Percy **68**
Roker, Al **12, 49**
Roker, Roxie **68**
Rolle, Esther **13, 21**
Rollins, Howard E., Jr. **16**
Ross, Diana **8, 27**
Ross, Tracee Ellis **35**
Roundtree, Richard **27**
Rowan, Carl T. **1, 30**
Rowell, Victoria **13, 68**
Rudolph, Maya **46**

Run **31, 73**
Rupaul **17**
Russell, Bill **8**
Russell, Nipsey **66**
Rust, Art, Jr. **8**
St. Jacques, Raymond **8**
St. John, Kristoff **25**
St. Patrick, Mathew **48**
Saldana, Zoe **72**
Salters, Lisa **71**
Sands, Diana **87**
Sanford, Isabel **53**
Santiago-Hudson, Ruben **85**
Schultz, Michael A. **6**
Scott, Hazel **66**
Scott, Jill **29, 83**
Scott, Stuart **34**
Shaw, Bernard **2, 28**
Shepherd, Sherri **55**
Simmons, Henry **55**
Simmons, Jamal **72**
Simmons, Kimora Lee **51, 83**
Simpson, Carole **6, 30**
Simpson, O. J. **15**
Sinbad **1, 16**
Sinclair, Madge **78**
Smiley, Tavis **20, 68**
Smith, Anjela Lauren **44**
Smith, B(arbara) **11**
Smith, Ian **62**
Smith, Roger Guenveur **12**
Smith, Tasha **73**
Smith, Will **8, 18, 53**
Stewart, Alison **13**
Stokes, Carl **10, 73**
Stone, Chuck **9**
Strahan, Michael **35, 81**
Stuart, Moira **82**
Sykes, Wanda **48, 81**
Syler, Rene **53**
Swann, Lynn **28**
Tate, Larenz **15**
Taylor, Jason **70**
Taylor, Karin **34**
Taylor, Meshach **4**
Taylor, Regina **9, 46**
Thigpen, Lynne **17, 41**
Thomas-Graham, Pamela **29**
Thomason, Marsha **47**
Thompson, Kenan **52**
Thoms, Tracie **61**
Tirico, Mike **68**
Torres, Gina **52**
Torry, Guy **31**
Toussaint, Lorraine **32**
Townsend, Robert **4, 23**
True, Rachel **82**
Tucker, Chris **13, 23, 62**
Tunie, Tamara **63**
Tyler, Aisha N. **36**
Tyson, Cicely **7, 51**
Uggams, Leslie **23**
Underwood, Blair **7, 27, 76**
Union, Gabrielle **31**
Usher **23, 56**
Van Peebles, Mario **2, 51**
Van Peebles, Melvin **7**
Vaughn, Countess **53**
Vereen, Ben **4**
Walker, Eamonn **37**
Ware, Andre **37**
Warfield, Marsha **2**
Warner, Malcolm-Jamal **22, 36**

Warren, Michael **27**
Warwick, Dionne **18**
Washington, Denzel **1, 16**
Washington, Hayma **86**
Washington, Isaiah **62**
Watson, Carlos **50**
Wattleton, Faye **9**
Watts, Rolonda **9**
Wayans, Damien **78**
Wayans, Damon **8, 41**
Wayans, Kim **80**
Wayans, Keenen Ivory **18**
Wayans, Marlon **29, 82**
Wayans, Shawn **29**
Weathers, Carl **10**
Wesley, Richard **73**
Whack, Rita Coburn **36**
Whitfield, Lynn **1, 18**
Wilbon, Michael **68**
Williams, Armstrong **29**
Williams, Billy Dee **8**
Williams, Clarence, III **26**
Williams, Juan **35, 80**
Williams, Malinda **57**
Williams, Montel **4, 57**
Williams, Russell, II **70**
Williams, Samm-Art **21**
Williams, Vanessa A. **32, 66**
Williams, Vanessa L. **4, 17**
Williams, Wendy **62**
Williamson, Mykelti **22**
Wills, Maury **73**
Wilson, Chandra **57**
Wilson, Debra **38**
Wilson, Dorien **55**
Wilson, Flip **21**
Winfield, Paul **2, 45**
Winfrey, Oprah **2, 15, 61**
Witherspoon, John **38**
Wright, Jeffrey **54**
Yarbrough, Cedric **51**
Yoba, Malik **11**

**Theater**
Adams, Osceola Macarthy **31**
Ailey, Alvin **8**
Alexander, Khandi **43**
Allen, Debbie **13, 42**
Amos, John **8, 62**
Anderson, Carl **48**
Andrews, Bert **13**
Angelou, Maya **1, 15**
Anthony, Trey **63**
Arkadie, Kevin **17**
Armstrong, Vanessa Bell **24**
Arnez J **53**
Babatunde, Obba **35**
Bandele, Biyi **68**
Baraka, Amiri **1, 38**
Barnett, Etta Moten **56**
Barrett, Lindsay **43**
Bassett, Angela **6, 23, 62**
Beach, Michael **26**
Beaton, Norman **14**
Belafonte, Harry **4, 65**
Belgrave, Cynthia **75**
Bennett, Louise **69**
Borders, James **9**
Branch, William Blackwell **39**
Brooks, Avery **9**
Brown, Oscar, Jr. **53**
Browne, Roscoe Lee **66**
Bruce, Bruce **56**

Caldwell, Benjamin 46
Calloway, Cab 14
Cameron, Earl 44
Campbell, Naomi 1
Cara, Irene 77
Carroll, Diahann 9
Carroll, Rocky 74
Carroll, Vinnette 29
Carter, Nell 39
Cash, Rosalind 28
Cheadle, Don 19, 52
Chenault, John 40
Childress, Alice 15
Clarke, Hope 14
Cleage, Pearl 17, 64
Cook, Will Marion 40
Cooper, Chuck 75
Corthron, Kia 43
Curtis-Hall, Vondie 17
Dadié, Bernard 34
David, Keith 27
Davis, Altovise 76
Davis, Eisa 68
Davis, Ossie 5, 50
Davis, Sammy, Jr. 18
Davis, Viola 34, 76
Dawn, Marpessa 75
De Shields, André 72
Dee, Ruby 8, 50, 68
Devine, Loretta 24
Dieudonné 67
Diggs, Taye 25, 63
Dixon, Ivan 69
Dodson, Owen Vincent 38
Duke, Bill 3
Dunham, Katherine 4, 59
Dutton, Charles S. 4, 22
Ejiofor, Chiwetel 67
Elba, Idris 49
Elder, Lonne, III 38
Emmanuel, Alphonsia 38
Epps, Mike 60
Esposito, Giancarlo 9
Europe, James Reese 10
Faison, Frankie 55
Falana, Lola 42
Fargas, Antonio 50
Fields, Felicia P. 60
Fishburne, Laurence 4, 22, 70
Franklin, J. E. 44
Freeman, Aaron 52
Freeman, Al, Jr. 11
Freeman, Morgan 2, 20, 62
Freeman, Yvette 27
Fuller, Charles 8
Gibson, John Trusty 87
Gilpin, Charles Sidney 81
Givens, Adele 62
Glover, Danny 1, 24
Glover, Keith 79
Glover, Savion 14
Goldberg, Whoopi 4, 33, 69
Gordone, Charles 15
Gossett, Louis, Jr. 7
Graves, Denyce Antoinette 19, 57
Greaves, William 38
Grier, Pam 9, 31, 86
Guillaume, Robert 3, 48
Gunn, Moses 10
Gurira, Danai 73
Guy, Jasmine 2
Hall, Juanita 62
Hamilton, Lisa Gay 71

Hamlin, Larry Leon 49, 62
Hansberry, Lorraine 6
Harewood, David 52
Harris, Bill 72
Harris, Robin 7
Hayes, Teddy 40
Hemsley, Sherman 19
Higginsen, Vy 65
Hill, Dulé 29
Hill, Errol 40
Hill, Hugh Morgan 83
Hines, Gregory 1, 42
Holder, Geoffrey 78
Holder, Laurence 34
Holland, Endesha Ida Mae 3, 57
Hooks, Robert 76
Hyman, Earle 25, 79
Hyman, Phyllis 19
Ingram, Rex 5
Jackson, Millie 25
Jackson, Samuel 8, 19, 63
Jamison, Judith 7, 67
Jean-Baptiste, Marianne 17, 46
Johnson, Je'Caryous 63
Jones, James Earl 3, 49, 79
Jones, Sarah 39
Joyner, Matilda Sissieretta 15
Kente, Gibson 52
Khumalo, Leleti 51
King, Woodie, Jr. 27
King, Yolanda 6
Kitt, Eartha 16, 75
Kotto, Yaphet 7
Kwei-Armah, Kwame 84
La Salle, Eriq 12
Lampley, Oni Faida 43, 71
Lathan, Sanaa 27
Lee, Canada 8
Lee, Leslie 85
Leggs, Kingsley 62
Lemmons, Kasi 20
LeNoire, Rosetta 37
Lenox, Adriane 59
Leon, Kenny 10
Lester, Adrian 46
Letson, Al 39
Lincoln, Abbey 3
Lindo, Delroy 18, 45
Lister, Marquita 65
Mabley, Jackie "Moms" 15
Marrow, Queen Esther 24
Martin, Helen 31
Martin, Jesse L. 31
McClinton, Marion Isaac 77
McDaniel, Hattie 5
McDonald, Audra 20, 62
McFarlan, Tyron 60
McKee, Lonette 12
McQueen, Butterfly 6, 54
Merkerson, S. Epatha 47, 83
Mickelbury, Penny 28
Mills, Florence 22
Milner, Ron 39
Mitchell, Brian Stokes 21
Mokae, Zakes 80
Mollel, Tololwa 38
Moore, Melba 21
Morgan, Tracy 61
Moses, Gilbert 12
Moss, Carlton 17
Moss, Preacher 63
Moten, Etta 18
Muse, Clarence Edouard 21

Ngaujah, Sahr 86
Nicholas, Fayard 20, 57
Nicholas, Harold 20
Norman, Maidie 20
Nottage, Lynn 66
Ntshona, Winston 52
Okonedo, Sophie 67
Orlandersmith, Dael 42
Oyelowo, David 82
Payne, Allen 13
Perrineau, Harold, Jr. 51
Perry, Tyler 54
Pounder, CCH 72
Powell, Maxine 8
Power, Will 83
Preer, Evelyn 82
Premice, Josephine 41
Primus, Pearl 6
Pryor, Rain 65
Ralph, Sheryl Lee 18
Randle, Theresa 16
Rashad, Phylicia 21
Raven 44
Redwood, John Henry 78
Reese, Della 6, 20
Reid, Tim 56
Rhames, Ving 14, 50
Richards, Beah 30
Richards, Lloyd 2
Richardson, Desmond 39
Richardson, LaTanya 71
Robeson, Paul 2
Rolle, Esther 13, 21
Rollins, Howard E., Jr. 16
Rose, Anika Noni 70
Rotimi, Ola 1
St. Jacques, Raymond 8
Salter, Nikkole 73
Sands, Diana 87
Sanford, Isabel 53
Santiago-Hudson, Ruben 85
Schultz, Michael A. 6
Scott, Harold Russell, Jr. 61
Shabazz, Attallah 6
Shange, Ntozake 8
Slocumb, Jonathan 52
Smiley, Rickey 59
Smith, Anjela Lauren 44
Smith, Anna Deavere 6, 44
Smith, Roger Guenveur 12
Snipes, Wesley 3, 24, 67
Sommore 61
Soyinka, Wole 4
Stew 69
Stewart, Tonea Harris 78
Sundiata, Sekou 66
Talbert, David 34
Taylor, Meshach 4
Taylor, Regina 9, 46
Taylor, Ron 35
Teer, Barbara Ann 81
Thigpen, Lynne 17, 41
Thompson, John Douglas 81
Thompson, Tazewell 13
Thurman, Wallace 16
Torres, Gina 52
Toussaint, Lorraine 32
Townsend, Robert 4, 23
Tyson, Cicely 7, 51
Uggams, Leslie 23
Underwood, Blair 7, 27, 76
Van Peebles, Melvin 7
Vance, Courtney B. 15, 60

Vereen, Ben 4
Verrett, Shirley 66
Walcott, Derek 5
Walker, Eamonn 37
Ward, Douglas Turner 42
Washington, Denzel 1, 16
Washington, Fredi 10
Waters, Ethel 7
Watts, Reggie 52
Whitaker, Forest 2, 49, 67
White, Terri 82
White, Willard 53
Whitfield, Lynn 18
Williams, Bert 18
Williams, Billy Dee 8
Williams, Clarence, III 26
Williams, Michelle 73
Williams, Samm-Art 21
Williamson, Mykelti 22
Wilson, August 7, 33, 55
Wilson, Dorien 55
Wilson, Tracey Scott 777
Winfield, Paul 2, 45
Withers-Mendes, Elisabeth 64
Wolfe, George C. 6, 43
Woodard, Alfre 9
Wright, Jeffrey 54
Yarbrough, Cedric 51

**Writing**
Abani, Chris 77
Abrahams, Peter 39
Abu-Jamal, Mumia 15
Achebe, Chinua 6
Adams, Jenoyne 60
Adams-Ender, Clara 40
Adichie, Chimamanda Ngozi 64
Aidoo, Ama Ata 38
Ake, Claude 30
Akpan, Uwem 70
Al-Amin, Jamil Abdullah 6
Alexander, Elizabeth 75
Alexander, Margaret Walker 22
Ali, Hana Yasmeen 52
Ali, Mohammed Naseehu 60
Allen, Robert L. 38
Allen, Samuel W. 38
Amadi, Elechi 40
Ames, Wilmer 27
Anderson, Ho Che 54
Andrews, Raymond 4
Andrews, Tina 74
Angelou, Maya 1, 15
Ansa, Tina McElroy 14
Anthony, Michael 29
Appiah, Kwame Anthony 67
Arac de Nyeko, Monica 66
Aristide, Jean-Bertrand 6, 45
Arkadie, Kevin 17
Armah, Ayi Kwei 49
Armah, Esther 87
Asante, Molefi Kete 3
Ashley-Ward, Amelia 23
Asim, Jabari 71
Atkins, Cholly 40
Atkins, Russell 45
Aubert, Alvin 41
Auguste, Arnold A. 47
Awoonor, Kofi 37
Azikiwe, Nnamdi 13
Ba, Mariama 30
Bahati, Wambui 60
Bailey, Chauncey 68

Baiocchi, Regina Harris 41
Baisden, Michael 25, 66
Baker, Augusta 38
Baker, Houston A., Jr. 6
Baldwin, James 1
Ballard, Allen Butler, Jr. 40
Bambara, Toni Cade 10
Bandele, Asha 36
Bandele, Biyi 68
Baquet, Dean 63
Baraka, Amiri 1, 38
Barnes, Steven 54
Barnett, Amy Du Bois 46
Barrax, Gerald William 45
Barrett, Lindsay 43
Bashir, Halima 73
Bass, Charlotta Spears 40
Baszile, Jennifer 79
Bates, Karen Grigsby 40
Beah, Ishmael 69
Beals, Melba Patillo 15
Bebey, Francis 45
Beckham, Barry 41
Bell, Derrick 6
Bell, James Madison 40
Benberry, Cuesta 65
Bennett, George Harold 45
Bennett, Gwendolyn B. 59
Bennett, Lerone, Jr. 5, 84
Bennett, Louise 69
Benson, Angela 34
Berry, James 41
Berry, Mary Frances 7
Best, Carrie 80
Beti, Mongo 36
Betts, R. Dwayne 86
Bishop, Maurice 39
Blackman, Toni 86
Blair, Jayson 50
Bland, Eleanor Taylor 39
Blassingame, John Wesley 40
Blockson, Charles L. 42
Blow, Charles M. 73
Bluitt, Juliann S. 14
Bolden, Tonya 32
Bontemps, Arna 8
Booker, Simeon 23
Borders, James 9
Boston, Lloyd 24
Boyd, Gerald M. 32, 59
Boyd, Melba Joyce 86
Boyd, Suzanne 52
Bradley, David Henry, Jr. 39
Bradley, Ed 2, 59
Braithwaite, William Stanley 52
Branch, William Blackwell 39
Brand, Dionne 32
Brathwaite, Kamau 36
Brawley, Benjamin 44
Breeze, Jean "Binta" 37
Bridges, Sheila 36
Brimmer, Andrew F. 2, 48
Briscoe, Connie 15
Britt, Donna 28
Brooks, Gwendolyn 1, 28
Brower, William 49
Brown, Cecil M. 46
Brown, Claude 38
Brown, Elaine 8
Brown, Les 5
Brown, Lloyd Louis 10, 42
Brown, Marie Dutton 12
Brown, Sterling Allen 10, 64

Brown, Tony 3
Brown, Wesley 23
Broyard, Anatole 68
Broyard, Bliss 68
Brutus, Dennis 38
Bryan, Ashley F. 41
Buckley, Gail Lumet 39
Bullins, Ed 25
Bunche, Ralph J. 5
Bunkley, Anita Richmond 39
Burgess, Marjorie L. 55
Burroughs, Margaret Taylor 9
Burwell, Bryan 83
Butler, Octavia 8, 43, 58
Bynum, Juanita 31, 71
Caldwell, Earl 60
Calhoun, Lillian Scott 87
Campbell, Bebe Moore 6, 24, 59
Carby, Hazel 27
Carmichael, Stokely 5, 26
Carroll, Vinnette 29
Carter, Joye Maureen 41
Carter, Martin 49
Carter, Stephen L. 4
Cartey, Wilfred 47
Cartiér, Xam Wilson 41
Cary, Lorene 3
Cary, Mary Ann Shadd 30
Cayton, Horace 26
Césaire, Aimé 48, 69
Chadiha, Jeffri 57
Channer, Colin 36
Chase-Riboud, Barbara 20, 46
Chenault, John 40
Cheney-Coker, Syl 43
Chesnutt, Charles 29
Chideya, Farai 14, 61
Childress, Alice 15
Christian, Barbara T. 44
Churchwell, Robert, Sr. 76
Clack, Zoanne 73
Clark, Kenneth B. 5, 52
Clark, Septima 7
Clark-Bekederemo, J. P. 44
Clarke, Austin C. 32
Clarke, Cheryl 32
Clarke, George 32
Cleage, Pearl 17, 64
Cleaver, Eldridge 5
Cliff, Michelle 42
Clifton, Lucille 14, 64
Coates, Ta-Nehisi 76
Cobb, William Jelani 59
Cobbs, Price M. 9
Cohen, Anthony 15
Cole, Johnnetta B. 5, 43
Coleman, Wanda 48
Collins, Patricia Hill 67
Colter, Cyrus J. 36
Comer, James P. 6
Common 31, 63
Cook, Suzan D. Johnson 22
Cooke, Marvel 31
Coombs, Orde M. 44
Cooper, Afua 53
Cooper, Andrew W. 36
Cooper, Anna Julia 20
Cooper, Helene 74
Cooper, J. California 12, 85
Cornish, Sam 50
Cortez, Jayne 43
Cosby, Bill 7, 26, 59
Cose, Ellis 5, 50

Cotter, Joseph Seamon, Sr. 40
Couto, Mia 45
Cox, Joseph Mason Andrew 51
Creagh, Milton 27
Croal, N'Gai 76
Crouch, Stanley 11, 87
Cruse, Harold 54
Crutchfield, James N. 55
Cullen, Countee 8
Cuney, William Waring 44
Cunningham, Evelyn 23, 85
Curry, George E. 23
Curtis, Christopher Paul 26
Curtis-Hall, Vondie 17
Dabydeen, David 48
Dadié, Bernard 34
D'Aguiar, Fred 50
Damas, Léon-Gontran 46
Dandridge, Raymond Garfield 45
Danner, Margaret Esse 49
Danticat, Edwidge 15, 68
Dash, Leon 47
Datcher, Michael 60
Dathorne, O. R. 52
Davis, Allison 12
Davis, Angela 5
Davis, Charles T. 48
Davis, Eisa 68
Davis, Frank Marshall 47
Davis, George 36
Davis, Nolan 45
Davis, Ossie 5, 50
Davis, Thulani 61
Dawkins, Wayne 20
de Passe, Suzanne 25
De Veaux, Alexis 44
Deggans, Eric 71
Delany, Martin R. 27
Delany, Samuel R., Jr. 9
DeLoach, Nora 30
Demby, William 51
Dent, Thomas C. 50
Dickerson, Debra J. 60
Dickey, Eric Jerome 21, 56
Diop, Birago 53
Diop, Cheikh Anta 4
Dodson, Howard, Jr. 7, 52
Dodson, Owen Vincent 38
Douglass, Frederick 87
Dove, Rita 6, 78
Draper, Sharon Mills 16, 43
Driskell, David C. 7
Driver, David E. 11
Drummond, William J. 40
Du Bois, David Graham 45
Du Bois, W. E. B. 3
DuBois, Shirley Graham 21
Due, Tananarive 30
Dumas, Henry 41
Dunbar, Paul Laurence 8
Dunbar-Nelson, Alice Ruth Moore 44
Dungy, Camille 86
Dunham, Katherine 4, 59
Dunnigan, Alice Allison 41
Duplechan, Larry 55
Dyson, Michael Eric 11, 40
Edmonds, Terry 17
Ekwensi, Cyprian 37
Elder, Lonne, III 38
Elliot, Lorris 37
Ellison, Ralph 7
Elmore, Ronn 21

Emanuel, James A. 46
Emecheta, Buchi 30
Equiano, Olaudah 78
Estes, Rufus 29
Evans, Diana 72
Evans, Mari 26
Fabio, Sarah Webster 48
Fair, Ronald L. 47
Fanon, Frantz 44
Farah, Nuruddin 27
Farley, Christopher John 54
Farrakhan, Louis 15
Fauset, Jessie 7
Feelings, Muriel 44
Feelings, Tom 11, 47
Fields, Julia 45
Figueroa, John J. 40
Files, Lolita 35
Finner-Williams, Paris Michele 62
Fisher, Antwone 40
Fisher, Rudolph 17
Fleming, Raymond 48
Fletcher, Bill, Jr. 41
Fletcher, Geoffrey 85
Forbes, Calvin 46
Ford, Clyde W. 40
Ford, Nick Aaron 44
Ford, Wallace 58
Forman, James 7, 51
Forrest, Leon 44
Fortune, T. Thomas 6
Foster, Cecil 32
Foster, Jylla Moore 45
Franklin, John Hope 5, 77
Franklin, Robert M. 13
Frazier, E. Franklin 10
Frazier, Oscar 58
French, Albert 18
Fuller, Charles 8
Fuller, Hoyt 44
Gabre-Medhin, Tsegaye 64
Gaines, Ernest J. 7
Gaiter, Dorothy J. 80
Gardner, Chris 65
Gaston, Marilyn Hughes 60
Gates, Henry Louis, Jr. 3, 38, 67
Gayle, Addison, Jr. 41
George, Nelson 12
Gibson, Donald Bernard 40
Giddings, Paula 11
Gilbert, Christopher 50
Gilliard, Steve 69
Giovanni, Nikki 9, 39, 85
Givhan, Robin Deneen 72
Gladwell, Malcolm 62
Glover, Donald 85
Goines, Donald 19
Golden, Marita 19
Gomez, Jewelle 30
Goodison, Lorna 71
Gordon-Reed, Annette 74
Graham, Lawrence Otis 12
Graham, Lorenz 48
Grant, Gwendolyn Goldsby 28
Gray, Darius 69
Greaves, William 38
Greenfield, Eloise 9
Greenlee, Sam 48
Greenwood, Monique 38
Griffith, Mark Winston 8
Grimké, Archibald H. 9
Guinier, Lani 7, 30
Guy, Rosa 5

Guy-Sheftall, Beverly 13
Haley, Alex 4
Halliburton, Warren J. 49
Hamblin, Ken 10
Hamilton, Virginia 10
Hansberry, Lorraine 6
Harding, Vincent 67
Hare, Nathan 44
Harkless, Necia Desiree 19
Harper, Frances Ellen Watkins 11
Harper, Michael S. 34
Harrington, Oliver W. 9
Harris, Bill 72
Harris, Claire 34
Harris, Eddy L. 18
Harris, Jay 19
Harris, Leslie 6
Harris, Monica 18
Harrison, Alvin 28
Harrison, Calvin 28
Haskins, James 36, 54
Hayden, Robert 12
Hayes, Teddy 40
Haygood, Wil 83
Haywood, Gar Anthony 43
Head, Bessie 28
Heard, Nathan C. 45
Hearne, John Edgar Caulwell 45
Hemphill, Essex 10
Henderson, David 53
Henderson, Stephen E. 45
Henries, A. Doris Banks 44
Henriques, Julian 37
Henry, Lenny 9, 52
Henson, Matthew 2
Herbert, Bob 63
Hercules, Frank 44
Hernton, Calvin C. 51
Hill, Donna 32
Hill, Errol 40
Hill, Leslie Pinckney 44
Hilliard, David 7
Hoagland, Everett H. 45
Hobson, Julius W. 44
Holland, Endesha Ida Mae 3, 57
Holmes, Shannon 70
Holt, Nora 38
Holton, Hugh, Jr. 39
hooks, bell 5
Horne, Frank 44
Hrabowski, Freeman A., III 22
Hudlin, Reginald 9, 86
Hudson, Cheryl 15
Hudson, Wade 15
Hughes, Langston 4
Hull, Akasha Gloria 45
Hunter-Gault, Charlayne 6, 31
Hurston, Zora Neale 3
Iceberg Slim 11
Ifill, Gwen 28
Ilibagiza, Immaculée 66
Jackson, Brenda 87
Jackson, Fred James 25
Jackson, George 14
Jackson, Sheneska 18
James, Marlon 85
Jarrett, Vernon D. 42
Jasper, Kenji 39
Jenkins, Beverly 14
Joachim, Paulin 34
Joe, Yolanda 21
Johnson, Angela 52
Johnson, Charles 1, 82

Johnson, Charles S. 12
Johnson, Georgia Douglas 41
Johnson, James Weldon 5
Johnson, John H. 3, 54
Johnson, Linton Kwesi 37
Johnson, Mat 31
Johnson, R. M. 36
Jolley, Willie 28
Jones, Edward P. 43, 67
Jones, Gayl 37
Jones, Orlando 30
Jones, Sarah 39
Jordan, June 7, 35
Josey, E. J. 10
July, William 27
Just, Ernest Everett 3
Kamau, Kwadwo Agymah 28
Karenga, Maulana 10, 71
Kariuki, J. M. 67
Kay, Jackie 37
Kayira, Legson 40
Kearney, Janis 54
Keene, John 73
Kendrick, Erika 57
Kennedy, Adrienne 11
Kennedy, Florynce 12, 33
Kennedy, Randall 40
Khanga, Yelena 6
Killens, John O. 54
Kimbro, Dennis 10
Kincaid, Jamaica 4
King, Colbert I. 69
King, Coretta Scott 3, 57
King, Preston 28
King, Woodie, Jr. 27
King, Yolanda 6
Kitt, Sandra 23
Kitwana, Bakari 86
Knight, Etheridge 37
Kobia, Samuel 43
Komunyakaa, Yusef 9
Kunjufu, Jawanza 3, 50
Lacy, Sam 30, 46
Ladner, Joyce A. 42
Laferriere, Dany 33
LaGuma, Alex 30
Lamming, George 35
Lampley, Oni Faida 43, 71
Larsen, Nella 10
Lawrence, Martin 6, 27, 60
Lawrence-Lightfoot, Sara 10
Lemmons, Kasi 20
Lester, Julius 9
Letson, Al 39
Lewis, David Levering 9
Lewis, Samella 25
Lincoln, C. Eric 38
Little, Benilde 21
Locke, Alain 10
Locke, Attica 85
Lorde, Audre 6
Louis, Errol T. 8
Loury, Glenn 36
Lowe, Herbert 57
Mabry, Marcus 70
Mabuza-Suttle, Felicia 43
Machado de Assis 74
Mackey, Nathaniel 75
Madhubuti, Haki 7, 85
Madison, Paula 37
Major, Clarence 9
Makeba, Miriam 2, 50, 74
Malveaux, Julianne 32, 70

Manley, Ruth 34
Marechera, Dambudzo 39
Markham, E. A. 37
Marshall, Paule 7, 77
Martin, Roland S. 49, 84
Mason, Felicia 31
Mason, Herman, Jr. 83
Massaquoi, Hans J. 30
Matejka, Adrian 87
Mathabane, Mark 5
Maynard, Nancy Hicks 73
Maynard, Robert C. 7
Mays, Benjamin E. 7
Mbaye, Mariétou 31
McBride, James 35, 87
McCall, Nathan 8
McCauley, Gina 76
McCrary Anthony, Crystal 70
McDuffie, Dwayne 62
McFadden, Bernice L. 39
McGruder, Robert 22, 35
McKay, Claude 6
McKinney Hammond, Michelle 51
McKinney-Whetstone, Diane 27
McMillan, Rosalynn A. 36
McMillan, Terry 4, 17, 53
McPherson, James Alan 70
Memmi, Albert 37
Mengestu, Dinaw 66
Meredith, James H. 11
Mfume, Kweisi 6, 41
Micheaux, Oscar 7
Mickelbury, Penny 28
Millner, Denene 76
Milner, Ron 39
Mitchell, Elvis 67
Mitchell, Loften 31
Mitchell, Russ 21, 73
Mitchell, Sharon 36
Mofolo, Thomas Mokopu 37
Mollel, Tololwa 38
Monroe, Bryan 71
Monroe, Mary 35
Moore, Jessica Care 30
Moore, Wes 86
Morrison, Toni 2, 15, 86
Mosley, Walter 5, 25, 68
Moss, Carlton 17
Mossell, Gertrude Bustill 40
Moutoussamy-Ashe, Jeanne 7
Mowry, Jess 7
Mphalele, Es'kia (Ezekiel) 40
Mudimbe, V.Y. 61
Mugo, Micere Githae 32
Mullen, Harryette 34
Murphy, John H. 42
Murray, Albert L. 33
Murray, Pauli 38
Mwangi, Meja 40
Myers, Walter Dean 8, 70
Nash, Shannon King 84
Naylor, Gloria 10, 42
Neal, Larry 38
Neal, Mark Anthony 74
Nelson, Jill 6, 54
Neto, António Agostinho 43
Newkirk, Pamela 69
Newton, Huey 2
Ngugi wa Thiong'o 29, 61
Nissel, Angela 42
Njawe, Pius 87
Nkosi, Lewis 46
Norris, Michele 83

Norton, Meredith 72
Nugent, Richard Bruce 39
Nunez, Elizabeth 62
Ojikutu, Bayo 66
Okara, Gabriel 37
Oliver, John J., Jr. 48
Onwueme, Tess Osonye 23
Orlandersmith, Dael 42
Oyono, Ferdinand 38
Packer, Z. Z. 64
Page, Clarence 4
Painter, Nell Irvin 24
Palmer, Everard 37
Parker, Pat 19
Parker, Star 70
Parks, Suzan-Lori 34, 85
Patterson, Orlando 4
Payne, Ethel L. 28
Peters, Lenrie 43
Petry, Ann 19
Philip, Marlene Nourbese 32
Phillips, Joseph C. 73
Piper, Adrian 71
Pitts, Leonard, Jr. 54, 85
Plaatje, Sol. T. 80
Polite, Carlene Hatcher 82
Poussaint, Alvin F. 5, 67
Poussaint, Renee 78
Powell, Adam Clayton, Jr. 3
Powell, Kevin 31, 74
Power, Will 83
Pressley, Condace L. 41
Prince, Richard E. 71
Pryor, Rain 65
Pryor, Richard 3, 24, 56
Quarles, Benjamin Arthur 18
Rahman, Aishah 37
Randall, Alice 38
Randall, Dudley 8, 55
Rapier, James T. 82
Raspberry, William 2
Reagon, Bernice Johnson 7
Reddick, Lawrence Dunbar 20
Redding, J. Saunders 26
Redmond, Eugene 23
Reed, Ishmael 8
Rhimes, Shonda Lynn 67
Rhoden, William C. 67
Rhodes, Jewell Parker 84
Rhone, Trevor 80
Richards, Beah 30
Ridley, John 69
Riggs, Marlon 5
Riley, Rochelle 50
Ringgold, Faith 4, 81
Robertson, Gil L., IV 85
Robeson, Eslanda Goode 13
Robinson, Aminah 50
Robinson, Eugene 77
Robinson, Matt 69
Roby, Kimberla Lawson 86
Rogers, Joel Augustus 30
Rollins, Charlamae Hill 27
Rotimi, Ola 1
Rowan, Carl T. 1, 30
Ruffin, Josephine St. Pierre 75
Run 31, 73
Rust, Art, Jr. 83
Sadlier, Rosemary 62
Saint James, Synthia 12
St. John, Kristoff 25
Salih, Al-Tayyib 37
Sanchez, Sonia 17, 51

Sanders, Dori 8
Sapphire 14
Saro-Wiwa, Kenule 39
Shelton, Paula Young 86
Schomburg, Arthur Alfonso 9
Schuyler, George Samuel 40
Seale, Bobby 3
Sembène, Ousmane 13, 62
Senghor, Léopold Sédar 12, 66
Sengstacke, John 18
Senior, Olive 37
Shabazz, Attallah 6
Shabazz, Ilyasah 36
Shakur, Assata 6
Shakur, Yusef 85
Shange, Ntozake 8
Shaw, Bernard 2, 28
Shipp, E. R. 15
Shockley, Ann Allen 84
Simone, Nina 15, 41
Simpson, Carole 6, 30
Singletary, Mike 4, 76
Singleton, John 2, 30
Sister Souljah 11
Skinner, Kiron K. 65
Smiley, Tavis 20, 68
Smith, Anna Deavere 6
Smith, B(arbara) 11
Smith, Barbara 28
Smith, Bruce W. 53
Smith, Danyel 40
Smith, Jessie Carney 35
Smith, Mary Carter 26
Smith, Stephen A. 69
Smith, Zadie 51
Snowden, Frank M., Jr. 67
Somé, Malidoma Patrice 10
Southgate, Martha 58
Sowell, Thomas 2

Soyinka, Wole 4
Spencer, Anne 27
Spriggs, William 67
Staples, Brent 8
Stewart, Alison 13
Stone, Chuck 9
Stringer, Vickie 58
Sundiata, Sekou 66
Tademy, Lalita 36
Talbert, David 34
Talley, André Leon 56
Tate, Eleanora E. 20, 55
Tatum, Beverly Daniel 42, 84
Tatum, Elinor R. 78
Tatum, Wilbert 76
Taulbert, Clifton Lemoure 19
Taylor, Kristin Clark 8
Taylor, Mildred D. 26
Taylor, Susan C. 62
Taylor, Susan L. 10, 86
Thomas, Michael 69
Thomas, Trisha R. 65
Thomas-Graham, Pamela 29
Thornton, Yvonne S. 69
Thurman, Howard 3
Thurston, Baratunde 79
Tillis, Frederick 40
Tolson, Melvin 37
Toomer, Jean 6
Touré, Askia (Muhammad Abu Bakr el) 47
Townsend, Robert 4
Trotter, Monroe 9
Troupe, Quincy 83
Tucker, Cynthia 15, 61
Turner, Henry McNeal 5
Tutuola, Amos 30
Tyree, Omar Rashad 21
Tyson, Asha 39

Tyson, Neil deGrasse 15, 65
Van Peebles, Melvin 7
van Sertima, Ivan 25
Vega, Marta Moreno 61
Vera, Yvonne 32
Verdelle, A. J. 26
Wade-Gayles, Gloria Jean 41
Walcott, Derek 5
Walker, Alice 1, 43
Walker, Margaret 29
Walker, Rebecca 50
Wallace, Michele Faith 13
Wallace, Phyllis A. 9
Walters, Ronald 83
Ward, Douglas Turner 42
Washington, Booker T. 4
Washington, Elsie B. 78
Washington, Harriet A. 69
Washington, James, Jr. 38
Washington, Laura S. 18
Wattleton, Faye 9
Wayans, Damon 8, 41
Weaver, Afaa Michael 37
Webb, Veronica 10
Weems, Renita J. 44
Wells-Barnett, Ida B. 8
Wesley, Dorothy Porter 19
Wesley, Richard 73
Wesley, Valerie Wilson 18
West, Cornel 5, 33, 80
West, Dorothy 12, 54
Whack, Rita Coburn 36
Wharton, Clifton R., Jr. 7
Whitaker, Mark 21, 47
White, Armond 80
White, Walter F. 4
Whitehead, Colson 77
Whitfield, LeRoy 84
Whitfield, Van 34

Whitlock, Jason 78
Wideman, John Edgar 5, 87
Wilbekin, Emil 63
Wiley, Ralph 8, 78
Wilkerson, Isabel 71
Wilkins, Roger 2, 84
Wilkins, Roy 4
Williams, Armstrong 29
Williams, George Washington 18
Williams, John A. 27
Williams, Juan 35, 80
Williams, Patricia 11, 54
Williams, Robert F. 11
Williams, Samm-Art 21
Williams, Saul 31
Williams, Sherley Anne 25
Williams, Stanley "Tookie" 29, 57
Williams, Wendy 62
Wilson, August 7, 33, 55
Wilson, Mary 28
Wilson, William Julius 22
Winans, Marvin L. 17
Wiwa, Ken 67
Wolfe, George C. 6, 43
Woods, Mattiebelle 63
Woods, Scott 55
Woods, Teri 69
Woodson, Carter G. 2
Worrill, Conrad 12
Wright, Bruce McMarion 3, 52
Wright, Richard 5
X, Marvin 45
Yarbrough, Camille 40
Yette, Samuel F. 63
Young, Al 82
Young, Whitney M., Jr. 4
Youngblood, Shay 32
Zane 71
Zook, Kristal Brent 62

# Cumulative Subject Index

*Volume numbers appear in **bold***

## A cappella

Cooke, Sam **17**
Reagon, Bernice Johnson **7**

## AA

See Alcoholics Anonymous

## AAAS

See American Association for the Advancement of Science

## AARP

Dixon, Margaret **14**
Smith, Marie F. **70**

## ABC

See American Broadcasting Company

## Abstract expressionism

Lewis, Norman **39**

## Academy awards

Austin, Patti **24**
Cara, Irene **77**
Fletcher, Geoffrey **85**
Freeman, Morgan **2, 20, 62**
Goldberg, Whoopi **4, 33, 69**
Gooding, Cuba, Jr. **16, 62**
Gossett, Louis, Jr. **7**
Jean-Baptiste, Marianne **17, 46**
McDaniel, Hattie **5**
Mo'Nique **35, 84**
Poitier, Sidney **11, 36**
Prince **18, 65**
Richie, Lionel **27, 65**
Washington, Denzel **1, 16**
Whitaker, Forest **2, 49, 67**
Williams, Russell, II **70**
Wonder, Stevie **11, 53**

## *Access Hollywood*

Robinson, Shaun **36**

## ACLU

See American Civil Liberties Union

## Acquired immune deficiency syndrome (AIDS)

Ashe, Arthur **1, 18**
Atim, Julian **66**
Broadbent, Hydeia **36**
Cargill, Victoria A. **43**
Fenton, Kevin **87**
Gayle, Helene D. **3, 46**
Hale, Lorraine **8**
Johnson, Earvin "Magic" **3, 39**

Lewis-Thornton, Rae **32**
Mboup, Souleymane **10**
Moutoussamy-Ashe, Jeanne **7**
Norman, Pat **10**
Ojikutu, Bisola **65**
Okaalet, Peter **58**
Pickett, Cecil **39**
Riggs, Marlon **5, 44**
Satcher, David **7, 57**
Seele, Pernessa **46**
Whitfield, LeRoy **84**
Wilson, Phill **9**
Zulu, Princess Kasune **54**

## ACT UP

See AIDS Coalition to Unleash Power

## Acting

Aaliyah **30**
Aaron, Quinton **82**
Adams, Osceola Macarthy **31**
Adebimpe, Tunde **75**
Akinnuoye-Agbaje, Adewale **56**
Alexander, Khandi **43**
Ali, Tatyana **73**
Allen, Debbie **13, 42**
Alonso, Laz **87**
Amos, John **8, 62**
Anderson, Anthony **51, 77**
Anderson, Carl **48**
Anderson, Eddie "Rochester" **30**
Andrews, Tina **74**
Angelou, Maya **1, 15**
Armstrong, Vanessa Bell **24**
Ashanti **37**
Babatunde, Obba **35**
Bahati, Wambui **60**
Baker, Josephine **3**
Banks, Michelle **59**
Banks, Tyra **11, 50**
Barnett, Etta Moten **56**
Bassett, Angela **6, 23, 62**
Beach, Michael **26**
Beals, Jennifer **12**
Beaton, Norman **14**
Beauvais, Garcelle **29**
Belgrave, Cynthia **75**
Bennett, Louise **69**
Bentley, Lamont **53**
Berry, Fred "Rerun" **48**
Berry, Halle **4, 19, 57**
Beyoncé **39, 70**
Bivins, Michael **72**

Blacque, Taurean **58**
Blanks, Billy **22**
Blige, Mary J. **20, 34, 60**
Bonet, Lisa **58**
Borders, James **9**
Bow Wow **35**
Brady, Wayne **32, 71**
Branch, William Blackwell **39**
Braugher, Andre **13, 58**
Bridges, Todd **37**
Brooks, Avery **9**
Brooks, Golden **62**
Brooks, Mehcad **62**
Brown, Chris **74**
Brown, Jim **11**
Browne, Roscoe Lee **66**
Byrd, Eugene **64**
Caesar, Shirley **19**
Calloway, Cab **14**
Cameron, Earl **44**
Campbell, Naomi **1, 31**
Campbell-Martin, Tisha **8, 42**
Cannon, Nick **47, 73**
Cara, Irene **77**
Carroll, Diahann **9**
Carroll, Rocky **74**
Carson, Lisa Nicole **21**
Carey, Mariah **32, 53, 69**
Cash, Rosalind **28**
Cedric the Entertainer **29, 60**
Cheadle, Don **19, 52**
Chestnut, Morris **31**
Childress, Alice **15**
Chong, Rae Dawn **62**
Chweneyagae, Presley **63**
Clarke, Hope **14**
Cliff, Jimmy **28**
Cole, Nat "King" **17**
Coleman, Gary **35, 86**
Combs, Sean "Puffy" **17, 43**
Cooper, Chuck **75**
Cosby, Bill **7, 26, 59**
Crothers, Scatman **19**
Curry, Mark **17**
Curtis-Hall, Vondie **17**
Dandridge, Dorothy **3**
David, Keith **27**
Davidson, Jaye **5**
Davis, Altovise **76**
Davis, Eisa **68**
Davis, Guy **36**
Davis, Ossie **5, 50**
Davis, Sammy, Jr. **18**
Davis, Viola **34, 76**

Dawn, Marpessa **75**
Dawson, Rosario **72**
De Bankolé, Isaach **78**
De Shields, André **72**
Dee, Ruby **8, 50, 68**
Devine, Loretta **24**
Diesel, Vin **29**
Diggs, Taye **25, 63**
Dixon, Ivan **69**
DMX **28, 64**
Dourdan, Gary **37**
Duke, Bill **3**
Duncan, Michael Clarke **26**
Dungey, Merrin **62**
Dutton, Charles S. **4, 22**
Ejiofor, Chiwetel **67**
Elba, Idris **49**
Elise, Kimberly **32**
Emmanuel, Alphonsia **38**
Epps, Mike **60**
Epps, Omar **23, 59**
Esposito, Giancarlo **9**
Everett, Francine **23**
Faison, Donald **50**
Faison, Frankie **55**
Falana, Lola **42**
Fargas, Antonio **50**
Fetchit, Stepin **32**
Fields, Felicia P. **60**
Fields, Kim **36**
Fishburne, Laurence **4, 22, 70**
Fisher, Gail **85**
Fox, Rick **27**
Fox, Vivica A. **15, 53**
Foxx, Jamie **15, 48**
Foxx, Redd **2**
Freeman, Al, Jr. **11**
Freeman, Morgan **2, 20, 62**
Freeman, Yvette **27**
Gaye, Nona **56**
Gibbs, Marla **86**
Gibson, Tyrese **27, 62**
Gilpin, Charles Sidney **81**
Ginuwine **35**
Givens, Adele **62**
Givens, Robin **4, 25, 58**
Glover, Danny **1, 24**
Glover, Donald **85**
Goldberg, Whoopi **4, 33, 69**
Gooding, Cuba, Jr. **16, 62**
Gordon, Dexter **25**
Gossett, Louis, Jr. **7**
Greaves, William **38**
Grier, David Alan **28**

Grier, Pam 9, 31, 86
Griffin, Angela 80
Guillaume, Robert 3, 48
Gunn, Moses 10
Gurira, Danai 73
Guy, Jasmine 2
Hall, Arsenio 58
Hamilton, Lisa Gay 71
Hamlin, Larry Leon 49, 62
Hammond, Fred 23
Hardison, Kadeem 22
Harewood, David 52
Harper, Hill 32, 65
Harris, Naomie 55
Harris, Robin 7
Harvey, Steve 18, 58
Hawkins, Screamin' Jay 30
Hayes, Isaac 20, 58, 73
Haysbert, Dennis 42
Hemsley, Sherman 19
Henry, Lenny 9, 52
Henson, Taraji P. 58, 77
Hill, Dulé 29
Hill, Lauryn 20, 53
Hines, Gregory 1, 42
Holder, Geoffrey 78
Hooks, Robert 76
Horne, Lena 5, 86
Hounsou, Djimon 19, 45
Houston, Whitney 7, 28, 83
Howard, Sherri 36
Howard, Terrence 59
Hudson, Ernie 72
Hudson, Jennifer 63, 83
Hughley, D. L. 23, 76
Hyman, Earle 25, 79
Ice Cube 8, 30, 60
Ingram, Rex 5
Ja Rule 35
Jackson, Janet 6, 30, 68
Jackson, Millie 25
Jackson, Samuel 8, 19, 63
Jean-Baptiste, Marianne 17, 46
Jean-Louis, Jimmy 76
Johnson, Rafer 33
Johnson, Rodney Van 28
Jones, James Earl 3, 49, 79
Jones, Orlando 30
Jorge, Seu 73
Kelley, Elijah 65
Kelley, Malcolm David 59
Kennedy-Overton, Jayne Harris 46
Khumalo, Leleti 51
Kid Cudi 83
King, Regina 22, 45
King, Woodie, Jr. 27
Kirby, George 14
Kitt, Eartha 16, 75
Knight, Gladys 16, 66
Kodhoe, Boris 34
Kotto, Yaphet 7
La Salle, Eriq 12
LaBelle, Patti 13, 30
Lampley, Oni Faida 43, 71
Lane, Charles 3
Lassiter, Roy 24
Lathan, Sanaa 27
Lawrence, Martin 6, 27, 60
Lee, Canada 8
Lee, Joie 1
Leggs, Kingsley 62
Lemmons, Kasi 20
LeNoire, Rosetta 37

Lenox, Adriane 59
Lester, Adrian 46
Lesure, James 64
Lewis, Emmanuel 36
Lil' Kim 28
Lincoln, Abbey 3
Lindo, Delroy 18, 45
LisaRaye 27
LL Cool J 16, 49
Love, Darlene 23
Luke, Derek 61
Lumbly, Carl 47
Mabley, Jackie "Moms" 15
Mac, Bernie 29, 61, 72
Malco, Romany 71
Mario 71
Marrow, Queen Esther 24
Martin, Helen 31
Martin, Jesse L. 31
Master P 21
Mayo, Whitman 32
M.C. Hammer 20, 80
McBride, Chi 73
McClinton, Marion Isaac 77
McDaniel, Hattie 5
McDonald, Audra 20, 62
McKee, Lonette 12
McKinney, Nina Mae 40
McQueen, Butterfly 6, 54
Meadows, Tim 30
Mello, Breno 73
Merkerson, S. Epatha 47, 83
Michele, Michael 31
Miller, Wentworth 75
Mitchell, Brian Stokes 21
Mitchell, Kel 66
Mokae, Zakes 80
Mo'Nique 35, 84
Moore, Chante 26
Moore, Juanita 83
Moore, Shemar 21
Morris, Garrett 31
Morris, Greg 28
Morton, Joe 18
Mos Def 30
Moten, Etta 18
Mowry, Tamera 79
Mowry, Tia 78
Murphy, Eddie 4, 20, 61
Muse, Clarence Edouard 21
Nash, Johnny 40
Nash, Niecy 66
Neal, Elise 29
Newton, Thandie 26
Ngaujah, Sahr 86
Nicholas, Fayard 20, 57
Nicholas, Harold 20
Nichols, Nichelle 11
Norman, Maidie 20
Notorious B.I.G. 20
Ntshona, Winston 52
Okonedo, Sophie 67
O'Neal, Ron 46
Orlandersmith, Dael 42
Orman, Roscoe 55
Oyelowo, David 82
Parker, Nicole Ari 52
Patton, Paula 62
Payne, Allen 13
Payne, Freda 58
Peete, Holly Robinson 20
Perrineau, Harold, Jr. 51
Perry, Tyler 40, 54

Phifer, Mekhi 25
Phillips, Joseph C. 73
Pickens, James, Jr. 59
Pinkett Smith, Jada 10, 41
Poitier, Sidney 11, 36
Poitier, Sydney Tamiia 65
Pounder, CCH 72
Pratt, Kyla 57
Preer, Evelyn 82
Premice, Josephine 41
Prince 18, 65
Pryor, Rain 65
Pryor, Richard 3, 24, 56
Queen Latifah 1, 16, 58
Randle, Theresa 16
Rashad, Phylicia 21
Raven 44
Ray, Gene Anthony 47
Reddick, Lance 52
Reed Hall, Alaina 83
Reese, Della 6, 20
Reid, Tim 56
Reuben, Gloria 15
Rhames, Ving 14, 50
Rhymes, Busta 31
Ribeiro, Alfonso 17
Richards, Beah 30
Richards, Lloyd 2
Richardson, LaTanya 71
Richardson, Salli 68
Robeson, Paul 2
Robinson, Shaun 36
Rock, Chris 3, 22, 66
Rock, The 29 66
Rodgers, Rod 36
Rodrigues, Percy 68
Roker, Roxie 68
Rolle, Esther 13, 21
Rose, Anika Noni 70
Ross, Diana 8, 27
Ross, Tracee Ellis 35
Roundtree, Richard 27
Rowell, Victoria 13, 68
Rudolph, Maya 46
Russell, Nipsey 66
St. Jacques, Raymond 8
St. John, Kristoff 25
St. Patrick, Mathew 48
Saldana, Zoe 72
Salter, Nikkole 73
Sands, Diana 87
Santiago-Hudson, Ruben 85
Scott, Hazel 66
Scott, Jill 29, 83
Shakur, Tupac 14
Short, Columbus 79
Sidibe, Gabourey 84
Simmons, Henry 55
Sinbad 1, 16
Sinclair, Madge 78
Sisqo 30
Smith, Anjela Lauren 44
Smith, Anna Deavere 6, 44
Smith, B(arbara) 11
Smith, Jaden 82
Smith, Roger Guenveur 12
Smith, Tasha 73
Smith, Will 8, 18, 53
Snipes, Wesley 3, 24, 67
Snoop Dogg 35, 84
Sommore 61
Stewart, Tonea Harris 78
Sticky Fingaz 86

Tamia 24, 55
Tate, Larenz 15
Taylor, Meshach 4
Taylor, Regina 9, 46
Taylor, Ron 35
Thomas, Sean Patrick 35
Thomason, Marsha 47
Thompson, John Douglas 81
Thompson, Kenan 52
Thompson, Tazewell 13
Thoms, Tracie 61
Torres, Gina 52
Torry, Guy 31
Toussaint, Lorraine 32
Townsend, Robert 4, 23
True, Rachel 82
Tucker, Chris 13, 23, 62
Tunie, Tamara 63
Turner, Tina 6, 27
Tyler, Aisha N. 36
Tyson, Cicely 7, 51
Uggams, Leslie 23
Underwood, Blair 7, 27, 76
Union, Gabrielle 31
Usher 23, 56
Van Peebles, Mario 2, 51
Van Peebles, Melvin 7
Vance, Courtney B. 15, 60
Vanity 67
Vereen, Ben 4
Walker, Eamonn 37
Ward, Douglas Turner 42
Warfield, Marsha 2
Warner, Malcolm-Jamal 22, 36
Warren, Michael 27
Washington, Denzel 1, 16
Washington, Fredi 10
Washington, Isaiah 62
Washington, Kerry 46
Waters, Ethel 7
Wayans, Damon 8, 41
Wayans, Keenen Ivory 18
Wayans, Kim 80
Wayans, Marlon 29, 82
Wayans, Shawn 29
Weathers, Carl 10
Webb, Veronica 10
Whitaker, Forest 2, 49, 67
White, Michael Jai 71
White, Terri 82
Whitfield, Lynn 18
Williams, Bert 18
Williams, Billy Dee 8
Williams, Clarence, III 26
Wilson, Chandra 57
Wilson, Dorien 55
Williams, Joe 5, 25
Williams, Malinda 57
Williams, Samm-Art 21
Williams, Saul 31
Williams, Vanessa A. 32, 66
Williams, Vanessa L. 4, 17
Williamson, Fred 67
Williamson, Mykelti 22
Wilson, Debra 38
Wilson, Flip 21
Winfield, Paul 2, 45
Winfrey, Oprah 2, 15, 61
Withers-Mendes, Elisabeth 64
Witherspoon, John 38
Woodard, Alfre 9
Wright, Jeffrey 54
Yarbrough, Cedric 51

Yoba, Malik 11

**Actuarial science**
Hill, Jesse, Jr. 13

**Adoption and foster care**
Baker, Josephine 3
Blacque, Taurean 58
Clements, George 2
Gossett, Louis, Jr. 7
Hale, Clara 16
Hale, Lorraine 8
Oglesby, Zena 12
Rowell, Victoria 13, 68

**Advertising**
Barboza, Anthony 10
Boyd, Edward 70
Burrell, Tom 21, 51
Campbell, E. Simms 13
Chisholm, Samuel J. 32
Coleman, Donald 24, 62
Cullers, Vincent T. 49
Gaskins, Rudy 74
Johnson, Beverly 2
Jones, Caroline R. 29
Jordan, Montell 23
Lewis, Byron E. 13
McKinney Hammond, Michelle 51
Mingo, Frank 32
Olden, Georg(e) 44
Pinderhughes, John 47
Roche, Joyce M. 17

**Affirmative action**
Arnwine, Barbara 28
Berry, Mary Frances 7
Carter, Stephen L. 4
Coleman, William T. 76
Edley, Christopher F., Jr. 48
Higginbotham, A. Leon, Jr. 13, 25
Maynard, Robert C. 7
Norton, Eleanor Holmes 7
Rand, A. Barry 6
Thompson, Bennie G. 26
Waters, Maxine 3, 67

**AFL-CIO**
See American Federation of Labor
  and Congress of Industrial Organizations

**African American art**
Jones, Paul R. 76

**African American Dance En-
semble**
Davis, Chuck 33

**African American folklore**
Bailey, Xenobia 11
Brown, Sterling Allen 10, 64
Driskell, David C. 7
Ellison, Ralph 7
Gaines, Ernest J. 7
Hamilton, Virginia 10
Hughes, Langston 4
Hurston, Zora Neale 3
Lester, Julius 9
Primus, Pearl 6
Tillman, George, Jr. 20
Williams, Bert 18
Yarbrough, Camille 40

**African American history**
Appiah, Kwame Anthony 67
Benberry, Cuesta 65

Bennett, Lerone, Jr. 5, 84
Berry, Mary Frances 7
Blackshear, Leonard 52
Blockson, Charles L. 42
Burroughs, Margaret Taylor 9
Camp, Kimberly 19
Chase-Riboud, Barbara 20, 46
Cheadle, Don 19, 52
Clarke, John Henrik 20
Clayton, Mayme Agnew 62
Cobb, William Jelani 59
Coombs, Orde M. 44
Cooper, Anna Julia 20
Dodson, Howard, Jr. 7, 52
Douglas, Aaron 7
Du Bois, W. E. B. 3
DuBois, Shirley Graham 21
Dyson, Michael Eric 11, 40
Feelings, Tom 11, 47
Franklin, John Hope 5, 77
Gaines, Ernest J. 7
Gates, Henry Louis, Jr. 3, 38, 67
Gill, Gerald 69
Gordon-Reed, Annette 74
Haley, Alex 4
Halliburton, Warren J. 49
Harkless, Necia Desiree 19
Harris, Richard E. 61
Hine, Darlene Clark 24
Hughes, Langston 4
Johnson, James Weldon 5
Jones, Edward P. 43, 67
Lewis, David Levering 9
Marable, Manning 10
Mason, Herman, Jr. 83
Painter, Nell Irvin 24
Pritchard, Robert Starling 21
Putney, Martha S. 75
Quarles, Benjamin Arthur 18
Reagon, Bernice Johnson 7
Richardson, Julieanna 81
Schomburg, Arthur Alfonso 9
Shadd, Abraham D. 81
Southern, Eileen 56
Tancil, Gladys Quander 59
Wilson, August 7, 33, 55
Woodson, Carter G. 2
Yarbrough, Camille 40

**African American literature**
Andrews, Raymond 4
Angelou, Maya 1, 15
Appiah, Kwame Anthony 67
Baisden, Michael 25, 66
Baker, Houston A., Jr. 6
Baldwin, James 1
Bambara, Toni Cade 1
Baraka, Amiri 1, 38
Bennett, George Harold "Hal" 45
Bontemps, Arna 8
Briscoe, Connie 15
Brooks, Gwendolyn 1, 28
Brown, Claude 38
Brown, Wesley 23
Burroughs, Margaret Taylor 9
Campbell, Bebe Moore 6, 24, 59
Cary, Lorene 3
Childress, Alice 15
Cleage, Pearl 17, 64
Cullen, Countee 8
Curtis, Christopher Paul 26
Davis, Arthur P. 41
Davis, Nolan 45

Dickey, Eric Jerome 21, 56
Dove, Rita 6, 78
Du Bois, W. E. B. 3
Dunbar, Paul Laurence 8
Ellison, Ralph 7
Evans, Mari 26
Fair, Ronald L. 47
Fauset, Jessie 7
Feelings, Tom 11, 47
Fisher, Rudolph 17
Ford, Nick Aaron 44
Fuller, Charles 8
Gaines, Ernest J. 7
Gates, Henry Louis, Jr. 3, 38, 67
Gayle, Addison, Jr. 41
Gibson, Donald Bernard 40
Giddings, Paula 11
Giovanni, Nikki 9, 39, 85
Goines, Donald 19
Golden, Marita 19
Guy, Rosa 5
Haley, Alex 4
Hansberry, Lorraine 6
Harper, Frances Ellen Watkins 11
Heard, Nathan C. 45
Himes, Chester 8
Holland, Endesha Ida Mae 3, 57
Holmes, Shannon 70
Hughes, Langston 4
Hull, Akasha Gloria 45
Hurston, Zora Neale 3
Iceberg Slim 11
Joe, Yolanda 21
Johnson, Charles 1, 82
Johnson, James Weldon 5
Jones, Gayl 37
Jordan, June 7, 35
July, William 27
Kitt, Sandra 23
Larsen, Nella 10
Lester, Julius 9
Little, Benilde 21
Lorde, Audre 6
Madhubuti, Haki 7, 85
Major, Clarence 9
Marshall, Paule 7, 77
McKay, Claude 6
McKay, Nellie Yvonne 17, 57
McKinney-Whetstone, Diane 27
McMillan, Terry 4, 17, 53
McPherson, James Alan 70
Morrison, Toni 2, 15, 86
Mowry, Jess 7
Myers, Walter Dean 8, 20
Naylor, Gloria 10, 42
Painter, Nell Irvin 24
Petry, Ann 19
Pinkney, Jerry 15
Rahman, Aishah 37
Randall, Dudley 8, 55
Redding, J. Saunders 26
Redmond, Eugene 23
Reed, Ishmael 8
Ringgold, Faith 4, 81
Sanchez, Sonia 17, 51
Schomburg, Arthur Alfonso 9
Schuyler, George Samuel 40
Shange, Ntozake 8
Smith, Mary Carter 26
Taylor, Mildred D. 26
Thomas, Trisha R. 65
Thurman, Wallace 16
Toomer, Jean 6

Tyree, Omar Rashad 21
Van Peebles, Melvin 7
Verdelle, A. J. 26
Villarosa, Clara 85
Walker, Alice 1, 43
Wesley, Valerie Wilson 18
Wideman, John Edgar 5, 87
Williams, John A. 27
Williams, Sherley Anne 25
Wilson, August 7, 33, 55
Wolfe, George C. 6, 43
Wright, Richard 5
Yarbrough, Camille 40

**African American studies**
Alexander, Elizabeth 75
Baszile, Jennifer 79
Brawley, Benjamin 44
Carby, Hazel 27
Christian, Barbara T. 44
De Veaux, Alexis 44
Ford, Nick Aaron 44
Hare, Nathan 44
Harris-Lacewell, Melissa 81
Henderson, Stephen E. 45
Huggins, Nathan Irvin 52
Long, Richard Alexander 65
Neal, Mark Anthony 74
Peterson, James 81
West, Cornel 5, 33, 80

**African Burial Ground Project**
Perry, Warren 56

**African Canadian literature**
Elliott, Lorris 37
Foster, Cecil 32
Senior, Olive 37

**African dance**
Acogny, Germaine 55
Adams, Jenoyne 60
Ailey, Alvin 8
Davis, Chuck 33
Fagan, Garth 18
Primus, Pearl 6

**African history**
Appiah, Kwame Anthony 67
Chase-Riboud, Barbara 20, 46
Clarke, John Henrik 20
Counter, S. Allen 74
Diop, Cheikh Anta 4
Dodson, Howard, Jr. 7, 52
DuBois, Shirley Graham 21
Feelings, Muriel 44
Halliburton, Warren J. 49
Hansberry, William Leo 11
Harkless, Necia Desiree 19
Henries, A. Doris Banks 44
Hilliard, Asa Grant, III 66
Jawara, Dawda Kairaba 11
Marshall, Paule 7, 77
van Sertima, Ivan 25

**African literature**
Aidoo, Ama Ata 38
Akpan, Uwem 70
Appiah, Kwame Anthony 67
Arac de Nyeko, Monica 66
Armah, Ayi Kwei 49
Awoonor, Kofi 37
Bandele, Biyi 68
Cartey, Wilfred 47
Cheney-Coker, Syl 43

Couto, Mia **45**
Dadié, Bernard **34**
Dathorne, O. R. **52**
Ekwensi, Cyprian **37**
Farah, Nuruddin **27**
Gabre-Medhin, Tsegaye **64**
Head, Bessie **28**
Kayira, Legson **40**
Memmi, Albert **37**
Mphalele, Es'kia **40**
Mwangi, Meja **40**
Oyono, Ferdinand **38**
Peters, Lenrie **43**
Salih, Al-Tayyib **37**

**African Methodist Episcopal Church (AME)**
Blanks, Deborah K. **69**
Bryant, John R. **45**
Flake, Floyd H. **18**
McKenzie, Vashti M. **29**
Mudimbe, V. Y. **61**
Murray, Cecil **12, 47**
Roundtree, Dovey **80**
Shuttlesworth, Fred **47**
Turner, Henry McNeal **5**
Youngblood, Johnny Ray **8**

**African music**
Ade, King Sunny **41**
Afro, Teddy **78**
Ashong, Derrick **86**
Fela **1, 42**
Keita, Salif **83**
Kidjo, Angelique **50**
Kolosoy, Wendo **73**
Kuti, Femi **47**
Maal, Baaba **66**
Mahlasela, Vusi **65**
Makeba, Miriam **2, 50, 74**
Nascimento, Milton **2 64**
Somi **85**

**African National Congress (ANC)**
Baker, Ella **5**
Hani, Chris **6**
Ka Dinizulu, Mcwayizeni **29**
Kaunda, Kenneth **2**
Kuzwayo, Ellen **68**
Luthuli, Albert **13**
Mandela, Nelson **1, 14, 77**
Mandela, Winnie **2, 35**
Masekela, Barbara **18**
Mbeki, Govan A. **80**
Mbeki, Thabo **14, 73**
Mhlaba, Raymond **55**
Motlanthe, Kgalema **74**
Nkomo, Joshua **4, 65**
Nyanda, Siphiwe **21**
Nzo, Alfred **15**
Ramaphosa, Cyril **3**
Sisulu, Albertina **57**
Sisulu, Walter **47**
Tutu, Desmond Mpilo **6, 44**
Weems, Renita J. **44**
Xuma, Madie Hall **59**
Zuma, Jacob **33, 75**
Zuma, Nkosazana Dlamini **34**

**Afro-Beat music**
Fela **1, 42**

**Afro-Brazilian music**
Brown, Carlinhos **81**
Caymmi, Dorival **72**
Gil, Gilberto **53**
Jorge, Seu **73**
Moura, Paulo **87**

**Afrocentricity**
Asante, Molefi Kete **3**
Biggers, John **20, 33**
Diop, Cheikh Anta **4**
Hansberry, Lorraine **6**
Hansberry, William Leo **11**
Sanchez, Sonia **17, 51**
Turner, Henry McNeal **5**

**Afro-Cuban music**
Lefel, Edith **41**
Rodríguez, Arsenio **87**
Santamaria, Mongo **81**

**Afro-Peruvian music**
Baca, Susana **80**

**Agency for International Development (AID)**
Gayle, Helene D. **3, 46**
Perkins, Edward **5**

**Agriculture**
Allen, Will **74**
Boyd, John W., Jr. **20, 72**
Carver, George Washington **4**
Hall, Lloyd A. **8**
Jones, Monty **66**
Masire, Quett **5**
Sanders, Dori **8**
Wambugu, Florence **42**

**AHA**
See American Heart Association

**AID**
See Agency for International Development

**AIDS**
See Acquired immune deficiency syndrome

**AIDS Coalition to Unleash Power (ACT UP)**
Norman, Pat **10**

***Akron Beacon Journal***
Crutchfield, James N. **55**

**Akwaaba Mansion Bed & Breakfast**
Greenwood, Monique **38**

**ALA**
See American Library Association

**Alabama state government**
Davis, Artur **41**
Ford, Johnny **70**
Gray, Fred **37**
Rapier, James T. **82**

**Alcoholics Anonymous (AA)**
Hilliard, David **7**
Lucas, John **7**

**All Afrikan People's Revolutionary Party**
Carmichael, Stokely **5, 26**
Moses, Robert Parris **11**

**Allied Arts Academy**
Bonds, Margaret **39**

**Alpha & Omega Ministry**
White, Reggie **6, 50**

**Alpha Kappa Alpha Sorority**
White, Linda M. **45**

**Alvin Ailey American Dance Theater**
Ailey, Alvin **8**
Clarke, Hope **14**
Dove, Ulysses **5**
Faison, George **16**
Jamison, Judith **7, 67**
Jefferson, Denise **87**
Primus, Pearl **6**
Rhoden, Dwight **40**
Richardson, Desmond **39**
Spears, Warren **52**
Tyson, Andre **40**
Williams, Dudley **60**

**Alvin Ailey Repertory Ensemble**
Ailey, Alvin **8**
Miller, Bebe **3**

**Ambassadors**
Braun, Carol Moseley **4, 42**
Carson, Johnnie **85**
Cook, Mercer **40**
Dudley, Edward R. **58**
Dymally, Mervyn **42**
Frazer, Jendayi **68**
Spearman, Leonard H. O., Sr. **81**
Stith, Charles R. **73**
Todman, Terence A. **55**
Watson, Diane **41**
Whitfield, Mal **60**

**AME**
See African Methodist Episcopal Church

**American Academy of Arts and Sciences**
Loury, Glenn **36**

**American Art Award**
Simpson, Lorna **4, 36**

**American Association for the Advancement of Science (AAAS)**
Cobb, W. Montague **39**
Massey, Walter E. **5, 45**
Pickett, Cecil **39**

**American Association of University Women**
Granville, Evelyn Boyd **36**

**American Ballet Theatre**
Dove, Ulysses **5**
Richardson, Desmond **39**

**American Bar Association**
Archer, Dennis **7, 36**
Pincham, R. Eugene, Sr. **69**
Thompson, Larry D. **39**
Walker, Cora T. **68**

**American Beach**
Betsch, MaVynee **28**

**American Book Award**
Baraka, Amiri **1, 38**
Bates, Daisy **13**
Bradley, David Henry, Jr. **39**
Clark, Septima **7**
Gates, Henry Louis, Jr. **3, 38, 67**
Lorde, Audre **6**
Loury, Glenn **36**
Marshall, Paule **7, 77**
Sanchez, Sonia **17, 51**
Troupe, Quincy **83**
Walker, Alice **1, 43**

**American Broadcasting Company (ABC)**
Christian, Spencer **15**
Goode, Mal **13**
Joyner, Tom **19**
Mickebury, Penny **28**
Reynolds, Star Jones **10, 27, 61**
Roberts, Robin **16, 54**
Robinson, Max **3**
Simpson, Carole **6, 30**
Winfrey, Oprah **2, 15, 61**

**American Cancer Society**
Ashe, Arthur **1, 18**
Leffall, Lasalle **3, 64**
Riperton, Minnie **32**
Thomas, Arthur Ray **52**

**American Choral Directors Association**
Adams, Leslie **39**

**American Civil Liberties Union (ACLU)**
Baugh, David **23**
Murphy, Laura M. **43**
Murray, Pauli **38**
Norton, Eleanor Holmes **7**
Pincham, R. Eugene, Sr. **69**

**American Communist Party**
Patterson, Louise **25**

**American Community Housing Associates, Inc.**
Lane, Vincent **5**

**American Composers Alliance**
Tillis, Frederick **40**

**American Counseling Association**
Mitchell, Sharon **36**

**American Economic Association**
Loury Glenn **36**

**American Enterprise Institute**
Woodson, Robert L. **10**

**American Express Company**
Adams, Eula L. **39**
Chenault, Kenneth I. **4, 36**

**American Federation of Labor and Congress of Industrial Organizations (AFL-CIO)**
Fletcher, Bill, Jr. **41**
Holt Baker, Arlene **73**

Randolph, A. Philip 3

**American Guild of Organists**
Adams, Leslie 39

**American Heart Association (AHA)**
Cooper, Edward S. 6
Grant, Augustus O. 71
Richardson, Donna 39

*American Idol*
Hudson, Jennifer 63, 83
Jackson, Randy 40

**American Institute for the Prevention of Blindness**
Bath, Patricia E. 37

**American Library Association (ALA)**
Franklin, Hardy R. 9, 87
Hayden, Carla D. 47
Jones, Clara Stanton 51
Josey, E. J. 10
McFadden, Bernice L. 39
Rollins, Charlamae Hill 27
Wedgeworth, Robert W. 42

**American Negro Academy**
Grimké, Archibald H. 9
Schomburg, Arthur Alfonso 9

**American Negro Theater**
Martin, Helen 31

**American Nuclear Society**
Wilkens, J. Ernest, Jr. 43

**American Nurses Association (ANA)**
Kennedy, Adrienne 11
Staupers, Mabel K. 7

**American Postal Workers Union**
Burrus, William Henry "Bill" 45

**American Psychological Association (APA)**
Anderson, Norman B. 45
Mitchell, Sharon 36

**American Red Cross**
Bullock, Steve 22
Drew, Charles Richard 7

**American Society of Magazine Editors**
Curry, George E. 23

**American Tennis Association**
Gibson, Althea 8, 43
Peters, Margaret and Matilda 43

**American Writers Association**
Schuyler, George Samuel 40

*Amsterdam News*
Cooper, Andrew W. 36
Holt, Nora 38
Tatum, Elinor R. 78
Tatum, Wilbert 76

**ANA**
See American Nurses Association

**ANC**
See African National Congress

**Anglican Church hierarchy**
Akinola, Peter Jasper 65
Tutu, Desmond Mpilo 6, 44

**Angolan government**
dos Santos, José Eduardo 43
Neto, António Agostinho 43

**Anheuser-Busch distribution**
Cherry, Deron 40

**Anthropology**
Asante, Molefi Kete 3
Bunche, Ralph J. 5
Cole, Johnnetta B. 5, 43
Davis, Allison 12
Diop, Cheikh Anta 4
Dunham, Katherine 4, 59
Hansberry, William Leo 11
Primus, Pearl 6
Robeson, Eslanda Goode 13
Rodriguez, Cheryl 64

**Antoinette Perry awards**
See Tony awards

**APA**
See American Psychological Association

**Apartheid**
Abrahams, Peter 39
Ashe, Arthur 18
Berry, Mary Frances 7
Biko, Steven 4
Brutus, Dennis 38
Butler, Jonathan 28
Howard, M. William, Jr. 26
Ka Dinizulu, Mcwayizeni 29
Kuzwayo, Ellen 68
LaGuma, Alex 30
Luthuli, Albert 13
Mahlasela, Vusi 65
Makeba, Miriam 2, 50, 74
Mandela, Nelson 1, 14, 77
Mandela, Winnie 2, 35
Masekela, Hugh 1
Mathabane, Mark 5
Mbeki, Thabo 14, 73
Mbuende, Kaire 12
McDougall, Gay J. 11, 43
Mhlaba, Raymond 55
Mphalele, Es'kia 40
Nkoli, Simon 60
Ntshona, Winston 52
Nyanda, Siphiwe 21
Nzo, Alfred 15
Plaatje, Sol. T. 80
Ramaphosa, Cyril 3
Ramphele, Mamphela 29
Robinson, Randall 7, 46
Sisulu, Albertina 57
Sisulu, Walter 47
Sullivan, Leon H. 13, 30
Tutu, Desmond Mpilo 6, 44

*Apollo*
Williams, O. S. 13

**Apollo Theater**
Sims, Howard 48
Sutton, Percy E. 42, 82

**APWU**
See American Postal Workers Union

**Arab-Israeli conflict**
Bunche, Ralph J. 5

**Architecture**
Abele, Julian 55
Adjaye, David 38, 78
Bond, J. Max, Jr. 76
Gantt, Harvey 1
Johnson, Jeh Vincent 44
King, Robert Arthur 58
McKissack, Leatrice 80
Sklarek, Norma Merrick 25
Taylor, Robert Robinson 80
Williams, Paul R. 9

**Argonne National Laboratory**
Massey, Walter E. 5, 45
Quarterman, Lloyd Albert 4

**Ariel Capital Management**
Hobson, Mellody 40
Rogers, John W., Jr. 5, 52

**Arista Records**
Lattimore, Kenny 35
Reid, Antonio "L.A." 28

**Arkansas government**
Elders, Joycelyn 6

**Art history**
Amaki, Amalia 76
Benjamin, Tritobia Hayes 53
Campbell, Mary Schmidt 43

**Arthur Andersen**
Scott, Milton 51

**Association of Tennis Professionals (ATP)**
Blake, James 43

**Astronauts**
Anderson, Michael P. 40
Bluford, Guy 2, 35
Bolden, Charles Frank, Jr. 7, 78
Gregory, Frederick 8, 51
Jemison, Mae C. 1, 35
Lawrence, Robert H., Jr. 16
McNair, Ronald 3, 58
Wilson, Stephanie 72

**Astronomy**
Pitts, Derrick 77

**Astrophysics**
Alcorn, George Edward, Jr. 59
Carruthers, George R. 40
Walker, Arthur, II 87

**Atco-EastWest**
Rhone, Sylvia 2

**ATD Publishing**
Tyson, Asha 39

**Athletic administration**
Goss, Tom 23
Littlepage, Craig 35

**Atlanta Association of Black Journalists**
Pressley, Condace L. 41

**Atlanta Baptist College**
See Morehouse College

**Atlanta Board of Education**
Mays, Benjamin E. 7

**Atlanta Braves baseball team**
Aaron, Hank 5
Baker, Dusty 8, 43, 72
Justice, David 18
McGriff, Fred 24
Sanders, Deion 4, 31

**Atlanta Chamber of Commerce**
Hill, Jesse, Jr. 13

**Atlanta city government**
Campbell, Bill 9, 76
Franklin, Shirley 34, 80
Jackson, Maynard 2, 41
Pitts, Robb 84
Reed, Kasim 82
Williams, Hosea Lorenzo 15, 31
Young, Andrew 3, 48

**Atlanta Falcons football team**
Anderson, Jamal 22
Buchanan, Ray 32
Sanders, Deion 4, 31
Vick, Michael 39, 65

**Atlanta Hawks basketball team**
Silas, Paul 24
Wilkens, Lenny 11
Wilkins, Dominique 74
Woodson, Mike 78

**Atlanta Negro Voters League**
Hill, Jesse, Jr. 13

**Atlanta Police Department**
Brown, Lee Patrick 1, 24
Harvard, Beverly 11

**Atlanta World**
Scott, C. A. 29

**Atlantic Records**
Franklin, Aretha 11, 44
Lil' Kim 28
Rhone, Sylvia 2

**ATP**
See Association of Tennis Professionals

**Audelco awards**
Holder, Laurence 34
Rodgers, Rod 36
Wesley, Richard 73

**Aurelian Honor Society Award**
Lewis, William M., Jr. 40

**Authors Guild**
Davis, George 36
Gayle, Addison, Jr. 41
Schuyler, George Samuel 40

**Authors League of America**
Abrahams, Peter 39
Cotter, Joseph Seamon, Sr. 40
Davis, George 36

Gayle, Addison, Jr. **41**

**Automobile dealership**
Farr, Mel **24**
Gidron, Richard D. **68**
Parker, Jim **64**

**Aviation**
Brown, Jesse Leroy **31**
Brown, Willa **40**
Bullard, Eugene **12**
Coleman, Bessie **9**
McLeod, Gus **27**
Petersen, Frank E. **31**
Roy, Kenny **51**

**"Back to Africa" movement**
Turner, Henry McNeal **5**

**Bad Boy Entertainment**
Combs, Sean "Puffy" **17, 43**
Harrell, Andre **9, 30**
Notorious B.I.G. **20**

**Bahamian government**
Christie, Perry Gladstone **53**
Pindling, Lynden **81**

**Ballet**
Ailey, Alvin **8**
Allen, Debbie **13, 42**
Anderson, Lauren **72**
Collins, Janet **33, 64**
Dove, Ulysses **5**
Faison, George **16**
Jamison, Judith **7, 67**
Johnson, Virginia **9**
Jones, Doris W. **62**
Mitchell, Arthur **2, 47**
Nichols, Nichelle **11**
Parks, Gordon **1, 35, 58**
Rhoden, Dwight **40**
Richardson, Desmond **39**
Rowell, Victoria **13, 68**
Tyson, Andre **40**

**Balm in Gilead, The**
Seele, Pernessa **46**

**Baltimore Black Sox baseball team**
Day, Leon **39**

**Baltimore city government**
Dixon, Sheila **68**
Robinson, Bishop L. **66**
Schmoke, Kurt **1, 48**

**Baltimore Colts football team**
Davis, Milt **74**
Parker, Jim **64**

**Baltimore Elite Giants baseball team**
Campanella, Roy **25**
Day, Leon **39**
Kimbro, Henry A. **25**

**Baltimore Orioles baseball team**
Baylor, Don **6**
Blair, Paul **36**
Carter, Joe **30**
Jackson, Reggie **15**

Robinson, Frank **9, 87**

**Banking**
Blaylock, Ronald **86**
Boyd, T. B., III **6**
Bradley, Jennette B. **40**
Bridgforth, Glinda **36**
Brimmer, Andrew F. **2, 48**
Bryant, John **26**
Chapman, Nathan A., Jr. **21**
Chappell, Emma **18**
Ferguson, Roger W. **25**
Forte, Linda Diane **54**
Funderburg, I. Owen **38**
Greene, Richard Thaddeus, Sr. **67**
Griffith, Mark Winston **8**
Harris, Carla A. **67**
Lawless, Theodore K. **8**
Louis, Errol T. **8**
March, William Carrington **56**
McGuire, Raymond J. **57**
Morgan, Rose **11**
Parsons, Richard Dean **11**
Utendahl, John **23**
Walker, Maggie Lena **17**
Watkins, Donald **35**
Watkins, Walter C. **24**
Willie, Louis, Jr. **68**
Wright, Deborah C. **25**

**Baptist**
Austin, Junius C. **44**
Bradley, J. Robert **65**
Braxton, Brad **77**
Davis, Gary **41**
Forbes, James A., Jr. **71**
Franklin, C. L. **68**
Gomes, Peter J. **15**
Hooks, Benjamin L. **2, 85**
Jemison, Major L. **48**
Jones, E. Edward, Sr. **45**
Long, Eddie L. **29**
Meek, Carrie **6**
Meek, Kendrick **41**
Moss, Otis, Jr. **72**
Rogers, Alan G. **72**
Taylor, Gardner C. **76**
Thurston, Stephen J. **49**
Walker, Wyatt Tee **80**

**Barnett-Ader Gallery**
Thomas, Alma **14**

**Baseball**
Aaron, Hank **5**
Allen, Dick **85**
Anderson, Elmer **25**
Ashford, Emmett **22**
Baines, Harold **32**
Baker, Dusty **8, 43, 72**
Banks, Ernie **33**
Barnhill, David **30**
Baylor, Don **6**
Bell, James "Cool Papa" **36**
Belle, Albert **10**
Black, Joe **75**
Blair, Paul **36**
Bonds, Barry **6, 34, 63**
Bonds, Bobby **43**
Brock, Lou **18**
Brown, Willard **36**
Campanella, Roy **25**
Carew, Rod **20**
Carter, Joe **30**

Charleston, Oscar **39**
Clendenon, Donn **26, 56**
Coleman, Leonard S., Jr. **12**
Cooper, Andy "Lefty" **63**
Cottrell, Comer **11**
Dandridge, Ray **36**
Davis, Piper **19**
Dawson, Andre **85**
Day, Leon **39**
Doby, Lawrence Eugene, Sr. **16**
Dye, Jermaine **58**
Ellis, Dock **78**
Fielder, Cecil **2**
Fielder, Prince Semien **68**
Flood, Curt **10**
Foster, Andrew **79**
Gaston, Cito **71**
Gibson, Bob **33**
Gibson, Josh **22**
Glanville, Douglas Metunwa **82**
Gooden, Dwight **20**
Granderson, Curtis **66**
Gregg, Eric **16**
Griffey, Ken, Jr. **12, 73**
Gwynn, Tony **18, 83**
Henderson, Rickey **28, 78**
Howard, Ryan **65**
Hunter, Torii **43**
Hyde, Cowan F. "Bubba" **47**
Irvin, Monte **31**
Jackson, Reggie **15**
Jenkins, Fergie **46**
Jeter, Derek **27**
Johnson, Clifford "Connie" **52**
Johnson, Mamie "Peanut" **40**
Justice, David **18**
Kaiser, Cecil **42**
Kimbro, Henry A. **25**
Lacy, Sam **30, 46**
Lankford, Ray **23**
Larkin, Barry **24**
Lloyd, John Henry "Pop" **30**
Lofton, Kenny **12**
Mackey, Biz **82**
Mariner, Jonathan **41**
Martinez, Pedro **81**
Mays, Willie **3**
McGriff, Fred **24**
McRae, Hal **84**
Morgan, Joe Leonard **9**
Murray, Eddie **12**
Newcombe, Don **24**
O'Neil, Buck **19, 59**
Ortiz, David **52, 82**
Paige, Satchel **7**
Payne, Ulice **42**
Pride, Charley **26**
Puckett, Kirby **4, 58**
Radcliffe, Ted **74**
Randolph, Willie **53**
Reese, Pokey **28**
Reynolds, Harold **77**
Rice, Jim **75**
Richard, J. R. **87**
Robinson, Frank **9, 87**
Robinson, Jackie **6**
Robinson, Sharon **22**
Rollins, Jimmy **70**
Sabathia, CC **74**
Sanders, Deion **4, 31**
Sheffield, Gary **16**
Smith, Hilton **29**
Smith, Ozzie **77**

Sosa, Sammy **21, 44**
Stargell, Willie **29**
Stearnes, Norman "Turkey" **31**
Stone, Toni **15**
Strawberry, Darryl **22**
Thomas, Frank **12, 51**
Trouppe, Quincy Thomas, Sr. **84**
Vaughn, Mo **16**
Virgil, Ozzie **48**
Watson, Bob **25**
White, Bill **1, 48**
Williams, Billy **86**
Williams, Ken **68**
Willis, Dontrelle **55**
Wills, Maury **73**
Winfield, Dave **5**

**Baseball Hall of Fame**
Banks, Ernie **33**
Bell, James "Cool Papa" **36**
Brown, Willard **36**
Campanella, Roy **25**
Charleston, Oscar **39**
Dandridge, Ray **36**
Dawson, Andre **85**
Day, Leon **39**
Doby, Lawrence Eugene, Sr. **16, 41**
Gibson, Josh **22**
Gwynn, Tony **18, 83**
Henderson, Rickey **28, 78**
Irvin, Monte **31**
Leonard, Buck **67**
Lloyd, John Henry "Pop" **30**
Morgan, Joe Leonard **9**
Paige, Satchel **7**
Rice, Jim **75**
Robinson, Frank **9, 87**
Robinson, Jackie **6**
Smith, Hilton **29**
Smith, Ozzie **77**
Stearnes, Norman "Turkey" **31**
Williams, Billy **86**

**Barbadian government**
Adams, Grantley **82**
Arthur, Owen **33**

**Basket making**
Jackson, Mary **73**

**Basketball**
Abdul-Jabbar, Kareem **8**
Abdur-Rahim, Shareef **28**
Allen, Ray **82**
Amaker, Tommy **62**
Anderson, Mike **63**
Anthony, Carmelo **46**
Arenas, Gilbert **84**
Artest, Ron **52**
Barkley, Charles **5, 66**
Bing, Dave **3, 59, 78**
Bogues, Tyrone "Muggsy" **56**
Bol, Manute **1**
Bolton-Holifield, Ruthie **28**
Bosh, Chris **85**
Brand, Elton **31**
Brandon, Terrell **16**
Brown, Mike **77**
Bryant, Kobe **15, 31, 71**
Bynoe, Peter C. B. **40**
Carter, Butch **27**
Carter, Kenneth **53**
Carter, Vince **26**
Catchings, Tamika **43**

Chamberlain, Wilt 18, 47
Chaney, John 67
Cheeks, Maurice 47
Clifton, Nathaniel "Sweetwater" 47
Cooper, Charles "Chuck" 47
Cooper, Cynthia 17
Cooper, Michael 31
Curry, Michael 85
Dantley, Adrian 72
Davis, Mike 41
Drexler, Clyde 4, 61
Dumars, Joe 16, 65
Duncan, Tim 20
Dunn, Jerry 27
Durant, Kevin 76
Edwards, Teresa 14
Ellerbe, Brian 22
Elliott, Sean 26
Erving, Julius 18, 47
Ewing, Patrick 17, 73
Fox, Rick 27
Freeman, Marianna 23
Gaines, Clarence E., Sr. 55
Garnett, Kevin 14, 70
Gentry, Alvin 23
Gossett, Louis, Jr. 7
Gourdine, Simon 11
Gray, Yeshimbra "Shimmy" 55
Green, A. C. 32
Griffith, Yolanda 25
Hardaway, Anfernee (Penny) 13
Hardaway, Tim 35
Haskins, Clem 23
Haynes, Marques 22
Heard, Gar 25
Hill, Grant 13
Holdsclaw, Chamique 24
Howard, Juwan 15
Hunter, Billy 22
Isaacs, John 76
Iverson, Allen 24, 46
James, LeBron 46, 78
Johnson, Avery 62
Johnson, Earvin "Magic" 3, 39
Johnson, Kevin 70
Johnson, Larry 28
Jones, K. C. 83
Jones, Merlakia 34
Jones, Roy, Jr. 22
Jones, Sam 85
Jordan, Eddie 83
Jordan, Michael 6, 21
Joyce, Dru 81
Justice, David 18
Kellogg, Clark 64
Kidd, Jason 86
Lanier, Bob 47
Lennox, Betty 31
Leslie, Lisa 16, 73
Lloyd, Earl 26
Lofton, Kenny 12
Lowe, Sidney 64
Lucas, John 7
Mahorn, Rick 60
Malone, Karl 18, 51
Malone, Moses 79
Manigault, Earl "The Goat" 15
Master P 21
McAdoo, Bob 75
McGrady, Tracy 80
Miller, Cheryl 10, 74
Milton, DeLisha 31
Mitchell, Sam 82

Mohammed, Nazr 64
Mourning, Alonzo 17, 44
Mutombo, Dikembe 7
Odom, Lamar 81
Olajuwon, Hakeem 2, 72
O'Neal, Shaquille 8, 30
Palmer, Violet 59
Parish, Robert 43
Parker, Candace 74
Parker, Tony 75
Paul, Chris 84
Peck, Carolyn 23
Phillips, Teresa L. 42
Pierce, Paul 71
Pippen, Scottie 15
Porter, Terry 75
Prince, Tayshaun 68
Reed, Willis, Jr. 86
Richardson, Nolan 9
Richmond, Mitch 19
Rivers, Doc 25, 81
Robertson, Oscar 26
Robinson, David 24
Robinson, Will 51, 69
Rodman, Dennis 12, 44
Rose, Derrick 82
Russell, Bill 8
Sanders, Satch 77
Silas, Paul 24
Smith, Randy 81
Smith, Stephen A. 69
Smith, Tubby 18, 83
Sprewell, Latrell 23
Stackhouse, Jerry 30
Staley, Dawn 57
Stoudemire, Amaré 59
Stringer, C. Vivian 13, 66
Swoopes, Sheryl 12, 56
Ussery, Terdema, II 29
Thomas, Isiah 7, 26, 65
Thompson, Tina 25, 75
Tisdale, Wayman 50
Unseld, Wes 23
Wade, Dwyane 61
Wallace, Ben 54
Wallace, Perry E. 47
Wallace, Rasheed 56
Webber, Chris 15, 30, 59
Wilkens, Lenny 11
Williams, Natalie 31
Woodard, Lynette 67
Woodson, Mike 78
Worthy, James 49

**Basketball Hall of Fame**
Abdul-Jabbar, Kareem 8
Barkley, Charles 5, 66
Bing, Dave 3, 59, 78
Chamberlain, Wilt 18, 47
Chaney, John 67
Dantley, Adrian 72
Drexler, Clyde 4, 61
Dumars, Joe 16, 65
Ewing, Patrick 17, 73
Gaines, Clarence E., Sr. 55
Gervin, George 80
Haynes, Marques 22
Johnson, Earvin "Magic"
Jones, K. C. 83
Jones, Sam 85
Lanier, Bob 47
Lloyd, Earl 26
Malone, Moses 79

McAdoo, Bob 75
Miller, Cheryl 10, 74
Olajuwon, Hakeem 2, 72
Parish, Robert 43
Reed, Willis, Jr. 86
Robertson, Oscar 26
Russell, Bill 8
Sanders, Satch 77
Thomas, Isiah 7, 26, 65
Unseld, Wes 23
Wilkens, Lenny 11
Wilkins, Dominique 74
Woodard, Lynette 67
Worthy, James 49

**Bass**
Foster, George "Pops" 40
Isley, Marvin 87
Jamerson, James 59

**BBC**
See British Broadcasting Company

**Beale Streeters**
Ace, Johnny 36
Bland, Bobby "Blue" 36
King, B. B. 7

**Bear, Stearns & Co.**
Fletcher, Alphonso, Jr. 16

**Beatrice International**
See TLC Beatrice International
    Holdings, Inc.

**Beauty salons and products**
Fine, Sam 60
Gibson, Ted 66
Stanford, Olivia Lee Dilworth 49

**Bebop**
Carter, Betty 19
Clarke, Kenny 27
Coltrane, John 19
Davis, Miles 4
Eckstine, Billy 28
Fitzgerald, Ella 8, 18
Gillespie, Dizzy 1
Gordon, Dexter 25
Hancock, Herbie 20, 67
Harris, Barry 68
Hawkins, Coleman 9
Jackson, Milt 26
Parker, Charlie 20
Powell, Bud 24
Roach, Max 21, 63
Vaughan, Sarah 13

**Ben & Jerry's Homemade Ice
Cream, Inc.**
Holland, Robert, Jr. 11

**Bennett College**
Cole, Johnnetta B. 5, 43
Player, Willa B. 43

**Benin government**
Kerekou, Ahmed 1933— 1
Soglo, Nicéphore 15
Yayi, Boni T. 84

**Bessie award**
Richardson, Desmond 39

**BET**
See Black Entertainment Television

**Bethune-Cookman College**
Bethune, Mary McLeod 4
Joyner, Marjorie Stewart 26

**A Better Chance**
Lewis, William M., Jr. 40

**Big Easy Award**
Adams, Johnny 39

**Bill and Melinda Gates Foundation**
Golston, Allan C. 55

**Billy Graham Evangelistic Association**
Bell, Ralph S. 5
Waters, Ethel 7

**Bing Group, The**
Bing, Dave 3, 59, 78
Lloyd, Earl 26

**Biology**
Cobb, Jewel Plummer 42
Emeagwali, Dale 31
Jarvis, Erich 67
Just, Ernest Everett 3
Malveaux, Floyd 54
Pickett, Cecil 39

**Biotechnology**
Juma, Calestous 57
Wambugu, Florence 42

**Birmingham (AL) city government**
Kincaid, Bernard 28
Langford, Larry P. 74
Nunn, Annetta 43

**Birmingham (AL) Police Department**
Nunn, Annetta 43
Woods, Abraham, Jr. 74

**Birth control**
Elders, Joycelyn 6
Williams, Maggie 7, 71

**Bishop College**
Cottrell, Comer 11

**Black Academy of Arts & Letters**
White, Charles 39

**Black Alliance for Educational Options**
Fuller, Howard L. 37

**Black American West Museum**
Stewart, Paul Wilbur 12

**Black Americans for Family Values**
Foster, Ezola 28

**Black arts movement**
Barrett, Lindsay 43
Caldwell, Benjamin 46
Cornish, Sam 50
Cortez, Jayne 43
Cruse, Harold 54
Dent, Thomas C. 50
Donaldson, Jeff 46
Dumas, Henry 41
Gayle, Addison, Jr. 41

Giovanni, Nikki **9, 39, 85**
Henderson, David **53**
Hoagland, Everett H. **45**
Neal, Larry **38**
Pomare, Eleo **72**
Smith, Vincent D. **48**
Touré, Askia (Muhammad Abu Bakr el) **47**
X, Marvin **45**

**Black Cabinet**
Hastie, William H. **8**

**Black Coaches Association (BCA)**
Freeman, Marianna **23**
Keith, Floyd A. **61**

**Black Consciousness movement**
Biko, Steven **4**
Fanon, Frantz **44**
Fuller, Hoyt **44**
Muhammad, Elijah **4**
Ramaphosa, Cyril **3**
Ramphele, Maphela **29**
Tutu, Desmond Mpilo **6, 44**

**Black Economic Union (BEU)**
Brown, Jim **11**

**Black Enterprise** magazine
Brimmer, Andrew F. **2, 48**
Graves, Butch **77**
Graves, Earl G. **1, 35**
Wallace, Phyllis A. **9**

**Black Enterprise** Corporate Executive of the Year
Chenault, Kenneth I. **5, 36**
Steward, David L. **36**

**Black Entertainment Television (BET)**
Ames, Wilmer **27**
Gordon, Ed **10, 53**
Greely, M. Gasby **27**
Johnson, Robert L. **3, 39**
Johnson, Sheila Crump **48**
Jones, Bobby **20**
Lee, Debra L. **62**
McCrary Anthony, Crystal **70**
Smiley, Tavis **20, 68**

**Black Filmmakers Hall of Fame**
Browne, Roscoe Lee **66**
Dee, Ruby **8, 50, 68**
Dixon, Ivan **69**
McKinney, Nina Mae **40**

**Black History Month**
Woodson, Carter G. **2**

**Black Horizons on the Hill**
Wilson, August **7, 33, 55**

**Black Manifesto**
Forman, James **7, 51**

**Black Music Center**
Moore, Undine Smith **28**

**Black Muslims**
Abdul-Jabbar, Kareem **8**
Ali, Muhammad **2, 16, 52**
Farrakhan, Louis **2**

Muhammad, Elijah **4**
Muhammed, W. Deen **27**
Redding, Ann Holmes **77**
X, Malcolm **1**

**Black nationalism**
Baker, Houston A., Jr. **6**
Baraka, Amiri **1, 38**
Caldwell, Benjamin **46**
Carmichael, Stokely **5, 26**
Donaldson, Jeff **46**
Farrakhan, Louis **2**
Forman, James **7, 51**
Garvey, Marcus **1**
Heard, Nathan C. **45**
Innis, Roy **5**
Muhammad, Elijah **4**
Obadele, Imari **84**
Turner, Henry McNeal **5**
X, Malcolm **1**
York, Dwight D. **71**

**Black Panther Party (BPP)**
Abu-Jamal, Mumia **15**
Al-Amin, Jamil Abdullah **6**
bin Wahad, Dhoruba **85**
Brown, Elaine **8**
Carmichael, Stokely **5**
Cleaver, Eldridge **5**
Cleaver, Kathleen Neal **29**
Coates, Ta-Nehisi **76**
Davis, Angela **5**
Forman, James **7, 51**
Hampton, Fred **18**
Hilliard, David **7**
Jackson, George Lester **14**
Kimbro, Warren **76**
Neal, Larry **38**
Newton, Huey **2**
Pratt, Geronimo **18**
Rush, Bobby **26, 76**
Seale, Bobby **3**
Shakur, Afeni **67**
Shakur, Assata **6**

**Black Power movement**
Al-Amin, Jamil Abdullah **6**
Baker, Houston A., Jr. **6**
Brown, Elaine **8**
Carmichael, Stokely **5, 26**
Dodson, Howard, Jr. **7, 52**
Donaldson, Jeff **46**
Dumas, Henry **41**
Hare, Nathan **44**
McKissick, Floyd B. **3**
Stone, Chuck **9**

**Black Think Tank**
Hare, Nathan **44**

**Blackvoices.com**
Cooper, Barry **33**

**Blackwell Consulting Services**
Blackwell, Robert D., Sr. **52**

**Black World** magazine
See *Negro Digest* magazine

**Black Writers Conference**
McMillan, Rosalynn A. **36**

**Blessed Martin House**
Riley, Helen Caldwell Day **13**

**Blind Boys of Alabama**
Scott, George **55**

**"Blood for Britain"**
Drew, Charles Richard **7**

**Blood plasma research/preservation**
Drew, Charles Richard **7**

**Blues**
Ace, Johnny **36**
Austin, Lovie **40**
Barnes, Roosevelt "Booba" **33**
Bibb, Eric **49**
Bland, Bobby "Blue" **36**
Broonzy, Big Bill **82**
Brown, Charles **23**
Brown, Nappy **73**
Burns, Eddie **44**
Burnside, R. L. **56**
Carr, Leroy **49**
Clarke, Kenny **27**
Collins, Albert **12**
Cox, Ida **42**
Cray, Robert **30**
Davis, Gary **41**
Davis, Guy **36**
Davis, Tyrone **54**
Dixon, Willie **4**
Dorsey, Thomas **15**
Estes, Sleepy John **33**
Evora, Cesaria **12**
Freeman, Yvette **27**
Fuller, Blind Boy **86**
Gaines, Grady **38**
Guy, Buddy **31**
Handy, W. C. **8**
Harris, Corey **39, 73**
Hemphill, Jessie Mae **33, 59**
Holiday, Billie **1**
Hooker, John Lee **30**
Hopkins, Lightnin' **83**
House, Son **8**
Howlin' Wolf **9**
Hunter, Alberta **42**
Hurt, Mississippi John **84**
Jackson, John **36**
James, Skip **38**
Jefferson, Blind Lemon **81**
Johnson, Buddy **36**
Johnson, Lonnie **85**
King, B. B. **7**
LaVette, Bettye **85**
Leadbelly **82**
Lipscomb, Mance **49**
Little Milton **36**
Little Walter **36**
Mahal, Taj **39**
Martin, Sara **38**
McGriff, Jimmy **72**
Mo', Keb' **36**
Moore, Johnny B. **38**
Muse, Clarence Edouard **21**
Neal, Raful **44**
Odetta **37, 74**
Owens, Jack **38**
Parker, Charlie **20**
Pena, Paul **58**
Perkins, Pinetop **70**
Peterson, James **38**
Rawls, Lou **17, 57**
Reed, A. C. **36**

Reed, Jimmy **38**
Reese, Della **6, 20**
Robinson, Fenton **38**
Rogers, Jimmy **38**
Ross, Isaiah "Doc" **40**
Rush, Bobby **78**
Rush, Otis **38**
Seals, Son **56**
Smith, Bessie **3**
Smith, Mamie **32**
Smith, Trixie **34**
Staples, Mavis **50**
Staples, "Pops" **32**
Streeter, Sarah **45**
Sykes, Roosevelt **20**
Tampa Red **63**
Taylor, Koko **40, 80**
Turner, Ike **68**
Wallace, Sippie **1**
Washington, Dinah **22**
Waters, Ethel **7**
Waters, Muddy **34**
Watson, Johnny "Guitar" **18**
Webster, Katie **29**
White, Josh, Jr. **52**
Williams, Joe **5, 25**
Williamson, Sonny Boy **84**
Wilson, August **7, 33, 55**

**Blues Hall of Fame**
Broonzy, Big Bill **82**
Hopkins, Lightnin' **83**
Hunter, Alberta **42**
Hurt, Mississippi John **84**
Little Milton **36**
Williamson, Sonny Boy **84**

**Blues vernacular**
Baker, Houston A., Jr. **6**

**Bobsledding**
Flowers, Vonetta **35**
Hines, Garrett **35**
Jones, Randy **35**
Moses, Edwin **8**

**Bodybuilding**
Haney, Lee **77**
Murray, Lenda **10**

**Boeing Company, The**
Bell, James A. **50**
Grooms, Henry R(andall) **50**
Mills, Joseph C. **51**

**Bola Press**
Cortez, Jayne **43**

**Bolero music**
Ferrer, Ibrahim **41**

**Boogie music**
Brooks, Hadda **40**

**The Boondocks**
McGruder, Aaron **28, 56**

**Boston Bruins hockey team**
O'Ree, Willie **5**

**Boston Celtics basketball team**
Allen, Ray **82**
Cooper, Charles "Chuck" **47**
Fox, Rick **27**
Garnett, Kevin **14, 70**

Parish, Robert **43**
Pierce, Paul **71**
Rivers, Doc **25, 81**
Russell, Bill **8**
Sanders, Satch **77**
Silas, Paul **24**

**Boston Red Sox baseball team**
Baylor, Don **6**
Ortiz, David **52, 82**
Rice, Jim **75**
Vaughn, Mo **16**

**Boston University**
Loury, Glenn **36**
Mitchell, Sharon **36**

**Botswanan government**
Masire, Quett **5**
Mogae, Festus Gontebanye **19, 79**

***Bountiful Blessings*** magazine
Patterson, Gilbert Earl **41**

**Bowling**
Branham, George, III **50**
Terrell-Kearney, Kim **83**

**Boxing**
Ali, Laila **27, 63**
Ali, Muhammad **2, 16, 52**
Bowe, Riddick **6**
Carter, Rubin **26**
DeGale, James **74**
Dixon, George **52**
Ellis, Jimmy **44**
Foreman, George **1, 15**
Forrest, Vernon **40, 79**
Frazier, Joe **19**
Frazier-Lyde, Jacqui **31**
Futch, Eddie **33**
Gibson, Truman K., Jr. **60**
Haye, David **82**
Hearns, Thomas **29**
Holmes, Larry **20, 68**
Holyfield, Evander **6**
Hopkins, Bernard **35, 69**
Johnson, Jack **8**
Jones, Roy, Jr. **22**
King, Don **14**
Lee, Canada **8**
Leonard, Sugar Ray **15**
Lewis, Butch **71**
Lewis, Lennox **27**
Louis, Joe **5**
Mayweather, Floyd, Jr. **57**
Moorer, Michael **19**
Mosley, Shane **32**
Muhammad, Jabir Herbert **72**
Mundine, Anthony **56**
Page, Greg **78**
Patterson, Floyd **19, 58**
Robinson, Sugar Ray **18**
Rose, Lionel **56**
Steward, Emanuel **18**
Taylor, Jermain **60**
Tyson, Mike **28, 44**
Ward, Andre **62**
Whitaker, Pernell **10**
Wills, Harry **80**
Wolfe, Ann **82**

Young, Jimmy **54**

**Boys and Girls Clubs**
Brooks, Derrick **43**
Gaines, Brenda **41**

**Boys Choir of Harlem**
Turnbull, Walter **13, 60**

**BPP**
See Black Panther Party

**Brazilian government**
da Silva, Benedita **5**
Silva, Marina **80**

**Breast cancer awareness**
Brown, Zora Kramer **12**
Norton, Meredith **72**
Riperton, Minnie **32**

**Bristol-Myers Squibb Inc.**
Potter, Myrtle **40**

**British Broadcasting Company (BBC)**
Armah, Esther **87**
Figueroa, John J. **40**
Stuart, Moira **82**

**British Film Institute**
Akomfrah, John **37**

**British government**
Abbott, Diane **9**
Amos, Valerie **41**
Boateng, Paul Yaw **56**
Grant, Bernie **57**
King, Oona **27**
Pitt, David Thomas **10**

**British Virgin Islands government**
Stoutt, H. Lavity **83**

**Broadcasting**
Allen, Byron **3, 24**
Ashley, Maurice **15, 47**
Banks, William **11**
Barden, Don H. **9, 20**
Bettis, Jerome **64**
Blackmon, Brenda **58**
Bradley, Ed **2, 59**
Branch, William Blackwell **39**
Brown, Les **5**
Brown, Tony **3**
Brown, Vivian **27**
Brunson, Dorothy **1, 87**
Clayton, Xernona **3, 45**
Cornelius, Don **4**
Davis, Ossie **5, 50**
Dee, Merri **55**
Elder, Larry **25**
Evans, Harry **25**
Figueroa, John J. **40**
Freeman, Aaron **52**
Goode, Mal **13**
Gumbel, Bryant **14, 80**
Gumbel, Greg **8**
Hamblin, Ken **10**
Hickman, Fred **11**
Holt, Lester **66**
Hunter-Gault, Charlayne **6, 31**
Jackson, Hal **41**
Johnson, Rafer **33**
Johnson, Robert L. **3, 39**

Jones, Bobby **20**
Joyner, Tom **19**
Kellogg, Clark **64**
Kennedy-Overton, Jayne Harris **46**
Langhart Cohen, Janet **19, 60**
Lawson, Jennifer **1, 50**
Lewis, Delano **7**
Lofton, James **42**
Long, Eddie L. **29**
Mabrey, Vicki **26**
Madison, Joseph E. **17**
Madison, Paula **37**
McEwen, Mark **5**
McFarland, Roland **49**
Melton, Frank **81**
Mickelbury, Penny **28**
Miller, Cheryl **10, 74**
Mitchell, Russ **21, 73**
Morgan, Joe Leonard **9**
Neville, Arthel **53**
Peete, Rodney **60**
Pinckney, Sandra **56**
Pinkston, W. Randall **24**
Quarles, Norma **25**
Reynolds, Star Jones **10, 27, 61**
Roberts, Deborah **35**
Roberts, Robin **16, 54**
Robinson, Max **3**
Rodgers, Johnathan **6, 51**
Russell, Bill **8**
Shaw, Bernard **2, 28**
Simmons, Jamal **72**
Simpson, Carole **6, 30**
Simpson, O. J. **15**
Smiley, Tavis **20, 68**
Stewart, Alison **13**
Swann, Lynn **28**
Syler, Rene **53**
Tirico, Mike **68**
Watts, Rolonda **9**
White, Bill **1, 48**
Williams, Armstrong **29**
Williams, Juan **35, 80**
Williams, Montel **4, 57**
Winfrey, Oprah **2, 15, 61**

**Broadside Press**
Hoagland, Everett H. **45**
Randall, Dudley **8, 55**

**Brookings Institute**
Ladner, Joyce A. **42**

**Brooklyn Academy of Music**
Miller, Bebe **3**

**Brooklyn Dodgers baseball team**
Black, Joe **75**
Campanella, Roy **25**
Newcombe, Don **24**
Robinson, Jackie **6**

**Brooklyn Eagles baseball team**
Day, Leon **39**

**Brotherhood of Sleeping Car Porters**
Randolph, A. Philip **3**
Tucker, Rosina **14**

**Brown University**
Beckham, Barry **41**
Gibson, Donald Bernard **40**

Simmons, Ruth **13, 38**

***Brown v. Board of Education of Topeka***
Bell, Derrick **6**
Carter, Robert L. **51**
Clark, Kenneth B. **5, 52**
Franklin, John Hope **5, 77**
Henderson, Zelma **71**
Hill, Oliver W. **24, 63**
Houston, Charles Hamilton **4**
Malone Jones, Vivian **59**
Marshall, Thurgood **1, 44**
Motley, Constance Baker **10, 55**
Redding, Louis L. **26**
Robinson, Spottswood W., III **22**

**Buena Vista Social Club**
Ferrer, Ibrahim **41**

**Buffalo Bills football team**
Lofton, James **42**
Simpson, O. J. **15**
Smith, Bruce **80**
Thomas, Thurman **75**

**Bull-riding**
Sampson, Charles **13**

**Burundian government**
Ndadaye, Melchior **7**
Nkurunziza, Pierre **78**
Ntaryamira, Cyprien **8**

**Busing (anti-busing legislation)**
Bosley, Freeman, Jr. **7**

**Cabinet**
See U.S. Cabinet

**Cable News Network (CNN)**
Chideya, Farai **14, 61**
Hickman, Fred **11**
Quarles, Norma **25**
Shaw, Bernard **2, 28**
Watson, Carlos **50**

**Calabash International Literary Festival**
Channer, Colin **36**

**Calgary Flames hockey team**
Iginla, Jarome **35**

**California Angels baseball team**
See Los Angeles Angels baseball team

***California Eagle*** newspaper
Bass, Charlotta Spears **40**
Jackson, Vera **40**

**California state government**
Bass, Karen **70**
Brown, Janice Rogers **43**
Brown, Willie **7, 85**
Dixon, Julian C. **24**
Dymally, Mervyn **42**
Hawkins, Augustus F. **68**
Lee, Barbara **25**
Millender-McDonald, Juanita **21, 61**
Richardson, Laura **81**
Riles, Wilson C. **79**
Waters, Maxine **3, 67**

Watson, Diane 41

**California State University**
Cobb, Jewel Plummer 42
Granville, Evelyn Boyd 36
Karenga, Maulana 10, 71

**California Supreme Court**
Brown, Janice Rogers 43

**Calypso**
Belafonte, Harry 4, 65
Premice, Josephine 41
Rhoden, Wayne 70
Rudder, David 79

**Cameroonian government**
Ahidjo, Ahmadou 81
Biya, Paul 28
Oyono, Ferdinand 38

**Canadian Agricultural Chemistry Association**
Donald, Arnold Wayne 36

**Canadian Football League (CFL)**
Clemons, Michael "Pinball" 64
Gilliam, Frank 23
Moon, Warren 8, 66
Thrower, Willie 35
Weathers, Carl 10

**Canadian government**
Augustine, Jean 53
Brown, Rosemary 62
Cools, Anne 64
Jean, Michaëlle; 70
Lewis, Daurene 72
Sparks, Corinne Etta 53

**Cancer research**
Adams-Campbell, Lucille L. 60
Chinn, May Edward 26
Clark, Celeste 15
Daly, Marie Maynard 37
Dunston, Georgia Mae 48
Freeman, Harold P. 23
Leffall, Lasalle 3, 64
Olopade, Olufunmilayo Falusi 58

**Capital punishment**
Hawkins, Steven 14

**Cardiac research**
Watkins, Levi, Jr. 9

**CARE**
Gossett, Louis, Jr. 7
Stone, Chuck 9

**Caribbean Artists' Movement**
Brathwaite, Kamau 36

**Caribbean dance**
Ailey, Alvin 8
Dunham, Katherine 4, 59
Fagan, Garth 18
Nichols, Nichelle 11
Primus, Pearl 6

**Caribbean literature**
Breeze, Jean "Binta" 37
Carter, Martin 49
Cartey, Wilfred 47
Dabydeen, David 48

Hearne, John Edgar Caulwell 45

**Caribbean music**
Ellis, Alton 74
Ranglin, Ernest 78

**Casting**
Cannon, Reuben 50

**Catalyst Award (American Express)**
Chenault, Kenneth I. 5, 36

**Cartoonists**
Armstrong, Robb 15
Bell, Darrin 77
Brandon, Barbara 3
Brown, Robert 65
Campbell, E. Simms 13
Fax, Elton 48
Harrington, Oliver W. 9
McDuffie, Dwayne 62
McGruder, Aaron 28, 56
Ormes, Jackie 73
Smith, Bruce W. 53

**Catholicism**
See Roman Catholic Church

**CBC**
See Congressional Black Caucus

**CBS**
See Columbia Broadcasting System

**CDC**
See Centers for Disease Control and Prevention

**CDF**
See Children's Defense Fund

**Celebrities for a Drug-Free America**
Vereen, Ben 4

**Censorship**
Butts, Calvin O., III 9
Ice-T 6, 31

**Centers for Disease Control and Prevention (CDC)**
Fenton, Kevin 87
Gayle, Helene D. 3
Satcher, David 7, 57
Wisdom, Kimberlydawn 57

**Central Intercollegiate Athletic Association (CIAA)**
Kerry, Leon G. 46
Yancy, Dorothy Cowser 42

**Certified public accountant**
Jones, Thomas W. 41
Washington, Mary T. 57

**CFL**
See Canadian Football League

**Chadian government**
Habré, Hissène 6

**Challenged Athletes Foundation**
Yeboah, Emmanuel Ofosu 53

*Challenger*
McNair, Ronald 3, 58

**Challenger Air Pilot's Association**
Brown, Willa 40

**Chama Cha Mapinduzi (Tanzania; Revolutionary Party)**
Kikwete, Jakaya Mrisho 73
Mkapa, Benjamin W. 16, 77
Mongella, Gertrude 11
Mwinyi, Ali Hassan 1, 77
Nyerere, Julius 5

**Charles H. Wright Museum of African American History**
Wright, Charles H. 35

**Charles R. Drew University**
Bath, Patricia E. 37

**Charlotte Hornets basketball team**
Bryant, Kobe 15, 31, 71
Parish, Robert 43

**Charter Schools USA**
Mariner, Jonathan 41

**Chemistry**
Daly, Marie Maynard 37
Hall, Lloyd A. 8
Humphries, Frederick 20
Julian, Percy Lavon 6
King, Reatha Clark 65
Massie, Samuel Proctor, Jr. 29
Mays, William G. 34
Mensah, Thomas 48

**Chesapeake and Potomac Telephone Company**
Lewis, Delano 7

**Chess**
Ashley, Maurice 15, 47

**Chicago American Giants baseball team**
Bell, James "Cool Papa" 36
Charleston, Oscar 39

**Chicago Art League**
Wilson, Ellis 39

**Chicago Bears football team**
Page, Alan 7
Payton, Walter 11, 25
Sayers, Gale 28
Singletary, Mike 4, 76
Thrower, Willie 35

**Chicago Black Arts Movement**
Cortor, Eldzier 42
Sebree, Charles 40

**Chicago Blaze basketball team**
Catchings, Tamika 43

**Chicago Bulls basketball team**
Brand, Elton 31
Jordan, Michael 6, 21
Parish, Robert 43
Pippen, Scottie 15
Rodman, Dennis 12, 44

**Chicago city government**
Berry, Edwin C. 81
De Priest, Oscar Stanton 80

Jones, Emil, Jr. 74
Kelley, Cliff 75
Lane, Vincent 5
Metcalfe, Ralph 26
Sawyer, Eugene 81
Tillman, Dorothy 76
Washington, Harold 6

**Chicago Cubs baseball team**
Baker, Dusty 8, 43, 72
Banks, Ernie 33
Bonds, Bobby 43
Carter, Joe 30
Sosa, Sammy 21, 44
Williams, Billy 86

*Chicago Defender*
Abbott, Robert Sengstacke 27
Holt, Nora 38
Martin, Roland S. 49, 84
Ormes, Jackie 73
Payne, Ethel L. 28

**Chicago Defender Charities**
Joyner, Marjorie Stewart 26

**Chicago Eight**
Seale, Bobby 3

**Chicago Library Board**
Williams, Fannie Barrier 27

**Chicago Negro Chamber of Commerce**
Fuller, S. B. 13

**Chicago Police Department**
Hillard, Terry 25
Holton, Hugh, Jr. 39

*Chicago Reporter*
Calhoun, Lillian Scott 87
Washington, Laura S. 18

*Chicago Tribune*
Page, Clarence 4

**Chicago White Sox baseball team**
Baines, Harold 32
Bonds, Bobby 43
Doby, Lawrence Eugene, Sr. 16, 41
Johnson, Clifford "Connie" 52
Thomas, Frank 12, 51
Williams, Ken 68

**Chicago Women's Club**
Williams, Fannie Barrier 27

**Child Welfare Administration**
Little, Robert L. 2

**Children's Defense Fund (CDF)**
Edelman, Marian Wright 5, 42
Williams, Maggie 7, 71

**Children's literature**
Asim, Jabari 71
Berry, James 41
Bryan, Ashley F. 41
Common 31, 63
De Veaux, Alexis 44
Feelings, Muriel 44
Graham, Lorenz 48
Greenfield, Eloise 9
Johnson, Angela 52

Mollel, Tololwa **38**
Myers, Walter Dean **8, 20**
Okara, Gabriel **37**
Palmer, Everard **37**
Shelton, Paula Young **86**
Yarbrough, Camille **40**

**Chi-Lites**
Record, Eugene **60**

**Chiropractics**
Ford, Clyde W. **40**
Reese, Milous J., Jr. **51**
Westbrooks, Bobby **51**

**Chisholm-Mingo Group, Inc.**
Chisholm, Samuel J. **32**
Mingo, Frank **32**

**Choreography**
Acogny, Germaine **55**
Ailey, Alvin **8**
Alexander, Khandi **43**
Allen, Debbie **13, 42**
Atkins, Cholly **40**
Babatunde, Obba **35**
Beatty, Talley **35**
Brooks, Avery **9**
Byrd, Donald **10**
Campbell-Martin, Tisha **8, 42**
Collins, Janet **33, 64**
Davis, Chuck **33**
de Lavallade, Carmen **78**
de Passe, Suzanne **25**
De Shields, André **72**
Dove, Ulysses **5**
Dunham, Katherine **4, 59**
Ellington, Mercedes **34**
Fagan, Garth **18**
Faison, George **16**
Glover, Savion **14**
Hall, Arthur **39**
Henson, Darrin **33**
Jamison, Judith **7, 67**
Johnson, Virginia **9**
Jones, Bill T. **1, 46, 80**
King, Alonzo **38**
LeTang, Henry **66**
Manning, Frankie **78**
Miller, Bebe **3**
Mitchell, Arthur **2, 47**
Nicholas, Fayard **20, 57**
Nicholas, Harold **20**
Pomare, Eleo **72**
Primus, Pearl **6**
Rhoden, Dwight **40**
Richardson, Desmond **39**
Robinson, Cleo Parker **38**
Robinson, Fatima **34**
Rodgers, Rod **36**
Spears, Warren **52**
Tyson, Andre **40**
Zollar, Jawole **28**

**Christian Financial Ministries, Inc.**
Ross, Charles **27**

*Christian Science Monitor*
Khanga, Yelena **6**

**Chrysler Corporation**
Colbert, Virgis William **17**
Farmer, Forest **1**
Gilles, Ralph **61**

Richie, Leroy C. **18**

**Church of God in Christ**
Blake, Charles E. **82**
Franklin, Robert M. **13**
Hayes, James C. **10**
Patterson, Gilbert Earl **41**

**CIAA**
See Central Intercollegiate Athletic Association

**Cincinnati city government**
Berry, Theodore M. **31**
Mallory, Mark **62**

**Cincinnati Reds baseball team**
Baker, Dusty **8, 43, 72**
Blair, Paul **36**
Larkin, Barry **24**
Morgan, Joe Leonard **9**
Reese, Pokey **28**
Robinson, Frank **9, 87**
Sanders, Deion **4, 31**

**Cinematography**
Dickerson, Ernest **6, 17**

**Circus**
McFarlan, Tyron **60**
Walker, Cedric "Ricky" **19**

**Citadel Press**
Achebe, Chinua **6**

**Citigroup**
Gaines, Brenda **41**
Jones, Thomas W. **41**
McGuire, Raymond J. **57**

**Citizens Federal Savings and Loan Association**
Gaston, Arthur George **3, 38, 59**
Willie, Louis, Jr. **68**

**Citizens for Affirmative Action's Preservation**
Dillard, Godfrey J. **45**

**City Capital Corporation**
Taylor, Ephren W., II **61**

**City government--U.S.**
Barden, Don H. **9, 20**
Bell, Michael **40**
Bellamy, Terry **58**
Bobb, Robert C. **83**
Bradley, Jennette B. **40**
Brown, Lee P. **1, 24**
Brown, Willie **7, 85**
Burris, Chuck **21**
Bush, Gordon **82**
Caesar, Shirley **19**
Clayton, Constance **1**
Cleaver, Emanuel **4, 45, 68**
Coleman, Michael **28, 79**
Craig-Jones, Ellen Walker **44**
Dellums, Ronald **2, 81**
Ford, Jack **39**
Ford, Johnny **70**
Foxx, Anthony **81**
Hatcher, Richard G. **55**
Hayes, James C. **10**
Herenton, Willie W. **24, 81**
Johnson, Harvey, Jr. **24, 82**
Lowery, Myron **80**
Mallett, Conrad, Jr. **16**

Marsh, Henry **32**
McPhail, Sharon **2**
Melton, Frank **81**
Millender-McDonald, Juanita **21, 61**
Morial, Ernest "Dutch" **26**
Morial, Marc H. **20, 51**
Murrell, Sylvia Marilyn **49**
Patterson, J. O., Jr. **80**
Perkins, James, Jr. **55**
Powell, Adam Clayton, Jr. **3**
Powell, Debra A. **23**
Usry, James L. **23**

*City Sun* newspaper
Cooper, Andrew W. **36**

**City University of New York**
Ballard, Allen Butler, Jr. **40**
Davis, George **36**
Gayle, Addison, Jr. **41**
Shabazz, Ilyasah **36**

**Civil rights**
Abbott, Diane **9**
Abernathy, Ralph **1**
Agyeman, Jaramogi Abebe **10, 63**
Al-Amin, Jamil Abdullah **6**
Alexander, Clifford **26**
Ali, Ayaan Hirsi **58**
Ali, Muhammad **2, 16, 52**
Amaker, Norman **63**
Angelou, Maya **1, 15**
Anthony, Wendell **25**
Aristide, Jean-Bertrand **6, 45**
Arnwine, Barbara **28**
Baker, Ella **5**
Baker, Houston A., Jr. **6**
Baker, Josephine **3**
Ballance, Frank W. **41**
Barbee, Lloyd Augustus **71**
Barrow, Willie T. **85**
Bashir, Halima **73**
Bass, Charlotta Spears **40**
Bates, Daisy **13**
Baugh, David **23**
Beals, Melba Patillo **15**
Belafonte, Harry **4, 65**
Bell, Derrick **6**
Bell, James Madison **40**
Berry, Mary Frances **7**
Berry, Theodore M. **31**
Bevel, James L. **75**
Biko, Steven **4**
Bishop, Sanford D., Jr. **24**
Bond, Julian **2, 35**
Booker, Simeon **23**
Boyd, John W., Jr. **20, 72**
Bradle, David Henry, Jr. **39**
Bridges, Ruby **77**
Brock, Roslyn McCallister **86**
Brooks, Tyrone **59**
Brown, Byrd **49**
Brown, Elaine **8**
Brown, Homer S. **47**
Brown, Tony **3**
Brown, Wesley **23**
Brown, Willa **40**
Burks, Mary Fair **40**
Caldwell, Earl **60**
Cameron, James **80**
Campbell, Bebe Moore **6, 24, 59**
Carmichael, Stokely **5, 26**
Carr, Johnnie **69**
Carter, Mandy **11**

Carter, Rubin **26**
Carter, Stephen L. **4**
Cary, Mary Ann Shadd **30**
Catto, Octavius V. **83**
Cayton, Horace **26**
Chambers, Julius **3**
Chavis, Benjamin **6**
Chestnut, J. L., Jr. **73**
Clark, Septima **7**
Clay, William Lacy **8**
Cleaver, Eldridge **5**
Cleaver, Kathleen Neal **29**
Clyburn, James E. **21, 71**
Cobb, W. Montague **39**
Cobbs, Price M. **9**
Cockrel, Kenneth Vern, Sr. **79**
Coleman, James E., Jr. **79**
Cooper, Anna Julia **20**
Cosby, Bill **7, 26, 59**
Crockett, George W., Jr. **10, 64**
Cunningham, Evelyn **23, 85**
Davis, Angela **5**
Davis, Artur **41**
Davis, James E. **50**
Days, Drew S., III **10**
Dee, Ruby **8, 50, 68**
Dent, Thomas C. **50**
Diallo, Amadou **27**
Diggs, Charles C. **21**
Diggs-Taylor, Anna **20**
Divine, Father **7**
Dodson, Howard, Jr. **7, 52**
Douglass, Frederick **87**
Du Bois, W. E. B. **3**
Dudley, Edward R. **58**
Dukes, Hazel Nell **56**
Dumas, Henry **41**
Edelman, Marian Wright **5, 42**
Ellison, Ralph **7**
Evers, Medgar **3**
Evers, Myrlie **8**
Farmer, James **2, 64**
Farmer-Paellmann, Deadria **43**
Fauntroy, Walter E. **11**
Fisher, Ada Lois Sipuel **76**
Fletcher, Bill, Jr. **41**
Forman, James **7, 51**
Fortune, T. Thomas **6**
Foster, Marie **48**
Franklin, C. L. **68**
Franklin, John Hope **5, 77**
Gaines, Ernest J. **7**
Gaines, Lloyd **79**
George, Zelma Watson **42**
Gibson, William F. **6**
Granger, Lester B. **75**
Gray, Fred **37**
Gregory, Dick **1, 54**
Grimké, Archibald H. **9**
Guinier, Lani **7, 30**
Haley, Alex **4**
Haley, George Williford Boyce **21**
Hall, Elliott S. **24**
Hamer, Fannie Lou **6**
Hampton, Fred **18**
Hampton, Henry **6**
Hansberry, Lorraine **6**
Harding, Vincent **67**
Harper, Frances Ellen Watkins **11**
Harris, Patricia Roberts **2**
Hastie, William H. **8**
Hatcher, Richard G. **55**
Hawkins, Augustus F. **68**

Hawkins, Steven **14**
Hayes, Dennis **54**
Hedgeman, Anna Arnold **22**
Height, Dorothy I. **2, 23, 78**
Henderson, Thelton E. **68**
Henderson, Wade J. **14**
Henry, Aaron **19**
Higginbotham, A. Leon, Jr. **13, 25**
Hill, Jesse, Jr. **13**
Hill, Oliver W. **24, 63**
Hilliard, David **7**
Hobson, Julius W. **44**
Holland, Endesha Ida Mae **3, 57**
Hollowell, Donald L. **57**
hooks, bell **5**
Hooks, Benjamin L. **2, 85**
Houston, Charles Hamilton **4**
Howard, M. William, Jr. **26**
Innis, Roy **5**
Irvis, K. Leroy **67**
Jackson, Alexine Clement **22**
Jackson, Jesse **1, 27, 72**
James, Daniel, Jr. **16**
Jarrett, Vernon D. **42**
Jenkins, Ray **77**
Johns, Vernon **38**
Johnson, Eddie Bernice **8**
Johnson, Georgia Douglas **41**
Johnson, James Weldon **5**
Johnson, Norma L. Holloway **17**
Jones, Elaine R. **7, 45**
Jones, William A., Jr. **61**
Jordan, Barbara **4, 78**
Jordan, June **7, 35**
Jordan, Vernon E. **3, 35**
Julian, Percy Lavon **6**
Karim, Benjamin **61**
Kennedy, Florynce **12, 33**
Kenyatta, Jomo **5**
Kidd, Mae Street **39**
King, Bernice **4, 81**
King, Coretta Scott **3, 57**
King, Martin Luther, Jr. **1**
King, Martin Luther, III **20**
King, Preston **28**
King, Robert Hillary **84**
King, Yolanda **6**
Ladner, Joyce A. **42**
Lampkin, Daisy **19**
Lester, Julius **9**
Lewis, John **2, 46, 83**
Logan, Rayford W. **40**
Lorde, Audre **6**
Loving, Mildred **69**
Lowery, Joseph **2**
Lowry, A. Leon **60**
Lucy Foster, Autherine **35**
Makeba, Miriam **2, 50, 74**
Malone Jones, Vivian **59**
Mandela, Nelson **1, 14, 77**
Mandela, Winnie **2, 35**
Martin, Louis E. **16**
Martin, Ruby Grant **49**
Mayfield, Curtis **2, 43**
Mays, Benjamin E. **7**
Mbeki, Thabo **14, 73**
McDonald, Gabrielle Kirk **20**
McDougall, Gay J. **11, 43**
McKissick, Floyd B. **3**
Meek, Carrie **6**
Meredith, James H. **11**
Metcalfe, Ralph **26**
Morgan, Irene **65**

Moore, Barbara C. **49**
Moore, Harry T. **29**
Morial, Ernest "Dutch" **26**
Moses, Robert Parris **11**
Moss, Otis, Jr. **72**
Motley, Constance Baker **10, 55**
Mowry, Jess **7**
Mukoko, Jestina **75**
Murphy, Laura M. **43**
Murray, Pauli **38**
Nash, Diane **72**
Ndadaye, Melchior **7**
Nelson, Jill **6, 54**
Newton, Huey **2**
Nkoli, Simon **60**
Nkomo, Joshua **4, 65**
Noble, Gil **76**
Norman, Pat **10**
Norton, Eleanor Holmes **7**
Nunn, Annetta **43**
Nzo, Alfred **15**
Orange, James **74**
Parker, Kellis E. **30**
Parks, Rosa **1, 35, 56**
Patrick, Deval **12, 61**
Patterson, Louise **25**
Patterson, Orlando **4**
Perkins, Edward **5**
Pincham, R. Eugene, Sr. **69**
Pinchback, P. B. S. **9**
Player, Willa B. **43**
Pleasant, Mary Ellen **9**
Plessy, Homer Adolph **31**
Poitier, Sidney **11, 36**
Powell, Adam Clayton, Jr. **3**
Price, Hugh B. **9, 54**
Ramaphosa, Cyril **3**
Randolph, A. Philip **3**
Reagon, Bernice Johnson **7**
Redding, Louis L. **26**
Riggs, Marlon **5, 44**
Rivers, Eugene F., III **81**
Robeson, Paul **2**
Robinson, Jackie **6**
Robinson, Rachel **16**
Robinson, Randall **7, 46**
Robinson, Sharon **22**
Robinson, Spottswood W., III **22**
Roundtree, Dovey **80**
Rowan, Carl T. **1, 30**
Rush, Bobby **26, 76**
Rustin, Bayard **4**
Sadlier, Rosemary **62**
Sanders, Malika **48**
Sané, Pierre Gabriel **21**
Saro-Wiwa, Kenule **39**
Seale, Bobby **3**
Shabazz, Attallah **6**
Shabazz, Betty **7, 26**
Shakur, Assata **6**
Shelton, Paula Young **86**
Shinhoster, Earl **32**
Shuttlesworth, Fred **47**
Simone, Nina **15, 41**
Sisulu, Albertina **57**
Sisulu, Sheila Violet Makate **24**
Sleet, Moneta, Jr. **5**
Smith, Barbara **28**
Staupers, Mabel K. **7**
Sullivan, Leon H. **3, 30**
Sutton, Percy E. **42, 82**
Sweet, Ossian **68**
Talbert, Mary B. **77**

Thompson, Bennie G. **26**
Thurman, Howard **3**
Till, Emmett **7**
Tillman, Dorothy **76**
Tolson, Melvin B. **37**
Touré, Faya Ora Rose **56**
Trotter, Monroe **9**
Tsvangirai, Morgan **26, 72**
Turner, Henry McNeal **5**
Tutu, Desmond Mpilo **6, 44**
Underwood, Blair **7, 27, 76**
Walker, Rebecca **50**
Washington, Booker T. **4**
Washington, Fredi **10**
Watt, Melvin **26**
Weaver, Robert C. **8, 46**
Wells, James Lesesne **10**
Wells-Barnett, Ida B. **8**
White, Walter F. **4**
Wilkins, Roy **4**
Williams, Evelyn **10**
Williams, Fannie Barrier **27**
Williams, Hosea Lorenzo **15, 31**
Williams, Robert F. **11**
Williams, Walter E. **4**
Wilson, August **7, 33, 55**
Wilson, Sunnie **7, 55**
Wilson, William Julius **22**
Woods, Abraham, Jr. **74**
Woodson, Robert L. **10**
Wright, Nathan, Jr. **56**
X, Malcolm **1**
Yoba, Malik **11**
Young, Andrew **3, 48**
Young, Jean Childs **14**
Young, Whitney M., Jr. **4**

**Civilian Pilots Training Program**
Brown, Willa **40**

**Clarinet**
Bechet, Sidney **18**
McGill, Anthony **76**

**Classical music**
Adams, Leslie **39**
Baiocchi, Regina Harris **41**
Bonds, Margaret **39**
Brown, Uzee **42**
Burleigh, Henry Thacker **56**
Coleridge-Taylor, Samuel **75**
Cook, Will Marion **40**
Dawson, William Levi **39**
DePreist, James **37**
Dixon, Dean **68**
Dunner, Leslie B. **45**
Freeman, Paul **39**
Kay, Ulysses **37**
Lewis, Henry **38**
McFerrin, Bobby **68**
McGill, Anthony **76**
Moore, Dorothy Rudd **46**
Murray, Tai **47**
Pratt, Awadagin **31**
Price, Florence **37**
Schuyler, Philippa **50**
Sowande, Fela **39**
Still, William Grant **37**
Tillis, Frederick **40**
Walker, George **37**
Wilkins, Thomas Alphonso **71**

Williams, Denise **40**

**Classical singers**
Anderson, Marian **2, 33**
Battle, Kathleen **70**
Bumbry, Grace **5**
Burleigh, Henry Thacker **56**
Hayes, Roland **4**
Hendricks, Barbara **3, 67**
Lister, Marquita **65**
Norman, Jessye **5**
Price, Leontyne **1**
Three Mo' Tenors **35**
Williams, Denise **40**

**Clearview Golf Club**
Powell, Renee **34**

**Cleo Parker Robinson Dance Ensemble**
Robinson, Cleo Parker **38**

**Clergy**
Agyeman, Jaramogi Abebe **10, 63**
Anthony, Wendell **25**
Austin, Junius C. **44**
Berry, Moses **84**
Black, Barry C. **47**
Bloomer, George **86**
Burgess, John **46**
Bynum, Juanita **31, 71**
Caesar, Shirley **19**
Caldwell, Kirbyjon **55**
Cleveland, James **19**
Cook, Suzan D. Johnson **22**
Dyson, Michael Eric **11, 40**
Ellis, Charles H., III **79**
Falana, Lola **42**
Gilmore, Marshall **46**
Gomes, Peter J. **15**
Gregory, Wilton **37**
Howard, M. William, Jr. **26**
Jakes, Thomas "T. D." **17, 43**
James, Skip **38**
Jemison, Major L. **48**
Johns, Vernon **38**
Jones, Absalom **52**
Jones, Alex **64**
Jones, William A., Jr. **61**
Karim, Benjamin **61**
Kee, John P. **43**
Kelly, Leontine **33**
King, Barbara **22**
King, Bernice **4, 81**
Kobia, Samuel **43**
Lee, Eric P. **79**
Lincoln, C. Eric **38**
Long, Eddie L. **29**
Maxis, Theresa **62**
McClurkin, Donnie **25**
McGuire, George Alexander **80**
McKenzie, Vashti M. **29**
Morgan, Gertrude **63**
Okaalet, Peter **58**
Otunga, Maurice Michael **55**
Peterson, Jesse Lee **81**
Phipps, Wintley **59**
Reems, Ernestine Cleveland **27**
Reese, Della **6, 20**
Reverend Ike **79**
Sentamu, John **58**
Shuttlesworth, Fred **47**
Taylor, Gardner C. **76**
Thurman, Howard **3**

Thurston, Stephen J. **49**
Tillard, Conrad **47**
Tolton, Augustine **62**
Ukpabio, Helen **86**
Walker, John T. **50**
Washington, James Melvin **50**
Watkins, Joe **86**
Weeks, Thomas, III **70**
Weems, Renita J. **44**
White-Hammond, Gloria **61**
Williams, David Rudyard **50**
Williams, Frederick (B.) **63**
Williams, Preston Warren, II **64**
Winans, Marvin L. **17**
Wright, Nathan, Jr. **56**

**Cleveland Browns football team**
Brown, Jim **11**
Crennel, Romeo **54**
Hill, Calvin **19**
Motley, Marion **26**
Newsome, Ozzie **26**
Willis, Bill **68**

**Cleveland Cavaliers basketball team**
Brandon, Terrell **16**
Brown, Mike **77**
James, LeBron **46, 78**
Wilkens, Lenny **11**

**Cleveland city government**
Jackson, Frank G. **76**
Stokes, Carl **10, 73**
White, Michael R. **5**

**Cleveland Foundation**
Adams, Leslie **39**

**Cleveland Indians baseball team**
Belle, Albert **10**
Bonds, Bobby **43**
Carter, Joe **30**
Doby, Lawrence Eugene, Sr. **16, 41**
Justice, David **18**
Lofton, Kenny **12**
Murray, Eddie **12**
Paige, Satchel **7**
Robinson, Frank **9, 87**
Sabathia, CC **74**

**Cleveland Rockers basketball team**
Jones, Merlakia **34**

**CLIO Awards**
Lewis, Emmanuel **36**

**Clothing design**
Aberra, Amsale **67**
Bailey, Xenobia **11**
Burrows, Stephen **31**
Gaskins, Eric **64**
Henderson, Gordon **5**
John, Daymond **23**
Jones, Carl **7**
Kani, Karl **10**
Kelly, Patrick **3**
Lars, Byron **32**
Malone, Maurice **32**
Pinkett Smith, Jada **10, 41**
Robinson, Patrick **19, 71**
Smith, Willi **8**

Walker, T. J. **7**
Williams, Serena **20, 41, 73**

**CNBC**
Epperson, Sharon **54**
Thomas-Graham, Pamela **29**

**CNN**
See Cable News Network

**Coaching**
Amaker, Tommy **62**
Anderson, Mike **63**
Ashley, Maurice **15, 47**
Baker, Dusty **8, 43, 72**
Baylor, Don **6**
Bickerstaff, Bernie **21**
Bonds, Bobby **43**
Brown, Mike **77**
Caldwell, Jim **81**
Campanella, Roy **25**
Carew, Rod **20**
Carter, Butch **27**
Carter, Kenneth **53**
Chaney, John **67**
Cheeks, Maurice **47**
Cooper, Michael **31**
Cox, Bryan **83**
Crennel, Romeo **54**
Curry, Michael **85**
Davis, Mike **41**
Dorrell, Karl **52**
Dungy, Tony **17, 42, 59**
Dunn, Jerry **27**
Edwards, Herman **51**
Ellerbe, Brian **22**
Freeman, Marianna **23**
Gaines, Clarence E., Sr. **55**
Gaither, Alonzo Smith (Jake) **14**
Gaston, Cito **71**
Gentry, Alvin **23**
Gibson, Althea **8, 43**
Gibson, Bob **33**
Gill, Turner **83**
Gorden, W. C. **71**
Graham, Trevor **84**
Gray, Yeshimbra "Shimmy" **55**
Green, Dennis **5, 45**
Greene, Joe **10**
Haskins, Clem **23**
Heard, Gar **25**
Johnson, Avery **62**
Jordan, Eddie **83**
Joyce, Dru **81**
Keith, Floyd A. **61**
Lewis, Marvin **51, 87**
Lofton, James **42**
Miller, Cheryl **10, 74**
Mitchell, Sam **82**
Morris, Raheem **77**
O'Neil, Buck **19, 59**
Parish, Robert **43**
Phillips, Teresa L. **42**
Rhodes, Ray **14**
Richardson, Nolan **9**
Rivers, Doc **25, 81**
Robinson, Eddie G. **10, 61**
Robinson, Frank **9, 87**
Robinson, Will **51, 69**
Russell, Bill **8**
Sanders, Satch **77**
Shannon, Randy **82**
Shell, Art **1, 66**
Silas, Paul **24**

Simmons, Bob **29**
Singletary, Mike **4, 76**
Smith, Lovie **66**
Smith, Tubby **18, 83**
Stringer, C. Vivian **13, 66**
Thomas, Emmitt **71**
Tunnell, Emlen **54**
White, Jesse **22, 75**
Williams, Doug **22**
Willingham, Tyrone **43**
Wills, Maury **73**

**Coalition of Black Trade Unionists**
Lucy, William **50**
Wyatt, Addie L. **56**

**Coca-Cola Company**
Llewellyn, J. Bruce **13, 85**
Ware, Carl T. **30**

**Coca-Cola Foundation**
Jones, Ingrid Saunders **18**

**Collage**
Andrews, Benny **22, 59**
Bearden, Romare **2, 50**
Driskell, David C. **7**
Pindell, Howardena **55**
Pinder, Jefferson **77**
Robinson, Aminah **50**
Saar, Betye **80**
Thomas, Mickalene **61**
Verna, Gelsy **70**

**College and university administration**
Ammons, James H. **81**
Archie-Hudson, Marguerite **44**
Barnett, Marguerite **46**
Bromery, Randolph Wilson **85**
Burnim, Mickey L. **48**
Christian, Barbara T. **44**
Davis, Erroll B., Jr. **57**
Ford, Nick Aaron **44**
Hill, Leslie Pinckney **44**
Hogan, Beverly Wade **50**
Horne, Frank **44**
Jackson, Edison O. **67**
King, Reatha Clark **65**
Lee, Joe A. **45**
Massey, Walter E. **5, 45**
Mell, Patricia **49**
Moody-Adams, Michele **76**
Nance, Cynthia **71**
Newman, Lester C. **51**
Page, Inman **82**
Ribeau, Sidney **70**
Trueheart, William E. **49**

**Colorado Rockies baseball team**
Baylor, Don **6**

**Colorado state government**
Brown, George Leslie **62**
Rogers, Joe **27**

**Columbia Broadcasting System (CBS)**
Bradley, Ed **2, 59**
Kellogg, Clark **64**
Mabrey, Vicki **26**
McEwen, Mark **5**
Mitchell, Russ **21, 73**

Olden, Georg(e) **44**
Pinkston, W. Randall **24**
Pitts, Byron **71**
Rodgers, Johnathan **6, 51**
Ware, Andre **37**

**Columbia Records**
Jackson, Randy **40**
Knowles, Tina **61**
Olatunji, Babatunde **36**
Williams, Deniece **36**

**Columbia University**
Huggins, Nathan Irvin **52**
Marable, Manning **10**
Moody-Adams, Michele **76**

**Comedy**
Allen, Byron **3, 24**
Amos, John **8, 62**
Anderson, Anthony **51, 77**
Anderson, Eddie "Rochester" **30**
Anthony, Trey **63**
Arnez J **53**
Beaton, Norman **14**
Bellamy, Bill **12**
Berry, Bertice **8, 55**
Brady, Wayne **32, 71**
Bruce, Bruce **56**
Cannon, Nick **47, 73**
Cedric the Entertainer **29, 60**
Chappelle, Dave **50**
Cosby, Bill **7, 26, 59**
Curry, Mark **17**
Davidson, Tommy **21**
Davis, Sammy, Jr. **18**
Dieudonné **67**
Earthquake **55**
Epps, Mike **60**
Foxx, Jamie **15, 48**
Foxx, Redd **2**
Freeman, Aaron **52**
Givens, Adele **62**
Glover, Donald **85**
Goldberg, Whoopi **4, 33, 69**
Harris, Robin **7**
Harvey, Steve **18, 58**
Henry, Lenny **9, 52**
Hughley, D. L. **23, 76**
Kirby, George **14**
Lawrence, Martin **6, 27, 60**
Mabley, Jackie "Moms" **15**
Mac, Bernie **29, 61, 72**
Mayo, Whitman **32**
McEwen, Mark **5**
Meadows, Tim **30**
Mooney, Paul **37**
Morgan, Tracy **61**
Morris, Garrett **31**
Moss, Preacher **63**
Murphy, Eddie **4, 20, 61**
Nash, Niecy **66**
Perry, Tyler **40, 54**
Pryor, Richard **3, 24, 56**
Rock, Chris **3, 22, 66**
Russell, Nipsey **66**
Schultz, Michael A. **6**
Slocumb, Jonathan **52**
Smiley, Rickey **59**
Sommore **61**
Sykes, Wanda **48, 81**
Thompson, Kenan **52**
Thurston, Baratunde **79**
Torry, Guy **31**

Townsend, Robert 4, 23
Tucker, Chris 13, 23, 62
Tyler, Aisha N. 36
Wayans, Damon 8, 41
Wayans, Keenen Ivory 18
Wayans, Kim 80
Wayans, Marlon 29, 82
Wayans, Shawn 29
Wilson, Debra 38
Wilson, Flip 21
Witherspoon, John 38
Yarbrough, Cedric 51

**Comerica Bank**
Forte, Linda Diane 54

**Commercial art**
Freeman, Leonard 27

**Communist Party**
Brown, Lloyd Louis 42
Davis, Angela 5
Du Bois, W. E. B. 3
Jagan, Cheddi 16
Wright, Richard 5

**Community activism**
Kimbro, Warren 76
Shakur, Yusef 85

**Complete Energy Partners**
Scott, Milton 51

**Complexions dance troupe**
Rhoden, Dwight 40
Richardson, Desmond 39
Tyson, Andre 40

**Computer graphics**
Coleman, Ken 57
Hannah, Marc 10

**Computer science**
Adkins, Rod 41
Auguste, Donna 29
Dean, Mark 35
Easley, Annie J. 61
Ellis, Clarence 38
Emeagwali, Philip 30
Hannah, Marc 10
Irvin, Vernon 65
Laryea, Thomas Davies, III 67
Mensah, Thomas 48
Millines Dziko, Trish 28
Zollar, Alfred 40

**Conceptual art**
Allen, Tina 22, 75
Bailey, Xenobia 11
Harris, Lyle Ashton 83
O'Grady, Lorraine 73
Piper, Adrian 71
Pope.L, William 72
Robinson, Aminah 50
Simpson, Lorna 4, 36

**Concerned Parents Association (Uganda)**
Atyam, Angelina 55

**Conductors**
Calloway, Cab 14
Cook, Will Marion 40
Dawson, William Levi 39
DePreist, James 37
Dixon, Dean 68

Dunner, Leslie B. 45
Freeman, Paul 39
Jackson, Isaiah 3
León, Tania 13
Lewis, Henry 38

**Congress of Racial Equality (CORE)**
Dee, Ruby 8, 50, 68
Farmer, James 2, 64
Hobson, Julius W. 44
Innis, Roy 5
Jackson, Jesse 1, 27, 72
McKissick, Floyd B. 3
Rustin, Bayard 4

**Congressional Black Caucus (CBC)**
Christian-Green, Donna M. 17
Clay, William Lacy 8
Clyburn, James E. 21, 71
Collins, Cardiss 10, 80
Conyers, John, Jr. 4, 45
Dellums, Ronald 2, 81
Diggs, Charles C. 21
Fauntroy, Walter E. 11
Gray, William H., III 3
Hastings, Alcee L. 16
Hawkins, Augustus F. 68
Johnson, Eddie Bernice 8
Mfume, Kweisi 6, 41
Mitchell, Parren J. 42, 66
Owens, Major 6
Payton, John 48
Rangel, Charles B. 3, 52, 85
Scott, Robert C. 23
Stokes, Louis 3
Thompson, Bennie G. 26
Towns, Edolphus 19, 75

**Contemporary Christian music**
Griffin, LaShell 51
Tait, Michael 57

**Continental Basketball Association (CBA)**
Davis, Mike 41
Thomas, Isiah 7, 26, 65
Ussery, Terdema, II 29

**Coppin State College**
Blair, Paul 36

**CORE**
See Congress of Racial Equality

**Coretta Scott King Awards**
Clifton, Lucille 14, 64
Curtis, Christopher Paul 26
Draper, Sharon Mills 16, 43
Fax, Elton 48
Greenfield, Eloise 9
Hamilton, Virginia 10
Haskins, James 36, 54
Johnson, Angela 52
Lester, Julius 9
Morrison, Toni 2, 15, 86
Rollins, Charlemae Hill 27
Taylor, Mildred D. 26

**Coronet**
Oliver, Joe "King" 42

**Corporation for Public Broadcasting (CPB)**
Brown, Tony 3

**Cosmetology**
Cottrell, Comer 11
Fuller, S. B. 13
McGrath, Pat 72
Morgan, Rose 11
Powell, Maxine 8
Roche, Joyce M. 17
Walker, A'lelia 14
Walker, Madame C. J. 7

**Cotton Club Revue**
Johnson, Buddy 36

**Council on Legal Education Opportunities (CLEO)**
Henderson, Wade J. 14
Henry, Aaron 19

**Count Basie Orchestra**
Eldridge, Roy 37
Johnson, J. J. 37
Powell, Benny 87
Rushing, Jimmy 37
Williams, Joe 5, 25
Young, Lester 37

**Country music**
Bailey, DeFord 33
Cowboy Troy 54
Palmer, Rissi 65
Pride, Charley 26
Randall, Alice 38
Rucker, Darius 34, 74

**Covad Communications**
Knowling, Robert 38

**Cowboys**
Love, Nat 9
Pickett, Bill 11

**CPB**
See Corporation for Public Broadcasting

**Creative Artists Agency**
Nelson Meigs, Andrea 48

**Credit Suisse First Boston, Inc.**
Ogunlesi, Adebayo 37

**Creole music**
Ardoin, Alphonse 65

**Cress Theory of Color Confrontation and Racism**
Welsing, Frances Cress 5

**Cricket**
Adams, Paul 50

**Critics' Choice Award**
Channer, Colin 36

**Cross Colours**
Jones, Carl 7
Kani, Karl 10
Walker, T. J. 7

**Crown Media**
Corbi, Lana 42

*Crusader*
Williams, Robert F. 11

**Cuban League**
Charleston, Oscar 39
Day, Leon 39

**Cuban military**
Maceo, Antonio 82

**Cuban music**
Ferrer, Ibrahim 41
Portuondo, Omara 53
Valdés, Bebo 75

**Cubism**
Bearden, Romare 2, 50
Green, Jonathan 54

**Culinary arts**
Allen, Eugene 79
Brown, Warren 61
Chase, Leah 57
Clark, Patrick 14
Estes, Rufus 29
Evans, Darryl 22
Garvin, Gerry 78
Henderson, Jeff 72
Ouattara, Morou 74
Samuelsson, Marcus 53

**Cultural Hangups**
Ham, Cynthia Parker 58

**Cultural pluralism**
Locke, Alain 10

**Cumulative voting**
Guinier, Lani 7, 30

**Curator/exhibition designer**
Amaki, Amalia 76
Camp, Kimberly 19
Campbell, Mary Schmidt 43
Golden, Thelma 10, 55
Hoyte, Lenon 50
Hutson, Jean Blackwell 16
Pindell, Howardena 55
Sanders, Joseph R., Jr. 11
Sims, Lowery Stokes 27
Stewart, Paul Wilbur 12

**Cy Young Award**
Gibson, Bob 33
Gooden, Dwight 20
Jenkins, Fergie 46
Martinez, Pedro 81
Newcombe, Don 24
Sabathia, CC 74

**Cycling**
Baugé, Grégory 86
Taylor, Marshall Walter "Major" 62
Yeboah, Emmanuel Ofosu 53

**Cytogenetics**
Satcher, David 7, 57

**Dallas city government**
Johnson, Eddie Bernice 8
Kirk, Ron 11, 75

**Dallas Cowboys football team**
Hayes, Bob 77
Hill, Calvin 19
Irvin, Michael 64
Jones, Ed "Too Tall" 46

Sanders, Deion **4, 31**
Smith, Emmitt **7, 87**
Wright, Rayfield **70**

**Dallas Police Department**
Bolton, Terrell D. **25**

**DanceAfrica**
Davis, Chuck **33**

**Dance Theatre of Harlem**
Johnson, Virginia **9**
King, Alonzo **38**
Mitchell, Arthur **2, 47**
Nicholas, Fayard **20, 57**
Nicholas, Harold **20**
Tyson, Cicely **7, 51**

**DAV**
See Disabled American Veterans

**Daytona Institute**
See Bethune-Cookman College

**D.C. sniper**
Moose, Charles **40**

**Death Row Records**
Dre, Dr. **10, 14, 30**
Knight, Suge **11, 30**
Shakur, Tupac **14**

**Decca Records**
Hardin Armstrong, Lil **39**

**Def Jam Records**
Jay-Z **27, 69**
Liles, Kevin **42**
Simmons, Russell **1, 30**

**Defense Communications Agency**
Gravely, Samuel L., Jr. **5, 49**

**Delta Sigma Theta Sorority**
Rice, Louise Allen **54**

**Democratic National Committee (DNC)**
Brown, Ron **5**
Dixon, Sharon Pratt **1**
Fattah, Chaka **11, 70**
Hamer, Fannie Lou **6**
Jackson, Maynard **2, 41**
Jordan, Barbara **4, 78**
Joyner, Marjorie Stewart **26**
Mallett, Conrad, Jr. **16**
Martin, Louis E. **16**
Moore, Minyon **45**
Waters, Maxine **3, 67**
Williams, Maggie **7, 71**

**Dentistry**
Bluitt, Juliann S. **14**
Delany, Bessie **12**
Gray, Ida **41**
Madison, Romell **45**
Sinkford, Jeanne C. **13**

**Denver Broncos football team**
Barnes, Ernie **16, 78**
Briscoe, Marlin **37**
Davis, Terrell **20**
Jackson, Tom **70**

Little, Floyd **86**

**Denver city government**
Webb, Wellington **3, 81**

**Denver Nuggets basketball team**
Bickerstaff, Bernie **21**
Bynoe, Peter C. B. **40**
Hardaway, Tim **35**
Lee, Bertram M., Sr. **46**
Mutombo, Dikembe **7**

**DePaul University**
Braun, Carol Moseley **4, 42**
Sizemore, Barbara A. **26**

**Depression/The Great Depression**
Hampton, Henry **6**

**Dermatology**
Taylor, Susan C. **62**

**Desert Shield/Desert Storm**
See Operation Desert Shield/Operation Desert Storm

**Destiny's Child**
Beyoncé **39, 70**
Knowles, Tina **61**
Luckett, Letoya **61**
Williams, Michelle **73**

**Detective fiction**
Bates, Karen Grigsby **40**
Bland, Eleanor Taylor **39**
DeLoach, Nora **30**
Hayes, Teddy **40**
Haywood, Gar Anthony **43**
Himes, Chester **8**
Holton, Hugh, Jr. **39**
Mosley, Walter **5, 25, 68**
Wesley, Valerie Wilson **18**

**Detroit Bible Institute**
Patterson, Gilbert Earl **41**

**Detroit city government**
Archer, Dennis **7, 36**
Bing, Dave **3, 59, 78**
Cockrel, Kenneth V., Jr. **79**
Cockrel, Kenneth Vern, Sr. **79**
Collins, Barbara-Rose **7, 87**
Conyers, Monica **85**
Crockett, George W., Jr. **10, 64**
Evans, Warren C. **76**
Garrett, Joyce Finley **59**
Kilpatrick, Kwame **34, 71**
Marshall, Bella **22**
Pugh, Charles **81**
Reeves, Martha **85**
Young, Coleman **1, 20**

**Detroit Golden Gloves**
Wilson, Sunnie **7, 55**

**Detroit Lions football team**
Barney, Lem **26**
Farr, Mel **24**
Johnson, Levi **48**
Mayhew, Martin R. **76**
Sanders, Barry **1, 53**
Ware, Andre **37**

**Detroit Pistons basketball team**
Bing, Dave **3, 59, 78**
Dumars, Joe **16, 65**
Gentry, Alvin **23**
Hill, Grant **13**
Lanier, Bob **47**
Lloyd, Earl **26**
Lowe, Sidney **64**
Mahorn, Rick **60**
Mohammed, Nazr **64**
Prince, Tayshaun **68**
Robinson, Will **51, 69**
Stackhouse, Jerry **30**
Thomas, Isiah **7, 26, 65**
Wallace, Ben **54**
Webber, Chris **15, 30, 59**

**Detroit Police Department**
Bully-Cummings, Ella **48**
Gomez-Preston, Cheryl **9**
McKinnon, Isaiah **9**
Napoleon, Benny N. **23**

**Detroit Public Schools**
Coleman, William F., III **61**

**Detroit Tigers baseball team**
Fielder, Cecil **2**
Granderson, Curtis **66**
Sheffield, Gary **16**
Virgil, Ozzie **48**

**Diabetes**
Fennoy, Ilene **72**
Wisdom, Kimberlydawn **57**

**Diamond mining**
Masire, Quett **5**

**Dictators**
Abacha, Sani **11, 70**
Ahidjo, Ahmadou **81**
Amin, Idi **42**
Biya, Paul **28**
Compaore, Blaise **87**
Eyadéma, Gnassingbé **7, 52**
Habré, Hissène **6**
Kabila, Laurent **20**
Meles Zenawi **3**
Mengistu, Haile Mariam **65**
Moi, Daniel Arap **1, 35**
Mswati III **56**
Mugabe, Robert **10, 71**
Touré, Sekou **6**

**Digital divide**
Adkins, Rod **41**

**Dillard University**
Cook, Samuel DuBois **14**
Lomax, Michael L. **58**

**Dime Savings Bank**
Parsons, Richard Dean **11**

**Diner's Club**
Gaines, Brenda **41**

**Diplomatic Corps**
See U.S. Department of State

**Director's Guild of America**
Barclay, Paris **37**

**Disabled American Veterans (DAV)**
Brown, Jesse **6, 41**

**Disco**
Gaynor, Gloria **36**
Payne, Freda **58**
Perren, Freddie **60**
Staton, Candi **27**
Summer, Donna **25**

**Distance running**
Cheruiyot, Robert **69**
Loroupe, Tegla **59**
Tergat, Paul **59**

**Diving**
Brashear, Carl **29**

**DJ**
Alert, Kool DJ Red **32**
Atkins, Juan **50**
Bond, Beverly **53**
DJ Jazzy Jeff **32**
Grandmaster Flash **33, 60**
Knuckles, Frankie **42**
Love, Ed **58**

**DNC**
See Democratic National Committee

**Documentary film**
Billops, Camille **82**
Blackwood, Maureen **37**
Branch, William Blackwell **39**
Byrd, Robert **11**
Dash, Julie **4**
Davis, Ossie **5, 50**
Gray, Darius **69**
Greaves, William **38**
Hampton, Henry **6**
Henry, Lenny **9, 52**
Hudlin, Reginald **9, 86**
Hudlin, Warrington **9**
Hurt, Byron **61**
Jean, Michaëlle; **70**
Julien, Isaac **3**
Lynch, Shola **61**
Peck, Raoul **32**
Riggs, Marlon **5, 44**
Roberts, Kimberly Rivers **72**
Whack, Rita Coburn **36**
Williams, Marco **53**

**Dollmaking**
El Wilson, Barbara **35**

**Dominica government**
Charles, Mary Eugenia **10, 55**
Charles, Pierre **52**
Skerrit, Roosevelt **72**

**Dove Award**
Baylor, Helen **36**
Winans, CeCe **14, 43**

***Down Beat*** Jazz Hall of Fame
Terry, Clark **39**

**Drama Desk Awards**
Carter, Nell **39**
Taylor, Ron **35**

Wesley, Richard 73

**Dreamland Orchestra**
Cook, Charles "Doc" 44

**Drug abuse prevention**
Clements, George 2
Creagh, Milton 27
Hale, Lorraine 8
Harris, Alice 7
Lucas, John 7

**Drug synthesis**
Julian, Percy Lavon 6
Pickett, Cecil 39

**Drums**
Ali, Rashied 79
Blakey, Art 37
Brown, Carlinhos 81
Durham, Bobby 73
Güines, Tata 69
Haynes, Roy 87
Jones, Elvin 14, 68
Locke, Eddie 44
Miles, Buddy 69
Purdie, Bernard 77
Rodríguez, Arsenio 87
Williams, Tony 67
Young, Lee 72

**Duke Ellington School of Arts**
Cooper Cafritz, Peggy 43

**Duke Records**
Bland, Bobby "Blue" 36

**Dunham Dance Company**
Dunham, Katherine 4, 59

**DuSable Museum of African American History**
Burroughs, Margaret Taylor 9
Wright, Antoinette 60

**Dynegy**
Scott, Milton 51

**E Street Band**
Clemons, Clarence 41

**East Harlem School at Exodus House**
Hageman, Hans 36
Hageman, Ivan 36

**Ebonics**
Cook, Toni 23

*Ebony* magazine
Bennett, Lerone, Jr. 5, 84
Branch, William Blackwell 39
Cullers, Vincent T. 49
Fuller, Hoyt 44
Johnson, Eunice W. 83
Johnson, John H. 3, 54
Massaquoi, Hans J. 30
Rice, Linda Johnson 9, 41
Sleet, Moneta, Jr. 5

**Ebony Museum of African American History**
See DuSable Museum of African American History

**Economic Community of West African States (ECOWAS)**
Sawyer, Amos 2

**Economic Regulatory Administration**
O'Leary, Hazel 6

**Economics**
Ake, Claude 30
Arthur, Owen 33
Boyd, T. B., III 6
Brimmer, Andrew F. 2, 48
Brown, Tony 3
Divine, Father 7
Fryer, Roland G. 56
Gibson, William F. 6
Hamer, Fannie Lou 6
Hampton, Henry 6
Juma, Calestous 57
Machel, Graca Simbine 16
Malveaux, Julianne 32, 70
Masire, Quett 5
Moyo, Dambisa 76
Pitta, Celso 17
Raines, Franklin Delano 14
Robinson, Randall 7, 46
Sowell, Thomas 2
Spriggs, William 67
Sullivan, Leon H. 3, 30
Van Peebles, Melvin 7
Wallace, Phyllis A. 9
Washington, Ebonya 79
Wharton, Clifton R., Jr. 7
White, Michael R. 5
Williams, Walter E. 4
Woodson, Robert L. 10

**ECOWAS**
See Economic Community of West African States

**Editing**
Abani, Chris 77
Aubert, Alvin 41
Bass, Charlotta Spears 40
Brown, Lloyd Louis 42
Curry, George E. 23
Delany, Martin R. 27
Dumas, Henry 41
Murphy, John H. 42
Schuyler, George Samuel 40

**Edmonton Oilers hockey team**
Fuhr, Grant 1, 49
Grier, Mike 43
Laraque, Georges 48

**Educational Testing Service**
Stone, Chuck 9

**EEC**
See European Economic Community

**EEOC**
See Equal Employment Opportunity Commission

**Egyptology**
Diop, Cheikh Anta 4

**Elder Foundation**
Elder, Lee 6

**Electronic music**
Craig, Carl 31, 71

**Elektra Records**
McPherson, David 32

*Emerge (Savoy)* magazine
Ames, Wilmer 27
Curry, George E. 23

**Emmy awards**
Allen, Debbie 13, 42
Amos, John 8, 62
Ashe, Arthur 1, 18
Barclay, Paris 37
Belafonte, Harry 4, 65
Bradley, Ed 2, 59
Branch, William Blackwell 39
Brown, James 22
Brown, Les 5
Browne, Roscoe Lee 66
Carter, Nell 39
Clayton, Xernona 3, 45
Cosby, Bill 7, 26, 59
Curtis-Hall, Vondie 17
De Shields, André 72
Dee, Ruby 8, 50, 68
Fisher, Gail 85
Foxx, Redd 2
Freeman, Al, Jr. 11
Goldberg, Whoopi 4, 33, 69
Gossett, Louis, Jr. 7
Guillaume, Robert 3, 48
Gumbel, Greg 8
Hunter-Gault, Charlayne 6, 31
Jones, James Earl 3, 49, 79
Kitt, Eartha 16, 75
La Salle, Eriq 12
Mabrey, Vicki 26
McQueen, Butterfly 6, 54
Moore, Shemar 21
Parks, Gordon 1, 35, 58
Pinkston, W. Randall 24
Quarles, Norma 25
Richards, Beah 30
Robinson, Max 3
Rock, Chris 3, 22, 66
Rolle, Esther 13, 21
St. John, Kristoff 25
Taylor, Billy 23
Thigpen, Lynne 17, 41
Tyson, Cicely 7, 51
Uggams, Leslie 23
Washington, Hayma 86
Wayans, Damon 8, 41
Whack, Rita Coburn 36
Whitfield, Lynn 18
Williams, Montel 4, 57
Williams, Russell, II 70
Williams, Sherley Anne 25
Winfrey, Oprah 2, 15, 61
Woodard, Alfre 9

**Emory University**
Cole, Johnnetta B. 5, 43

**Endocrinology**
Elders, Joycelyn 6
Fennoy, Ilene 72

**Energy**
Cose, Ellis 5, 50
Lawal, Kase L. 45

O'Leary, Hazel 6

**Engineering**
Alexander, Archie Alphonso 14
Anderson, Charles Edward 37
Auguste, Donna 29
Benson, Angela 34
Boyd, Gwendolyn 49
Burns, Ursula 60
Emeagwali, Philip 30
Ericsson-Jackson, Aprille 28
Gibson, Kenneth Allen 6
Gourdine, Meredith 33
Grooms, Henry R(andall) 50
Hannah, Marc 10
Harris, Gary L. 87
Henderson, Cornelius Langston 26
Howard, Ayanna 65
Jones, Wayne 53
Laroche, Joseph Philippe Lemercier 85
Laryea, Thomas Davies, III 67
McCoy, Elijah 8
Miller, Warren F., Jr. 53
Mills, Joseph C. 51
Pierre, Percy Anthony 46
Price, Richard 51
Sigur, Wanda 44
Slaughter, John Brooks 53
Spencer, Michael G. 87
Trotter, Lloyd G. 56
West, James E. 87
Wilkens, J. Ernest, Jr. 43
Williams, O. S. 13

**Entertainment promotion**
Bowen, Ruth 83
Lewis, Butch 71

**Environmental issues**
Carter, Majora 77
Eugene-Richard, Margie 63
Hill, Bonnie Guiton 20
Jackson, Lisa 77
Jones, Van 70
Miller-Travis, Vernice 64
Osborne, Na'taki 54

**Epic Records**
McPherson, David 32
Mo', Keb' 36

**Epidemiology**
Fenton, Kevin 87
Gayle, Helene D. 3
Poindexter, Hildrus A. 87

**Episcopalian**
Burgess, John 46
Harris, Barbara 12
Jones, Absalom 52
Redding, Ann Holmes 77
Walker, John T. 50
Williams, Frederick (B.) 63

**Equal Employment Opportunity Commission (EEOC)**
Alexander, Clifford 26
Hill, Anita 5, 65
Lewis, Delano 7
Norton, Eleanor Holmes 7
Thomas, Clarence 2, 39, 65

Wallace, Phyllis A. 9

**Equality Now**
Jones, Sarah 39

**Esalen Institute**
Olatunji, Babatunde 36

**ESPN**
Jackson, Tom 70
Roberts, Robin 16, 54
Salters, Lisa 71
Scott, Stuart 34
Smith, Stephen A. 69
Tirico, Mike 68
Wilbon, Michael 68

*Essence* magazine
Bandele, Asha 36
Burt-Murray, Angela 59
Channer, Colin 36
De Veaux, Alexis 44
Ebanks, Michelle 60
Grant, Gwendolyn Goldsby 28
Greenwood, Monique 38
Lewis, Edward T. 21
Parks, Gordon 1, 35, 58
Smith, Clarence O. 21
Taylor, Susan L. 10, 86
Wesley, Valerie Wilson 18

*Essence* Award
Broadbent, Hydeia 36
McMurray, Georgia L. 36

**Ethiopian government**
Haile Selassie 7
Meles Zenawi 3
Mengistu, Haile Mariam 65

**Etiquette**
Bates, Karen Grigsby 40

**Eugene O'Neill Theater**
Richards, Lloyd 2

**European Economic Community (EEC)**
Diouf, Abdou 3

**Event planning**
Bailey, Preston 64
Williams, Lindsey 75

**Executive Leadership Council**
Jackson, Mannie 14

**Exiled heads of state**
Aristide, Jean-Bertrand 6, 45

**Exploration**
Henson, Matthew 2

**Fair Share Agreements**
Gibson, William F. 6

**Famine relief**
See World hunger

**FAN**
See Forces Armées du Nord (Chad)

**Fannie Mae**
Jackson, Maynard 2, 41
Raines, Franklin Delano 14

**Fashion**
Aberra, Amsale 67
Boateng, Ozwald 35

Boyd, Suzanne 52
Darego, Agbani 52
Delice, Ronald 48
Delice, Rony 48
Evans, Etu 55
Fine, Sam 60
Gaskins, Eric 64
Givhan, Robin Deneen 72
Hall, Kevan 61
Hendy, Francis 47
Knowles, Tina 61
Lars, Byron 32
Malone, Maurice 32
McGrath, Pat 72
Reese, Tracy 54
Sade 15
Simmons, Kimora Lee 51, 83
Smaltz, Audrey 12
Steele, Lawrence 28
Stoney, Michael 50
Sy, Oumou 65
Talley, André Leon 56
White, Jessica 83

**Fashion Institute of Technology (FIT)**
Brown, Joyce F. 25

**Fast 50 Awards**
Steward, David L. 36

**FCC**
See Federal Communications Commission

**Federal Bureau of Investigation (FBI)**
Gibson, Johnnie Mae 23
Harvard, Beverly 11

**Federal Communications Commission (FCC)**
Barrett, Andrew C. 12
Clyburn, Mignon 78
Hughes, Cathy 27
Kennard, William Earl 18
Powell, Michael 32
Russell-McCloud, Patricia A. 17

**Federal Court of Canada**
Isaac, Julius 34

**Federal Energy Administration**
O'Leary, Hazel 6

**Federal Reserve Bank**
Brimmer, Andrew F. 2, 48
Ferguson, Roger W. 25
Layton, William 87

**Federation of Nigeria**
Sowande, Fela 39

**Feed the Hungry program**
Williams, Hosea Lorenzo 15, 31

**Fellowship of Reconciliation (FOR)**
Farmer, James 2, 64
Rustin, Bayard 4

**Feminist studies**
Carby, Hazel 27
Christian, Barbara T. 44
De Veaux, Alexis 44
Hull, Akasha Gloria 45

Smith, Barbara 28
Walker, Rebecca 50

**Fencing**
Westbrook, Peter 20

**Fiction**
Adams, Jenoyne 60
Adichie, Chimamanda Ngozi 64
Alexander, Margaret Walker 22
Ali, Mohammed Naseehu 60
Amadi, Elechi 40
Anthony, Michael 29
Ansa, Tina McElroy 14
Armah, Ayi Kwei 49
Ba, Mariama 30
Baiocchi, Regina Harris 41
Baisden, Michael 25, 66
Ballard, Allen Butler, Jr. 40
Bandele, Biyi 68
Barrett, Lindsay 43
Bates, Karen Grigsby 40
Beckham, Barry 41
Benson, Angela 34
Berry, James 41
Bland, Eleanor Taylor 39
Bolden, Tonya 32
Bradley, David Henry, Jr. 39
Brand, Dionne 32
Briscoe, Connie 15
Brown, Cecil M. 46
Brown, Lloyd Louis 42
Bunkley, Anita Richmond 39
Butler, Octavia 8, 43, 58
Campbell, Bebe Moore 6, 24, 59
Cartiér, Xam Wilson 41
Chase-Riboud, Barbara 20, 46
Cheney-Coker, Syl 43
Chesnutt, Charles 29
Clarke, Austin 32
Cleage, Pearl 17, 64
Cliff, Michelle 42
Cooper, J. California 12, 85
Creagh, Milton 27
Curtis, Christopher Paul 26
Danticat, Edwidge 15, 68
Dathorne, O. R. 52
Demby, William 51
Diop, Birago 53
Draper, Sharon Mills 16, 43
Due, Tananarive 30
Dumas, Henry 41
Dunbar-Nelson, Alice Ruth Moore 44
Duplechan, Larry 55
Emecheta, Buchi 30
Evans, Diana 72
Fair, Ronald L. 47
Farah, Nuruddin 27
Farley, Christopher John 54
Files, Lolita 35
Ford, Nick Aaron 44
Ford, Wallace 58
Forrest, Leon 44
Gomez, Jewelle 30
Gray, Darius 69
Greenlee, Sam 48
Harris, E. Lynn 12, 33
Haywood, Gar Anthony 43
Hercules, Frank 44
Hill, Donna 32
Holton, Hugh, Jr. 39
Horne, Frank 44

Jackson, Sheneska 18
Jakes, Thomas "T. D." 17, 43
James, Marlon 85
Jasper, Kenji 39
Jenkins, Beverly 14
Johnson, Georgia Douglas 41
Johnson, Mat 31
Jones, Edward P. 43, 67
Jones, Gayl 37
Kamau, Kwadwo Agymah 28
Kay, Jackie 37
Kayira, Legson 40
Keene, John 73
Kendrick, Erika 57
Killens, John O. 54
Laferriere, Dany 33
LaGuma, Alex 30
Lamming, George 35
Locke, Attica 85
Machado de Assis 74
Marechera, Dambudzo 39
Markham, E. A. 37
Mason, Felicia 31
Mbaye, Mariétou 31
McCrary Anthony, Crystal 70
McFadden, Bernice L. 39
McKinney-Whetstone, Diane 27
McMillan, Terry 4, 17, 53
Memmi, Albert 37
Mengestu, Dinaw 66
Monroe, Mary 35
Mosley, Walter 5, 25, 68
Mossell, Gertrude Bustill 40
Mphalele, Es'kia 40
Mwangi, Meja 40
Naylor, Gloria 10, 42
Ngugi wa Thiong'o 29, 61
Nkosi, Lewis 46
Nugent, Richard Bruce 39
Nunez, Elizabeth 62
Okara, Gabriel 37
Ojikutu, Bayo 66
Packer, Z. Z. 64
Peters, Lenrie 43
Philip, Marlene Nourbese 32
Polite, Carlene Hatcher 82
Randall, Alice 38
Ridley, John 69
Roby, Kimberla Lawson 86
Saro-Wiwa, Kenule 39
Schuyler, George Samuel 40
Senior, Olive 37
Smith, Danyel 40
Smith, Zadie 51
Southgate, Martha 58
Tate, Eleanora E. 20, 55
Taylor, Mildred D. 26
Thomas, Michael 69
Thomas-Graham, Pamela 29
Tutuola, Amos 30
Vera, Yvonne 32
Verdelle, A. J. 26
Walker, Margaret 29
Weaver, Afaa Michael 37
Whitehead, Colson 77
Whitfield, Van 34
Williams, Sherley Anne 25
Williams, Stanley "Tookie" 29, 57
Woods, Teri 69
Yarbrough, Camille 40
Young, Al 82
Youngblood, Shay 32

Zane 71

**Figure skating**
Bonaly, Surya 7
Bonheur, Yannick 84
James, Vanessa 84
Thomas, Debi 26
Vanessa James and Yannick Bonheur 84

**Film criticism**
Mitchell, Elvis 67

**Film direction/video direction**
Akomfrah, John 37
Allain, Stephanie 49
Barclay, Paris 37
Blackwood, Maureen 37
Burnett, Charles 16, 68
Byrd, Robert 11
Cortez, Jayne 43
Curtis-Hall, Vondie 17
Daniels, Lee 36, 76
Dash, Julie 4
Davis, Ossie 5, 50
Dickerson, Ernest 6, 17
Duke, Bill 3
Franklin, Carl 11
Freeman, Al, Jr. 11
Fuqua, Antoine 35
Gerima, Haile 38, 80
Gray, Darius 69
Gray, F. Gary 14, 49
Greaves, William 38
Harris, Leslie 6
Hayes, Teddy 40
Henriques, Julian 37
Hines, Gregory 1, 42
Hudlin, Reginald 9, 86
Hudlin, Warrington 9
Hughes, Albert 7
Hughes, Allen 7
Hurt, Byron 61
Jackson, George 19
Julien, Isaac 3
Lane, Charles 3
Lee, Malcolm D. 75
Lee, Spike 5, 19, 86
Lemmons, Kasi 20
Lewis, Samella 25
Martin, Darnell 43, 78
McQueen, Steve 84
Micheaux, Oscar 7
Morton, Joe 18
Moses, Gilbert 12
Moss, Carlton 17
Mwangi, Meja 40
Onwurah, Ngozi 38
Peck, Raoul 32
Perry, Tyler 40, 54
Pinkett Smith, Jada 10, 41
Poitier, Sidney 11, 36
Prince-Bythewood, Gina 31, 77
Riggs, Marlon 5, 44
Roberts, Darryl 70
St. Jacques, Raymond 8
Schultz, Michael A. 6
Sembène, Ousmane 13, 62
Singleton, John 2, 30
Smith, Roger Guenveur 12
Souleymane, Mahamane 78
Tillman, George, Jr. 20
Townsend, Robert 4, 23
Tyler, Aisha N. 36

Underwood, Blair 7, 27, 76
Van Peebles, Mario 2, 51
Van Peebles, Melvin 7
Wallace, William 75
Ward, Douglas Turner 42
Wayans, Damon 8, 41
Wayans, Keenen Ivory 18
Whitaker, Forest 2, 49, 67

**Film production**
Allain, Stephanie 49
Chase, Debra Martin 49
Daniels, Lee 36, 76
Gerima, Haile 38, 80
Greaves, William 38
Hines, Gregory 1, 42
Lewis, Emmanuel 36
Morrison, Vanessa 84
Onwurah, Ngozi 38
Packer, Will 71
Patton, Paula 62
Poitier, Sidney 11, 36
Randall, Alice 38
Robinson, Matt 69
Tyler, Aisha N. 36
Van Lierop, Robert 53
Ward, Douglas Turner 42
Wayans, Damien 78
Whitaker, Forest 2, 49, 67
Williams, Marco 53
Williams, Russell, II 70
Williamson, Fred 67

**Film scores**
Blanchard, Terence 43
Crouch, Andraé 27
Hancock, Herbie 20, 67
Jones, Quincy 8, 30
Prince 18, 65
RZA 80

**Finance**
Adams, Eula L. 39
Banks, Jeffrey 17
Bell, James A. 50
Boston, Kelvin E. 25
Brown, Eddie C. 35
Bryant, John 26
Chapman, Nathan A., Jr. 21
Doley, Harold, Jr. 26
Epperson, Sharon 54
Ferguson, Roger W. 25
Fletcher, Alphonse, Jr. 16
Funderburg, I. Owen 38
Gaines, Brenda 41
Griffith, Mark Winston 8
Hall, Alvin D. 86
Harris, Carla A. 67
Hobson, Mellody 40
Jones, Thomas W. 41
Lawless, Theodore K. 8
Lewis, William M., Jr. 40
Louis, Errol T. 8
Marshall, Bella 22
Moyo, Dambisa 76
Nash, Shannon King 84
O'Neal, Stanley 38, 67
Rogers, John W., Jr. 5, 52
Ross, Charles 27
Shank, Suzanne F. 77
Thompson, William C. 35

**Firefighters**
Barlow, Roosevelt 49
Bell, Michael 40

**First Data Corporation**
Adams, Eula L. 39

**Fisk University**
Harvey, William R. 42
Imes, Elmer Samuel 39
Johnson, Charles S. 12
Phillips, Teresa L. 42
Smith, John L. 22

**Fitness**
Richardson, Donna 39
Smith, Ian 62

**Florida A & M University**
Ammons, James H. 81
Gaither, Alonzo Smith (Jake) 14
Humphries, Frederick 20
Meek, Kendrick 41

**Florida Marlins baseball team**
Mariner, Jonathan 41
Sheffield, Gary 16

**Florida state government**
Brown, Corrine 24
Meek, Carrie 6
Meek, Kendrick 41
Tribble, Israel, Jr. 8

**Florida State Supreme Court**
Quince, Peggy A. 69

**Fluoride chemistry**
Quarterman, Lloyd Albert 4

**Focus Detroit Electronic Music Festival**
May, Derrick 41

**Folk music**
Bailey, DeFord 33
Broonzy, Big Bill 82
Chapman, Tracy 26
Charlemagne, Manno 11
Cuney, William Waring 44
Davis, Gary 41
Dawson, William Levi 39
Handy, W. C. 8
Harper, Ben 34, 62
House, Son 8
Jenkins, Ella 15
Johnson, James Weldon 5
Lester, Julius 9
Love, Laura 50
Odetta 37, 74
Reagon, Toshi 76
Southern, Eileen 56
Spence, Joseph 49
White, Josh 86
Williams, Denise 40

**Food products**
Amos, Wally 9
Briggs, Curtis 84

**Football**
Buchanan, Ray 32
Bush, Reggie 59
Carter, Cris 21
Clemons, Michael "Pinball" 64
Davis, Ernie 48

Dorrell, Karl 52
Dungy, Tony 17, 42, 59
Gaither, Alonzo Smith (Jake) 14
Gill, Turner 83
Gorden, W. C. 71
Grier, Roosevelt 13
Jones, Ed "Too Tall" 46
Keith, Floyd A. 61
Lanier, Willie 33
Lewis, Marvin 51, 87
McNabb, Donovan 29
Parker, Jim 64
Perry, Lowell 30
Pollard, Fritz 53
Prince, Ron 64
Robinson, Eddie G. 10, 61
Shannon, Randy 82
Simmons, Bob 29
Smith, Lovie 66
Watts, J. C., Jr. 14, 38
Weathers, Carl 10
Willingham, Tyrone 43
Willis, Bill 68
Woodson, Rod 79

**Football Hall of Fame, professional**
Allen, Marcus 20
Barney, Lem 26
Briscoe, Marlin 37
Brown, Jim 11
Dickerson, Eric 27
Green, Darrell 39, 74
Greene, Joe 10
Hayes, Bob 77
Irvin, Michael 64
Lanier, Willie 33
Little, Floyd 86
Lofton, James 42
Lott, Ronnie 9
McDaniel, Randall Cornell 81
Monk, Art 38, 73
Moon, Warren 8, 66
Motley, Marion 26
Newsome, Ozzie 26
Page, Alan (Cedric) 7
Parker, Jim 64
Payton, Walter (Jerry) 11, 25
Pollard, Fritz 53
Randle, John 87
Sanders, Barry 1, 53
Sayers, Gale 28
Shell, Art 1, 66
Simpson, O. J. 15
Singletary, Mike 4, 76
Smith, Bruce 80
Smith, Emmitt 7, 87
Swann, Lynn 28
Taylor, Lawrence 25
Thomas, Derrick 25
Thomas, Emmitt 71
Thomas, Thurman 75
Tunnell, Emlen 54
Upshaw, Gene 18, 47, 72
White, Reggie 1961-2004 6, 50
Willis, Bill 68
Winslow, Kellen 83
Woodson, Rod 79
Wright, Rayfield 70

**FOR**
See Fellowship of Reconciliation

**Forces Armées du Nord (Chad; FAN)**
Déby, Idriss 30
Habré, Hissène 6

**Ford Foundation**
Franklin, Robert M. 13
Thomas, Franklin A. 5, 49

**Ford Motor Company**
Cherry, Deron 40
Dawson, Matel, Jr. 39
Goldsberry, Ronald 18
Hazel, Darryl B. 50
McMillan, Rosalynn A. 36

**Fordham University**
Blair, Paul 36
McMurray, Georgia L. 36

**Foreign policy**
Bunche, Ralph J. 5
Frazer, Jendayi 68
Rice, Condoleezza 3, 28, 72
Robinson, Randall 7, 46

**Forensic science**
Griffin, Bessie Blout 43

**Forest Club**
Wilson, Sunnie 7, 55

**Foster care**
Hale, Clara 16
Hale, Lorraine 8

**Fox Broadcasting Company**
Corbi, Lana 42
McFarland, Roland 49
Oliver, Pam 54
Strahan, Michael 35, 81

**FPI**
See Ivorian Popular Front

**Frank H. Williams Caribbean Cultural Center African Diaspora Institute**
Vega, Marta Moreno 61

**Freddie Mac**
Baker, Maxine 28

**Frederick Douglass Caring Award**
Broadbent, Hydeia 36

**Frederick Douglass Memorial Hospital**
Mossell, Gertrude Bustill 40

**French West Africa**
Camara, Moussa Dadis 76
Diouf, Abdou 3
Ndiaye, Iba 74

**Funeral homes**
March, William Carrington 56

**Funk music**
Ayers, Roy 16
Brown, James 15, 60
Clinton, George 9
Collins, Bootsy 31
Collins, Lyn 53
Love, Laura 50
Monáe, Janelle 86
Parker, Maceo 72

Parker, Ray, Jr. 85
Purdie, Bernard 77
Richie, Lionel 27, 65
Shider, Garry 87
Stone, Sly 85
Watson, Johnny "Guitar" 18

**Fusion**
Davis, Miles 4
Jones, Quincy 8, 30
Williams, Tony 67

**Gabonese government**
Bongo, Ali Ben 80
Bongo, Omar 1, 79

**Gambling**
Ivey, Phil 72

**Gangs**
Taylor, Bo 72
Shakur, Yusef 85
Williams, Stanley "Tookie" 29, 57

*Gary Post-Tribune*
Ross, Don 27

**Gassaway, Crosson, Turner & Parsons**
Parsons, James 14

**Gay and Lesbian Activism**
De Veaux, Alexis 44

**Gay Men of Color Consortium**
Wilson, Phill 9

**Genealogy**
Allen, Lucy 85
Blockson, Charles L. 42
Dash, Julie 4
Haley, Alex 4

*General Hospital* TV series
Cash, Rosalind 28

**General Motors Corporation**
O'Neal, Stanley 38, 67
Roberts, Roy S. 14
Welburn, Edward T. 50

**Genetech**
Potter, Myrtle 40

**Genetics**
Dunston, Georgia Mae 48
Harris, Mary Styles 31
Kittles, Rick 51
Olopade, Olufunmilayo Falusi 58

**Geometric symbolism**
Douglas, Aaron 7

**Geophysics**
Person, Waverly 9, 51

**George Foster Peabody Broadcasting Award**
Bradley, Ed 2, 59
Hunter-Gault, Charlayne 6, 31
Mac, Bernie 29, 61, 72
Shaw, Bernard 2

**George Mason University**
Dunn, Jerry 27
Wilkins, Roger 2, 84

**George Washington University**
Carter, Joye Maureen 41

**Georgia state government**
Baker, Thurbert 22
Bishop, Sanford D., Jr. 24
Bond, Julian 2, 35
Brooks, Tyrone 59
Johnson, Hank, Jr. 80
Majette, Denise 41
McKinney, Cynthia 11, 52, 74
Reed, Kasim 82
Scott, David 41
Williams, Hosea Lorenzo 15, 31

**Georgia State Supreme Court**
Benham, Robert 78
Melton, Harold D. 79
Sears, Leah Ward 5, 79

**Ghanaian government**
Atta Mills, John 75
Awoonor, Kofi 37
Bartels, Peggielene 80
Kufuor, John Agyekum 54, 82
Nkrumah, Kwame 3
Rawlings, Jerry 9

**Girl Scouts of the USA**
Thompson, Cynthia Bramlett 50

**Goddard Space Flight Center**
Ericsson-Jackson, Aprille 28

**Gold Mind, Inc.**
Elliott, Missy 31

**Golden Globe awards**
Allen, Debbie 13, 42
Bassett, Angela 6, 23, 62
Cara, Irene 77
Carroll, Diahann 9
Fisher, Gail 85
Freeman, Morgan 2, 20, 62
Ross, Diana 8, 27
Taylor, Regina 9, 46

**Golden Pen award**
McFadden, Bernice L. 39

**Golden State Warriors basketball team**
Lucas, John 7
Parish, Robert 43
Sprewell, Latrell 23

**Golf**
Elder, Lee 6
Gibson, Althea 8, 43
Gregory, Ann 63
Jackson, Fred James 25
Peete, Calvin 11
Powell, William J. 82
Richmond, Mitch 19
Shippen, John 43
Sifford, Charlie 4, 49
Spiller, Bill 64
Woods, Tiger 14, 31, 81

**Goodwill ambassador**
Terry, Clark 39

**Gospel music**
Adams, Oleta 18
Adams, Yolanda 17, 67

Armstrong, Vanessa Bell 24
Baylor Helen 36
Bonds, Margaret 39
Bradley, J. Robert 65
Caesar, Shirley 19
Cage, Byron 53
Clark, Mattie Moss 61
Clark-Cole, Dorinda 66
Clark-Sheard, Karen 22
Cleveland, James 19
Christie, Angella 36
Cooke, Sam 17
Crouch, Andraé 27
Davis, Gary 41
Dorsey, Thomas 15
Franklin, Aretha 11, 44
Franklin, Kirk 15, 49
Gaynor, Gloria 36
Green, Al 13, 47, 74
Haddon, Dietrick 55
Hammond, Fred 23
Hawkins, Tramaine 16
Hawkins, Walter 87
Higginsen, Vy 65
Houston, Cissy 20, 83
Jackson, Mahalia 5
Jakes, Thomas "T. D." 17, 43
Jeter, Claude 75
Jones, Bobby 20
Kee, John P. 43
Kenoly, Ron 45
Killings, Debra 57
Knight, Gladys 16, 66
Knight, Marie 80
Lassiter, Roy 24
Little Richard 15
Majors, Jeff 41
Marrow, Queen Esther 24
Martin, Roberta 58
Mary Mary 34
Mayfield, Curtis 2, 43
McClendon, Lisa 61
McClurkin, Donnie 25
Mills, Stephanie 36
Monica 21
Moss, J 64
Mullen, Nicole C. 45
Peoples, Dottie 22
Phipps, Wintley 59
Preston, Billy 39, 59
Reagon, Bernice Johnson 7
Reese, Della 6, 20
Sapp, Marvin 74
Scott, George 55
Sheard, Kierra "Kiki" 61
Stampley, Micah 54
Staples, Mavis 50
Staples, "Pops" 32
Staton, Candi 27
Steinberg, Martha Jean "The Queen" 28
Tharpe, Rosetta 65
Tonex 54
Tribbett, Tye 81
Walker, Albertina 10, 58
Walker, Hezekiah 34
Washington, Dinah 22
West, Kanye 52
Whalum, Kirk 37, 64
Williams, Deniece 36
Williams, Michelle 73
Wilson, Natalie 38
Winans, Angie 36

Winans, BeBe 14
Winans, CeCe 14, 43
Winans, David 77
Winans, Debbie 36
Winans, Marvin L. 17
Winans, Ronald 54
Winans, Vickie 24
Wright, Timothy 74

**Graffiti art**
White, Dondi 34

**Grambling State University**
Favors, Steve 23

**Grammy awards**
Adams, Oleta 18
Adderley, Nat 29
Babyface 10, 31, 82
Badu, Erykah 22
Battle, Kathleen 70
Belafonte, Harry 4, 65
Beyoncé 39, 70
Blige, Mary J. 20, 34, 60
Brandy 14, 34, 72
Caesar, Shirley 19
Cara, Irene 77
Chapman, Tracy 26
Cleveland, James 19
Cole, Natalie 17, 60, 84
Combs, Sean "Puffy" 17, 43
Cosby, Bill 7, 26, 59
Cray, Robert 30
Crouch, Andraé 27
Davis, Miles 4
Dee, Ruby 8, 50, 68
Ellington, Duke 5
Estelle 75
Ferrer, Ibrahim 41
Fitzgerald, Ella 8
Forté, John 74
Franklin, Aretha 11, 44
Gamble, Kenny 85
Gaye, Marvin 2
Gaynor, Gloria 36
Gibson, Tyrese 27, 62
Glover, Corey 34
Goldberg, Whoopi 4, 33, 69
Gray, Macy 29
Guy, Buddy 31
Hathaway, Donny 18
Hawkins, Tramaine 16
Hawkins, Walter 87
Hayes, Isaac 20, 58, 73
Hill, Lauryn 20, 53
Holland-Dozier-Holland 36
Hooker, John Lee 30
Houston, Cissy 20, 83
Houston, Whitney 7, 28, 83
Hubbard, Freddie 75
Isley, Ronald 25, 56
Jackson, Janet 6, 30, 68
Jackson, Michael 19, 53, 76
James, Etta 13, 52
Jay-Z 27, 69
Jean, Wyclef 20, 86
Jimmy Jam 13
Jones, Bobby 20
Jones, Quincy 8, 30
Kee, John P. 43
Kelly, R. 18, 44, 71
Keys, Alicia 32, 68
Knight, Gladys 16, 66
Knuckles, Frankie 42

LaBelle, Patti 13, 30
Legend, John 67
Lewis, Terry 13
Lopes, Lisa "Left Eye" 36
Mahal, Taj 39
Maitreya, Sananda 85
Makeba, Miriam 2, 50, 74
Marley, Ziggy 41
Marsalis, Branford 34
M.C. Hammer 20, 80
Method Man 81
Mills, Stephanie 36
Mo', Keb' 36
Moore, LeRoi 72
Murphy, Eddie 4, 20, 61
Norman, Jessye 5
Olatunji, Babatunde 36
Perkins, Pinetop 70
Poitier, Sidney 11, 36
Price, Leontyne 1
Pride, Charley 26
Prince 18, 65
Queen Latifah 1, 16, 58
?uestlove 74
Reagon, Bernice Johnson 7
Redding, Otis 16
Reid, Vernon 34
Richie, Lionel 27, 65
Robinson, Smokey 3, 49
Ross, Isaiah "Doc" 40
Rucker, Darius 34, 74
Sade 15
Scott, Jill 29, 83
Seal 14, 75
Shaggy 31
Shorter, Wayne 75
Slash 75
Smith, Will 8, 18
Summer, Donna 25
Turner, Tina 6, 27
Walker, Hezekiah 34
Warwick, Dionne 18
White, Barry 13, 41
White, Maurice 29
Whitfield, Norman 73
Williams, Deniece 36
Williams, Joe 5, 25
Williams, Michelle 73
Wilson, Nancy 10
Winans, CeCe 14, 43
Winans, Marvin L. 17
Wonder, Stevie 11, 53

**Grand Ole Opry**
Bailey, DeFord 33

**Graphic novels**
Anderson, Ho Che 54
McDuffie, Dwayne 62
Tooks, Lance 62

**Green Bay Packers football team**
Brooks, Aaron 33
Butler, Leroy, III 17
Howard, Desmond 16, 58
Lofton, James 42
Sharper, Darren 32
White, Reggie 6, 50

**Green Belt Movement**
Maathai, Wangari 43

**Green Party**
Clemente, Rosa 74
McKinney, Cynthia 11, 52, 74

**Grenadian government**
Bishop, Maurice 39
Gairy, Eric Matthew 83
Mitchell, Keith 82

**Groupe de Recherche Choréographique de**
Dove, Ulysses 5

*Guardian*
Trotter, Monroe 9

**Guggenheim fellowship**
Pope.L, William 72
Rollins, Sonny 37
Taylor, Cecil 70
Wilson, Ellis 39

**Guinea government**
Camara, Moussa Dadis 76
Conté, Lansana 7, 76
Touré, Sekou 6

**Guinea-Bissau government**
Sanhá Malam Bacai 84
Vieira, João 14, 84

**Guitar**
Ade, King Sunny 41
Barker, Danny 32
Barnes, Roosevelt "Booba" 33
Bibb, Eric 49
Brown, Clarence Gatemouth 59
Butler, Jonathan 28
Burns, Eddie 44
Burnside, R. L. 56
Caymmi, Dorival 72
Collins, Bootsy 31
Cray, Robert 30
Davis, Gary 41
Diddley, Bo 39, 72
Estes, Sleepy John 33
Fuller, Blind Boy 86
Green, Grant 56
Guy, Buddy 31
Harris, Corey 39, 73
Hemphill, Jessie Mae 33, 59
Hendrix, Jimi 10
House, Son 8
Hooker, John Lee 30
Hopkins, Lightnin' 83
Howlin' Wolf 9
Johnson, Robert 2
Jordan, Ronny 26
Killings, Debra 57
King, B. B. 7
Klugh, Earl 59
Kolosoy, Wendo 73
Kravitz, Lenny 10, 34
Leadbelly 82
Lipscomb, Mance 49
Long, Huey 79
Marley, Bob 5
Mayfield, Curtis 2, 43
Ndegeocello, Meshell 15, 83
Ongala, Remmy 9
Parker, Ray, Jr. 85
Pena, Paul 58
Ranglin, Ernest 78
Rodríguez, Arsenio 87
Rush, Bobby 78

Seals, Son 56
Shider, Garry 87
Slash 75
Spence, Joseph 49
Staples, Mavis 50
Staples, "Pops" 32
Ulmer, James 79
Watson, Johnny "Guitar" 18
White, Josh 86

**Gulf War**
Powell, Colin 1, 28, 75
Shaw, Bernard 2
Von Lipsey, Roderick K. 11

**Gurdjieff Institute**
Toomer, Jean 6

**Guyanese government**
Burnham, Forbes 66

**Gymnastics**
Dawes, Dominique 11
Hilliard, Wendy 53
White, Jesse 22, 75

**Hair care**
Cottrell, Comer 11
Fuller, S. B. 13
Gibson, Ted 66
Johnson, George E. 29
Joyner, Marjorie Stewart 26
Malone, Annie 13
Roche, Joyce M. 17
Walker, Madame C. J. 7

**Haitian government**
Aristide, Jean-Bertrand 6, 45
Pascal-Trouillot, Ertha 3
Pierre-Louis, Michèle 75
Préval, René 87

**Hale House**
Hale, Clara 16
Hale, Lorraine 8

**Hallmark Channel**
Corbi, Lana 42

**Hampton University**
Harvey, William R. 42

**Handy Award**
Hunter, Alberta 42

**Harlem Artist Guild**
Nugent, Richard Bruce 39
Wilson, Ellis 39

**Harlem Globetrotters**
Chamberlain, Wilt 18, 47
Haynes, Marques 22
Jackson, Mannie 14
Woodard, Lynette 67

**Harlem Junior Tennis League**
Blake, James 43

**Harlem Renaissance**
Alexander, Margaret Walker 22
Bennett, Gwendolyn B. 59
Christian, Barbara T. 44
Crichlow, Ernest 75
Cullen, Countee 8
Cuney, William Waring 44
Dandridge, Raymond Garfield 45
Davis, Arthur P. 41

Delaney, Beauford 19
Ellington, Duke 5
Fauset, Jessie 7
Fisher, Rudolph 17
Frazier, E. Franklin 10
Horne, Frank 44
Hughes, Langston 4
Hurston, Zora Neale 3
Imes, Elmer Samuel 39
Johnson, Georgia Douglas 41
Johnson, James Weldon 5
Johnson, William Henry 3
Larsen, Nella 10
Locke, Alain 10
McKay, Claude 6
Mills, Florence 22
Nugent, Richard Bruce 39
Petry, Ann 19
Thurman, Wallace 16
Toomer, Jean 6
VanDerZee, James 6
West, Dorothy 12, 54
Wilson, Ellis 39

**Harlem Writers Guild**
Guy, Rosa 5
Killens, John O. 54
Wesley, Valerie Wilson 18

**Harlem Youth Opportunities
Unlimited (HARYOU)**
Clark, Kenneth B. 5, 52

**Harmonica**
Bailey, DeFord 33
Barnes, Roosevelt "Booba" 33
Burns, Eddie 44
Howlin' Wolf 9
Neal, Raful 44
Ross, Isaiah "Doc" 40

**Harness racing**
Minor, DeWayne 32

**Harp**
Coltrane, Alice 70
Majors, Jeff 41

**Harriet Tubman Home for
Aged and Indigent Colored
People**
Tubman, Harriet 9

**Harrisburg Giants baseball
team**
Charleston, Oscar 39

**Harvard Law School**
Bell, Derrick 6
Dickerson, Debra J. 60
Ogletree, Charles, Jr. 12, 47
Wilkins, David 77

**Harvard University**
Amaker, Tommy 62
Epps, Archie C., III 45
Ferguson, Ronald F. 75
Hammonds, Evelynn 69
Huggins, Nathan Irvin 52
Loury, Glenn 36
Poindexter, Hildrus A. 87

**HARYOU**
See Harlem Youth Opportunities
Unlimited

**Hazelitt Award for Excellence
in Arts**
Bradley, David Henry, Jr. 39

**Head Start**
Edelman, Marian Wright 5, 42
Taylor, Helen 30

**Health care reform**
Adams-Campbell, Lucille L. 60
Berrysmith, Don Reginald 49
Brown, Jesse 6, 41
Carroll, L. Natalie 44
Cole, Lorraine 48
Cooper, Edward S. 6
Dirie, Waris 56
Gibson, Kenneth A. 6
Hughes, Ebony 57
Kintaudi, Leon 62
Lavizzo-Mourey, Risa 48
Norman, Pat 10
Potter, Myrtle 40
Richardson, Rupert 67
Satcher, David 7, 57
Tuckson, Reed V. 71
Vaughn, Viola 70
Williams, Daniel Hale 2
Williams, David Rudyard 50

**Heart disease**
Cooper, Edward S. 6
Grant, Augustus O. 71

**Heidelberg Project**
Guyton, Tyree 9

**Heisman Trophy**
Allen, Marcus 20
Bush, Reggie 59
Davis, Ernie 48
George, Eddie 80
Howard, Desmond 16, 58
Sanders, Barry 1, 53
Simpson, O. J. 15
Walker, Herschel 1, 69
Ware, Andre 37
Williams, Ricky 85

**Heritage Network, The**
Mercado-Valdes, Frank 43

**Heroism**
Autrey, Wesley 68
Delaney, Joe 76

**HEW**
See U.S. Department of Health,
Education, and Welfare

**HHS**
See U.S. Department of Health and
Human Services

**Hip-hop music**
Akon 68
apl.de.ap 84
Ashanti 37
Benjamin, Andre 45
Blackman, Toni 86
Estelle 75
Fiasco, Lupe 64
Forté, John 74
Garrett, Sean 57
Guru 84
Jean, Wyclef 20, 86
Jennings, Lyfe 56, 69

Kid Cudi 83
Kitwana, Bakari 86
K-Swift 73
Lil Wayne 66, 84
Method Man 81
Minaj, Nicki 86
Patton, Antwan 45
Peterson, James 81
?uestlove 74
Rascal, Dizzee 82
Redman 81
Run 31, 73
Sermon, Erick 81
Smith, Danyel 40
will.i.am 64
Williams, Pharrell 47, 82

**Hip-hop theater**
Power, Will 83

**Historians**
Ballard, Allen Butler, Jr. 40
Berry, Mary Frances 7
Blassingame, John Wesley 40
Blockson, Charles L. 42
Bogle, Donald 34
Chase-Riboud, Barbara 20, 46
Cooper, Afua 53
Cooper, Anna Julia 20
Cruse, Harold 54
Diop, Cheikh Anta 4
Dodson, Howard, Jr. 7, 52
Du Bois, W. E. B. 3
Franklin, John Hope 5, 77
Gates, Henry Louis, Jr. 3, 38, 67
Giddings, Paula 11
Gill, Gerald 69
Gordon-Reed, Annette 74
Hammonds, Evelynn 69
Hansberry, William Leo 11
Harkless, Necia Desiree 19
Hine, Darlene Clark 24
Horton, James Oliver 58
Huggins, Nathan Irvin 52
Logan, Rayford W. 40
Nash, Joe 55
Marable, Manning 10
Moore, Wes 86
Painter, Nell Irvin 24
Patterson, Orlando 4
Quarles, Benjamin Arthur 18
Querino, Manuel Raimundo 84
Reagon, Bernice Johnson 7
Reddick, Lawrence Dunbar 20
Rogers, Joel Augustus 30
Sadlier, Rosemary 62
Schomburg, Arthur Alfonso 9
Skinner, Kiron K. 65
Snowden, Frank M., Jr. 67
van Sertima, Ivan 25
Washington, James Melvin 50
Williams, George Washington 18
Williams, Rhonda Y. 86
Woodson, Carter G. 2

**Hitman Records**
Brae, C. Michael 61

**Hockey**
Brashear, Donald 39
Brathwaite, Fred 35
Brown, Sean 52
Carnegie, Herbert 25
Doig, Jason 45

Fuhr, Grant 1, 49
Grand-Pierre, Jean-Luc 46
Grier, Mike 43
Iginla, Jarome 35
Mayers, Jamal 39
McBride, Bryant 18
McCarthy, Sandy 64
McKegney, Tony 3
O'Ree, Willie 5
Salvador, Bryce 51
Weekes, Kevin 67

**Homestead Grays baseball
team**
Charleston, Oscar 39
Day, Leon 39

**Homosexuality**
Carter, Mandy 11
Clarke, Cheryl 32
Delany, Samuel R., Jr. 9
Gomes, Peter J. 15
Harris, E. Lynn 12, 33
Hemphill, Essex 10
Julien, Isaac 3
Lorde, Audre 6
Norman, Pat 10
Nugent, Richard Bruce 39
Parker, Pat 19
Riggs, Marlon 5, 44
Rupaul 17
Wilson, Phill 9

**Honeywell Corporation**
Jackson, Mannie 14

**Horse racing**
Harris, Sylvia 70
St. Julien, Marlon 29
Winkfield, Jimmy 42

**House music**
Knuckles, Frankie 42

**House of Representatives**
See U.S. House of Representatives

**Houston Astros baseball team**
Morgan, Joe Leonard 9
Richard, J. R. 87
Watson, Bob 25

**Houston Oilers football team**
McNair, Steve 22, 47, 79
Moon, Warren 8, 66

**Houston Rockets basketball
team**
Lucas, John 7
Olajuwon, Hakeem 2, 72

**Howard University**
Adams-Campbell, Lucille L. 60
Benjamin, Tritobia Hayes 53
Branson, Herman 87
Cardozo, Francis L. 33
Carter, Joye Maureen 41
Cobb, W. Montague 39
Davis, Arthur P. 41
Dodson, Owen 38
Gerima, Haile 38, 80
Harris, Gary L. 87
Jenifer, Franklyn G. 2
Johnson, Mordecai Wyatt 79
Ladner, Joyce A. 42
Locke, Alain 10

Logan, Rayford W. 40
Malveaux, Floyd 54
Mays, Benjamin E. 7
Neal, Larry 38
Payton, Benjamin F. 23
Porter, James A. 11
Reid, Irvin D. 20
Ribeau, Sidney 70
Robinson, Spottswood W., III 22
Snowden, Frank M., Jr. 67
Sowande, Fela 39
Spriggs, William 67
Swygert, H. Patrick 22
Wells, James Lesesne 10
Wesley, Dorothy Porter 19
White, Charles 39
Young, Roger Arliner 29

**HUD**
See U.S. Department of Housing
  and Urban Development

**Hugo awards**
Butler, Octavia 8, 43, 58
Delany, Samuel R., Jr. 9

**Hull-Ottawa Canadiens
hockey team**
O'Ree, Willie 5

**Human resources**
Howroyd, Janice Bryant 42

**Human rights**
Bond, Julian 2, 35
Carter, Mandy 11
McDougall, Gay J. 11, 43
Williams, Robert F. 11

**Hunter College**
DeCarava, Roy 42, 81
Mayhew, Richard 39
Thomas, Michael 69

**IBF**
See International Boxing Federation

**IBM**
Adkins, Rod 41
Blackwell, Robert D., Sr. 52
Chenault, Kenneth I. 5, 36
Dean, Mark 35
Foster, Jylla Moore 45
Thompson, John W. 26
Zollar, Alfred 40

**IBM's National Black Family
Technology Awareness**
Adkins, Rod 41

**Ice Hockey in Harlem**
Mayers, Jamal 39

**Ice skating**
See Figure skating

**Igbo people/traditions**
Achebe, Chinua 6

**Illinois state government**
Braun, Carol Moseley 4, 42
Burris, Roland W. 25, 75
Colter, Cyrus J. 36
Jones, Emil, Jr. 74
Obama, Barack 49, 74
Raoul, Kwame 55
Trotter, Donne E. 28

Washington, Harold 6
White, Jesse 22, 75

**Illustrations**
Anderson, Ho Che 54
Baker, Matt 76
Biggers, John 20, 33
Bryan, Ashley F. 41
Campbell, E. Simms 13
Crichlow, Ernest 75
Fax, Elton 48
Honeywood, Varnette P. 54
Hudson, Cheryl 15
Kitt, Sandra 23
Pinkney, Jerry 15
Saint James, Synthia 12
Simmons, Gary 58

**IMF**
See International Monetary Fund

**Indecorp, Inc.**
Johnson, George E. 29

**Indiana Fever basketball team**
Catchings, Tamika 43

**Indiana state government**
Carson, Julia 23, 69
Carter, Pamela Lynn 67

**Indianapolis ABCs baseball
team**
Charleston, Oscar 39

**Indianapolis Clowns baseball
team**
Charleston, Oscar 39
Johnson, Mamie "Peanut" 40

**Indianapolis Colts football
team**
Caldwell, Jim 81
Dickerson, Eric 27
Dungy, Tony 17, 42, 59
Sanders, Bob 72

**Indianapolis Crawfords base-
ball team**
Charleston, Oscar 39
Kaiser, Cecil 42

**Indianapolis 500**
Ribbs, Willy T. 2

**Industrial design**
Harrison, Charles 72

**Information technology**
Blackwell, Robert D., Sr. 52
Coleman, Ken 57
Pinkett, Randal 61
Smith, Joshua 10
Woods, Jacqueline 52
Zollar, Alfred 40

**Insurance**
Gaston, Arthur George 3, 38, 59
Hill, Jesse, Jr. 13
James, Donna A. 51
Kidd, Mae Street 39
Killingsworth, Cleve, Jr. 54
Procope, Ernesta 23
Procope, John Levy 56
Scott, Tim 87
Spaulding, Charles Clinton 9
Vaughns, Cleopatra 46

Williams, Ronald A. 57
Willie, Louis, Jr. 68

**Interior design**
Ashford, Calvin, Jr. 74
Bridges, Sheila 36
De' Alexander, Quinton 57
Ham, Cynthia Parker 58
Hayes, Cecil N. 46
King, Robert Arthur 58
Myles, Kim 69
Steave-Dickerson, Kia 57
Taylor, Karin 34

**Internal Revenue Service**
Colter, Cyrus J. 36

**International ambassadors**
Davis, Ruth 37
Poitier, Sidney 11, 36
Smythe Haith, Mabel 61
Todman, Terence A. 55
Wharton, Clifton Reginald, Sr. 36

**International Association of
Fire Chiefs**
Bell, Michael 40
Day, Leon 39

**International Boxing Federa-
tion (IBF)**
Ali, Muhammad 2, 16, 52
Hearns, Thomas 29
Hopkins, Bernard 35, 69
Lewis, Lennox 27
Moorer, Michael 19
Mosley, Shane 32
Tyson, Mike 28, 44
Whitaker, Pernell 10

**International Federation of
Library Associations and In-
stitutions**
Wedgeworth, Robert W. 42

**International Free and Ac-
cepted Masons and Eastern
Star**
Banks, William 11

**International Ladies' Auxiliary**
Tucker, Rosina 14

**International law**
Payne, Ulice 42

**International Monetary Fund
(IMF)**
Babangida, Ibrahim 4
Chissano, Joaquim 7, 55, 67
Diouf, Abdou 3
Patterson, P. J. 6, 20

**International Workers Organi-
zation (IWO)**
Patterson, Louise 25

**Internet**
Cooper, Barry 33
Gilliard, Steve 69
Knowling, Robert 38
Thomas-Graham, Pamela 29

**Internet security**
Thompson, John W. 26

**Interpol**
Noble, Ronald 46

**Interscope Geffen A & M
Records**
Stoute, Steve 38

*In the Black* television show
Jones, Caroline R. 29

**Inventions**
Johnson, Lonnie G. 32
Jones, Frederick McKinley 68
Julian, Percy Lavon 6
Latimer, Lewis H. 4
McCoy, Elijah 8
Morgan, Garrett 1
West, James E. 87
Woods, Granville T. 5

**Investment management**
Beal, Bernard B. 46
Bryant, John 26
Ford, Wallace 58
Gardner, Chris 65
Goings, Russell 59
Green, Isaac H. 79
Harris, Carla A. 67
Procope, Ernesta 23
Rogers, John W., Jr. 5, 52
Utendahl, John 23

**Island Def Jam Music Group**
Liles, Kevin 42

**Ivorian Popular Front (FPI)**
Gbagbo, Laurent 43

**Ivory Coast government**
Gbagbo, Laurent 43
Guéï, Robert 66

**Jackie Robinson Foundation**
Robinson, Rachel 16

**Jackson University**
Mason, Ronald 27

**Jamaican government**
Golding, Bruce 78
Simpson-Miller, Portia 62

**Jazz**
Adderley, Julian "Cannonball" 30
Adderley, Nat 29
Albright, Gerald 23
Ali, Rashied 79
Anderson, Carl 48
Anderson, Fred 87
Armstrong, Louis 2
Astatke, Mulatu 81
Austin, Lovie 40
Austin, Patti 24
Ayers, Roy 16
Bailey, Buster 38
Bailey, Philip 63
Barker, Danny 32
Basie, Count 23
Batiste, Alvin 66
Bechet, Sidney 18
Belgrave, Marcus 77
Belle, Regina 1, 51
Betts, Keter 85
Blakey, Art 37
Blanchard, Terence 43
Bolden, Buddy 39

Bridgewater, Dee Dee **32**
Brooks, Avery **9**
Brown, Clifford **86**
Butler, Jonathan **28**
Calloway, Cab **14**
Carter, Benny **46**
Carter, Betty **19**
Carter, Regina **23**
Carter, Warrick L. **27**
Cartiér, Xam Wilson **41**
Charles, Ray **16, 48**
Cheatham, Doc **17**
Clarke, Kenny **27**
Cole, Nat "King" **17**
Cole, Natalie **17, 60, 84**
Coleman, Ornette **39, 69**
Coltrane, Alice **70**
Coltrane, John **19**
Coltrane, Ravi **71**
Cook, Charles "Doc" **44**
Count Basie **23**
Crawford, Hank **77**
Crawford, Randy **19**
Crothers, Scatman **19**
Crouch, Stanley **11, 87**
Crowder, Henry **16**
Daemyon, Jerald **64**
Dara, Olu **35**
Davis, Anthony **11**
Davis, Frank Marshall **47**
Davis, Miles **4**
Dickenson, Vic **38**
Dixon, Bill **87**
Donegan, Dorothy **19**
Downing, Will **19**
Duke, George **21**
Dumas, Henry **41**
Durham, Bobby **73**
Eckstine, Billy **28**
Eldridge, Roy **37**
Ellington, Duke **5**
Ellison, Ralph **7**
Eubanks, Kevin **15**
Farmer, Art **38**
Ferrell, Rachelle **29**
Fitzgerald, Ella **8, 18**
Flanagan, Tommy **69**
Foster, George "Pops" **40**
Freelon, Nnenna **32**
Freeman, Yvette **27**
Fuller, Arthur **27**
Garner, Erroll **76**
Gillespie, Dizzy **1**
Golson, Benny **37**
Gordon, Dexter **25**
Green, Grant **56**
Greene, Jimmy **74**
Griffin, Johnny **71**
Güines, Tata **69**
Hampton, Lionel **17, 41**
Hancock, Herbie **20, 67**
Hardin Armstrong, Lil **39**
Harris, Barry **68**
Hathaway, Lalah **57**
Hawkins, Coleman **9**
Haynes, Roy **87**
Henderson, Fletcher **32**
Higginbotham, J. C. **37**
Hill, Andrew **66**
Hines, Earl "Fatha" **39**
Hinton, Milt **30**
Holiday, Billie **1**
Horn, Shirley **32, 56**

Hubbard, Freddie **75**
Hyman, Phyllis **19**
Jackson, Milt **26**
Jacquet, Illinois **49**
Jamal, Ahmad **69**
James, Etta **13, 52**
Jarreau, Al **21, 65**
Johnson, Buddy **36**
Johnson, J. J. **37**
Johnson, Lonnie **85**
Jones, Elvin **14, 68**
Jones, Etta **35**
Jones, Hank **57, 86**
Jones, Jonah **39**
Jones, Quincy **8, 30**
Jones, Thad **68**
Jordan, Ronny **26**
Kenyatta, Robin **54**
Klugh, Earl **59**
Ledisi **73**
Lee, Consuela **84**
Lewis, Ramsey **35, 70**
Lincoln, Abbey **3**
Locke, Eddie **44**
Long, Huey **79**
Lucie, Lawrence **80**
Lucien, Jon **66**
Marsalis, Branford **34**
Marsalis, Delfeayo **41**
Marsalis, Wynton **16**
McBride, James **35, 87**
McGriff, Jimmy **72**
McLean, Jackie **78**
McRae, Carmen **77**
Miller, Marcus **84**
Mills, Florence **22**
Mingus, Charles **15**
Mitchell, Nicole **66**
Monk, Thelonious **1**
Moody, James **83**
Moore, Melba **21**
Morton, Jelly Roll **29**
Muse, Clarence Edouard **21**
Nascimento, Milton **2, 64**
Newman, David **76**
Oliver, Joe "King" **42**
Parker, Charlie **20**
Parker, Maceo **72**
Payne, Freda **58**
Peterson, Marvin "Hannibal" **27**
Peterson, Oscar **52**
Powell, Benny **87**
Powell, Bud **24**
Purdie, Bernard **77**
Redman, Joshua **30**
Reese, Della **6, 20**
Reeves, Dianne **32**
Roach, Max **21, 63**
Roberts, Marcus **19**
Rollins, Sonny **37**
Ruffins, Kermit **85**
Rushing, Jimmy **37**
Sample, Joe **51**
Santamaria, Mongo **81**
Scarlett, Millicent **49**
Scott, Hazel **66**
Scott, "Little" Jimmy **48**
Shorter, Wayne **75**
Silver, Horace **26**
Simpson-Hoffman, N'kenge **52**
Sissle, Noble **29**
Smith, Bessie **3**
Smith, Cladys "Jabbo" **32**

Smith, Dr. Lonnie **49**
Smith, Lonnie Liston **49**
Smith, Stuff **37**
Somi **85**
Staton, Dakota **62**
Strayhorn, Billy **31**
Sullivan, Maxine **37**
Sun Ra **60**
Swann, Lynn **28**
Tampa Red **63**
Taylor, Billy **23**
Taylor, Cecil **70**
Terry, Clark **39**
Tisdale, Wayman **50**
Ulmer, James **79**
Valdés, Bebo **75**
Vaughan, Sarah **13**
Waller, Fats **29**
Washington, Dinah **22**
Washington, Grover, Jr. **17, 44**
Waters, Benny **26**
Watson, Johnny "Guitar" **18**
Watts, Reggie **52**
Webster, Katie **29**
Wein, Joyce **62**
Whalum, Kirk **37, 64**
White, Maurice **29**
Williams, Claude **80**
Williams, Joe **5, 25**
Williams, Mary Lou **15**
Williams, Tony **67**
Wilson, Cassandra **16**
Wilson, Gerald **49**
Wilson, Nancy **10**
York, Vincent **40**
Young, Lee **72**
Young, Lester **37**

**Jet magazine**
Johnson, John H. **3, 54**
Massaquoi, Hans J. **30**
Sleet, Moneta, Jr. **5**

**Jive Records**
McPherson, David **32**

**Jockeys**
Harris, Sylvia **70**
Lewis, Oliver **56**
Winkfield, Jimmy **42**

**Johnson C. Smith University**
Yancy, Dorothy Cowser **42**

**Johnson Products**
Johnson, George E. **29**

**Johnson Publishing Company, Inc.**
Booker, Simeon **23**
Johnson, Eunice W. **83**
Johnson, John H. **3, 54**
Monroe, Bryan **71**
Rice, Linda Johnson **9, 41**
Sleet, Moneta, Jr. **5**

**Joint Center for Political Studies**
Williams, Eddie N. **44**

**Joint Chiefs of Staff**
See U.S. Joint Chiefs of Staff

**Jones Haywood School of Ballet**
Jones, Doris W. **62**

**Journalism**
Abbott, Robert Sengstacke **27**
Abrahams, Peter **39**
Abu-Jamal, Mumia **15**
Ansa, Tina McElroy **14**
Ashley-Ward, Amelia **23**
Asim, Jabari **71**
Auguste, Arnold A. **47**
Azikiwe, Nnamdi **13**
Bailey, Chauncey **68**
Baquet, Dean **63**
Barden, Don H. **9, 20**
Barnett, Amy Du Bois **46**
Barrett, Lindsay **43**
Bass, Charlotta Spears **40**
Bates, Karen Grigsby **40**
Bennett, Gwendolyn B. **59**
Bennett, Lerone, Jr. **5, 84**
Best, Carrie **80**
Blair, Jayson **50**
Blake, Asha **26**
Blow, Charles M. **73**
Bolden, Frank E. **44**
Booker, Simeon **23**
Borders, James **9**
Boyd, Gerald M. **32, 59**
Boyd, Suzanne **52**
Bradley, Ed **2, 59**
Britt, Donna **28**
Brower, William **49**
Brown, George Leslie **62**
Brown, Lloyd Louis **42**
Brown, Tony **3**
Buckley, Gail Lumet **39**
Burt-Murray, Angela **59**
Burwell, Bryan **83**
Caldwell, Earl **60**
Campbell, Bebe Moore **6, 24, 59**
Cary, Mary Ann Shadd **30**
Cayton, Horace **26**
Chadiha, Jeffri **57**
Chideya, Farai **14, 61**
Churchwell, Robert, Sr. **76**
Ciara, Barbara **69**
Cooke, Marvel **31**
Cooper, Barry **33**
Cooper, Helene **74**
Cose, Ellis **5, 50**
Croal, N'Gai **76**
Crouch, Stanley **11, 87**
Crutchfield, James N. **55**
Cullen, Countee **8**
Cunningham, Evelyn **23, 85**
Dash, Leon **47**
Datcher, Michael **60**
Davis, Belva **61**
Davis, Frank Marshall **47**
Davis, Thulani **61**
Dawkins, Wayne **20**
Deggans, Eric **71**
Douglass, Frederick **87**
Drummond, William J. **40**
Due, Tananarive **30**
Dunbar, Paul Laurence **8**
Dunnigan, Alice Allison **41**
Edmonds, Terry **17**
Epperson, Sharon **54**
Farley, Christopher John **54**
Forman, James **7, 51**

Fortune, T. Thomas 6
Fuller, Hoyt 44
Gaiter, Dorothy J. 80
Giddings, Paula 11
Gilliard, Steve 69
Givhan, Robin Deneen 72
Goode, Mal 13
Gordon, Ed 10, 53
Grimké, Archibald H. 9
Gumbel, Bryant 14, 80
Gumbel, Greg 8
Hansberry, Lorraine 6
Hare, Nathan 44
Harrington, Oliver W. 9
Harris, Claire 34
Harris, Jay 19
Harris, Richard E. 61
Haygood, Wil 83
Haynes, Trudy 44
Henriques, Julian 37
Herbert, Bob 63
Hickman, Fred 11
Holt, Lester 66
Huggins, Edie 71
Hunter-Gault, Charlayne 6, 31
Ifill, Gwen 28
Jarrett, Vernon D. 42
Jasper, Kenji 39
Jealous, Benjamin 70
Joachim, Paulin 34
Johnson, Georgia Douglas 41
Johnson, James Weldon 5
Kaufman, Monica 66
Kearney, Janis 54
Khanga, Yelena 6
Killens, John O. 54
King, Colbert I. 69
Kitwana, Bakari 86
Knight, Etheridge 37
LaGuma, Alex 30
Lacy, Sam 30, 46
Lampkin, Daisy 19
Leavell, Dorothy R. 17
Lewis, Edward T. 21
Lowe, Herbert 57
Mabrey, Vicki 26
Mabry, Marcus 70
Mabuza-Suttle, Felicia 43
Madison, Paula 37
Martin, Louis E. 16
Mason, Felicia 31
Maynard, Nancy Hicks 73
Maynard, Robert C. 7
Mbeki, Govan A. 80
McBride, James 35, 87
McCall, Nathan 8
McGruder, Robert 22, 35
McKay, Claude 6
Mickelbury, Penny 28
Mitchell, Elvis 67
Mitchell, Russ 21, 73
Mkapa, Benjamin W. 16, 77
Monroe, Bryan 71
Mossell, Gertrude Bustill 40
Mukoko, Jestina 75
Murphy, John H. 42
Murray, Pauli 38
Nelson, Jill 6, 54
Neville, Arthel 53
Newkirk, Pamela 69
Njawe, Pius 87
Nkosi, Lewis 46
Noble, Gil 76

Norris, Michele 83
Oliver, Pam 54
Olojede, Dele 59
Page, Clarence 4
Palmer, Everard 37
Parham, Marjorie B. 71
Parker, Star 70
Parks, Gordon 1, 35, 58
Payne, Ethel L. 28
Perez, Anna 1
Perkins, Tony 24
Phillips, Joseph C. 73
Pinkston, W. Randall 24
Pitts, Byron 71
Pitts, Leonard, Jr. 54, 85
Plaatje, Sol. T. 80
Poussaint, Renee 78
Pressley, Condace L. 41
Price, Hugh B. 9, 54
Prince, Richard E. 71
Pugh, Charles 81
Quarles, Norma 25
Rapier, James T. 82
Raspberry, William 2
Reed, Ishmael 8
Reeves, Rachel J. 23
Rhoden, William C. 67
Riley, Rochelle 50
Roberts, Robin 16, 54
Robertson, Gil L., IV 85
Robinson, Eugene 77
Robinson, Max 3
Rodgers, Johnathan 6, 51
Rowan, Carl T. 1, 30
Rust, Art, Jr. 83
Salih, Al-Tayyib 37
Salters, Lisa 71
Sanders, Pharoah 64
Schuyler, George Samuel 40
Schuyler, Philippa 50
Senior, Olive 37
Shaw, Bernard 2, 28
Shipp, E. R. 15
Simpson, Carole 6, 30
Smith, Clarence O. 21
Smith, Danyel 40
Smith, Stephen A. 69
Sowell, Thomas 2
Staples, Brent 8
Stewart, Alison 13
Stokes, Carl 10, 73
Stone, Chuck 9
Syler, Rene 53
Tate, Eleanora E. 20, 55
Tatum, Elinor R. 78
Tatum, Wilbert 76
Taylor, Kristin Clark 8
Thurman, Wallace 16
Tolson, Melvin B. 37
Trotter, Monroe 9
Tucker, Cynthia 15, 61
Wallace, Michele Faith 13
Washington, Elsie B. 78
Washington, Harriet A. 69
Watson, Carlos 50
Watts, Rolonda 9
Webb, Veronica 10
Wells-Barnett, Ida B. 8
Wesley, Valerie Wilson 18
Whitaker, Mark 21, 47
White, Armond 80
Whitfield, LeRoy 84
Whitlock, Jason 78

Wilbekin, Emil 63
Wilbon, Michael 68
Wiley, Ralph 8, 78
Wilkerson, Isabel 71
Wilkins, Roger 2, 84
Williams, Armstrong 29
Williams, Clarence 70
Williams, Juan 35, 80
Williams, Patricia 11, 54
Wiwa, Ken 67
Woods, Mattiebelle 63
Yette, Samuel F. 63
Zook, Kristal Brent 62

**Judaism**
Funnye, Capers C., Jr. 73
Stanton, Alysa 78

**Judiciary**
Hatchett, Glenda 32
Sampson, Edith S. 4

**Just Us Books**
Hudson, Cheryl 15
Hudson, Wade 15

**Kansas City Athletics base-ball team**
Paige, Satchel 7

**Kansas City Chiefs football team**
Allen, Marcus 20
Cherry, Deron 40
Delaney, Joe 76
Dungy, Tony 17, 42, 59
Thomas, Derrick 25
Thomas, Emmitt 71

**Kansas City (MO) government**
Cleaver, Emanuel 4, 45, 68

**Kansas City Monarchs base-ball team**
Bell, James "Cool Papa" 36
Brown, Willard 36

**Kansas State University**
Prince, Ron 64

**KANU**
See Kenya African National Union

**Kappa Alpha Psi**
Hamilton, Samuel C. 47

**Karl Kani Infinity**
Kani, Karl 10

**KAU**
See Kenya African Union

**Kentucky Derby**
Winkfield, Jimmy 42

**Kentucky Negro Educational Association**
Cotter, Joseph Seamon, Sr. 40

**Kentucky state government**
Kidd, Mae Street 39

**Kenya African National Union (KANU)**
Kariuki, J. M. 67
Kenyatta, Jomo 5
Kibaki, Mwai 60
Moi, Daniel Arap 1, 35

Ngilu, Charity 58
Odinga, Raila 67

**Kenya African Union (KAU)**
Kenyatta, Jomo 5

**Kenya National Council of Churches (NCCK)**
Kobia, Samuel 43

**Kenyan government**
Kariuki, J. M. 67
Kibaki, Mwai 60
Maathai, Wangari 43
Moi, Daniel Arap 1, 35
Ngilu, Charity 58
Odinga, Raila 67

**King Center**
See Martin Luther King Jr. Center for Nonviolent Social Change

**King Oliver's Creole Band**
Armstrong, Louis 2
Hardin Armstrong, Lil 39
Oliver, Joe "King" 42

**King's Troop of the Royal Horse Artillery**
Scantlebury, Janna 47

**Kitchen Table: Women of Color Press**
Smith, Barbara 28

**Kmart Holding Corporation**
Lewis, Aylwin 51

**Kraft General Foods**
Fudge, Ann (Marie) 11, 55
Sneed, Paula A. 18

**Kunta Kinte–Alex Haley Foundation**
Blackshear, Leonard 52

**Kwanzaa**
Karenga, Maulana 10, 71

**Kwazulu Territorial Authority**
Buthelezi, Mangosuthu Gatsha 9

**Labour Party**
Amos, Valerie 41

**Ladies Professional Golfers' Association (LPGA)**
Gibson, Althea 8, 43
Powell, Renee 34

**LaFace Records**
Babyface 10, 31, 82
Benjamin, Andre 45
OutKast 35
Patton, Antwan 45
Reid, Antonio "L.A." 28

**LAPD**
See Los Angeles Police Department

**Latin American folk music**
Nascimento, Milton 2, 64

**Latin baseball leagues**
Kaiser, Cecil 42

**Law enforcement**
Alexander, Joyce London 18
Barrett, Jacquelyn 28

Bolton, Terrell D. **25**
Bradley, Thomas **2**, **20**
Brown, Lee P. **1**, **24**
Bully-Cummings, Ella **48**
Evans, Warren C. **76**
Feemster, Herbert **72**
Freeman, Charles **19**
Gibson, Johnnie Mae **23**
Glover, Nathaniel, Jr. **12**
Gomez-Preston, Cheryl **9**
Harvard, Beverly **11**
Hillard, Terry **25**
Holton, Hugh, Jr. **39**
Hurtt, Harold **46**
Johnson, Norma L. Holloway **17**
Johnson, Robert T. **17**
Jordan, Eddie **82**
McKinnon, Isaiah **9**
Moose, Charles **40**
Napoleon, Benny N. **23**
Noble, Ronald **46**
Oliver, Jerry **37**
Parks, Bernard C. **17**
Ramsey, Charles H. **21**, **69**
Robinson, Bishop L. **66**
Schmoke, Kurt **1**, **48**
Smith, Richard **51**
Thomas, Franklin A. **5**, **49**
Wainwright, Joscelyn **46**
Ward, Benjamin **68**
Williams, Willie L. **4**
Wilson, Jimmy **45**

**Lawyers' Committee for Civil Rights under Law**
Arnwine, Barbara **28**
Hubbard, Arnette **38**
McDougall, Gay J. **11**, **43**

**LDF**
See NAACP Legal Defense and Educational Fund

**League of Nations**
Haile Selassie **7**

**League of Women Voters**
Meek, Carrie **36**

**Legal Defense Fund**
See NAACP Legal Defense and Educational Fund

**Lexicography**
Major, Clarence **9**

**Liberian government**
Henries, A. Doris Banks **44**
Sawyer, Amos **2**
Sirleaf, Ellen Johnson **71**
Weah, George **58**

**Liberians United for Reconciliation and Democracy (LURD)**
Conneh, Sekou Damate, Jr. **51**

**Library science**
Bontemps, Arna **8**
Franklin, Hardy R. **9**, **87**
Harsh, Vivian Gordon **14**
Hutson, Jean Blackwell **16**
Jones, Clara Stanton **51**
Josey, E. J. **10**
Kitt, Sandra **23**
Larsen, Nella **10**

Morrison, Sam **50**
Owens, Major **6**
Rollins, Charlemae Hill **27**
Schomburg, Arthur Alfonso **9**
Shockley, Ann Allen **84**
Smith, Jessie Carney **35**
Spencer, Anne **27**
Wedgeworth, Robert W. **42**
Wesley, Dorothy Porter **19**

**Librettos**
Chenault, John **40**

**Lincoln University (MO)**
Page, Inman **82**
Randall, Dudley **8**, **55**

**Lincoln University (PA)**
Cuney, William Waring **44**
Sudarkasa, Niara **4**

**Listen Up Foundation**
Jones, Quincy **8**, **30**

**Literacy Volunteers of America**
Amos, Wally **9**

**Literary criticism**
Baker, Houston A., Jr. **6**
Braithwaite, William Stanley **52**
Brown, Sterling Allen **10**, **64**
Broyard, Anatole **68**
Cartey, Wilfred **47**
Christian, Barbara T. **44**
Cook, Mercer **40**
De Veaux, Alexis **44**
Emanuel, James A. **46**
Fleming, Raymond **48**
Ford, Nick Aaron **44**
Fuller, Hoyt **44**
Joachim, Paulin **34**
Mackey, Nathaniel **75**
Mugo, Micere Githae **32**
Ngugi wa Thiong'o **29**, **61**
Redding, J. Saunders **26**
Reed, Ishmael **8**
Smith, Barbara **28**
Wesley, Valerie Wilson **18**
West, Cornel **5**, **33**, **80**

**Literary Hall of Fame for Writers of African Descent**
Colter, Cyrus J. **36**

**Lithography**
White, Charles **39**

**Litigation**
Allen, Lucy **85**
Baldwin, Cynthia A. **74**
Cochran, Johnnie **11**, **39**, **52**
Gary, Willie E. **12**
Worthy, Kym **84**

**"Little Rock Nine"**
Bates, Daisy **13**

**Liver research**
Leevy, Carrol M. **42**

**Lobbying**
Boyd, John W., Jr. **20**, **72**
Brooke, Edward **8**
Brown, Elaine **8**
Brown, Jesse **6**, **41**

Brown, Ron **5**
Christie, Ron **83**
Edelman, Marian Wright **5**, **42**
Lee, Canada **8**
Mallett, Conrad, Jr. **16**
Reeves, Gregory **49**
Robinson, Randall **7**, **46**
Wynn, Albert R. **25**, **77**

**Los Angeles Angels baseball team**
Baylor, Don **6**
Bonds, Bobby **43**
Winfield, Dave **5**

**Los Angeles city government**
Bradley, Thomas **2**, **20**
Evers, Myrlie **8**

**Los Angeles Clippers basketball team**
Brand, Elton **31**

**Los Angeles Dodgers baseball team**
Baker, Dusty **8**, **43**, **72**
Newcombe, Don **24**
Strawberry, Darryl **22**
Wills, Maury **73**

**Los Angeles Lakers basketball team**
Abdul-Jabbar, Kareem **8**
Bryant, Kobe **15**, **31**, **71**
Chamberlain, Wilt **18**, **47**
Fox, Rick **27**
Green, A. C. **32**
Johnson, Earvin "Magic" **3**, **39**
Odom, Lamar **81**
O'Neal, Shaquille **8**, **30**
Worthy, James **49**

**Los Angeles Philharmonic**
Lewis, Henry **38**

**Los Angeles Police Department (LAPD)**
Parks, Bernard C. **17**
Smith, Richard **51**
Williams, Willie L. **4**

**Los Angeles Raiders football team**
Allen, Marcus **20**
Lofton, James **42**
Lott, Ronnie **9**
Shell, Art **1**, **66**

**Los Angeles Rams football team**
Bryant, Cullen **81**
Dickerson, Eric **27**
Washington, Kenny **50**

**Los Angeles Sparks basketball team**
Leslie, Lisa **16**, **73**

**Los Angeles Times** newspaper
Baquet, Dean **63**
Drummond, William J. **40**

**Lost-Found Nation of Islam**
Ali, Muhammad **2**, **16**, **52**
Ellison, Keith **59**
Farrakhan, Louis **2**, **15**

Heard, Nathan C. **45**
Karim, Benjamin **61**
Muhammad, Ava **31**
Muhammad, Elijah **4**
Muhammad, Jabir Herbert **72**
Muhammad, Khallid Abdul **10**, **31**
Muhammed, W. Deen **27**
Sutton, Percy E. **42**, **82**
Tillard, Conrad **47**
X, Malcolm **1**
X, Marvin **45**

**Louisiana Disaster Recovery Authority**
Francis, Norman (C.) **60**

**Louisiana state government**
Fields, Cleo **13**
Jefferson, William J. **25**, **72**
Morial, Ernest "Dutch" **26**
Pinchback, P. B. S. **9**
Richardson, Rupert **67**

**LPGA**
See Ladies Professional Golfers' Association

**Lunar surface ultraviolet camera**
See Ultraviolet camera/spectrograph

**Lynching (anti-lynching legislation)**
Johnson, James Weldon **5**
Moore, Harry T. **29**
Till, Emmett **7**

**Lyrics**
Crouch, Andraé **27**
D'Angelo **27**
Dunbar, Paul Laurence **8**
Fitzgerald, Ella **8**
Jefferson, Blind Lemon **81**
Johnson, James Weldon **5**
KRS-One **34**
Lil' Kim **28**
MC Lyte **34**
Randall, Alice **38**
Run-DMC **31**, **75**

**MacArthur Foundation Fellowship**
Allen, Will **74**
Benjamin, Regina **20**, **75**
Butler, Octavia **8**, **43**, **58**
Carter, Majora **77**
Cooper, Lisa **73**
Hammons, David **69**
Harris, Corey **39**, **73**
Jackson, Mary **73**
Johnson, Charles **1**, **82**
Lee, Raphael C. **87**
Lovell, Whitfield **74**
Mehretu, Julie **85**
Olopade, Olufunmilayo Falusi **58**
Parks, Suzan-Lori **34**, **85**
Taylor, Cecil **70**
Whitehead, Colson **77**

**MacNeil/Lehrer NewsHour**
Hunter-Gault, Charlayne **6**, **31**

**Mad TV**
Jones, Orlando **30**
Wilson, Debra **38**

**Madame C. J. Walker Manufacturing Company**
Joyner, Marjorie Stewart 26
Walker, A'lelia 14
Walker, Madame C. J. 7

**Major League Baseball administration**
Solomon, Jimmie Lee 38

**Maktub**
Watts, Reggie 52

**Malaco Records**
Bland, Bobby "Blue" 36

**Malawi Congress Party (MCP)**
Banda, Hastings Kamuzu 6, 54

**Malawian government**
Muluzi, Bakili 14, 76

**Manhattan Project**
Quarterman, Lloyd Albert 4
Wilkens, J. Ernest, Jr. 43

**MARC Corp.**
See Metropolitan Applied Research Center

**March on Washington/Freedom March**
Baker, Josephine 3
Belafonte, Harry 4, 65
Bunche, Ralph J. 5
Davis, Ossie 5, 50
Fauntroy, Walter E. 11
Forman, James 7, 51
Franklin, John Hope 5, 77
Hedgeman, Anna Arnold 22
Jackson, Mahalia 5
King, Coretta Scott 3, 57
King, Martin Luther, Jr. 1
Lewis, John 2, 46, 83
Meredith, James H. 11
Randolph, A. Philip 3
Rustin, Bayard 4
Sleet, Moneta, Jr. 5
Wilkins, Roy 4
Woods, Abraham, Jr. 74
Young, Whitney M., Jr. 4

**Marketing**
DeVard, Jerri 61
Edwards, Trevor 54
Fils-Aimé, Reggie 74
Gaskins, Rudy 74
Kaigler, Denise 63
Kendrick, Erika 57
Moyo, Karega Kofi 36
Moyo, Yvette Jackson 36

**Martial arts**
Barnes, Steven 54
Copeland, Michael 47
Slice, Kimbo 73

**Martin Luther King Jr. Center for Nonviolent Social Change**
Dodson, Howard, Jr. 7, 52
Farris, Isaac Newton, Jr. 63
King, Bernice 4, 81
King, Coretta Scott 3, 57
King, Dexter 10
King, Martin Luther, Jr. 1

King, Yolanda 6

**Martin Luther King Jr. Drum Major Award**
Broadbent, Hydeia 36
Mfume, Kweisi 6, 41

**Martin Luther King Jr. National Memorial Project**
Johnson, Harry E. 57

**Marxism**
Baraka, Amiri 1, 38
Bishop, Maurice 39
Jagan, Cheddi 16
Machel, Samora Moises 8
Nkrumah, Kwame 3
Sankara, Thomas 17

**Maryland Mustangs basketball team**
Parish, Robert 43

**Maryland state government**
Brown, Anthony G. 72
Currie, Ulysses 73
Steele, Michael 38, 73

**Massachusetts state government**
Brooke, Edward 8

**Masters Golf Tournament**
Elder, Lee 6
Woods, Tiger 14, 31, 81

**Mathematics**
Alcorn, George Edward, Jr. 59
Blackwell, David 79
Deconge-Watson, Lovenia 55
Emeagwali, Philip 30
Falconer, Etta Zuber 59
Gates, Sylvester James, Jr. 15
Johnson, Katherine (Coleman Goble) 61
Price, Richard 51
Wilkens, J. Ernest, Jr. 43

**MAXIMA Corporation**
Smith, Joshua 10

**Maxwell House Coffee Company**
Fudge, Ann (Marie) 11, 55

**McCall Pattern Company**
Lewis, Reginald F. 6

**McDonald's Corporation**
Thompson, Don 56

**McGill University (Canada)**
Elliott, Lorris 37

**MCP**
See Malawi Congress Party

**Medical examiners**
Carter, Joye Maureen 41

**Medicine**
Adams-Campbell, Lucille L. 60
Anderson, William G(ilchrist) 57
Atim, Julian 66
Banda, Hastings Kamuzu 6, 54
Bashir, Halima 73
Benjamin, Regina 20, 75
Black, Keith Lanier 18, 84

Callender, Clive O. 3
Canady, Alexa 28
Carroll, L. Natalie 44
Carson, Benjamin 1, 35, 76
Carter, Joye Maureen 41
Chatard, Peter 44
Chinn, May Edward 26
Christian-Green, Donna M. 17
Cobb, W. Montague 39
Cole, Rebecca 38
Comer, James P. 6
Coney, PonJola 48
Cooper, Edward S. 6
Cooper, Lisa 73
Cornwell, Edward E., III 70
Counter, S. Allen 74
Dailey, Ulysses Grant 87
Deas, Gerald 85
Dickens, Helen Octavia 14, 64
Drew, Charles Richard 7
Edwards, Lena Frances 76
Edwards, Willarda V. 59
Elders, Joycelyn 6
Fennoy, Ilene 72
Fisher, Ada M. 76
Fisher, Rudolph 17
Flowers, Sylester 50
Foster, Henry W., Jr. 26
Freeman, Harold P. 23
Fuller, Solomon Carter, Jr. 15
Gayle, Helene D. 3
Gibson, William F. 6
Grant, Augustus O. 71
Griffin, Anthony 71
Griffith, Patrick A. 64
Hamburg, Margaret 78
Hinton, William Augustus 8
Holmes, Hamilton E. 82
Hutcherson, Hilda Yvonne 54
Jemison, Mae C. 1, 35
Johnson, R. M. 36
Jones, Edith Mae Irby 65
Joseph, Kathie-Ann 56
Keith, Rachel Boone 63
Kenney, John A., Jr. 48
Kintaudi, Leon 62
Kong, B. Waine 50
Kountz, Samuel L. 10
Lavizzo-Mourey, Risa 48
Lawless, Theodore K. 8
Lee, Raphael C. 87
Leffall, Lasalle 3, 64
Logan, Onnie Lee 14
Malveaux, Floyd 54
Maxey, Randall 46
Naki, Hamilton 63
Nour, Nawal M. 56
Okaalet, Peter 58
Olopade, Olufunmilayo Falusi 58
Pace, Betty 59
Pinn, Vivian Winona 49
Pitt, David Thomas 10
Poussaint, Alvin F. 5, 67
Rabb, Maurice F., Jr. 58
Randolph, Linda A. 52
Reece, E. Albert 63
Ross-Lee, Barbara 67
Satcher, David 7, 57
Scantlebury-White, Velma 64
Smith, Ian 62
Stewart, Ella 39
Sullivan, Louis 8
Sweet, Ossian 68

Taylor, Susan C. 62
Thomas, Claudia Lynn 64
Thomas, Vivien 9
Thornton, Yvonne S. 69
Tuckson, Reed V. 71
Washington, Harriet A. 69
Watkins, Levi, Jr. 9
Welsing, Frances Cress 5
White-Hammond, Gloria 61
Williams, Daniel Hale 2
Witt, Edwin T. 26
Wright, Charles H. 35
Wright, Louis Tompkins 4

**Meharry Medical College**
Coney, PonJola 48
Foster, Henry W., Jr. 26
Griffith, Patrick A. 64
Lyttle, Hulda Margaret 14

**Melanin theory of racism**
See Cress Theory of Color Confrontation and Racism

**Melody Makers**
Marley, Ziggy 41

**Men's movement**
Somé, Malidoma Patrice 10

**Merce Cunningham Dance Company**
Dove, Ulysses 5

**Merrill Lynch & Co., Inc.**
Ford, Harold E(ugene), Jr. 16, 70
Matthews Shatteen, Westina 51
O'Neal, Stanley 38, 67

**Meteorology**
Anderson, Charles Edward 37
Bacon-Bercey, June 38

**Metropolitan Applied Research Center (MARC Corp.)**
Clark, Kenneth B. 5, 52

**Mexican baseball league**
Bell, James "Cool Papa" 36
Dandridge, Ray 36

**Miami Dolphins football team**
Cox, Bryan 83
Greene, Joe 10
Williams, Ricky 85

**Michigan state government**
Brown, Cora 33
Collins, Barbara-Rose 7, 87
Kilpatrick, Carolyn Cheeks 16
Kilpatrick, Kwame 34, 71
Reeves, Triette Lipsey 27
Wisdom, Kimberlydawn 57

**Michigan State Supreme Court**
Archer, Dennis 7, 36
Mallett, Conrad, Jr. 16

**Michigan State University**
Wharton, Clifton R., Jr. 7
Willingham, Tyrone 43

**Microsoft Corporation**
Millines Dziko, Trish 28

**Midwest Stamping**
Thompson, Cynthia Bramlett **50**

**Midwifery**
Logan, Onnie Lee **14**
Robinson, Sharon **22**

**Military police**
Cadoria, Sherian Grace **14**

**Militia**
Nkunda, Laurent **75**

**Millennium Digital Media**
Westbrook, Kelvin **50**

**Miller Brewing Company**
Colbert, Virgis William **17**
Shropshire, Thomas B. **49**

**Millinery**
Bailey, Xenobia **11**

**Million Man March**
Farrakhan, Louis **2, 15**
Hawkins, La-Van **17, 54**
Worrill, Conrad **12**

**Milwaukee Braves baseball team**
Aaron, Hank **5**

**Milwaukee Brewers baseball team**
Aaron, Hank **5**
Baylor, Don **6**
Fielder, Prince Semien **68**
Payne, Ulice **42**
Sheffield, Gary **16**

**Milwaukee Bucks basketball team**
Abdul-Jabbar, Kareem **8**
Lucas, John **7**
Robertson, Oscar **26**

**Mingo-Jones Advertising**
Chisholm, Samuel J. **32**
Jones, Caroline R. **29**
Mingo, Frank **32**

**Minneapolis city government**
Sayles Belton, Sharon **9, 16**

**Minnesota State Supreme Court**
Page, Alan **7**

**Minnesota Timberwolves basketball team**
Garnett, Kevin **14, 70**

**Minnesota Twins baseball team**
Baylor, Don **6**
Carew, Rod **20**
Hunter, Torii **43**
Puckett, Kirby **4, 58**
Winfield, Dave **5**

**Minnesota Vikings football team**
Carter, Cris **21**
Culpepper, Daunte **32, 85**
Cunningham, Randall **23**
Dungy, Tony **17, 42, 59**
Fowler, Reggie **51**
Gilliam, Frank **23**

Green, Dennis **5, 45**
McDaniel, Randall Cornell **81**
Moon, Warren **8, 66**
Moss, Randy **23**
Page, Alan **7**
Randle, John **87**
Rashad, Ahmad **18**
Stringer, Korey **35**

**Minority Business Enterprise Legal Defense and Education Fund**
Mitchell, Parren J. **42, 66**

**Minority Business Resource Center**
Hill, Jesse, Jr. **13**

**Minstrel shows**
McDaniel, Hattie **5**

**Miracle Network Telethon**
Warner, Malcolm-Jamal **22, 36**

**Miss America**
Dunlap, Ericka **55**
Harold, Erika **54**
Vincent, Marjorie Judith **2**
Williams, Vanessa L. **4, 17**

**Miss USA**
Gist, Carole **1**

**Miss World**
Darego, Agbani **52**

**Mississippi state government**
Anderson, Reuben V. **81**
Fleming, Erik R. **75**
Hamer, Fannie Lou **6**

**Missouri state government**
Wilson, Margaret Bush **79**

**Mixed martial arts**
Jackson, Rampage **83**

**MLA**
See Modern Language Association of America

**Model Inner City Community Organization (MICCO)**
Fauntroy, Walter E. **11**

**Modeling**
Allen-Buillard, Melba **55**
Banks, Tyra **11, 50**
Beckford, Tyson **11, 68**
Berry, Halle **4, 19, 57**
Campbell, Naomi **1, 31**
Darego, Agbani **52**
Dirie, Waris **56**
Ebanks, Selita **67**
Gibson, Tyrese **27, 62**
Hardison, Bethann **12**
Hounsou, Djimon **19, 45**
Iman **4, 33, 87**
Iman, Chanel **66**
Johnson, Beverly **2**
Kebede, Liya **59**
Kodjoe, Boris **34**
Langhart Cohen, Janet **19, 60**
Leslie, Lisa **16, 73**
LisaRaye **27**
McKenzie, Jaunel **73**
Michele, Michael **31**

Niane, Katoucha **70**
Onwurah, Ngozi **38**
Powell, Maxine **8**
Rochon, Lela **16**
Simmons, Kimora Lee **51, 83**
Sims, Naomi **29, 79**
Smith, B(arbara) **11**
Tamia **24, 55**
Taylor, Karin **34**
Tyson, Cicely **7, 51**
Watley, Jody **54**
Webb, Veronica **10**
Wek, Alek **18, 63**

**Modern dance**
Ailey, Alvin **8**
Allen, Debbie **13, 42**
Byrd, Donald **10**
Collins, Janet **33, 64**
Davis, Chuck **33**
Diggs, Taye **25, 63**
Dove, Ulysses **5**
Fagan, Garth **18**
Faison, George **16**
Henson, Darrin **33**
Jamison, Judith **7, 67**
Jones, Bill T. **1, 46, 80**
King, Alonzo **38**
Kitt, Eartha **16, 75**
Miller, Bebe **3**
Pomare, Eleo **72**
Primus, Pearl **6**
Spears, Warren **52**
Vereen, Ben **4**
Williams, Dudley **60**

**Modern Language Association of America (MLA)**
Baker, Houston A., Jr. **6**

**Modern Records**
Brooks, Hadda **40**

**Monoprinting**
Honeywood, Varnette P. **54**

**Montgomery bus boycott**
Abernathy, Ralph David **1**
Baker, Ella **5**
Burks, Mary Fair **40**
Carr, Johnnie **69**
Jackson, Mahalia **5**
Killens, John O. **54**
King, Martin Luther, Jr. **1**
Parks, Rosa **1, 35, 56**
Rustin, Bayard **4**

**Montgomery County (MD) Police Department**
Moose, Charles **40**

**Montreal Canadiens hockey team**
Brashear, Donald **39**

**Montreal Expos baseball team**
Dawson, Andre **85**
Doby, Lawrence Eugene, Sr. **16, 41**

**Morehouse College**
Brown, Uzee **42**
Hope, John **8**
Mays, Benjamin E. **7**

**Morgan Stanley**
Lewis, William M., Jr. **40**

*Morna*
Evora, Cesaria **12**

**Morris Brown College**
Cross, Dolores E. **23**

*Moscow World News*
Khanga, Yelena **6**
Sullivan, Louis **8**

**Motivational speaking**
Bahati, Wambui **60**
Baisden, Michael **66**
Brown, Les **5**
Bunkley, Anita Richmond **39**
Creagh, Milton **27**
Gardner, Chris **65**
Grant, Gwendolyn Goldsby **28**
Gray, Farrah **59**
Jolley, Willie **28**
July, William **27**
Kimbro, Dennis **10**
Russell-McCloud, Patricia **17**
Tyson, Asha **39**

**Motorcycle racing**
Brown, Antron **85**
Showers, Reggie **30**
Stewart, James "Bubba," Jr. **60**

**Motown Records**
Atkins, Cholly **40**
Avant, Clarence **19, 86**
Bizimungu, Pasteur **19**
Busby, Jheryl **3, 74**
de Passe, Suzanne **25**
Edwards, Esther Gordy **43**
Gaye, Marvin **2**
Gordy, Berry, Jr. **1**
Harrell, Andre **9, 30**
Holland-Dozier-Holland **36**
Holloway, Brenda **65**
Hutch, Willie **62**
Jackson, George **19**
Jamerson, James **59**
Jones, Robert G. **81**
Kendricks, Eddie **22**
Knight, Gladys **16, 66**
Massenburg, Kedar **23**
Powell, Maxine **8**
Richie, Lionel **27, 65**
Robinson, Smokey **3, 49**
Ross, Diana **8, 27**
Sanders, Angelia **86**
Terrell, Tammi **32**
Wells, Mary **28**
Whitfield, Norman **73**
Wilson, Mary **28**
Wonder, Stevie **11, 53**

**Mt. Holyoke College**
Tatum, Beverly Daniel **42, 84**

**Mouvement Revolutionnaire National pour le Developpement (Rwanda; MRND)**
Habyarimana, Juvenal **8**

**Movement for Assemblies of the People**
Bishop, Maurice **39**

**Movement for Democratic Change (MDC)**
Moyo, Lovemore **76**
Tsvangirai, Morgan **26, 72**

**Movement for the Survival of the Ogoni People**
Saro-Wiwa, Kenule 39
Wiwa, Ken 67

**Movimento Popular de Libertação de Angola (MPLA)**
dos Santos, José Eduardo 43
Neto, António Agostinho 43

**Mozambican government**
Chissano, Joaquim 7, 55, 67
Diogo, Luisa Dias 63
Guebuza, Armando 81
Machel, Samora Moises 8

**MPLA**
See Movimento Popular de Libertação de Angola

**MPS**
See Patriotic Movement of Salvation

**MRND**
See Mouvement Revolutionnaire National pour le Developpement

**MTV Jams**
Bellamy, Bill 12

**Multimedia art**
Amaki, Amalia 76
Bailey, Xenobia 11
Lovell, Whitfield 74
Pinder, Jefferson 77
Robinson, Aminah 50
Simpson, Lorna 4, 36

**Muppets, The**
Clash, Kevin 14

**Murals**
Alston, Charles 33
Biggers, John 20, 33
Douglas, Aaron 7
Lee-Smith, Hughie 5
Walker, Kara 16, 80

**Murder Inc.**
Ashanti 37
Gotti, Irv 39
Ja Rule 35

**Museum of Modern Art**
Pindell, Howardena 55

**Music Critics Circle**
Holt, Nora 38

**Music One, Inc.**
Majors, Jeff 41

**Music publishing**
Combs, Sean "Puffy" 17, 43
Cooke, Sam 17
Edmonds, Tracey 16, 64
Gordy, Berry, Jr. 1
Handy, W. C. 8
Holland-Dozier-Holland 36
Humphrey, Bobbi 20
Ice Cube 8, 30, 60
Jackson, George 19
Jackson, Michael 19, 53, 76
James, Rick 17
Knight, Suge 11, 30
Lewis, Emmanuel 36

Master P 21
Mayfield, Curtis 2, 43
Otis, Clyde 67
Prince 18, 65
Redding, Otis 16
Ross, Diana 8, 27
Shakur, Afeni 67
Shorty, Ras, I 47

**Music Television (MTV)**
Bellamy, Bill 12
Chideya, Farai 14, 61
Norman, Christina 47
Powell, Kevin 31, 74
Run 31, 73

**Musical composition**
Armatrading, Joan 32
Ashford, Nickolas 21
Baiocchi, Regina Harris 41
Ballard, Hank 41
Bebey, Francis 45
Blanchard, Terence 43
Blige, Mary J. 20, 34, 60
Bonds, Margaret 39
Bonga, Kuenda 13
Braxton, Toni 15, 61
Bridgetower, George 78
Brown, Patrick "Sleepy" 50
Brown, Uzee 42
Burke, Solomon 31, 86
Burleigh, Henry Thacker 56
Caesar, Shirley 19
Carter, Warrick L. 27
Chapman, Tracy 26
Charlemagne, Manno 11
Charles, Ray 16, 48
Cleveland, James 19
Cole, Natalie 17, 60, 84
Coleman, Ornette 39, 69
Collins, Bootsy 31
Combs, Sean "Puffy" 17, 43
Cook, Will Marion 40
Davis, Anthony 11
Davis, Miles 4
Davis, Sammy, Jr. 18
Dawson, William Levi 39
Diddley, Bo 39, 72
Domino, Fats 20
Ellington, Duke 5
Elliott, Missy 31
Europe, James Reese 10
Evans, Faith 22
Freeman, Paul 39
Fuller, Arthur 27
Gamble, Kenny 85
Garrett, Sean 57
Gaynor, Gloria 36
George, Nelson 12
Gillespie, Dizzy 1
Golson, Benny 37
Gordy, Berry, Jr. 1
Green, Al 13, 47, 74
Hailey, JoJo 22
Hailey, K-Ci 22
Handy, W. C. 8
Harris, Corey 39, 73
Hathaway, Donny 18
Hayes, Isaac 20, 58, 73
Hayes, Teddy 40
Hill, Lauryn 20, 53
Holland-Dozier-Holland 36
Holmes, Clint 57

Holt, Nora 38
Humphrey, Bobbi 20
Hutch, Willie 62
Isley, Ronald 25, 56
Jackson, Fred James 25
Jackson, Michael 19, 53, 76
Jackson, Randy 40
James, Rick 17
Jerkins, Rodney 31
Johnson, Buddy 36
Johnson, Georgia Douglas 41
Jones, Jonah 39
Jones, Quincy 8, 30
Jones, Thad 68
Joplin, Scott 6
Jordan, Montell 23
Jordan, Ronny 26
Kay, Ulysses 37
Kee, John P. 43
Kelly, R. 18, 44, 71
Keys, Alicia 32, 68
Kidjo, Angelique 50
Killings, Debra 57
King, B. B. 7
León, Tania 13
Lincoln, Abbey 3
Little Milton 36, 54
Little Walter 36
Lopes, Lisa "Left Eye" 36
Mahlasela, Vusi 65
Majors, Jeff 41
Marsalis, Delfeayo 41
Marsalis, Wynton 16
Martin, Roberta 58
Master P 21
Maxwell 20, 81
Mayfield, Curtis 2, 43
M.C. Hammer 20, 80
McClurkin, Donnie 25
McFerrin, Bobby 68
Mills, Stephanie 36
Mitchell, Brian Stokes 21
Mo', Keb' 36
Monica 21
Moore, Chante 26
Moore, Dorothy Rudd 46
Moore, Undine Smith 28
Muse, Clarence Edouard 21
Nash, Johnny 40
Ndegeocello, Meshell 15, 83
Osborne, Jeffrey 26
Otis, Clyde 67
Parker, Ray, Jr. 85
Pratt, Awadagin 31
Price, Florence 37
Prince 18, 65
Pritchard, Robert Starling 21
Reagon, Bernice Johnson 7
Redding, Otis 16
Reed, A. C. 36
Reid, Antonio "L.A." 28
Roach, Max 21, 63
Robinson, Reginald R. 53
Run-DMC 31, 75
Rushen, Patrice 12
Russell, Brenda 52
Sangare, Oumou 18
Seal 14, 75
Shorty, Ras, I 47
Silver, Horace 26
Simone, Nina 15, 41
Simpson, Valerie 21
Somi 85

Sowande, Fela 39
Still, William Grant 37
Strayhorn, Billy 31
Sundiata, Sekou 66
Sweat, Keith 19
Tillis, Frederick 40
Usher 23, 56
Van Peebles, Melvin 7
Walker, George 37
Warwick, Dionne 18
Washington, Grover, Jr. 17, 44
Williams, Deniece 36
Williams, Tony 67
Winans, Angie 36
Winans, Debbie 36
Withers, Bill 61

**Musicology**
George, Zelma Watson 42

**Muslim Mosque, Inc.**
X, Malcolm 1

**Mysteries**
Bland, Eleanor Taylor 39
Creagh, Milton 27
DeLoach, Nora 30
Himes, Chester 8
Holton, Hugh, Jr. 39
Mickelbury, Penny 28
Mosley, Walter 5, 25, 68
Thomas-Graham 29
Wesley, Valerie Wilson 18

**The Mystery**
Delany, Martin R. 27

**Mystic Seaport Museum**
Pinckney, Bill 42

**NAACP**
See National Association for the Advancement of Colored People

**NAACP Image Awards**
Brandy 14, 34, 72
Fields, Kim 36
Lawrence, Martin 6, 27, 60
Mac, Bernie 29, 61, 72
McRae, Carmen 77
Okonedo, Sophie 67
Prince-Bythewood, Gina 31, 77
Rhimes, Shonda Lynn 67
Warner, Malcolm-Jamal 22, 36
Wesley, Richard 73

**NAACP Legal Defense and Educational Fund (LDF)**
Bell, Derrick 6
Carter, Robert L. 51
Chambers, Julius 3
Coleman, James E., Jr. 79
Coleman, William T. 76
Edelman, Marian Wright 5, 42
Fisher, Ada Lois Sipuel 76
Guinier, Lani 7, 30
Jones, Elaine R. 7, 45
Julian, Percy Lavon 6
Marshall, Thurgood 1, 44
Motley, Constance Baker 10, 55
Rice, Constance LaMay 60
Smith, Kemba 70

Smythe Haith, Mabel **61**

**NABJ**
See National Association of Black
Journalists

**NAC**
See Nyasaland African Congress

**NACW**
See National Association of Colored Women

**Namibian government**
Nujoma, Samuel **10**

**NASA**
See National Aeronautics and
Space Administration

**NASCAR**
See National Association of Stock
Car Auto Racing

**Nation of Islam**
See Lost-Found Nation of Islam

**National Academy of Design**
White, Charles **39**

**National Action Council for
Minorities in Engineering**
Pierre, Percy Anthony **46**
Slaughter, John Brooks **53**

**National Action Network**
Sharpton, Al **21**

**National Aeronautics and
Space Administration (NASA)**
Anderson, Michael P. **40**
Bluford, Guy **2, 35**
Bolden, Charles Frank, Jr. **7, 78**
Campbell, Donald J. **66**
Carruthers, George R. **40**
Drew, Alvin, Jr. **67**
Easley, Annie J. **61**
Gregory, Frederick **8, 51**
Jemison, Mae C. **1, 35**
Johnson, Katherine (Coleman
Goble) **61**
McNair, Ronald **3, 58**
Mills, Joseph C. **51**
Nichols, Nichelle **11**
Sigur, Wanda **44**
Wilson, Stephanie **72**

**National Afro-American Council**
Fortune, T. Thomas **6**
Mossell, Gertrude Bustill **40**

**National Airmen's Association
of America**
Brown, Willa **40**

**National Alliance of Postal
and Federal Employees**
McGee, James Madison **46**

**National Alliance Party (NAP)**
Fulani, Lenora **11**

**National Association for the
Advancement of Colored
People (NAACP)**
Anderson, Reuben V. **81**
Anderson, William G(ilchrist) **57**

Anthony, Wendell **25**
Austin, Junius C. **44**
Baker, Ella **5**
Ballance, Frank W. **41**
Bates, Daisy **13**
Bell, Derrick **6**
Bond, Julian **2, 35**
Bontemps, Arna **8**
Brock, Roslyn McCallister **86**
Brooks, Gwendolyn **1**
Brown, Homer S. **47**
Bunche, Ralph J. **5**
Chambers, Julius **3**
Chavis, Benjamin **6**
Clark, Kenneth B. **5, 52**
Clark, Septima **7**
Cobb, W. Montague **39**
Colter, Cyrus, J. **36**
Cotter, Joseph Seamon, Sr. **40**
Creagh, Milton **27**
Days, Drew S., III **10**
Dee, Ruby **8, 50, 68**
Du Bois, W. E. B. **3**
DuBois, Shirley Graham **21**
Dukes, Hazel Nell **56**
Edelman, Marian Wright **5, 42**
Evers, Medgar **3**
Evers, Myrlie **8**
Farmer, James **2, 64**
Ford, Clyde W. **40**
Fuller, S. B. **13**
Gibson, William F. **6**
Grimké, Archibald H. **9**
Hampton, Fred **18**
Harrington, Oliver W. **9**
Hayes, Dennis **54**
Henderson, Wade **14**
Hobson, Julius W. **44**
Hollowell, Donald L. **57**
Hooks, Benjamin L. **2, 85**
Houston, Charles Hamilton **4**
Jackson, Vera **40**
Jealous, Benjamin **70**
Johnson, James Weldon **5**
Jordan, Vernon E. **3, 35**
Kidd, Mae Street **39**
Lampkin, Daisy **19**
Madison, Joseph E. **17**
Marshall, Thurgood **1, 44**
McKissick, Floyd B. **3**
McPhail, Sharon **2**
Meek, Carrie **36**
Meredith, James H. **11**
Mfume, Kweisi **6, 41**
Mitchell, Sharon **36**
Moore, Harry T. **29**
Morgan, Irene **65**
Moses, Robert Parris **11**
Motley, Constance Baker **10, 55**
Moyo, Yvette Jackson **36**
Owens, Major **6**
Payton, John **48**
Richardson, Rupert **67**
Rustin, Bayard **4**
Sutton, Percy E. **42, 82**
Talbert, Mary B. **77**
Terrell, Mary Church **9**
Tobias, Channing H. **79**
Tucker, C. Delores **12, 56**
Van Lierop, Robert **53**
White, Walter F. **4**
Wilkins, Roy **4**
Williams, Hosea Lorenzo **15, 31**

Williams, Robert F. **11**
Wilson, Margaret Bush **79**
Wright, Louis Tompkins **4**

**National Association of Black
Journalists (NABJ)**
Curry, George E. **23**
Dawkins, Wayne **20**
Harris, Jay T. **19**
Jarrett, Vernon D. **42**
Lowe, Herbert **57**
Madison, Paula **37**
Pressley, Condace L. **41**
Rice, Linda Johnson **9, 41**
Shipp, E. R. **15**
Stone, Chuck **9**
Washington, Laura S. **18**

**National Association of Colored Women (NACW)**
Bethune, Mary McLeod **4**
Cooper, Margaret J. **46**
Harper, Frances Ellen Watkins **11**
Lampkin, Daisy **19**
Ruffin, Josephine St. Pierre **75**
Stewart, Ella **39**
Talbert, Mary B. **77**
Terrell, Mary Church **9**

**National Association of Negro
Business and Professional
Women's Clubs**
Vaughns, Cleopatra **46**

**National Association of Negro
Musicians**
Bonds, Margaret **39**
Brown, Uzee **42**

**National Association of Regulatory Utility Commissioners**
Colter, Cyrus, J. **36**

**National Association of Social
Workers**
Jackson, Judith D. **57**
McMurray, Georgia L. **36**

**National Association for Stock
Car Auto Racing**
Lester, Bill **42, 85**

**National Baptist Convention
USA**
Bradley, J. Robert **65**
Jones, E. Edward, Sr. **45**
Lyons, Henry **12**
Shaw, William J. **30**
Thurston, Stephen J. **49**

**National Bar Association**
Alexander, Joyce London **18**
Alexander, Sadie Tanner Mossell
**22**
Archer, Dennis **7, 36**
Bailey, Clyde **45**
Hubbard, Arnette **38**
McPhail, Sharon **2**
Pincham, R. Eugene, Sr. **69**
Quince, Peggy A. **69**
Ray, Charlotte E. **60**
Robinson, Malcolm S. **44**
Thompson, Larry D. **39**

Walker, Cora T. **68**

**National Basketball Players
Association**
Erving, Julius **18, 47**
Ewing, Patrick **17, 73**
Gourdine, Simon **11**
Hunter, Billy **22**

**National Black Arts Festival
(NBAF)**
Borders, James **9**
Brooks, Avery **9**

**National Black College Hall of
Fame**
Dortch, Thomas W., Jr. **45**

**National Black Farmers Association (NBFA)**
Boyd, John W., Jr. **20, 72**

**National Black Fine Art Show**
Wainwright, Joscelyn **46**

**National Black Gay and Lesbian Conference**
Wilson, Phill **9**

**National Black Gay and Lesbian Leadership Forum (NBGLLF)**
Boykin, Keith **14**
Carter, Mandy **11**
Wilson, Phill **9**

**National Black Women's
Health Project**
Avery, Byllye Y. **66**

**National Book Award**
Ellison, Ralph **7**
Haley, Alex **4**
Johnson, Charles **1, 82**
Mackey, Nathaniel **75**
Patterson, Orlando **4**

**National Broadcasting Company (NBC)**
Allen, Byron **3, 24**
Gumbel, Bryant **14, 80**
Hinderas, Natalie **5**
Holt, Lester **66**
Ifill, Gwen **28**
Johnson, Rodney Van **28**
Madison, Paula **37**
Reynolds, Star Jones **10, 27, 61**
Roker, Al **12, 49**
Simpson, Carole **6, 30**
Thomas-Graham, Pamela **29**
Williams, Montel **4, 57**

**National Brotherhood of Skiers (NBS)**
Horton, Andre **33**
Horton, Suki **33**

**National Center for Neighborhood Enterprise (NCNE)**
Woodson, Robert L. **10**

**National Coalition of 100
Black Women (NCBW)**
Mays, Leslie A. **41**
McCabe, Jewell Jackson **10**

**National Coalition to Abolish the Death Penalty (NCADP)**
Hawkins, Steven 14

**National Conference on Black Lawyers (NCBL)**
McDougall, Gay J. 11, 43

**National Council of Churches**
Howard, M. William, Jr. 26

**National Council of Negro Women (NCNW)**
Bethune, Mary McLeod 4
Blackwell, Unita 17
Cole, Johnnetta B. 5, 43
Hamer, Fannie Lou 6
Height, Dorothy I. 2, 23, 78
Lampkin, Daisy 19
Sampson, Edith S. 4
Smith, Jane E. 24
Staupers, Mabel K. 7

**National Council of Nigeria and the Cameroons (NCNC)**
Azikiwe, Nnamdi 13

**National Council of Teachers of Mathematics**
Granville, Evelyn Boyd 36

**National Council on the Arts**
Robinson, Cleo Parker 38

**National Cowboys of Color Museum and Hall of Fame**
Austin, Gloria 63
Austin, Jim 63

**National Dental Association**
Madison, Romell 45

**National Earthquake Information Center**
Person, Waverly 9, 51

**National Education Association (NEA)**
Futrell, Mary Hatwood 33

**National Endowment for the Arts (NEA)**
Barthé, Earl 78
Bradley, David Henry, Jr. 39
Brown, Chuck 78
Hall, Arthur 39
Hemphill, Essex 10
Pope.L, William 72
Serrano, Andres 3
Williams, John A. 27
Williams, William T. 11

**National Endowment for the Arts Jazz Hall of Fame**
Terry, Clark 39

**National Endowment for the Humanities**
Gibson, Donald Bernard 40

**National Equal Rights League**
Trotter, Monroe 9

**National Football League (NFL)**
Alexander, Shaun 58
Allen, Marcus 20

Anderson, Jamal 22
Barber, Ronde 41
Barber, Tiki 57
Barney, Lem 26
Bettis, Jerome 64
Briscoe, Marlin 37
Brooks, Aaron 33
Brooks, Derrick 43
Brown, Jim 11
Bruce, Isaac 26
Bryant, Cullen 81
Butler, Leroy, III 17
Caldwell, Jim 81
Cherry, Deron 40
Cox, Bryan 83
Crennel, Romeo 54
Croom, Sylvester 50
Culpepper, Daunte 32, 85
Cunningham, Randall 23
Davis, Milt 74
Davis, Terrell 20
Delaney, Joe 76
Dickerson, Eric 27
Edwards, Herman 51
Farr, Mel 24
Faulk, Marshall 35
Fowler, Reggie 51
George, Eddie 80
Gilliam, Frank 23
Gilliam, Joe 31
Green, Darrell 39, 74
Green, Dennis 5, 45
Greene, Joe 10
Harris, James 79
Hill, Calvin 19
Holmes, Santonio 87
Howard, Desmond 16, 58
Irvin, Michael 64
Jackson, Tom 70
Johnson, Levi 48
Ladd, Ernie 64
Little, Floyd 86
Lofton, James 42
Lott, Ronnie 9
Mayhew, Martin R. 76
McDaniel, Randall Cornell 81
McNair, Steve 22, 47, 79
Monk, Art 38, 73
Moon, Warren 8, 66
Moss, Randy 23
Motley, Marion 26
Newsome, Ozzie 26
Oliver, Pam 54
Owens, Terrell 53
Pace, Orlando 21
Page, Alan 7
Payton, Walter 11, 25
Peete, Rodney 60
Randle, John 87
Rashad, Ahmad 18
Rhodes, Ray 14
Rice, Jerry 5, 55
Sanders, Barry 1, 53
Sanders, Bob 72
Sanders, Deion 4, 31
Sapp, Warren 38
Sayers, Gale 28
Sharper, Darren 32
Shell, Art 1, 66
Simpson, O.J. 15
Singletary, Mike 4, 76
Smith, Bruce 80
Smith, Emmitt 7, 87

Smith, Rick 72
Stewart, Kordell 21
Stingley, Darryl 69
Strahan, Michael 35, 81
Stringer, Korey 35
Swann, Lynn 28
Tatum, Jack 87
Taylor, Jason 70
Taylor, Lawrence 25
Thomas, Derrick 25
Thomas, Emmitt 71
Thomas, Thurman 75
Thrower, Willie 35
Toler, Burl 80
Tomlinson, LaDainian 65
Tunnell, Emlen 54
Upshaw, Gene 18, 47, 72
Vick, Michael 39, 65
Walker, Herschel 1, 69
Ward, Hines 84
Ware, Andre 37
Washington, Kenny 50
White, Reggie 6, 50
Williams, Doug 22
Williams, J. Mayo 83
Williams, Ricky 85
Williamson, Fred 67
Winslow, Kellen 83
Wright, Rayfield 70

**National Heritage "Living Treasure" Fellowship**
Jackson, John 36

**National Hockey League (NHL)**
Brashear, Donald 39
Brathwaite, Fred 35
Brown, Sean 52
Fuhr, Grant 1, 49
Grier, Mike 43
Iginla, Jarome 35
Laraque, Georges 48
Mayers, Jamal 39
McBride, Bryant 18
McCarthy, Sandy 64
McKegney, Tony 3
O'Ree, Willie 5
Salvador, Bryce 51
Weekes, Kevin 67

**National Immigration Forum**
Jones, Sarah 39

**National Information Infrastructure**
Lewis, Delano 7

**National Institute of Arts & Letters**
Lewis, Norman 39
White, Charles 39

**National Institute of Education**
Baker, Gwendolyn Calvert 9

**National Institutes of Health (NIH)**
Anderson, Norman B. 45
Cargill, Victoria A. 43
Dunston, Georgia Mae 48
Pinn, Vivian Winona 49

**National Inventors Hall of Fame**
Carruthers, George R. 40

**National Lawn & Garden Distributor Association**
Donald, Arnold Wayne 36

**National Medical Association**
Cole, Lorraine 48
Maxey, Randall 46
Ojikutu, Bisola 65

**National Minority Business Council**
Leary, Kathryn D. 10

**National Museum of American History**
Crew, Spencer R. 55
Reagon, Bernice Johnson 7

**National Negro Congress**
Bunche, Ralph J. 5

**National Negro Suffrage League**
Trotter, Monroe 9

**National Network for African American Women and the Law**
Arnwine, Barbara 28

**National Newspaper Publishers Association**
Cooper, Andrew W. 36
Jealous, Benjamin 70
Oliver, John J., Jr. 48

**National Oceanic and Atmospheric Administration**
Bacon-Bercey, June 38
Fields, Evelyn J. 27

**National Organization for Women (NOW)**
Hernandez, Aileen Clarke 13
Kennedy, Florynce 12, 33
Meek, Carrie 6, 36
Murray, Pauli 38

**National Political Congress of Black Women**
Chisholm, Shirley 2, 50
Tucker, C. Delores 12, 56
Waters, Maxine 3, 67

**National Public Radio (NPR)**
Abu-Jamal, Mumia 15
Bates, Karen Grigsby 40
Drummond, William J. 40
Early, Gerald 15
Lewis, Delano 7
Mitchell, Elvis 67
Norris, Michele 83
Smiley, Tavis 20, 68
Williams, Juan 35, 80
Zook, Kristal Brent 62

**National Resistance Army (Uganda; NRA)**
Museveni, Yoweri 4

**National Resistance Movement**
Museveni, Yoweri 4

**National Revolutionary Movement for Development**
See Mouvement Revolutionnaire National pour le Developpement

**National Rifle Association (NRA)**
Williams, Robert F. **11**

**National Science Foundation (NSF)**
Massey, Walter E. **5, 45**

**National Security Council**
Frazer, Jendayi **68**
Powell, Colin **1, 28, 75**
Rice, Condoleezza **3, 28, 72**
Rice, Susan E. **74**
Sutphen, Mona **77**

**National Society of Black Engineers**
Donald, Arnold Wayne **36**
Price, Richard **51**

**National Union for the Total Independence of Angola (UNITA)**
Roberto, Holden **65**
Savimbi, Jonas **2, 34**

**National Union of Mineworkers (South Africa)**
Motlanthe, Kgalema **74**
Ramaphosa, Cyril **3**

**National Urban Coalition (NUC)**
Edelin, Ramona Hoage **19**

**National Urban League**
Barrow, Willie T. **85**
Berry, Edwin C. **81**
Brown, Ron **5**
Gordon, Bruce S. **41, 53, 82**
Granger, Lester B. **75**
Greely, M. Gasby **27**
Haynes, George Edmund **8**
Jacob, John E. **2**
Jones, Eugene Kinckle **79**
Jordan, Vernon E. **3, 35**
Price, Hugh B. **9, 54**
Spriggs, William **67**
Young, Whitney M., Jr. **4**

**National War College**
Clemmons, Reginal G. **41**

**National Wildlife Federation**
Osborne, Na'taki **54**

**National Women's Basketball League (NWBL)**
Catchings, Tamika **43**

**National Women's Hall of Fame**
Cary, Mary Ann Shadd **30**
Kelly, Leontine **33**
Talbert, Mary B. **77**

**National Youth Administration (NYA)**
Bethune, Mary McLeod **4**
Primus, Pearl **6**

**Nationwide**
James, Donna A. **51**

**Naval Research Laboratory (NRL)**
Carruthers, George R. **40**

**NBAF**
See National Black Arts Festival

**NBC**
See National Broadcasting Company

**NBGLLF**
See National Black Gay and Lesbian Leadership Forum

**NCBL**
See National Conference on Black Lawyers

**NCBW**
See National Coalition of 100 Black Women

**NCCK**
See Kenya National Council of Churches

**NCNE**
See National Center for Neighborhood Enterprise

**NCNW**
See National Council of Negro Women

**NEA**
See National Education Association; National Endowment for the Arts

**Nebula awards**
Butler, Octavia **8, 43, 58**
Delany, Samuel R., Jr. **9**

**Négritude**
Césaire, Aimé **48, 69**
Damas, Léon-Gontran **46**
Ndiaye, Iba **74**

**Negro American Political League**
Trotter, Monroe **9**

*Negro Digest* magazine
Fuller, Hoyt **44**
Johnson, John H. **3, 54**

**Negro Ensemble Company**
Cash, Rosalind **28**
Gordon, Carl **87**
Hooks, Robert **76**
Rolle, Esther **13, 21**
Schultz, Michael A. **6**
Ward, Douglas Turner **42**

**Negro Leagues**
Banks, Ernie **33**
Barnhill, David **30**
Bell, James "Cool Papa" **36**
Black, Joe **75**
Brown, Willard **36**
Campanella, Roy **25**
Charleston, Oscar **39**
Dandridge, Ray **36**
Davis, Piper **19**
Day, Leon **39**

Foster, Andrew **79**
Gibson, Josh **22**
Hyde, Cowan F. "Bubba" **47**
Irvin, Monte **31**
Johnson, Clifford "Connie" **52**
Johnson, Mamie "Peanut" **40**
Kaiser, Cecil **42**
Kimbro, Henry A. **25**
Leonard, Buck **67**
Lloyd, John Henry "Pop" **30**
Mackey, Biz **82**
O'Neil, Buck **19, 59**
Paige, Satchel **7**
Pride, Charley **26**
Radcliffe, Ted **74**
Smith, Hilton **29**
Stearnes, Norman "Turkey" **31**
Stone, Toni **15**

**Neo-hoodoo**
Reed, Ishmael **8**

**Netherlands Antilles**
Liberia-Peters, Maria Philomena **12**

**Netherlands government**
Ali, Ayaan Hirsi **58**

**NetNoir Inc.**
CasSelle, Malcolm **11**
Ellington, E. David **11**

**Neurosurgery**
Black, Keith Lanier **18, 84**
Canady, Alexa **28**
Carson, Benjamin **1, 35, 76**

**Neustadt International Prize for Literature**
Brathwaite, Kamau **36**

**New Dance Group**
Primus, Pearl **6**

**New Edition**
Bivins, Michael **72**
Gill, Johnny **51**

**New Jack Swing music**
Brown, Bobby **58**
Hall, Aaron **57**

**New Jersey Family Development Act**
Bryant, Wayne R. **6**

**New Jersey General Assembly**
Bryant, Wayne R. **6**
Payne, William D. **60**

**New Jersey Nets**
Doby, Lawrence Eugene, Sr. **16, 41**

**New Jewel Movement**
Bishop, Maurice **39**

**New Life Community Choir**
Kee, John P. **43**

**New Negro movement**
See Harlem Renaissance

**New Orleans city government**
Henry, Troy **85**
Mason, Ronald **27**
Nagin, C. Ray **42, 57**

Perry, James **83**

**New Orleans Saints football team**
Brooks, Aaron **33**
Mills, Sam **33**

**New York City government**
Campbell, Mary Schmidt **43**
Crew, Rudolph F. **16**
Davis, Gordon J. **76**
Dinkins, David **4**
Farrell, Herman D., Jr. **81**
Fields, C. Virginia **25**
Ford, Wallace **58**
Hageman, Hans **36**
Paterson, Basil A. **69**
Spigner, Archie **81**
Sutton, Percy E. **42**
Thompson, William **35**
Tolbert, Terence **74**

**New York Coalition of 100 Black Woman**
Wein, Joyce **62**

*New York Daily News*
Cose, Ellis **5, 50**

**New York Drama Critics Circle Award**
Hansberry, Lorraine **6**

**New York Giants baseball team**
Dandridge, Ray **36**
Mays, Willie **3**
Tunnell, Emlen **54**

**New York Giants football team**
Barber, Tiki **57**
Strahan, Michael **35, 81**
Taylor, Lawrence **25**

**New York Hip Hop Theater Festival**
Jones, Sarah **39**

**New York Institute for Social Therapy and Research**
Fulani, Lenora **11**

**New York Jets football team**
Lott, Ronnie **9**

**New York Knicks basketball team**
Ewing, Patrick **17, 73**
Johnson, Larry **28**
Reed, Willis, Jr. **86**
Sprewell, Latrell **23**

**New York Mets baseball team**
Clendenon, Donn **26, 56**

**New York Philharmonic**
DePreist, James **37**

**New York Public Library**
Baker, Augusta **38**
Dodson, Howard, Jr. **7, 52**
Schomburg, Arthur Alfonso **9**

**New York Shakespeare Festival**
Browne, Roscoe Lee **66**
Gunn, Moses **10**

Wolfe, George C. **6, 43**

**New York state government**
Brown, Byron W. **72**
Farrell, Herman D., Jr. **81**
McCall, H. Carl **27**
Motley, Constance Baker **10, 55**
Owens, Major **6**
Paterson, Basil A. **69**
Paterson, David A. **59**
Smith, Malcolm A. **75**

**New York State Supreme Court**
Dudley, Edward R. **58**
Wright, Bruce McMarion **3, 52**

**New York Stock Exchange**
Doley, Harold, Jr. **26**

**New York Times**
Blair, Jayson **50**
Blow, Charles M. **73**
Boyd, Gerald M. **32, 59**
Broyard, Anatole **68**
Caldwell, Earl **60**
Cooper, Helene **74**
Davis, George **36**
Hunter-Gault, Charlayne **6, 31**
Ifill, Gwen **28**
Mabry, Marcus **70**
Price, Hugh B. **9, 54**
Rhoden, William C. **67**
Wilkins, Roger **2, 84**

**New York University**
Brathwaite, Kamau **36**
Campbell, Mary Schmidt **43**
Newkirk, Pamela **69**

**New York Yankees baseball team**
Baylor, Don **6**
Bonds, Bobby **43**
Jackson, Reggie **15**
Jeter, Derek **27**
Sabathia, CC **74**
Strawberry, Darryl **22**
Watson, Bob **25**
Winfield, Dave **5**

**Newark (NJ) city government**
Booker, Cory Anthony **68**
Gibson, Kenneth Allen **6**
James, Sharpe **23, 69**

**Newark Housing Authority**
Gibson, Kenneth Allen **6**

**The News Hour with Jim Lehrer** TV series
Ifill, Gwen **28**

**Newsday**
Olojede, Dele **59**

**Newsweek**
Mabry, Marcus **70**

**NFL**
See National Football League

**NHL**
See National Hockey League

**Niagara movement**
Du Bois, W. E. B. **3**
Hope, John **8**

Talbert, Mary B. **77**
Trotter, Monroe **9**

**Nickelodeon**
Thompson, Kenan **52**

**Nigerian Armed Forces**
Abacha, Sani **11, 70**
Abiola, Moshood **70**
Babangida, Ibrahim **4**
Obasanjo, Olusegun **5, 22**

**Nigerian Association of Patriotic Writers and Artists**
Barrett, Lindsay **43**

**Nigerian government**
Abiola, Moshood **70**
Abubakar, Abdulsalami **66**
Akunyili, Dora Nkem **58**
Jonathan, Goodluck **83**
Obasanjo, Olusegun **5**
Yar'adua, Umaru **69**

**Nigerian literature**
Achebe, Chinua **6**
Akpan, Uwem **70**
Amadi, Elechi **40**
Bandele, Biyi **68**
Barrett, Lindsay **43**
Ekwensi, Cyprian **37**
Onwueme, Tess Osonye **23**
Rotimi, Ola **1**
Saro-Wiwa, Kenule **39**
Soyinka, Wole **4**

**Nigerien government**
Tandja, Mamadou **33, 78**

**NIH**
See National Institutes of Health

**Nike, Inc.**
Edwards, Trevor **54**
Miller, Larry G. **72**

**Nobel Peace Prize**
Annan, Kofi Atta **15, 48**
Bunche, Ralph J. **5**
King, Martin Luther, Jr. **1**
Luthuli, Albert **13**
Tutu, Desmond Mpilo **6, 44**

**Nobel Prize for Literature**
Morrison, Toni **2, 15, 86**
Soyinka, Wole **4**
Walcott, Derek **5**

**Noma Award for Publishing in African**
Ba, Mariama **30**

**Nonfiction**
Abrahams, Peter **39**
Adams-Ender, Clara **40**
Ali, Hana Yasmeen **52**
Allen, Debbie **13, 42**
Allen, Robert L. **38**
Andrews, Tina **74**
Atkins, Cholly **40**
Baisden, Michael **66**
Ballard, Allen Butler, Jr. **40**
Bashir, Halima **73**
Beah, Ishmael **69**
Blassingame, John Wesley **40**
Blockson, Charles L. **42**

Bogle, Donald **34**
Brown, Cecil M. **46**
Brown, Lloyd Louis **42**
Broyard, Bliss **68**
Buckley, Gail Lumet **39**
Carby, Hazel **27**
Carter, Joye Maureen **41**
Cashin, Sheryll **63**
Cobb, William Jelani **59**
Cole, Johnnetta B. **5, 43**
Cook, Mercer **40**
Cox, Joseph Mason Andrew **51**
Crew, Spencer R. **55**
Cruse, Harold **54**
Datcher, Michael **60**
Davis, Arthur P. **41**
Davis, Thulani **61**
Dickerson, Debra J. **60**
Dunnigan, Alice Allison **41**
Edelman, Marian Wright **5, 42**
Elliott, Lorris **37**
Fax, Elton **48**
Fine, Sam **60**
Finner-Williams, Paris Michele **62**
Fisher, Antwone **40**
Fletcher, Bill, Jr. **41**
Ford, Clyde W. **40**
Foster, Cecil **32**
Gayle, Addison, Jr. **41**
Gibson, Donald Bernard **40**
Gladwell, Malcolm **62**
Greenwood, Monique **38**
Harrison, Alvin **28**
Harrison, Calvin **28**
Henderson, David **53**
Henries, A. Doris Banks **44**
Henriques, Julian **37**
Hercules, Frank **44**
Hernton, Calvin C. **51**
Hill, Errol **40**
Hobson, Julius W. **44**
Horne, Frank **44**
Ilibagiza, Immaculée **66**
Jakes, Thomas "T. D." **17, 43**
Jolley, Willie **28**
Jordan, Vernon E. **7, 35**
Kayira, Legson **40**
Kearney, Janis **54**
Kennedy, Randall **40**
Knight, Etheridge **37**
Kobia, Samuel **43**
Ladner, Joyce A. **42**
Lampley, Oni Faida **43, 71**
Lincoln, C. Eric **38**
Long, Eddie L. **29**
Mabuza-Suttle, Felicia **43**
Malveaux, Julianne **32, 70**
Manley, Ruth **34**
Matthews Shatteen, Westina **51**
McKenzie, Vashti M. **29**
McKinney Hammond, Michelle **51**
McWhorter, John **35**
Mossell, Gertrude Bustill **40**
Murray, Pauli **38**
Myers, Walter Dean **8, 20**
Naylor, Gloria **10, 42**
Neal, Mark Anthony **74**
Newkirk, Pamela **69**
Nissel, Angela **42**
Norton, Meredith **72**
Parks, Rosa **1, 35, 56**
Pitts, Leonard, Jr. **54, 85**
Run **31, 73**

Rusesabagina, Paul **60**
Sadlier, Rosemary **62**
Shakur, Yusef **85**
Smith, Jessie Carney **35**
Steele, Shelby **13, 82**
Thornton, Yvonne S. **69**
Tillis, Frederick **40**
Wade-Gayles, Gloria Jean **41**
Walker, Rebecca **50**
Wambugu, Florence **42**
Wilkens, J. Ernest, Jr. **43**
Williams, Terrie **35**
Williams, Wendy **62**
Wiwa, Ken **67**
Wright, Nathan, Jr. **56**
Zook, Kristal Brent **62**

**North Carolina state government**
Ballance, Frank W. **41**

**North Carolina State University**
Lowe, Sidney **64**

**North Pole**
Counter, S. Allen **74**
Delany, Martin R. **27**
Henson, Matthew **2**
Hillary, Barbara **65**
McLeod, Gus **27**

**NOW**
See National Organization for Women

**NPR**
See National Public Radio

**NRA**
See National Resistance Army (Uganda); National Rifle Association

**NRL**
See Naval Research Laboratory

**NSF**
See National Science Foundation

**Nuclear energy**
O'Leary, Hazel **6**
Packer, Daniel **56**
Quarterman, Lloyd Albert **4**

**Nuclear Regulatory Commission**
Jackson, Shirley Ann **12**

**Nucleus**
King, Yolanda **6**
Shabazz, Attallah **6**

**Nursing**
Adams-Ender, Clara **40**
Auguste, Rose-Anne **13**
Hillary, Barbara **65**
Hughes, Ebony **57**
Hunter, Alberta **42**
Johnson, Eddie Bernice **8**
Johnson, Hazel **22**
Johnson, Mamie "Peanut" **40**
Larsen, Nella **10**
Lewis, Daurene **72**
Lyttle, Hulda Margaret **14**
Richards, Hilda **49**
Riley, Helen Caldwell Day **13**

Robinson, Rachel **16**
Robinson, Sharon **22**
Seacole, Mary **54**
Shabazz, Betty **7, 26**
Staupers, Mabel K. **7**
Taylor, Susie King **13**

**Nutrition**
Clark, Celeste **15**
Gregory, Dick **1, 54**
Smith, Ian **62**
Watkins, Shirley R. **17**

**Nuwaubianism**
York, Dwight D. **71**

**NWBL**
See National Women's Basketball
League

**NYA**
See National Youth Administration

**Nyasaland African Congress (NAC)**
Banda, Hastings Kamuzu **6, 54**

**Oakland Athletics baseball team**
Baylor, Don **6**
Henderson, Rickey **28, 78**
Jackson, Reggie **15**
Morgan, Joe Leonard **9**

**Oakland Raiders football team**
Howard, Desmond **16, 58**
Tatum, Jack **87**
Upshaw, Gene **18, 47, 72**

*Oakland Tribune*
Bailey, Chauncey **68**
Maynard, Nancy Hicks **73**
Maynard, Robert C. **7**

**OAU**
See Organization of African Unity

**Obie awards**
Browne, Roscoe Lee **66**
Carter, Nell **39**
De Shields, André **72**
Freeman, Yvette **27**
Orlandersmith, Dael **42**
Sands, Diana **87**
Thigpen, Lynne **17, 41**

**Office of Civil Rights**
See U.S. Department of Education

**Office of Management and Budget**
Raines, Franklin Delano **14**

**Ohio state government**
Brown, Les **5**
Ford, Jack **39**
Stokes, Carl **10, 73**
White, Michael R. **5**
Williams, George Washington **18**

**Ohio Women's Hall of Fame**
Craig-Jones, Ellen Walker **44**
Stewart, Ella **39**

**OKeh record label**
Brooks, Hadda **40**
Mo', Keb' **36**

*Oklahoma Eagle*
Ross, Don **27**

**Oklahoma Hall of Fame**
Mitchell, Leona **42**

**Oklahoma state government**
Ross, Don **27**

**Olatunji Center for African Culture**
Olatunji, Babatunde **36**

**Olympics**
Ali, Muhammad **2, 16, 52**
Beamon, Bob **30**
Bekele, Kenenisa **75**
Bolt, Usain **73**
Bonaly, Surya **7**
Bonheur, Yannick **84**
Bowe, Riddick **6**
Christie, Linford **8**
Clay, Bryan **57, 74**
Coachman, Alice **18**
Davis, Shani **58, 84**
Dawes, Dominique **11**
DeFrantz, Anita **37**
DeGale, James **74**
Devers, Gail **7, 87**
Dibaba, Tirunesh **73**
Edwards, Teresa **14**
Ervin, Anthony **66**
Eto'o, Samuel **73**
Felix, Allyson **48**
Flowers, Vonetta **35**
Freeman, Cathy **29**
Garrison, Zina **2**
Gebrselassie, Haile **70**
Gourdine, Meredith **33**
Greene, Maurice **27, 77**
Griffith, Yolanda **25**
Griffith-Joyner, Florence **28**
Harrison, Alvin **28**
Harrison, Calvin **28**
Hayes, Bob **77**
Hines, Garrett **35**
Holmes, Kelly **47**
Holyfield, Evander **6**
Howard, Sherri **36**
Iginla, Jarome **35**
James, G. Larry **74**
James, Vanessa **84**
Johnson, Ben **1**
Johnson, Michael **13**
Johnson, Rafer **33**
Jones, Cullen **73**
Jones, Lou **64**
Jones, Randy **35**
Joyner-Kersee, Jackie **5**
Keflezighi, Meb **49**
Kidd, Jason **86**
Lewis, Carl **4**
Malone, Karl **18, 51**
Metcalfe, Ralph **26**
Miller, Cheryl **10, 74**
Montgomery, Tim **41**
Moses, Edwin **8**
Mutola, Maria **12**
Owens, Jesse **2**
Powell, Mike **7**
Quirot, Ana **13**
Richards, Sanya **66**
Rudolph, Wilma **4**
Scurry, Briana **27**

Thomas, Debi **26**
Thugwane, Josia **21**
Vanessa James and Yannick Bonheur **84**
Ward, Andre **62**
Ward, Lloyd **21, 46**
Westbrook, Peter **20**
Whitaker, Pernell **10**
White, Willye **67**
Whitfield, Mal **60**
Wilkens, Lenny **11**
Williams, Lauryn **58**
Woodruff, John **68**

*On a Roll* Radio
Smith, Greg **28**

**Oncology**
Leffall, Lasalle **3, 64**

**100 Black Men of America**
Dortch, Thomas W., Jr. **45**
Llewellyn, J. Bruce **13, 85**

**Ontario Legislature**
Curling, Alvin **34**

**Onyx Opera**
Brown, Uzee **42**

**Opera**
Adams, Leslie **39**
Allen, Betty **83**
Anderson, Marian **2, 33**
Arroyo, Martina **30**
Battle, Kathleen **70**
Brooks, Avery **9**
Brown, Angela M. **54**
Brown, Anne **76**
Brown, Uzee **42**
Bumbry, Grace **5**
Collins, Janet **33, 64**
Davis, Anthony **11**
Dobbs, Mattiwilda **34**
Duncan, Todd **76**
Estes, Simon **28**
Freeman, Paul **39**
Graves, Denyce Antoinette **19, 57**
Greely, M. Gasby **27**
Grist, Reri **84**
Hendricks, Barbara **3, 67**
Joplin, Scott **6**
Joyner, Matilda Sissieretta **15**
Lister, Marquita **65**
Maynor, Dorothy **19**
McDonald, Audra **20, 62**
Mitchell, Leona **42**
Norman, Jessye **5**
Phillips, Helen L. **63**
Price, Leontyne **1**
Ragin, Derek Lee **84**
Simpson-Hoffman, N'kenge **52**
Still, William Grant **37**
Three Mo' Tenors **35**
Verrett, Shirley **66**
White, Willard **53**

**Operation Desert Shield/Operation Desert Storm**
Powell, Colin **1, 28, 75**

**Operation HOPE**
Bryant, John **26**

**Ophthalmology**
Bath, Patricia E. **37**

**Oracle Corporation**
Phillips, Charles E., Jr. **57**
Woods, Jacqueline **52**

**Organ**
McGriff, Jimmy **72**

**Organization of African States**
Museveni, Yoweri **4**

**Organization of African Unity (OAU)**
Diouf, Abdou **3**
Haile Selassie **7**
Kaunda, Kenneth **2**
Kenyatta, Jomo **5**
Nkrumah, Kwame **3**
Nujoma, Samuel **10**
Nyerere, Julius **5**
Touré, Sekou **6**

**Organization of Afro-American Unity**
Feelings, Muriel **44**
X, Malcolm **1**

**Organization of Women Writers of African Descent**
Cortez, Jayne **43**

**Organization Us**
Karenga, Maulana **10, 71**

**Orlando Magic basketball team**
Erving, Julius **18, 47**
O'Neal, Shaquille **8, 30**

**Orlando Miracle basketball team**
Peck, Carolyn **23**

**Osteopathy**
Allen, Ethel D. **13**
Anderson, William G(ilchrist) **57**
Ross-Lee, Barbara **67**

**Overbrook Entertainment**
Pinkett Smith, Jada **10, 41**

**Page Education Foundation**
Page, Alan **7**

**Paine College**
Lewis, Shirley A. R. **14**

**Painting**
Alston, Charles **33**
Amos, Emma **63**
Andrews, Benny **22, 59**
Bailey, Radcliffe **19**
Barnes, Ernie **16, 78**
Barthe, Richmond **15**
Basquiat, Jean-Michel **5**
Bearden, Romare **2, 50**
Beasley, Phoebe **34**
Biggers, John **20, 33**
Campbell, E. Simms **13**
Colescott, Robert **69**
Collins, Paul **61**
Cortor, Eldzier **42**
Cowans, Adger W. **20**
Crichlow, Ernest **75**
Crite, Alan Rohan **29**

Davis, Bing 84
Delaney, Beauford 19
Delaney, Joseph 30
Delsarte, Louis 34
Douglas, Aaron 7
Driskell, David C. 7
Ferguson, Amos 81
Flood, Curt 10
Freeman, Leonard 27
Gilliam, Sam 16
Goodnight, Paul 32
Green, Jonathan 54
Guyton, Tyree 9
Harkless, Necia Desiree 19
Hayden, Palmer 13
Holder, Geoffrey 78
Honeywood, Varnette P. 54
Hunter, Clementine 45
Jackson, Earl 31
Johnson, William Henry 3
Jones, Lois Mailou 13
Knight, Gwendolyn 63
Knox, Simmie 49
Lawrence, Jacob 4, 28
Lee, Annie Frances 22
Lee-Smith, Hughie 5, 22
Lewis, Norman 39
Lewis, Samella 25
Ligon, Glenn 82
Loving, Alvin, Jr. 35, 53
Major, Clarence 9
Marshall, Kerry James 59
Mayhew, Richard 39
McGee, Charles 10
Mehretu, Julie 85
Mitchell, Corinne 8
Motley, Archibald, Jr. 30
Mutu, Wangechi 44
Ndiaye, Iba 74
Neals, Otto 73
Nugent, Richard Bruce 39
Ouattara 43
Pierre, Andre 17
Pindell, Howardena 55
Pippin, Horace 9
Porter, James A. 11
Reid, Senghor 55
Ringgold, Faith 4, 81
Ruley, Ellis 38
Sallee, Charles 38
Sebree, Charles 40
Smith, Vincent D. 48
Sudduth, Jimmy Lee 65
Tanksley, Ann 37
Tanner, Henry Ossawa 1
Thomas, Alma 14
Thomas, Mickalene 61
Tolliver, Mose 60
Tolliver, William 9
Verna, Gelsy 70
Wagner, Albert 78
Washington, James, Jr. 38
Wells, James Lesesne 10
White, Charles 39
Wiley, Kehinde 62
Williams, Billy Dee 8
Williams, William T. 11
Wilson, Ellis 39
Woodruff, Hale 9

**Pan African Congress**
Logan, Rayford W. 40

**Pan African Orthodox Christian Church**
Agyeman, Jaramogi Abebe 10, 63

**Pan-Africanism**
Carmichael, Stokely 5, 26
Clarke, John Henrik 20
Du Bois, David Graham 45
Du Bois, W. E. B. 3
Garvey, Marcus 1
Haile Selassie 7
Kenyatta, Jomo 5
Madhubuti, Haki 7, 85
Marshall, Paule 7, 77
Nkrumah, Kwame 3
Nyerere, Julius 5
Touré, Sekou 6
Turner, Henry McNeal 5

**Papal Medal**
Hampton, Lionel 17, 41

**Parents of Watts**
Harris, Alice 7

**Parti Démocratique de la Côte d'Ivoire (Democratic Party of the Ivory Coast; PDCI)**
Bedie, Henri Konan 21
Houphouët-Boigny, Félix 4, 64

**Party for Unity and Progress (Guinea; PUP)**
Conté, Lansana 7, 76

**PATC**
See Performing Arts Training Center

**Pathology**
Fuller, Solomon Carter, Jr. 15

**Patriot Party**
Fulani, Lenora 11

**Patriotic Alliance for Reconstruction and Construction (PARC)**
Jammeh, Yahya 23

**Patriotic Movement of Salvation (MPS)**
Déby, Idriss 30

**PBS**
See Public Broadcasting Service

**PDCI**
See Parti Démocratique de la Côte d'Ivoire (Democratic Party of the Ivory Coast)

**PDP**
See People's Democratic Party

**Peace and Freedom Party**
Cleaver, Eldridge 5

**Peace Corps**
See U.S. Peace Corps

**Peck School of the Fine Arts**
Tyson, Andre 40

**Pediatrics**
Carson, Benjamin 1, 35, 76
Elders, Joycelyn 6
Fennoy, Ilene 72

Witt, Edwin T. 26
Zuma, Nkosazana Dlamini 34

**Peg Leg Bates Country Club**
Bates, Peg Leg 14

**PEN/Faulkner award**
Bradley, David Henry, Jr. 39
Mayhew, Richard 39
Wideman, John Edgar 5, 87

**Pennsylvania state government**
Allen, Ethel D. 13
Brown, Homer S. 47
Fattah, Chaka 11, 70
Irvis, K. Leroy 67
Nix, Robert N. C., Jr. 51

**Pennsylvania State University**
Dunn, Jerry 27

**Pennsylvania Supreme Court**
Baldwin, Cynthia A. 74

**Pentecostal church**
Patterson, J. O., Jr. 80
Rivers, Eugene F., III 81
Sapp, Marvin 74
Wright, Timothy 74

**People United to Serve Humanity (PUSH)**
Barrow, Willie T. 85
Jackson, Jesse 1, 27, 72
Jackson, Jesse, Jr. 14, 45, 81

**People's Choice Awards**
Flo Rida 78
Lewis, Emmanuel 36

**People's Democratic Party (Nigeria; PDP)**
Jonathan, Goodluck 83
Obasanjo, Stella 32
Yar'adua, Umaru 69

**People's National Party (Jamaica; PNP)**
Patterson, P. J. 6, 20

**People's Progressive Party (Gambia; PPP)**
Jagan, Cheddi 16
Jawara, Dawda Kairaba 11

**People's Revolutionary government**
Bishop, Maurice 39

**PepsiCo Inc.**
Banks, Paula A. 68
Boyd, Edward 70
Harvey, William R. 42

**Performing Arts Training Center (PATC)**
Dunham, Katherine 4, 59

**Perkins Prize**
Jones, Thomas W. 41

**PGA**
See Professional Golfers' Association

**Pharmaceutical research**
Pickett, Cecil 39

**Pharmaceuticals**
Flowers, Sylester 50
Potter, Myrtle 40

**Pharmacist**
Akunyili, Dora Nkem 58
Flowers, Sylester 50
Pickett, Cecil 39
Stewart, Ella 39

**Phelps Stokes Fund**
Patterson, Frederick Douglass 12

**Phi Beta Sigma Fraternity**
Thomas, Arthur Ray 52

**Philadelphia city government**
Allen, Ethel D. 13
Goode, W. Wilson 4
Nutter, Michael 69
Street, John F. 24

**Philadelphia Eagles football team**
Cunningham, Randall 23
McNabb, Donovan 29
Rhodes, Ray 14
White, Reggie 6, 50

**Philadelphia Flyers hockey team**
Brashear, Donald 39
Charleston, Oscar 39

**Philadelphia Phillies baseball team**
Howard, Ryan 65
Morgan, Joe Leonard 9
Rollins, Jimmy 70

**Philadelphia public schools**
Clayton, Constance 1

**Philadelphia 76ers basketball team**
Barkley, Charles 5, 66
Bol, Manute 1
Chamberlain, Wilt 18, 47
Erving, Julius 18, 47
Iverson, Allen 24, 46
Lucas, John 7
Stackhouse, Jerry 30

**Philadelphia Stars baseball team**
Charleston, Oscar 39

**Philadelphia Warriors**
Chamberlain, Wilt 18, 47

**Philanthropy**
Banks, Paula A. 68
Brown, Eddie C. 35
Cooper, Evern 40
Cosby, Bill 7, 26, 59
Cosby, Camille 14, 80
Dawson, Matel, Jr. 39
Edley, Christopher 2, 48
Gardner, Chris 65
Golden, Marita 19
Gray, Willie 46
Johnson, Kevin 70
Johnson, Sheila Crump 48
Jones, Paul R. 76
Lavizzo-Mourey, Risa 48
Malone, Annie 13

McCarty, Osceola **16**
Millines Dziko, Trish **28**
Pleasant, Mary Ellen **9**
Reeves, Rachel J. **23**
Thomas, Franklin A. **5, 49**
Waddles, Charleszetta "Mother" **10, 49**
Walker, Madame C. J. **7**
Washington, Pauletta Pearson **86**
Wein, Joyce **62**
White, Reggie **6, 50**
Williams, Fannie Barrier **27**
Wonder, Stevie **11, 53**

**Philosophy**
Appiah, Kwame Anthony **67**
Baker, Houston A., Jr. **6**
Hall, Stuart **78**
Piper, Adrian **71**
Toomer, Jean **6**
West, Cornel **5, 33, 80**

**Phoenix Suns basketball team**
Barkley, Charles **5, 66**
Heard, Gar **25**
Johnson, Kevin **70**

**Photography**
Andrews, Bert **13**
Barboza, Anthony **10**
Cowans, Adger W. **20**
Cox, Renée **67**
DeCarava, Roy **42, 81**
Harris, Lyle Ashton **83**
Hinton, Milt **30**
Jackson, Vera **40**
Lester, Julius **9**
Moutoussamy-Ashe, Jeanne **7**
Parks, Gordon **1, 35, 58**
Pinderhughes, John **47**
Robeson, Eslanda Goode **13**
Roble, Abdi **71**
Serrano, Andres **3**
Simpson, Lorna **4, 36**
Sleet, Moneta, Jr. **5**
Smith, Marvin **46**
Smith, Morgan **46**
Tanner, Henry Ossawa **1**
Thomas, Mickalene **61**
VanDerZee, James **6**
Weems, Carrie Mae **63**
White, John H. **27**
Williams, Clarence **70**
Willis, Deborah **85**
Withers, Ernest C. **68**

**Photojournalism**
Ashley-Ward, Amelia **23**
du Cille, Michel **74**
Jackson, Vera **40**
Moutoussamy-Ashe, Jeanne **7**
Parks, Gordon **1, 35, 58**
Sleet, Moneta, Jr. **5**
Van Lierop, Robert **53**
Wallace, William **75**
White, John H. **27**
Williams, Clarence **70**
Withers, Ernest C. **68**
Yette, Samuel F. **63**

**Physical therapy**
Elders, Joycelyn **6**
Griffin, Bessie Blout **43**

**Physics**
Adkins, Rutherford H. **21**
Branson, Herman **87**
Carruthers, George R. **40**
Gates, Sylvester James, Jr. **15**
Gourdine, Meredith **33**
Imes, Elmer Samuel **39**
Jackson, Shirley Ann **12**
Massey, Walter E. **5, 45**
Tyson, Neil deGrasse **15, 65**

**Piano**
Adams, Leslie **39**
Austin, Lovie **40**
Basie, Count **23**
Bonds, Margaret **39**
Brooks, Hadda **40**
Cartiér, Xam Wilson **41**
Cole, Nat "King" **17**
Coltrane, Alice **70**
Cook, Charles "Doc" **44**
Domino, Fats **20**
Donegan, Dorothy **19**
Duke, George **21**
Ellington, Duke **5**
Flanagan, Tommy **69**
Garner, Erroll **76**
Hancock, Herbie **20, 67**
Hardin Armstrong, Lil **39**
Harris, Barry **68**
Hayes, Isaac **20, 58, 73**
Hinderas, Natalie **5**
Hines, Earl "Fatha" **39**
Horn, Shirley **32, 56**
Jamal, Ahmad **69**
Johnson, Johnnie **56**
Jones, Hank **57, 86**
Joplin, Scott **6**
Keys, Alicia **32, 68**
Lee, Consuela **84**
McRae, Carmen **77**
Monk, Thelonious **1**
Perkins, Pinetop **70**
Peterson, Oscar **52**
Powell, Bud **24**
Pratt, Awadagin **31**
Preston, Billy **39, 59**
Price, Florence **37**
Pritchard, Robert Starling **21**
Roberts, Marcus **19**
Robinson, Reginald R. **53**
Sample, Joe **51**
Schuyler, Philippa **50**
Scott, Hazel **66**
Silver, Horace **26**
Simone, Nina **15, 41**
Sun Ra **60**
Swann, Lynn **28**
Southern, Eileen **56**
Sykes, Roosevelt **20**
Taylor, Billy **23**
Taylor, Cecil **70**
Turner, Ike **68**
Valdés, Bebo **75**
Vaughan, Sarah **13**
Walker, George **37**
Waller, Fats **29**
Watts, Andre **42**
Webster, Katie **29**
Williams, Mary Lou **15**

**Pittsburgh Crawfords**
See Indianapolis Crawfords

**Pittsburgh Homestead Grays baseball team**
Charleston, Oscar **39**
Kaiser, Cecil **42**
Leonard, Buck **67**

**Pittsburgh Pirates baseball team**
Bonds, Barry **6, 34, 63**
Clendenon, Donn **26, 56**
Ellis, Dock **78**
Stargell, Willie **29**

**Pittsburgh Steelers football team**
Dungy, Tony **17, 42, 59**
Gilliam, Joe **31**
Greene, Joe **10**
Perry, Lowell **30**
Stargell, Willie **29**
Stewart, Kordell **21**
Swann, Lynn **28**
Ward, Hines **84**
Woodson, Rod **79**

**Planned Parenthood Federation of America Inc.**
Wattleton, Faye **9**

*Playboy*
Brown, Robert **65**
Taylor, Karin **34**

**Playwright**
Anthony, Trey **63**
Arkadie, Kevin **17**
Armah, Esther **87**
Baldwin, James **1**
Bandele, Biyi **68**
Barrett, Lindsay **43**
Beckham, Barry **41**
Branch, William Blackwell **39**
Brown, Cecil M. **46**
Brown, Oscar, Jr. **53**
Bullins, Ed **25**
Caldwell, Benjamin **46**
Carroll, Vinnette **29**
Césaire, Aimé **48, 69**
Chenault, John **40**
Childress, Alice **15**
Clark-Bekedermo, J. P. **44**
Clarke, George **32**
Cleage, Pearl **17, 64**
Corthron, Kia **43**
Cotter, Joseph Seamon, Sr. **40**
Cox, Joseph Mason Andrew **51**
Dadié, Bernard **34**
Davis, Eisa **68**
De Veaux, Alexis **44**
Dent, Thomas C. **50**
Dodson, Owen **38**
Elder, Larry, III **38**
Evans, Mari **26**
Farah, Nuruddin **27**
Franklin, J. E. **44**
Glover, Keith **79**
Gordone, Charles **15**
Gurira, Danai **73**
Hansberry, Lorraine **6**
Harris, Bill **72**
Hayes, Teddy **40**
Hill, Errol **40**
Hill, Leslie Pinckney **44**
Holder, Laurence **34**

Hughes, Langston **4**
Johnson, Georgia Douglas **41**
Johnson, Je'Caryous **63**
Jones, Sarah **39**
Kennedy, Adrienne **11**
Kente, Gibson **52**
King, Woodie, Jr. **27**
Kwei-Armah, Kwame **84**
Lampley, Oni Faida **43, 71**
Lee, Leslie **85**
Long, Richard Alexander **65**
Marechera, Dambudzo **39**
McClinton, Marion Isaac **77**
Milner, Ron **39**
Mitchell, Loften **31**
Moss, Carlton **17**
Mugo, Micere Githae **32**
Nottage, Lynn **66**
Onwueme, Tess Osonye **23**
Orlandersmith, Dael **42**
Parks, Suzan-Lori **34, 85**
Perry, Tyler **40, 54**
Rahman, Aishah **37**
Redwood, John Henry **78**
Rhone, Trevor **80**
Salter, Nikkole **73**
Sanchez, Sonia **17, 51**
Santiago-Hudson, Ruben **85**
Schuyler, George Samuel **40**
Sebree, Charles **40**
Smith, Anna Deavere **6, 44**
Talbert, David **34**
Taylor, Regina **9, 46**
Teer, Barbara Ann **81**
Thurman, Wallace **17**
Tolson, Melvin B. **37**
Walcott, Derek **5**
Ward, Douglas Turner **42**
Wesley, Richard **73**
Williams, Samm-Art **21**
Wilson, August **7, 33, 55**
Wilson, Tracey Scott **777**
Wolfe, George C. **6, 43**
Youngblood, Shay **32**

**PNP**
See People's National Party (Jamaica)

**Podium Records**
Patterson, Gilbert Earl **41**

**Poet laureate (U.S.)**
Dove, Rita **6, 78**

**Poetry**
Abani, Chris **77**
Adams, Jenoyne **60**
Alexander, Elizabeth **75**
Alexander, Margaret Walker **22**
Allen, Samuel L. **38**
Angelou, Maya **1, 15**
Atkins, Russell **45**
Aubert, Alvin **41**
Baiocchi, Regina Harris **41**
Bandele, Asha **36**
Barrax, Gerald William **45**
Barrett, Lindsay **43**
Bell, James Madison **40**
Bennett, Gwendolyn B. **59**
Bennett, Louise **69**
Berry, James **41**
Bontemps, Arna **8**
Boyd, Melba Joyce **86**

Braithwaite, William Stanley 52
Brand, Dionne 32
Breeze, Jean "Binta" 37
Brooks, Gwendolyn 1, 28
Brown, Cecil M. 46
Brutus, Dennis 38
Burgess, Marjorie L. 55
Carter, Martin 49
Cartey, Wilfred 47
Césaire, Aimé 48, 69
Chenault, John 40
Cheney-Coker, Syl 43
Clark-Bekedermo, J. P. 44
Clarke, Cheryl 32
Clarke, George 32
Cleage, Pearl 17, 64
Cliff, Michelle 42
Clifton, Lucille 14, 64
Coleman, Wanda 48
Cooper, Afua 53
Cornish, Sam 50
Cortez, Jayne 43
Cotter, Joseph Seamon, Sr. 40
Cox, Joseph Mason Andrew 51
Cuney, William Waring 44
Dabydeen, David 48
Dadié, Bernard 34
D'Aguiar, Fred 50
Damas, Léon-Gontran 46
Dandridge, Raymond Garfield 45
Danner, Margaret Esse 49
Datcher, Michael 60
Davis, Charles T. 48
Davis, Frank Marshall 47
De Veaux, Alexis 44
Dent, Thomas C. 50
Dodson, Owen 38
Dove, Rita 6, 78
Draper, Sharon Mills 16, 43
Dumas, Henry 41
Dunbar-Nelson, Alice Ruth Moore 44
Dungy, Camille 86
Emanuel, James A. 46
Evans, Mari 26
Fabio, Sarah Webster 48
Fair, Ronald L. 47
Figueroa, John J. 40
Fisher, Antwone 40
Fleming, Raymond 48
Forbes, Calvin 46
Ford, Nick Aaron 44
Frazier, Oscar 58
Gabre-Medhin, Tsegaye 64
Gilbert, Christopher 50
Goings, Russell 59
Goodison, Lorna 71
Harkless, Necia Desiree 19
Harper, Frances Ellen Watkins 11
Harper, Michael S. 34
Harris, Bill 72
Harris, Claire 34
Hayden, Robert 12
Henderson, David 53
Hernton, Calvin C. 51
Hill, Leslie Pinckney 44
Hoagland, Everett H. 45
Horne, Frank 44
Hughes, Langston 7
Jackson, Fred James 25
Joachim, Paulin 34
Johnson, Georgia Douglas 41
Johnson, Linton Kwesi 37

Jones, Sarah 39
Kay, Jackie 37
Keene, John 73
Knight, Etheridge 37
Laraque, Paul 67
Letson, Al 39
Lorde, Audre 6
Mackey, Nathaniel 75
Manley, Ruth 34
Marechera, Dambudzo 39
Matejka, Adrian 87
Moore, Jessica Care 30
Mugo, Micere Githae 32
Mullen, Harryette 34
Naylor, Gloria 10, 42
Neto, António Agostinho 43
Nugent, Richard Bruce 39
Okara, Gabriel 37
Parker, Pat 19
Peters, Lenrie 43
Philip, Marlene Nourbese 32
Powell, Kevin 31, 74
Quigless, Helen G. 49
Randall, Dudley 8, 55
Redmond, Eugene 23
Richards, Beah 30
Sanchez, Sonia 17, 51
Sapphire 14
Senghor, Léopold Sédar 12
Senior, Olive 37
Smith, Mary Carter 26
Spencer, Anne 27
Sundiata, Sekou 66
Tillis, Frederick 40
Tolson, Melvin B. 37
Touré, Askia (Muhammad Abu Bakr el) 47
Troupe, Quincy 83
van Sertima, Ivan 25
Walker, Margaret 29
Washington, James, Jr. 38
Weaver, Afaa Michael 37
Williams, Saul 31
Williams, Sherley Anne 25
Woods, Scott 55
Young, Al 82

**Poetry Slam, Inc.**
Woods, Scott 55

**Political science**
Ake, Claude 30
Dawson, Michael C. 63
Harris-Lacewell, Melissa 81
Skinner, Kiron K. 65
Walters, Ronald 83
Watson, Carlos 50

**Politics**
Adebari, Rotimi 83
Alexander, Archie Alphonso 14
Allen, Claude 68
Arthur, Owen 33
Austin, Junius C. 44
Avant, Clarence 19, 86
Baker, Thurbert 22
Ballance, Frank W. 41
Barnes, Melody 75
Barrow, Dean 69
Bass, Charlotta Spears 40
Belton, Sharon Sayles 9, 16
Bishop, Sanford D., Jr. 24
Blackwell, Unita 17
Boateng, Paul Yaw 56

Booker, Cory Anthony 68
Boye, Madior 30
Brazile, Donna 25, 70
Brown, Corrine 24
Brown, Oscar, Jr. 53
Buckley, Victoria (Vikki) 24
Burris, Chuck 21
Burris, Roland W. 25, 75
Butler, Jerry 26
Césaire, Aimé 48, 69
Chideya, Farai 14, 61
Christian-Green, Donna M. 17
Clayton, Eva M. 20
Coleman, Mary 46
Compton, John 65
Connerly, Ward 14
Cummings, Elijah E. 24
Curling, Alvin 34
Currie, Betty 21
Davis, Artur 41
Davis, James E. 50
Dixon, Julian C. 24
Dixon, Sheila 68
dos Santos, José Eduardo 43
Dymally, Mervyn 42
Edmonds, Terry 17
Ellison, Keith 59
Fields, C. Virginia 25
Fields, Julia 45
Fleming, Erik R. 75
Ford, Jack 39
Gbagbo, Laurent 43
Gordon, Pamela 17
Greenlee, Sam 48
Hatcher, Richard G. 55
Henry, Aaron 19
Hilliard, Earl F. 24
Holmes, Amy 69
Ingraham, Hubert A. 19
Isaac, Julius 34
Jackson, Mae 57
Jackson Lee, Sheila 20
James, Sharpe 23, 69
Jammeh, Yahya 23
Jarrett, Valerie 73
Jarvis, Charlene Drew 21
Jefferson, William J. 25, 72
Kabbah, Ahmad Tejan 23
Kabila, Joseph 30
Kariuki, J. M. 67
Kelley, Cliff 75
Lee, Barbara 25
Lumumba, Patrice 33
Maathai, Wangari 43
Magloire, Paul Eugène 68
Majette, Denise 41
McGlowan, Angela 64, 86
Meek, Carrie 6, 36
Meek, Kendrick 41
Meeks, Gregory 25
Metcalfe, Ralph 26
Millender-McDonald, Juanita 21, 61
Moore, Gwendolynne S. 55
Moore, Harry T. 29
Morial, Ernest "Dutch" 26
Morial, Marc H. 20, 51
Nagin, C. Ray 42, 57
Pereira, Aristides 30
Perry, Ruth 15
Pitta, Celso 17
Powell, Debra A. 23
Sankoh, Foday 74

Saro-Wiwa, Kenule 39
Scott, David 41
Scott, Robert C. 23
Simmons, E. Denise 79
Simmons, Jamal 72
Sisulu, Sheila Violet Makate 24
Smith, Jennifer 21
Smith, Princella 86
Spencer, Winston Baldwin 68
Thompson, Bennie G. 26
Thurston, Baratunde 79
Touré, Amadou Toumani 18
Watkins, Joe 86
Watt, Melvin 38
Watts, J. C., Jr. 14, 38
Wheat, Alan 14
Williams, Anthony 21
Williams, Eddie N. 44
Williams, Eric Eustace 65
Williams, George Washington 18
Wiwa, Ken 67
Yar'adua, Umaru 69

**Pop music**
Ashanti 37
Ashford, Nickolas 21
Babyface 10, 31, 82
Bailey Rae, Corinne 83
Barrino, Fantasia 53
Bassey, Shirley 25
Bleu, Corbin 65
Blige, Mary J. 20, 34, 60
Brown, Bobby 58
Brown, Melanie 73
Butler, Jonathan 28
Cannon, Nick 47, 73
Carey, Mariah 32, 53, 69
Cee-Lo 70
Chanté, Keshia 50
Checker, Chubby 28
Cole, Nat "King" 17
Combs, Sean "Puffy" 17, 43
Coppola, Imani Francesca 82
Cox, Deborah 28
David, Craig 31, 53
Duke, George 21
Ferrell, Rachelle 29
Franklin, Aretha 11, 44
Franklin, Kirk 15, 49
Gray, Macy 29
Hailey, JoJo 22
Hailey, K-Ci 22
Hathaway, Lalah 57
Hawkins, Screamin' Jay 30
Hayes, Isaac 20, 58, 73
Hill, Lauryn 20, 53
Holmes, Clint 57
Houston, Whitney 7, 28, 83
Hudson, Jennifer 63, 83
Humphrey, Bobbi 20
Isley, Ronald 25, 56
Ja Rule 35
Jackson, Janet 6, 30, 68
Jackson, Jermaine 79
Jackson, Michael 19, 53, 76
James, Rick 17
Jarreau, Al 21, 65
Jones, Booker T. 84
Jones, Quincy 8, 30
Jordan, Montell 23
Kelis 58
Kendricks, Eddie 22
Keys, Alicia 32, 68

Khan, Chaka **12, 50**
LaBelle, Patti **13, 30**
Lewis, Leona **75**
Love, Darlene **23**
Luckett, Letoya **61**
Massenburg, Kedar **23**
Mathis, Johnny **20**
McFerrin, Bobby **68**
Monica **21**
Moore, Chante **26**
Mumba, Samantha **29**
Mya **35**
Neville, Aaron **21**
Ne-Yo **65**
Noah, Yannick **4, 60**
Osborne, Jeffrey **26**
Otis, Clyde **67**
Palmer, Keke **68**
P.M. Dawn **54**
Preston, Billy **39, 59**
Prince **18, 65**
Reid, Antonio "L.A." **28**
Reid, Vernon **34**
Richie, Lionel **27, 65**
Rihanna **65**
Robinson, Smokey **3, 49**
Rucker, Darius **34, 74**
Rupaul **17**
Sade **15**
Seal **14, 75**
Senghor, Léopold Sédar **12**
Short, Bobby **52**
Simpson, Valerie **21**
Sisqo **30**
Staton, Candi **27**
Summer, Donna **25**
Supremes, The **33**
Sweat, Keith **19**
Temptations, The **33**
The-Dream **74**
Thomas, Irma **29**
TLC **34**
Turner, Tina **6, 27**
Usher **23, 56**
Vanity **67**
Washington, Dinah **22**
Washington, Grover, Jr. **17, 44**
Washington, Val **12**
Welch, Elisabeth **52**
White, Barry **13, 41**
White, Josh, Jr. **52**
White, Maurice **29**
will.i.am **64**
Williams, Vanessa L. **4, 17**
Wilson, Jackie **60**
Wilson, Mary **28**
Wilson, Nancy **10**
Withers-Mendes, Elisabeth **64**
Wonder, Stevie **11, 53**

**Portland (OR) Police Department**
Moose, Charles **40**

**Portland Trail Blazers basketball team**
Drexler, Clyde **4, 61**
Miller, Larry G. **72**
Porter, Terry **75**
Wilkens, Lenny **11**

**PPP**
See People's Progressive Party (Gambia)

**Pratt Institute**
Mayhew, Richard **39**

**Presbyterianism**
Cannon, Katie **10**

**Pride Economic Enterprises**
Barry, Marion S. **7, 44**

**Princeton University**
Blanks, Deborah K. **69**
Harris-Lacewell, Melissa **81**
Simmons, Ruth **13, 38**

**Printmaking**
Blackburn, Robert **28**
Crichlow, Ernest **75**
Neals, Otto **73**
Tanksley, Ann **37**
Thrash, Dox **35**
Wells, James Lesesne **10**

**Printmaking Workshop**
Blackburn, Robert **28**
Tanksley, Ann **37**

**Prison ministry**
Bell, Ralph S. **5**

**Prison reform**
Betts, R. Dwayne **86**

**Professional Golfers' Association (PGA)**
Elder, Lee **6**
Powell, Renee **34**
Sifford, Charlie **4, 49**
Woods, Tiger **14, 31, 81**

**Professional Women's Club of Chicago**
Gray, Ida **41**

**Progressive Labour Party**
Smith, Jennifer **21**

**Progressive Party**
Bass, Charlotta Spears **40**

**Pro-Line Corp.**
Cottrell, Comer **11**

**Proposition 209**
Connerly, Ward **14**

**Prosecution**
Darden, Christopher **13**
Worthy, Kym **84**

*Provincial Freeman*
Cary, Mary Ann Shadd **30**

**Psychiatry**
Cobbs, Price M. **9**
Comer, James P. **6**
Fanon, Frantz **44**
Fuller, Solomon Carter, Jr. **15**
Hamburg, Beatrix **84**
Poussaint, Alvin F. **5, 67**
Welsing, Frances Cress **5**

**Psychic health**
Ford, Clyde W. **40**

**Psychology**
Anderson, Norman B. **45**
Archie-Hudson, Marguerite **44**
Brown, Joyce F. **25**

Clark, Mamie Phipps **79**
Edwards, Harry **2**
Finner-Williams, Paris Michele **62**
Fulani, Lenora **11**
Gardere, Jeffrey **76**
Gilbert, Christopher **50**
Hale, Lorraine **8**
Hare, Nathan **44**
Hilliard, Asa Grant, III **66**
Staples, Brent **8**
Steele, Claude Mason **13**
Tatum, Beverly Daniel **42, 84**

**Psychotheraphy**
Berrysmith, Don Reginald **49**
Ford, Clyde W. **40**

**Public Broadcasting Service (PBS)**
Brown, Les **5**
Brown, Tony **3**
Creagh, Milton **27**
Davis, Ossie **5, 50**
Duke, Bill **3**
Hampton, Henry **6**
Hunter-Gault, Charlayne **6, 31**
Ifill, Gwen **28**
Lawson, Jennifer **1, 50**
Long, Loretta **58**
Lynch, Shola **61**
Riggs, Marlon **5, 44**
Roker, Al **12, 49**

**Public housing**
Hamer, Fannie Lou **6**
Lane, Vincent **5**
Perry, James **83**
Reems, Ernestine Cleveland **27**

**Public relations**
Barden, Don H. **9, 20**
Barrett, Andrew C. **12**
Calhoun, Lillian Scott **87**
Compton-Rock, Malaak **86**
Edmonds, Terry **17**
Graham, Stedman **13**
Hedgeman, Anna Arnold **22**
Jones, Robert G. **81**
McCabe, Jewell Jackson **10**
Perez, Anna **1**
Pritchard, Robert Starling **21**
Rowan, Carl T. **1, 30**
Taylor, Kristin Clark **8**
Tobin, Patricia **75**
Williams, Maggie **7, 71**

**Public speaking**
Bell, James Madison **40**
Douglass, Frederick **87**
Kennedy, Randall **40**

**Publishing**
Abbott, Robert Sengstacke **27**
Achebe, Chinua **6**
Ames, Wilmer **27**
Ashley-Ward, Amelia **23**
Aubert, Alvin **41**
Auguste, Arnold A. **47**
Baisden, Michael **25, 66**
Barden, Don H. **9, 20**
Bass, Charlotta Spears **40**
Bates, Daisy **13**
Boston, Lloyd **24**
Boyd, T. B., III **6**
Brown, Marie Dutton **12**

Cary, Mary Ann Shadd **30**
Coombs, Orde M. **44**
Cox, William E. **68**
Dawkins, Wayne **20**
Driver, David E. **11**
Ducksworth, Marilyn **12**
Dumas, Henry **41**
Fuller, Hoyt **44**
Giddings, Paula **11**
Graves, Butch **77**
Graves, Earl G. **1, 35**
Harris, Jay **19**
Harris, Monica **18**
Hill, Bonnie Guiton **20**
Hudson, Cheryl **15**
Hudson, Wade **15**
James, Juanita **13**
Johnson, John H. **3, 54**
Jones, Quincy **8, 30**
Kunjufu, Jawanza **3, 50**
Lawson, Jennifer **1, 50**
Leavell, Dorothy R. **17**
Lewis, Edward T. **21**
Lorde, Audre **6**
Madhubuti, Haki **7, 85**
Maynard, Nancy Hicks **73**
Maynard, Robert C. **7**
McDonald, Erroll **1**
Moore, Jessica Care **30**
Morgan, Garrett **1**
Murphy, John H. **42**
Myers, Walter Dean **8, 20**
Parks, Gordon **1, 35, 58**
Perez, Anna **1**
Randall, Dudley **8, 55**
Scott, C. A. **29**
Sengstacke, John **18**
Smith, Clarence O. **21**
Stinson, Denise L. **59**
Stringer, Vickie **58**
Tyree, Omar Rashad **21**
Vanzant, Iyanla **17, 47**
Walker, Alice **1, 43**
Washington, Alonzo **29**
Washington, Laura S. **18**
Wells-Barnett, Ida B. **8**
Williams, Armstrong **29**
Williams, Patricia **11, 54**
Woods, Teri **69**

**Pulitzer Prize**
Brooks, Gwendolyn **1, 28**
Dove, Rita **6, 78**
Fuller, Charles **8**
Givhan, Robin Deneen **72**
Gordone, Charles **15**
Haley, Alex **4**
Komunyakaa, Yusef **9**
Lewis, David Levering **9**
McPherson, James Alan **70**
Morrison, Toni **2, 15, 86**
Newkirk, Pamela **69**
Page, Clarence **4**
Parks, Suzan-Lori **34, 85**
Pitts, Leonard, Jr. **54, 85**
Robinson, Eugene **77**
Shipp, E. R. **15**
Sleet, Moneta, Jr. **5**
Walker, Alice **1, 43**
Walker, George **37**
White, John H. **27**
Wilkins, Roger **2, 84**

Wilson, August **7, 33, 55**

**PUP**
See Party for Unity and Progress (Guinea)

**Puppeteer**
Clash, Kevin **14**

**PUSH**
See People United to Serve Humanity

**Quiltmaking**
Benberry, Cuesta **65**
Ringgold, Faith **4, 81**

**Qwest Records**
Jones, Quincy **8, 30**

**Race car driving**
Brown, Antron **85**
Hamilton, Lewis **66**
Lester, Bill **42, 85**
Ribbs, Willy T. **2**
Scott, Wendell Oliver, Sr. **19**

**Race relations**
Abbott, Diane **9**
Achebe, Chinua **6**
Alexander, Clifford **26**
Anthony, Wendell **25**
Asante, Molefi Kete **3**
Baker, Ella **5**
Baker, Houston A., Jr. **6**
Baldwin, James **1**
Beals, Melba Patillo **15**
Bell, Derrick **6**
Bethune, Mary McLeod **4**
Bobo, Lawrence **60**
Booker, Simeon **23**
Bosley, Freeman, Jr. **7**
Boyd, T. B., III **6**
Bradley, David Henry, Jr. **39**
Branch, William Blackwell **39**
Brown, Elaine **8**
Bunche, Ralph J. **5**
Butler, Paul D. **17**
Butts, Calvin O., III **9**
Carter, Stephen L. **4**
Cary, Lorene **3**
Cashin, Sheryll **63**
Cayton, Horace **26**
Chavis, Benjamin **6**
Clark, Kenneth B. **5, 52**
Clark, Septima **7**
Cobbs, Price M. **9**
Cochran, Johnnie **11, 39, 52**
Cole, Johnnetta B. **5, 43**
Comer, James P. **6**
Cone, James H. **3, 82**
Conyers, John, Jr. **4, 45**
Cook, Suzan D. Johnson **22**
Cook, Toni **23**
Cosby, Bill **7, 26, 59**
Davis, Angela **5**
Davis, Benjamin O., Jr. **2, 43**
Davis, Benjamin O., Sr. **4**
Dee, Ruby **8, 50, 68**
Delany, Martin R. **27**
Diallo, Amadou **27**
Dickerson, Debra J. **60**
Divine, Father **7**
DuBois, Shirley Graham **21**
Dunbar, Paul Laurence **8**

Dunbar-Nelson, Alice Ruth Moore **44**
Dyson, Michael Eric **11, 40**
Edelman, Marian Wright **5, 42**
Elder, Lee **6**
Ellison, Ralph **7**
Esposito, Giancarlo **9**
Farmer, James **2, 64**
Farmer-Paellmann, Deadria **43**
Farrakhan, Louis **2**
Fauset, Jessie **7**
Franklin, John Hope **5, 77**
Fuller, Charles **8**
Gaines, Ernest J. **7**
Gibson, William F. **6**
Goode, W. Wilson **4**
Graham, Lawrence Otis **12**
Gregory, Dick **1, 54**
Grimké, Archibald H. **9**
Guinier, Lani **7, 30**
Guy, Rosa **5**
Haley, Alex **4**
Hall, Elliott S. **24**
Hampton, Henry **6**
Hansberry, Lorraine **6**
Harris, Alice **7**
Hastie, William H. **8**
Haynes, George Edmund **8**
Hedgeman, Anna Arnold **22**
Henry, Aaron **19**
Henry, Lenny **9, 52**
Hill, Oliver W. **24, 63**
hooks, bell **5**
Hope, John **8**
Howard, M. William, Jr. **26**
Ingram, Rex **5**
Jeffries, Leonard **8**
Johnson, James Weldon **5**
Jones, Elaine R. **7, 45**
Jordan, Vernon E. **3, 35**
Khanga, Yelena **6**
King, Bernice **4, 81**
King, Coretta Scott **3, 57**
King, Martin Luther, Jr. **1**
King, Yolanda **6**
Lane, Charles **3**
Lee-Smith, Hughie **5, 22**
Lorde, Audre **6**
Mabuza-Suttle, Felicia **43**
Mandela, Nelson **1, 14, 77**
Martin, Louis E. **16**
Mathabane, Mark **5**
Maynard, Robert C. **7**
Mays, Benjamin E. **7**
McDougall, Gay J. **11, 43**
McKay, Claude **6**
Meredith, James H. **11**
Micheaux, Oscar **7**
Moore, Harry T. **29**
Mosley, Walter **5, 25, 68**
Muhammad, Khallid Abdul **10, 31**
Norton, Eleanor Holmes **7**
Page, Clarence **4**
Perkins, Edward **5**
Pitt, David Thomas **10**
Poussaint, Alvin F. **5, 67**
Price, Frederick K. C. **21**
Price, Hugh B. **9, 54**
Robeson, Paul **2**
Robinson, Spottswood W., III **22**
Sampson, Edith S. **4**
Shabazz, Attallah **6**

Sifford, Charlie **4, 49**
Simpson, Carole **6, 30**
Sister Souljah **11**
Sisulu, Sheila Violet Makate **24**
Smith, Anna Deavere **6, 44**
Sowell, Thomas **2**
Spaulding, Charles Clinton **9**
Staples, Brent **8**
Steele, Claude Mason **13**
Steele, Shelby **13, 82**
Taulbert, Clifton Lemoure **19**
Till, Emmett **7**
Tutu, Desmond Mpilo **6, 44**
Tutu, Nontombi Naomi **57**
Tyree, Omar Rashad **21**
Walcott, Derek **5**
Walker, Maggie **17**
Washington, Booker T. **4**
Washington, Harold **6**
Wells-Barnett, Ida B. **8**
Welsing, Frances Cress **5**
Wiley, Ralph **8, 78**
Wilkins, Roy **4**
Williams, Fannie Barrier **27**
Williams, Gregory **11**
Williams, Hosea Lorenzo **15, 31**
Williams, Patricia **11, 54**
Williams, Walter E. **4**
Wilson, Sunnie **7, 55**
Wright, Richard **5**
Young, Whitney M., Jr. **4**

**Radio**
Abrahams, Peter **39**
Abu-Jamal, Mumia **15**
Alert, Kool DJ Red **33**
Anderson, Eddie "Rochester" **30**
Ashong, Derrick **86**
Banks, William **11**
Bates, Karen Grigsby **40**
Beasley, Phoebe **34**
Blayton, Jesse B., Sr. **55**
Booker, Simeon **23**
Branch, William Blackwell **39**
Crocker, Frankie **29**
Dee, Ruby **8, 50, 68**
Dre, Dr. **10, 14, 30**
Elder, Larry **25**
Fuller, Charles **8**
Gibson, Truman K., Jr. **60**
Goode, Mal **13**
Greene, Petey **65**
Gumbel, Greg **8**
Hamblin, Ken **10**
Haynes, Trudy **44**
Holt, Nora **38**
Hughes, Cathy **27**
Jackson, Hal **41**
Jarrett, Vernon D. **42**
Joe, Yolanda **21**
Joyner, Tom **19**
Kelley, Cliff **75**
Keyes, Alan L. **11**
Lewis, Delano **7**
Lewis, Ramsey **35, 70**
Ligging, Alfred, III **43**
Love, Ed **58**
Lover, Ed **10**
Ludacris **37, 60**
Madison, Joseph E. **17**
Majors, Jeff **41**
Mickelbury, Penny **28**
Moss, Carlton **17**

Parr, Russ **51**
Pressley, Condace L. **41**
Pugh, Charles **81**
Quivers, Robin **61**
Samara, Noah **15**
Smiley, Rickey **59**
Smiley, Tavis **20, 68**
Smith, Greg **28**
Steinberg, Martha Jean "The Queen" **28**
Stuart, Moira **82**
Taylor, Billy **23**
Tirico, Mike **68**
Whack, Rita Coburn **36**
Williams, Armstrong **29**
Williams, Wendy **62**
Woods, Georgie **57**
Yarbrough, Camille **40**

**Radio-Television News Directors Association**
Pressley, Condace L. **41**

**Ragtime**
Blake, Eubie **29**
Europe, James Reese **10**
Joplin, Scott **6**
Robinson, Reginald R. **53**
Sissle, Noble **29**

**Rainbow Coalition**
Chappell, Emma **18**
Jackson, Jesse **1, 27, 72**
Jackson, Jesse, Jr. **14, 45, 81**
Moore, Minyon **45**

**Rap music**
Alert, Kool DJ Red **33**
Baker, Houston A., Jr. **6**
Bambaataa, Afrika **34**
Banner, David **55**
Benjamin, Andre **45**
Big Daddy Kane **79**
Black Thought **63**
Blackman, Toni **86**
Blow, Kurtis **31**
Bow Wow **35**
Brown, Foxy **25**
Butts, Calvin O., III **9**
Cee-Lo **70**
Chamillionaire **82**
Chuck D. **9**
Combs, Sean "Puffy" **17, 43**
Common **31, 63**
Da Don, Polow **86**
Deezer D **53**
DJ Jazzy Jeff **32**
DMX **28, 64**
Drake **86**
Dre, Dr. **10, 14, 30**
Dupri, Jermaine **13, 46**
Dyson, Michael Eric **11, 40**
Elliott, Missy **31**
Eve **29**
50 Cent **46, 83**
Flavor Flav **67**
Flo Rida **78**
Gotti, Irv **39**
Grae, Jean **51**
Grandmaster Flash **33, 60**
Gray, F. Gary **14, 49**
Harrell, Andre **9, 30**
Heavy D **58**
Hill, Lauryn **20, 53**

Ice Cube **8, 30, 60**
Ice-T **6, 31**
Ja Rule **35**
Jay-Z **27, 69**
Jones, Quincy **8, 30**
Kid Cudi **83**
K'naan **76**
Knight, Suge **11, 30**
KRS-One **34**
Lil' Kim **28**
Lil Wayne **66, 84**
Liles, Kevin **42**
Lopes, Lisa "Left Eye" **36**
Lover, Ed **10**
Ludacris **37, 60**
Mase **24**
Master P **21**
MC Breed **75**
M.C. Hammer **20, 80**
MC Lyte **34**
McDaniels, Ralph **79**
Method Man **81**
Mos Def **30**
Nelly **32**
Notorious B.I.G. **20**
Ol' Dirty Bastard **52**
OutKast **35**
Peterson, James **81**
Queen Latifah **1, 16, 58**
?uestlove **74**
Ray J **86**
Redman **81**
Rhymes, Busta **31**
Roberts, Kimberly Rivers **72**
Ross, Rick **79**
Run-DMC **31, 75**
RZA **80**
Sermon, Erick **81**
Shakur, Afeni **67**
Shakur, Tupac **14**
Simmons, Russell **1, 30**
Sir Mix-A-Lot **82**
Sister Souljah **11**
Slim Thug **86**
Smith, Will **8, 18, 53**
Snoop Dogg **35, 84**
Speech **82**
Sticky Fingaz **86**
Sugarhill Gang, The **79**
Timbaland **32**
T-Pain **73**
West, Kanye **52**
Xzibit **78**
Yarbrough, Camille **40**
Young Jeezy **63**

**Rassemblement Démocratique Africain (African Democratic Rally; RDA)**
Houphouët-Boigny, Félix **4, 64**
Touré, Sekou **6**

**Rastafarianism**
Burning Spear **79**
Dube, Lucky **77**
Haile Selassie **7**
Marley, Bob **5**
Marley, Rita **32, 70**
Tosh, Peter **9**

**RDA**
See Rassemblement Démocratique Africain (African Democratic
Rally)

**Reader's Choice Award**
Holton, Hugh, Jr. **39**

**Reading Is Fundamental**
Trueheart, William E. **49**

**Real estate development**
Barden, Don H. **9, 20**
Brooke, Edward **8**
Holmes, Larry **20, 68**
Lane, Vincent **5**
Marshall, Bella **22**
Russell, Herman Jerome **17**
Toote, Gloria E. A. **64**

**Record producer**
Albright, Gerald **23**
Ayers, Roy **16**
Babyface **10, 31, 82**
Bambaataa, Afrika **34**
Barnes, Lloyd **77**
Bivins, Michael **72**
Blige, Mary J. **20, 34, 60**
Butler, George, Jr. **70**
Coleman, Ornette **39, 69**
Combs, Sean "Puffy" **17, 43**
Da Don, Polow **86**
de Passe, Suzanne **25**
DJ Jazzy Jeff **32**
Dre, Dr. **10, 14, 30**
Duke, George **21**
Dupri, Jermaine **13, 46**
Elliott, Missy **31**
Gotti, Irv **39**
Hailey, JoJo **22**
Hailey, K-Ci **22**
Hammond, Fred **23**
Hawkins, Walter **87**
Hill, Lauryn **20, 53**
Huff, Leon **86**
Ice Cube **8, 30, 60**
Ja Rule **35**
Jackson, George **19**
Jackson, Joe **78**
Jackson, Michael **19, 53, 76**
Jackson, Randy **40**
Jean, Wyclef **20, 86**
Jerkins, Rodney **31**
Jimmy Jam **13**
Jones, Quincy **8, 30**
Kelly, R. **18, 44, 71**
Lewis, Terry **13**
Liles, Kevin **42**
Marley, Rita **32, 70**
Master P **21**
Mayfield, Curtis **2, 43**
Minott, Sugar **86**
Osborne, Jeffrey **26**
Prince **18, 65**
Queen Latifah **1, 16, 58**
Reid, Antonio "L.A." **28**
Robinson, Sylvia **79**
Sermon, Erick **81**
Sweat, Keith **19**
Timbaland **32**
Turner, Ike **68**
Vandross, Luther **13, 48, 59**
White, Barry **13, 41**
Whitfield, Norman **73**
Williams, J. Mayo **83**
Williams, Pharrell **47, 82**
Yabby You **83**

Young, Lee **72**

**Recording executives**
Busby, Jheryl **3, 74**
Butler, George, Jr. **70**
Combs, Sean "Puffy" **17, 43**
de Passe, Suzanne **25**
Dupri, Jermaine **13, 46**
Gordy, Berry, Jr. **1**
Gotti, Irv **39**
Harrell, Andre **9, 30**
Jackson, George **19**
Jackson, Randy **40**
Jimmy Jam **13**
Jones, Quincy **8, 30**
Knight, Suge **11, 30**
Lewis, Terry **13**
Liles, Kevin **42**
Massenburg, Kedar **23**
Master P **21**
Mayfield, Curtis **2, 43**
Queen Latifah **1, 16, 58**
Reid, Antonio "L.A." **28**
Rhone, Sylvia **2**
Robinson, Smokey **3, 49**
Sanders, Angelia **86**
Simmons, Russell **1, 30**
Williams, J. Mayo **83**

**Reform Party**
Foster, Ezola **28**

**Reggae**
Afro, Teddy **78**
Barnes, Lloyd **77**
Beenie Man **32**
Blondy, Alpha **30**
Burning Spear **79**
Cliff, Jimmy **28**
Dube, Lucky **77**
Ellis, Alton **74**
Ford, Vincent **75**
Griffiths, Marcia **29**
Hammond, Lenn **34**
Johnson, Linton Kwesi **37**
Marley, Bob **5**
Marley, Rita **32, 70**
Marley, Ziggy **41**
Minott, Sugar **86**
Mowatt, Judy **38**
Perry, Ruth **19**
Rhoden, Wayne **70**
Shaggy **31**
Sly & Robbie **34**
Steely **80**
Tosh, Peter **9**
Yabby You **83**

**Republic of New Afrika (RNA)**
Williams, Robert F. **11**

**Republican Party**
Allen, Ethel D. **13**
Fisher, Ada M. **76**
Scott, Tim **87**
Steele, Michael **38, 73**
Toote, Gloria E. A. **64**

**Restaurants**
Armstrong, Govind **81**
Cain, Herman **15**
Daniels-Carter, Valerie **23**
Garvin, Gerry **78**
Hawkins, La-Van **17, 54**
James, Charles H., III **62**

Otis, Clarence, Jr. **55**
Ouattara, Morou **74**
Pierce, Harold **75**
Rodriguez, Jimmy **47**
Samuelsson, Marcus **53**
Smith, B(arbara) **11**
Thompson, Don **56**
Washington, Regynald G. **44**
Williams, Lindsey **75**

**Rheedlen Centers for Children and Families**
Canada, Geoffrey **23**

**Rhode Island School of Design**
Prophet, Nancy Elizabeth **42**

**Rhodes scholar**
Braxton, Brad **77**
Kennedy, Randall **40**
Locke, Alain **10**
Rice, Susan E. **74**

**Rhythm and blues/soul music**
Aaliyah **30**
Ace, Johnny **36**
Adams, Johnny **39**
Adams, Oleta **18**
Akon **68**
Amerie **52**
Ashanti **37**
Ashford, Nickolas **21**
Austin, Patti **24**
Ayers, Roy **16**
Babyface **10, 31, 82**
Badu, Erykah **22**
Bailey, Philip **63**
Baker, Anita **21, 48**
Baker, LaVern **26**
Ballard, Hank **41**
Baylor, Helen **36**
Belgrave, Marcus **77**
Belle, Regina **1, 51**
Benét, Eric **28, 77**
Berry, Chuck **29**
Beverly, Frankie **25**
Beyoncé **39, 70**
Bivins, Michael **72**
Blige, Mary J. **20, 34, 60**
Boyz II Men **82**
Brandy **14, 34, 72**
Braxton, Toni **15, 61**
Brooks, Hadda **40**
Brown, Bobby **58**
Brown, Charles **23**
Brown, Chris **74**
Brown, Chuck **78**
Brown, Clarence Gatemouth **59**
Brown, James **15, 60**
Brown, Nappy **73**
Brown, Oscar, Jr. **53**
Burke, Solomon **31, 86**
Busby, Jheryl **3, 74**
Butler, Jerry **26**
Carey, Mariah **32, 53, 69**
Charles, Ray **16, 48**
Ciara **56**
Clinton, George **9**
Cole, Keyshia **63**
Cole, Natalie **17, 60, 84**
Combs, Sean "Puffy" **17, 43**
Cooke, Sam **17**
Cox, Deborah **28**

Crawford, Hank 77
D'Angelo 27
David, Craig 31, 53
Davis, Tyrone 54
Diddley, Bo 39, 72
Domino, Fats 20
Dorsey, Lee 65
Downing, Will 19
Dre, Dr. 14, 30
Dupri, Jermaine 13, 46
Elliott, Missy 31
Escobar, Damien 56
Escobar, Tourie 56
Evans, Faith 22
Feemster, Herbert 72
Fiona, Melanie 84
Franklin, Aretha 11, 44
Gamble, Kenny 85
Garrett, Sean 57
Gaye, Marvin 2
Gaynor, Gloria 36
Gibson, Tyrese 27, 62
Gill, Johnny 51
Ginuwine 35
Goapele 55
Goodman, Al 87
Gotti, Irv 39
Gray, Macy 29
Green, Al 13, 47, 74
Hailey, JoJo 22
Hailey, K-Ci 22
Hall, Aaron 57
Hamilton, Anthony 61
Harris, Corey 39, 73
Hart, Alvin Youngblood 61
Hathaway, Donny 18
Hathaway, Lalah 57
Hayes, Isaac 20, 58, 73
Hendryx, Nona 56
Henry, Clarence "Frogman" 46
Hill, Lauryn 20, 53
Hilson, Keri 84
Holloway, Brenda 65
Houston, Cissy 20, 83
Houston, Whitney 7, 28, 83
Huff, Leon 86
Hyman, Phyllis 19
India.Arie 34
Ingram, James 84
Isley, Marvin 87
Isley, Ronald 25, 56
Ja Rule 35
Jackson, Janet 6, 30, 68
Jackson, Michael 19, 53, 76
Jackson, Millie 25
Jackson, Tito 81
Jaheim 58
Jamelia 51
James, Etta 13, 52
James, Rick 17
Jarreau, Al 21, 65
Jennings, Lyfe 56, 69
Johnson, Robert 2
Johnson-George, Tamara 79
Jones, Booker T. 84
Jones, Donell 29
Jones, Quincy 8, 30
Jones, Sharon 86
Jordan, Montell 23
Kandi 83
Kelly, R. 18, 44, 71
Kem 47
Kendricks, Eddie 22

Keys, Alicia 32, 68
Knight, Gladys 16, 66
Knight, Marie 80
LaBelle, Patti 13, 30
Larrieux, Amel 63
Lattimore, Kenny 35
LaVette, Bettye 85
Ledisi 73
Legend, John 67
Levert, Eddie 70
Levert, Gerald 22, 59
Little Richard 15
Lopes, Lisa "Left Eye" 36
Luckett, Letoya 61
Maitreya, Sananda 85
Mario 71
Massenburg, Kedar 23
Master P 21
Maxwell 20, 81
Mayfield, Curtis 2, 43
McCoo, Marilyn 53
McKnight, Brian 18, 34
Miles, Buddy 69
Monáe, Janelle 86
Monica 21
Moore, Chante 26
Moore, Melba 21
Musiq 37, 84
Mya 35
Nash, Johnny 40
Ndegeocello, Meshell 15, 83
Neale, Haydain 52
Neville, Aaron 21
Ne-Yo 65
Notorious B.I.G. 20
Otis, Clyde 67
Parker, Maceo 72
Parker, Ray, Jr. 85
Pendergrass, Teddy 22, 83
Pinkney, Fayette 80
Pleasure P 84
Preston, Billy 39, 59
Price, Kelly 23
Prince 18, 65
Reagon, Toshi 76
Record, Eugene 60
Redding, Otis 16
Reed, A. C. 36
Reeves, Martha 85
Richie, Lionel 27, 65
Rihanna 65
Riperton, Minnie 32
Robinson, Smokey 3, 49
Ross, Diana 8, 27
Russell, Brenda 52
Sade 15
Sample, Joe 51
Scott, Jill 29, 83
Scott, "Little" Jimmy 48
Siji 56
Simpson, Valerie 21
Sisqo 30
Sledge, Percy 39
Sparks, Jordin 66
Staples, Mavis 50
Staples, "Pops" 32
Staton, Candi 27
Steinberg, Martha Jean "The
    Queen" 28
Stone, Angie 31
Studdard, Ruben 46
Sullivan, Jazmine 81
Supremes, The 33

Sweat, Keith 19
Tamia 24, 55
Temptations, The 33
Terrell, Tammi 32
The-Dream 74
Thomas, Irma 29
Thomas, Rozonda 34, 78
Thomas, Rufus 20
TLC 34
Tresvant, Ralph 57
Turner, Ike 68
Turner, Tina 6, 27
Ulmer, James 79
Usher 23, 56
Valentino, Bobby 62
Vandross, Luther 13, 48, 59
Watley, Jody 54
Watts, Reggie 52
Wells, Mary 28
West, Kanye 52
White, Barry 13, 41
Williams, Michelle 73
Williams, Vanessa L. 4, 17
Wilson, Cassandra 16
Wilson, Charlie 31, 77
Wilson, Mary 28
Wilson, Nancy 10
Withers, Bill 61
Womack, Bobby 60
Wonder, Stevie 11, 53

**RNA**
See Republic of New Afrika

**Robert C. Maynard Institute
for Journalism Education**
Harris, Jay T. 19
Maynard, Nancy Hicks 73
Maynard, Robert C. 7

**Roberts Companies, The**
Roberts, Mike 57

**Roc-A-Fella**
Dash, Damon 31
Jay-Z 27, 69

**Rock and Roll Hall of Fame**
Ballard, Hank 41
Bennett, Estelle 77
Berry, Chuck 29
Bland, Bobby "Blue" 36
Brown, Charles 23
Burke, Solomon 31, 86
Cole, Nat "King" 17
Davis, Miles 4
Diddley, Bo 39, 72
Franklin, Aretha 11, 44
Gamble, Kenny 85
Grandmaster Flash 33, 60
Green, Al 13, 47, 74
Guy, Buddy 31
Hayes, Isaac 20, 58, 73
Holiday, Billie 1
Holland-Dozier-Holland 36
Hooker, John Lee 30
Isley, Marvin 87
Isley, Ronald 25, 56
Jackson, Mahalia 5
Jackson, Michael 19, 53, 76
Jackson, Tito 81
Jamerson, James 59
James, Etta 13, 52
Johnson, Johnnie 56

Jones, Booker T. 84
Knight, Gladys 16, 66
Mayfield, Curtis 2, 43
Morton, Jelly Roll 29
Prince 18, 65
Reeves, Martha 85
Run-DMC 31, 75
Shider, Garry 87
Sledge, Percy 39
Spector, Ronnie 77
Steinberg, Martha Jean "The
    Queen" 28
Stone, Sly 85
Toussaint, Allen 60
Turner, Ike 68
Turner, Tina 6, 27
Wilson, Jackie 60
Wilson, Mary 28
Wonder, Stevie 11, 53

**Rock music**
Adebimpe, Tunde 75
Ballard, Hank 41
Bennett, Estelle 77
Berry, Chuck 29
Clemons, Clarence 41
Clinton, George 9
Diddley, Bo 39, 72
Domino, Fats 20
Edwards, Esther Gordy 43
Glover, Corey 34
Hendrix, Jimi 10
Ice-T 6, 31
Johnson, Johnnie 56
Kravitz, Lenny 10, 34
Little Richard 15
Lymon, Frankie 22
Mayfield, Curtis 2, 43
Miles, Buddy 69
Moore, LeRoi 72
Preston, Billy 39, 59
Prince 18, 65
Reagon, Toshi 76
Reid, Vernon 34
Run-DMC 31, 75
Slash 75
Spector, Ronnie 77
Stew 69
Stone, Sly 85
Tait, Michael 57
Tamar-kali 63
Tinsley, Boyd 50
Toussaint, Allen 60
Turner, Ike 68
Turner, Tina 6, 27
will.i.am 64
Wilson, Jackie 60

**Rockefeller Foundation**
Price, Hugh B. 9, 54

**Rockets**
Williams, O. S. 13

**Rodeo**
Nash, Johnny 40
Pickett, Bill 11
Sampson, Charles 13
Whitfield, Fred 23

**Roman Catholic Church**
Akpan, Uwem 70
Arinze, Francis 19
Aristide, Jean-Bertrand 6, 45

Chineworth, Mary Alice **79**
Clements, George **2**
DeLille, Henriette **30**
Fabre, Shelton **71**
Gantin, Bernardin **70**
Gregory, Wilton D. **37**
Guy, Rosa **5**
Healy, James Augustine **30**
Jean-Juste, Gérard **78**
Jones, Alex **64**
Marino, Eugene Antonio **30**
Otunga, Maurice Michael **55**
Rugambwa, Laurean **20**
Senghor, Augustin Diamacoune **66**
Stallings, George A., Jr. **6**

**Romance fiction**
Bunkley, Anita Richmond **39**
Hill, Donna **32**
Jackson, Brenda **87**
Washington, Elsie B. **78**

**Royalty**
Christophe, Henri **9**
Ka Dinizulu, Mcwayizeni **29**
Mswati III **56**
Mutebi, Ronald **25**

**RPT**
See Togolese People's Rally

**Ruff Ryders Records**
Eve **29**

**Rugby**
Mundine, Anthony **56**

**Rush Artists Management Co.**
Simmons, Russell **1, 30**

**Rutgers University**
Davis, George **36**
Gibson, Donald Bernard **40**

**Rwandan government**
Kagame, Paul **54**

**Rwandese Patriotic Front**
Kagame, Paul **54**

**SAA**
See Syndicat Agricole Africain

**SACC**
See South African Council of
Churches

**Sacramento Kings basketball
team**
Russell, Bill **8**
Webber, Chris **15, 30, 59**

**Sacramento Monarchs basket-
ball team**
Griffith, Yolanda **25**

**SADCC**
See Southern African Development
Coordination Conference

**Sailing**
Pinckney, Bill **42**

**St. Kitts and Nevis govern-
ment**
Douglas, Denzil Llewellyn **53**

**St. Louis Blues hockey team**
Brathwaite, Fred **35**
Mayers, Jamal **39**

**St. Louis Browns baseball
team**
Brown, Willard **36**
Paige, Satchel **7**

**St. Louis Cardinals baseball
team**
Baylor, Don **6**
Bonds, Bobby **43**
Brock, Lou **18**
Flood, Curt **10**
Gibson, Bob **33**
Lankford, Ray **23**
Smith, Ozzie **77**

**St. Louis city government**
Bosley, Freeman, Jr. **7**
Harmon, Clarence **26**

**St. Louis Giants baseball
team**
Charleston, Oscar **39**

**St. Louis Hawks basketball
team**
See Atlanta Hawks basketball team

**St. Louis Rams football team**
Bruce, Isaac **26**
Faulk, Marshall **35**
Pace, Orlando **21**

**St. Louis Stars baseball team**
Bell, James "Cool Papa" **36**

**Sainte Beuve Prize**
Beti, Mongo **36**

**Salvation Army**
Gaither, Israel L. **65**

**Sammy Davis Jr. National
Liver Institute University Hos-
pital**
Leevy, Carrol M. **42**

**San Antonio Spurs basketball
team**
Duncan, Tim **20**
Elliott, Sean **26**
Gervin, George **80**
Lucas, John **7**
Mohammed, Nazr **64**
Parker, Tony **75**
Robinson, David **24**

**San Diego Chargers football
team**
Barnes, Ernie **16, 78**
Lofton, James **42**
Tomlinson, LaDainian **65**
Winslow, Kellen **83**

**San Diego Conquistadors**
Chamberlain, Wilt **18, 47**

**San Diego Gulls hockey team**
O'Ree, Willie **5**

**San Diego Hawks hockey
team**
O'Ree, Willie **5**

**San Diego Padres baseball
team**
Carter, Joe **30**
Gwynn, Tony **18, 83**
McGriff, Fred **24**
Smith, Ozzie **77**
Winfield, Dave **5**

**San Francisco 49ers football
team**
Green, Dennis **5, 45**
Hayes, Bob **77**
Lott, Ronnie **9**
Rice, Jerry **5, 55**
Simpson, O. J. **15**
Singletary, Mike **4, 76**
Washington, Gene **63**

**San Francisco Giants base-
ball team**
Baker, Dusty **8, 43, 72**
Bonds, Barry **6, 34, 63**
Bonds, Bobby **43**
Carter, Joe **30**
Mays, Willie **3**
Morgan, Joe Leonard **9**
Strawberry, Darryl **22**

**San Francisco Opera**
Mitchell, Leona **42**

**San Francisco public schools**
Coleman, William F., III **61**

**Saturday Night Live**
Meadows, Tim **30**
Morgan, Tracy **61**
Morris, Garrett **31**
Murphy, Eddie **4, 20, 61**
Rock, Chris **3, 22, 66**
Rudolph, Maya **46**
Thompson, Kenan **52**

**Savoy Ballroom**
Johnson, Buddy **36**

**Saxophone**
Adderley, Julian "Cannonball" **30**
Albright, Gerald **23**
Anderson, Fred **87**
Bechet, Sidney **18**
Clemons, Clarence **41**
Coltrane, John **19**
Coltrane, Ravi **71**
Crawford, Hank **77**
Golson, Benny **37**
Gordon, Dexter **25**
Greene, Jimmy **74**
Griffin, Johnny **71**
Hawkins, Coleman **9**
Jacquet, Illinois **49**
Kay, Ulysess **37**
Kenyatta, Robin **54**
McLean, Jackie **78**
Moody, James **83**
Moore, LeRoi **72**
Moura, Paulo **87**
Newman, David **76**
Parker, Charlie **20**
Parker, Maceo **72**
Redman, Joshua **30**
Rollins, Sonny **37**
Sanders, Pharoah **64**
Shider, Garry **87**
Shorter, Wayne **75**

**Washington, Grover, Jr. 17, 44**
Waters, Benny **26**
Whalum, Kirk **37, 64**
York, Vincent **40**
Young, Lester **37**

**Schomburg Center for Re-
search in Black Culture**
Andrews, Bert **13**
Dodson, Howard, Jr. **7, 52**
Hutson, Jean Blackwell **16**
Morrison, Sam **50**
Reddick, Lawrence Dunbar **20**
Schomburg, Arthur Alfonso **9**

**School desegregation**
Bridges, Ruby **77**
Chestnut, J. L., Jr. **73**
Fortune, T. Thomas **6**
Hamer, Fannie Lou **6**
Hobson, Julius W. **44**
Holmes, Hamilton E. **82**

**Science fiction**
Barnes, Steven **54**
Bell, Derrick **6**
Butler, Octavia **8, 43, 58**
Delany, Samuel R., Jr. **9**

**SCLC**
See Southern Christian Leadership
Conference

**Scotland Yard**
Griffin, Bessie Blout **43**

**Screenplay writing**
Akil, Mara Brock **60, 82**
Brown, Cecil M. **46**
Clack, Zoanne **73**
Davis, Thulani **61**
Elder, Lonne, III **38**
Fisher, Antwone **40**
Fletcher, Geoffrey **85**
Greaves, William **38**
Jones, Orlando **30**
Lumet, Jenny **80**
Nissel, Angela **42**
Prince-Bythewood, Gina **31, 77**
Rhimes, Shonda Lynn **67**
Rhone, Trevor **80**
Ridley, John **69**
Robinson, Matt **69**
Singleton, John **2, 30**
Wesley, Richard **73**

**Sculpture**
Allen, Tina **22, 75**
Amos, Emma **63**
Bailey, Radcliffe **19**
Barthe, Richmond **15**
Biggers, John **20, 33**
Biggers, Sanford **62**
Billops, Camille **82**
Brown, Donald **19**
Burke, Selma **16**
Catlett, Elizabeth **2**
Chase-Riboud, Barbara **20, 46**
Cortor, Eldzier **42**
Dwight, Edward **65**
Edwards, Melvin **22**
Fuller, Meta Vaux Warrick **27**
Guyton, Tyree **9**
Hammons, David **69**
Hathaway, Isaac Scott **33**

Hunt, Richard 6
Lewis, Edmonia 10
Lewis, Samella 25
Manley, Edna 26
Marshall, Kerry James 59
McCullough, Geraldine 58, 79
McGee, Charles 10
Moody, Ronald 30
Neals, Otto 73
Perkins, Marion 38
Pierce, Elijah 84
Prophet, Nancy Elizabeth 42
Puryear, Martin 42
Ringgold, Faith 4, 81
Saar, Alison 16
Saar, Betye 80
Savage, Augusta 12
Scott, John T. 65
Shabazz, Attallah 6
Simmons, Gary 58
Stout, Renee 63
Washington, James, Jr. 38

**Sean John clothing line**
Combs, Sean "Puffy" 17, 43

**Seattle city government**
Rice, Norm 8

**Seattle Mariners baseball team**
Griffey, Ken, Jr. 12, 73
Reynolds, Harold 77

**Seattle Supersonics basket-ball team**
Bickerstaff, Bernie 21
Durant, Kevin 76
Lucas, John 7
Russell, Bill 8
Silas, Paul 24
Wilkens, Lenny 11

**Security and defense services**
Garrett, James F. 78

**Seismology**
Person, Waverly 9, 51

**Senegalese government**
Senghor, Léopold Sédar 66
Wade, Abdoulaye 66

*Sesame Street*
Byrd, Eugene 64
Clash, Kevin 14
Glover, Savion 14
Long, Loretta 58
Orman, Roscoe 55
Reed Hall, Alaina 83
Robinson, Matt 69

**Sexual harassment**
Gomez-Preston, Cheryl 9
Hill, Anita 5, 65
McCauley, Gina 76
Thomas, Clarence 2, 39, 65

*Share*
Auguste, Arnold A. 47

**Sheila Bridges Design Inc.**
Bridges, Sheila 36

**Shell Oil Company**
Mays, Leslie A. 41

**Shrine of the Black Madonna**
Agyeman, Jaramogi Abebe 10, 63

**Sickle cell anemia**
Edwards, Willarda V. 59
Pace, Betty 59
Satcher, David 7, 57

**Sierra Leone government**
Kabbah, Ahmad Tejan 23
Koroma, Ernest Bai 84

**Silicon Graphics Incorporated**
Coleman, Ken 57
Hannah, Marc 10

**Siméus Foods International**
Siméus, Dumas M. 25

**Skateboarding**
Williams, Stevie 71

**Sketches**
Crite, Alan Rohan 29
Sallee, Charles 38

**Skiing**
Horton, Andre 33
Horton, Suki 33

**Skillman Foundation**
Goss, Carol A. 55

**Slavery**
Asante, Molefi Kete 3
Bibb, Henry and Mary 54
Blackshear, Leonard 52
Blassingame, John Wesley 40
Chase-Riboud, Barbara 20, 46
Cooper, Anna Julia 20
Douglas, Aaron 7
Du Bois, W. E. B. 3
Dunbar, Paul Laurence 8
Equiano, Olaudah 78
Farmer-Paellmann, Deadria 43
Gaines, Ernest J. 7
Gordon-Reed, Annette 74
Haley, Alex 4
Harper, Frances Ellen Watkins 11
Huggins, Nathan Irvin 52
Johnson, Charles 1, 82
Jones, Edward P. 43, 67
Muhammad, Elijah 4
Patterson, Orlando 4
Pleasant, Mary Ellen 9
Stephens, Charlotte Andrews 14
Stewart, Maria W. Miller 19
Tancil, Gladys Quander 59
Taylor, Susie King 13
Tubman, Harriet 9
X, Malcolm 1

**Small Business Association Hall of Fame**
Steward, David L. 36

**Smart Books**
Pinkett Smith, Jada 10, 41

**Smith College**
Mayhew, Richard 39
Simmons, Ruth 13, 38

**SNCC**
See Student Nonviolent Coordinating Committee

**Soccer**
Adu, Freddy 67
Anderson, Viv 58
Barnes, John 53
Beasley, Jamar 29
Crooks, Garth 53
dos Santos, Manuel Francisco 65
Drogba, Didier 78
Eto'o, Samuel 73
Ferdinand, Rio 82
Gyan, Asamoah 87
Henry, Thierry 66
Ince, Paul 83
James, David 84
Jones, Cobi N'Gai 18
Kanouté, Fred 68
Mello, Breno 73
Mensah, John 87
Milla, Roger 2
Nakhid, David 25
Onyewu, Oguchi 60
Pelé 7
Regis, Cyrille 51
Ronaldinho 69
Scurry, Briana 27
Sono, Jomo 86
Weah, George 58

**Social science**
Berry, Mary Frances 7
Black, Albert 51
Bobo, Lawrence 60
Bunche, Ralph J. 5
Cayton, Horace 26
Clark, Kenneth B. 5, 52
Cobbs, Price M. 9
Collins, Patricia Hill 67
Frazier, E. Franklin 10
George, Zelma Watson 42
Hall, Stuart 78
Hare, Nathan 44
Harris, Eddy L. 18
Haynes, George Edmund 8
Ladner, Joyce A. 42
Lawrence-Lightfoot, Sara 10
Marable, Manning 10
Steele, Claude Mason 13
Williams, David Rudyard 50
Woodson, Robert L. 10

**Social Service Auxiliary**
Mossell, Gertrude Bustill 40

**Social work**
Auguste, Rose-Anne 13
Berry, Bertice 8, 55
Berrysmith, Don Reginald 49
Brown, Cora 33
Canada, Geoffrey 23
Coles, Alice 80
Colston, Hal 72
Compton-Rock, Malaak 86
Dunham, Katherine 4, 59
Fields, C. Virginia 25
Finner-Williams, Paris Michele 62
Gbowee, Leymah 76
Granger, Lester B. 75
Hale, Clara 16
Hale, Lorraine 8
Harris, Alice 7
Haynes, George Edmund 8
Jackson, Judith D. 57
Jackson, Mae 57

King, Barbara 22
Lewis, Thomas 19
Little, Robert L. 2
Robinson, Rachel 16
Sears, Stephanie 53
Smith, Damu 54
Vaughn, Viola 70
Waddles, Charleszetta "Mother" 10, 49
Walker, Bernita Ruth 53
Wallace, Joaquin 49
Wells, Henrietta Bell 69
White-Hammond, Gloria 61
Williams, Fannie Barrier 27
Thrower, Willie 35
Young, Whitney M., Jr. 4

**Socialist Party of Senegal**
Diouf, Abdou 3

**Sociology**
Edwards, Harry 2

**Soft Sheen Products**
Gardner, Edward G. 45

**Soledad Brothers**
Jackson, George Lester 14

**Somalian government**
Ahmed, Sharif 80

**Soul City, NC**
McKissick, Floyd B. 3

**Soul food**
Williams, Lindsey 75
Woods, Sylvia 34

*Soul Train*
Baylor, Helen 36
Cornelius, Don 4
D'Angelo 27
Lil' Kim 28
Winans, CeCe 14, 43

*Source* music awards
Nelly 32

**South African Communist Party**
Hani, Chris 6
Mhlaba, Raymond 55

**South African Council of Churches (SACC)**
Tutu, Desmond Mpilo 6, 44

**South African government**
Dandala, Mvume 77
Mhlaba, Raymond 55
Motlanthe, Kgalema 74
Sisulu, Walter 47
Zuma, Jacob 33, 75
Zuma, Nkosazana Dlamini 34

**South African literature**
Abrahams, Peter 39
Brutus, Dennis 38
Head, Bessie 28
Mathabane, Mark 5
Mofolo, Thomas 37
Mphalele, Es'kia 40

**South African Students' Organization**
Biko, Steven 4

**South Carolina state government**
Cardozo, Francis L. 33
Scott, Tim 87

**Southeastern University**
Jarvis, Charlene Drew 21

**Southern African Development Community (SADC)**
Mbuende, Kaire 12

**Southern African Development Coordination Conference (SADCC)**
Masire, Quett 5
Nujoma, Samuel 10

**Southern African Project**
McDougall, Gay J. 11, 43

**Southern Christian Leadership Conference (SCLC)**
Abernathy, Ralph 1
Angelou, Maya 1, 15
Baker, Ella 5
Barrow, Willie T. 85
Brooks, Tyrone 59
Chavis, Benjamin 6
Dee, Ruby 8, 50, 68
Fauntroy, Walter E. 11
Hooks, Benjamin L. 2, 85
Jackson, Jesse 1, 27, 72
Jones, William A., Jr. 61
King, Bernice 4, 81
King, Martin Luther, Jr. 1
King, Martin Luther, III 20
Lee, Eric P. 79
Lowery, Joseph 2
Moses, Robert Parris 11
Moss, Otis, Jr. 72
Nash, Diane 72
Orange, James 74
Rustin, Bayard 4
Shuttlesworth, Fred 47
Walker, Wyatt Tee 80
Williams, Hosea Lorenzo 15, 31
Young, Andrew 3, 48

**Southern Syncopated Orchestra**
Cook, Will Marion 40

**Space shuttle**
Gregory, Frederick 8, 51
Jemison, Mae C. 1, 35
McNair, Ronald 3, 58
Wilson, Stephanie 72

**Special Olympics**
Clairborne, Loretta 34

**Spectroscopy**
Quarterman, Lloyd Albert 4

**Speedskating**
Davis, Shani 58, 84

**Spelman College**
Cobb, William Jelani 59
Cole, Johnnetta B. 5, 43
Falconer, Etta Zuber 59
Price, Glenda 22
Simmons, Ruth 13, 38
Tatum, Beverly Daniel 42, 84

Wade-Gayles, Gloria Jean 41

**Sphinx Organization**
Dworkin, Aaron P. 52

**Spingarn medal**
Aaron, Hank 5
Ailey, Alvin 8
Anderson, Marian 2, 33
Angelou, Maya 1, 15
Bates, Daisy 13
Bethune, Mary McLeod 4
Bradley, Thomas 2, 20
Brooke, Edward 8
Bunche, Ralph J. 5
Carver, George Washington 4
Chesnutt, Charles 29
Clark, Kenneth B. 5, 52
Cosby, Bill 7, 26, 59
Davis, Sammy, Jr. 18
Drew, Charles Richard 7
Du Bois, W. E. B. 3
Ellington, Duke 5
Evers, Medgar 3
Franklin, John Hope 5, 77
Grimké, Archibald H. 9
Haley, Alex 4
Hastie, William H. 8
Hayes, Roland 4
Height, Dorothy I. 2, 23, 78
Higginbotham, A. Leon, Jr. 13, 25
Hinton, William Augustus 8
Hooks, Benjamin L. 2, 85
Horne, Lena 5, 86
Houston, Charles Hamilton 4
Hughes, Langston 4
Jackson, Jesse 1, 27, 72
Johnson, James Weldon 5
Johnson, John H. 3, 54
Jordan, Barbara 4, 78
Julian, Percy Lavon 6
Just, Ernest Everett 3
Keith, Damon J. 16, 74
King, Martin Luther, Jr. 1
Lawless, Theodore K. 8
Lawrence, Jacob 4
Logan, Rayford 40
Marshall, Thurgood 1, 44
Mays, Benjamin E. 7
Moore, Harry T. 29
Parks, Gordon 1, 35, 58
Parks, Rosa 1, 35, 56
Powell, Colin 1, 28, 75
Price, Leontyne 1
Randolph, A. Philip 3
Robeson, Paul 2
Robinson, Jackie 6
Staupers, Mabel K. 7
Sullivan, Leon H. 3, 30
Tobias, Channing H. 79
Weaver, Robert C. 8, 46
White, Walter F. 4
Wilder, L. Douglas 3, 48
Wilkins, Roy 4
Williams, Paul R. 9
Woodson, Carter G. 2
Wright, Louis Tompkins 4
Wright, Richard 5
Young, Andrew 3, 48
Young, Coleman 1, 20

**Spirituals**
Anderson, Marian 2, 33
Carr, Kurt 56

Hayes, Roland 4
Jackson, Mahalia 5
Joyner, Matilda Sissieretta 15
Norman, Jessye 5
Reese, Della 6, 20
Robeson, Paul 2
Williams, Denise 40

**Sports administration**
Fuller, Vivian 33
Kerry, Leon G. 46
Lee, Bertram M., Sr. 46
Mills, Steve 47
Phillips, Teresa L. 42
Randolph, Willie 53
Ussery, Terdema, II 29

**Sports agent**
Holland, Kimberly N. 62

**Stanford University**
Bobo, Lawrence 60
Rice, Condoleezza 3, 28, 72
Walker, Arthur, II 87
Washington, Gene 63
Willingham, Tyrone 43

**Starcom**
McCann, Renetta 44

**State University of New York System**
Ballard, Allen Butler, Jr. 40
Baraka, Amiri 1, 38
Clemente, Rosa 74
Wharton, Clifton R., Jr. 7

**Stellar Awards**
Baylor, Helen 36
Hawkins, Walter 87
Sapp, Marvin 74
Tribbett, Tye 81
Walker, Hezekiah 34

**Stonewall 25**
Norman, Pat 10

**Stop the Violence Movement**
KRS-One 34
MC Lyte 34

**Storytelling**
Baker, Augusta 38
Bennett, Louise 69
Hill, Hugh Morgan 83

**Student Nonviolent Coordinating Committee (SNCC)**
Al-Amin, Jamil Abdullah 6
Anderson, William G(ilchrist) 57
Baker, Ella 5
Barry, Marion S. 7, 44
Blackwell, Unita 17
Bond, Julian 2, 35
Carmichael, Stokely 5, 26
Clark, Septima 7
Davis, Angela 5
Forman, James 7, 51
Hamer, Fannie Lou 6
Holland, Endesha Ida Mae 3, 57
Lester, Julius 9
Lewis, John 2, 46, 83
Moses, Robert Parris 11
Nash, Diane 72
Norton, Eleanor Holmes 7
Poussaint, Alvin F. 5, 67

Reagon, Bernice Johnson 7
Touré, Askia (Muhammad Abu Bakr el) 47

**Sudan government**
Bashir, Omar al- 77
Cham, Adongo Agada Akway 77
Kiir, Salva 85

**Sun Microsystems**
Tademy, Lalita 36

**Sundance Film Festival**
Harris, Leslie 6

**Sunni Muslim**
Kalbani, Adil 77
Muhammed, W. Deen 27

**Sunny Alade Records**
Ade, King Sunny 41

**Supreme Court**
See U.S. Supreme Court

**Surfing**
Corley, Tony 62

**Surrealism**
Ellison, Ralph 7
Lee-Smith, Hughie 5, 22

**Swaziland government**
Mswati III 56

**Sweet Honey in the Rock**
Reagon, Bernice Johnson 7

**Swimming**
Jones, Cullen 73

**Sylvia's Restaurant**
Washington, Regynald G. 44
Woods, Sylvia 34

**Syndicat Agricole Africain (SAA)**
Houphouët-Boigny, Félix 4, 64

***Talk Soup***
Tyler, Aisha N. 36

**Talladega College**
Archie-Hudson, Marguerite 44

**Tampa Bay Buccaneers football team**
Barber, Ronde 41
Brooks, Derrick 43
Dungy, Tony 17, 42, 59
McDaniel, Randall Cornell 81
Morris, Raheem 77
Sapp, Warren 38
Williams, Doug 22

**Tanganyikan African National Union (TANU)**
Kikwete, Jakaya Mrisho 73
Nyerere, Julius 5

**TANU**
See Tanganyikan African National Union

**Tanzanian African National Union (TANU)**
See Tanganyikan African National Union

**Tap dancing**
Atkins, Cholly 40
Bates, Peg Leg 14

Brown, Ernest **80**
Glover, Savion **14**
Hines, Gregory **1, 42**
Robinson, LaVaughn **69**
Sims, Howard "Sandman" **48**
Slyde, Jimmy **70**
Walker, Dianne **57**

**TBS**
See Turner Broadcasting System

**Teacher of the Year Award**
Draper, Sharon Mills **16, 43**
Oliver, Kimberly **60**

**Teachers Insurance and Annuity Association and the College Retirement Equities Fund (TIAA-CREF)**
Wharton, Clifton R., Jr. **7**

**Teaching**
Abani, Chris **77**
Adams-Ender, Clara **40**
Alexander, Margaret Walker **22**
Amadi, Elechi **40**
Archie-Hudson, Marguerite **44**
Aubert, Alvin **41**
Baiocchi, Regina Harris **41**
Ballard, Allen Butler, Jr. **40**
Belgrave, Marcus **77**
Bibb, Henry and Mary **54**
Blassingame, John Wesley **40**
Branch, William Blackwell **39**
Brawley, Benjamin **44**
Brown, Uzee **42**
Brown, Willa **40**
Bryan, Ashley F. **41**
Campbell, Mary Schmidt **43**
Cardozo, Francis L. **33**
Carruthers, George R. **40**
Carter, Joye Maureen **41**
Chenault, John **40**
Cheney-Coker, Syl **43**
Clarke, John Henrik **20**
Clemmons, Reginal G. **41**
Cobb, Jewel Plummer **42**
Cobb, W. Montague **39**
Cole, Johnnetta B. **5, 43**
Colescott, Robert **69**
Collins, Patricia Hill **67**
Cook, Mercer **40**
Cooper Cafritz, Peggy **43**
Cortez, Jayne **43**
Cortor, Eldzier **42**
Cotter, Joseph Seamon, Sr. **40**
Dailey, Ulysses Grant **87**
Davis, Arthur P. **41**
Davis, Gary **41**
Davis, Milt **74**
De Veaux, Alexis **44**
Dennard, Brazeal **37**
Draper, Sharon Mills **16, 43**
Drummond, William J. **40**
Dumas, Henry **41**
Dunnigan, Alice Allison **41**
Dymally, Mervyn **42**
Early, Gerald **15**
Falconer, Etta Zuber **59**
Feelings, Muriel **44**
Ferguson, Ronald F. **75**
Figueroa, John J. **40**
Fletcher, Bill, Jr. **41**
Ford, Nick Aaron **44**

Forrest, Leon **44**
Fuller, A. Oveta **43**
Fuller, Arthur **27**
Fuller, Howard L. **37**
Gates, Sylvester James, Jr. **15**
Gayle, Addison, Jr. **41**
George, Zelma Watson **42**
Gibson, Donald Bernard **40**
Gill, Gerald **69**
Hall, Arthur **39**
Hamburg, Beatrix **84**
Hammonds, Evelynn **69**
Harding, Vincent **67**
Hare, Nathan **44**
Harris, Barry **68**
Harvey, William R. **42**
Henries, A. Doris Banks **44**
Hill, Errol **40**
Hill, Leslie Pinckney **44**
Horne, Frank **44**
Humphries, Frederick **20**
Imes, Elmer Samuel **39**
Jackson, Fred James **25**
Jarrett, Vernon D. **42**
Jarvis, Erich **67**
Kennedy, Randall **40**
Ladner, Joyce A. **42**
Leevy, Carrol M. **42**
Lewis, Norman **39**
Lindsey, Tommie **51**
Logan, Rayford W. **40**
Maathai, Wangari **43**
McCullough, Geraldine **58, 79**
Mitchell, Parren J. **42, 66**
Moore, Harry T. **29**
Mphalele, Es'kia **40**
Naylor, Gloria **10, 42**
Norman, Maidie **20**
Oliver, Kimberly **60**
Owens, Helen **48**
Palmer, Everard **37**
Patterson, Mary Jane **54**
Peters, Margaret and Matilda **43**
Player, Willa B. **43**
Prophet, Nancy Elizabeth **42**
Puryear, Martin **42**
Putney, Martha S. **75**
Querino, Manuel Raimundo **84**
Ray, Charlotte E. **60**
Redmond, Eugene **23**
Reid, Senghor **55**
Rhodes, Jewell Parker **84**
Ross-Lee, Barbara **67**
Shockley, Ann Allen **84**
Simpson-Hoffman, N'kenge **52**
Smith, Anna Deavere **6, 44**
Smith, John L. **22**
Tillis, Frederick **40**
Toler, Burl **80**
Tutu, Nontombi Naomi **57**
Tyson, Andre **40**
Wambugu, Florence **42**
Watson, Diane **41**
Wells, Henrietta Bell **69**
Wesley, Richard **73**
Wilkens, J. Ernest, Jr. **43**
Yancy, Dorothy Cowser **42**
Yarbrough, Camille **40**
York, Vincent **40**

**Techno music**
Atkins, Juan **50**
Craig, Carl **31, 71**

May, Derrick **41**

**Technology Access Foundation**
Millines Dziko, Trish **28**

**TEF**
See Theological Education Fund

**Telecommunications**
Clyburn, Mignon **78**
Gordon, Bruce S. **41, 53, 82**
Ibrahim, Mo **67**
Irvin, Vernon **65**
Wilkins, Ray **47**

**Television**
Akil, Mara Brock **60, 82**
Anderson, Eddie "Rochester" **30**
Andrews, Tina **74**
Arkadie, Kevin **17**
Arnold, Tichina **63**
Banks, Tyra **11, 50**
Barclay, Paris **37**
Barrino, Fantasia **53**
Beach, Michael **26**
Bentley, Lamont **53**
Blacque, Taurean **58**
Blake, Asha **26**
Bonet, Lisa **58**
Bowser, Yvette Lee **17**
Brady, Wayne **32, 71**
Branch, William Blackwell **39**
Bridges, Todd **37**
Brooks, Golden **62**
Brooks, Hadda **40**
Brooks, Mehcad **62**
Brown, Bobby **58**
Brown, James **22**
Brown, Joe **29**
Brown, Vivian **27**
Burnett, Charles **16, 68**
Carson, Lisa Nicole **21**
Carter, Nell **39**
Cash, Rosalind **28**
Cedric the Entertainer **29, 60**
Cheadle, Don **19, 52**
Clack, Zoanne **73**
Coleman, Gary **35, 86**
Corbi, Lana **42**
Cosby, Bill **7, 26, 59**
Creagh, Milton **27**
Curtis-Hall, Vondie **17**
Davis, Viola **34, 76**
de Passe, Suzanne **25**
Deezer D **53**
Diggs, Taye **25, 63**
Dourdan, Gary **37**
Dungey, Merrin **62**
Earthquake **55**
Elba, Idris **49**
Elder, Larry **25**
Ephriam, Mablean **29**
Eubanks, Kevin **15**
Evans, Harry **25**
Faison, Donald **50**
Falana, Lola **42**
Fields, Kim **36**
Flavor Flav **67**
Fox, Rick **27**
Frazier, Kevin **58**
Freeman, Yvette **27**
Gardere, Jeffrey **76**
Gibbs, Marla **86**

Givens, Robin **4, 25, 58**
Gray, Willie **46**
Greely, M. Gasby **27**
Greene, Petey **65**
Grier, David Alan **28**
Griffin, Angela **80**
Hall, Arsenio **58**
Hardison, Kadeem **22**
Harewood, David **52**
Hatchett, Glenda **32**
Haynes, Trudy **44**
Haysbert, Dennis **42**
Hemsley, Sherman **19**
Henriques, Julian **37**
Hill, Lauryn **20, 53**
Hill, Marc Lamont **80**
Hughley, D. L. **23, 76**
Hyman, Earle **25, 79**
Jackson, George **19**
Jackson, Randy **40**
Jackson, Tom **70**
Jarrett, Vernon D. **42**
Jean-Louis, Jimmy **76**
Joe, Yolanda **21**
Johnson, Rodney Van **28**
Jones, Bobby **20**
Kandi **83**
Kodjoe, Boris **34**
Lathan, Sanaa **27**
Lesure, James **64**
Lewis, Emmanuel **36**
Long, Loretta **58**
Lumbly, Carl **47**
Mabuza-Suttle, Felicia **43**
Mac, Bernie **29, 61, 72**
Mahorn, Rick **60**
Manigault-Stallworth, Omarosa **69**
Marsalis, Branford **34**
Martin, Helen **31**
Martin, Jesse L. **31**
Mathis, Greg **26**
McCrary Anthony, Crystal **70**
McFarland, Roland **49**
McGlowan, Angela **64, 86**
McKenzie, Vashti M. **29**
McKinney, Nina Mae **40**
Meadows, Tim **30**
Mercado-Valdes, Frank **43**
Michele, Michael **31**
Miller, Wentworth **75**
Mitchell, Brian Stokes **21**
Mitchell, Russ **21, 73**
Moss, Carlton **16**
Nash, Johnny **40**
Nash, Niecy **66**
Neal, Elise **29**
Neville, Arthel **53**
Nicholas, Denise **82**
Nissel, Angela **42**
Norman, Christina **47**
Orman, Roscoe **55**
Palmer, Keke **68**
Parker, Nicole Ari **52**
Perry, Tyler **40, 54**
Phifer, Mekhi **25**
Pickens, James, Jr. **59**
Pitts, Byron **71**
Poussaint, Renee **78**
Pratt, Kyla **57**
Premice, Josephine **41**
Price, Frederick K. C. **21**
Prince-Bythewood, Gina **31, 77**
Quarles, Norma **25**

Ray, Gene Anthony 47
Reddick, Lance 52
Reynolds, Star Jones 10, 27, 61
Rhimes, Shonda Lynn 67
Richards, Beah 30
Richardson, Salli 68
Ridley, John 69
Roberts, Deborah 35
Robinson, Shaun 36
Rock, Chris 3, 22, 66
Rodrigues, Percy 68
Roker, Al 12, 49
Roker, Roxie 68
Rollins, Howard E., Jr. 17
Russell, Nipsey 66
St. Patrick, Mathew 48
Salters, Lisa 71
Sanford, Isabel 53
Shepherd, Sherri 55
Simmons, Henry 55
Simmons, Kimora Lee 51, 83
Smiley, Tavis 20, 68
Snipes, Wesley 3, 24, 67
Stuart, Moira 82
Sykes, Wanda 48, 81
Taylor, Jason 70
Taylor, Karin 34
Taylor, Regina 9, 46
Thigpen, Lynne 17, 41
Thompson, Kenan 52
Torres, Gina 52
Tyler, Aisha N. 36
Union, Gabrielle 31
Usher 23, 56
Vaughn, Countess 53
Wainwright, Joscelyn 46
Warner, Malcolm-Jamal 22, 36
Warren, Michael 27
Washington, Hayma 86
Watson, Carlos 50
Wayans, Damien 78
Wayans, Damon 8, 41
Wayans, Marlon 29, 82
Wayans, Shawn 29
Whitaker, Forest 2, 49, 67
Williams, Armstrong 29
Williams, Clarence, III 26
Williams, Serena 20, 41, 73
Williams, Vanessa A. 32, 66
Williams, Wendy 62
Williamson, Mykelti 22
Wilson, Chandra 57
Wilson, Dorien 55

**Television direction**
Barclay, Paris 37
Warner, Malcolm-Jamal 22, 36
Whack, Rita Coburn 36

**Tennessee state government**
Ford, Harold E(ugene) 42

**Tennessee State University**
Phillips, Teresa L. 42

**Tennessee Supreme Court**
Birch, Adolpho A., Jr. 85

**Tennessee Titans football team**
George, Eddie 80
McNair, Steve 22, 47, 79

**Tennis**
Ashe, Arthur 1, 18
Blake, James 43

Garrison, Zina 2
Gibson, Althea 8, 43
Jackson, Jamea 64
Lucas, John 7
McNeil, Lori 1
Noah, Yannick 4, 60
Peters, Margaret and Matilda 43
Rubin, Chanda 37
Washington, MaliVai 8
Williams, Samm-Art 21
Williams, Serena 20, 41, 73
Williams, Venus 17, 34, 62
Young, Donald, Jr. 57

**Texas Rangers baseball team**
Bonds, Bobby 43
Cottrell, Comer 11

**Texas state government**
Delco, Wilhemina 33
Johnson, Eddie Bernice 8
Jordan, Barbara 4, 78

**Theater administration/ownership**
Austin, Lovie 40
Banks, Michelle 59
Borders, James 9
Cortez, Jayne 43
Cox, Ida 42
Gibson, John Trusty 87
Hamlin, Larry Leon 49, 62
Leggs, Kingsley 62
LeNoire, Rosetta 37
Leon, Kenny 10
Marsalis, Delfeayo 41
Spears, Warren 52

**Theatrical direction/production**
Belgrave, Cynthia 75
Glover, Keith 79
Hall, Juanita 62
Hayes, Teddy 40
McClinton, Marion Isaac 77
Milner, Ron 39
Perry, Tyler 40, 54
Scott, Harold Russell, Jr. 61
Teer, Barbara Ann 81
Thompson, Tazewell 13
Wolfe, George C. 6, 43

**Thelonius Monk Institute of Jazz Performance**
Blanchard, Terence 43

**Theological Education Fund (TEF)**
Gordon, Pamela 17
Tutu, Desmond Mpilo 6, 44

**Theology**
Cone, James H. 3, 82
Franklin, Robert M. 13
Harding, Vincent 67
Wright, Jeremiah A., Jr. 45, 69

**They All Played Baseball Foundation**
Johnson, Mamie "Peanut" 40

**Threads 4 Life**
Jones, Carl 7
Kani, Karl 10

Walker, T. J. 7

**Three Fifths Productions**
Marsalis, Delfeayo 41

**TIAA-CREF**
See Teachers Insurance and Annuity Association and the College Retirement Equities Fund

**Time Warner Inc.**
Ames, Wilmer 27
Parsons, Richard Dean 11, 33

**TLC Beatrice International Holdings, Inc.**
Lewis, Reginald F. 6

**TLC Group L.P.**
Lewis, Reginald F. 6

**Togolese Army**
Eyadéma, Gnassingbé 7, 52

**Togolese People's Rally (RPT)**
Eyadéma, Gnassingbé 7, 52
Gnassingbé, Faure 67

**Toledo Civic Hall of Fame**
Stewart, Ella 39

*The Tonight Show*
Eubanks, Kevin 15

**Tony awards**
Allen, Debbie 13, 42
Belafonte, Harry 4, 65
Carroll, Diahann 9
Carter, Nell 39
Clarke, Hope 14
Davis, Viola 34, 76
Faison, George 16
Falana, Lola 42
Fishburne, Laurence 4, 22, 70
Hall, Juanita 62
Horne, Lena 5, 86
Hyman, Phyllis 19
Jones, James Earl 3, 49, 79
McDonald, Audra 20, 62
Mokae, Zakes 80
Moore, Melba 21
Premice, Josephine 41
Richards, Lloyd 2
Rose, Anika Noni 70
Santiago-Hudson, Ruben 85
Thigpen, Lynne 17, 41
Uggams, Leslie 23
Vereen, Ben 4
Wilson, August 7, 33, 55
Wolfe, George C. 6, 43

**Toronto Blue Jays baseball team**
Carter, Joe 30
Gaston, Cito 71
McGriff, Fred 24
Winfield, Dave 5

**Toronto Raptors basketball team**
Carter, Butch 27
Carter, Vince 26
Olajuwon, Hakeem 2, 72
Thomas, Isiah 7, 26, 65

**Tourism**
Edmunds, Gladys 48

**Track and field**
Ashford, Evelyn 63
Beamon, Bob 30
Bekele, Kenenisa 75
Bolt, Usain 73
Christie, Linford 8
Clay, Bryan 57, 74
Devers, Gail 7, 87
Dibaba, Tirunesh 73
Felix, Allyson 48
Freeman, Cathy 29
Gebrselassie, Haile 70
Graham, Trevor 84
Greene, Maurice 27, 77
Griffith-Joyner, Florence 28
Harrison, Alvin 28
Harrison, Calvin 28
Hayes, Bob 77
Holmes, Kelly 47
Jacobs, Regina 38
James, G. Larry 74
Johnson, Michael 13
Johnson, Rodney Van 28
Jones, Lou 64
Jones, Marion 21, 66
Joyner-Kersee, Jackie 5
Keflezighi, Meb 49
Lewis, Carl 4
Metcalfe, Ralph 26
Montgomery, Tim 41
Moses, Edwin 8
Mutola, Maria 12
Owens, Jesse 2
Pollard, Fritz 53
Powell, Mike 7
Quirot, Ana 13
Richards, Sanya 66
Rudolph, Wilma 4
Thugwane, Josia 21
White, Willye 67
Whitfield, Mal 60
Williams, Lauryn 58
Woodruff, John 68

**TransAfrica Forum, Inc.**
Fletcher, Bill, Jr. 41
Robinson, Randall 7, 46

**Transplant surgery**
Callender, Clive O. 3
Kountz, Samuel L. 10

**Transport and General Workers' Union**
Morris, William "Bill" 51

**"Trial of the Century"**
Cochran, Johnnie 11, 39, 52
Darden, Christopher 13
Simpson, O. J. 15

**Trombone**
Marsalis, Delfeayo 41
Powell, Benny 87

**Trumpet**
Adderley, Nat 29
Armstrong, Louis 2
Belgrave, Marcus 77
Blanchard, Terence 43
Brown, Clifford 86
Dara, Olu 35
Davis, Miles 4
Dixon, Bill 87

Eldridge, Roy 37
Ellison, Ralph 7
Farmer, Art 38
Gillespie, Dizzy 1
Hubbard, Freddie 75
Jones, Jonah 39
Jones, Thad 68
Smith, Cladys "Jabbo" 32
Terry, Clark 39
Wilson, Gerald 49

**Tulane University**
Mason, Ronald 27

**Turner Broadcasting System (TBS)**
Clayton, Xernona 3, 45

**Tuskegee Airmen**
Archer, Lee, Jr. 79
Bromery, Randolph Wilson 85
Brown, Willa 40
Davis, Benjamin O., Jr. 2, 43
Haysbert, Raymond V., Sr. 87
James, Daniel, Jr. 16
Patterson, Frederick Douglass 12

**Tuskegee University**
Carver, George Washington 4
Dawson, William Levi 39
Harvey, William R. 42
Moton, Robert Russa 83
Payton, Benjamin F. 23
Taylor, Robert Robinson 80

**TV One**
Ligging, Alfred, III 43

**UAW**
See United Auto Workers

**UCC**
See United Church of Christ

**UFBL**
See Universal Foundation for Better Living

**UGA**
See United Golf Association

**Ugandan government**
Amin, Idi 42
Museveni, Yoweri 4
Obote, Milton 63

**Ultraviolet camera/spectrograph (UVC)**
Carruthers, George R. 40

***Umkhonto we Sizwe***
Hani, Chris 6
Mandela, Nelson 1, 14, 77
Motlanthe, Kgalema 74
Zuma, Jacob 33, 75

**UN**
See United Nations

**UNCF**
See United Negro College Fund

**Underground Railroad**
Blockson, Charles L. 42
Cohen, Anthony 15
Crew, Spencer R. 55
DeBaptiste, George 32

Shadd, Abraham D. 81

**Unemployment and Poverty Action Committee**
Forman, James 7, 51

**UNESCO**
See United Nations Educational, Scientific, and Cultural Organization

**UNESCO Medals**
Dadié, Bernard 34

**UNIA**
See Universal Negro Improvement Association

**UNICEF**
See United Nations Children's Fund

**Unions**
Brown, Lloyd Louis 42
Clay, William Lacy 8
Crockett, George W., Jr. 10, 64
Europe, James Reese 10
Farmer, James 2, 64
Fletcher, Bill, Jr. 41
Hilliard, David 7
Holt Baker, Arlene 73
Lucy, William 50
Morris, William "Bill" 51
Ramaphosa, Cyril 3
Randolph, A. Philip 3
Roberts, Lillian 83
Smith, Nate 49
Touré, Sekou 6
Wyatt, Addie L. 56

**UNIP**
See United National Independence Party

**UNITA**
See National Union for the Total Independence of Angola

**United Auto Workers (UAW)**
Fletcher, Bill, Jr. 41

**United Bermuda Party**
Gordon, Pamela 17

**United Church of Christ (UCC)**
Chavis, Benjamin 6
Forbes, James A., Jr. 71
Moss, Otis, III 72

**United Democratic Front (UDF; Malawi)**
Muluzi, Bakili 14, 76

**United Golf Association (UGA)**
Elder, Lee 6
Sifford, Charlie 4, 49

**United Methodist Church**
Caldwell, Kirbyjon 55
Lewis, Shirley A. R. 14
Muzorewa, Abel 85
Stith, Charles R. 73

**United National Independence Party (UNIP)**
Kaunda, Kenneth 2

**United Nations (UN)**
Annan, Kofi Atta 15, 48
Bunche, Ralph J. 5

Cleaver, Emanuel 4, 45, 68
Diouf, Abdou 3
Juma, Calestous 57
Lafontant, Jewel Stradford 3, 51
McDonald, Gabrielle Kirk 20
McHenry, Donald F. 83
Mongella, Gertrude 11
Perkins, Edward 5
Sampson, Edith S. 4
Young, Andrew 3, 48

**United Nations Children's Fund (UNICEF)**
Baker, Gwendolyn Calvert 9
Belafonte, Harry 4, 65
Machel, Graca Simbine 16
Weah, George 58

**United Nations Educational, Scientific, and Cultural Organization (UNESCO)**
Diop, Cheikh Anta 4
Frazier, E. Franklin 10
Machel, Graca Simbine 16
Smythe Haith, Mabel 61

**United Negro College Fund (UNCF)**
Boyd, T. B., III 6
Bunkley, Anita Richmond 39
Creagh, Milton 27
Dawson, Matel, Jr. 39
Edley, Christopher 2, 48
Gray, William H., III 3
Jordan, Vernon E. 3, 35
Lomax, Michael L. 58
Mays, Benjamin E. 7
Patterson, Frederick Douglass 12
Tillis, Frederick 40

**United Parcel Service**
Cooper, Evern 40
Darden, Calvin 38
Washington, Patrice Clarke 12

**United Parcel Service Foundation**
Cooper, Evern 40

**United Somali Congress**
Ali Mahdi Mohamed 5

**United States Delegations**
Shabazz, Ilyasah 36

**United States Football League (USFL)**
White, Reggie 6, 50
Williams, Doug 22

**United Way**
Donald, Arnold Wayne 36
Steward, David L. 36

**United Workers Union of South Africa (UWUSA)**
Buthelezi, Mangosuthu Gatsha 9

**Universal Foundation for Better Living (UFBL)**
Colemon, Johnnie 11
Reese, Della 6, 20

**Universal Negro Improvement Association (UNIA)**
Austin, Junius C. 44
Garvey, Marcus 1

McGuire, George Alexander 80

**University administration**
See College and university administration

**University of Alabama**
Davis, Mike 41
Lucy Foster, Autherine 35

**University of California–Berkeley**
Blackwell, David 79
Drummond, William J. 40
Edley, Christopher F., Jr. 48

**University of Cape Town**
Ramphele, Maphela 29

**University of Chicago Hospitals**
Lee, Raphael C. 87
Obama, Michelle 61

**University of Colorado**
Berry, Mary Frances 7

**University of Delaware**
Mitchell, Sharon 36

**University of Florida**
Haskins, James 36, 54

**University of Michigan**
Amaker, Tommy 62
Dillard, Godfrey J. 45
Fuller, A. Oveta 43
Goss, Tom 23
Gray, Ida 41
Imes, Elmer Samuel 39

**University of Missouri**
Anderson, Mike 63
Floyd, Elson S. 41

**University of North Carolina**
Floyd, Elson S. 41

**University of Notre Dame**
Willingham, Tyrone 43

**University of Texas**
Granville, Evelyn Boyd 36

**University of the West Indies**
Brathwaite, Kamau 36
Hill, Errol 40

**University of Virginia**
Littlepage, Craig 35

***Upscale magazine***
Bronner, Nathaniel H., Sr. 32

**Urban Bush Women**
Zollar, Jawole 28

**Urban League (regional)**
Adams, Sheila J. 25
Clayton, Xernona 3, 45
Jacob, John E. 2
Layton, William 87
Mays, Benjamin E. 7
Young, Whitney M., Jr. 4

**Urban renewal**
Allen, Will 74
Archer, Dennis 7, 36
Bosley, Freeman, Jr. 7

Carter, Majora 77
Harris, Alice 7
Lane, Vincent 5
Waters, Maxine 3, 67

**U.S. Air Force**
Anderson, Michael P. 40
Carter, Joye Maureen 41
Davis, Benjamin O., Jr. 2, 43
Drew, Alvin, Jr. 67
Dwight, Edward 65
Gregory, Frederick 8, 51
Harris, Marcelite Jordan 16
James, Daniel, Jr. 16
Johnson, Lonnie G. 32
Jones, Wayne 53
Lyles, Lester 31

**U.S. Army**
Adams-Ender, Clara 40
Baker, Vernon Joseph 65, 87
Brown, Anthony G. 72
Cadoria, Sherian Grace 14
Clemmons, Reginal G. 41
Davis, Benjamin O., Sr. 4
Delany, Martin R. 27
Flipper, Henry O. 3
Greenhouse, Bunnatine "Bunny" 57
Honoré, Russel L. 64
Jackson, Fred James 25
Johnson, Hazel 22
Johnson, Shoshana 47
King, Teresa 80
Matthews, Mark 59
Poindexter, Hildrus A. 87
Powell, Colin 1, 28, 75
Rogers, Alan G. 72
Snow, Samuel 71
Stanford, John 20
Watkins, Perry 12
West, Togo D., Jr. 16
Young, Charles 77

**U.S. Army Air Corps**
Anderson, Charles Edward 37

**U.S. Atomic Energy Commission**
Nabrit, Samuel Milton 47

**U.S. Attorney's Office**
Jordan, Eddie 82
Lafontant, Jewel Stradford 3, 51

**U.S. Basketball League (USBL)**
Lucas, John 7

**U.S. Bureau of Engraving and Printing**
Felix, Larry R. 64

**U.S. Cabinet**
Brown, Ron 5
Elders, Joycelyn 6
Espy, Mike 6
Harris, Patricia Roberts 2
Herman, Alexis M. 15
Kirk, Ron 11, 75
O'Leary, Hazel 6
Powell, Colin 1, 28, 75
Rice, Condoleezza 3, 28, 72
Slater, Rodney E. 15
Sullivan, Louis 8

Weaver, Robert C. 8, 46

**U.S. Coast Guard**
Brown, Erroll M. 23
Rochon, Stephen W. 78

**U.S. Commission on Civil Rights**
Berry, Mary Frances 7
Edley, Christopher 2, 48
Fletcher, Arthur A. 63

**U.S. Conference of Catholic Bishops**
Gregory, Wilton D. 37

**U.S. Court of Appeals**
Hastie, William H. 8
Higginbotham, A. Leon, Jr. 13, 25
Kearse, Amalya Lyle 12
Keith, Damon J. 16, 74
Rawlinson, Johnnie B. 79
Williams, Ann Claire 82

**U.S. Department of Agriculture (USDA)**
Espy, Mike 6
Layton, William 87
Sherrod, Shirley 87
Vaughn, Gladys Gary 47
Watkins, Shirley R. 17
Williams, Hosea Lorenzo 15, 31

**U.S. Department of Commerce**
Brown, Ron 5
Irving, Larry, Jr. 12
Person, Waverly 9, 51
Shavers, Cheryl 31

**U.S. Department of Defense**
Greenhouse, Bunnatine "Bunny" 57
Johnson, Jeh C. 76
Tribble, Israel, Jr. 8

**U.S. Department of Education**
Hill, Anita 5, 65
Hill, Bonnie Guiton 20
Paige, Rod 29
Purnell, Silas 59
Thomas, Clarence 2, 39, 65
Tribble, Israel, Jr. 8
Velez-Rodriguez, Argelia 56

**U.S. Department of Energy**
O'Leary, Hazel 6

**U.S. Department of Health and Human Services (HHS)**
See also U.S. Department of Health, Education, and Welfare
Gaston, Marilyn Hughes 60
Hamburg, Margaret 78

**U.S. Department of Health, Education, and Welfare (HEW)**
Bell, Derrick 6
Berry, Mary Frances 7
Harris, Patricia Roberts 2
Johnson, Eddie Bernice 8
Randolph, Linda A. 52
Spearman, Leonard H. O., Sr. 81
Sullivan, Louis 8

**U.S. Department of Housing and Urban Development (HUD)**
Blackwell, J. Kenneth, Sr. 61
Gaines, Brenda 41

Harris, Patricia Roberts 2
Jackson, Alphonso R. 48
Weaver, Robert C. 8, 46

**U.S. Department of Justice**
Bell, Derrick 6
Campbell, Bill 9, 76
Days, Drew S., III 10
Guinier, Lani 7, 30
Holder, Eric H., Jr. 9, 76
Lafontant, Jewel Stradford 3, 51
Lewis, Delano 7
Patrick, Deval 12, 61
Payton, John 48
Thompson, Larry D. 39
Williams, Michael L. 86

**U.S. Department of Labor**
Crockett, George W., Jr. 10, 64
Fletcher, Arthur A. 63
Herman, Alexis M. 15

**U.S. Department of Social Services**
Little, Robert L. 2

**U.S. Department of State**
Baltimore, Richard Lewis, III 71
Bethune, Mary McLeod 4
Bunche, Ralph J. 5
Davis, Ruth 37
Dougherty, Mary Pearl 47
Frazer, Jendayi 68
Garrett, Joyce Finley 59
Grimké, Archibald H. 9
Haley, George Williford Boyce 21
Harris, Patricia Roberts 2
Keyes, Alan L. 11
Lafontant, Jewel Stradford 3, 51
McGee, James D. 74
Perkins, Edward 5
Powell, Colin 1, 28, 75
Rice, Condoleezza 3, 28, 72
Rice, Susan E. 74
Stokes, Carl 10, 73
Sutphen, Mona 77
Van Lierop, Robert 53
Wharton, Clifton R., Jr. 7
Wharton, Clifton Reginald, Sr. 36

**U.S. Department of the Interior**
Person, Waverly 9, 51

**U.S. Department of the Treasury**
Morton, Azie Taylor 48

**U.S. Department of Transportation**
Coleman, William T. 76
Davis, Benjamin O., Jr. 2, 43

**U.S. Department of Veterans Affairs**
Brown, Jesse 6, 41

**U.S. Diplomatic Corps**
See U.S. Department of State

**U.S. District Attorney**
Harris, Kamala D. 64
Lloyd, Reginald 64

**U.S. District Court judge**
Bryant, William Benson 61
Carter, Robert L. 51

Cooke, Marcia 60
Diggs-Taylor, Anna 20
Henderson, Thelton E. 68
Keith, Damon J. 16, 74
Parsons, James 14
Williams, Ann Claire 82

**U.S. Dream Academy**
Phipps, Wintley 59

**U.S. Environmental Protection Agency**
Jackson, Lisa 77

**U.S. Foreign Service**
See U.S. Department of State

**U.S. Geological Survey**
Bromery, Randolph Wilson 85
Person, Waverly 9, 51

**U.S. House of Representatives**
Archie-Hudson, Marguerite 44
Ballance, Frank W. 41
Bishop, Sanford D., Jr. 24
Brown, Corrine 24
Burke, Yvonne Brathwaite 42
Carson, André 69
Carson, Julia 23, 69
Chisholm, Shirley 2, 50
Clay, William Lacy 8
Clayton, Eva M. 20
Cleaver, Emanuel 4, 45, 68
Clyburn, James E. 21, 71
Collins, Barbara-Rose 7, 87
Collins, Cardiss 10, 80
Conyers, John, Jr. 4, 45
Crockett, George W., Jr. 10, 64
Cummings, Elijah E. 24
Davis, Artur 41
Davis, Danny K. 24, 79
De Priest, Oscar Stanton 80
Dellums, Ronald 2, 81
Diggs, Charles C. 21
Dixon, Julian C. 24
Dymally, Mervyn 42
Edwards, Donna 77
Ellison, Keith 59
Espy, Mike 6
Fattah, Chaka 11, 70
Fauntroy, Walter E. 11
Fields, Cleo 13
Flake, Floyd H. 18
Ford, Harold E(ugene) 42
Ford, Harold E(ugene), Jr. 16, 70
Franks, Gary 2
Fudge, Marcia L. 76
Gray, William H., III 3
Hastings, Alcee L. 16
Hawkins, Augustus F. 68
Hilliard, Earl F. 24
Jackson, Jesse, Jr. 14, 45, 81
Jackson Lee, Sheila 20
Jefferson, William J. 25, 72
Johnson, Eddie Bernice 8
Johnson, Hank, Jr. 80
Jordan, Barbara 4, 78
Kilpatrick, Carolyn Cheeks 16
Lee, Barbara 25
Leland, Mickey 2
Lewis, John 2, 46, 83
Majette, Denise 41
McKinney, Cynthia 11, 52, 74

Meek, Carrie 6
Meek, Kendrick 41
Meeks, Gregory 25
Metcalfe, Ralph 26
Mfume, Kweisi 6, 41
Millender-McDonald, Juanita 21, 61
Mitchell, Parren J. 42, 66
Moore, Gwendolynne S. 55
Norton, Eleanor Holmes 7
Owens, Major 6
Payne, Donald M. 2, 57
Pinchback, P. B. S. 9
Powell, Adam Clayton, Jr. 3
Rangel, Charles B. 3, 52, 85
Rapier, James T. 82
Richardson, Laura 81
Rush, Bobby 26, 76
Scott, David 41
Scott, Robert C. 23
Smalls, Robert 82
Stokes, Louis 3
Towns, Edolphus 19, 75
Tubbs Jones, Stephanie 24, 72
Washington, Harold 6
Waters, Maxine 3, 67
Watson, Diane 41
Watt, Melvin 26
Watts, J. C., Jr. 14, 38
Wheat, Alan 14
Wynn, Albert R. 25, 77
Young, Andrew 3, 48

**U.S. Information Agency**
Allen, Samuel 38

**U.S. Joint Chiefs of Staff**
Howard, Michelle 28
Powell, Colin 1, 28, 75
Rice, Condoleezza 3, 28, 72

**U.S. Marines**
Bolden, Charles Frank, Jr. 7, 78
Brown, Jesse 6, 41
Petersen, Franke E. 31
Von Lipsey, Roderick K. 11

**U.S. Navy**
Black, Barry C. 47
Brashear, Carl 29
Brown, Jesse Leroy 31
Doby, Lawrence Eugene, Sr. 16, 41
Fields, Evelyn J. 27
Gravely, Samuel L., Jr. 5, 49
Howard, Michelle 28
Miller, Dorie 29
Pinckney, Bill 42
Reason, J. Paul 19
Wright, Lewin 43

**U.S. Open tennis tournament**
Williams, Venus 17, 34, 62

**U.S. Peace Corps**
Days, Drew S., III 10
Johnson, Rafer 33
Lewis, Delano 7

**U.S. presidency**
Obama, Barack 49, 74

**U.S. Register of the Treasury**
Bruce, Blanche Kelso 33

**U.S. Senate**
Black, Barry C. 47
Bowman, Bertie 71

Braun, Carol Moseley 4, 42
Brooke, Edward 8
Bruce, Blanche Kelso 33
Burris, Roland W. 25, 75
Obama, Barack 49, 74
Pinchback, P. B. S. 9

**U.S. State Department**
See U.S. Department of State

**U.S. Supreme Court**
Marshall, Thurgood 1, 44
Thomas, Clarence 2, 39, 65

**U.S. Surgeon General**
Elders, Joycelyn 6
Satcher, David 7, 57

**U.S. Virgin Islands government**
DeJongh, John, Jr. 85
Hastie, William H. 8
Turnbull, Charles Wesley 62

**USDA**
See U.S. Department of Agriculture

**USFL**
See United States Football League

**U.S.S. *Constitution***
Wright, Lewin 43

**UVC**
See Ultraviolet
    camera/spectrograph

**UWUSA**
See United Workers Union of South
    Africa

**Vancouver Canucks hockey team**
Brashear, Donald 39

**Vancouver Grizzlies basketball team**
Abdur-Rahim, Shareef 28

**Vaudeville**
Anderson, Eddie "Rochester" 30
Austin, Lovie 40
Bates, Peg Leg 14
Cox, Ida 42
Davis, Sammy, Jr. 18
Gilpin, Charles Sidney 81
Johnson, Jack 8
Martin, Sara 38
McDaniel, Hattie 5
Mills, Florence 22
Robinson, Bill "Bojangles" 11
Waters, Ethel 7

**Veterans's issues**
Carr, Keela 74

**Veterinary science**
Jawara, Dawda Kairaba 11
Lushington, Augustus Nathaniel 56
Maathai, Wangari 43
Patterson, Frederick Douglass 12
Thomas, Vivien 9

***Vibe***
Jones, Quincy 8, 30
Smith, Danyel 40

Wilbekin, Emil 63

**Vibraphone**
Hampton, Lionel 17, 41

**Victim's Bill of Rights**
Dee, Merri 55

**Video gaming**
Croal, N'Gai 76
Fils-Aimé, Reggie 74

**Vietnam Veterans of America**
Duggins, George 64

***Village Voice***
Cooper, Andrew W. 36
Crouch, Stanley 11

**Violin**
Bridgetower, George 78
Daemyon, Jerald 64
Dworkin, Aaron P. 52
Escobar, Damien 56
Escobar, Tourie 56
Murray, Tai 47
Smith, Stuff 37
Tinsley, Boyd 50
Williams, Claude 80

***VIP Memphis*** magazine
McMillan, Rosalynn A. 36

**Virgin Records**
Brooks, Hadda 40
Sledge, Percy 39

**Virginia state government**
Marsh, Henry 32
Martin, Ruby Grant 49
Wilder, L. Douglas 3, 48

**Virginia State Supreme Court**
Hassell, Leroy Rountree, Sr. 41

**Virology**
Fuller, A. Oveta 43

***Vogue*** magazine
Talley, André Leon 56

**Volleyball**
Blanton, Dain 29

**Voodoo**
Beauvoir, Max 74
Dunham, Katherine 4, 59
Guy, Rosa 5
Hurston, Zora Neale 3
Pierre, Andre 17

**Voting rights**
Cary, Mary Ann Shadd 30
Chestnut, J. L., Jr. 73
Clark, Septima 7
Forman, James 7, 51
Guinier, Lani 7, 30
Hamer, Fannie Lou 6
Harper, Frances Ellen Watkins 11
Hill, Jesse, Jr. 13
Johnson, Eddie Bernice 8
Lampkin, Daisy 19
Mandela, Nelson 1, 14, 77
Moore, Harry T. 29
Moses, Robert Parris 11
Terrell, Mary Church 9
Touré, Faya Ora Rose 56

Trotter, Monroe 9
Tubman, Harriet 9
Wells-Barnett, Ida B. 8
Williams, Fannie Barrier 27
Williams, Hosea Lorenzo 15, 31
Woodard, Alfre 9

**WAAC (Women's Auxiliary Army Corps)**
See Women's Army Corps (WAC)

**WAC**
See Women's Army Corps

**Wall Street**
Lewis, William M., Jr. 40
McGuire, Raymond J. 57
Phillips, Charles E., Jr. 57

**War criminals**
Sankoh, Foday 74

**War Resisters League (WRL)**
Carter, Mandy 11

**Washington Capitols hockey team**
Grier, Mike 43

**Washington Color Field group**
Thomas, Alma 14

**Washington, D.C., city government**
Barry, Marion S. 7, 44
Cooper Cafritz, Peggy 43
Dixon, Sharon Pratt 1
Fauntroy, Walter E. 11
Fenty, Adrian 60
Hobson, Julius W. 44
Jarvis, Charlene Drew 21
Norton, Eleanor Holmes 7
Washington, Walter 45
Williams, Anthony 21

**Washington, D.C., Commission on the Arts and Humanities**
Neal, Larry 38

**Washington Mystics basketball team**
McCray, Nikki 18

***Washington Post***
Britt, Donna 28
Davis, George 36
Givhan, Robin Deneen 72
Haygood, Wil 83
Ifill, Gwen 28
King, Colbert I. 69
Maynard, Robert C. 7
McCall, Nathan 8
Nelson, Jill 6, 54
Raspberry, William 2

**Washington Redskins football team**
Green, Darrell 39, 74
Monk, Art 38, 73
Sanders, Deion 4, 31

**Washington State Higher Education Coordinating Board**
Floyd, Elson S. 41

***Washington Week in Review***
TV Series
Ifill, Gwen **28**

**Washington Wizards basketball team**
Bickerstaff, Bernie **21**
Heard, Gar **25**
Howard, Juwan **15**
Lucas, John **7**
Unseld, Wes **23**
Webber, Chris **15, 30, 59**

**WBA**
See World Boxing Association

**WBC**
See World Boxing Council

**WCC**
See World Council of Churches

**Weather**
Brown, Vivian **27**
Christian, Spencer **15**
McEwen, Mark **5**
Roker, Al **12, 49**

**Welfare reform**
Bryant, Wayne R. **6**
Carson, Julia **23, 69**
Parker, Star **70**
Wallace, Joaquin **49**
Williams, Walter E. **4**

**Wellspring Gospel**
Winans, CeCe **14, 43**

**WERD (radio station)**
Blayton, Jesse B., Sr. **55**

**West Indian folk songs**
Belafonte, Harry **4, 65**
Rhoden, Wayne **70**

**West Indian literature**
Coombs, Orde M. **44**
Guy, Rosa **5**
Kincaid, Jamaica **4**
Markham, E. A. **37**
Marshall, Paule **7, 77**
McKay, Claude **6**
Walcott, Derek **5**

**West Point**
Davis, Benjamin O., Jr. **2, 43**
Flipper, Henry O. **3**
Young, Charles **77**

**West Side Preparatory School**
Collins, Marva **3, 71**

**Western Michigan University**
Floyd, Elson S. **41**

**White House**
Allen, Eugene **79**
Butts, Cassandra **78**
Christie, Ron **83**
Gaspard, Patrick **84**
Jarvis, Kristen **85**
Love, Reggie **77**
Rochon, Stephen W. **78**
Strautmanis, Michael **87**

**Whitney Museum of American Art**
Golden, Thelma **10, 55**
Simpson, Lorna **4, 36**

**Wimbledon**
Williams, Venus **17, 34, 62**

**Wine and winemaking**
Allen-Buillard, Melba **55**
Rideau, Iris **46**

**Wisconsin State Supreme Court**
Butler, Louis **70**

**Women Helping Offenders**
Holland, Endesha Ida Mae **3, 57**

**Women's Army Corps (WAC)**
Adams Earley, Charity **13, 34**
Cadoria, Sherian Grace **14**

**Women's Auxiliary Army Corps**
See Women's Army Corps

**Women's issues**
Allen, Ethel D. **13**
Angelou, Maya **1, 15**
Avery, Byllye Y. **66**
Ba, Mariama **30**
Baker, Ella **5**
Bashir, Halima **73**
Berry, Mary Frances **7**
Brown, Elaine **8**
Campbell, Bebe Moore **6, 24, 59**
Cannon, Katie **10**
Cary, Mary Ann Shadd **30**
Charles, Mary Eugenia **10, 55**
Chinn, May Edward **26**
Christian, Barbara T. **44**
Christian-Green, Donna M. **17**
Clark, Septima **7**
Cole, Johnnetta B. **5, 43**
Cooper, Anna Julia **20**
Davis, Angela **5**
Edelman, Marian Wright **5, 42**
Edwards, Lena Frances **76**
Elders, Joycelyn **6**
Evans, Diana **72**
Fauset, Jessie **7**
Giddings, Paula **11**
Goldberg, Whoopi **4, 33, 69**
Gomez, Jewelle **30**
Grimké, Archibald H. **9**
Guy-Sheftall, Beverly **13**
Hale, Clara **16**
Hale, Lorraine **8**
Hamer, Fannie Lou **6**
Harper, Frances Ellen Watkins **11**
Harris, Alice **7**
Harris, Leslie **6**
Harris, Patricia Roberts **2**
Height, Dorothy I. **2, 23, 78**
Hernandez, Aileen Clarke **13**
Hill, Anita **5, 65**
Hine, Darlene Clark **24**
Holland, Endesha Ida Mae **3, 57**
hooks, bell **5**
Hughes, Ebony **57**
Hussein, Lubna **80**
Jackson, Alexine Clement **22**
Joe, Yolanda **21**
Jordan, June **7, 35**

Lampkin, Daisy **19**
Larsen, Nella **10**
Lorde, Audre **6**
Maathai, Wangari **43**
Marshall, Paule **7, 77**
Mbaye, Mariétou **31**
McCabe, Jewell Jackson **10**
McCauley, Gina **76**
McKenzie, Vashti M. **29**
McMillan, Terry **4, 17, 53**
Meek, Carrie **6**
Millender-McDonald, Juanita **21, 61**
Millner, Denene **76**
Mongella, Gertrude **11**
Mossell, Gertrude Bustill **40**
Naylor, Gloria **10, 42**
Nelson, Jill **6, 54**
Niane, Katoucha **70**
Nichols, Nichelle **11**
Norman, Pat **10**
Norton, Eleanor Holmes **7**
Ormes, Jackie **73**
Painter, Nell Irvin **24**
Parker, Pat **19**
Rawlings, Nana Konadu Agyeman **13**
Ruffin, Josephine St. Pierre **75**
Shange, Ntozake **8**
Sherrod, Shirley **87**
Simpson, Carole **6, 30**
Smith, Jane E. **24**
Talbert, Mary B. **77**
Terrell, Mary Church **9**
Tubman, Harriet **9**
Vanzant, Iyanla **17, 47**
Walker, Alice **1, 43**
Walker, Maggie Lena **17**
Wallace, Michele Faith **13**
Waters, Maxine **3, 67**
Wattleton, Faye **9**
Williams, Fannie Barrier **27**
Winfrey, Oprah **2, 15, 61**
Xuma, Madie Hall **59**

**Women's Leadership Forum**
Shabazz, Ilyasah **36**

**Women's National Basketball Association (WNBA)**
Bolton-Holifield, Ruthie **28**
Cash, Swin **59**
Catchings, Tamika **43**
Cooper, Cynthia **17**
Edwards, Teresa **14**
Ford, Cheryl **45**
Griffith, Yolanda **25**
Holdsclaw, Chamique **24**
Jones, Merlakia **34**
Lennox, Betty **31**
Leslie, Lisa **16, 73**
McCray, Nikki **18**
Miller, Cheryl **10, 74**
Milton, DeLisha **31**
Palmer, Violet **59**
Parker, Candace **74**
Peck, Carolyn **23**
Perrot, Kim **23**
Staley, Dawn **57**
Swoopes, Sheryl **12, 56**
Thompson, Tina **25, 75**
Williams, Natalie **31**

Woodard, Lynette **67**

**Workplace equity**
Clark, Septima **7**
Hill, Anita **5, 65**
Nelson, Jill **6, 54**
Simpson, Carole **6, 30**

**Works Progress (Projects) Administration (WPA)**
Alexander, Margaret Walker **22**
Baker, Ella **5**
Blackburn, Robert **28**
DeCarava, Roy **42, 81**
Douglas, Aaron **7**
Dunham, Katherine **4, 59**
Hall, Juanita **62**
Lawrence, Jacob **4, 28**
Lee-Smith, Hughie **5, 22**
Murray, Pauli **38**
Sallee, Charles **38**
Sebree, Charles **40**
Winkfield, Jimmy **42**
Wright, Richard **5**

**World African Hebrew Israelite Community**
Ben-Israel, Ben Ami **11**

**World Bank**
Soglo, Nicéphore **15**

**World beat**
Belafonte, Harry **4, 65**
Fela **1, 42**
Maal, Baaba **66**
N'Dour, Youssou **1, 53, 79**
Okosuns, Sonny **71**
Ongala, Remmy **9**

**World Boxing Association (WBA)**
Ellis, Jimmy **44**
Hearns, Thomas **29**
Hopkins, Bernard **35, 69**
Lewis, Lennox **27**
Tyson, Mike **28, 44**
Whitaker, Pernell **10**

**World Boxing Council (WBC)**
Mosley, Shane **32**
Tyson, Mike **28, 44**
Whitaker, Pernell **10**

**World Council of Churches (WCC)**
Kobia, Samuel **43**
Mays, Benjamin E. **7**
Tutu, Desmond Mpilo **6, 44**

**World Cup**
dos Santos, Manuel Francisco **65**
Gyan, Asamoah **87**
Mensah, John **87**
Milla, Roger **2**
Pelé **7**
Scurry, Briana **27**

**World hunger**
Belafonte, Harry **4, 65**
Iman **4, 33, 87**
Jones, Quincy **8, 30**
Leland, Mickey **2**

Masire, Quett **5**

**World Wide Technology**
Steward, David L. **36**

**World Wrestling Entertainment (WWE) Hall of Fame**
Ladd, Ernie **64**

**World Wrestling Federation (WWF)**
Ladd, Ernie **64**
Lashley, Bobby **63**
Rock, The **29, 66**

**WPA**
See Works Progress (Projects) Administration

**Wrestling**
Ladd, Ernie **64**
Lashley, Bobby **63**
Rock, The **29, 66**

**WRL**
See War Resisters League

**WSB Radio**
Pressley, Condace L. **41**

**WWF**
See World Wrestling Federation

**Xavier University of Louisiana**
Francis, Norman (C.) **60**

**Xerox Corp.**
Burns, Ursula **60**
Rand, A. Barry **6**

**Yab Yum Entertainment**
Edmonds, Tracey **16, 64**

**Yale Repertory Theater**
Dutton, Charles S. **4, 22**
Richards, Lloyd **2**
Wilson, August **7, 33, 55**

**Yale School of Drama**
Dutton, Charles S. **4, 22**
Richards, Lloyd **2**

**Yale University**
Blassingame, John Wesley **40**
Carby, Hazel **27**
Davis, Charles T. **48**
Hill, Errol **40**
Neal, Larry **38**

**YMCA**
See Young Men's Christian Association

**Yoruban folklore**
Soyinka, Wole **4**
Vanzant, Iyanla **17, 47**

**Young adult literature**
Anderson, Ho Che **54**
Bolden, Tonya **32**

Ekwensi, Cyprian **37**
Johnson, Angela **52**
Millner, Denene **76**

**Young British Artists**
Shonibare, Yinka **58**

**Young Men's Christian Association (YMCA)**
Butts, Calvin O., III **9**
Goode, Mal **13**
Hope, John **8**
Mays, Benjamin E. **7**
Tobias, Channing H. **79**

**Young Women's Christian Association (YWCA)**
Baker, Ella **5**
Baker, Gwendolyn Calvert **9**
Clark, Septima **7**
Claytor, Helen **14, 52**
Hedgeman, Anna Arnold **22**
Height, Dorothy I. **2, 23, 78**
Jackson, Alexine Clement **22**
Jenkins, Ella **15**
Sampson, Edith S. **4**
Stewart, Ella **39**
Xuma, Madie Hall **59**

**Youth Services Administration**
Little, Robert L. **2**

**YWCA**
See Young Women's Christian Association

**Zairian government**
Mobutu Sese Seko **1, 56**

**Zambian government**
Chiluba, Frederick **56, 80**
Mwanawasa, Levy **72**

**ZCTU**
See Zimbabwe Congress of Trade Unions

**Zimbabwe Congress of Trade Unions (ZCTU)**
Tsvangirai, Morgan **26, 72**
Young, Roger Arliner **29**

**Zimbabwean government**
Moyo, Lovemore **76**
Mugabe, Robert **10, 71**
Mukoko, Jestina **75**
Muzorewa, Abel **85**
Nkomo, Joshua **4, 65**

**Zouk music**
Lefel, Edith **41**

**ZTA**
See Zululand Territorial Authority

**Zululand Territorial Authority (ZTA)**
Buthelezi, Mangosuthu Gatsha **9**

# Cumulative Name Index

*Volume numbers appear in* **bold**

Aaliyah 1979–2001 **30**

Aaron, Hank 1934— **5**

Aaron, Henry Louis *See Aaron, Hank*

Aaron, Quinton 1984— **82**

Abacha, Sani 1943–1998 **11, 70**

Abani, Chris 1966— **77**

Abbott, Diane (Julie) 1953— **9**

Abbott, Robert Sengstacke 1868–1940 **27**

Abdul-Jabbar, Kareem 1947— **8**

Abdullah, Imaam Isa *See York, Dwight D.*

Abdulmajid, Iman Mohamed *See Iman*

Abdur-Rahim, Shareef 1976— **28**

Abele, Julian 1881–1950 **55**

Abernathy, Ralph David 1926–1990 **1**

Aberra, Amsale 1954— **67**

Abiola, Moshood 1937–1998 **70**

Abrahams, Peter 1919— **39**

Abu-Jamal, Mumia 1954— **15**

Abubakar, Abdulsalami 1942— **66**

Ace, Johnny 1929–1954 **36**

Achebe, (Albert) Chinua(lumogu) 1930— **6**

Acogny, Germaine 1944— **55**

Adams, Eula L. 1950— **39**

Adams, Floyd, Jr. 1945— **12**

Adams, Grantley 1898–1971 **82**

Adams, H. Leslie *See Adams, Leslie*

Adams, Jenoyne (?)— **60**

Adams, Johnny 1932–1998 **39**

Adams, Leslie 1932— **39**

Adams, Oleta 19(?)(?)— **18**

Adams, Osceola Macarthy 1890–1983 **31**

Adams, Paul 1977— **50**

Adams, Sheila J. 1943— **25**

Adams, Yolanda 1961— **17, 67**

Adams-Campbell, Lucille L. 1953— **60**

Adams Earley, Charity (Edna) 1918— **13, 34**

Adams-Ender, Clara 1939— **40**

Adderley, Julian "Cannonball" 1928–1975 **30**

Adderley, Nat 1931–2000 **29**

Adderley, Nathaniel *See Adderley, Nat*

Ade, Sunny King 1946— **41**

Adebari, Rotimi 1963(?)— **83**

Adebimpe, Tunde 1975— **75**

Adeniyi, Sunday *See Ade, Sunny King*

Adichie, Chimamanda Ngozi 1977— **64**

Adjaye, David 1966— **38, 78**

Adkins, Rod 1958— **41**

Adkins, Rutherford H. 1924–1998 **21**

Adu, Freddy 1989— **67**

Adu, Fredua Koranteng *See Adu, Freddy*

Adu, Helen Folasade *See Sade*

Afro, Teddy 1976— **78**

Agyeman, Jaramogi Abebe 1911–2000 **10, 63**

Agyeman Rawlings, Nana Konadu 1948— **13**

Ahidjo, Ahmadou 1924–1989 **81**

Ahmed, Sharif 1964— **80**

Aidoo, Ama Ata 1942— **38**

Aiken, Loretta Mary *See Mabley, Jackie "Moms"*

Ailey, Alvin 1931–1989 **8**

Ake, Claude 1939–1996 **30**

Akil, Mara Brock 1970— **60, 82**

Akinnuoye-Agbaje, Adewale 1967— **56**

Akinola, Peter Jasper 1944— **65**

Akomfrah, John 1957— **37**

Akon 1973(?)— **68**

Akpan, Uwem 1971— **70**

Akunyili, Dora Nkem 1954— **58**

Al-Amin, Jamil Abdullah 1943— **6**

Albright, Gerald 1947— **23**

Alcindor, Ferdinand Lewis *See Abdul-Jabbar, Kareem*

Alcorn, George Edward, Jr. 1940— **59**

Alert, Kool DJ Red 19(?)(?)— **33**

Alexander, Archie Alphonso 1888–1958 **14**

Alexander, Clifford 1933— **26**

Alexander, Elizabeth 1962— **75**

Alexander, John Marshall *See Ace, Johnny*

Alexander, Joyce London 1949— **18**

Alexander, Khandi 1957— **43**

Alexander, Margaret Walker 1915–1998 **22**

Alexander, Sadie Tanner Mossell 1898–1989 **22**

Alexander, Shaun 1977— **58**

Ali, Ayaan Hirsi 1969— **58**

Ali, Hana Yasmeen 1976— **52**

Ali, Laila 1977— **27, 63**

Ali, Mohammed Naseehu 1971— **60**

Ali, Muhammad 1942— **2, 16, 52**

Ali, Rashied 1935–2009 **79**

Ali, Tatyana 1979— **73**

Ali Mahdi Mohamed 1940— **5**

Allain, Stephanie 1959— **49**

Allen, Betty 1927–2009 **83**

Allen, Byron 1961— **3, 24**

Allen, Claude 1960— **68**

Allen, Debbie 1950— **13, 42**

Allen, Dick 1942— **85**

Allen, Ethel D. 1929–1981 **13**

Allen, Eugene 1919— **79**

Allen, Fulton *See Fuller, Blind Boy*

Allen, Lucy 1932— **85**

Allen, Marcus 1960— **20**

Allen, Ray 1975— **82**

Allen, Richard 1760–1831 **14**

Allen, Robert L. 1942— **38**

Allen, Samuel W. 1917— **38**

Allen, Tina 1949–2008 **22, 75**

Allen, Will 1949— **74**

Allen-Buillard, Melba 1960— **55**

Alonso, Laz 1974— **87**

Alston, Charles Henry 1907–1997 **33**

Amadi, Elechi 1934— **40**

Amaker, Harold Tommy, Jr. *See Amaker, Tommy*

Amaker, Norman 1935–2000 **63**

Amaker, Tommy 1965— **62**

Amaki, Amalia 1949— **76**

Amerie 1980— **52**

Ames, Wilmer 1950–1993 **27**

Amin, Idi 1925–2003 **42**

Ammons, James H. 1952(?)— **81**

Amos, Emma 1938— **63**

Amos, John 1941— **8, 62**

Amos, Valerie 1954— **41**

Amos, Wally 1937— **9**

Anderson, Anthony 1970— **51, 77**

Anderson, Carl 1945–2004 **48**

Anderson, Charles Edward 1919–1994 **37**

Anderson, Eddie "Rochester" 1905–1977 **30**

Anderson, Elmer 1941— **25**

Anderson, Fred 1929–2010 **87**

Anderson, Ho Che 1969— **54**

Anderson, Jamal 1972— **22**

Anderson, Lauren 1965— **72**

Anderson, Marian 1902— **2, 33**

Anderson, Michael P. 1959–2003 **40**

Anderson, Mike 1959— **63**

Anderson, Norman B. 1955— **45**

Anderson, Reuben V. 1942— **81**

Anderson, Viv 1956— **58**

Anderson, William G(ilchrist) 1927— **57**

Andre 3000 *See Benjamin, Andre*

Andrews, Benny 1930–2006 **22, 59**

Andrews, Bert 1929–1993 **13**

Andrews, Mark *See Sisqo*

Andrews, Raymond 1934–1991 **4**

Andrews, Tina 1951— **74**

Angelou, Maya 1928— **1, 15**

Anna Marie *See Lincoln, Abbey*

Annan, Kofi Atta 1938— **15, 48**

Ansa, Tina McElroy 1949— **14**

Anthony, Carmelo 1984— **46**

Anthony, Crystal *See McCrary Anthony, Crystal*

Anthony, Michael 1930(?)— **29**

Anthony, Trey 1974— **63**

Anthony, Wendell 1950— **25**

apl.de.ap 1974— **84**

Appiah, Kwame Anthony 1954— **67**

Arac de Nyeko, Monica 1979— **66**

Arach, Monica *See Arac de Nyeko, Monica*

Archer, Dennis (Wayne) 1942— **7, 36**

Archer, Lee, Jr. 1919— **79**

Archer, Michael D'Angelo *See D'Angelo*

Archer, Osceola *See Adams, Osceola Macarthy*

Archie-Hudson, Marguerite 1937— **44**

Ardoin, Alphonse 1915–2007 **65**

Arenas, Gilbert 1982— **84**

Arinze, Francis 1932— **19**

Aristide, Jean-Bertrand 1953— **6, 45**

Arkadie, Kevin 1957— **17**

Armah, Ayi Kwei 1939— **49**

Armah, Esther 1963— **87**

Armatrading, Joan 1950— **32**

Armstrong, Govind 1968— **81**

Armstrong, (Daniel) Louis 1900–1971 **2**

Armstrong, Robb 1962— **15**

Armstrong, Vanessa Bell 1953— **24**

Arnez J, 1966(?)— **53**

Arnold, Monica *See Monica*

Arnold, Tichina 1971— **63**

Arnwine, Barbara 1951(?)— **28**

Arrington, Richard 1934— **24**

Arroyo, Martina 1936— **30**

Artest, Ron 1979— **52**

Arthur, Owen 1949— **33**

Asante, Molefi Kete 1942— **3**

Ashanti 1980— **37**

Ashe, Arthur Robert, Jr. 1943–1993 **1, 18**

Ashford, Calvin, Jr. 1935(?)–2008 **74**

Ashford, Emmett 1914–1980 **22**

Ashford, Evelyn 1957— **63**

Ashford, Nickolas 1942— **21**

Ashley, Maurice 1966— **15, 47**

Ashley-Ward, Amelia 1957— **23**

Ashong, Derrick 1975— **86**

Asim, Jabari 1962— **71**

Astatke, Mulatu 1942(?)— **81**

Atim, Julian 1980(?)— **66**

Atkins, Cholly 1930–2003 **40**

Atkins, David See Sinbad

Atkins, Erica 1972(?)— See Mary Mary

Atkins, Jeffrey See Ja Rule

Atkins, Juan 1962— **50**

Atkins, Russell 1926— **45**

Atkins, Tina 1975(?)— See Mary Mary

Atta Mills, John 1944— **75**

Atyam, Angelina 1946— **55**

Aubert, Alvin 1930— **41**

Auguste, Arnold A. 1946— **47**

Auguste, Donna 1958— **29**

Auguste, (Marie Carmele) Rose-Anne 1963— **13**

Augustine, Jean 1937— **53**

Austin, Gloria 1956— **63**

Austin, Jim 1951— **63**

Austin, Junius C. 1887–1968 **44**

Austin, Lovie 1887–1972 **40**

Austin, Patti 1948— **24**

Autrey, Wesley 1956— **68**

Avant, Clarence 1931— **19, 86**

Avery, Byllye Y. 1937— **66**

Awoonor, Kofi 1935— **37**

Awoonor-Williams, George See Awoonor, Kofi

Awoyinka, Adesiji See Siji

Ayers, Roy 1940— **16**

Azikiwe, Nnamdi 1904–1996 **13**

Ba, Mariama 1929–1981 **30**

Babangida, Ibrahim (Badamasi) 1941— **4**

Babatunde, Obba 19(?)(?)— **35**

Babyface 1959— **10, 31, 82**

Baca, Susana 1954— **80**

Bacon-Bercey, June 1942— **38**

Badu, Erykah 1971(?)— **22**

Bahati, Wambui 1950(?)— **60**

Bailey, Buster 1902–1967 **38**

Bailey, Chauncey 1949–2007 **68**

Bailey, Clyde 1946— **45**

Bailey, DeFord 1899–1982 **33**

Bailey, Pearl Mae 1918–1990 **14**

Bailey, Philip 1951— **63**

Bailey, Preston 1948(?)— **64**

Bailey, Radcliffe 1968— **19**

Bailey, William C. See Bailey, Buster

Bailey, Xenobia 1955(?)— **11**

Bailey Rae, Corinne 1979— **83**

Baines, Harold 1959— **32**

Baiocchi, Regina Harris 1956— **41**

Baisden, Michael 1963— **25, 66**

Baker, Anita 1957— **21, 48**

Baker, Arlene Holt See Holt Baker, Arlene

Baker, Augusta 1911–1998 **38**

Baker, Constance See Motley, Constance Baker

Baker, Dusty 1949— **8, 43, 72**

Baker, Ella 1903–1986 **5**

Baker, George See Divine, Father

Baker, Gwendolyn Calvert 1931— **9**

Baker, Houston A(lfred), Jr. 1943— **6**

Baker, Johnnie B., Jr. See Baker, Dusty

Baker, Josephine 1906–1975 **3**

Baker, LaVern 1929–1997 **26**

Baker, Matt 1921–1959 **76**

Baker, Maxine 1952— **28**

Baker, Thurbert 1952— **22**

Baker, Vernon Joseph 1919–2010 **65, 87**

Balance, Frank W. 1942— **41**

Baldwin, Cynthia A. 1945— **74**

Baldwin, James 1924–1987 **1**

Ballard, Allen B(utler), Jr. 1930— **40**

Ballard, Hank 1927–2003 **41**

Baltimore, Richard Lewis, III 1946— **71**

Bambaataa, Afrika 1958— **34**

Bambara, Toni Cade 1939— **10**

Banda, Hastings Kamuzu 1898(?)–1997 **6, 54**

Bandele, Asha 1970(?)— **36**

Bandele, Biyi 1967— **68**

Bandele-Thomas, Biyi See Bandele, Biyi

Banks, A. Doris See Henries, A. Doris Banks

Banks, Ernie 1931— **33**

Banks, Jeffrey 1953— **17**

Banks, Michelle 1968(?)— **59**

Banks, Paula A. 1950— **68**

Banks, Tyra 1973— **11, 50**

Banks, William (Venoid) 1903–1985 **11**

Banner, David 1975(?)— **55**

Baquet, Dean 1956— **63**

Baraka, Amiri 1934— **1, 38**

Barbee, Lloyd Augustus 1925–2002 **71**

Barber, Atiim Kiambu See Barber, Tiki

Barber, Ronde 1975— **41**

Barber, Tiki 1975— **57**

Barboza, Anthony 1944— **10**

Barclay, Paris 1957— **37**

Barden, Don H. 1943— **9, 20**

Barker, Danny 1909–1994 **32**

Barkley, Charles 1963— **5, 66**

Barlow, Roosevelt 1917–2003 **49**

Barnes, Ernie 1938–2009 **16, 78**

Barnes, John 1963— **53**

Barnes, Lloyd 1944— **77**

Barnes, Melody 1964— **75**

Barnes, Roosevelt "Booba" 1936–1996 **33**

Barnes, Steven 1952— **54**

Barnett, Amy Du Bois 1969— **46**

Barnett, Etta Moten 1901–2004 **18, 56**

Barnett, Marguerite 1942–1992 **46**

Barney, Lem 1945— **26**

Barnhill, David 1914–1983 **30**

Barrax, Gerald William 1933— **45**

Barrett, Andrew C. 1942(?)— **12**

Barrett, Jacqueline 1950— **28**

Barrett, Lindsay 1941— **43**

Barrett, Mario Dewar See Mario

Barrino, Fantasia 1984— **53**

Barrow, Dean 1951— **69**

Barrow, Joseph Louis See Louis, Joe

Barrow, Willie T. 1924— **85**

Barry, Marion S(hepilov, Jr.) 1936— **7, 44**

Bartels, Peggielene 1953(?)— **80**

Barthé, Earl 19(?)(?)— **78**

Barthe, Richmond 1901–1989 **15**

Bashir, Halima 1979— **73**

Bashir, Omar al- 1944— **77**

Basie, William James See Count Basie

Basquiat, Jean-Michel 1960–1988 **5**

Bass, Charlotta Amanda Spears 1874–1969 **40**

Bass, Karen 1953— **70**

Bassett, Angela 1958— **6, 23, 62**

Bassey, Shirley 1937— **25**

Baszile, Jennifer 1969(?)— **79**

Bates, Clayton See Bates, Peg Leg

Bates, Daisy (Lee Gatson) 1914(?)— **13**

Bates, Elias See Diddley, Bo

Bates, Karen Grigsby 19(?)(?)— **40**

Bates, Peg Leg 1907— **14**

Bath, Patricia E. 1942— **37**

Batiste, Alvin 1932–2007 **66**

Battle, Kathleen 1948— **70**

Baugé, Grégory 1985— **86**

Baugh, David 1947— **23**

Baylor, Don(ald Edward) 1949— **6**

Baylor, Helen 1953— **36**

Beach, Michael 1963— **26**

Beah, Ishmael 1980— **69**

Beal, Bernard B. 1954(?)— **46**

Beals, Jennifer 1963— **12**

Beals, Melba Patillo 1941— **15**

Beamon, Bob 1946— **30**

Bearden, Romare 1912–1988 **2, 50**

Beasley, Jamar 1979— **29**

Beasley, Myrlie See Evers, Myrlie

Beasley, Phoebe 1943— **34**

Beaton, Norman Lugard 1934–1994 **14**

Beatty, Talley 1923(?)–1995 **35**

Beauvais, Garcelle 1966— **29**

Beauvoir, Max 1936(?)— **74**

Bebey, Francis 1929–2001 **45**

Bechet, Sidney 1897–1959 **18**

Beck, Robert See Iceberg Slim

Beckford, Tyson 1970— **11, 68**

Beckham, Barry 1944— **41**

Bedie, Henri Konan 1934— **21**

Beenie Man 1973— **32**

Bekele, Kenenisa 1982— **75**

Belafonte, Harold George, Jr. See Belafonte, Harry

Belafonte, Harry 1927— **4, 65**

Belgrave, Cynthia 1920–1997 **75**

Belgrave, Marcus 1936— **77**

Bell, Darrin 1975— **77**

Bell, Derrick (Albert, Jr.) 1930— **6**

Bell, James "Cool Papa" 1901–1991 **36**

Bell, James A. 1948— **50**

Bell, James Madison 1826–1902 **40**

Bell, Michael 1955— **40**

Bell, Ralph S. 1934— **5**

Bell, Robert Mack 1943— **22**

Bellamy, Bill 1967— **12**

Bellamy, Terry 1972— **58**

Belle, Albert (Jojuan) 1966— **10**

Belle, Regina 1963— **1, 51**

Belton, Sharon Sayles 1951— **9, 16**

Benberry, Cuesta 1923–2007 **65**

Benét, Eric 1966— **28, 77**

Benham, Robert 1946— **78**

Ben-Israel, Ben Ami 1940(?)— **11**

Benjamin, Andre 1975— **45**

Benjamin, Andre (3000) 1975(?)— See OutKast

Benjamin, Regina 1956— **20, 75**

Benjamin, Tritobia Hayes 1944— **53**

Bennett, Estelle 1941–2009 **77**

Bennett, George Harold "Hal" 1930— **45**

Bennett, Gwendolyn B. 1902–1981 **59**

Bennett, Lerone, Jr. 1928— **5, 84**

Bennett, Louise 1919–2006 **69**

Benson, Angela 19(?)(?)— **34**

Bentley, Lamont 1973–2005 **53**

Berry, Bertice 1960— **8, 55**

Berry, Bill See Berry, Edwin C.

Berry, Charles Edward Anderson See Berry, Chuck

Berry, Chuck 1926— **29**

Berry, Edwin C. 1910–1987 **81**

Berry, Fred "Rerun" 1951–2003 **48**

Berry, Halle 1966— **4, 19, 57**

Berry, James 1925— **41**

Berry, Mary Frances 1938— **7**

Berry, Moses 1950(?)— **84**

Berry, Theodore M. 1905–2000 **31**

Berrysmith, Don Reginald 1936— **49**

Best, Carrie 1903–2001 **80**

Betha, Mason Durrell 1977(?)— **24**

Bethune, Mary (Jane) McLeod 1875–1955 **4**

Beti, Mongo 1932–2001 **36**

Betsch, MaVynee 1935— **28**

Bettis, Jerome 1972— **64**

Betts, Keter 1928–2005 **85**

Betts, R. Dwayne 1979(?)— **86**

Bevel, James L. 1936–2008 **75**

Beverly, Frankie 1946— **25**

Beyoncé 1981— **39, 70**

Beze, Dante Terrell See Mos Def

Bibb, Eric 1951— **49**

Bibb, Henry 1815–1854 **54**

Bibb, Mary 1820–1877 **54**

Bickerstaff, Bernard Tyrone 1944— **21**

Big Bank Hank See Sugarhill Gang, The

Big Boi See Patton, Antwan

Big Daddy Kane 1968— **79**

Biggers, John 1924–2001 **20, 33**

Biggers, Sanford 1970— **62**

Biko, Stephen See Biko, Steven (Bantu)

Biko, Steven (Bantu) 1946–1977 **4**

Billops, Camille 1933— **82**
bin Wahad, Dhoruba 1943— **85**
Bing, Dave 1943— **3, 59, 78**
Birch, Adolpho A., Jr. 1932— **85**
Birch, Glynn R. 195(?)— **61**
Bishop, Eric See Foxx, Jamie
Bishop, Maurice 1944–1983 **39**
Bishop, Sanford D. Jr. 1947— **24**
Bivins, Michael 1968— **72**
Biya, Paul 1933— **28**
Biyidi-Awala, Alexandre See Beti, Mongo
Bizimungu, Pasteur 1951— **19**
Black, Albert 1940— **51**
Black, Barry C. 1948— **47**
Black, Joe 1924–2002 **75**
Black, Keith Lanier 1957— **18, 84**
Black Kold Madina See Roberts, Kimberly Rivers
Black Thought 1972— **63**
Blackburn, Robert 1920— **28**
Blackman, Toni 1968— **86**
Blackmon, Brenda 1952— **58**
Blackshear, Leonard 1943— **52**
Blackwell, David 1919— **79**
Blackwell, Kenneth, Sr. 1948— **61**
Blackwell, Robert D., Sr. 1937— **52**
Blackwell, Unita 1933— **17**
Blackwood, Maureen 1960— **37**
Blacque, Taurean 1941— **58**
Blair, Jayson 1976— **50**
Blair, Maxine See Powell, Maxine
Blair, Paul 1944— **36**
Blake, Asha 1961(?)— **26**
Blake, Charles E. 1940— **82**
Blake, Eubie 1883–1983 **29**
Blake, James 1979— **43**
Blake, James Hubert See Blake, Eubie
Blakey, Art(hur) 1919–1990 **37**
Blanchard, Terence 1962— **43**
Bland, Bobby "Blue" 1930— **36**
Bland, Eleanor Taylor 1944— **39**
Bland, Robert Calvin See Bland, Bobby "Blue"
Blanks, Billy 1955(?)— **22**
Blanks, Deborah K. 1958— **69**
Blanton, Dain 1971— **29**
Blassingame, John Wesley 1940–2000 **40**
Blaylock, Ronald 1960(?)— **86**
Blayton, Jesse B., Sr. 1897–1977 **55**
Bleu, Corbin 1989— **65**
Blige, Mary J. 1971— **20, 34, 60**
Blockson, Charles L. 1933— **42**
Blondy, Alpha 1953— **30**
Bloomer, George 1963— **86**
Blow, Charles M. 1968(?)— **73**
Blow, Kurtis 1959— **31**
Bluford, Guion Stewart, Jr. See Bluford, Guy
Bluford, Guy 1942— **2, 35**
Bluitt, Juliann Stephanie 1938— **14**
Boateng, Ozwald 1968— **35**
Boateng, Paul Yaw 1951— **56**
Bobb, Robert C. 1945— **83**
Bobo, Lawrence 1958— **60**
Bogle, Donald 19(?)(?)— **34**
Bogues, Tyrone "Muggsy" 1965— **56**
Bol, Manute 1963— **1**
Bolden, Buddy 1877–1931 **39**

Bolden, Charles Frank, Jr. 1946— **7, 78**
Bolden, Charles Joseph See Bolden, Buddy
Bolden, Frank E. 1913–2003 **44**
Bolden, Tonya 1959— **32**
Bolin, Jane 1908–2007 **22, 59**
Bolt, Usain 1986— **73**
Bolton, Terrell D. 1959(?)— **25**
Bolton-Holifield, Ruthie 1967— **28**
Bonaly, Surya 1973— **7**
Bond, Beverly 1970— **53**
Bond, J. Max, Jr. 1935— **76**
Bond, (Horace) Julian 1940— **2, 35**
Bonds, Barry 1964— **6, 34, 63**
Bonds, Bobby 1946— **43**
Bonds, Margaret 1913–1972 **39**
Bonet, Lisa 1967— **58**
Boney, Lisa Michelle See Bonet, Lisa
Bonga, Kuenda 1942— **13**
Bongo, Albert-Bernard See Bongo, Omar
Bongo, Ali Ben 1959— **80**
Bongo, Omar 1935–2009 **1, 79**
Bonheur, Yannick 1982— **84**
Bontemps, Arna(ud Wendell) 1902–1973 **8**
Booker, Cory Anthony 1969— **68**
Booker, Simeon 1918— **23**
Borders, James (Buchanan, IV) 1949— **9**
Bosh, Chris 1984— **85**
Bosley, Freeman (Robertson), Jr. 1954— **7**
Boston, Kelvin E. 1955(?)— **25**
Boston, Lloyd 1970(?)— **24**
Bow Wow 1987— **35**
Bowe, Riddick (Lamont) 1967— **6**
Bowen, Ruth 1924–2009 **83**
Bowman, Bertie 1931— **71**
Bowman, Herbert See Bowman, Bertie
Bowser, Yvette Lee 1965(?)— **17**
Boyd, Edward 1914–2007 **70**
Boyd, Gerald M. 1950–2006 **32, 59**
Boyd, Gwendolyn 1955— **49**
Boyd, John W., Jr. 1965— **20, 72**
Boyd, Melba Joyce 1950— **86**
Boyd, Suzanne 1963— **52**
Boyd, T(heophilus) B(artholomew), III 1947— **6**
Boye, Madior 1940— **30**
Boykin, Keith 1965— **14**
Boyz II Men **82**
Bradley, David Henry, Jr. 1950— **39**
Bradley, Ed 1941–2006 **2, 59**
Bradley, J. Robert 1919–2007 **65**
Bradley, Jennette B. 1952— **40**
Bradley, Thomas 1917— **2, 20**
Brady, Wayne 1972— **32, 71**
Brae, C. Michael 1963(?)— **61**
Braithwaite, William Stanley 1878–1962 **52**
Branch, William Blackwell 1927— **39**
Brand, Dionne 1953— **32**
Brand, Elton 1979— **31**
Brandon, Barbara 1960(?)— **3**
Brandon, Thomas Terrell 1970— **16**
Brandy 1979— **14, 34, 72**
Branham, George, III 1962— **50**
Branson, Herman 1914–1995 **87**
Brashear, Carl Maxie 1931— **29**

Brashear, Donald 1972— **39**
Brathwaite, Fred 1972— **35**
Brathwaite, Kamau 1930— **36**
Brathwaite, Lawson Edward See Kamau Brathwaite
Braugher, Andre 1962— **13, 58**
Braun, Carol Moseley 1947— **4, 42**
Brawley, Benjamin 1882–1939 **44**
Braxton, Brad 1969(?)— **77**
Braxton, Toni 1968(?)— **15, 61**
Brazile, Donna 1959— **25, 70**
Breed, Eric T. See MC Breed
Breed, MC See MC Breed
Breedlove, Sarah See Walker, Madame C. J.
Breeze, Jean "Binta" 1956— **37**
Bridges, Christopher See Ludacris
Bridges, Ruby 1954— **77**
Bridges, Sheila 1964— **36**
Bridges, Todd 1965— **37**
Bridgetower, George 1780(?)–1860 **78**
Bridgewater, Dee Dee 1950— **32**
Bridgforth, Glinda 1952— **36**
Briggs, Curtis 1952(?)— **84**
Brimmer, Andrew F. 1926— **2, 48**
Briscoe, Connie 1952— **15**
Briscoe, Marlin 1946(?)— **37**
Britt, Donna 1954(?)— **28**
Broadbent, Hydeia 1984— **36**
Brock, Lou 1939— **18**
Brock, Roslyn McCallister 1965— **86**
Bromery, Randolph Wilson 1926— **85**
Bronner, Nathaniel H., Sr. 1914–1993 **32**
Brooke, Edward (William, III) 1919— **8**
Brooks, Aaron 1976— **33**
Brooks, Avery 1949— **9**
Brooks, Derrick 1973— **43**
Brooks, Golden 1970— **62**
Brooks, Gwendolyn 1917–2000 **1, 28**
Brooks, Hadda 1916–2002 **40**
Brooks, Mehcad 1980— **62**
Brooks, Tyrone 1945— **59**
Broonzy, Big Bill 1893–1958 **82**
Brother Blue See Hill, Hugh Morgan
Brower, William 1916–2004 **49**
Brown, Andre See Dre, Dr.
Brown, Angela M. 1964(?)— **54**
Brown, Anne 1912–2009 **76**
Brown, Anthony G. 1961— **72**
Brown, Antron 1976— **85**
Brown, Bobby 1969— **58**
Brown, Buck See Brown, Robert
Brown, Byrd 1930–2001 **49**
Brown, Byron W. 1958— **72**
Brown, Carlinhos 1962— **81**
Brown, Cecil M. 1943— **46**
Brown, Charles 1922–1999 **23**
Brown, Chris 1989— **74**
Brown, Chuck 1939— **78**
Brown, Clarence Gatemouth 1924–2005 **59**
Brown, Claude 1937–2002 **38**
Brown, Clifford 1930–1956 **86**
Brown, Cora 1914–1972 **33**
Brown, Corrine 1946— **24**
Brown, Cupcake 1964— **63**

Brown, Donald 1963— **19**
Brown, Eddie C. 1940— **35**
Brown, Elaine 1943— **8**
Brown, Ernest 1916–2009 **80**
Brown, Erroll M. 1950(?)— **23**
Brown, Foxy 1979— **25**
Brown, George Leslie 1926–2006 **62**
Brown, H. Rap See Al-Amin, Jamil Abdullah
Brown, Homer S. 1896–1977 **47**
Brown, Hubert Gerold See Al-Amin, Jamil Abdullah
Brown, James 1933–2006 **15, 60**
Brown, James 1951— **22**
Brown, James Nathaniel See Brown, Jim
Brown, James Willie, Jr. See Komunyakaa, Yusef
Brown, Janice Rogers 1949— **43**
Brown, Jesse 1944–2003 **6, 41**
Brown, Jesse Leroy 1926–1950 **31**
Brown, Jim 1936— **11**
Brown, Joe 19(?)(?)— **29**
Brown, Joyce F. 1946— **25**
Brown, Lee P(atrick) 1937— **1, 24**
Brown, Les(lie Calvin) 1945— **5**
Brown, Lloyd Louis 1913–2003 **42**
Brown, Melanie 1975— **73**
Brown, Mike 1970— **77**
Brown, Nappy 1929–2008 **73**
Brown, Oscar, Jr. 1926–2005 **53**
Brown, Patrick "Sleepy" 1970— **50**
Brown, Robert 1936–2007 **65**
Brown, Ron(ald Harmon) 1941— **5**
Brown, Rosemary 1930–2003 **62**
Brown, Sean 1976— **52**
Brown, Sterling Allen 1901–1989 **10, 64**
Brown, Tony 1933— **3**
Brown, Uzee 1950— **42**
Brown, Vivian 1964— **27**
Brown, Warren 1971(?)— **61**
Brown, Wesley 1945— **23**
Brown, Willa Beatrice 1906–1992 **40**
Brown, Willard 1911(?)–1996 **36**
Brown, William Anthony See Brown, Tony
Brown, Willie 1934— **7, 85**
Brown, Zora Kramer 1949— **12**
Brown Bomber, The See Louis, Joe
Browne, Roscoe Lee 1925–2007 **66**
Broyard, Anatole 1920–1990 **68**
Broyard, Bliss 1966— **68**
Bruce, Blanche Kelso 1849–1898 **33**
Bruce, Bruce 19(?)(?)— **56**
Bruce, Isaac 1972— **26**
Brunson, Dorothy 1938— **1, 87**
Brutus, Dennis 1924— **38**
Bryan, Ashley F. 1923— **41**
Bryant, Cullen 1951–2009 **81**
Bryant, John 1966— **26**
Bryant, John R. 1943— **45**
Bryant, Kobe 1978— **15, 31, 71**
Bryant, Wayne R(ichard) 1947— **6**
Bryant, William Benson 1911–2005 **61**
Bryant, William Cullen See Bryant, Cullen
Buchanan, Ray 1971— **32**
Buckley, Gail Lumet 1937— **39**

Buckley, Victoria (Vikki) 1947–1999 24

Bullard, Eugene Jacques 1894–1961 12

Bullins, Ed 1935— 25

Bullock, Anna Mae See Turner, Tina

Bullock, Steve 1936— 22

Bully-Cummings, Ella 1957(?)— 48

Bumbry, Grace (Ann) 1937— 5

Bunche, Ralph J(ohnson) 1904–1971 5

Bunkley, Anita Richmond 19(?)(?)— 39

Burgess, John 1909–2003 46

Burgess, Marjorie L. 1929— 55

Burke, Selma Hortense 1900–1995 16

Burke, Solomon 1940— 31, 86

Burke, Yvonne Brathwaite 1932— 42

Burks, Mary Fair 1920–1991 40

Burleigh, Henry Thacker 1866–1949 56

Burley, Mary Lou See Williams, Mary Lou

Burnett, Charles 1944— 16, 68

Burnett, Chester Arthur See Howlin' Wolf

Burnett, Dorothy 1905–1995 19

Burnham, Forbes 1923–1985 66

Burnim, Mickey L. 1949— 48

Burning Spear 194(?)— 79

Burns, Eddie 1928— 44

Burns, Jesse Louis See Jackson, Jesse

Burns, Ursula 1958— 60

Burnside, R. L. 1926–2005 56

Burrell, Orville Richard See Shaggy

Burrell, Stanley Kirk See M.C. Hammer

Burrell, Tom 1939— 21, 51

Burris, Chuck 1951— 21

Burris, Roland W. 1937— 25, 75

Burroughs, Margaret Taylor 1917— 9

Burrows, Stephen 1943— 31

Burrus, William Henry "Bill" 1936— 45

Burruss, Kandi See Kandi

Burt-Murray, Angela 1970— 59

Burton, LeVar 1957— 8

Burwell, Bryan 1955— 83

Busby, Jheryl 1949–2008 3, 74

Bush, Gordon 1942— 82

Bush, Reggie 1985— 59

Buthelezi, Mangosuthu Gatsha 1928— 9

Butler, George, Jr. 1931–2008 70

Butler, Jerry 1939— 26

Butler, Jonathan 1961— 28

Butler, Leroy, III 1968— 17

Butler, Louis 1952— 70

Butler, Octavia 1947–2006 8, 43, 58

Butler, Paul D. 1961— 17

Butts, Calvin O(tis), III 1950— 9

Butts, Cassandra 1965— 78

Bynoe, Peter C. B. 1951— 40

Bynum, Juanita 1959— 31, 71

Byrd, Donald 1949— 10

Byrd, Eugene 1975— 64

Byrd, Michelle 1965— 19

Byrd, Robert (Oliver Daniel, III) 1952— 11

Byron, JoAnne Deborah See Shakur, Assata

Cade, Toni See Bambara, Toni Cade

Cadoria, Sherian Grace 1940— 14

Caesar, Shirley 1938— 19

Cage, Byron 1965(?)— 53

Cain, Herman 1945— 15

Caldwell, Benjamin 1937— 46

Caldwell, Earl 1941(?)— 60

Caldwell, Jim 1955— 81

Caldwell, Kirbyjon 1953(?)— 55

Calhoun, Cora See Austin, Lovie

Calhoun, Lillian Scott 1923–2006 87

Callaway, Thomas DeCarlo See Cee-Lo

Callender, Clive O(rville) 1936— 3

Calloway, Cab 1907–1994 14

Camara, Moussa Dadis 1964— 76

Cameron, Earl 1917— 44

Cameron, James 1914–2006 80

Camp, Georgia Blanche Douglas See Johnson, Georgia Douglas

Camp, Kimberly 1956— 19

Campanella, Roy 1921–1993 25

Campbell, Bebe Moore 1950–2006 6, 24, 59

Campbell, Bill 1954— 9, 76

Campbell, Charleszetta Lena See Waddles, Charleszetta (Mother)

Campbell, Donald J. 1935— 66

Campbell, E(lmer) Simms 1906–1971 13

Campbell, Mary Schmidt 1947— 43

Campbell, Milton See Little Milton

Campbell, Naomi 1970— 1, 31

Campbell, Tisha See Campbell-Martin, Tisha

Campbell-Martin, Tisha 1969— 8, 42

Canada, Geoffrey 1954— 23

Canady, Alexa 1950— 28

Canegata, Leonard Lionel Cornelius See Lee, Canada

Cannon, Katie 1950— 10

Cannon, Nick 1980— 47, 73

Cannon, Reuben 1946— 50

Cara, Irene 1959— 77

Carby, Hazel 1948— 27

Cardozo, Francis L. 1837–1903 33

Carew, Rod 1945— 20

Carey, Mariah 1970— 32, 53, 69

Cargill, Victoria A. 19(?)(?)— 43

Carmichael, Stokely 1941–1998 5, 26

Carnegie, Herbert 1919— 25

Carr, Johnnie 1911–2008 69

Carr, Keela 1973— 74

Carr, Kurt 196(?)— 56

Carr, Leroy 1905–1935 49

Carroll, Diahann 1935— 9

Carroll, L. Natalie 1950— 44

Carroll, Rocky 1963— 74

Carroll, Vinnette 1922— 29

Carruthers, George R. 1939— 40

Carson, André 1974— 69

Carson, Benjamin 1951— 1, 35, 76

Carson, Johnnie 1943— 85

Carson, Josephine See Baker, Josephine

Carson, Julia 1938–2007 23, 69

Carson, Lisa Nicole 1969— 21

Carter, Anson 1974— 24

Carter, Ben See Ben-Israel, Ben Ami

Carter, Benny 1907–2003 46

Carter, Betty 1930— 19

Carter, Butch 1958— 27

Carter, Cris 1965— 21

Carter, Dwayne Michael, Jr. See Lil Wayne

Carter, Joe 1960— 30

Carter, Joye Maureen 1957— 41

Carter, Kenneth 1959(?)— 53

Carter, Majora 1966— 77

Carter, Mandy 1946— 11

Carter, Martin 1927–1997 49

Carter, Nell 1948–2003 39

Carter, Pamela Lynn 1949— 67

Carter, Regina 1966(?)— 23

Carter, Robert L. 1917— 51

Carter, Rubin 1937— 26

Carter, Shawn See Jay-Z

Carter, Stephen L(isle) 1954— 4

Carter, Vince 1977— 26

Carter, Warrick L. 1942— 27

Cartey, Wilfred 1931–1992 47

Cartiér, Xam Wilson 1949— 41

Carver, George Washington 1861(?)–1943 4

Cary, Lorene 1956— 3

Cary, Mary Ann Shadd 1823–1893 30

Cash, Rosalind 1938–1995 28

Cash, Swin 1979— 59

Cashin, Sheryll 1962— 63

CasSelle, Malcolm 1970— 11

Catchings, Tamika 1979— 43

Catlett, Elizabeth 1919— 2

Catto, Octavius V. 1839–1871 83

Caymmi, Dorival 1914–2008 72

Cayton, Horace 1903–1970 26

Cedric the Entertainer 1964— 29, 60

Cee-Lo 1974— 70

Césaire, Aimé 1913–2008 48, 69

Chadiha, Jeffri 1970— 57

Cham, Adongo Agada Akway 1954(?)— 77

Chamberlain, Wilt 1936–1999 18, 47

Chambers, James See Cliff, Jimmy

Chambers, Julius (LeVonne) 1936— 3

Chamillionaire 1979— 82

Chaney, John 1932— 67

Channer, Colin 1963— 36

Chanté, Keshia 1988— 50

Chapman, Nathan A., Jr. 1957— 21

Chapman, Tracy 1964— 26

Chappell, Emma C. 1941— 18

Chappelle, Dave 1973— 50

Charlemagne, Emmanuel See Charlemagne, Manno

Charlemagne, Manno 1948— 11

Charles, Mary Eugenia 1919–2005 10, 55

Charles, Pierre 1954–2004 52

Charles, Ray 1930–2004 16, 48

Charleston, Oscar 1896–1954 39

Chase, Debra Martin 1956(?)— 49

Chase, Leah 1923— 57

Chase-Riboud, Barbara 1939— 20, 46

Chatard, Peter 1936— 44

Chavis, Benjamin (Franklin, Jr.) 1948— 6

Cheadle, Don 1964— 19, 52

Cheatham, Doc 1905–1997 17

Checker, Chubby 1941— 28

Cheeks, Maurice 1956— 47

Chenault, John 1952— 40

Chenault, Kenneth I. 1952— 4, 36

Cheney-Coker, Syl 1945— 43

Cheruiyot, Robert 1978— 69

Cherry, Deron 1959— 40

Chesimard, JoAnne (Deborah) See Shakur, Assata

Chesnutt, Charles 1858–1932 29

Chestnut, J. L., Jr. 1930–2008 73

Chestnut, Morris 1969— 31

Chideya, Farai 1969— 14, 61

Chief Black Thunderbird Eagle See York, Dwight D.

Childress, Alice 1920–1994 15

Chiluba, Frederick 1943— 56, 80

Chineworth, Mary Alice 1917— 79

Chinn, May Edward 1896–1980 26

Chisholm, Samuel J. 1942— 32

Chisholm, Shirley 1924–2005 2, 50

Chissano, Joaquim 1939— 7, 55, 67

Chong, Rae Dawn 1961— 62

Christian, Barbara T. 1946–2000 44

Christian, Spencer 1947— 15

Christian-Green, Donna M. 1945— 17

Christie, Angella 36

Christie, Linford 1960— 8

Christie, Perry Gladstone 1944— 53

Christie, Ron 1969(?)— 83

Christophe, Henri 1767–1820 9

Chuck D 1960— 9

Church, Bruce See Bruce, Bruce

Churchwell, Robert, Sr. 1917–2009 76

Chweneyagae, Presley 1984— 63

Ciara 1985— 56

Ciara, Barbara 195(?)— 69

Cissé, Souleymane See Souleymane, Mahamane

Clack, Zoanne 1968(?)— 73

Claiborne, Loretta 1953— 34

Clark, Celeste (Clesteen) Abraham 1953— 15

Clark, Joe 1939— 1

Clark, John Pepper See Clark-Bekedermo, J. P.

Clark, Kenneth B. 1914–2005 5, 52

Clark, Kristin See Taylor, Kristin Clark

Clark, Mamie Phipps 1917–1983 79

Clark, Mattie Moss 1925–1994 61

Clark, Patrick 1955— 14

Clark, Septima (Poinsette) 1898–1987 7

Clark-Bekedermo, J. P. 1935— 44

Clark-Cole, Dorinda 1957— 66

Clarke, Austin C. 1934— 32

Clarke, Cheryl 1932— 32

Clarke, George Elliott 1960— 32

Clarke, Hope 1943(?)— 14

Clarke, John Henrik 1915–1998 20

Clarke, Kenny 1914–1985 27

Clarke, Patrice Francise See Washington, Patrice Clarke

Clark-Sheard, Karen 19(?)(?)— 22

Clash, Kevin 1961(?)— **14**

Clay, Bryan 1980— **57, 74**

Clay, Cassius Marcellus, Jr. *See Ali, Muhammad*

Clay, William Lacy 1931— **8**

Clayton, Constance 1937— **1**

Clayton, Eva M. 1934— **20**

Clayton, Mayme Agnew 1923–2006 **62**

Clayton, Xernona 1930— **3, 45**

Claytor, Helen 1907–2005 **14, 52**

Cleage, Albert B., Jr. *See Agyeman, Jaramogi Abebe*

Cleage, Pearl 1948— **17, 64**

Cleaver, (Leroy) Eldridge 1935— **5, 45**

Cleaver, Emanuel (II) 1944— **4, 68**

Cleaver, Kathleen Neal 1945— **29**

Clemente, Rosa 1972— **74**

Clements, George (Harold) 1932— **2**

Clemmons, Reginal G. 19(?)(?)— **41**

Clemons, Clarence 1942— **41**

Clemons, Michael "Pinball" 1965— **64**

Clendenon, Donn 1935–2005 **26, 56**

Cleveland, James 1932(?)–1991 **19**

Cliff, Jimmy 1948— **28**

Cliff, Michelle 1946— **42**

Clifton, Lucille 1936— **14, 64**

Clifton, Nathaniel "Sweetwater" 1922(?)–1990 **47**

Clinton, George (Edward) 1941— **9**

Clyburn, James E. 1940— **21, 71**

Clyburn, Mignon 1962— **78**

Coachman, Alice 1923— **18**

Coates, Ta-Nehisi 1975— **76**

Cobb, Jewel Plummer 1924— **42**

Cobb, Monty *See Cobb, W. Montague*

Cobb, W. Montague 1904–1990 **39**

Cobb, William Jelani 1969— **59**

Cobbs, Price M(ashaw) 1928— **9**

Cochran, Johnnie 1937–2005 **11, 39, 52**

Cockrel, Kenneth V., Jr. 1965— **79**

Cockrel, Kenneth Vern, Sr. 1938–1989 **79**

Cohen, Anthony 1963— **15**

Colbert, Virgis William 1939— **17**

Cole, Johnnetta B(etsch) 1936— **5, 43**

Cole, Keyshia 1983— **63**

Cole, Lorraine 195(?)— **48**

Cole, Nat "King" 1919–1965 **17**

Cole, Natalie 1950— **17, 60, 84**

Cole, Rebecca 1846–1922 **38**

Coleman, Bessie 1892–1926 **9**

Coleman, Donald 1952— **24, 62**

Coleman, Gary 1968–2010 **35, 86**

Coleman, James E., Jr. 1948(?)— **79**

Coleman, Ken 1942— **57**

Coleman, Leonard S., Jr. 1949— **12**

Coleman, Mary 1946— **46**

Coleman, Michael B. 1954— **28, 79**

Coleman, Ornette 1930— **39, 69**

Coleman, Troy *See Cowboy Troy*

Coleman, Wanda 1946— **48**

Coleman, William F., III 1955(?)— **61**

Coleman, William T. 1920— **76**

Colemon, Johnnie 1921(?)— **11**

Coleridge-Taylor, Samuel 1875–1912 **75**

Coles, Alice 1951(?)— **80**

Colescott, Robert 1925— **69**

Collins, Albert 1932–1993 **12**

Collins, Barbara-Rose 1939— **7, 87**

Collins, Bootsy 1951— **31**

Collins, Cardiss 1931— **10, 80**

Collins, Janet 1917–2003 **33, 64**

Collins, Lyn 1948–2005 **53**

Collins, Marva 1936— **3, 71**

Collins, Patricia Hill 1948— **67**

Collins, Paul 1936— **61**

Collins, William *See Collins, Bootsy*

Colston, Hal 1953(?)— **72**

Colter, Cyrus J. 1910–2002 **36**

Coltrane, Alice 1937–2007 **70**

Coltrane, John William 1926–1967 **19**

Coltrane, Ravi 1965— **71**

Combs, Sean "Puffy" 1969— **17, 43**

Comer, James P(ierpont) 1934— **6**

Common 1972— **31, 63**

Compaore, Blaise 1951— **87**

Compton, John 1925–2007 **65**

Compton-Rock, Malaak 1969— **86**

Cone, James H. 1938— **3, 82**

Coney, PonJola 1951— **48**

Conneh, Sekou Damate, Jr. 1960— **51**

Connerly, Ward 1939— **14**

Conté, Lansana 1934(?)–2008 **7, 76**

Conyers, John, Jr. 1929— **4, 45**

Conyers, Monica 1964— **85**

Conyers, Nathan G. 1932— **24**

Cook, Charles "Doc" 1891–1958 **44**

Cook, (Will) Mercer 1903–1987 **40**

Cook, Sam 1931–1964 **17**

Cook, Samuel DuBois 1928— **14**

Cook, Suzan D. Johnson 1957— **22**

Cook, Toni 1944— **23**

Cook, Victor Trent 19(?)(?)— *See Three Mo' Tenors*

Cook, Wesley *See Abu-Jamal, Mumia*

Cook, Will Marion 1869–1944 **40**

Cooke, Charles L. *See Cook, Charles "Doc"*

Cooke, Marcia 1954— **60**

Cooke, Marvel 1901(?)–2000 **31**

Cooks, Patricia 1944–1989 **19**

Cool Papa Bell *See Bell, James "Cool Papa"*

Cools, Anne 1943— **64**

Coombs, Orde M. 1939–1984 **44**

Cooper, Afua 1957— **53**

Cooper, Andrew Lewis *See Cooper, Andy "Lefty"*

Cooper, Andrew W. 1928–2002 **36**

Cooper, Andy "Lefty" 1898–1941 **63**

Cooper, Anna Julia 1858–1964 **20**

Cooper, Barry 1956— **33**

Cooper, Charles "Chuck" 1926–1984 **47**

Cooper, Chuck 1954— **75**

Cooper, Cynthia 1963— **17**

Cooper, Edward S(awyer) 1926— **6**

Cooper, Evern 19(?)(?)— **40**

Cooper, Helene 1966— **74**

Cooper, J. California 1932(?)— **12, 85**

Cooper, Lisa 1963— **73**

Cooper, Marcus *See Pleasure P*

Cooper, Margaret J. 194(?)— **46**

Cooper, Michael 1956— **31**

Cooper Cafritz, Peggy 1947— **43**

Copeland, Michael 1954— **47**

Coppola, Imani Francesca 1978— **82**

Corbi, Lana 1955— **42**

Corley, Tony 1949— **62**

Cornelius, Don 1936— **4**

Cornish, Sam 1935— **50**

Cornwell, Edward E., III 1956— **70**

Cortez, Jayne 1936— **43**

Corthron, Kia 1961— **43**

Cortor, Eldzier 1916— **42**

Cosby, Bill 1937— **7, 26, 59**

Cosby, Camille 1945— **14, 80**

Cosby, William Henry, Jr. *See Cosby, Bill*

Cose, Ellis 1951— **5, 50**

Cotter, Joseph Seamon, Sr. 1861–1949 **40**

Cottrell, Comer 1931— **11**

Count Basie 1904–1984 **23**

Counter, S. Allen 1944— **74**

Couto, Mia 1955— **45**

Coverley, Louise Bennett *See Bennett, Louise*

Cowans, Adger W. 1936— **20**

Cowboy Troy, 1970— **54**

Cox, Bryan 1968— **83**

Cox, Deborah 1974(?)— **28**

Cox, Ida 1896–1967 **42**

Cox, Joseph Mason Andrew 1930— **51**

Cox, Renée 1960— **67**

Cox, William E. 1942— **68**

Craig, Carl 1969— **31, 71**

Craig-Jones, Ellen Walker 1906–2000 **44**

Crawford, Hank 1934–2009 **77**

Crawford, Randy 1952— **19**

Crawford, Veronica *See Crawford, Randy*

Cray, Robert 1953— **30**

Creagh, Milton 1957— **27**

Crennel, Romeo 1947— **54**

Crew, Rudolph F. 1950(?)— **16**

Crew, Spencer R. 1949— **55**

Crichlow, Ernest 1914–2005 **75**

Crite, Alan Rohan 1910— **29**

Croal, N'Gai 1972— **76**

Crocker, Frankie 1937–2000 **29**

Crockett, George W., Jr. 1909–1997 **10, 64**

Crooks, Garth 1958— **53**

Croom, Sylvester 1954— **50**

Cross, Dolores E. 1938— **23**

Crothers, Benjamin Sherman *See Crothers, Scatman*

Crothers, Scatman 1910–1986 **19**

Crouch, Andraé 1942— **27**

Crouch, Stanley 1945— **11, 87**

Crowder, Henry 1895–1954(?) **16**

Crump, Lavell *See Banner, David*

Cruse, Harold 1916–2005 **54**

Crutchfield, James N. 1947— **55**

Cullen, Countee 1903–1946 **8**

Cullers, Vincent T. 1924(?)–2003 **49**

Culp, Napoleon Brown Goodson *See Brown, Nappy*

Culpepper, Daunte 1977— **32, 85**

Cummings, Elijah E. 1951— **24**

Cuney, William Waring 1906–1976 **44**

Cunningham, Evelyn 1916–2010 **23, 85**

Cunningham, Randall 1963— **23**

Curling, Alvin 1939— **34**

Currie, Betty 1939(?)— **21**

Currie, Ulysses 1937— **73**

Curry, George E. 1947— **23**

Curry, Mark 1964— **17**

Curry, Michael 1968— **85**

Curtis, Christopher Paul 1954(?)— **26**

Curtis-Hall, Vondie 1956— **17**

Da Don, Polow 1978— **86**

da Silva, Benedita 1942— **5**

da Silva, Jorge Mário *See Jorge, Seu*

Dabydeen, David 1956— **48**

Dadié, Bernard 1916— **34**

Daemyon, Jerald 1970(?)— **64**

D'Aguiar, Fred 1960— **50**

Dailey, Ulysses Grant 1885–1961 **87**

Daly, Marie Maynard 1921— **37**

Damas, Léon-Gontran 1912–1978 **46**

Dance, Kelvin *See Kitwana, Bakari*

Dandala, Mvume 1951— **77**

Dandridge, Dorothy 1922–1965 **3**

Dandridge, Ray 1913–1994 **36**

Dandridge, Raymond Garfield 1882–1930 **45**

D'Angelo 1974— **27**

Daniels, Gertrude *See Haynes, Trudy*

Daniels, Lee 1959— **36, 76**

Daniels-Carter, Valerie 19(?)(?)— **23**

Danner, Margaret Esse 1915–1986 **49**

Danticat, Edwidge 1969— **15, 68**

Dantley, Adrian 1956— **72**

Dara, Olu 1941— **335**

D'Arby, Terence Trent *See Maitreya, Sananda*

Darden, Calvin 1950— **38**

Darden, Christopher 1957— **13**

Darego, Agbani 1982— **52**

Dash, Damon 19(?)(?)— **31**

Dash, Darien 1972(?)— **29**

Dash, Julie 1952— **4**

Dash, Leon 1944— **47**

Datcher, Michael 1967— **60**

Dathorne, O. R. 1934— **52**

Davenport, Arthur *See Fattah, Chaka*

David, Craig 1981— **31, 53**

David, Keith 1954— **27**

Davidson, Jaye 1967(?)— **5**

Davidson, Tommy 1963(?)— **21**

Davis, Allison 1902–1983 **12**

Davis, Altovise 1943–2009 **76**

Davis, Angela (Yvonne) 1944— **5**

Davis, Anthony 1951— **11**

Davis, Anthony Moses *See Beenie Man*

Davis, Arthur P. 1904–1996 **41**

Davis, Artur 1967— **41**

Davis, Belva 1932— **61**

Davis, Benjamin O(liver), Jr. 1912–2002 **2, 43**
Davis, Benjamin O(liver), Sr. 1877–1970 **4**
Davis, Bing 1937— **84**
Davis, Charles T. 1918–1981 **48**
Davis, Chuck 1937— **33**
Davis, Danny K. 1941— **24, 79**
Davis, Ed 1911–1999 **24**
Davis, Eisa 1971— **68**
Davis, Ernie 1939–1963 **48**
Davis, Erroll B., Jr. 1944— **57**
Davis, Frank Marshall 1905–1987 **47**
Davis, Gary 1896–1972 **41**
Davis, George 1939— **36**
Davis, Gordon J. 1941— **76**
Davis, Guy 1952— **36**
Davis, Jamelia Niela See Jamelia
Davis, James E. 1962–2003 **50**
Davis, Lorenzo "Piper" 1917–1997 **19**
Davis, Mike 1960— **41**
Davis, Miles (Dewey, III) 1926–1991 **4**
Davis, Milt 1929–2008 **74**
Davis, Nolan 1942— **45**
Davis, Ossie 1917–2005 **5, 50**
Davis, Ruth 1943— **37**
Davis, Sammy, Jr. 1925–1990 **18**
Davis, Shani 1982— **58, 84**
Davis, Terrell 1972— **20**
Davis, Thulani 1948— **61**
Davis, Tyrone 1938–2005 **54**
Davis, Viola 1965— **34, 76**
Dawes, Dominique (Margaux) 1976— **11**
Dawkins, Wayne 1955— **20**
Dawn, Marpessa 1934–2008 **75**
Dawson, Andre 1954— **85**
Dawson, Matel "Mat," Jr. 1921–2002 **39**
Dawson, Michael C. 1951— **63**
Dawson, Rosario 1979— **72**
Dawson, William Levi 1899–1900 **39**
Day, Leon 1916–1995 **39**
Days, Drew S(aunders, III) 1941— **10**
De' Alexander, Quinton 19??— **57**
de Assís Moreira, Ronaldo See Ronaldinho
De Bankolé, Isaach 1957— **78**
de Carvalho, Barcelo See Bonga, Kuenda
de Lavallade, Carmen 1931— **78**
de Passe, Suzanne 1948(?)— **25**
De Priest, Oscar Stanton 1871–1951 **80**
De Shields, André 1946— **72**
De Veaux, Alexis 1948— **44**
"Deadwood Dick" See Love, Nat
Dean, Mark E. 1957— **35**
Deas, Gerald 1931— **85**
DeBaptiste, George 1814(?)–1875 **32**
Déby, Idriss 1952— **30**
DeCarava, Roy 1919–2009 **42, 81**
Deconge-Watson, Lovenia 1933— **55**
Dee, Merri 1936— **55**
Dee, Ruby 1924— **8, 50, 68**
Deezer D 1965— **53**
DeFrantz, Anita 1952— **37**

DeGale, James 1986— **74**
Deggans, Eric 1965— **71**
DeJongh, John, Jr. 1957— **85**
Delaney, Beauford 1901–1979 **19**
Delaney, Joe 1958–1983 **76**
Delaney, Joseph 1904–1991 **30**
Delany, Annie Elizabeth 1891–1995 **12**
Delany, Martin R. 1812–1885 **27**
Delany, Samuel R(ay), Jr. 1942— **9**
Delany, Sarah (Sadie) 1889— **12**
Delco, Wilhemina R. 1929— **33**
Delice, Ronald 1966— **48**
Delice, Rony 1966— **48**
DeLille, Henriette 1813–1862 **30**
Dellums, Ronald 1935— **2, 81**
DeLoach, Nora 1940–2001 **30**
Delsarte, Louis 1944— **34**
Demby, William 1922— **51**
Dennard, Brazeal 1929— **37**
Dent, Thomas C. 1932–1998 **50**
Dent, Tom See Dent, Thomas C.
DePreist, James 1936— **37**
DeVard, Jerri 1957(?)— **61**
Devers, Gail 1966— **7, 87**
Devine, Loretta 1953— **24**
Devine, Major J. See Divine, Father
DeWese, Mohandas See Kool Moe Dee
Diallo, Amadou 1976–1999 **27**
Dibaba, Tirunesh 1985— **73**
Dickens, Helen Octavia 1909–2001 **14, 64**
Dickenson, Vic 1906–1984 **38**
Dickerson, Debra J. 1959— **60**
Dickerson, Eric 1960— **27**
Dickerson, Ernest 1952(?)— **6, 17**
Dickey, Eric Jerome 1961— **21, 56**
Diddley, Bo 1928–2008 **39, 72**
Diesel, Vin 1967(?)— **29**
Dieudonné 1966— **67**
Diggs, Charles C. 1922–1998 **21**
Diggs, Robert Fitzgerald See RZA
Diggs, Scott See Diggs, Taye
Diggs, Taye 1972— **25, 63**
Diggs-Taylor, Anna 1932— **20**
Dillard, Godfrey J. 1948— **45**
Dillard, Tramar See Flo Rida
Dinkins, David (Norman) 1927— **4**
Diogo, Luisa Dias 1958— **63**
Diop, Birago 1906–1989 **53**
Diop, Cheikh Anta 1923–1986 **4**
Diouf, Abdou 1935— **3**
Dirie, Waris 1965(?)— **56**
Divine, Father 1877(?)–1965 **7**
Dixon, Bill 1925–2010 **87**
Dixon, Dean 1915–1976 **68**
Dixon, George 1870–1909 **52**
Dixon, Ivan 1931–2008 **69**
Dixon, Julian C. 1934— **24**
Dixon, Margaret 192(?)— **14**
Dixon, Rodrick 19(?)(?)— See Three Mo' Tenors
Dixon, Sharon Pratt 1944— **1**
Dixon, Sheila 1953— **68**
Dixon, Willie (James) 1915–1992 **4**
DJ Jazzy Jeff 1965— **32**
DJ Red Alert See Alert, Kool DJ Red
DMC See Run-DMC
DMX 1970— **28, 64**
do Nascimento, Edson Arantes See Pelé

Dobbs, Mattiwilda 1925— **34**
Doby, Larry See Doby, Lawrence Eugene, Sr.
Doby, Lawrence Eugene, Sr. 1924–2003 **16, 41**
Dodson, Howard, Jr. 1939— **7, 52**
Dodson, Owen 1914–1983 **38**
Doig, Jason 1977— **45**
Doley, Harold, Jr. 1947— **26**
Domini, Rey See Lorde, Audre (Geraldine)
Domino, Fats 1928— **20**
Donald, Arnold Wayne 1954— **36**
Donaldson, Jeff 1932–2004 **46**
Donegan, Dorothy 1922–1998 **19**
Donovan, Kevin See Bambaataa, Afrika
Dorrell, Karl 1963— **52**
Dorsey, Lee 1926–1986 **65**
Dorsey, Thomas Andrew 1899–1993 **15**
Dortch, Thomas W., Jr. 1950— **45**
dos Santos, José Eduardo 1942— **43**
dos Santos, Manuel Francisco 1933 **65**
Dougherty, Mary Pearl 1915–2003 **47**
Douglas, Aaron 1899–1979 **7**
Douglas, Ashanti See Ashanti
Douglas, Denzil Llewellyn 1953— **53**
Douglas, Lizzie See Memphis Minnie
Douglass, Frederick 1817(?)–1895 **87**
Dourdan, Gary 1966— **37**
Dove, Rita 1952— **6, 78**
Dove, Ulysses 1947— **5**
Downing, Will 19(?)(?)— **19**
Dozier, Lamont See Holland-Dozier-Holland
Dr. J See Erving, Julius
Drake 1986— **86**
Draper, Sharon Mills 1952— **16, 43**
Drayton, William Jonathan, Jr. See Flavor Flav
Dre, Dr. 1965(?)— **10, 14, 30**
Dream, The See The-Dream
Drew, Alvin, Jr. 1962— **67**
Drew, Charles Richard 1904–1950 **7**
Drexler, Clyde 1962— **4, 61**
Driskell, David C(lyde) 1931— **7**
Driver, David E. 1955— **11**
Drogba, Didier 1978— **78**
Drummond, William J. 1944— **40**
Du Bois, David Graham 1925— **45**
Du Bois, W(illiam) E(dward) B(urghardt) 1868–1963 **3**
du Cille, Michel 1955(?)— **74**
Dube, Lucky 1964–2007 **77**
DuBois, Shirley Graham 1907–1977 **21**
Duchemin, Alamaine See Maxis, Theresa
Duchemin, Marie See Maxis, Theresa
Duchemin, Theresa Maxis See Maxis, Theresa
Ducksworth, Marilyn 1957— **12**
Dudley, Edward R. 1911–2005 **58**
Due, Tananarive 1966— **30**
Duggins, George 1943–2005 **64**

Duke, Bill 1943— **3**
Duke, George 1946— **21**
Dukes, Hazel Nell 1932— **56**
Dumars, Joe 1963— **16, 65**
Dumas, Henry 1934–1968 **41**
Dunbar, Alice See Dunbar-Nelson, Alice Ruth Moore
Dunbar, Paul Laurence 1872–1906 **8**
Dunbar, Sly 1952— See Sly & Robbie
Dunbar-Nelson, Alice Ruth Moore 1875–1935 **44**
Duncan, Michael Clarke 1957— **26**
Duncan, Tim 1976— **20**
Duncan, Todd 1903–1998 **76**
Dungey, Merrin 1971— **62**
Dungy, Camille 1972— **86**
Dungy, Tony 1955— **17, 42, 59**
Dunham, Katherine 1910–2006 **4, 59**
Dunlap, Ericka 1982(?)— **55**
Dunn, Jerry 1953— **27**
Dunner, Leslie B. 1956— **45**
Dunnigan, Alice Allison 1906–1983 **41**
Dunston, Georgia Mae 1944— **48**
Duplechan, Larry 1956— **55**
Dupri, Jermaine 1972— **13, 46**
Durant, Kevin 1988— **76**
Durham, Bobby 1937–2008 **73**
Durham, Robert Joseph See Durham, Bobby
Dutton, Charles S. 1951— **4, 22**
Dutton, Marie Elizabeth 1940— **12**
Dwight, Edward 1933— **65**
Dworkin, Aaron P. 1970— **52**
Dye, Jermaine 1974— **58**
Dymally, Mervyn 1926— **42**
Dyson, Michael Eric 1958— **11, 40**
Early, Deloreese Patricia See Reese, Della
Early, Gerald (Lyn) 1952— **15**
Earthquake, 1963— **55**
Easley, Annie J. 1933— **61**
Ebanks, Michelle 1962— **60**
Ebanks, Selita 1983— **67**
Eckstein, William Clarence See Eckstine, Billy
Eckstine, Billy 1914–1993 **28**
Edelin, Ramona Hoage 1945— **19**
Edelman, Marian Wright 1939— **5, 42**
Edgerton, Khia Danielle See K-Swift
Edley, Christopher 1928–2003 **2, 48**
Edley, Christopher F., Jr. 1953— **48**
Edmonds, Kenneth See Babyface
Edmonds, Terry 1950(?)— **17**
Edmonds, Tracey 1967— **16, 64**
Edmunds, Gladys 1951(?)— **48**
Edwards, Donna 1958— **77**
Edwards, Eli See McKay, Claude
Edwards, Esther Gordy 1920(?)— **43**
Edwards, Harry 1942— **2**
Edwards, Herman 1954— **51**
Edwards, Lena Frances 1900–1986 **76**
Edwards, Melvin 1937— **22**
Edwards, Teresa 1964— **14**
Edwards, Trevor 1962— **54**
Edwards, Willarda V. 1951— **59**

Eikerenkoetter, Frederick J., II *See Reverend Ike*
Ejiofor, Chiwetal 1977(?)— 67
Ekwensi, Cyprian 1921— 37
El Wilson, Barbara 1959— 35
Elam, Keith *See Guru*
Elba, Idris 1972— 49
Elder, Larry 1952— 25
Elder, (Robert) Lee 1934— 6
Elder, Lonne, III 1931–1996 38
Elders, Joycelyn (Minnie) 1933— 6
Eldridge, Roy 1911–1989 37
El-Hajj Malik El-Shabazz *See X, Malcolm*
Elise, Kimberly 1967— 32
Ellerbe, Brian 1963— 22
Ellington, Duke 1899–1974 5
Ellington, E. David 1960— 11
Ellington, Edward Kennedy *See Ellington, Duke*
Ellington, Mercedes 1939— 34
Elliott, Lorris 1931–1999 37
Elliott, Missy "Misdemeanor" 1971— 31
Elliott, Sean 1968— 26
Ellis, Alton 1938–2008 74
Ellis, Charles H., III 1958(?)— 79
Ellis, Clarence A. 1943— 38
Ellis, Dock 1945–2008 78
Ellis, Jimmy 1940— 44
Ellison, Keith 1963— 59
Ellison, Ralph (Waldo) 1914–1994 7
Elmore, Ronn 1957— 21
El-Shabazz, El-Hajj Malik *See X, Malcolm*
Emanuel, James A. 1921— 46
Emeagwali, Dale 1954— 31
Emeagwali, Philip 1954— 30
Emecheta, Buchi 1944— 30
Emmanuel, Alphonsia 1956— 38
Ensley, Carol Denis *See Nash, Niecy*
Ephriam, Mablean 1949(?)— 29
Epperson, Sharon 1969(?)— 54
Epps, Archie C., III 1937–2003 45
Epps, Mike 1970— 60
Epps, Omar 1973— 23, 59
Equiano, Olaudah 1745(?)–1797 78
Ericsson-Jackson, Aprille 19(?)(?)— 28
Ervin, Anthony 1981— 66
Ervin, Clark Kent 1959— 82
Erving, Julius 1950— 18, 47
Escobar, Damien 1987— 56
Escobar, Tourie 1985— 56
Esposito, Giancarlo (Giusseppi Alessandro) 1958— 9
Espy, Alphonso Michael *See Espy, Mike*
Espy, Mike 1953— 6
Estelle 1980— 75
Esters, Monica Ann *See Conyers, Monica*
Estes, Rufus 1857–19(?)(?) 29
Estes, Simon 1938— 28
Estes, Sleepy John 1899–1977 33
Eto'o, Samuel 1981— 73
Eubanks, Kevin 1957— 15
Eugene-Richard, Margie 1941— 63
Europe, (William) James Reese 1880–1919 10
Evans, Darryl 1961— 22
Evans, Diana 1972(?)— 72

Evans, Ernest *See Checker, Chubby*
Evans, Etu 1969— 55
Evans, Faith 1973(?)— 22
Evans, Harry 1956(?)— 25
Evans, Mari 1923— 26
Evans, Warren C. 1948— 76
Eve 1979— 29
Everett, Francine 1917–1999 23
Everett, Ronald McKinley *See Karenga, Maulana*
Evers, Medgar (Riley) 1925–1963 3
Evers, Myrlie 1933— 8
Evora, Cesaria 1941— 12
Ewing, Patrick 1962— 17, 73
Eyadéma, Gnassingbé 1937–2005 7, 52
Fabio, Sarah Webster 1928–1979 48
Fabre, Shelton 1963— 71
Fagan, Garth 1940— 18
Fair, Ronald L. 1932— 47
Faison, Donald 1974— 50
Faison, Frankie 1949— 55
Faison, George William 1946— 16
Falana, Lola 1942— 42
Falconer, Etta Zuber 1933–2002 59
Fanon, Frantz 1925–1961 44
Farah, Nuruddin 1945— 27
Fargas, Antonio 1946(?)— 50
Farley, Christopher John 1966— 54
Farmer, Art(hur Stewart) 1928–1999 38
Farmer, Forest J(ackson) 1941— 1
Farmer, James 1920–1999 2, 64
Farmer-Paellmann, Deadria 1966— 43
Farr, Mel 1944— 24
Farrakhan, Louis 1933— 2, 15
Farrell, Herman D., Jr. 1932— 81
Farris, Isaac Newton, Jr. 1962— 63
Father Goose *See Rhoden, Wayne*
Fattah, Chaka 1956— 11, 70
Faulk, Marshall 1973— 35
Fauntroy, Walter E(dward) 1933— 11
Fauset, Jessie (Redmon) 1882–1961 7
Favors, Steve 1948— 23
Fax, Elton 1909–1993 48
Feaster, Robert Franklin *See Sundiata, Sekou*
Feelings, Muriel 1938— 44
Feelings, Tom 1933–2003 11, 47
Feemster, Herbert 1942— 72
Fela 1938–1997 1, 42
Felix, Allyson 1985— 48
Felix, Larry R. (?)— 64
Fennoy, Ilene 1947— 72
Fenton, Kevin 1966(?)— 87
Fentry, Robyn *See Rihanna*
Fenty, Adrian 1970— 60
Ferdinand, Rio 1978— 82
Ferguson, Amos 1920–2009 81
Ferguson, Kevin *See Slice, Kimbo*
Ferguson, Roger W. 1951— 25
Ferguson, Ronald F. 1950(?)— 75
Ferrell, Rachelle 1961— 29
Ferrer, Ibrahim 1927— 41
Fetchit, Stepin 1892–1985 32
Fiasco, Lupe 1982— 64
Fielder, Cecil (Grant) 1963— 2
Fielder, Prince Semien 1984— 68

Fields, C. Virginia 1946— 25
Fields, Cleo 1962— 13
Fields, Evelyn J. 1949— 27
Fields, Felicia P. (?)— 60
Fields, Julia 1938— 45
Fields, Kim 1969— 36
50 Cent 1976— 46, 83
Figueroa, John J. 1920–1999 40
Files, Lolita 1964(?)— 35
Fils-Aimé, Reggie 1961— 74
Fine, Sam 1969— 60
Finner-Williams, Paris Michele 1951— 62
Fiona, Melanie 1983— 84
Fishburne, Larry *See Fishburne, Laurence*
Fishburne, Laurence 1961— 4, 22, 70
Fisher, Ada Lois Sipuel 1924–1995 76
Fisher, Ada M. 1947— 76
Fisher, Antwone Quenton 1959— 40
Fisher, Gail 1935–2000 85
Fisher, Rudolph John Chauncey 1897–1934 17
Fitzgerald, Ella 1918–1996 8, 18
Flack, Roberta 1940— 19
Flake, Floyd H. 1945— 18
Flanagan, Tommy 1930–2001 69
Flash, Grandmaster *See Grandmaster Flash*
Flavor Flav 1959— 67
Fleming, Erik R. 1965— 75
Fleming, Raymond 1945— 48
Fletcher, Alphonse, Jr. 1965— 16
Fletcher, Arthur A. 1924–2005 63
Fletcher, Bill, Jr. 1954— 41
Fletcher, Geoffrey 1970— 85
Flipper, Henry O(ssian) 1856–1940 3
Flo Rida 1979— 78
Flood, Curt(is) 1963— 10
Flowers, Sylester 1935— 50
Flowers, Vonetta 1973— 35
Floyd, Elson S. 1956— 41
Folks, Byron *See Allen, Byron*
Forbes, Audrey Manley 1934— 16
Forbes, Calvin 1945— 46
Forbes, James A., Jr. 1935— 71
Ford, Cheryl 1981— 45
Ford, Clyde W. 1951— 40
Ford, Harold E(ugene) 1945— 42
Ford, Harold E(ugene), Jr. 1970— 16, 70
Ford, Jack 1947— 39
Ford, Johnny 1942— 70
Ford, Nick Aaron 1904–1982 44
Ford, Vincent 1940(?)–2008 75
Ford, Wallace 1950— 58
Foreman, George 1948— 1, 15
Forman, James 1928–2005 7, 51
Forrest, Leon 1937–1997 44
Forrest, Vernon 1971–2009 40, 79
Forté, John 1975— 74
Forte, Linda Diane 1952— 54
Fortune, T(imothy) Thomas 1856–1928 6
Foster, Andrew 1879–1930 79
Foster, Cecil (A.) 1954— 32
Foster, Ezola 1938— 28
Foster, George "Pops" 1892–1969 40
Foster, Henry W., Jr. 1933— 26

Foster, Jylla Moore 1954— 45
Foster, Marie 1917–2003 48
Foster, Rube *See Foster, Andrew*
Fowler, Reggie 1959— 51
Fowles, Gloria *See Gaynor, Gloria*
Fox, Rick 1969— 27
Fox, Ulrich Alexander *See Fox, Rick*
Fox, Vivica A. 15, 53
Foxx, Anthony 1971— 81
Foxx, Jamie 1967— 15, 48
Foxx, Redd 1922–1991 2
Francis, Norman (C.) 1931— 60
Franklin, Aretha 1942— 11, 44
Franklin, C. L. 1915–1984 68
Franklin, Carl 1949— 11
Franklin, Hardy R. 1929–2004 9, 87
Franklin, J. E. 1937— 44
Franklin, John Hope 1915–2009 5, 77
Franklin, Kirk 1970(?)— 15, 49
Franklin, Robert M(ichael) 1954— 13
Franklin, Shirley 1945— 34, 80
Franks, Gary 1954(?)— 2
Frazer, Jendayi 196(?)— 68
Frazier, Edward Franklin 1894–1962 10
Frazier, Joe 1944— 19
Frazier, Kevin 1964— 58
Frazier, Oscar 1956–2005 58
Frazier-Lyde, Jacqui 1961— 31
Fredericks, Henry Saint Claire *See Mahal, Taj*
Freelon, Nnenna 1954— 32
Freeman, Aaron 1956— 52
Freeman, Al(bert Cornelius), Jr. 1934— 11
Freeman, Cathy 1973— 29
Freeman, Charles Eldridge 1933— 19
Freeman, Harold P. 1933— 23
Freeman, Leonard 1950— 27
Freeman, Marianna 1957— 23
Freeman, Morgan 1937— 2, 20, 62
Freeman, Paul 1936— 39
Freeman, Yvette 27
French, Albert 1943— 18
Fresh Prince, The *See Smith, Will*
Friday, Jeff 1964(?)— 24
Fryer, Roland G. 1977— 56
Fudge, Ann (Marie) 1951— 11, 55
Fudge, Marcia L. 1952— 76
Fuhr, Grant 1962— 1, 49
Fulani, Lenora (Branch) 1950— 11
Fuller, A. Oveta 1955— 43
Fuller, Arthur 1972— 27
Fuller, Blind Boy 1907(?)–1941 86
Fuller, Charles (Henry) 1939— 8
Fuller, Howard L. 1941— 37
Fuller, Hoyt 1923–1981 44
Fuller, Meta Vaux Warrick 1877–1968 27
Fuller, S. B. 1895–1988 13
Fuller, Solomon Carter, Jr. 1872–1953 15
Fuller, Vivian 1954— 33
Funderburg, I. Owen 1924–2002 38
Funnye, Capers C., Jr. 1952(?)— 73
Fuqua, Antoine 1966— 35
Futch, Eddie 1911–2001 33
Gabre-Medhin, Tsegaye 1936–2006 64

Gaines, Brenda 19(?)(?)— 41
Gaines, Clarence E., Sr. 1923–2005 55
Gaines, Ernest J(ames) 1933— 7
Gaines, Grady 1934— 38
Gaines, Lloyd 1911–19(?)(?) 79
Gairy, Eric Matthew 1922–1997 83
Gaiter, Dorothy J. 1950(?)— 80
Gaither, Israel L. 1944— 65
Gaither, Jake 1903–1994 14
Gamble, Kenny 1943— 85
Gantin, Bernardin 1922–2008 70
Gantt, Harvey (Bernard) 1943— 1
Gardere, Jeffrey 1956— 76
Gardner, Chris 1954— 65
Gardner, Edward G. 1925— 45
Garner, Erroll 1921–1977 76
Garnett, Kevin (Maurice) 1976— 14, 70
Garrett, James F. 1942— 78
Garrett, Joyce Finley 1931–1997 59
Garrett, Sean 1979— 57
Garrincha See dos Santos, Manuel Francisco
Garrison, Zina 1963— 2
Garvey, Marcus 1887–1940 1
Garvin, Gerry 1967(?)— 78
Gary, Willie Edward 1947— 12
Gaskins, Eric 1958— 64
Gaskins, Rudy 1960(?)— 74
Gaspard, Patrick 1967— 84
Gaston, Arthur George 1892–1996 3, 38, 59
Gaston, Cito 1944— 71
Gaston, Clarence Edwin See Gaston, Cito
Gaston, Marilyn Hughes 1939— 60
Gates, Henry Louis, Jr. 1950— 3, 38, 67
Gates, Sylvester James, Jr. 1950— 15
Gay, Marvin Pentz, Jr. See Gaye, Marvin
Gaye, Marvin 1939–1984 2
Gaye, Nona 1974— 56
Gayle, Addison, Jr. 1932–1991 41
Gayle, Helene D. 1955— 3, 46
Gaynor, Gloria 1947— 36
Gbagbo, Laurent 1945— 43
Gbowee, Leymah 1971(?)— 76
Gebrselassie, Haile 1973— 70
Gentry, Alvin 1954— 23
George, Eddie 1973— 80
George, Nelson 1957— 12
George, Zelma Watson 1903–1994 42
Gerima, Haile 1946— 38, 80
Gervin, George 1952— 80
Gibbs, Marla 1931— 86
Gibson, Althea 1927–2003 8, 43
Gibson, Bob 1935— 33
Gibson, Donald Bernard 1933— 40
Gibson, John Trusty 1878–1937 87
Gibson, Johnnie Mae 1949— 23
Gibson, Josh 1911–1947 22
Gibson, Kenneth Allen 1932— 6
Gibson, Ted 1965— 66
Gibson, Truman K., Jr. 1912–2005 60
Gibson, Tyrese 1978— 27, 62
Gibson, William F(rank) 1933— 6
Giddings, Paula (Jane) 1947— 11
Gidron, Richard D. 1939–2007 68
Gil, Gilberto 1942— 53

Gilbert, Christopher 1949— 50
Gill, Gerald 1948–2007 69
Gill, Johnny 1966— 51
Gill, Turner 1962— 83
Gilles, Ralph 1970— 61
Gillespie, Dizzy 1917–1993 1
Gillespie, John Birks See Gillespie, Dizzy
Gilliam, Frank 1934(?)— 23
Gilliam, Joe, Jr. 1950–2000 31
Gilliam, Sam 1933— 16
Gilliard, Steve 1964–2007 69
Gilmore, Marshall 1931— 46
Gilpin, Charles Sidney 1878–1930 81
Ginuwine 1975(?)— 35
Giovanni, Nikki 1943— 9, 39, 85
Gist, Carole 1970(?)— 1
Givens, Adele 19(?)(?)— 62
Givens, Robin 1964— 4, 25, 58
Givhan, Robin Deneen 1964— 72
Gladwell, Malcolm 1963— 62
Glanville, Douglas Metunwa 1970— 82
Glover, Corey 1964— 34
Glover, Danny 1948— 1, 24
Glover, Donald 1983— 85
Glover, Keith 1966— 79
Glover, Nathaniel, Jr. 1943— 12
Glover, Savion 1974— 14
Gnassingbé, Faure 1966— 67
Goapele 1977— 55
"The Goat" See Manigault, Earl "The Goat"
Godbolt, James Titus See Slyde, Jimmy
Goines, Donald 1937(?)–1974 19
Goings, Russell 1932(?)— 59
Goldberg, Whoopi 1955— 4, 33, 69
Golden, Marita 1950— 19
Golden, Thelma 1965— 10, 55
Golding, Bruce 1947— 78
Goldsberry, Ronald 1942— 18
Golson, Benny 1929— 37
Golston, Allan C. 1967(?)— 55
Gomes, Peter J(ohn) 1942— 15
Gomez, Jewelle 1948— 30
Gomez-Preston, Cheryl 1954— 9
Goode, Mal(vin Russell) 1908–1995 13
Goode, W(oodrow) Wilson 1938— 4
Gooden, Dwight 1964— 20
Gooden, Lolita See Roxanne Shante
Gooding, Cuba, Jr. 1968— 16, 62
Goodison, Lorna 1947— 71
Goodman, Al 1943–2010 87
Goodnight, Paul 1946— 32
Gorden, W. C. 1930— 71
Gorden, William C. See Gorden, W. C.
Gordon, Bruce S. 1946— 41, 53, 82
Gordon, Carl 1932–2010 87
Gordon, Dexter 1923–1990 25
Gordon, Ed 1960— 10, 53
Gordon, Pamela 1955— 17
Gordone, Charles 1925–1995 15
Gordon-Reed, Annette 1958— 74
Gordy, Berry, Jr. 1929— 1
Goreed, Joseph See Williams, Joe
Goss, Carol A. 1947— 55

Goss, Tom 1946— 23
Gossett, Louis, Jr. 1936— 7
Gotti, Irv 1971— 39
Gourdine, Meredith 1929–1998 33
Gourdine, Simon (Peter) 1940— 11
Grace, George H. 1948— 48
Grae, Jean 1976— 51
Graham, Aubrey Drake See Drake
Graham, Lawrence Otis 1962— 12
Graham, Lorenz 1902–1989 48
Graham, Stedman 1951(?)— 13
Graham, Trevor 1962(?)— 84
Granderson, Curtis 1981— 66
Grandmaster Flash 1958— 33, 60
Grand-Pierre, Jean-Luc 1977— 46
Granger, Lester B. 1896–1976 75
Grant, Augustus O. 1946(?)— 71
Grant, Bernie 1944–2000 57
Grant, Gwendolyn Goldsby 19(?)(?)— 28
Granville, Evelyn Boyd 1924— 36
Gravely, Samuel L., Jr. 1922–2004 5, 49
Graves, Butch 1962— 77
Graves, Denyce Antoinette 1964— 19, 57
Graves, Earl G(ilbert) 1935— 1, 35
Graves, Earl Gilbert, Jr. See Graves, Butch
Gray, Darius 1945— 69
Gray, F. Gary 1969— 14, 49
Gray, Farrah 1984— 59
Gray, Fred Sr. 1930— 37
Gray, Frizzell See Mfume, Kweisi
Gray (Nelson Rollins), Ida 1867–1953 41
Gray, Macy 1970— 29
Gray, William H., III 1941— 3
Gray, Willie 1947— 46
Gray, Yeshimbra "Shimmy" 1972— 55
Greaves, William 1926— 38
Greely, M. Gasby 1946— 27
Greely, Margaret Gasby See Greely, M. Gasby
Green, A. C. 1963— 32
Green, Al 1946— 13, 47, 74
Green, Cee-Lo See Cee-Lo
Green, Darrell 1960— 39, 74
Green, Dennis 1949— 5, 45
Green, Grant 1935–1979 56
Green, Isaac H. 1959— 79
Green, Jonathan 1955— 54
Greene, Jimmy 1975— 74
Greene, Joe 1946— 10
Greene, Maurice 1974— 27, 77
Greene, Petey 1931–1984 65
Greene, Ralph Waldo See Greene, Petey
Greene, Richard Thaddeus, Sr. 1913–2006 67
Greenfield, Eloise 1929— 9
Greenfield, Ronnie Spector See Spector, Ronnie
Greenhouse, Bunnatine "Bunny" 1944— 57
Greenlee, Sam 1930— 48
Greenwood, Monique 1959— 38
Gregg, Eric 1951— 16
Gregory, Ann 1912–1990 63
Gregory, Dick 1932— 1, 54
Gregory, Frederick 1941— 8, 51
Gregory, Wilton 1947— 37

Grier, David Alan 1955— 28
Grier, Mike 1975— 43
Grier, Pam 1949— 9, 31, 86
Grier, Roosevelt (Rosey) 1932— 13
Griffey, Ken, Jr. 1969— 12, 73
Griffin, Angela 1976— 80
Griffin, Anthony 1960— 71
Griffin, Bessie Blout 1914— 43
Griffin, John Arnold, III See Griffin, Johnny
Griffin, Johnny 1928–2008 71
Griffin, LaShell 1967— 51
Griffith, Mark Winston 1963— 8
Griffith, Patrick A. 1944— 64
Griffith, Yolanda 1970— 25
Griffith-Joyner, Florence 1959–1998 28
Griffiths, Marcia 1948(?)— 29
Grimké, Archibald H(enry) 1849–1930 9
Grist, Reri 1932— 84
Grooms, Henry R(andall) 1944— 50
Guarionex See Schomburg, Arthur Alfonso
Guebuza, Armando 1943— 81
Guéï, Robert 1941–2002 66
Guillaume, Robert 1927— 3, 48
Güines, Tata 1930–2008 69
Guinier, (Carol) Lani 1950— 7, 30
Gumbel, Bryant 1948— 14, 80
Gumbel, Greg 1946— 8
Gunn, Moses 1929–1993 10
Gurira, Danai 1978(?)— 73
Guru 1961–2010 84
Guy, (George) Buddy 1936— 31
Guy, Jasmine 1964(?)— 2
Guy, Rosa 1925(?)— 5
Guy-Sheftall, Beverly 1946— 13
Guyton, Tyree 1955— 9
Gwynn, Tony 1960— 18, 83
Gyan, Asamoah 1985— 87
Habré, Hissène 1942— 6
Habyarimana, Juvenal 1937–1994 8
Haddon, Dietrick 1973(?)— 55
Hageman, Hans 19(?)(?)— 36
Hageman, Ivan 19(?)(?)— 36
Haile Selassie 1892–1975 7
Hailey, JoJo 1971— 22
Hailey, K-Ci 1969— 22
Hale, Clara 1902–1992 16
Hale, Lorraine 1926(?)— 8
Haley, Alex (Palmer) 1921–1992 4
Haley, George Williford Boyce 1925— 21
Hall, Aaron 1963— 57
Hall, Alvin D. 1952— 86
Hall, Arsenio 1955— 58
Hall, Arthur 1943–2000 39
Hall, Elliott S. 1938(?)— 24
Hall, Juanita 1901–1968 62
Hall, Kevan 19(?)(?)— 61
Hall, Lloyd A(ugustus) 1894–1971 8
Hall, Syren See Fiona, Melanie
Hall, Stuart 1932— 78
Halliburton, Warren J. 1924— 49
Hallim, Melanie Fiona See Fiona, Melanie
Ham, Cynthia Parker 1970(?)— 58
Hamblin, Ken 1940— 10
Hamburg, Beatrix 1923— 84
Hamburg, Margaret 1955— 78

Hamer, Fannie Lou (Townsend) 1917–1977 **6**
Hamilton, Anthony 1971— **61**
Hamilton, Lewis 1985— **66**
Hamilton, Lisa Gay 1964— **71**
Hamilton, Samuel C. 19(?)(?)— **47**
Hamilton, Virginia 1936— **10**
Hamlin, Larry Leon 1948–2007 **49, 62**
Hammer, M. C. *See M.C. Hammer*
Hammond, Fred 1960— **23**
Hammond, Lenn 1970(?)— **34**
Hammonds, Evelynn 1953— **69**
Hammons, David 1943— **69**
Hampton, Fred 1948–1969 **18**
Hampton, Henry (Eugene, Jr.) 1940— **6**
Hampton, Lionel 1908(?)–2002 **17, 41**
Hancock, Herbie 1940— **20, 67**
Handy, W(illiam) C(hristopher) 1873–1937 **8**
Haney, Lee 1959— **77**
Hani, Chris 1942–1993 **6**
Hani, Martin Thembisile *See Hani, Chris*
Hannah, Marc (Regis) 1956— **10**
Hansberry, Lorraine (Vivian) 1930–1965 **6**
Hansberry, William Leo 1894–1965 **11**
Hardaway, Anfernee (Penny) 1971— **13**
Hardaway, Penny *See Hardaway, Anfernee (Penny)*
Hardaway, Tim 1966— **35**
Hardin Armstrong, Lil 1898–1971 **39**
Hardin, Lillian Beatrice *See Hardin Armstrong, Lil*
Harding, Vincent 1931— **67**
Hardison, Bethann 19(?)(?)— **12**
Hardison, Kadeem 1966— **22**
Hardy, Antonio *See Big Daddy Kane*
Hardy, Nell *See Carter, Nell*
Hare, Nathan 1934— **44**
Harewood, David 1965— **52**
Harkless, Necia Desiree 1920— **19**
Harmon, Clarence 1940(?)— **26**
Harold, Erika 1980(?)— **54**
Harper, Ben 1969— **34, 62**
Harper, Frances E(llen) W(atkins) 1825–1911 **11**
Harper, Frank *See Harper, Hill*
Harper, Hill 1966— **32, 65**
Harper, Michael S. 1938— **34**
Harrell, Andre (O'Neal) 1962(?)— **9, 30**
Harrington, Oliver W(endell) 1912— **9**
Harris, Alice 1934— **7**
Harris, Barbara 1930— **12**
Harris, Barry 1929— **68**
Harris, Bill 1941— **72**
Harris, Carla A. 1962— **67**
Harris, Ciara Princess *See Ciara*
Harris, Claire 1937— **34**
Harris, Corey 1969— **39, 73**
Harris, E. Lynn 1957— **12, 33**
Harris, Eddy L. 1956— **18**
Harris, Gary L. 1953— **87**
Harris, James 1947— **79**
Harris, James, III *See Jimmy Jam*

Harris, Jay **19**
Harris, Kamala D. 1964— **64**
Harris, Leslie 1961— **6**
Harris, Lyle Ashton 1965— **83**
Harris, Marcelite Jordon 1943— **16**
Harris, Mary Styles 1949— **31**
Harris, Monica 1968— **18**
Harris, Naomie 1976— **55**
Harris, Patricia Roberts 1924–1985 **2**
Harris, Richard E. 1912(?)— **61**
Harris, Robin 1953–1990 **7**
Harris, Shack *See Harris, James*
Harris, "Sweet" Alice *See Harris, Alice*
Harris, Sylvia 1967(?)— **70**
Harris, William Anthony *See Harris, Bill*
Harris-Lacewell, Melissa 1973— **81**
Harrison, Alvin 1974— **28**
Harrison, Calvin 1974— **28**
Harrison, Charles 1931— **72**
Harrison, Mya *See Mya*
Harsh, Vivian Gordon 1890–1960 **14**
Hart, Alvin Youngblood 1963— **61**
Hart, Gregory Edward *See Hart, Alvin Youngblood*
Harvard, Beverly (Joyce Bailey) 1950— **11**
Harvey, Steve 1956— **18, 58**
Harvey, William R. 1941— **42**
Haskins, Clem 1943— **23**
Haskins, James 1941–2005 **36, 54**
Hassell, Leroy Rountree, Sr. 1955— **41**
Hastie, William H(enry) 1904–1976 **8**
Hastings, Alcee Lamar 1936— **16**
Hatcher, Richard G. 1933— **55**
Hatchett, Glenda 1951(?)— **32**
Hathaway, Donny 1945–1979 **18**
Hathaway, Isaac Scott 1874–1967 **33**
Hathaway, Lalah 1969— **57**
Haughton, Aaliyah *See Aaliyah*
Hawkins, Adrienne Lita *See Kennedy, Adrienne*
Hawkins, Augustus F. 1907–2007 **68**
Hawkins, Coleman 1904–1969 **9**
Hawkins, Erskine Ramsey 1914–1993 **14**
Hawkins, Jamesetta *See James, Etta*
Hawkins, La-Van 1960— **17, 54**
Hawkins, "Screamin'" Jay 1929–2000 **30**
Hawkins, Steven Wayne 1962— **14**
Hawkins, Tramaine Aunzola 1951— **16**
Hawkins, Walter 1949–2010 **87**
Hayden, Carla D. 1952— **47**
Hayden, Palmer 1890–1973 **13**
Hayden, Robert Earl 1913–1980 **12**
Haye, David 1980— **82**
Hayes, Bob 1942–2002 **77**
Hayes, Cecil N. 1945— **46**
Hayes, Dennis 1951— **54**
Hayes, Isaac 1942–2008 **20, 58, 73**
Hayes, James C. 1946— **10**
Hayes, Robert Lee *See Hayes, Bob*
Hayes, Roland 1887–1977 **4**
Hayes, Teddy 1951— **40**

Haygood, Wil 1954— **83**
Haynes, Cornell, Jr. *See Nelly*
Haynes, George Edmund 1880–1960 **8**
Haynes, Marques 1926— **22**
Haynes, Roy 1925— **87**
Haynes, Trudy 1926— **44**
Haysbert, Dennis 1955— **42**
Haysbert, Raymond V., Sr. 1920–2010 **87**
Haywood, Gar Anthony 1954— **43**
Haywood, Jimmy 1993(?)— **58**
Haywood, Margaret A. 1912— **24**
Hazel, Darryl B. 1949— **50**
Head, Bessie 1937–1986 **28**
Healy, James Augustine 1830–1900 **30**
Heard, Gar 1948— **25**
Heard, Nathan C. 1936–2004 **45**
Hearne, John Edgar Caulwell 1926–1994 **45**
Hearns, Thomas 1958— **29**
Heavy D 1967— **58**
Hedgeman, Anna Arnold 1899–1990 **22**
Hedgeman, Peyton Cole *See Hayden, Palmer*
Height, Dorothy I. 1912— **2, 23, 78**
Hemphill, Essex 1957— **10**
Hemphill, Jessie Mae 1923–2006 **33, 59**
Hemsley, Sherman 1938— **19**
Henderson, Cornelius Langston 1888(?)–1976 **26**
Henderson, David 1942— **53**
Henderson, Fletcher 1897–1952 **32**
Henderson, Gordon 1957— **5**
Henderson, Jeff 1964— **72**
Henderson, Natalie Leota *See Hinderas, Natalie*
Henderson, Rickey 1958— **28, 78**
Henderson, Stephen E. 1925–1997 **45**
Henderson, Thelton E. 1933— **68**
Henderson, Wade 1944(?)— **14**
Henderson, Zelma 1920–2008 **71**
Hendricks, Barbara 1948— **3, 67**
Hendrix, James Marshall *See Hendrix, Jimi*
Hendrix, Jimi 1942–1970 **10**
Hendrix, Johnny Allen *See Hendrix, Jimi*
Hendryx, Nona 1944— **56**
Hendy, Francis 195(?)— **47**
Henries, A. Doris Banks 1913–1981 **44**
Henriques, Julian 1955(?)— **37**
Henry, Aaron Edd 1922–1997 **19**
Henry, Clarence "Frogman" 1937— **46**
Henry, Lenny 1958— **9, 52**
Henry, Richard Bullock *See Obadele, Imari*
Henry, Thierry 1977— **66**
Henry, Troy 1960(?)— **85**
Henson, Darrin 1970(?)— **33**
Henson, Matthew (Alexander) 1866–1955 **2**
Henson, Taraji P. 1970— **58, 77**
Herbert, Bob 1945— **63**
Hercules, Frank 1911–1996 **44**
Herenton, Willie W. 1940— **24, 81**
Herman, Alexis Margaret 1947— **15**

Hernandez, Aileen Clarke 1926— **13**
Hernton, Calvin C. 1932–2001 **51**
Hickman, Fred(erick Douglass) 1951— **11**
Hicks Maynard, Nancy *See Maynard, Nancy Hicks*
Higginbotham, A(loyisus) Leon, Jr. 1928–1998 **13, 25**
Higginbotham, Jack *See Higginbotham, Jay C.*
Higginbotham, Jay C. 1906–1973 **37**
Higginsen, Vy 1945(?)— **65**
Hightower, Dennis F(owler) 1941— **13**
Hill, Andrew 1931–2007 **66**
Hill, Anita 1956— **5, 65**
Hill, Beatrice *See Moore, Melba*
Hill, Bonnie Guiton 1941— **20**
Hill, Calvin 1947— **19**
Hill, Donna 1955— **32**
Hill, Dulé 1975(?)— **29**
Hill, Errol 1921— **40**
Hill, Grant (Henry) 1972— **13**
Hill, Hugh Morgan 1921–2009 **83**
Hill, Janet 1947— **19**
Hill, Jesse, Jr. 1927— **13**
Hill, Lauryn 1975— **20, 53**
Hill, Leslie Pinckney 1880–1960 **44**
Hill, Marc Lamont 1978— **80**
Hill, Oliver W. 1907–2007 **24, 63**
Hill, Tamia *See Tamia*
Hillard, Terry 1954— **25**
Hillary, Barbara 1923(?)— **65**
Hilliard, Asa Grant, III 1933–2007 **66**
Hilliard, David 1942— **7**
Hilliard, Earl F. 1942— **24**
Hilliard, Wendy 196(?)— **53**
Hilson, Keri 1982— **84**
Himes, Chester 1909–1984 **8**
Hinderas, Natalie 1927–1987 **5**
Hine, Darlene Clark 1947— **24**
Hines, Earl "Fatha" 1905–1983 **39**
Hines, Garrett 1969— **35**
Hines, Gregory (Oliver) 1946–2003 **1, 42**
Hinton, Milt 1910–2000 **30**
Hinton, William Augustus 1883–1959 **8**
Hoagland, Everett H. 1942— **45**
Hoagland, Jaheim *See Jaheim*
Hobson, Julius W. 1919–1977 **44**
Hobson, Mellody 1969— **40**
Hogan, Beverly Wade 1951— **50**
Holder, Eric H., Jr. 1951— **9, 76**
Holder, Geoffrey 1930— **78**
Holder, Laurence 1939— **34**
Holdsclaw, Chamique 1977— **24**
Holiday, Billie 1915–1959 **1**
Holland, Brian *See Holland-Dozier-Holland*
Holland, Eddie *See Holland-Dozier-Holland*
Holland, Endesha Ida Mae 1944–2006 **3, 57**
Holland, Kimberly N. 19(?)(?)— **62**
Holland, Robert, Jr. 1940— **11**
Holland-Dozier-Holland **36**
Holloway, Brenda 1946— **65**
Hollowell, Donald L. 1917–2004 **57**
Holmes, Amy 1973— **69**
Holmes, Clint 1946— **57**

Holmes, Hamilton E. 1941–1995 **82**
Holmes, Kelly 1970— **47**
Holmes, Larry 1949— **20, 68**
Holmes, Santonio 1984— **87**
Holmes, Shannon 1973(?)— **70**
Holt, Lester 1959— **66**
Holt, Nora 1885(?)–1974 **38**
Holt Baker, Arlene 1951— **73**
Holte, Patricia Louise *See LaBelle, Patti*
Holton, Hugh, Jr. 1947–2001 **39**
Holyfield, Evander 1962— **6**
Honeywood, Varnette P. 1950— **54**
Honoré, Russel L. 1947— **64**
Hooker, John Lee 1917–2000 **30**
hooks, bell 1952— **5**
Hooks, Benjamin L. 1925–2010 **2, 85**
Hooks, Robert 1937— **76**
Hope, John 1868–1936 **8**
Hopgood, Hadda *See Brooks, Hadda*
Hopkins, Bernard 1965— **35, 69**
Hopkins, Lightnin' 1912–1982 **83**
Hopkins, Sam *See Hopkins, Lightnin'*
Horn, Shirley 1934–2005 **32, 56**
Horne, Frank 1899–1974 **44**
Horne, Lena 1917–2010 **5, 86**
Horton, Andre 1979— **33**
Horton, James Oliver 1943— **58**
Horton, (Andreana) "Suki" 1982— **33**
Hounsou, Djimon 1964— **19, 45**
Houphouët, Dia *See Houphouët-Boigny, Félix*
Houphouët-Boigny, Félix 1905–1993 **4, 64**
House, Eddie James, Jr. *See House, Son*
House, Eugene *See House, Son*
House, Son 1902–1988 **8**
Houston, Charles Hamilton 1895–1950 **4**
Houston, Cissy 1933— **20, 83**
Houston, Whitney 1963— **7, 28, 83**
Howard, Ayanna 1972— **65**
Howard, Corinne *See Mitchell, Corinne*
Howard, Desmond 1970— **16, 58**
Howard, Juwan Antonio 1973— **15**
Howard, M. William, Jr. 1946— **26**
Howard, Michelle 1960— **28**
Howard, Ryan 1979— **65**
Howard, Sherri 1962— **36**
Howard, Terrence Dashon 1969— **59**
Howlin' Wolf 1910–1976 **9**
Howroyd, Janice Bryant 1953— **42**
Hoyte, Lenon 1905–1999 **50**
Hrabowski, Freeman A., III 1950— **22**
Hubbard, Arnette 19(?)(?)— **38**
Hubbard, Freddie 1948–2008 **75**
Hubbard, Frederick DeWayne *See Hubbard, Freddie*
Hudlin, Reginald 1961— **9, 86**
Hudlin, Warrington, Jr. 1953(?)— **9**
Hudson, Cheryl 19(?)(?)— **15**
Hudson, Ernie 1945— **72**
Hudson, Jennifer 1981— **63, 83**
Hudson, Saul *See Slash*
Hudson, Wade 1946— **15**
Huff, Leon 1942— **86**

Huggins, Edie 1935–2008 **71**
Huggins, Larry 1950— **21**
Huggins, Nathan Irvin 1927–1989 **52**
Hughes, Albert 1972— **7**
Hughes, Allen 1972— **7**
Hughes, Cathy 1947(?)— **27**
Hughes, Ebony 1948— **57**
Hughes, (James Mercer) Langston 1902–1967 **4**
Hughley, D. L. 1963— **23, 76**
Hughley, Darryl Lynn *See Hughley, D. L.*
Hull, Akasha Gloria 1944— **45**
Humphrey, Bobbi 1950— **20**
Humphries, Frederick 1935— **20**
Hunt, Richard (Howard) 1935— **6**
Hunter, Alberta 1895–1984 **42**
Hunter, Billy 1943— **22**
Hunter, Charlayne *See Hunter-Gault, Charlayne*
Hunter, Clementine 1887–1988 **45**
Hunter, George William *See Hunter, Billy*
Hunter, Torii 1975— **43**
Hunter-Gault, Charlayne 1942— **6, 31**
Hurston, Zora Neale 1891–1960 **3**
Hurt, Byron 1970— **61**
Hurt, Mississippi John 1892(?)—1966 **84**
Hurtt, Harold 1947(?)— **46**
Hussein, Lubna 1970(?)— **80**
Hutch, Willie 1944–2005 **62**
Hutcherson, Hilda Yvonne 1955— **54**
Hutchinson, Earl Ofari 1945— **24**
Hutson, Jean Blackwell 1914— **16**
Hyde, Cowan F. "Bubba" 1908–2003 **47**
Hyman, Earle 1926— **25, 79**
Hyman, Phyllis 1949(?)–1995 **19**
Ibrahim, Mo 1946— **67**
Ice Cube 1969— **8, 30, 60**
Iceberg Slim 1918–1992 **11**
Ice-T 1958(?)— **6, 31**
Ifill, Gwen 1955— **28**
Iginla, Jarome 1977— **35**
Ilibagiza, Immaculée 1972(?)— **66**
Iman 1955— **4, 33, 87**
Iman, Chanel 1989— **66**
Imes, Elmer Samuel 1883–1941 **39**
Ince, Paul 1967— **83**
India.Arie 1975— **34**
Ingraham, Hubert A. 1947— **19**
Ingram, James 1952— **84**
Ingram, Rex 1895–1969 **5**
Innis, Roy (Emile Alfredo) 1934— **5**
Irvin, Michael 1966— **64**
Irvin, (Monford Merrill) Monte 1919— **31**
Irvin, Vernon 1961— **65**
Irving, Clarence (Larry) 1955— **12**
Irvis, K. Leroy 1917(?)–2006 **67**
Isaac, Julius 1928— **34**
Isaacs, John 1915–2009 **76**
Isley, Marvin 1953–2010 **87**
Isley, Ronald 1941— **25, 56**
Iverson, Allen 1975— **24, 46**
Ivey, Phil 1976— **72**
Ja Rule 1976— **35**
Jackson, Alexine Clement 1936— **22**
Jackson, Alphonso R. 1946— **48**

Jackson, Brenda 1953— **87**
Jackson, Earl 1948— **31**
Jackson, Edison O. 1943(?)— **67**
Jackson, Frank G. 1946— **76**
Jackson, Fred James 1950— **25**
Jackson, George 1960(?)— **19**
Jackson, George Lester 1941–1971 **14**
Jackson, Hal 1915— **41**
Jackson, Isaiah (Allen) 1945— **3**
Jackson, Jamea 1986— **64**
Jackson, James Curtis, III *See 50 Cent*
Jackson, Janet 1966— **6, 30, 68**
Jackson, Jermaine 1954— **79**
Jackson, Jesse 1941— **1, 27, 72**
Jackson, Jesse, Jr. 1965— **14, 45, 81**
Jackson, Joe 1929— **78**
Jackson, John 1924–2002 **36**
Jackson, Judith D. 1950— **57**
Jackson, Lisa 1962— **77**
Jackson, Mae 1941–2005 **57**
Jackson, Mahalia 1911–1972 **5**
Jackson, Mannie 1939— **14**
Jackson, Mary 1945— **73**
Jackson, Maynard (Holbrook, Jr.) 1938–2003 **2, 41**
Jackson, Michael 1958–2009 **19, 53, 76**
Jackson, Millie 1944— **25**
Jackson, Milt 1923–1999 **26**
Jackson, O'Shea *See Ice Cube*
Jackson, Quinton *See Jackson, Rampage*
Jackson, Rampage 1978— **83**
Jackson, Randy 1956— **40**
Jackson, Reginald Martinez 1946— **15**
Jackson, Samuel 1948— **8, 19, 63**
Jackson, Sheneska 1970(?)— **18**
Jackson, Shirley Ann 1946— **12**
Jackson, Tito 1953— **81**
Jackson, Tom 1951— **70**
Jackson, Vera 1912— **40**
Jackson, Vivian *See Yabby You*
Jackson, Zelda Mavin *See Ormes, Jackie*
Jackson Lee, Sheila 1950— **20**
Jaco, Wasalu Muhammad *See Fiasco, Lupe*
Jacob, John E(dward) 1934— **2**
Jacobs, Marion Walter *See Little Walter*
Jacobs, Regina 1963— **38**
Jacquet, Illinois 1922(?)–2004 **49**
Jagan, Cheddi 1918–1997 **16**
Jaheim 1978— **58**
Jakes, Thomas "T.D." 1957— **17, 43**
Jam, Jimmy *See Jimmy Jam*
Jam Master Jay *See Run-DMC*
Jamal, Ahmad 1930— **69**
Jamelia 1981— **51**
Jamerson, James 1936–1983 **59**
James, Charles H., III 1959(?)— **62**
James, Daniel "Chappie," Jr. 1920–1978 **16**
James, David 1970— **84**
James, Donna A. 1957— **51**
James, Etta 1938— **13, 52**
James, G. Larry 1947–2008 **74**
James, Juanita (Therese) 1952— **13**

James, LeBron 1984— **46, 78**
James, Marlon 1970— **85**
James, Sharpe 1936— **23, 69**
James, Skip 1902–1969 **38**
James, Vanessa 1987— **84**
Jamison, Judith 1943— **7, 67**
Jammeh, Yahya 1965— **23**
Jarreau, Al 1940— **21, 65**
Jarrett, Valerie 1956— **73**
Jarrett, Vernon D. 1921— **42**
Jarvis, Charlene Drew 1941— **21**
Jarvis, Erich 1965— **67**
Jarvis, Kristen 1981(?)— **85**
Jasper, Kenji 1976(?)— **39**
Jawara, Dawda Kairaba 1924— **11**
Jay-Z 1970— **27, 69**
Jealous, Benjamin 1973— **70**
Jean, Michaëlle 1957— **70**
Jean, Wyclef 1970— **20, 86**
Jean-Baptiste, Marianne 1967— **17, 46**
Jean-Juste, Gérard 1946–2009 **78**
Jean-Louis, Jimmy 1968— **76**
Jeffers, Eve Jihan *See Eve*
Jefferson, Blind Lemon 1893(?)–1929 **81**
Jefferson, Denise 1944–2010 **87**
Jefferson, William J. 1947— **25, 72**
Jeffries, Leonard 1937— **8**
Jemison, Mae C. 1957— **1, 35**
Jemison, Major L. 1955(?)— **48**
Jenifer, Franklyn G(reen) 1939— **2**
Jenkins, Beverly 1951— **14**
Jenkins, Ella (Louise) 1924— **15**
Jenkins, Fergie 1943— **46**
Jenkins, Jay *See Young Jeezy*
Jenkins, Ray 1920–2009 **77**
Jennings, Chester *See Jennings, Lyfe*
Jennings, Lyfe 1973— **56, 69**
Jerkins, Rodney 1978(?)— **31**
Jeter, Claude 1914–2009 **75**
Jeter, Derek 1974— **27**
Jimmy Jam 1959— **13**
Joachim, Paulin 1931— **34**
Joe, Yolanda 19(?)(?)— **21**
John, Daymond 1969(?)— **23**
Johns, Vernon 1892–1965 **38**
Johnson, Angela 1961— **52**
Johnson, Arnez *See Arnez J*
Johnson, Avery 1965— **62**
Johnson, Ben 1961— **1**
Johnson, Beverly 1952— **2**
Johnson, Buddy 1915–1977 **36**
Johnson, Carol Diann *See Carroll, Diahann*
Johnson, Caryn E. *See Goldberg, Whoopi*
Johnson, Charles 1948— **1, 82**
Johnson, Charles Arthur *See St. Jacques, Raymond*
Johnson, Charles Spurgeon 1893–1956 **12**
Johnson, Clifford "Connie" 1922–2004 **52**
Johnson, Dwayne *See Rock, The*
Johnson, Earvin "Magic" 1959— **3, 39**
Johnson, Eddie Bernice 1935— **8**
Johnson, Eunice W. 1916–2010 **83**
Johnson, George E. 1927— **29**
Johnson, Georgia Douglas 1880–1966 **41**

Johnson, Hank, Jr. 1954— **80**
Johnson, Harry E. 1954— **57**
Johnson, Harvey, Jr. 1947(?)— **24, 82**
Johnson, Hazel 1927— **22**
Johnson, J. J. 1924–2001 **37**
Johnson, Jack 1878–1946 **8**
Johnson, James Louis *See Johnson, J. J.*
Johnson, James Weldon 1871–1938 **5**
Johnson, James William *See Johnson, James Weldon*
Johnson, Je'Caryous 1977— **63**
Johnson, Jeh C. 1957— **76**
Johnson, Jeh Vincent 1931— **44**
Johnson, John Arthur *See Johnson, Jack*
Johnson, John H. 1918–2005 **3, 54**
Johnson, Johnnie 1924–2005 **56**
Johnson, Katherine (Coleman Goble) 1918— **61**
Johnson, Kevin 1966— **70**
Johnson, Larry 1969— **28**
Johnson, Levi 1950— **48**
Johnson, Linton Kwesi 1952— **37**
Johnson, Lonnie 1899(?)–1970 **85**
Johnson, Lonnie G. 1949— **32**
Johnson, "Magic" *See Johnson, Earvin "Magic"*
Johnson, Mamie "Peanut" 1932— **40**
Johnson, Marguerite *See Angelou, Maya*
Johnson, Mat 1971(?)— **31**
Johnson, Michael (Duane) 1967— **13**
Johnson, Michelle *See Ndegeocello, Meshell*
Johnson, Mordecai Wyatt 1890–1976 **79**
Johnson, Norma L. Holloway 1932— **17**
Johnson, R. M. 1968— **36**
Johnson, Rafer 1934— **33**
Johnson, Robert 1911–1938 **2**
Johnson, Robert L. 1946(?)— **3, 39**
Johnson, Robert T. 1948— **17**
Johnson, Rodney Van 19(?)(?)— **28**
Johnson, Sheila Crump 1949(?)— **48**
Johnson, Shoshana 1973— **47**
Johnson, Taalib *See Musiq*
Johnson, Virginia (Alma Fairfax) 1950— **9**
Johnson, William Henry 1901–1970 **3**
Johnson, Woodrow Wilson *See Johnson, Buddy*
Johnson, Wyclffe *See Steely*
Johnson-Brown, Hazel W. *See Johnson, Hazel*
Johnson-George, Tamara 1971— **79**
Joiner, Alvin Nathaniel *See Xzibit*
Jolley, Willie 1956— **28**
Jonathan, Goodluck 1957— **83**
Jones, Absalom 1746–1818 **52**
Jones, Alex 1941— **64**
Jones, Anthony *See Jones, Van*
Jones, Bill T. 1952— **1, 46, 80**
Jones, Bob *See Jones, Robert G.*
Jones, Bobby 1939(?)— **20**

Jones, Booker T. 1944— **84**
Jones, Carl 1955(?)— **7**
Jones, Caroline R. 1942— **29**
Jones, Clara Stanton 1913— **51**
Jones, Cobi N'Gai 1970— **18**
Jones, Cullen 1984— **73**
Jones, Donell 1973— **29**
Jones, Doris W. 1914(?)–2006 **62**
Jones, E. Edward, Sr. 1931— **45**
Jones, Ed "Too Tall" 1951— **46**
Jones, Edith Mae Irby 1927— **65**
Jones, Edward P. 1950— **43, 67**
Jones, Elaine R. 1944— **7, 45**
Jones, Elvin 1927–2004 **14, 68**
Jones, Emil, Jr. 1935— **74**
Jones, Etta 1928–2001 **35**
Jones, Eugene Kinckle 1885–1954 **79**
Jones, Frederick McKinley 1893–1961 **68**
Jones, Frederick Russell *See Jamal, Ahmad*
Jones, Gayl 1949— **37**
Jones, Hank 1918–2010 **57, 86**
Jones, Ingrid Saunders 1945— **18**
Jones, James Earl 1931— **3, 49, 79**
Jones, Jonah 1909–2000 **39**
Jones, K. C. 1932— **83**
Jones, Kelis *See Kelis*
Jones, Kimberly Denise *See Lil' Kim*
Jones, Kirk *See Sticky Fingaz*
Jones, Le Roi *See Baraka, Amiri*
Jones, Lillie Mae *See Carter, Betty*
Jones, Lois Mailou 1905— **13**
Jones, Lou 1932–2006 **64**
Jones, Marion 1975— **21, 66**
Jones, Merlakia 1973— **34**
Jones, Monty 1951(?)— **66**
Jones, Nasir *See Nas*
Jones, Orlando 1968— **30**
Jones, Paul R. 1928— **76**
Jones, Quincy (Delight) 1933— **8, 30**
Jones, Randy 1969— **35**
Jones, Robert Elliott *See Jones, Jonah*
Jones, Robert G. 1936–2008 **81**
Jones, Roy Jr. 1969— **22**
Jones, Russell *See Ol' Dirty Bastard*
Jones, Ruth Lee *See Washington, Dinah*
Jones, Sam 1933— **85**
Jones, Sarah 1974— **39**
Jones, Sharon 1955(?)— **86**
Jones, Sissieretta *See Joyner, Matilda Sissieretta*
Jones, Star *See Reynolds, Star Jones*
Jones, Thad 1923–1986 **68**
Jones, Thomas W. 1949— **41**
Jones, Van 1968— **70**
Jones, Wayne 1952— **53**
Jones, William A., Jr. 1934–2006 **61**
Joplin, Scott 1868–1917 **6**
Jordan, Barbara 1936–1996 **4, 78**
Jordan, Eddie 1952— **82**
Jordan, Eddie 1955— **83**
Jordan, Eric Benét *See Benét, Eric*
Jordan, June 1936— **7, 35**

Jordan, Michael (Jeffrey) 1963— **6, 21**
Jordan, Montell 1968(?)— **23**
Jordan, Ronny 1962— **26**
Jordan, Vernon E(ulion, Jr.) 1935— **3, 35**
Jorge, Seu 1970— **73**
Joseph, Kathie-Ann 1970(?)— **56**
Josey, E. J. 1924— **10**
Joyce, Dru 1955— **81**
Joyner, Jacqueline *See Joyner-Kersee, Jackie*
Joyner, Marjorie Stewart 1896–1994 **26**
Joyner, Matilda Sissieretta 1869(?)–1933 **15**
Joyner, Tom 1949(?)— **19**
Joyner-Kersee, Jackie 1962— **5**
Julian, Percy Lavon 1899–1975 **6**
Julien, Isaac 1960— **3**
July, William II 19(?)(?)— **27**
Juma, Calestous 1953— **57**
Just, Ernest Everett 1883–1941 **3**
Justice, David Christopher 1966— **18**
Ka Dinizulu, Israel *See Ka Dinizulu, Mcwayizeni*
Ka Dinizulu, Mcwayizeni 1932–1999 **29**
Kabbah, Ahmad Tejan 1932— **23**
Kabila, Joseph 1968(?)— **30**
Kabila, Laurent 1939— **20**
Kagame, Paul 1957— **54**
Kaigler, Denise 1962— **63**
Kaiser, Cecil 1916— **42**
Kalbani, Adil 1959(?)— **77**
Kamau, Johnstone *See Kenyatta, Jomo*
Kamau, Kwadwo Agymah 1960(?)— **28**
Kandi 1976— **83**
Kani, Karl 1968(?)— **10**
Kanouté, Fred 1977— **68**
Karenga, Maulana 1941— **10, 71**
Karim, Benjamin 1932–2005 **61**
Kariuki, J. M. 1929–1975 **67**
Kassahun, Tewodros *See Afro, Teddy*
Katoucha *See Niane, Katoucha*
Kaufman, Monica 1948(?)— **66**
Kaunda, Kenneth (David) 1924— **2**
Kay, Jackie 1961— **37**
Kay, Ulysses 1917–1995 **37**
Kayira, Legson 1942— **40**
Kearney, Janis 1953— **54**
Kearse, Amalya Lyle 1937— **12**
Kebede, Liya 1978— **59**
Kee, John P. 1962— **43**
Keene, John 1965— **73**
Keflezighi, Meb 1975— **49**
Keita, Salif 1949— **83**
Keith, Damon J. 1922— **16, 74**
Keith, Floyd A. 1948— **61**
Keith, Rachel Boone 1924–2007 **63**
Kelis 1979— **58**
Kelley, Cliff 1941— **75**
Kelley, Elijah 1986— **65**
Kelley, Malcolm David 1992— **59**
Kellogg, Clark 1961— **64**
Kelly, Leontine 1920— **33**
Kelly, Patrick 1954(?)–1990 **3**
Kelly, R. 1967— **18, 44, 71**
Kelly, Robert Sylvester *See Kelly, R.*

Kelly, Sharon Pratt *See Dixon, Sharon Pratt*
Kem 196(?)— **47**
Kendrick, Erika 1975— **57**
Kendricks, Eddie 1939–1992 **22**
Kennard, William Earl 1957— **18**
Kennedy, Adrienne 1931— **11**
Kennedy, Florynce Rae 1916–2000 **12, 33**
Kennedy, Lelia McWilliams Robinson 1885–1931 **14**
Kennedy, Randall 1954— **40**
Kennedy-Overton, Jayne Harris 1951— **46**
Kenney, John A., Jr. 1914–2003 **48**
Kenoly, Ron 1944— **45**
Kente, Gibson 1932–2004 **52**
Kenyatta, Jomo 1891(?)–1978 **5**
Kenyatta, Robin 1942–2004 **54**
Kerekou, Ahmed (Mathieu) 1933— **1**
Kerry, Leon G. 1949(?)— **46**
Keyes, Alan L(ee) 1950— **11**
Keys, Alicia 1981— **32, 68**
Khan, Chaka 1953— **12, 50**
Khanga, Yelena 1962— **6**
Khumalo, Leleti 1970— **51**
Kibaki, Mwai 1931— **60**
Kid Cudi 1984— **83**
Kidd, Jason 1973— **86**
Kidd, Mae Street 1904–1995 **39**
Kidjo, Angelique 1960— **50**
Kiir, Salva 1951— **85**
Kikwete, Jakaya Mrisho 1950— **73**
Killens, John O. 1967–1987 **54**
Killings, Debra 196(?)— **57**
Killingsworth, Cleve, Jr. 1952— **54**
Kilpatrick, Carolyn Cheeks 1945— **16**
Kilpatrick, Kwame 1970— **34, 71**
Kimbro, Dennis (Paul) 1950— **10**
Kimbro, Henry A. 1912–1999 **25**
Kimbro, Warren 1934–2009 **76**
Kincaid, Bernard 1945— **28**
Kincaid, Jamaica 1949— **4**
King, Alonzo 19(?)(?)— **38**
King, B. B. 1925— **7**
King, Barbara 19(?)(?)— **22**
King, Bernice 1963— **4, 81**
King, Colbert I. 1939— **69**
King, Coretta Scott 1927–2006 **3, 57**
King, Dexter (Scott) 1961— **10**
King, Don 1931— **14**
King, Gayle 1956— **19**
King, Martin Luther, III 1957— **20**
King, Martin Luther, Jr. 1929–1968 **1**
King, Oona 1967— **27**
King, Preston 1936— **28**
King, Reatha Clark 1938— **65**
King, Regina 1971— **22, 45**
King, Riley B. *See King, B. B.*
King, Robert Arthur 1945— **58**
King, Robert Hillary 1942— **84**
King, Teresa 1961— **80**
King, Woodie Jr. 1937— **27**
King, Yolanda (Denise) 1955— **6**
Kintaudi, Leon 1949(?)— **62**
Kintaudi, Ngoma Miezi *See Kintaudi, Leon*
Kirby, George 1924–1995 **14**
Kirk, Ron 1954— **11, 75**

Kitt, Eartha 1927–2008 **16, 75**

Kitt, Sandra 1947— **23**

Kittles, Rick 1976(?)— **51**

Kitwana, Bakari 19(?)(?)— **86**

Klugh, Earl 1953— **59**

K'naan 1978— **76**

Knight, Etheridge 1931–1991 **37**

Knight, Gladys 1944— **16, 66**

Knight, Gwendolyn 1913–2005 **63**

Knight, Marie 1925(?)–2009 **80**

Knight, Marion, Jr. See Knight, Suge

Knight, Suge 1966— **11, 30**

Knowles, Beyoncé See Beyoncé

Knowles, Tina 1954(?)— **61**

Knowling, Robert Jr. 1955(?)— **38**

Knox, Simmie 1935— **49**

Knuckles, Frankie 1955— **42**

Kobia, Samuel 1947— **43**

Kodjoe, Boris 1973— **34**

Kolosoy, Wendo 1925–2008 **73**

Komunyakaa, Yusef 1941— **9**

Kone, Seydou See Blondy, Alpha

Kong, B. Waine 1943— **50**

Kool DJ Red Alert See Alert, Kool DJ Red

Kool Moe Dee 1963— **37**

Koroma, Ernest Bai 1953— **84**

Kotto, Yaphet (Fredrick) 1944— **7**

Kountz, Samuel L(ee) 1930–1981 **10**

Kravitz, Lenny 1964— **10, 34**

Kravitz, Leonard See Kravitz, Lenny

KRS-One 1965— **34**

Krute, Fred See Alert, Kool DJ Red

K-Swift 1978–2008 **73**

Kufuor, John Agyekum 1938— **54, 82**

Kunjufu, Jawanza 1953— **3, 50**

Kuti, Fela Anikulapo See Fela

Kuti, Femi 1962— **47**

Kuzwayo, Ellen 1914–2006 **68**

Kwei-Armah, Kwame 1967— **84**

Kyles, Cedric See Cedric the Entertainer

La Menthe, Ferdinand Joseph See Morton, Jelly Roll

La Salle, Eriq 1962— **12**

LaBelle, Patti 1944— **13, 30**

Lacy, Sam 1903–2003 **30, 46**

Ladd, Ernie 1938–2007 **64**

Ladner, Joyce A. 1943— **42**

Laferriere, Dany 1953— **33**

Lafontant, Jewel Stradford 1922–1997 **3, 51**

Lafontant-MANkarious, Jewel Stradford See Lafontant, Jewel Stradford

LaGuma, Alex 1925–1985 **30**

Lamming, George 1927— **35**

Lampkin, Daisy 1883(?)–1965 **19**

Lampley, Oni Faida 1959–2008 **43, 71**

Lampley, Vera See Lampley, Oni Faida

Lane, Charles 1953— **3**

Lane, Vincent 1942— **5**

Langford, Larry P. 1948— **74**

Langhart Cohen, Janet 1941— **19, 60**

Lanier, Bob 1948— **47**

Lanier, Willie 1945— **33**

Lankford, Raymond Lewis 1967— **23**

Laraque, Georges 1976— **48**

Laraque, Paul 1920–2007 **67**

Larkin, Barry 1964— **24**

Laroche, Joseph Philippe Lemercier 1889–1912 **85**

Larrieux, Amel 1973(?)— **63**

Lars, Byron 1965— **32**

Larsen, Nella 1891–1964 **10**

Laryea, Thomas Davies III 1979— **67**

Lashley, Bobby 1976— **63**

Lashley, Franklin Roberto See Lashley, Bobby

Lassiter, Roy 1969— **24**

Lathan, Sanaa 1971— **27**

Latimer, Lewis H(oward) 1848–1928 **4**

Lattimore, Kenny 1970(?)— **35**

LaVette, Bettye 1946— **85**

Lavizzo-Mourey, Risa 1954— **48**

Lawal, Kase L. 19(?)(?)— **45**

Lawless, Theodore K(enneth) 1892–1971 **8**

Lawrence, Jacob (Armstead) 1917–2000 **4, 28**

Lawrence, Martin 1965— **6, 27, 60**

Lawrence, Robert Henry, Jr. 1935–1967 **16**

Lawrence-Lightfoot, Sara 1944— **10**

Lawson, Jennifer 1946— **1, 50**

Layton, William 1915–2007 **87**

Leadbelly 1885–1949 **82**

Leary, Kathryn D. 1952— **10**

Leavell, Dorothy R. 1944— **17**

Ledbetter, Hudson William See Leadbelly

Ledisi 197(?)— **73**

Lee, Annie Frances 1935— **22**

Lee, Barbara 1946— **25**

Lee, Bertram M., Sr. 1939–2003 **46**

Lee, Canada 1907–1952 **8**

Lee, Consuela 1926–2009 **84**

Lee, Debra L. 1954— **62**

Lee, Don Luther See Madhubuti, Haki R.

Lee, Eric P. 1958— **79**

Lee, Gabby See Lincoln, Abbey

Lee, Joe A. 1946(?)— **45**

Lee, Joie 1962(?)— **1**

Lee, Leslie 1935— **85**

Lee, Malcolm D. 1970— **75**

Lee, Raphael C. 1949— **87**

Lee, Shelton Jackson See Lee, Spike

Lee, Spike 1957— **5, 19, 86**

Lee-Smith, Hughie 1915— **5, 22**

Leevy, Carrol M. 1920— **42**

Lefel, Edith 1963–2003 **41**

Leffall, Lasalle, Jr. 1930— **3, 64**

Legend, John 1978— **67**

Leggs, Kingsley 196(?)— **62**

Leland, George Thomas See Leland, Mickey

Leland, Mickey 1944–1989 **2**

Lemmons, Kasi 1961— **20**

Lennox, Betty 1976— **31**

LeNoire, Rosetta 1911–2002 **37**

Lenox, Adriane 1956— **59**

Leon, Kenny 1957(?)— **10**

León, Tania 1943— **13**

Leonard, Buck 1907— **67**

Leonard, Sugar Ray 1956— **15**

Leonard, Walter Fenner See Leonard, Buck

Leslie, Lisa 1972— **16, 73**

Lester, Adrian 1968— **46**

Lester, Bill 1961— **42, 85**

Lester, Julius 1939— **9**

Lesure, James 1975— **64**

LeTang, Henry 1915–2007 **66**

Letson, Al 1972— **39**

Levert, Eddie 1942— **70**

Levert, Gerald 1966–2006 **22, 59**

Lewis, Aylwin 1954(?)— **51**

Lewis, Butch 1946— **71**

Lewis, Byron E(ugene) 1931— **13**

Lewis, (Frederick) Carl(ton) 1961— **4**

Lewis, Daurene 194(?)— **72**

Lewis, David Levering 1936— **9**

Lewis, Delano (Eugene) 1938— **7**

Lewis, Denise 1972— **33**

Lewis, (Mary) Edmonia 1845(?)–1911(?) **10**

Lewis, Edward T. 1940— **21**

Lewis, Emmanuel 1971— **36**

Lewis, Henry 1932–1996 **38**

Lewis, John 1940— **2, 46, 83**

Lewis, Lennox 1965— **27**

Lewis, Leona 1985— **75**

Lewis, Marvin 1958— **51, 87**

Lewis, Norman 1909–1979 **39**

Lewis, Oliver 1856–1924 **56**

Lewis, Ramsey 1935— **35, 70**

Lewis, Ray 1975— **33**

Lewis, Reginald F. 1942–1993 **6**

Lewis, Ronald See Lewis, Butch

Lewis, Samella 1924— **25**

Lewis, Shirley Ann Redd 1937— **14**

Lewis, Terry 1956— **13**

Lewis, Thomas 1939— **19**

Lewis, William M., Jr. 1956— **40**

Lewis-Thornton, Rae 1962— **32**

Ligging, Alfred III 1965— **43**

Ligon, Glenn 1960— **82**

Lil' Bow Wow See Bow Wow

Lil' Kim 1975— **28**

Lil Wayne 1982— **66, 84**

Lilakoi Moon See Bonet, Lisa

Liles, Kevin 1968— **42**

Lincoln, Abbey 1930— **3**

Lincoln, C(harles) Eric 1924–2000 **38**

Lindo, Allen Pineda See apl.de.ap

Lindo, Delroy 1952— **18, 45**

Lindsey, Tommie 1951— **51**

Lipscomb, Mance 1895–1976 **49**

LisaRaye 1967— **27**

Lister, Marquita 1965(?) **65**

Liston, (Charles) Sonny 1928(?)–1970 **33**

Little, Benilde 1958— **21**

Little, Floyd 1942— **86**

Little, Malcolm See X, Malcolm

Little, Robert L(angdon) 1938— **2**

Little Milton 1934–2005 **36, 54**

Little Richard 1932— **15**

Little Walter 1930–1968 **36**

Little Warrior See Barrow, Willie T.

Littlepage, Craig 1951— **35**

LL Cool J 1968— **16, 49**

Llewellyn, J. Bruce 1927–2010 **13, 85**

Lloyd, Earl 1928(?)— **26**

Lloyd, John Henry "Pop" 1884–1965 **30**

Lloyd, Reginald 1967— **64**

Locke, Alain (LeRoy) 1886–1954 **10**

Locke, Attica 1974— **85**

Locke, Eddie 1930— **44**

Lofton, James 1956— **42**

Lofton, Kenneth 1967— **12**

Lofton, Ramona 1950— **14**

Logan, Onnie Lee 1910(?)–1995 **14**

Logan, Rayford W. 1897–1982 **40**

Lomax, Michael L. 1947— **58**

Long, Eddie L. 19(?)(?)— **29**

Long, Huey 1904–2009 **79**

Long, Loretta 1940— **58**

Long, Nia 1970— **17**

Long, Richard Alexander 1927— **65**

Lopes, Lisa " Left Eye" 1971–2002 **36**

Lord Pitt of Hampstead See Pitt, David Thomas

Lorde, Audre (Geraldine) 1934–1992 **6**

Lorenzo, Irving See Gotti, Irv

Loroupe, Tegla 1973— **59**

Lott, Ronnie 1959— **9**

Louis, Errol T. 1962— **8**

Louis, Joe 1914–1981 **5**

Loury, Glenn 1948— **36**

Love, Darlene 1941— **23**

Love, Ed 1932(?)— **58**

Love, Laura 1960— **50**

Love, Nat 1854–1921 **9**

Love, Reggie 1982— **77**

Lovell, Whitfield 1959— **74**

Lover, Ed **10**

Loving, Alvin, Jr., 1935–2005 **35, 53**

Loving, Mildred 1939–2008 **69**

Lowe, Herbert 1962— **57**

Lowe, Sidney 1960— **64**

Lowery, Joseph E. 1924— **2**

Lowery, Myron 1946(?)— **80**

Lowry, A. Leon 1913–2005 **60**

Lucas, John 1953— **7**

Lucie, Lawrence 1907–2009 **80**

Lucien, Jon 1942–2007 **66**

Luckett, Letoya 1981— **61**

Lucy, William 1933— **50**

Lucy Foster, Autherine 1929— **35**

Ludacris, 1978— **37, 60**

Luke, Derek 1974— **61**

Lumbly, Carl 1952— **47**

Lumet, Jenny 1967— **80**

Lumpkin, Elgin Baylor See Ginuwine

Lumumba, Patrice 1925–1961 **33**

Lushington, Augustus Nathaniel 1869–1939 **56**

Luthuli, Albert (John Mvumbi) 1898(?)–1967 **13**

Lyfe See Jennings, Lyfe

Lyle, Marcenia See Stone, Toni

Lyles, Lester Lawrence 1946— **31**

Lymon, Frankie 1942–1968 **22**

Lynch, Shola 1969— **61**

Lynn, Lonnie Rashid See Common

Lyons, Henry 1942(?)— **12**

Lyttle, Hulda Margaret 1889–1983 **14**

Maal, Baaba 1953— **66**

Maathai, Wangari 1940— **43**

Mabley, Jackie "Moms" 1897(?)–1975 **15**

Mabrey, Vicki 1957(?)— 26
Mabry, Marcus 1967— 70
Mabuza, Lindiwe 1938— 18
Mabuza-Suttle, Felicia 1950— 43
Mac, Bernie 1957–2008 29, 61, 72
Maceo, Antonio 1845–1896 82
Machado de Assis 1839–1908 74
Machel, Graca Simbine 1945— 16
Machel, Samora Moises
   1933–1986 8
Mackey, Biz 1897–1965 82
Mackey, Nathaniel 1947— 75
Madhubuti, Haki R. 1942— 7, 85
Madikizela, Nkosikazi Nobandle
   Nomzamo Winifred See Mandela,
   Winnie
Madison, Joseph E. 1949— 17
Madison, Paula 1952— 37
Madison, Romell 1952— 45
Magloire, Paul Eugène 1907–2001
   68
Mahal, Taj 1942— 39
Mahlasela, Vusi 1965— 65
Mahorn, Rick 1958— 60
Mainor, Dorothy Leigh
   1910(?)–1996 19
Maitreya, Sananda 1962— 85
Majette, Denise 1955— 41
Major, Clarence 1936— 9
Majors, Jeff 1960(?)— 41
Makeba, Miriam 1932–2008 2, 50,
   74
Malco, Romany 1968— 71
Malcolm X See X, Malcolm
Mallett, Conrad, Jr. 1953— 16
Mallory, Mark 1962— 62
Malone, Annie (Minerva Turnbo
   Pope) 1869–1957 13
Malone, Karl 1963— 18, 51
Malone, Maurice 1965— 32
Malone, Moses 1955— 79
Malone Jones, Vivian 1942–2005
   59
Malveaux, Floyd 1940— 54
Malveaux, Julianne 1953— 32, 70
Mandela, Nelson 1918— 1, 14, 77
Mandela, Winnie 1934— 2, 35
Manigault, Earl "The Goat" 1943—
   15
Manigault-Stallworth, Omarosa
   1974— 69
Manley, Audrey Forbes 1934— 16
Manley, Edna 1900–1987 26
Manley, Ruth 1947— 34
Manning, Frankie 1914–2009 78
Marable, Manning 1950— 10
March, William Carrington
   1923–2002 56
Marchand, Inga See Foxy Brown
Marechera, Charles William See
   Marechera, Dambudzo
Marechera, Dambudzo 1952–1987
   39
Marechera, Tambudzai See Mare-
   chera, Dambudzo
Mariner, Jonathan 1954(?)— 41
Marino, Eugene Antonio 1934–2000
   30
Mario 1986— 71
Markham, E(dward) A(rchibald)
   1939— 37
Marley, Bob 1945–1981 5
Marley, David See Marley, Ziggy
Marley, Rita 1947— 32, 70

Marley, Robert Nesta See Marley,
   Bob
Marley, Ziggy 1968— 41
Marrow, Queen Esther 1943(?)—
   24
Marrow, Tracey See Ice-T
Marsalis, Branford 1960— 34
Marsalis, Delfeayo 1965— 41
Marsalis, Wynton 1961— 16
Marsh, Henry L., III 1934(?)— 32
Marshall, Bella 1950— 22
Marshall, Gloria See Sudarkasa,
   Niara
Marshall, Kerry James 1955— 59
Marshall, Paule 1929— 7, 77
Marshall, Thurgood 1908–1993 1,
   44
Marshall, Valenza Pauline Burke
   See Marshall, Paule
Martha Jean "The Queen" See
   Steinberg, Martha Jean
Martin, Darnell 1964— 43, 78
Martin, Helen 1909–2000 31
Martin, Jesse L. 19(?)(?)— 31
Martin, Louis Emanuel 1912–1997
   16
Martin, Roberta 1907–1969 58
Martin, Roland S. 1968— 49, 84
Martin, Ruby Grant 1933–2003 49
Martin, Sara 1884–1955 38
Martinez, Pedro 1971— 81
Marvin X See X, Marvin
Mary Mary 34
Mase 1977(?)— 24
Masekela, Barbara 1941— 18
Masekela, Hugh (Ramopolo)
   1939— 1
Masire, Quett (Ketumile Joni)
   1925— 5
Mason, Felicia 1963(?)— 31
Mason, Herman, Jr. 1962— 83
Mason, Ronald 1949— 27
Massaquoi, Hans J. 1926— 30
Massenburg, Kedar 1964(?)— 23
Massey, Brandon 1973— 40
Massey, Walter E(ugene) 1938— 5,
   45
Massie, Samuel Proctor, Jr. 1919—
   29
Master Gee See Sugarhill Gang,
   The
Master P 1970— 21
Matejka, Adrian 1971(?)— 87
Mathabane, Johannes See Matha-
   bane, Mark
Mathabane, Mark 1960— 5
Mathis, Greg 1960— 26
Mathis, Johnny 1935— 20
Matthews, Denise See Vanity
Matthews, Mark 1894–2005 59
Matthews Shatteen, Westina
   1948— 51
Mauldin, Jermaine Dupri See Dupri,
   Jermaine
Maxey, Randall 1941— 46
Maxis, Theresa 1810–1892 62
Maxwell 1973— 20, 81
May, Derrick 1963— 41
Mayers, Jamal 1974— 39
Mayfield, Curtis (Lee) 1942–1999 2,
   43
Mayhew, Martin R. 1965— 76
Mayhew, Richard 1924— 39

Maynard, Nancy Hicks 1946–2008
   73
Maynard, Robert C(lyve)
   1937–1993 7
Maynor, Dorothy 1910–1996 19
Mayo, Whitman 1930–2001 32
Mays, Benjamin E(lijah) 1894–1984
   7
Mays, Leslie A. 19(?)(?)— 41
Mays, William G. 1946— 34
Mays, William Howard, Jr. See
   Mays, Willie
Mays, Willie 1931— 3
Mayweather, Floyd, Jr. 1977— 57
Mazrui, Ali Al'Amin 1933— 12
M'bala M'bala, Dieudonné See
   Dieudonné
Mbaye, Mariétou 1948— 31
Mbeki, Govan A. 1910–2001 80
Mbeki, Thabo 1942— 14, 73
Mboup, Souleymane 1951— 10
Mbuende, Kaire Munionganda
   1953— 12
MC Breed 1971–2008 75
M.C. Hammer 1963— 20, 80
MC Lyte 1971— 34
McAdoo, Bob 1951— 75
McAnulty, William E., Jr.
   1947–2007 66
McBride, Bryant Scott 1965— 18
McBride, Chi 1961— 73
McBride, James 1957— 35, 87
McCabe, Jewell Jackson 1945— 10
McCall, H. Carl 1938(?)— 27
McCall, Nathan 1955— 8
McCann, Renetta 1957(?)— 44
McCarthy, Sandy 1972— 64
McCarty, Osceola 1908— 16
McCary, Michael S. See Boyz II
   Men
McCauley, Gina 1976(?)— 76
McClendon, Lisa 1975(?)— 61
McClinton, Marion Isaac 1954— 77
McClurkin, Donnie 1961— 25
McCoo, Marilyn 1943— 53
McCoy, Elijah 1844–1929 8
McCrary, Crystal See McCrary An-
   thony, Crystal
McCrary Anthony, Crystal 1969—
   70
McCray, Nikki 1972— 18
McCullough, Bernard Jeffrey See
   Mac, Bernie
McCullough, Geraldine 1917–2008
   58, 79
McDaniel, Hattie 1895–1952 5
McDaniel, Randall Cornell 1964—
   81
McDaniels, Darryl See DMC
McDaniels, Ralph 19(?)(?)— 79
McDonald, Audra 1970— 20, 62
McDonald, Erroll 1954(?)— 1
McDonald, Gabrielle Kirk 1942—
   20
McDougall, Gay J. 1947— 11, 43
McDuffie, Dwayne 1962— 62
McEwen, Mark 1954— 5
McFadden, Bernice L. 1966— 39
McFarlan, Tyron 1971(?)— 60
McFarland, Roland 1940— 49
McFerrin, Bobby 1950— 68
McFerrin, Robert, Jr. See McFerrin,
   Bobby
McGee, Charles 1924— 10

McGee, James D. 1949— 74
McGee, James Madison 1940— 46
McGill, Anthony 1979— 76
McGlowan, Angela 1970— 64, 86
McGrady, Tracy 1979— 80
McGrath, Pat 1970— 72
McGriff, Fred 1963— 24
McGriff, James Harrell See McGriff,
   Jimmy
McGriff, Jimmy 1936–2008 72
McGruder, Aaron 1974— 28, 56
McGruder, Robert 1942— 22, 35
McGuire, George Alexander
   1866–1934 80
McGuire, Raymond J. 1957(?)(—)
   57
McHenry, Donald F. 1936— 83
McIntosh, Winston Hubert See
   Tosh, Peter
McIntyre, Natalie See Gary, Macy
McKay, Claude 1889–1948 6
McKay, Festus Claudius See
   McKay, Claude
McKay, Nellie Yvonne
   19(?)(?)–2006 17, 57
McKee, Lonette 1952— 12
McKegney, Tony 1958— 3
McKenzie, Jaunel 1986— 73
McKenzie, Vashti M. 1947— 29
McKinney, Cynthia 1955— 11, 52,
   74
McKinney, Nina Mae 1912–1967 40
McKinney Hammond, Michelle
   1957— 51
McKinney-Whetstone, Diane
   1954(?)— 27
McKinnon, Ike See McKinnon,
   Isaiah
McKinnon, Isaiah 1943— 9
McKissack, Leatrice 1930— 80
McKissick, Floyd B(ixler)
   1922–1981 3
McKnight, Brian 1969— 18, 34
McLean, Jackie 1931–2006 78
McLeod, Gus 1955(?)— 27
McLeod, Gustavus See McLeod,
   Gus
McMillan, Rosalynn A. 1953— 36
McMillan, Terry 1951— 4, 17, 53
McMurray, Georgia L. 1934–1992
   36
McNabb, Donovan 1976— 29
McNair, Ronald 1950–1986 3, 58
McNair, Steve 1973–2009 22, 47,
   79
McNeil, Lori 1964(?)— 1
McPhail, Sharon 1948— 2
McPherson, David 1968— 32
McPherson, James Alan 1943— 70
McQueen, Butterfly 1911–1995 6,
   54
McQueen, Steve 1969— 84
McRae, Carmen 1920–1994 77
McRae, Hal 1945— 84
McWhorter, John 1965— 35
Meadows, Tim 1961— 30
Meek, Carrie (Pittman) 1926— 6,
   36
Meek, Kendrick 1966— 41
Meeks, Gregory 1953— 25
Mehretu, Julie 1970— 85
Meles Zenawi 1955(?)— 3
Mell, Patricia 1953— 49
Mello, Breno 1931–2008 73

Melton, Frank 1949–2009 **81**

Melton, Harold D. 1966— **79**

Memmi, Albert 1920— **37**

Memphis Minnie 1897–1973 **33**

Mengestu, Dinaw 1978— **66**

Mengistu, Haile Mariam 1937— **65**

Mensah, John 1982— **87**

Mensah, Thomas 1950— **48**

Mercado-Valdes, Frank 1962— **43**

Meredith, James H(oward) 1933— **11**

Merkerson, S. Epatha 1952— **47, 83**

Mescudi, Scott Ramon Seguro See Kid Cudi

Messenger, The See Divine, Father

Metcalfe, Ralph 1910–1978 **26**

Method Man 1971— **81**

Meyer, June See Jordan, June

Mfume, Kweisi 1948— **6, 41**

Mhlaba, Raymond 1920–2005 **55**

Micheaux, Oscar (Devereaux) 1884–1951 **7**

Michele, Michael 1966— **31**

Mickelbury, Penny 1948— **28**

Miles, Buddy 1947–2008 **69**

Miles, George Allen, Jr. See Miles, Buddy

Milla, Roger 1952— **2**

Millender-McDonald, Juanita 1938–2007 **21, 61**

Miller, Bebe 1950— **3**

Miller, Cheryl 1964— **10, 74**

Miller, Dorie 1919–1943 **29**

Miller, Doris See Miller, Dorie

Miller, Larry G. 1950(?)— **72**

Miller, Marcus 1959— **84**

Miller, Maria 1803–1879 **19**

Miller, Percy See Master P

Miller, Reggie 1965— **33**

Miller, Rice See Williamson, Sonny Boy

Miller, Warren F., Jr. 1943— **53**

Miller, Wentworth 1972— **75**

Miller-Travis, Vernice 1959— **64**

Millines Dziko, Trish 1957— **28**

Millner, Denene 1969(?)— **76**

Mills, Dylan Kwabena See Rascal, Dizzee

Mills, Florence 1896–1927 **22**

Mills, Joseph C. 1946— **51**

Mills, Sam 1959— **33**

Mills, Stephanie 1957— **36**

Mills, Steve 1960(?)— **47**

Milner, Ron 1938— **39**

Milton, DeLisha 1974— **31**

Minaj, Nicki 1984— **86**

Mingo, Frank L. 1939–1989 **32**

Mingus, Charles Jr. 1922–1979 **15**

Minor, DeWayne 1956— **32**

Minott, Sugar 1956–2010 **86**

Mitchell, Arthur 1934— **2, 47**

Mitchell, Brian Stokes 1957— **21**

Mitchell, Corinne 1914–1993 **8**

Mitchell, Elvis 1958— **67**

Mitchell, Keith 1946— **82**

Mitchell, Kel 1978— **66**

Mitchell, Leona 1949— **42**

Mitchell, Loften 1919–2001 **31**

Mitchell, Nicole 1967(?)— **66**

Mitchell, Parren J. 1922–2007 **42, 66**

Mitchell, Russ 1960— **21, 73**

Mitchell, Sam 1963— **82**

Mitchell, Sharon 1962— **36**

Mizell, Jason See Run-DMC

Mkapa, Benjamin W. 1938— **16, 77**

Mo', Keb' 1952— **36**

Mobutu Sese Seko 1930–1997 **1, 56**

Mofolo, Thomas (Mokopu) 1876–1948 **37**

Mogae, Festus Gontebanye 1939— **19, 79**

Mohamed, Ali Mahdi See Ali Mahdi Mohamed

Mohammed, Nazr 1977— **64**

Mohammed, W. Deen 1933— **27**

Mohammed, Warith Deen See Mohammed, W. Deen

Mohlabane, Goapele See Goapele

Moi, Daniel Arap 1924— **1, 35**

Mokae, Zakes 1934–2009 **80**

Mollel, Tololwa 1952— **38**

Monáe, Janelle 1985— **86**

Mongella, Gertrude 1945— **11**

Monica 1980— **21**

Mo'Nique 1967— **35, 84**

Monk, Art 1957— **38, 73**

Monk, Thelonious (Sphere, Jr.) 1917–1982 **1**

Monroe, Bryan 1965— **71**

Monroe, Mary 19(?)(?)— **35**

Montgomery, Tim 1975— **41**

Moody, James 1925— **83**

Moody, Ronald 1900–1984 **30**

Moody-Adams, Michele 1956— **76**

Moon, Warren 1956— **8, 66**

Mooney, Paul 19(?)(?)— **37**

Moore, Alice Ruth See Dunbar-Nelson, Alice Ruth Moore

Moore, Barbara C. 1949— **49**

Moore, Bobby See Rashad, Ahmad

Moore, Chante 1970(?)— **26**

Moore, Dorothy Rudd 1940— **46**

Moore, Gwendolynne S. 1951— **55**

Moore, Harry T. 1905–1951 **29**

Moore, Jessica Care 1971— **30**

Moore, Johnny B. 1950— **38**

Moore, Juanita 1922— **83**

Moore, Kevin See Mo', Keb'

Moore, LeRoi 1961–2008 **72**

Moore, Melba 1945— **21**

Moore, Minyon 19(?)(?)— **45**

Moore, Richard See bin Wahad, Dhoruba

Moore, Shemar 1970— **21**

Moore, Undine Smith 1904–1989 **28**

Moore, Wes 1978— **86**

Moorer, Lana See MC Lyte

Moorer, Michael 1967— **19**

Moose, Charles 1953— **40**

Morgan, Garrett (Augustus) 1877–1963 **1**

Morgan, Gertrude 1900–1986 **63**

Morgan, Irene 1917–2007 **65**

Morgan, Joe Leonard 1943— **9**

Morgan, Rose (Meta) 1912(?)— **11**

Morgan, Tracy 1968— **61**

Morganfield, McKinley See Muddy Waters

Morial, Ernest "Dutch" 1929–1989 **26**

Morial, Marc H. 1958— **20, 51**

Morris, Garrett 1937— **31**

Morris, Greg 1934–1996 **28**

Morris, Nathan See Boyz II Men

Morris, Raheem 1976— **77**

Morris, Wanya See Boyz II Men

Morris, William "Bill" 1938— **51**

Morris, Stevland Judkins See Wonder, Stevie

Morrison, Keith 1942— **13**

Morrison, Mary Thelma See Washington, Mary T.

Morrison, Sam 1936— **50**

Morrison, Toni 1931— **2, 15, 86**

Morrison, Vanessa 1969(?)— **84**

Morton, Azie Taylor 1936–2003 **48**

Morton, Jelly Roll 1885(?)–1941 **29**

Morton, Joe 1947— **18**

Mos Def 1973— **30**

Moseka, Aminata See Lincoln, Abbey

Moseley-Braun, Carol See Braun, Carol Moseley

Moses, Edwin 1955— **8**

Moses, Gilbert, III 1942–1995 **12**

Moses, Robert Parris 1935— **11**

Mosley, "Sugar" Shane 1971— **32**

Mosley, Tim See Timbaland

Mosley, Walter 1952— **5, 25, 68**

Moss, Bryant See Moss, Preacher

Moss, Carlton 1909–1997 **17**

Moss, J. (?)— **64**

Moss, Otis, Jr. 1935— **72**

Moss, Otis, III 1971(?)— **72**

Moss, Preacher 1967— **63**

Moss, Randy 1977— **23**

Moss, Shad Gregory See Lil' Bow Wow

Mossell, Gertrude Bustill 1855–1948 **40**

Moten, Etta See Barnett, Etta Moten

Motlanthe, Kgalema 1949— **74**

Motley, Archibald, Jr. 1891–1981 **30**

Motley, Constance Baker 1921–2005 **10, 55**

Motley, Marion 1920–1999 **26**

Moton, Robert Russa 1867–1940 **83**

Moura, Paulo 1932–2010 **87**

Mourning, Alonzo 1970— **17, 44**

Moutoussamy-Ashe, Jeanne 1951— **7**

Mowatt, Judy 1952(?)— **38**

Mowry, Jess 1960— **7**

Mowry, Tamera 1978— **79**

Mowry, Tia 1978— **78**

Moyo, Dambisa 1970(?)— **76**

Moyo, Karega Kofi 19(?)(?)— **36**

Moyo, Lovemore 1965— **76**

Moyo, Yvette Jackson 1953— **36**

Mphalele, Es'kia (Ezekiel) 1919— **40**

Mswati III 1968— **56**

Mudimbe, V. Y. 1941— **61**

Mugabe, Robert 1924— **10, 71**

Mugo, Madeleine See Mugo, Micere Githae

Mugo, Micere Githae 1942— **32**

Muhajir, El See X, Marvin

Muhammad, Ava 1951— **31**

Muhammad, Elijah 1897–1975 **4**

Muhammad, Jabir Herbert 1929–2008 **72**

Muhammad, Khallid Abdul 1951(?)— **10, 31**

Mukoko, Jestina 1957(?)— **75**

Mullen, Harryette 1953— **34**

Mullen, Nicole C. 1967— **45**

Muluzi, Bakili 1943— **14, 76**

Mumba, Samantha 1983— **29**

Mundine, Anthony 1975— **56**

Murphy, Eddie 1961— **4, 20, 61**

Murphy, Edward Regan See Murphy, Eddie

Murphy, John H. 1916— **42**

Murphy, Laura M. 1955— **43**

Murphy McKenzie, Vashti See McKenzie, Vashti M.

Murray, Albert L. 1916— **33**

Murray, Cecil 1929— **12, 47**

Murray, Eddie 1956— **12**

Murray, Lenda 1962— **10**

Murray, Pauli 1910–1985 **38**

Murray, Tai 1982— **47**

Murrell, Sylvia Marilyn 1947— **49**

Muse, Clarence Edouard 1889–1979 **21**

Museveni, Yoweri (Kaguta) 1944(?)— **4**

Musiq 1977— **37, 84**

Mutebi, Ronald 1956— **25**

Mutola, Maria de Lurdes 1972— **12**

Mutombo, Dikembe 1966— **7**

Mutu, Wangechi 19(?)(?)— **44**

Muzorewa, Abel 1925–2010 **85**

Mwanawasa, Levy 1948–2008 **72**

Mwangi, Meja 1948— **40**

Mwinyi, Ali Hassan 1925— **1, 77**

Mya 1979— **35**

Myers, Dwight See Heavy D

Myers, Walter Dean 1937— **8, 70**

Myers, Walter Milton See Myers, Walter Dean

Myles, Kim 1974— **69**

Nabrit, Samuel Milton 1905–2003 **47**

Nagin, C. Ray 1956— **42, 57**

Nagin, Ray See Nagin, C. Ray

Najm, Faheem Rasheed See T-Pain

Nakhid, David 1964— **25**

Naki, Hamilton 1926–2005 **63**

Nance, Cynthia 1958— **71**

Nanula, Richard D. 1960— **20**

Napoleon, Benny N. 1956(?)— **23**

Nas 1973— **33**

Nascimento, Milton 1942— **2, 64**

Nash, Diane 1938— **72**

Nash, Joe 1919–2005 **55**

Nash, Johnny 1940— **40**

Nash, Niecy 1970— **66**

Nash, Shannon King 1971— **84**

Nash, Terius Youngdell See The-Dream

Naylor, Gloria 1950— **10, 42**

Nazario, Zoe Yadira Zaldaña See Saldana, Zoe

Ndadaye, Melchior 1953–1993 **7**

Ndegeocello, Meshell 1968— **15, 83**

Ndiaye, Iba 1928–2008 **74**

N'Dour, Youssou 1959— **1, 53, 79**

Ndungane, Winston Njongonkulu 1941— **16**

Neal, Elise 1970— **29**

Neal, Larry 1937–1981 **38**

Neal, Mark Anthony 1965(?)— **74**
Neal, Raful 1936— **44**
Neale, Haydain 1970— **52**
Neals, Otto 1930— **73**
Nelly 1978— **32**
Nelson, Jill 1952— **6, 54**
Nelson, Prince Rogers *See Prince*
Nelson Meigs, Andrea 1968— **48**
Neto, António Agostinho 1922— **43**
Nettles, Marva Deloise *See Collins, Marva*
Neville, Aaron 1941— **21**
Neville, Arthel 1962— **53**
Newcombe, Don 1926— **24**
Newkirk, Pamela 1957— **69**
Newman, David 1933–2009 **76**
Newman, Lester C. 1952— **51**
Newsome, Ozzie 1956— **26**
Newton, Huey (Percy) 1942–1989 **2**
Newton, Thandie 1972— **26**
Ne-Yo 1982— **65**
Ngaujah, Sahr 1976— **86**
Ngengi, Kamau wa *See Kenyatta, Jomo*
Ngilu, Charity 1952— **58**
Ngubane, (Baldwin Sipho) Ben 1941— **33**
Ngugi wa Thiong'o 1938— **29, 61**
Ngugi, James wa Thiong'o *See Ngugi wa Thiong'o*
Niane, Katoucha 1960–2008 **70**
Nicholas, Denise 1944— **82**
Nicholas, Fayard 1914–2006 **20, 57, 61**
Nicholas, Harold 1921— **20**
Nichols, Grace *See Nichols, Nichelle*
Nichols, James Thomas *See Bell, James "Cool Papa"*
Nichols, Nichelle 1933(?)— **11**
Nissel, Angela 1974— **42**
Nix, Robert N. C., Jr. 1928–2003 **51**
Njawe, Pius 1957–2010 **87**
Njongonkulu, Winston Ndungane 1941— **16**
Nkoli, Simon 1957–1998 **60**
Nkomo, Joshua 1917–1999 **4, 65**
Nkosi, Lewis 1936— **46**
Nkrumah, Kwame 1909–1972 **3**
Nkunda, Laurent 1967— **75**
Nkurunziza, Pierre 1963— **78**
N'Namdi, George R. 1946— **17**
Noah, Yannick 1960— **4, 60**
Noble, Gil 1932— **76**
Noble, Reginald *See Redman*
Noble, Ronald 1957— **46**
Norman, Christina 1960(?)— **47**
Norman, Jessye 1945— **5**
Norman, Maidie 1912–1998 **20**
Norman, Pat 1939— **10**
Norris, Michele 1961— **83**
Norton, Eleanor Holmes 1937— **7**
Norton, Meredith 1970(?)— **72**
Norwood, Brandy *See Brandy*
Norwood, William Raymond, Jr. *See Ray J*
Notorious B.I.G. 1972–1997 **20**
Nottage, Cynthia DeLores *See Tucker, C. DeLores*
Nottage, Lynn 1964— **66**
Nour, Nawal M. 1965(?)— **56**
Ntaryamira, Cyprien 1955–1994 **8**

Ntshona, Winston 1941— **52**
Nugent, Richard Bruce 1906–1987 **39**
Nujoma, Samuel 1929— **10**
Nunez, Elizabeth 1944(?)— **62**
Nunn, Annetta 1959— **43**
Nutter, Michael 1958— **69**
Nuttin' but Stringz *See Escobar, Tourie, and Escobar, Damien*
Nyanda, Siphiwe 1950— **21**
Nyerere, Julius (Kambarage) 1922— **5**
Nzo, Alfred (Baphethuxolo) 1925— **15**
Obadele, Imari 1930–2010 **84**
Obama, Barack 1961— **49, 74**
Obama, Michelle 1964— **61**
Obasanjo, Olusegun 1937— **5, 22**
Obasanjo, Stella 1945–2005 **32, 56**
Obote, Milton 1925–2005 **63**
ODB *See Ol' Dirty Bastard*
Odetta 1930— **37, 74**
Odinga, Raila 1945— **67**
Odom, Lamar 1979— **81**
Oglesby, Zena 1947— **12**
Ogletree, Charles, Jr. 1952— **12, 47**
O'Grady, Lorraine 1934— **73**
Ogunlesi, Adebayo O. 19(?)(?)— **37**
Ojikutu, Bayo 1971— **66**
Ojikutu, Bisola 1974— **65**
Okaalet, Peter 1953— **58**
Okara, Gabriel 1921— **37**
Okonedo, Sophie 1969— **67**
Okosuns, Sonny 1947–2008 **71**
Ol' Dirty Bastard 1968–2004 **52**
Olajuwon, Akeem *See Olajuwon, Hakeem*
Olajuwon, Hakeem 1963— **2, 72**
Olatunji, Babatunde 1927— **36**
Olden, Georg(e) 1920–1975 **44**
O'Leary, Hazel (Rollins) 1937— **6**
Oliver, Jerry 1947— **37**
Oliver, Joe "King" 1885–1938 **42**
Oliver, John J., Jr. 1945— **48**
Oliver, Kimberly 1976— **60**
Oliver, Pam 1961— **54**
Olojede, Dele 1961— **59**
Olopade, Olufunmilayo Falusi 1957(?)— **58**
O'Neal, Ron 1937–2004 **46**
O'Neal, Shaquille (Rashaun) 1972— **8, 30**
O'Neal, Stanley 1951— **38, 67**
O'Neil, Buck 1911–2006 **19, 59**
O'Neil, John Jordan *See O'Neil, Buck*
Ongala, Ramadhani Mtoro *See Ongala, Remmy*
Ongala, Remmy 1947— **9**
Onwueme, Tess Osonye 1955— **23**
Onwurah, Ngozi 1966(?)— **38**
Onyewu, Oguchi 1982— **60**
Orange, James 1942–2008 **74**
O'Ree, William Eldon *See O'Ree, Willie*
O'Ree, Willie 1935— **5**
Orlandersmith, Dael 1959— **42**
Orman, Roscoe 1944— **55**
Ormes, Jackie 1911–1985 **73**
Ortiz, David 1975— **52, 82**
Osborne, Jeffrey 1948— **26**
Osborne, Na'taki 1974— **54**

Otis, Clarence, Jr. 1956— **55**
Otis, Clyde 1924— **67**
Otunga, Maurice Michael 1923–2003 **55**
Ouattara 1957— **43**
Ouattara, Morou 1966— **74**
Ousmane, Sembène *See Sembène, Ousmane*
OutKast **35**
Owens, Dana *See Queen Latifah*
Owens, Helen 1937— **48**
Owens, J. C. *See Owens, Jesse*
Owens, Jack 1904–1997 **38**
Owens, James Cleveland *See Owens, Jesse*
Owens, Jesse 1913–1980 **2**
Owens, Major (Robert) 1936— **6**
Owens, Terrell 1973— **53**
Oyelowo, David 1976— **82**
Oyono, Ferdinand 1929— **38**
P. Diddy *See Combs, Sean "Puffy"*
Pace, Betty 1954— **59**
Pace, Orlando 1975— **21**
Packer, Daniel 1947— **56**
Packer, Will 1974(?)— **71**
Packer, Z. Z. 1973— **64**
Page, Alan (Cedric) 1945— **7**
Page, Clarence 1947— **4**
Page, Greg 1958–2009 **78**
Page, Inman 1853–1935 **82**
Paige, Leroy Robert *See Paige, Satchel*
Paige, Rod 1933— **29**
Paige, Satchel 1906–1982 **7**
Painter, Nell Irvin 1942— **24**
Palmer, Everard 1930— **37**
Palmer, Keke 1993— **68**
Palmer, Rissi 1981— **65**
Palmer, Violet 1964— **59**
Papa Wendo *See Kolosoy, Wendo*
Parham, Marjorie B. 1918— **71**
Parish, Robert 1953— **43**
Parker, Candace 1986— **74**
Parker, Charlie 1920–1955 **20**
Parker, Jim 1934–2005 **64**
Parker, Kellis E. 1942–2000 **30**
Parker, (Lawrence) Kris(hna) *See KRS-One*
Parker, LarStella Irby *See Parker, Star*
Parker, Maceo 1943— **72**
Parker, Nicole Ari 1970— **52**
Parker, Ray, Jr. 1954— **85**
Parker, Star 1956— **70**
Parker, Tony 1982— **75**
Parks, Bernard C. 1943— **17**
Parks, Gordon 1912–2006 **1, 35, 58**
Parks, Rosa 1913–2005 **1, 35, 56**
Parks, Suzan-Lori 1963— **34, 85**
Parr, Russ 196(?)— **51**
Parsons, James Benton 1911–1993 **14**
Parsons, Richard Dean 1948— **11, 33**
Pascal-Trouillot, Ertha 1943— **3**
Paterson, Basil A. 1926— **69**
Paterson, David A. 1954— **59**
Patillo, Melba Joy 1941— **15**
Patrick, Deval 1956— **12, 61**
Patterson, Floyd 1935–2006 **19, 58**
Patterson, Frederick Douglass 1901–1988 **12**

Patterson, Gilbert Earl 1939— **41**
Patterson, J. O., Jr. 1935— **80**
Patterson, Louise 1901–1999 **25**
Patterson, Mary Jane 1840–1894 **54**
Patterson, Orlando 1940— **4**
Patterson, P(ercival) J(ames) 1936(?)— **6, 20**
Patterson, Robert, Jr. *See Ali, Rashied*
Patton, Antwan 1975— **45**
Patton, Antwan "Big Boi" 1975(?)— *See OutKast*
Patton, Paula 1975— **62**
Paul, Chris 1985— **84**
Payne, Allen 1962(?)— **13**
Payne, Donald M. 1934— **2, 57**
Payne, Ethel L. 1911–1991 **28**
Payne, Freda 1942— **58**
Payne, Ulice 1955— **42**
Payne, William D. 1932— **60**
Payton, Benjamin F. 1932— **23**
Payton, John 1946— **48**
Payton, Walter (Jerry) 1954–1999 **11, 25**
Pearman, Raven-Symone Christina *See Raven*
Peck, Carolyn 1966(?)— **23**
Peck, Raoul 1953— **32**
Peete, Calvin 1943— **11**
Peete, Holly Robinson 1965— **20**
Peete, Rodney 1966— **60**
Pelé 1940— **7**
Pena, Paul 1950–2005 **58**
Pendergrass, Teddy 1950–2010 **22, 83**
Penniman, Richard Wayne *See Little Richard*
Peoples, Dottie 19(?)(?)— **22**
Pereira, Aristides 1923— **30**
Perez, Anna 1951— **1**
Perkins, Anthony 1959(?)— **24**
Perkins, Edward (Joseph) 1928— **5**
Perkins, James, Jr. 1953(?)— **55**
Perkins, Joe Willie *See Perkins, Pinetop*
Perkins, Marion 1908–1961 **38**
Perkins, Pinetop 1913— **70**
Perren, Freddie 1943–2004 **60**
Perrineau, Harold, Jr. 1968— **51**
Perrot, Kim 1967–1999 **23**
Perry, Emmitt, Jr. *See Perry, Tyler*
Perry, James 1975— **83**
Perry, Laval 195(?)— **64**
Perry, Lee "Scratch" 1936— **19**
Perry, Lincoln *See Fetchit, Stepin*
Perry, Lowell 1931–2001 **30**
Perry, Rainford Hugh *See Perry, Lee "Scratch"*
Perry, Ruth 1936— **19**
Perry, Ruth Sando 1939— **15**
Perry, Tyler 1969— **40, 54**
Perry, Warren 1942(?)— **56**
Person, Waverly 1927— **9, 51**
Peters, Lenrie 1932— **43**
Peters, Margaret 1915— **43**
Peters, Maria Philomena 1941— **12**
Peters, Matilda 1917— **43**
Petersen, Frank E. 1932— **31**
Peterson, Hannibal *See Peterson, Marvin "Hannibal"*
Peterson, James 19(?)(?)— **81**
Peterson, James 1937— **38**

Peterson, Jesse Lee 1949— **81**
Peterson, Marvin "Hannibal" 1948— **27**
Peterson, Oscar 1925— **52**
Petry, Ann 1909–1997 **19**
Phifer, Mekhi 1975— **25**
Philip, M. Nourbese See Philip, Marlene Nourbese
Philip, Marlene Nourbese 1947— **32**
Phillips, Charles E., Jr. 1959— **57**
Phillips, Helen L. 1919–2005 **63**
Phillips, Joseph C. 1962— **73**
Phillips, Teresa L. 1958— **42**
Phipps, Wintley 1955— **59**
Pickens, James, Jr. 1954— **59**
Pickett, Bill 1870–1932 **11**
Pickett, Cecil 1945— **39**
Pierce, Elijah 1892–1984 **84**
Pierce, Harold 1917-1988 **75**
Pierce, Paul 1977— **71**
Pierre, Andre 1915— **17**
Pierre, Percy Anthony 1939— **46**
Pierre-Louis, Michèle 1947— **75**
Pincham, R. Eugene, Sr. 1925–2008 **69**
Pinchback, P(inckney) B(enton) S(tewart) 1837–1921 **9**
Pinckney, Bill 1935— **42**
Pinckney, Sandra 194(?)— **56**
Pindell, Howardena 1943— **55**
Pinder, Jefferson 1970— **77**
Pinderhughes, John 1946— **47**
Pindling, Lynden 1930–2000 **81**
Pinkett, Jada See Pinkett Smith, Jada
Pinkett, Randal 1971— **61**
Pinkett Smith, Jada 1971— **10, 41**
Pinkney, Fayette 1948–2009 **80**
Pinkney, Jerry 1939— **15**
Pinkston, W. Randall 1950— **24**
Pinn, Vivian Winona 1941— **49**
Piper, Adrian 1948— **71**
Pippen, Scottie 1965— **15**
Pippin, Horace 1888–1946 **9**
Pitt, David Thomas 1913–1994 **10**
Pitta (do Nascimento), Celso (Roberto) 19(?)(?)— **17**
Pitts, Byron 1960— **71**
Pitts, Derrick 1956(?)— **77**
Pitts, Leonard, Jr. 1957— **54, 85**
Pitts, Robb 1941— **84**
Pitts, Robert Lee See Pitts, Robb
Plaatje, Sol. T. 1876–1932 **80**
Player, Willa B. 1909–2003 **43**
Pleasant, Mary Ellen 1814–1904 **9**
Pleasure P 1984— **84**
Plessy, Homer Adolph 1862–1925 **31**
P.M. Dawn, **54**
Poindexter, Hildrus A. 1901–1987 **87**
Poitier, Sidney 1927— **11, 36**
Poitier, Sydney Tamiia 1973— **65**
Polite, Carlene Hatcher 1932–2009 **82**
Pollard, Fritz 1894–1986 **53**
Pomare, Eleo 1937–2008 **72**
Poole, Elijah See Muhammad, Elijah
Pope.L, William 1955— **72**
Porter, Countee Leroy See Cullin, Countee

Porter, Dorothy See Wesley, Dorothy Porter
Porter, James A(mos) 1905–1970 **11**
Porter, Terry 1963— **75**
Portuondo, Omara 1930— **53**
Potter, Myrtle 1958— **40**
Pough, Terrell 1987(?)–2005 **58**
Pounder, Carol Christine Hilaria See Pounder, CCH
Pounder, CCH 1952— **72**
Poussaint, Alvin F. 1934— **5, 67**
Poussaint, Renee 1944— **78**
Powell, Adam Clayton, Jr. 1908–1972 **3**
Powell, Benny 1930–2010 **87**
Powell, Bud 1924–1966 **24**
Powell, Colin 1937— **1, 28, 75**
Powell, Debra A. 1964— **23**
Powell, Kevin 1966— **31, 74**
Powell, Maxine 1924— **8**
Powell, Michael Anthony See Powell, Mike
Powell, Michael K. 1963— **32**
Powell, Mike 1963— **7**
Powell, Renee 1946— **34**
Powell, William J. 1916–2009 **82**
Power, Will 1970— **83**
Pratt, Awadagin 1966— **31**
Pratt, Geronimo 1947— **18**
Pratt, Kyla 1986— **57**
Pratt Dixon, Sharon See Dixon, Sharon Pratt
Preer, Evelyn 1896–1932 **82**
Premice, Josephine 1926–2001 **41**
Pressley, Condace L. 1964— **41**
Preston, Billy 1946–2006 **39, 59**
Preston, William Everett See Preston, Billy
Préval, René 1943— **87**
Price, Florence 1887–1953 **37**
Price, Frederick K.C. 1932— **21**
Price, Glenda 1939— **22**
Price, Hugh B. 1941— **9, 54**
Price, Kelly 1973(?)— **23**
Price, Leontyne 1927— **1**
Price, Richard 1930(?)— **51**
Pride, Charley 1938(?)— **26**
Primus, Pearl 1919— **6**
Prince 1958— **18, 65**
Prince, Richard E. 1947— **71**
Prince, Ron 1969— **64**
Prince, Tayshaun 1980— **68**
Prince-Bythewood, Gina 1969— **31, 77**
Pritchard, Robert Starling 1927— **21**
Procope, Ernesta 19(?)(?)— **23**
Procope, John Levy 1925–2005 **56**
Prophet, Nancy Elizabeth 1890–1960 **42**
Prothrow, Deborah Boutin See Prothrow-Stith, Deborah
Prothrow-Stith, Deborah 1954— **10**
Pryor, Rain 1969— **65**
Pryor, Richard 1940–2005 **3, 24, 56**
Puckett, Kirby 1960–2006 **4, 58**
Puff Daddy See Combs, Sean "Puffy"
Pugh, Charles 197199— **81**
Purdie, Bernard 1939— **77**
Purnell, Silas 1923–2003 **59**
Puryear, Martin 1941— **42**

Putney, Martha S. 1916–2008 **75**
Quarles, Benjamin Arthur 1904–1996 **18**
Quarles, Norma 1936— **25**
Quarterman, Lloyd Albert 1918–1982 **4**
Queen Latifah 1970— **1, 16, 58**
Querino, Manuel Raimundo 1851–1923 **84**
?uestlove 1971— **74**
Quigless, Helen G. 1944–2004 **49**
Quince, Peggy A. 1948— **69**
Quirot, Ana (Fidelia) 1963— **13**
Quivers, Robin 1952— **61**
Rabb, Maurice F., Jr. 1932–2005 **58**
Rabia, Aliyah See Staton, Dakota
Radcliffe, Ted 1902–2005 **74**
Radcliffe, Theodore Roosevelt See Radcliffe, Ted
Ragin, Derek Lee 1958— **84**
Rahman, Aishah 1936— **37**
Raines, Franklin Delano 1949— **14**
Rainey, Ma 1886–1939 **33**
Ralph, Sheryl Lee 1956— **18**
Ramaphosa, (Matamela) Cyril 1952— **3**
Rambough, Lori Ann See Sommore
Ramphele, Mamphela 1947— **29**
Ramsey, Charles H. 1948— **21, 69**
Rand, A(ddison) Barry 1944— **6**
Randall, Alice 1959— **38**
Randall, Dudley 1914–2000 **8, 55**
Randle, John 1967— **87**
Randle, Theresa 1967— **16**
Randolph, A(sa) Philip 1889–1979 **3**
Randolph, Linda A. 1941— **52**
Randolph, Willie 1954— **53**
Rangel, Charles B. 1930— **3, 52, 85**
Ranglin, Ernest 1932— **78**
Rankin Don See Rhoden, Wayne
Raoul, Kwame 1964— **55**
Rapier, James T. 1837–1883 **82**
Ras Tafari See Haile Selassie
Rascal, Dizzee 1985— **82**
Rashad, Ahmad 1949— **18**
Rashad, Phylicia 1948— **21**
Raspberry, William 1935— **2**
Raven, 1985— **44**
Raven-Symone See Raven
Rawlings, Jerry (John) 1947— **9**
Rawlinson, Johnnie B. 1952— **79**
Rawls, Lou 1936–2006 **17, 57**
Ray, Charlotte E. 1850–1911 **60**
Ray, Gene Anthony 1962–2003 **47**
Ray J 1981— **86**
Raymond, Usher, IV See Usher
Razaf, Andy 1895–1973 **19**
Razafkeriefo, Andreamentania Paul See Razaf, Andy
Ready, Stephanie 1975— **33**
Reagon, Bernice Johnson 1942— **7**
Reagon, Toshi 1964— **76**
Reason, Joseph Paul 1943— **19**
Record, Eugene 1940–2005 **60**
Reddick, Lance 19(?)(?)— **52**
Reddick, Lawrence Dunbar 1910–1995 **20**
Redding, Ann Holmes 1951— **77**
Redding, J. Saunders 1906–1988 **26**
Redding, Louis L. 1901–1998 **26**

Redding, Otis, Jr. 1941— **16**
Redman 1970— **81**
Redman, Joshua 1969— **30**
Redmond, Eugene 1937— **23**
Redwood, John Henry 1942–2003 **78**
Reece, E. Albert 1950— **63**
Reed, A. C. 1926— **36**
Reed, Alaina See Reed Hall, Alaina
Reed, Ishmael 1938— **8**
Reed, Jimmy 1925–1976 **38**
Reed, Kasim 1969— **82**
Reed, Willis, Jr. 1942— **86**
Reed Amini, Alaina See Reed Hall, Alaina
Reed Hall, Alaina 1946–2009 **83**
Reems, Ernestine Cleveland 1932— **27**
Reese, Calvin See Reese, Pokey
Reese, Della 1931— **6, 20**
Reese, Milous J., Jr. 1904— **51**
Reese, Pokey 1973— **28**
Reese, Tracy 1964— **54**
Reeves, Dianne 1956— **32**
Reeves, Gregory 1952— **49**
Reeves, Martha 1941— **85**
Reeves, Rachel J. 1950(?)— **23**
Reeves, Triette Lipsey 1963— **27**
Regis, Cyrille 1958— **51**
Reid, Antonio "L.A." 1958(?)— **28**
Reid, Irvin D. 1941— **20**
Reid, L.A. See Reid, Antonio "L.A."
Reid, Senghor 1976— **55**
Reid, Tim 1944— **56**
Reid, Vernon 1958— **34**
Reivers, Corbin Bleu See Corbin Bleu
Reuben, Gloria 19(?)(?)— **15**
Rev Run See Run; Run-DMC
Reverend Ike 1935–2009 **79**
Reynolds, Harold 1960— **77**
Reynolds, Star Jones 1962(?)— **10, 27, 61**
Rhames, Ving 1959— **14, 50**
Rhimes, Shonda Lynn 1970— **67**
Rhoden, Dwight 1962— **40**
Rhoden, Wayne 1966— **70**
Rhoden, William C. 1950(?)— **67**
Rhodes, Jewell Parker 1954— **84**
Rhodes, Ray 1950— **14**
Rhone, Sylvia 1952— **2**
Rhone, Trevor 1940–2009 **80**
Rhymes, Busta 1972— **31**
Ribbs, William Theodore, Jr. See Ribbs, Willy T.
Ribbs, Willy T. 1956— **2**
Ribeau, Sidney 1947(?)— **70**
Ribeiro, Alfonso 1971— **17**
Rice, Condoleezza 1954— **3, 28, 72**
Rice, Constance LaMay 1956— **60**
Rice, Jerry 1962— **5, 55**
Rice, Jim 1953— **75**
Rice, Linda Johnson 1958— **9, 41**
Rice, Louise Allen 1941— **54**
Rice, Norm(an Blann) 1943— **8**
Rice, Susan E. 1964— **74**
Richard, J. R. 1950— **87**
Richards, Beah 1926–2000 **30**
Richards, Hilda 1936— **49**
Richards, Lloyd 1923(?)— **2**
Richards, Sanya 1985— **66**
Richardson, Desmond 1969— **39**

Richardson, Donna 1962— **39**

Richardson, Elaine Potter *See Kincaid, Jamaica*

Richardson, Julieanna 1954— **81**

Richardson, LaTanya 1949— **71**

Richardson, Laura 1962— **81**

Richardson, Nolan 1941— **9**

Richardson, Pat *See Norman, Pat*

Richardson, Rupert 1930–2008 **67**

Richardson, Salli 1967— **68**

Richie, Leroy C. 1941— **18**

Richie, Lionel 1949— **27, 65**

Richmond, Mitchell James 1965— **19**

Rideau, Iris 1940(?)— **46**

Ridenhour, Carlton *See Chuck D.*

Ridley, John 1965— **69**

Riggs, Marlon 1957–1994 **5, 44**

Rihanna 1988— **65**

Riles, Wilson C. 1917–1999 **79**

Riley, Helen Caldwell Day 1926— **13**

Riley, Rochelle 1959(?)— **50**

Ringgold, Faith 1930— **4, 81**

Riperton, Minnie 1947–1979 **32**

Rivers, Doc 1961— **25, 81**

Rivers, Eugene F., III 1950— **81**

Rivers, Glenn *See Rivers, Doc*

Rivers, Kim *See Roberts, Kimberly Rivers*

Roach, Max 1924–2007 **21, 63**

Roberto, Holden 1923–2007 **65**

Roberts, Darryl 1962(?)— **70**

Roberts, Deborah 1960— **35**

Roberts, Ian *See Kwei-Armah, Kwame*

Roberts, James *See Lover, Ed*

Roberts, Kimberly Rivers 1981(?)— **72**

Roberts, Kristina LaFerne *See Zane*

Roberts, Lillian 1928— **83**

Roberts, Marcus 1963— **19**

Roberts, Marthaniel *See Roberts, Marcus*

Roberts, Mike 1948— **57**

Roberts, Robin 1960— **16, 54**

Roberts, Roy S. 1939(?)— **14**

Roberts, William Leonard, II *See Ross, Rick*

Robertson, Gil L., IV 1964— **85**

Robertson, Oscar 1938— **26**

Robeson, Eslanda Goode 1896–1965 **13**

Robeson, Paul (Leroy Bustill) 1898–1976 **2**

Robinson, Aminah 1940— **50**

Robinson, Bill "Bojangles" 1878–1949 **11**

Robinson, Bishop L. 1927— **66**

Robinson, Cleo Parker 1948(?)— **38**

Robinson, David 1965— **24**

Robinson, Eddie G. 1919–2007 **10, 61**

Robinson, Eugene 1955— **77**

Robinson, Fatima 19(?)(?)— **34**

Robinson, Fenton 1935–1997 **38**

Robinson, Frank 1935— **9, 87**

Robinson, Jack Roosevelt *See Robinson, Jackie*

Robinson, Jackie 1919–1972 **6**

Robinson, LaVaughn 1927–2008 **69**

Robinson, Luther *See Robinson, Bill "Bojangles"*

Robinson, Malcolm S. 1948— **44**

Robinson, Matt 1937–2002 **69**

Robinson, Matthew, Jr. *See Robinson, Matt*

Robinson, Max 1939–1988 **3**

Robinson, Patrick 1966— **19, 71**

Robinson, Rachel 1922— **16**

Robinson, Randall 1941— **7, 46**

Robinson, Reginald R. 1972— **53**

Robinson, Sharon 1950— **22**

Robinson, Shaun 19(?)(?)— **36**

Robinson, Smokey 1940— **3, 49**

Robinson, Spottswood W., III 1916–1998 **22**

Robinson, Sugar Ray 1921— **18**

Robinson, Sylvia 1936— **79**

Robinson, Will 1911–2008 **51, 69**

Robinson, William, Jr. *See Robinson, Smokey*

Roble, Abdi 1964— **71**

Roby, Kimberla Lawson 1965— **86**

Roche, Joyce M. 1947— **17**

Rochester *See Anderson, Eddie "Rochester"*

Rochon, Lela 1965(?)— **16**

Rochon, Stephen W. 1950(?)— **78**

Rock, Chris 1967(?)— **3, 22, 66**

Rock, The 1972— **29, 66**

Rodgers, Johnathan 1946— **6, 51**

Rodgers, Rod 1937–2002 **36**

Rodman, Dennis 1961— **12, 44**

Rodney, Winston *See Burning Spear*

Rodrigues, Percy 1918–2007 **68**

Rodríguez, Arsenio 1911–1970 **87**

Rodriguez, Jimmy 1963(?)— **47**

Rodriguez, Cheryl 1952— **64**

Rogers, Alan G. 1967–2008 **72**

Rogers, Jimmy 1924–1997 **38**

Rogers, Joe 1964— **27**

Rogers, Joel Augustus 1883(?)–1996 **30**

Rogers, John W., Jr. 1958— **5, 52**

Rogers, Kelis *See Kelis*

Rojas, Don 1949— **33**

Roker, Al 1954— **12, 49**

Roker, Roxie 1929–1995 **68**

Rolle, Esther 1920–1998 **13, 21**

Rollins, Charlemae Hill 1897–1979 **27**

Rollins, Howard E., Jr. 1950–1996 **16**

Rollins, Ida Gray Nelson *See Gray (Nelson Rollins), Ida*

Rollins, James Calvin, III *See Rollins, Jimmy*

Rollins, Jimmy 1978— **70**

Rollins, Sonny 1930— **37**

Ronaldinho 1980— **69**

Rooakhptah, Amunnubi *See York, Dwight D.*

Rose, Anika Noni 1972— **70**

Rose, Derrick 1988— **82**

Rose, Lionel 1948— **56**

Ross, Araminta *See Tubman, Harriet*

Ross, Charles 1957— **27**

Ross, Diana 1944— **8, 27**

Ross, Don 1941— **27**

Ross, Isaiah "Doc" 1925–1993 **40**

Ross, Rick 1976— **79**

Ross, Tracee Ellis 1972— **35**

Ross-Lee, Barbara 1942— **67**

Rotimi, (Emmanuel Gladstone) Ola-(wale) 1938— **1**

Roundtree, Dovey 1914— **80**

Roundtree, Richard 1942— **27**

Rowan, Carl T(homas) 1925— **1, 30**

Rowell, Victoria 1960— **13, 68**

Roxanne Shante 1969— **33**

Roy, Kenny 1990(?)— **51**

Rubin, Chanda 1976— **37**

Rucker, Darius 1966— **34, 74**

Rudder, David 1953— **79**

Rudolph, Maya 1972— **46**

Rudolph, Wilma (Glodean) 1940— **4**

Ruffin, Joseph Lee *See Shakur, Yusef*

Ruffin, Josephine St. Pierre 1842–1924 **75**

Ruffins, Kermit 1964— **85**

Rugambwa, Laurean 1912–1997 **20**

Ruley, Ellis 1882–1959 **38**

Run 1964— **31, 73, 75**

Run-DMC **31, 75**

Rupaul 1960— **17**

Rusesabagina, Paul 1954— **60**

Rush, Bobby 1940— **78**

Rush, Bobby 1946— **26, 76**

Rush, Otis 1934— **38**

Rushen, Patrice 1954— **12**

Rushing, Jimmy 1903–1972 **37**

Russell, Bill 1934— **8**

Russell, Brenda 1944(?)— **52**

Russell, Herman Jerome 1931(?)— **17**

Russell, Nipsey 1924–2005 **66**

Russell, William Felton *See Russell, Bill*

Russell-McCloud, Patricia 1946— **17**

Rust, Art, Jr. 1927–2010 **83**

Rustin, Bayard 1910–1987 **4**

RZA 1969— **80**

Saar, Alison 1956— **16**

Saar, Betye 1926— **80**

Sabathia, Carsten Charles, Jr. *See Sabathia, CC*

Sabathia, CC 1980— **74**

Sade 1959— **15**

Sadler, Joseph *See Grandmaster Flash*

Sadlier, Rosemary 19(?)(?)— **62**

St. Jacques, Raymond 1930–1990 **8**

Saint James, Synthia 1949— **12**

St. John, Kristoff 1966— **25**

St. Julien, Marlon 1972— **29**

St. Patrick, Mathew 1969— **48**

Saldana, Zoe 1978— **72**

Salih, Al-Tayyib 1929— **37**

Sallee, Charles 1911— **38**

Salter, Nikkole 1979(?)— **73**

Salters, Alisia *See Salters, Lisa*

Salters, Lisa 1966(?)— **71**

Salvador, Bryce 1976— **51**

Samara, Noah 1956— **15**

SAMO *See Basquiat, Jean-Michel*

Sample, Joe 1939— **51**

Sampson, Charles 1957— **13**

Sampson, Edith S(purlock) 1901–1979 **4**

Samuel, Sealhenry Olumide *See Seal*

Samuelsson, Marcus 1970— **53**

Sanchez, Sonia 1934— **17, 51**

Sanders, Angelia 1961(?)— **86**

Sanders, Barry 1968— **1, 53**

Sanders, Bob 1981— **72**

Sanders, Deion (Luwynn) 1967— **4, 31**

Sanders, Demond *See Sanders, Bob*

Sanders, Dori(nda) 1935— **8**

Sanders, Joseph R(ichard, Jr.) 1954— **11**

Sanders, Malika 1973— **48**

Sanders, Pharoah 1940— **64**

Sanders, Rose M. *See Touré, Faya Ora Rose*

Sanders, Satch 1938— **77**

Sanders, Thomas Ernest *See Sanders, Satch*

Sands, Diana 1934–1973 **87**

Sané, Pierre Gabriel 1948–1998 **21**

Sanford, Isabel 1917–2004 **53**

Sanford, John Elroy *See Foxx, Redd*

Sangare, Oumou 1968— **18**

Sanhá Malam Bacai 1947— **84**

Sankara, Thomas 1949–1987 **17**

Sankoh, Foday 1937–2003 **74**

Santamaria, Mongo 1917–2003 **81**

Santiago-Hudson, Ruben 1956— **85**

Santos de Freitas, Antonio Carlos *See Brown, Carlinhos*

Sapp, Marvin 1966(?)— **74**

Sapp, Warren 1972— **38**

Saro-Wiwa, Kenule 1941–1995 **39**

Satcher, David 1941— **7, 57**

Satchmo *See Armstrong, (Daniel) Louis*

Savage, Augusta Christine 1892(?)–1962 **12**

Savimbi, Jonas (Malheiro) 1934–2002 **2, 34**

Sawyer, Amos 1945— **2**

Sawyer, Eugene 1934–2008 **81**

Sayers, Gale 1943— **28**

Sayles Belton, Sharon 1952(?)— **9, 16**

Scantlebury, Janna 1984(?)— **47**

Scantlebury-White, Velma 1955— **64**

Scarlett, Millicent 1971— **49**

Schmoke, Kurt 1949— **1, 48**

Schomburg, Arthur Alfonso 1874–1938 **9**

Schomburg, Arturo Alfonso *See Schomburg, Arthur Alfonso*

Schultz, Michael A. 1938— **6**

Schuyler, George Samuel 1895–1977 **40**

Schuyler, Philippa 1931–1967 **50**

Scott, C. A. 1908–2000 **29**

Scott, Coretta *See King, Coretta Scott*

Scott, Cornelius Adolphus *See Scott, C. A.*

Scott, David 1946— **41**

Scott, George 1929–2005 **55**

Scott, Harold Russell, Jr. 1935–2006 **61**

Scott, Hazel 1920–1981 **66**

Scott, Jill 1972— **29, 83**

Scott, John T. 1940–2007 **65**

Scott, "Little" Jimmy 1925— **48**

Scott, Milton 1956— **51**

Scott, Robert C. 1947— **23**

Scott, Stuart 1965— **34**

Scott, Tim 1965— **87**

Scott, Wendell Oliver, Sr. 1921–1990 **19**

Scruggs, Mary Elfrieda See Williams, Mary Lou

Scurry, Briana 1971— **27**

Seacole, Mary 1805–1881 **54**

Seal **14, 75**

Seale, Bobby 1936— **3**

Seale, Robert George See Seale, Bobby

Seals, Frank See Seals, Son

Seals, Son 1942–2004 **56**

Sears, Leah Ward 1955— **5, 79**

Sears, Stephanie 1964— **53**

Sears-Collins, Leah J(eanette) See Sears, Leah Ward

Sebree, Charles 1914–1985 **40**

Seele, Pernessa 1954— **46**

Selassie, Haile See Haile Selassie

Sembène, Ousmane 1923–2007 **13, 62**

Senghor, Augustin Diamacoune 1928–2007 **66**

Senghor, Léopold Sédar 1906–2001 **12, 66**

Sengstacke, John Herman Henry 1912–1997 **18**

Senior, Olive 1941— **37**

Sentamu, John 1949— **58**

Sermon, Erick 1968— **81**

Serrano, Andres 1951(?)— **3**

Shabazz, Attallah 1958— **6**

Shabazz, Betty 1936–1997 **7, 26**

Shabazz, Ilyasah 1962— **36**

Shadd, Abraham D. 1801–1882 **81**

Shaggy 1968— **31**

Shakespeare, Robbie 1953— See Sly & Robbie

Shakur, Afeni 1947— **67**

Shakur, Assata 1947— **6**

Shakur, Meshell Suihailia Bashir See Ndegeocello, Meshell

Shakur, Tupac Amaru 1971–1996 **14**

Shakur, Yusef 1973— **85**

Shange, Ntozake 1948— **8**

Shank, Suzanne F. 1962(?)— **77**

Shannon, Randy 1966— **82**

Sharper, Darren 1975— **32**

Sharpton, Al 1954— **21**

Shavers, Cheryl 19(?)(?)— **31**

Shaw, Bernard 1940— **2, 28**

Shaw, William J. 1934— **30**

Sheard, Kierra "Kiki" 1987— **61**

Sheffey, Asa Bundy See Hayden, Robert Earl

Sheffield, Gary Antonian 1968— **16**

Shell, Art 1946— **1, 66**

Shelton, Paula Young 1961— **86**

Shepherd, Sherri 1970— **55**

Sherrod, Clayton 1944— **17**

Sherrod, Shirley 1948— **87**

Shider, Garry 1953–2010 **87**

Shinhoster, Earl 1950(?)–2000 **32**

Shipp, E. R. 1955— **15**

Shippen, John 1879–1968 **43**

Shirley, George I. 1934— **33**

Shockley, Ann Allen 1927— **84**

Shonibare, Yinka 1962— **58**

Short, Bobby 1924–2005 **52**

Short, Columbus 1982— **79**

Shorter, Wayne 1933— **75**

Shorty, Ras, I 1941–2000 **47**

Showers, Reggie 1964— **30**

Shropshire, Thomas B. 1925–2003 **49**

Shuttlesworth, Fred 1922— **47**

Sidibe, Gabourey 1983— **84**

Sifford, Charlie 1922— **4, 49**

Sigur, Wanda 1958— **44**

Siji 1971(?)— **56**

Silas, Paul 1943— **24**

Silva, Marina 1958— **80**

Silver, Horace 1928— **26**

Siméus, Dumas M. 1940— **25**

Simmons, Bob 1948— **29**

Simmons, E. Denise 19(?)(?)— **79**

Simmons, Gary 1964— **58**

Simmons, Henry 1970— **55**

Simmons, Jamal 1971— **72**

Simmons, Joseph See Run; Run-DMC

Simmons, Kimora Lee 1975— **51, 83**

Simmons, Russell 1957(?)— **1, 30**

Simmons, Ruth J. 1945— **13, 38**

Simone, Nina 1933–2003 **15, 41**

Simpson, Carole 1940— **6, 30**

Simpson, Lorna 1960— **4, 36**

Simpson, O. J. 1947— **15**

Simpson, Valerie 1946— **21**

Simpson-Hoffman, N'kenge 1975(?)— **52**

Simpson-Miller, Portia 1945— **62**

Sims, Howard "Sandman" 1917–2003 **48**

Sims, Lowery Stokes 1949— **27**

Sims, Naomi 1948–2009 **29, 79**

Sinbad 1957(?)— **1, 16**

Sinclair, Madge 1938–1995 **78**

Singletary, Mike 1958— **4, 76**

Singleton, John 1968— **2, 30**

Sinkford, Jeanne C. 1933— **13**

Sir Mix-A-Lot 1963— **82**

Sirleaf, Ellen Johnson 1938— **71**

Sisqo 1976— **30**

Sissle, Noble 1889–1975 **29**

Sister Souljah 1964— **11**

Sisulu, Albertina 1918— **57**

Sisulu, Sheila Violet Makate 1948(?)— **24**

Sisulu, Walter 1912–2003 **47**

Sizemore, Barbara A. 1927— **26**

Skerrit, Roosevelt 1972— **72**

Skinner, Kiron K. 1962(?) **65**

Sklarek, Norma Merrick 1928— **25**

Slash 1975— **75**

Slater, Rodney Earl 1955— **15**

Slaughter, John Brooks 1934— **53**

Sledge, Percy 1940— **39**

Sleet, Moneta (J.), Jr. 1926— **5**

Slice, Kimbo 1974— **73**

Slim Thug 1980— **86**

Slocumb, Jonathan 19(?)(?)— **52**

Sly & Robbie **34**

Slyde, Jimmy 1927–2008 **70**

Smalls, Robert 1839–1915 **82**

Smaltz, Audrey 1937(?)— **12**

Smiley, Rickey 1968— **59**

Smiley, Tavis 1964— **20, 68**

Smith, Anjela Lauren 1973— **44**

Smith, Anna Deavere 1950— **6, 44**

Smith, Arthur Lee, See Asante, Molefi Kete

Smith, B. See Smith, B(arbara)

Smith, B(arbara) 1949(?)— **11**

Smith, Barbara 1946— **28**

Smith, Bessie 1894–1937 **3**

Smith, Bruce 1984— **80**

Smith, Bruce W. 19(?)(?)— **53**

Smith, Cladys "Jabbo" 1908–1991 **32**

Smith, Clarence O. 1933— **21**

Smith, Clifford See Method Man

Smith, Damu 1951— **54**

Smith, Danyel 1966(?)— **40**

Smith, Dr. Lonnie 1942— **49**

Smith, Emmitt 1969— **7, 87**

Smith, Greg 1964— **28**

Smith, Hezekiah Leroy Gordon See Smith, Stuff

Smith, Hilton 1912–1983 **29**

Smith, Ian 1970(?)— **62**

Smith, Jabbo See Smith, Cladys "Jabbo"

Smith, Jaden 1998— **82**

Smith, Jane E. 1946— **24**

Smith, Jennifer 1947— **21**

Smith, Jessie Carney 1930— **35**

Smith, John L. 1938— **22**

Smith, Joshua (Isaac) 1941— **10**

Smith, Kemba 1971— **70**

Smith, Lonnie Liston 1940— **49**

Smith, Lovie 1958— **66**

Smith, Malcolm A. 1956— **75**

Smith, Mamie 1883–1946 **32**

Smith, Marie F. 1939— **70**

Smith, Marvin 1910–2003 **46**

Smith, Mary Carter 1919— **26**

Smith, Morgan 1910–1993 **46**

Smith, Nate 1929— **49**

Smith, Orlando See Smith, Tubby

Smith, Ozzie 1954— **77**

Smith, Princella 1983— **86**

Smith, Randy 1948–2009 **81**

Smith, Richard 1957— **51**

Smith, Rick 1969— **72**

Smith, Roger Guenveur 1960— **12**

Smith, Shaffer Chimere See Ne-Yo

Smith, Stephen A. 1967— **69**

Smith, Stuff 1909–1967 **37**

Smith, Tasha 1971— **73**

Smith, Trevor, Jr. See Rhymes, Busta

Smith, Trixie 1895–1943 **34**

Smith, Tubby 1951— **18, 83**

Smith, Vincent D. 1929–2003 **48**

Smith, Walker, Jr. See Robinson, Sugar Ray

Smith, Will 1968— **8, 18, 53**

Smith, Willi (Donnell) 1948–1987 **8**

Smith, Zadie 1975— **51**

Smythe Haith, Mabel 1918–2006 **61**

Sneed, Paula A. 1947— **18**

Snipes, Wesley 1962— **3, 24, 67**

Snoop Dogg 1971— **35, 84**

Snow, Samuel 1923–2008 **71**

Snowden, Frank M., Jr. 1911–2007 **67**

Soglo, Nicéphore 1935— **15**

Solomon, Jimmie Lee 1947(?)— **38**

Somé, Malidoma Patrice 1956— **10**

Somi 1979— **85**

Sommore, 1966— **61**

Sono, Jomo 1955— **86**

Sosa, Sammy 1968— **21, 44**

Soto Alejo, Federico Arístides See Güines, Tata

Soulchild, Musiq See Musiq

Souleymane, Mahamane 1940— **78**

Southern, Eileen 1920–2002 **56**

Southgate, Martha 1960(?)— **58**

Sowande, Fela 1905–1987 **39**

Sowande, Olufela Obafunmilayo See Sowande, Fela

Sowell, Thomas 1930— **2**

Soyinka, (Akinwande Olu) Wole 1934— **4**

Sparks, Corinne Etta 1953— **53**

Sparks, Jordin 1989— **66**

Spaulding, Charles Clinton 1874–1952 **9**

Spearman, Leonard H. O., Sr. 1929–2008 **81**

Spears, Warren 1954–2005 **52**

Spector, Ronnie 1943— **77**

Speech 1968— **82**

Spence, Joseph 1910–1984 **49**

Spencer, Anne 1882–1975 **27**

Spencer, Michael G. 1952— **87**

Spencer, Winston Baldwin 1948— **68**

Spigner, Archie 1928— **81**

Spikes, Dolores Margaret Richard 1936— **18**

Spiller, Bill 1913–1988 **64**

Sprewell, Latrell 1970— **23**

Spriggs, William 195(?)— **67**

Stackhouse, Jerry 1974— **30**

Staley, Dawn 1970— **57**

Stallings, George A(ugustus), Jr. 1948— **6**

Stampley, Micah 1971— **54**

Stanford, John 1938— **20**

Stanford, Olivia Lee Dilworth 1914–2004 **49**

Stanton, Alysa 1963— **78**

Stanton, Robert 1940— **20**

Staples, Brent 1951— **8**

Staples, Mavis 1939(?)— **50**

Staples, "Pops" 1915–2000 **32**

Staples, Roebuck See Staples, "Pops"

Stargell, Willie 1940(?)–2001 **29**

Staton, Candi 1940(?)— **27**

Staton, Dakota 1930(?)–2007 **62**

Staupers, Mabel K(eaton) 1890–1989 **7**

Stearnes, Norman "Turkey" 1901–1979 **31**

Steave-Dickerson, Kia 1970— **57**

Steele, Claude Mason 1946— **13**

Steele, Lawrence 1963— **28**

Steele, Michael 1958— **38, 73**

Steele, Shelby 1946— **13, 82**

Steely 1962–2009 **80**

Steinberg, Martha Jean 1930(?)–2000 **28**

Stephens, Charlotte Andrews 1854–1951 **14**

Stephens, John See Legend, John

Stephens, Myrtle See Potter, Myrtle

Stevens, Yvette See Khan, Chaka

Stew 1961— **69**

Steward, David L. 19(?)(?)— **36**

Steward, Emanuel 1944— **18**

Stewart, Alison 1966(?)— **13**

Stewart, Ella 1893–1987 **39**
Stewart, James "Bubba," Jr. 1985— **60**
Stewart, Kordell 1972— **21**
Stewart, Mark *See Stew*
Stewart, Paul Wilbur 1925— **12**
Stewart, Sylvester *See Stone, Sly*
Stewart, Tonea Harris 1947— **78**
Sticky Fingaz 1970— **86**
Still, William Grant 1895–1978 **37**
Stingley, Darryl 1951–2007 **69**
Stinson, Denise L. 1954— **59**
Stith, Charles R. 1949— **73**
Stockman, Shawn *See Boyz II Men*
Stokes, Carl 1927–1996 **10, 73**
Stokes, Louis 1925— **3**
Stone, Angie 1965(?)— **31**
Stone, Charles Sumner, Jr. *See Stone, Chuck*
Stone, Chuck 1924— **9**
Stone, Sly 1943— **85**
Stone, Toni 1921–1996 **15**
Stoney, Michael 1969— **50**
Stott, Dorothy M. *See Stout, Renee*
Stott, Dot *See Stout, Renee*
Stoudemire, Amaré 1982— **59**
Stout, Juanita Kidd 1919–1998 **24**
Stout, Renee 1958— **63**
Stoute, Steve 1971(?)— **38**
Stoutt, H. Lavity 1929–1995 **83**
Strahan, Michael 1971— **35, 81**
Strautmanis, Michael 1969— **87**
Strawberry, Darryl 1962— **22**
Strayhorn, Billy 1915–1967 **31**
Street, John F. 1943(?)— **24**
Streeter, Sarah 1953— **45**
Stringer, C. Vivian 1948— **13, 66**
Stringer, Korey 1974–2001 **35**
Stringer, Vickie 196(?)— **58**
Stroman, Nathaniel *See Earthquake*
Stuart, Moira 1949— **82**
Studdard, Ruben 1978— **46**
Sudarkasa, Niara 1938— **4**
Sudduth, Jimmy Lee 1910–2007 **65**
Sugarhill Gang, The **79**
Sullivan, Jazmine 1987— **81**
Sullivan, Leon H(oward) 1922— **3, 30**
Sullivan, Louis (Wade) 1933— **8**
Sullivan, Maxine 1911–1987 **37**
Summer, Donna 1948— **25**
Sun Ra, 1914–1993 **60**
Sundiata, Sekou 1948–2007 **66**
Supremes, The **33**
Sutphen, Mona 1967— **77**
Sutton, Percy E. 1920–2009 **42, 82**
Swann, Lynn 1952— **28**
Swaray, Fanta Estelle *See Estelle*
Sweat, Keith 1961(?)— **19**
Sweet, Ossian 1895–1960 **68**
Swoopes, Sheryl 1971— **12, 56**
Swygert, H. Patrick 1943— **22**
Sy, Oumou 1952— **65**
Sykes, Roosevelt 1906–1984 **20**
Sykes, Wanda 1964— **48, 81**
Syler, Rene 1963— **53**
Tademy, Lalita 1948— **36**
Tafari Makonnen *See Haile Selassie*
Tait, Michael 1966— **57**
Talbert, David 1966(?)— **34**
Talbert, Mary B. 1866–1923 **77**

Talley, André Leon 1949(?)— **56**
Tamar-kali 1973(?)— **63**
Tamia 1975— **24, 55**
Tampa Red 1904(?)–1980 **63**
Tancil, Gladys Quander 1921–2002 **59**
Tandja, Mamadou 1938— **33, 78**
Tanksley, Ann (Graves) 1934— **37**
Tanner, Henry Ossawa 1859–1937 **1**
Tate, Eleanora E. 1948— **20, 55**
Tate, Larenz 1975— **15**
Tatum, Art 1909–1956 **28**
Tatum, Beverly Daniel 1954— **42, 84**
Tatum, Elinor R. 197(?)— **78**
Tatum, Jack 1948— **87**
Tatum, Wilbert 1933–2009 **76**
Taulbert, Clifton Lemoure 1945— **19**
Taylor, Billy 1921— **23**
Taylor, Bo 1966–2008 **72**
Taylor, Cecil 1929— **70**
Taylor, Charles 1948— **20**
Taylor, Darren *See Taylor, Bo*
Taylor, Ephren W., II 1982— **61**
Taylor, Gardner C. 1918— **76**
Taylor, Helen (Lavon Hollingshed) 1942–2000 **30**
Taylor, Jason 1974— **70**
Taylor, Jermain 1978— **60**
Taylor, John (David Beckett) 1952— **16**
Taylor, Karin 1971— **34**
Taylor, Koko 1928–2009 **40, 80**
Taylor, Kristin Clark 1959— **8**
Taylor, Lawrence 1959— **25**
Taylor, Marshall Walter "Major" 1878–1932 **62**
Taylor, Meshach 1947(?)— **4**
Taylor, Mildred D. 1943— **26**
Taylor, Natalie 1959— **47**
Taylor, Regina 1959(?)— **9, 46**
Taylor, Robert Robinson 1868–194280
Taylor, Ron 1952–2002 **35**
Taylor, Susan C. 1957— **62**
Taylor, Susan L. 1946— **10, 86**
Taylor, Susie King 1848–1912 **13**
Teer, Barbara Ann 1937–2008 **81**
Temptations, The **33**
Tergat, Paul 1969— **59**
Terrell, Dorothy A. 1945— **24**
Terrell, Mary (Elizabeth) Church 1863–1954 **9**
Terrell, Tammi 1945–1970 **32**
Terrell-Kearney, Kim 1965— **83**
Terry, Clark 1920— **39**
Tharpe, Rosetta 1915–1973 **65**
The Artist *See Prince*
The-Dream 1982— **74**
Thiam, Aliaune Akon *See Akon*
Thigpen, Lynne 1948–2003 **17, 41**
Thomas, Alma Woodsey 1891–1978 **14**
Thomas, Arthur Ray 1951— **52**
Thomas, Clarence 1948— **2, 39, 65**
Thomas, Claudia Lynn 1950— **64**
Thomas, Debi 1967— **26**
Thomas, Derrick 1967–2000 **25**
Thomas, Emmitt 1943— **71**
Thomas, Frank 1968— **12, 51**
Thomas, Franklin A. 1934— **5, 49**
Thomas, Irma 1941— **29**

Thomas, Isiah 1961— **7, 26, 65**
Thomas, Michael 1967— **69**
Thomas, Mickalene 1971— **61**
Thomas, Rozonda 1971— **34, 78**
Thomas, Rufus 1917— **20**
Thomas, Sean Patrick 1970— **35**
Thomas, Stayve Jerome *See Slim Thug*
Thomas, Thurman 1966— **75**
Thomas, Todd *See Speech*
Thomas, Trisha R. 1964— **65**
Thomas, Vivien (T.) 1910–1985 **9**
Thomas-Graham, Pamela 1963(?)— **29**
Thomason, Marsha 1976— **47**
Thompson, Ahmir *See ?uestlove*
Thompson, Bennie G. 1948— **26**
Thompson, Cynthia Bramlett 1949— **50**
Thompson, Dearon *See Deezer D*
Thompson, Don 1963— **56**
Thompson, John Douglas 1964— **81**
Thompson, John W. 1949— **26**
Thompson, Kenan 1978— **52**
Thompson, Larry D. 1945— **39**
Thompson, Tazewell (Alfred, Jr.) 1954— **13**
Thompson, Tina 1975— **25, 75**
Thompson, William C. 1953(?)— **35**
Thoms, Tracie 1975— **61**
Thornton, Big Mama 1926–1984 **33**
Thornton, Yvonne S. 1947— **69**
Thrash, Dox 1893–1965 **35**
Three Mo' Tenors **35**
Thrower, Willie 1930–2002 **35**
Thugwane, Josia 1971— **21**
Thurman, Howard 1900–1981 **3**
Thurman, Wallace Henry 1902–1934 **16**
Thurston, Baratunde 1977— **79**
Thurston, Stephen J. 1952— **49**
Till, Emmett (Louis) 1941–1955 **7**
Tillard, Conrad 1964— **47**
Tillis, Frederick 1930— **40**
Tillman, Dorothy 1947— **76**
Tillman, George, Jr. 1968— **20**
Timbaland 1971— **32**
Tinsley, Boyd 1964— **50**
Tirico, Michael *See Tirico, Mike*
Tirico, Mike 1966— **68**
Tisdale, Wayman 1964— **50**
TLC **34**
Tobias, Channing H. 1882–1961 **79**
Tobin, Patricia 1943–2008 **75**
Todman, Terence A. 1926— **55**
Tolbert, Terence 1964— **74**
Toler, Burl 1928–2009 **80**
Tolliver, Mose 1915(?)–2006 **60**
Tolliver, William (Mack) 1951— **9**
Tolson, Melvin B(eaunorus) 1898–1966 **37**
Tolton, Augustine 1854–1897 **62**
Tomlinson, LaDainian 1979— **65**
Tonex, 1978(?)— **54**
Tooks, Lance 1962— **62**
Toomer, Jean 1894–1967 **6**
Toomer, Nathan Pinchback *See Toomer, Jean*
Toote, Gloria E. A. 1931— **64**
Torres, Gina 1969— **52**
Torry, Guy 19(?)(?)— **31**
Tosh, Peter 1944–1987 **9**

Touré, Amadou Toumani 1948(?)— **18**
Touré, Askia (Muhammad Abu Bakr el) 1938— **47**
Touré, Faya Ora Rose 1945— **56**
Touré, Sekou 1922–1984 **6**
Toussaint, Allen 1938— **60**
Toussaint, Lorraine 1960— **32**
Townes, Jeffrey Allan *See DJ Jazzy Jeff*
Towns, Edolphus 1934— **19, 75**
Townsend, Robert 1957— **4, 23**
T-Pain 1985— **73**
Trammell, Kimberly N. *See Holland, Kimberly N.*
Tresvant, Ralph 1968— **57**
Tribbett, Tye 1977— **81**
Tribble, Israel, Jr. 1940— **8**
Trotter, Donne E. 1950— **28**
Trotter, Lloyd G. 1945(?)— **56**
Trotter, (William) Monroe 1872–1934 **9**
Trotter, Tariq Luqmaan *See Black Thought*
Trouillot, Ertha Pascal *See Pascal-Trouillot, Ertha*
Troupe, Quincy 1943— **83**
Trouppe, Quincy Thomas, Sr. 1912–1993 **84**
True, Rachel 1966— **82**
Trueheart, William E. 1942— **49**
Tsvangirai, Morgan 1952— **26, 72**
Tubbs Jones, Stephanie 1949–2008 **24, 72**
Tubman, Harriet 1820(?)–1913 **9**
Tucker, C. Delores 1927–2005 **12, 56**
Tucker, Chris 1972— **13, 23, 62**
Tucker, Cynthia 1955— **1561**
Tucker, Rosina Budd Harvey Corrothers 1881–1987 **14**
Tuckson, Reed V. 1951(?)— **71**
Tunie, Tamara 1959— **63**
Tunnell, Emlen 1925–1975 **54**
Ture, Kwame *See Carmichael, Stokely*
Turnbull, Charles Wesley 1935— **62**
Turnbull, Walter 1944— **13, 60**
Turner, Henry McNeal 1834–1915 **5**
Turner, Ike 1931–2007 **68**
Turner, Izear *See Turner, Ike*
Turner, Tina 1939— **6, 27**
Tutu, Desmond (Mpilo) 1931— **6, 44**
Tutu, Nontombi Naomi 1960— **57**
Tutuola, Amos 1920–1997 **30**
Tyler, Aisha N. 1970— **36**
Tyree, Omar Rashad 1969— **21**
Tyrese *See Gibson, Tyrese*
Tyson, Andre 1960— **40**
Tyson, Asha 1970— **39**
Tyson, Cicely 1933— **7, 51**
Tyson, Mike 1966— **28, 44**
Tyson, Neil deGrasse 1958— **15, 65**
Uggams, Leslie 1943— **23**
Ukpabio, Helen 1969— **86**
Ulmer, James 1942— **79**
Underwood, Blair 1964— **7, 27, 76**
Union, Gabrielle 1973— **31**
Unseld, Wes 1946— **23**
Upshaw, Gene 1945–2008 **18, 47, 72**

Usher 1978— **23, 56**

Usry, James L. 1922— **23**

Ussery, Terdema Lamar, II 1958— **29**

Utendahl, John 1956— **23**

Valdés, Bebo 1918— **75**

Valdés, Dionisio Ramón Emilio *See Valdés, Bebo*

Valentino, Bobby 1980— **62**

Van Lierop, Robert 1939— **53**

Van Peebles, Mario 1957— **2, 51**

Van Peebles, Melvin 1932— **7**

van Sertima, Ivan 1935— **25**

Vance, Courtney B. 1960— **15, 60**

VanDerZee, James (Augustus Joseph) 1886–1983 **6**

Vandross, Luther 1951–2005 **13, 48, 59**

Vanessa James and Yannick Bonheur **84**

Vanity 1959— **67**

Vann, Harold Moore *See Muhammad, Khallid Abdul*

Vanzant, Iyanla 1953— **17, 47**

Vaughan, Sarah (Lois) 1924–1990 **13**

Vaughn, Countess 1978— **53**

Vaughn, Gladys Gary 1942(?)— **47**

Vaughn, Mo 1967— **16**

Vaughn, Viola 1947— **70**

Vaughns, Cleopatra 1940— **46**

Vega, Marta Moreno 1942(?)— **61**

Velez-Rodriguez, Argelia 1936— **56**

Vera, Yvonne 1964— **32**

Verdelle, A. J. 1960— **26**

Vereen, Ben(jamin Augustus) 1946— **4**

Verna, Gelsy 1961–2008 **70**

Verrett, Shirley 1931— **66**

Vick, Michael 1980— **39, 65**

Vieira, João Bernardo 1939–2009 **14, 84**

Villarosa, Clara 1930(?)— **85**

Vincent, Marjorie Judith 1965(?)— **2**

Vincent, Mark *See Diesel, Vin*

Virgil, Ozzie 1933— **48**

Von Lipsey, Roderick 1959— **11**

wa Ngengi, Kamau *See Kenyatta, Jomo*

Waddles, Charleszetta "Mother" 1912–2001 **10, 49**

Waddles, Mother *See Waddles, Charleszetta "Mother"*

Wade, Abdoulaye 1926— **66**

Wade, Dwyane 1982— **61**

Wade-Gayles, Gloria Jean 1937(?)— **41**

Wagner, Albert 1924–2006 **78**

Wagner, Annice 1937— **22**

Wainwright, Joscelyn 1941— **46**

Walcott, Derek (Alton) 1930— **5**

Walcott, Louis Eugene 1933— **2, 15**

Walker, Albertina 1929— **10, 58**

Walker, Alice 1944— **1, 43**

Walker, Arthur, II 1936–2001 **87**

Walker, Bernita Ruth 1946— **53**

Walker, Cedric "Ricky" 1953— **19**

Walker, Cora T. 1922–2006 **68**

Walker, Dianne 1951— **57**

Walker, Eamonn 1961(?)— **37**

Walker, George 1922— **37**

Walker, Herschel 1962— **1, 69**

Walker, Hezekiah 1962— **34**

Walker, John T. 1925–1989 **50**

Walker, Kara 1969— **16, 80**

Walker, Kurt *See Blow, Kurtis*

Walker, Madame C. J. 1867–1919 **7**

Walker, Maggie Lena 1867(?)–1934 **17**

Walker, Margaret 1915–1998 **29**

Walker, Nellie Marian *See Larsen, Nella*

Walker, Rebecca 1969— **50**

Walker, T. J. 1961(?)— **7**

Walker, Thomas "T. J." *See Walker, T. J.*

Walker, Wyatt Tee 1929— **80**

Wallace, Ben 1974— **54**

Wallace, Joaquin 1965— **49**

Wallace, Michele Faith 1952— **13**

Wallace, Perry E. 1948— **47**

Wallace, Phyllis A(nn) 1920(?)–1993 **9**

Wallace, Rasheed 1974— **56**

Wallace, Ruby Ann *See Dee, Ruby*

Wallace, Sippie 1898–1986 **1**

Wallace, William 1939–2008 **75**

Waller, Fats 1904–1943 **29**

Waller, Thomas Wright *See Waller, Fats*

Walters, Ronald 1938— **83**

Walton, Cora *See Taylor, Koko*

Wambugu, Florence 1953— **42**

Wamutombo, Dikembe Mutombo Mpolondo Mukamba Jean Jacque *See Mutombo, Dikembe*

Ward, Andre 1984— **62**

Ward, Benjamin 1926–2002 **68**

Ward, Douglas Turner 1930— **42**

Ward, Hines 1976— **84**

Ward, Lloyd 1949— **21, 46**

Ware, Andre 1968— **37**

Ware, Carl H. 1943— **30**

Warfield, Marsha 1955— **2**

Warner, Malcolm-Jamal 1970— **22, 36**

Warren, Michael 1946— **27**

Warren, Mike *See Warren, Michael*

Warsame, Keinan Abdi *See K'naan*

Warwick, Dionne 1940— **18**

Washington, Alonzo 1967— **29**

Washington, Booker T(aliaferro) 1856–1915 **4**

Washington, Denzel 1954— **1, 16**

Washington, Dinah 1924–1963 **22**

Washington, Ebonya 1973(?)— **79**

Washington, Elsie B. 1942–2009 **78**

Washington, Fred(er)i(cka Carolyn) 1903–1994 **10**

Washington, Gene 1947— **63**

Washington, Grover, Jr. 1943–1999 **17, 44**

Washington, Harold 1922–1987 **6**

Washington, Harriet A. 1951— **69**

Washington, Hayma 19(?)(?)— **86**

Washington, Isaiah 1963— **62**

Washington, James, Jr. 1909(?)–2000 **38**

Washington, James Melvin 1948–1997 **50**

Washington, Kenny 1918–1971 **50**

Washington, Kerry 1977— **46**

Washington, Laura S. 1956(?)— **18**

Washington, MaliVai 1969— **8**

Washington, Mary T. 1906–2005 **57**

Washington, Patrice Clarke 1961— **12**

Washington, Pauletta Pearson 1950— **86**

Washington, Regynald G. 1954(?)— **44**

Washington, Tamia Reneé *See Tamia*

Washington, Valores James 1903–1995 **12**

Washington, Walter 1915–2003 **45**

Washington Wylie, Mary T. *See Washington, Mary T.*

Wasow, Omar 1970— **15**

Waters, Benny 1902–1998 **26**

Waters, Ethel 1895–1977 **7**

Waters, Maxine 1938— **3, 67**

Waters, Muddy 1915–1983 **34**

Watkins, Donald 1948— **35**

Watkins, Frances Ellen *See Harper, Frances Ellen Watkins*

Watkins, Gloria Jean *See hooks, bell*

Watkins, Joe 1953— **86**

Watkins, Levi, Jr. 1945— **9**

Watkins, Perry James Henry 1948–1996 **12**

Watkins, Shirley R. 1938— **17**

Watkins, Tionne "T-Boz" 1970— *See TLC*

Watkins, Walter C. 1946— **24**

Watley, Jody 1959— **54**

Watson, Bob 1946— **25**

Watson, Carlos 1970— **50**

Watson, Diane 1933— **41**

Watson, Johnny "Guitar" 1935–1996 **18**

Watt, Melvin 1945— **26**

Wattleton, (Alyce) Faye 1943— **9**

Watts, Andre 1946— **42**

Watts, J(ulius) C(aesar), Jr. 1957— **14, 38**

Watts, Reggie 1972(?)— **52**

Watts, Rolonda 1959— **9**

Wayans, Damien 198(?)— **78**

Wayans, Damon 1961— **8, 41**

Wayans, Keenen Ivory 1958— **18**

Wayans, Kim 1961— **80**

Wayans, Marlon 1972— **29, 82**

Wayans, Shawn 1971— **29**

Waymon, Eunice Kathleen *See Simone, Nina*

Weah, George 1966— **58**

Weathers, Carl 1948— **10**

Weaver, Afaa Michael 1951— **37**

Weaver, Michael S. *See Weaver, Afaa Michael*

Weaver, Robert C. 1907–1997 **8, 46**

Webb, Veronica 1965— **10**

Webb, Wellington 1941— **3, 81**

Webber, Chris 1973— **15, 30, 59**

Webster, Katie 1936–1999 **29**

Wedgeworth, Robert W. 1937— **42**

Weekes, Kevin 1975— **67**

Weeks, Thomas, III 1967— **70**

Weems, Carrie Mae 1953— **63**

Weems, Renita J. 1954— **44**

Wein, Joyce 1928–2005 **62**

Wek, Alek 1977— **18, 63**

Welburn, Edward T. 1950— **50**

Welch, Elisabeth 1908–2003 **52**

Welles, Rosalind *See Washington, Elsie B.*

Wells, Henrietta Bell 1912–2008 **69**

Wells, James Lesesne 1902–1993 **10**

Wells, Mary 1943–1992 **28**

Wells-Barnett, Ida B(ell) 1862–1931 **8**

Welsing, Frances (Luella) Cress 1935— **5**

Wendo *See Kolosoy, Wendo*

Wesley, Dorothy Porter 1905–1995 **19**

Wesley, Richard 1945— **73**

Wesley, Valerie Wilson 194(?)— **18**

West, Cornel 1953— **5, 33, 80**

West, Dorothy 1907–1998 **12, 54**

West, James E. 1931— **87**

West, Kanye 1977— **52**

West, Togo Dennis, Jr. 1942— **16**

Westbrook, Kelvin 1955— **50**

Westbrook, Peter 1952— **20**

Westbrooks, Bobby 1930(?)–1995 **51**

Whack, Rita Coburn 1958— **36**

Whalum, Kirk 1958— **37, 64**

Wharton, Clifton R(eginald), Jr. 1926— **7**

Wharton, Clifton Reginald, Sr. 1899–1990 **36**

Wheat, Alan Dupree 1951— **14**

Whitaker, Forest 1961— **2, 49, 67**

Whitaker, Mark 1957— **21, 47**

Whitaker, Pernell 1964— **10**

Whitaker, "Sweet Pea" *See Whitaker, Pernell*

White, Armond 1954(?)— **80**

White, Barry 1944–2003 **13, 41**

White, Bill 1933(?)— **1, 48**

White, Charles 1918–1979 **39**

White, (Donald) Dondi 1961–1998 **34**

White, Jesse 1934— **22, 75**

White, Jessica 1984— **83**

White, John H. 1945— **27**

White, Josh 1914(?)–1969 **86**

White, Josh, Jr. 1940— **52**

White, Linda M. 1942— **45**

White, Lois Jean 1938— **20**

White, Maurice 1941— **29**

White, Michael Jai 1967— **71**

White, Michael R(eed) 1951— **5**

White, Reggie 1961–2004 **6, 50**

White, Reginald Howard *See White, Reggie*

White, Terri 1948— **82**

White, Walter F(rancis) 1893–1955 **4**

White, Willard 1946— **53**

White, William DeKova *See White, Bill*

White, Willye 1939— **67**

White-Hammond, Gloria 1951(?)— **61**

Whitehead, Colson 1969— **77**

Whitfield, Fred 1967— **23**

Whitfield, LeRoy 1969–2005 **84**

Whitfield, Lynn 1954— **18**

Whitfield, Mal 1924— **60**

Whitfield, Norman 1940–2008 **73**

Whitfield, Van 1960(?)— **34**

Whitlock, Jason 1967— **78**

Whittaker, Hudson *See Tampa Red*

Wideman, John Edgar 1941— **5, 87**

Wilbekin, Emil 1968— **63**

Wilbon, Michael 1958— **68**

Wilder, L. Douglas 1931— **3, 48**

Wiley, Kehinde 1977— **62**

Wiley, Ralph 1952–2004 **8, 78**

Wilkens, J. Ernest, Jr. 1923— **43**

Wilkens, Lenny 1937— **11**

Wilkens, Leonard Randolph See
Wilkens, Lenny

Wilkerson, Isabel 1961— **71**

Wilkerson, Robert King See King,
Robert Hillary

Wilkins, David 1956— **77**

Wilkins, Dominique 1960— **74**

Wilkins, Ray 1951— **47**

Wilkins, Roger 1932— **2, 84**

Wilkins, Roy 1901–1981 **4**

Wilkins, Thomas Alphonso 1956—
**71**

will.i.am 1975— **64**

Williams, Alice Faye See Shakur,
Afeni

Williams, Ann Claire 1949— **82**

Williams, Anthony 1951— **21**

Williams, Anthony Charles See
Tonex

Williams, Armstrong 1959— **29**

Williams, Bert 1874–1922 **18**

Williams, Billy 1938— **86**

Williams, Billy Dee 1937— **8**

Williams, Carl See Kani, Karl

Williams, Clarence 1893(?)–1965
**33**

Williams, Clarence 1967— **70**

Williams, Clarence, III 1939— **26**

Williams, Claude 1908–2004 **80**

Williams, Daniel Hale (III)
1856–1931 **2**

Williams, David Rudyard 1954— **50**

Williams, Deniece 1951— **36**

Williams, Denise 1958— **40**

Williams, Doug 1955— **22**

Williams, Dudley 1938— **60**

Williams, Eddie N. 1932— **44**

Williams, Eric Eustace 1911–1981
**65**

Williams, Evelyn 1922(?)— **10**

Williams, Fannie Barrier 1855–1944
**27**

Williams, Frederick (B.) 1939–2006
**63**

Williams, George Washington
1849–1891 **18**

Williams, Gertrude See Morgan,
Gertrude

Williams, Gregory (Howard) 1943—
**11**

Williams, Hosea Lorenzo 1926—
**15, 31**

Williams, J. Mayo 1894–1980 **83**

Williams, Joe 1918–1999 **5, 25**

Williams, John A. 1925— **27**

Williams, Juan 1954— **35, 80**

Williams, Ken 1964— **68**

Williams, Lauryn 1983— **58**

Williams, Lindsey 1966— **75**

Williams, Maggie 1954— **7, 71**

Williams, Malinda 1975— **57**

Williams, Marco 1956— **53**

Williams, Margaret Ann See Williams, Maggie

Williams, Mary Lou 1910–1981 **15**

Williams, Michael L. 1953— **86**

Williams, Michelle 1980— **73**

Williams, Montel 1956— **4, 57**

Williams, Natalie 1970— **31**

Williams, O(swald) S. 1921— **13**

Williams, Patricia 1951— **11, 54**

Williams, Paul R(evere) 1894–1980
**9**

Williams, Paulette Linda See
Shange, Ntozake

Williams, Pharrell 1973— **47, 82**

Williams, Preston Warren, II
1939(?)— **64**

Williams, Rhonda Y. 1967(?)— **86**

Williams, Ricky 1977— **85**

Williams, Robert F(ranklin) 1925—
**11**

Williams, Robert Peter See Guillaume, Robert

Williams, Ronald A. 1949— **57**

Williams, Russell, II 1952— **70**

Williams, Samuel Arthur 1946— **21**

Williams, Saul 1972— **31**

Williams, Serena 1981— **20, 41, 73**

Williams, Sherley Anne 1944–1999
**25**

Williams, Stanley "Tookie"
1953–2005 **29, 57**

Williams, Stevie 1979— **71**

Williams, Terrie M. 1954— **35**

Williams, Tony 1945–1997 **67**

Williams, Vanessa A. 1963— **32, 66**

Williams, Vanessa L. 1963— **4, 17**

Williams, Venus 1980— **17, 34, 62**

Williams, Walter E(dward) 1936— **4**

Williams, Wendy 1964— **62**

Williams, William December See
Williams, Billy Dee

Williams, William T(homas) 1942—
**11**

Williams, Willie L(awrence) 1943—
**4**

Williamson, Fred 1938— **67**

Williamson, Lisa See Sister Souljah

Williamson, Mykelti 1957— **22**

Williamson, Sonny Boy
1899(?)–1965 **84**

Willie, Louis, Jr. 1923–2007 **68**

Willingham, Tyrone 1953— **43**

Willis, Bill 1921–2007 **68**

Willis, Cheryl See Hudson, Cheryl

Willis, Deborah 1948— **85**

Willis, Dontrelle 1982— **55**

Willis, William Karnet See Willis,
Bill

Wills, Harry 1889(?)–1958 **80**

Wills, Maury 1932— **73**

Wilson, August 1945–2005 **7, 33,
55**

Wilson, Cassandra 1955— **16**

Wilson, Chandra 1969— **57**

Wilson, Charlie 1953— **31, 77**

Wilson, Debra 1970(?)— **38**

Wilson, Dorien 1962(?)— **55**

Wilson, Ellis 1899–1977 **39**

Wilson, Flip 1933–1998 **21**

Wilson, Gerald 1918— **49**

Wilson, Jackie 1934–1984 **60**

Wilson, Jimmy 1946— **45**

Wilson, Margaret Bush 1919–2009
**79**

Wilson, Mary 1944 **28**

Wilson, Nancy 1937— **10**

Wilson, Natalie 1972(?)— **38**

Wilson, Phill 1956— **9**

Wilson, Stephanie 1966— **72**

Wilson, Sunnie 1908–1999 **7, 55**

Wilson, Tracey Scott 1967(?)— **77**

Wilson, William Julius 1935— **22**

Wilson, William Nathaniel See Wilson, Sunnie

Winans, Angie 1968— **36**

Winans, Benjamin 1962— **14**

Winans, CeCe 1964— **14, 43**

Winans, David 1934–2009 **77**

Winans, Debbie 1972— **36**

Winans, Marvin L. 1958— **17**

Winans, Ronald 1956–2005 **54**

Winans, Vickie 1953(?)— **24**

Winfield, Dave 1951— **5**

Winfield, David Mark See Winfield,
Dave

Winfield, Paul (Edward) 1941–2004
**2, 45**

Winfrey, Oprah 1954— **2, 15, 61**

Winkfield, Jimmy 1882–1974 **42**

Winslow, Kellen 1957— **83**

Wisdom, Kimberlydawn 1956— **57**

Withers, Bill 1938— **61**

Withers, Ernest C. 1922–2007 **68**

Withers-Mendes, Elisabeth
1973(?)— **64**

Witherspoon, John 1942— **38**

Witt, Edwin T. 1920— **26**

Wiwa, Ken 1968— **67**

Wofford, Chloe Anthony See Morrison, Toni

Wolfe, Ann 1971— **82**

Wolfe, George C. 1954— **6, 43**

Womack, Bobby 1944— **60**

Wonder, Stevie 1950— **11, 53**

Wonder Mike See Sugarhill Gang,
The

Woodard, Alfre 1953— **9**

Woodard, Lynette 1959— **67**

Woodbridge, Hudson See Tampa
Red

Woodruff, Hale (Aspacio)
1900–1980 **9**

Woodruff, John 1915–2007 **68**

Woods, Abraham, Jr. 1928–2008
**74**

Woods, Eldrick See Woods, Tiger

Woods, Georgie 1927–2005 **57**

Woods, Granville T. 1856–1910 **5**

Woods, Jacqueline 1962— **52**

Woods, Mattiebelle 1902–2005 **63**

Woods, Scott 1971— **55**

Woods, Sylvia 1926— **34**

Woods, Teri 1968— **69**

Woods, Tiger 1975— **14, 31, 81**

Woodson, Carter G(odwin)
1875–1950 **2**

Woodson, Mike 1958— **78**

Woodson, Robert L. 1937— **10**

Woodson, Rod 1965— **79**

Wooldridge, Anna Marie See Lincoln, Abbey

Worrill, Conrad 1941— **12**

Worthy, James 1961— **49**

Worthy, Kym 1956— **84**

Wright, Antoinette 195(?)— **60**

Wright, Bruce McMarion
1918–2005 **3, 52**

Wright, Charles H. 1918–2002 **35**

Wright, Deborah C. 1958— **25**

Wright, Jeffrey 1966— **54**

Wright, Jeremiah A., Jr. 1941— **45,
69**

Wright, Lewin 1962— **43**

Wright, Louis Tompkins 1891–1952
**4**

Wright, Nathan, Jr. 1923–2005 **56**

Wright, Rayfield 1945— **70**

Wright, Richard 1908–1960 **5**

Wright, Timothy 1947— **74**

Wyatt, Addie L. 1924— **56**

Wynn, Albert R. 1951— **25, 77**

X, Malcolm 1925–1965 **1**

X, Marvin 1944— **45**

Xuma, Madie Hall 1894–1982 **59**

Xzibit 1974— **78**

Yabby You 1946–2010 **83**

Yancy, Dorothy Cowser 1944— **42**

Yar'adua, Umaru 1951— **69**

Yarbrough, Camille 1938— **40**

Yarbrough, Cedric 1971— **51**

Yayi, Boni T. 1952— **84**

Yeboah, Emmanuel Ofosu 1977—
**53**

Yette, Samuel F. 1929— **63**

Yoba, (Abdul-)Malik (Kashie)
1967— **11**

York, Dwight D. 1945— **71**

York, Malachi Z. See York, Dwight
D.

York, Vincent 1952— **40**

Young, Al 1939— **82**

Young, Andre Ramelle See Dre, Dr.

Young, Andrew 1932— **3, 48**

Young, Charles 1864–1922 **77**

Young, Coleman 1918–1997 **1, 20**

Young, Donald, Jr. 1989— **57**

Young, Jean Childs 1933–1994 **14**

Young, Jimmy 1948–2005 **54**

Young, Ledisi Anibade See Ledisi

Young, Lee 1914–2008 **72**

Young, Leonidas Raymond See
Young, Lee

Young, Roger Arliner 1899–1964 **29**

Young, Thomas 194(?)— See
Three Mo' Tenors

Young, Whitney M(oore), Jr.
1921–1971 **4**

Young Jeezy 1977— **63**

Youngblood, Johnny Ray 1948— **8**

Youngblood, Shay 1959— **32**

Zane 1967(?)— **71**

Zollar, Alfred 1955(?)— **40**

Zollar, Jawole Willa Jo 1950— **28**

Zook, Kristal Brent 1966(?)— **62**

Zulu, Princess Kasune 1977— **54**

Zuma, Jacob 1942— **33, 75**

Zuma, Nkosazana Dlamini 1949—
**34**